ACCOUNTING ISSUES FOR LAWYERS

TEACHING MATERIALS

Fourth Edition

By

Ted J. Fiflis

Professor of Law, University of Colorado

AMERICAN CASEBOOK SERIES®

WEST PUBLISHING CO.
ST. PAUL, MINN., 1991

COPYRIGHT © 1971 WEST PUBLISHING CO.
COPYRIGHT © 1977 FIFLIS, KRIPKE
COPYRIGHT © 1984 FIFLIS, KRIPKE & FOSTER
COPYRIGHT © 1991 By WEST PUBLISHING CO.
                    610 Opperman Drive
                    P.O. Box 64526
                    St. Paul, MN 55164–0526
                    1–800–328–9352

Library of Congress Cataloging-in-Publication Data

Fiflis, Ted J., 1933–
    Accounting issues for lawyers : teaching materials / by Ted J.
Fiflis. — 4th ed.
     p.   cm. — (American casebook series)
    Rev. ed. of: Accounting for business lawyers.
    Includes index.
    ISBN 0–314–86280–3
    1. Accounting—Law and legislation—United States. I. Fiflis,
Ted. J., 1933– Accounting for business lawyers. II. Title.
III. Series.
KF1446.A7F53   1991
657'02434—dc20   91–17631
                                              CIP

ISBN 0–314–86280–3

3rd Reprint — 2001

To
Timothy, Christopher, Rose, Brendan,
Alexandra, Kayla and Sean

*

Preface

Accounting issues have always been of great concern to business lawyers, whether they advise on general corporate law, taxation, securities regulation, pension planning, acquisitions, or any of a myriad of other subjects which make up a business practice. These issues are changing rapidly, as are other areas of law, and a comprehensive revision of this book was necessary to cover developments of recent years in dividend law, the new cash flow statement, the SEC's required management discussion and analysis of financial statements, auditors' new responsibilities, and other matters.

In this fourth edition the materials have been pared to their leanest, consistently with providing the essentials for practicing business law in the next several years. Over 400 pages of the prior edition have been replaced with new materials. The contents are no more nor less complex than, say, a course in securities law or taxation. That is to say, they are difficult. But every effort has been made to make them teachable and learnable. As one measure to assist in this purpose, I have marked with asterisks in the Table of Contents the materials which I delete from my own one-semester, three-hour offering. Much more of the non-deleted material must be only lightly touched upon in the classroom in order to provide full coverage. I vary this treatment from year to year.

Chapters I to X provide the core law school course. Chapters XI to XIV are for lawyers who wish additional background for their business practice. They need not be covered in the course.

I spend the first three weeks on Chapter I, on bookkeeping. Some teachers place less emphasis on this topic on one ground or another. Others, using other texts, do *nothing but* teach the equivalent of this first chapter for the full course. Since the chapter covers the same ground as an undergraduate one or two semester introductory course, without the details, this may be deemed a sufficient basis for law students. But I do not believe so. I am firmly of the view that more is required. The remaining chapters provide the extras.

Chapter II, dealing with basic background material—i.e., the distinction between accounting and auditing, the sources of authority, the application of principles, and the meaning of internal controls—is largely for students' at-home study and requires minimal classroom time.

I emphasize Chapter III, again for about three weeks because most securities and tax law issues are in this realm—recognition and realization of revenue and income. Every week's law reports contain a half dozen cases concerning the problems dealt with in this chapter. And perhaps more importantly, lawyers advising on disclosure documents must understand its contents. Again not every aspect of the chapter can be thoroughly examined in the classroom in only three weeks, so selective treatment is necessary.

Then in the next four or five weeks Chapters IV through VII (dealing with cost allocations for inventories, depreciation, intangibles and contingent costs, all of which parallel each other) may be considered, again touching some parts only lightly.

The last three chapters I use for the course are on stockholders' equity, mergers and acquisitions, and financial analysis.

Case and statute citations, as well as footnotes, of courts and commentators have been omitted without so specifying; numbered footnotes are from the original materials and retain the original numbering. Lettered footnotes are those of the author.

It is impossible to adequately acknowledge the contributions of all those who have affected my thinking on accounting matters over the years. My co-authors on prior editions, Homer Kripke and Paul Foster, provided immense knowledge from the real worlds of finance and accounting as well as securities and creditors' rights law. In addition, numerous colleagues from law schools and business schools as well as corporate practitioners have provided advice which has found its way into this edition. Several members of Coopers & Lybrand read every chapter of the prior edition, providing many helpful suggestions which continue here.

Special thanks are owing to Professor Richard L. Kaplan, not only for his suggestion of the new title to the book, but also for his insights and suggestions over the years, many of which have found their way into this edition.

My student assistant, Leroy Llewellyn, worked tirelessly in preparing the final manuscript for publication, for which I am grateful. Finally, I wish to acknowledge the superb assistance from the cheerful and professional secretarial staff of the University of Colorado Law School, Kay Wilkie, Marge Brunner and Anne Guthrie, who were always gracious in typing and retyping what I have sometimes suspected may have been less interesting to them than they were willing to reveal.

TJF

Foreword

The technicalities of accounting are often beyond the interests and needs of most lawyers-to-be. In recent years, these technicalities have increased geometrically, reflecting the more general trend toward increased complexity in our various forms of business regulation, of which financial accounting is an integral part. Accordingly, the book's title emphasizes two interrelated focal points. First are accounting *issues*, those questions of financial practice that generate controversy, spawn differences, and have consequences beyond the mechanics. The second area of focus is on what *lawyers* need to know, can use, or will encounter in their professional activities as lawyers.

An analogy might be drawn to the study of a foreign language, for accounting is often described as the language of business. No one would expect to master a new language after a two or three hour course, and one should not expect to master all the intricacies of financial accounting in that span either. But the assumption of this book, which differentiates it from texts prepared for accountants, is that such mastery is not really necessary. The endeavor is to make lawyers conversant with accounting, but not fluent in it.

As a result, the consequences of accounting issues are emphasized over the technical refinements. This focus should not be taken to imply superficial treatment, however. The importance of accounting information will vary with the context, of course, but it will still be considerable for a contract drafter working on executive compensation agreements, a labor lawyer advising on profit-sharing proposals, a regulator of environmental conduct, a tax attorney, or a litigator disputing an insurance claim for destroyed assets.

Other perspectives are included as well. Strange as it may seem to many law students, there are very important public policy implications of most financial accounting issues. For better or worse, the resolution of these issues affects how our society responds to energy shortages, fiscal debacles like the savings and loan mess, concerns for corporate social responsibility, general problems of capital allocation, and other wealth distribution issues. These implications are often paramount in assessing the paths that financial accounting has taken or is contemplating.

More generally, the development of financial accounting can be seen as a microcosm of society's relationship to business entities. The role of private management of corporations, the different pressures that public stock ownership brings to bear, the use or non-use of government resources, and the decisions actually reached say much about how business is regulated in the post-capitalist society of the 1990's. This perspective is particularly important to lawyers who expect to serve as informed citizens advocating various views in the full range of forums available—from town meetings to corporate boardrooms to rate commissions to legislatures at every level.

Finally, but by no means least (if however somewhat less lofty), is the role of accounting information in managing financial investments. Whether for oneself, one's family, one's clients, or persons to whom one owes a fiduciary duty, lawyers regularly use financial information in making and monitoring personal investments. While this book makes no pretense to being a course in "Personal Financial Planning," accounting implications for that subject are never far away, and items of significance to that perspective are regularly highlighted. Indeed, certain questions of financial statement presentation and disclosure can be understood only in the context of personal investment decision-making.

Summary of Contents

Table of Contents

*See first page, paragraph 2 of the Preface.

PART C. COST ALLOCATION

*See first page, paragraph 2 of the Preface.

*See first page, paragraph 2 of the Preface.

*See first page, paragraph 2 of the Preface.

*See first page, paragraph 2 of the Preface.

PART E. MERGERS, ACQUISITIONS AND INVESTMENTS

*See first page, paragraph 2 of the Preface.

PART G. ADVANCED PROBLEMS

*See first page, paragraph 2 of the Preface.

*See first page, paragraph 2 of the Preface.

*

Table of Abbreviations

A number of abbreviations are used throughout this book, as follows:

AAA: American Accounting Association, an organization principally of teachers of accounting.

AAER: An Accounting and Auditing Enforcement Release, published by the Securities and Exchange Commission.

AcSEC: Accounting Standards Executive Committee, (of the AICPA—see below).

AICPA: The American Institute of Certified Public Accountants, the principle organization of practicing accountants.

APB: The Accounting Principles Board of the AICPA.

APB STATEMENT: These are statements of the APB which do not have the mandatory force given to APB Opinions as discussed in the Appendix to APB Opinion No. 6.

ARB: An Accounting Research Bulletin issued by a predecessor of the Accounting Principles Board. All of the ARB's were adopted by the APB with some modifications, in APB Opinion No. 6.

ARS: Accounting Research Study: one of a series of studies, many of them of book length, published by the Director of Accounting Research of the AICPA, but not having the status of pronouncements of the APB. Their purpose is to provide the research leading to Opinions of the APB.

ASR: An Accounting Series Release of the SEC, many of which have been incorporated in the SEC's Codification of Financial Reporting Policies (instituted in 1982). Other ASR's have been rescinded as obsolete or otherwise superseded. We continue to cite to ASR's as their original text is valuable. CCH has preserved the ASR's intact in a separate Transfer Binder volume. For an explanation of the codification process and the status of ASR's and FRR's, see FRR No. 1 (1982) at 5 Fed.Sec.L.Rep. (CCH) ¶ 72,401.

ATB: An Accounting Terminology Bulletin issued by a predecessor of the Accounting Priniples Board. ATB's have not been formally adopted by the APB.

AudSEC: Auditing Standards Executive Committee (of AICPA).

FASB: Financial Accounting Standards Board.

FRR: A Financial Reporting Release of the SEC, replacing the ASR series.

GAAP: Generally Accepted Accounting Principles.

GAAS: Generally Accepted Auditing Standards.

IRC: Internal Revenue Code of 1954.

IRS: Internal Revenue Service.

J. ACCOUNTANCY: The Journal of Accountancy, the monthly publication of the AICPA.

Reg. S–X: Regulation S–X issued by the SEC, governing the form and content of financial statements filed with it under the Securities Act of 1933 and the Securities Exchange Act of 1934. Reg. S–X is published in the Code of Federal Regulations as CFR Part 210, Title 17.

SAB: Staff Accounting Bulletin (SEC staff).

SAP: Statement of Auditing Procedure (AICPA).

SAS: Statement of Auditing Standards (AICPA).

SFAC: Statement of Financial Accounting Concepts of the FASB.

SFAS: Statement of Financial Accounting Standards, of the FASB.

SOP: Statement of Position by AcSEC.

Table of Cases

The principal cases are in bold type. Cases cited or discussed in the text are roman type. References are to pages. Cases cited in principal cases and within other quoted materials are not included.

ACCOUNTING ISSUES FOR LAWYERS

TEACHING MATERIALS

Fourth Edition

*

Part A

INTRODUCTION

Chapter I

FUNDAMENTALS OF BOOKKEEPING

OBJECTIVES

1. Understand the fundamentals of the recordkeeping process, from recording individual business transactions to preparing a company's financial statements.

2. Decipher the jargon of basic accounting, including the accrual method that recognizes income and expense independently of the receipt or payment of cash.

RELEVANCE FOR LAWYERS

Financial statements describe the economic status of a commercial enterprise and are used by lawyers in the entire range of business transactions, including the borrowing and lending of funds, mergers and acquisitions, the formation and liquidation of business entities, the negotiation of labor agreements and compensation contracts, and securities and utility regulation and taxation of business activities, as well as the evaluation of investment opportunities. Understanding the mechanics of the accounting process and its terminology is critical to using and interpreting financial statements in these contexts and to appreciating their limitations.

A. INTRODUCTION

Because balance sheets, some using numbers running into the hundreds of millions of dollars, appear to balance perfectly, a newcomer to accounting might approach it with the assumption that the apparent precision of the numbers indicates that accounting is an exact science. In a sense this appearance of scientific precision is justified, for the technique of accounting (known as double-entry bookkeeping) insures that the numbers on the balance sheet will balance. But the *source* of these numbers is anything but scientific. While the numbers must be rooted in events in the real world, the *interpretation* of the events and their translation into numbers, and the circumstances under which new numbers will be recognized and recorded are matters not of science but of policy, although the underlying policies have not been fully developed as yet. Accounting rules based on shifting policy grounds are being continually legislated.

Yes, *legislated*! This is largely a *legislative* course, in which most of the rules we study are *codified* and *enacted* by a quasi-public body known as the Financial Accounting Standards Board (FASB) (and its predecessors) under the pressures of, with the support of, and with enforcement of the rules by a United States public administrative agency, the Securities and Exchange Commission (SEC).

We have said the policy grounds are shifting. The accounting profession has from time to time attempted to develop a coherent organizing theory for accounting and in fact has published something known as the "Conceptual Framework Study," which involves what may result in major changes in accounting in the future. On the other hand many old hands of accounting do not believe the study to be useful. In any event, the beginning reader will not be able to follow a discussion of the Conceptual Framework or the relationship of the FASB and the SEC until he or she first gets a feel for our subject by learning the *technique* of maintaining books of account and producing financial statements, that is, the art of bookkeeping. We turn to that technique and will return to these other matters in the following chapters.

B. A PRELIMINARY VIEW OF FINANCIAL STATEMENTS

Any enterprise, commercial, governmental, charitable or other, would quickly slip out of control if its financial status were unknown to its managers.[a] Even the smallest sole proprietor finds it necessary to calculate receipts and expenditures, to check inventory and to perform other accounting functions regularly for purposes of making decisions

---

a. These materials are concerned principally with accounting for business enterprises not non-businesses like governments or charitable hospitals, etc. Nevertheless, most of what is said applies to accounting for these non-business entities.

and reports to governmental agencies. When an enterprise achieves a size entailing the employment of several persons, it quickly becomes apparent that management would be at sea without a system of collecting and summarizing data in financial terms.

But accounting is of value not only to management in aiding it to make business decisions; as any business grows in size, accounting information becomes important for others, such as employee-beneficiaries of profit sharing plans, labor union bargaining agents, Internal Revenue agents, state and local government taxing officers, present and prospective shareholders or bondholders, numerous state and national regulatory commissions, bank loan officers, economists, antitrust administrators, the Securities and Exchange Commission and state securities commissions. Lawyers as representatives of such users are expected to have a working knowledge of accounting.

Lawyers also have a need to understand accounting as policy makers and advisors. It is one of our important instruments of social regulation, like law, economics, or religion. We could not function without a system of abstraction by which the diverse worlds of agriculture, manufacturing, transportation, communication, distribution, retailing, finance and banking can be reduced to a system of numbers for comparison of companies and for comparison of the same company at different periods. Accounting is that system. As in the case of other disciplines, it must be understood by lawyers so that it may be utilized in the numerous tasks lawyers perform in these various aspects of social regulation. A distinctive benefit of the study of accounting is that it provides a comparative study of another system. Much may be learned from accounting which is relevant to law with its many parallels.

Two sets of data are of great importance to users of financial information: (1) the worth of the business and its assets and liabilities at a given time; and (2) the extent to which that worth has increased or decreased over a period, i.e., its income or loss (sometimes referred to as "negative income") for a period. For the moment we will assume that these terms are unambiguous and the subject of general agreement. Their meaning will be our major concern in the subsequent chapters, but in this first chapter we are interested in the mechanism by which these concepts are recorded and summarized.

The financial accounting with which lawyers are principally concerned and which we will study chiefly in this book is that for commercial businesses usually in corporate form. The same bookkeeping is done for businesses operated by individuals (called "sole proprietors") and for partnerships. To illustrate in the simplest possible context the basic accounting concepts of net worth and income, let us start with the case of a sole proprietor. We shall exclude the proprietor's personal income from his or her job, such activities as investing in securities or bank accounts, and personal expenses, and shall include only the business of owning and renting a small apartment building because it is that business in which we are interested.

A computation of net worth of the proprietorship (here called "Owner's Equity") may be made by taking the difference between assets and liabilities. It might look like this:

Joan Proprietor, Doing Business as Crest Apartments: Computation of Owner's Equity, December 31, 19X1 [b]

Land and apartment building	$100,000	(Assets)
Less Debt (mortgage note)	65,000	(Liabilities)
Equals Owners' Equity	$ 35,000	(Net Worth)

One may see that this is simply the expression:

ASSETS minus LIABILITIES = OWNER'S EQUITY
(or NET WORTH)

This is the fundamental accounting equation; it merely states the simple logical fact that the net worth of an entity *must* be the difference between its assets and liabilities. The terms of the equation may be rearranged to say the same thing in a different mode:

ASSETS = LIABILITIES plus NET WORTH

In this format it parallels the typical form of the accounting balance sheet, so named because the two sides are equal, or "balance." It is portrayed as follows:

Joan Proprietor, d.b.a. Crest Apartments Balance Sheet at December 31, 19X1

Assets		**Liabilities & Owner's Equity**	
		Liabilities:	
Land and apartment building	$100,000	Mortgage notes	$ 65,000
		Owner's Equity	35,000
	$100,000		$100,000

Another, perhaps less common form, will list assets, liabilities and net worth as in the initial form of the equation above.

Joan Proprietor, d.b.a. Crest Apartments Balance Sheet at December 31, 19X1

Assets:	
Land and Apartment Building	$100,000
Less Liabilities:	
Mortgage Notes	65,000
Owner's Equity	$ 35,000

All bookkeeping is based on this formula and has as its ultimate goal the preparation of a balance sheet for the particular entity. See infra p. 526 for a much more complex balance sheet which nevertheless follows the same

---

b. In this explanation, to aid exposition we sometimes shall designate years by no- tations such as 19X1 to indicate the first of a series, 19X2 for the second, etc.

basic format. One may see that he or she could feed in incorrect or badly estimated numbers as to any of these terms, and the subtraction shown above would take place, resulting in an owner's equity which always balances perfectly regardless of such errors. For the time being, as stated, we shall ignore the problems implied by this fact.

Now let us consider the second item of interest we noted above—the extent of increase or decrease in net worth over a period of time. This may be described as the "income" of the entity for the period (whether positive or negative), assuming no dividends have been paid. We shall see that the increase or decrease may be calculated merely by finding net increase or decrease in net worth from the balance sheet at the beginning to that at the ending of the period. Or, again, by simple logic it may be calculated by finding the difference between revenues and expenses for the period. [You may see the equivalence of the two techniques of determining income by noting that, if revenues exceed expenses for the period, the net worth of the entity must have increased by precisely that amount.]

Fundamentally, every business receives an inflow of revenues from sales, from performance of services, from rents for the use of property, from interest for the use of money, etc. And it suffers an outflow of expenses, such as those listed below. For Joan Proprietor, in the next year after 19X1, we might have:

Joan Proprietor, d.b.a. Crest Apartments Income Statement for the Year Ended December 31, 19X2

Rent Revenues		$60,000
Less Expenses:		
Heat and hot water	$25,000	
Janitor, cleaning and repairs	25,000	
Interest on mortgage note	1,500	
Real estate taxes	5,000	
Depreciation	1,500	
		58,000
Net Income		$ 2,000

Given the net income for 19X2, the December 31, 19X2 balance sheet might [c] appear as follows:

Joan Proprietor, d.b.a. Crest Apartments Balance Sheet at December 31, 19X2

Assets:			Liabilities & Owner's Equity:	
Cash		$ 3,500	Liabilities:	
Land and Apartment			Mortgage Notes	$ 65,000
Building	100,000			
Less Depreciation	1,500		Owner's Equity	37,000
	$ 98,500			
		$102,000		$102,000

c. We say "might" because the $3,500 shown here as "Cash" might instead have been used to, say, purchase another asset, or pay off some of the mortgage note, or to

As may be seen, the difference in Owner's Equity from the beginning of year, 19X2 (which is identical with the end of year 19X1), is also the amount of the $2,000 Net Income shown on the Income Statement.

The accounting for a corporation is basically no different from the above. The owner's equity or net worth of a corporation is divided into shares, or classes of shares, called shares of stock, which can be held by one or a few or a vast number of persons. It is called Shareholders' Equity or Stockholders' Equity on the balance sheet. A simplified corporate balance sheet and corporate income statement appear below.

Plimpton Paper Clip Corporation Balance Sheet at December 31, 19X1

Assets:		Liabilities:	
Cash	$ 12,000	Accounts Payable	$ 20,000
Accounts Receivable	20,000	Bonds Payable	40,000
Inventory	10,000		
Plant and Equipment	75,000		
		Total Liabilities	$ 60,000
		Stockholders' Equity:	
		Common Stock	$ 50,000
		Retained Earnings	7,000
		Total Stockholders' Equity	$ 57,000
		Total Liabilities and Stock-	
Total Assets	$117,000	holders' Equity	$117,000

Plimpton Paper Clip Corporation Income Statement for the Year Ending December 31, 19X1

Sales Revenue		$150,000
Less: Cost of Goods Sold	$75,000	
Office Expense	10,000	
Supplies Expense	4,000	
Wage Expense	12,000	
Tax Expense	20,000	
		121,000
Earnings		$ 29,000

Notice that the balance sheet purports to be a statement of financial condition at a particular instant in time—the end of the accounting period—and that the income statement reflects the results of operations over a period of time. Note also that the difference between Assets ($117,000) and Liabilities ($60,000) is the Stockholders' Equity, or Net Worth, ($57,000) composed of the original investment ($50,000) plus earnings from inception retained in the business and not yet paid out to stockholders ($7,000).

make a distribution to Joan Proprietor, or any combination of these transactions, each of which would have resulted in a different configuration of numbers on the balance sheet.

But there seems to be an inconsistency between the two statements. The income statement shows Earnings of $29,000 while the balance sheet shows Retained Earnings of only $7,000.

A third statement should clarify the reason for the discrepancy:

Plimpton Paper Clip Corporation Statement of Earnings Retained in the Business for the Year Ending December 31, 19X1

Balance of Retained Earnings, beginning of year	$ 0
Earnings for the year	29,000
Less: Dividends distributed to shareholders	22,000
Balance of Retained Earnings, December 31, 19X1	$ 7,000

This statement reconciles the income statement amount of Earnings ($29,000) with the balance sheet amount of *Retained* Earnings by showing that $22,000 of Earnings were not retained but were paid out as dividends to shareholders.

Note that the amount of cash shown in the balance sheet does not coincide with either the amount of Earnings ($29,000) or the amount of Retained Earnings ($7,000). It is important to recognize that Retained Earnings are seldom present as cash, for the cash has usually been reinvested in other assets of the business. A fourth statement, the "statement of cash flows," reconciles these changes. This statement will be discussed later in Chapter X as it is extremely difficult to understand without more background than it is now efficient to set forth.

C.   DOUBLE–ENTRY BOOKKEEPING

The technique for collecting data in a form suitable for making up the financial statements is known as "double-entry bookkeeping." It is the only form of bookkeeping acceptable in common use.

One can best understand the conveniences of double-entry bookkeeping if we illustrate some of the difficulties of attempting to get along without it. For this purpose, we will work with the balance sheet, since it expresses the fundamental accounting equation from which double-entry bookkeeping is derived and on which it depends.

As has been seen, the balance sheet sets forth assets, liabilities, and the difference between these two, net worth. The term "net worth" is passing out of use because, as we shall see in later chapters, under currently accepted concepts the difference between assets and liabilities bears little relation to the actual worth of a business. For this reason accountants use terms such as "equity" or, more specifically, to designate equity in a particular type of business organization, "proprietorship" or "owner's equity" when referring to the net worth of a sole proprietor, "partnership equity" for partnerships, or "stockholders' equity" and "equity" for corporations.

As we have said, changing to the corporate terminology, the most common form of balance sheet arranges the terms of the accounting equation as follows:

$$\text{Assets} = \text{Liabilities} + \text{Stockholders' Equity}$$

with the consequence that the form of the statement shows an equality of these elements, balancing like weights on a chemist's scale.

Assets:		Liabilities:	
Cash	$2,000	Accounts Payable	$2,000
Inventory	1,000	Notes Payable	2,000
Land	2,000	Total Liabilities	$4,000
Machinery	3,000		
		Stockholders' Equity:	
		Capital Stock	$3,000
		Retained Earnings	1,000
		Total Stockholders' Equity	$4,000
		Total Liabilities	
Total Assets	$8,000	and Stockholders' Equity	$8,000

[D615]

Numerous things can be done to the balance sheet and it will still balance. Pursuing our analogy to weights on a chemist's scale, we might practice maintaining the balance while adding and removing weights:

(1) Take away $500 of Cash and use it to buy $500 of Inventory. Both sides will still balance at a weight of $8,000 because one asset, Inventory, has been increased and another asset, Cash, correspondingly decreased, leaving the total at the bottom of the left side unchanged and leaving the entire right side unchanged. We may show this transaction directly on the balance sheet. (In this and the following examples, the new dollar figures resulting from each transaction are denoted by the parenthetic numbers to their left, with those parenthetic numbers corresponding to the numbers of paragraphs in the text.)

Assets:			**Liabilities:**	
Cash		$2,000	Accounts Payable	$2,000
	(1)	$1,500		
			Notes Payable	2,000
Inventory		1,000		
	(1)	1,500	Total Liabilities	$4,000
Land		2,000	**Stockholders' Equity:**	
Machinery		3,000	Capital Stock	$3,000
			Retained Earnings	1,000
			Total Equity	$4,000
			Total Liabilities and Stockholders'	
Total Assets		$8,000	Equity	$8,000

(2) Now use $200 of Cash to pay Accounts Payable of $200. This leaves Cash of $1,300 and Accounts Payable of $1,800. The balance sheet now balances with each side weighing a total of $7,800, i.e., the same amount or weight has been taken away from each side.

Assets:			Liabilities:		
Cash		~~$2,000~~	Accounts Payable		~~$2,000~~
	(1)	~~$1,500~~		(2)	$1,800
	(2)	$1,300			
Inventory		~~1,000~~	Notes Payable		2,000
	(1)	1,500			
			Total Liabilities		~~$4,000~~
Land		2,000		(2)	$3,800
Machinery		3,000	Stockholders' Equity:		
			Capital Stock		$3,000
			Retained Earnings		1,000
			Total Equity		$4,000
			Total Liabilities and Stockholders'		
Total Assets		~~$8,000~~	Equity		~~$8,000~~
	(2)	$7,800		(2)	$7,800

(3) Next we obtain new Inventory for $400 and agree to pay for it next month, creating an Account Payable. Inventory is now up to $1,900 and Accounts Payable up to $2,200. Our balance sheet will still balance, now at $8,200 on each side.

Assets:			Liabilities:		
Cash		~~$2,000~~	Accounts Payable		~~$2,000~~
	(1)	~~$1,500~~		(2)	~~$1,800~~
	(2)	$1,300		(3)	$2,200
Inventory		~~1,000~~	Notes Payable		2,000
	(1)	~~1,500~~			
	(3)	1,900	Total Liabilities		~~$4,000~~
				(2)	~~$3,800~~
Land		2,000		(3)	$4,200
Machinery		3,000	Stockholders' Equity:		
			Capital Stock		$3,000
			Retained Earnings		1,000
			Total Equity		$4,000
			Total Liabilities and Stockholders'		
Total Assets		~~$8,000~~	Equity		~~$8,000~~
	(2)	~~$7,800~~		(2)	~~$7,800~~
	(3)	$8,200		(3)	$8,200

(4) Then a creditor holding a note payable for $1,000 accepts capital stock in payment. Notes Payable goes down to $1,000 and Capital Stock goes up to $4,000. These transactions are offsetting

transactions on the right side of the balance sheet, leaving the total of each side unchanged at $8,200.

Assets:			Liabilities:		
Cash		~~$2,000~~	Accounts Payable		~~$2,000~~
	(1)	~~$1,500~~		(2)	~~$1,800~~
	(2)	$1,300		(3)	$2,200
Inventory		~~1,000~~	Notes Payable		~~2,000~~
	(1)	~~1,500~~		(4)	1,000
	(3)	1,900			
			Total Liabilities		~~$4,000~~
Land		2,000		(2)	~~$3,800~~
				(3)	~~$4,200~~
Machinery		3,000		(4)	$3,200
			Stockholders' Equity:		
			Capital Stock		~~$3,000~~
				(4)	$4,000
			Retained Earnings		1,000
			Total Equity		~~$4,000~~
				(4)	$5,000
			Total Liabilities and Stockholders'		
Total Assets		~~$8,000~~	Equity		~~$8,000~~
	(2)	~~$7,800~~		(2)	~~$7,800~~
	(3)	$8,200		(3)	$8,200

The two sides *always* stay in balance. This is because Net Worth is a residual figure which is *always* the difference between Assets and Liabilities no matter what their amounts. It follows that every change in an account is counterbalanced by a contra entry, thus maintaining the basic accounting equation. If one of the three elements of the equation changes, there may be an offsetting change elsewhere in the same element (e.g., in transaction (1) above, Cash is reduced, but Inventory is increased, leaving the total of the element, Assets, unchanged). But if only one component of the element (say, Assets) changes, the equation *requires* one of the other elements (either Liabilities or Stockholders' Equity) to change, as in transactions (2), (3) and (4) above.

Let us test this. Assume that the business has a wastebasket fire, and $500 of office furniture is destroyed. Surely this must be a case where nothing has changed except that assets have been reduced? Not so. If there is full recovery of the loss through insurance, the total of assets remains unchanged because the asset, Furniture, is replaced by another asset, an Account Receivable (or, eventually, Cash) from the insurance company. Even if there is no insurance, assets have indeed been reduced by $500, but so has Net Worth or Proprietor's Equity been correspondingly reduced!

The fact that the system is based on the accounting equation, means that *two* balancing events *must* and *do* happen in every transaction, to keep the balance sheet balancing. This is much of what is meant by the term "*double-entry* bookkeeping." We shall now explore the remainder of the concept of "double-entry."

By this time our balance sheet appears rather cluttered. It is obvious that a General Motors Corporation or even a neighborhood retail store cannot keep its records by constantly marking up the balance sheet as above. So we should take each of the items off the balance sheet and transfer it to a separate piece of paper where we have room to deal with it. The separate record of each item is called an "account." But if all we do is transfer items from our balance sheet to separate pieces of paper, we still have a problem. It would not be satisfactory to have a Cash account look like this:

Cash

	$~~$2,000~~
(1)	~~1,500~~
(2)	1,300

This is still cluttered. A permanent legible record of the changes is as important as showing the present balance of an item; so we adopt the practice of having a separate page for each item and two sides to each page, one for additions, the other for reductions, thus:

Cash

$2,000	$500 (1)
	200 (2)

A permanent record is needed to enable the company to reconstruct its business activities. Such reconstructions are used in filing tax returns and in preparing reports to securities officials, utility rate boards, and other interested parties, including creditors and stockholders. For such purposes, the final "bottom line" result, in the above example, $1,300, is not sufficiently informative. That figure could have been the result of an opening cash balance of $100,000 and expenditures of $98,700—obviously a very different situation than the example given. Accordingly, being able to reconstruct the flow of money transactions requires records that disclose more than just a net final balance.

The $2,000 figure is from our opening balance sheet on page 9. The numbers in parentheses refer to the transactions numbered (1) and (2) above.

Since the Cash account appears on the left side of the balance sheet, the additions are on the left side, and the reductions are on the right side. The balance in an asset account at any moment is the sum of the items on the left side of the account less the sum of the items on the right side, which you can verify from the Cash account on the balance sheet on page 10.

Since liabilities and equities are on the right side of the balance sheet, opposite to assets, additions to items in these categories are on the right side and reductions are on the left side, thus:

Accounts Payable

(2) $200	$2,000
	400 (3)

The balance in a liability or equity account at any moment is the sum of the items on the right side less the sum of the items on the left side, which you can verify from the Accounts Payable account on the balance sheet on page 10.

Accounting terminology uses the term "debit" (abbreviated "Dr." from the Renaissance Italian, "debitor") for an entry on the left side of any account, and the term "credit" (abbreviated "Cr.") for an entry on the right side of any account. The term "charge" is sometimes used instead of "debit." [d] It is counterproductive to seek to find meanings for these terms other than "left" or "right". This terminology applies to all left side and all right side entries, respectively. But note that a debit to an asset account is an increase in the account, while a debit to a liability account or to an equity account is a decrease in the account. The reverse is true for credits.

Using the three types of accounts we have identified—assets, liabilities, and equities—and remembering their positions on the balance sheet, it is apparent that only a limited number of types of offsetting entries are possible. To illustrate, if any asset (e.g., Inventory) increases, then one of three balancing changes must occur: (1) another asset is reduced (e.g., Cash is paid for the Inventory); or (2) a liability increases (e.g., a liability to pay for the Inventory, called an Account Payable, arises); or (3) equity increases (e.g., the Inventory was contributed by the owner and increases the Owner's Worth).

We may chart all the possibilities as follows, each dotted line connecting the two aspects of any one transaction:

d. When you deposit money in your checking account, the bank "credits" its own Deposits Payable Account, a liability (of the bank to you), giving rise to the expression, "we have credited your account." When you write a check, on receipt, the bank "charges" or "debits" that same account. It is not a "charge to your account" although so described in notices to you. It is a charge to the bank's own account for the Deposits Payable to you; the bank keeps its own books, not yours.

Similarly a department store "charge account" is on the store's books. Hence also the expression, "charge it to my account" means, "on your books." On your own books, if you kept such, you would charge or debit an asset account for whatever you had bought, and credit the liability to the store.

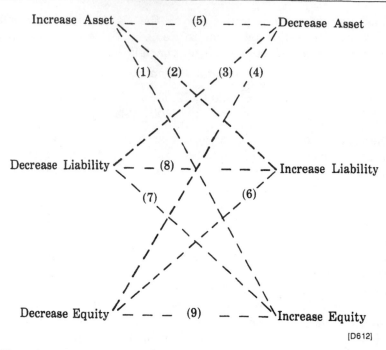

[D612]

The nine possible combinations, or transactions, are numbered in the chart to correspond to the descriptions below. Taking each of the nine separately, then, let us see the effects on a balance sheet. Observe the double aspect of each transaction as well as the change of date on each balance sheet.

(1) Let us assume that X Corp. is incorporated in the state of Delaware on January 3, 19X1, with authority to issue 1,000 shares of common stock with a par value of $10 per share and 1,000 shares of preferred stock with a par value of $5 per share.[e] Sam Stockholder pays $1,000 cash for 100 shares of common stock. At this point a balance sheet would appear as follows:

X Corp. Balance Sheet at Jan. 3, 19X1

Assets:		Liabilities:	$ 0
Cash	$1,000	Stockholders' Equity:	
		Preferred Stock:	
		Authorized: 1,000 shares, $5 par; none issued.	
		Common Stock:	
		Authorized: 1,000 shares, $10 par; Issued and Outstanding: 100 shares	1,000
Total	$1,000	Total	$1,000

Note the comparative amounts of the debits and credits that are used in this opening transaction and in each one of the other transactions that we will record. This one corresponds to the line marked (1) on our chart. We may record the transaction as follows:

Jan. 3, 19X1   Dr. Cash [increase
           asset] $1,000
       Cr. Common Stock
       [increase equity] $1,000

For present purposes, it is sufficient to note that when a corporation is formed, a charter (or articles of incorporation) is certified by a state official (who may be titled "Corporations Commissioner," "Secretary of State" or the like, depending on the state) when it is filed. That charter authorizes the corporation to issue stock on certain terms and in certain numbers. That is the "authorized stock" (or "authorized capital" or "authorized capital stock").

Corporation codes usually provide that the board of directors may cause issuance by the officers of any or all of the authorized stock, which, when issued, is referred to as "issued" stock.

If there is only one class of stock, it is designated "common stock," or "capital stock." If more than one class is authorized, the difference will be in terms of prior rights on liquidation or some other contractual term such as a prior right to receive a stated annual dividend before any dividend may be paid on the other class of stock. The most junior class of stock usually will be referred to as "common" stock and the senior classes as "preferred" because of their preferential rights. There are sometimes sub-classes of stock which, because it is hard to say that one is junior to the other, are often designated as "Class A common," "Class B common," etc.

"Par" value refers to the dollar amount, if any, designated in the charter for the stock (common or preferred). The function of par is largely of historical interest now, as will be seen in Chapter VIII.[f]

(2) On January 4, X Corp. borrows $5,000 from James Creditor on open account (that is, without a note or other instrument evidencing the liability). The balance sheet then appears:

Jan. 4, 19X1

X Corp. Balance Sheet at ~~**Jan. 3, 19X1**~~

Assets:			Liabilities:		$ ~~0~~
Cash		~~$1,000~~	Account Payable		
	(2)	$6,000	J. Creditor	(2)	$5,000
			Stockholders' Equity:		
			Common Stock:		
			Authorized: 1,000 shares,		
			$10 par; Issued and		
			Outstanding: 100		
			shares		1,000
Total		~~$1,000~~	Total		~~$1,000~~
		$6,000			$6,000

f. For a more detailed description of "authorized stock," "par value," "common" and "preferred" stock, see Chapter VIII infra.

The debit and credit for this transaction, classified on the chart at line (2), are:

Jan. 4, 19X1　　Dr. Cash [increase
　　　　　　　　　　　asset]　　　$5,000
　　　　　　　Cr. Account Payable
　　　　　　　　[increase liability]　　　$5,000

(3) On January 15, X Corp. repays Creditor $3,000 of the $5,000 owed to him.

Jan. 15, 19X1
~~**Jan. 4, 19X1**~~

X Corp. Balance Sheet at ~~**Jan. 3, 19X1**~~

Assets:			Liabilities:		$　0
Cash		~~$1,000~~	Account Payable		
	(2)	~~$6,000~~	J. Creditor	(2)	~~$5,000~~
	(3)	$3,000		(3)	2,000
			Stockholders' Equity:		
			Common Stock:		
			Authorized: 1,000 shares,		
			$10 par; Issued and		
			Outstanding: 100		
			shares		1,000
Total		~~$1,000~~	Total		~~$1,000~~
		~~$6,000~~			~~$6,000~~
		$3,000			$3,000

The debit and credit for this transaction, classified on the chart at line (3), are:

Jan. 15, 19X1 Dr. Accounts Payable
　　　　　　　　[decrease liability] $3,000
　　　　　　　Cr. Cash [decrease
　　　　　　　　　asset]　　　　$3,000

(4) (For this and the following five entries, since it is cumbersome to show by crossed-out figures how the original balance sheet is changed, we shall simply make up a new balance sheet for each transaction without depicting and then crossing out the old figures. The figures that have been changed from the last balance sheet are shown with asterisks (*).)

On January 16, Sam Stockholder sells back five of his shares for $50 cash to X Corp. which immediately elects to cancel them.

X Corp. Balance Sheet at Jan. 16, 19X1

Assets:		Liabilities:	
Cash	$2,950*	Account Payable	
		J. Creditor	$2,000
		Stockholders' Equity:	
		Common Stock:	
		Authorized: 1,000 shares, $10 par; Issued and Outstanding: 95* shares	950*
Total	$2,950*	Total	$2,950*

The debit and credit for this transaction are classified on the chart at line (4):

Jan. 16, 19X1 Dr. Common Stock
              [decrease equity] $ 50
       Cr. Cash [decrease asset] $ 50

(5) On January 17, X Corp. buys a desk for $200 cash.

X Corp. Balance Sheet at Jan. 17, 19X1

Assets:		Liabilities:	
Cash	$2,750*	Account Payable	
Office Equipment	200*	J. Creditor	$2,000
		Stockholders' Equity:	
		Common Stock:	
		Authorized: 1,000 shares, $10 par; Issued and Outstanding: 95 shares	950
Total	$2,950	Total	$2,950

The debit and credit for this transaction, classified on the chart at line (5), are:

Jan. 17, 19X1   Dr. Office Equipment
              [increase asset] $ 200
       Cr. Cash [decrease asset] $ 200

(6) January 19, Sam Stockholder sells back to X Corp. another five shares on open account. X Corp. immediately elects to cancel these shares.

X Corp. Balance Sheet at Jan. 19, 19X1

Assets:		Liabilities:	
Cash	$2,750	Account Payable	
Office Equipment	200	J. Creditor	$2,000
		Account Payable	
		S. Stockholder	50*
		Stockholders' Equity:	
		Common Stock:	
		Authorized: 1,000	
		shares, $10 par; Is-	
		sued and Outstand-	
		ing: 90* shares	900*
Total	$2,950	Total	$2,950

Note the debit and credit for this transaction, classified on the chart at line (6):

Jan. 19, 19X1   Dr. Common Stock
                [decrease equity] $ 50
             Cr. Account Payable
                [increase liability] $ 50

(7) On January 21, X Corp. issues ten shares of preferred stock to Sam Stockholder in full payment of his claim for $50.

X Corp. Balance Sheet at Jan. 21, 19X1

Assets:		Liabilities:	
Cash	$2,750	Account Payable	
Office Equipment	200	J. Creditor	$2,000
		Account Payable	
		S. Stockholder	0*
		Stockholders' Equity:	
		Preferred Stock:	
		Authorized: 1,000 shares,	
		$5 par; Issued and Out-	
		standing: 10 shares	50*
		Common Stock:	
		Authorized: 1,000 shares,	
		$10 par; Issued and Out-	
		standing: 90 shares	900
Total	$2,950	Total	$2,950

The debit and credit for this transaction are classified on the chart at line (7):

Jan. 21, 19X1   Dr. Account Payable
               [decrease liability] $ 50
            Cr. Preferred Stock
              [increase equity] $ 50

(8) On January 25, James Creditor requests and receives a promissory note for $2,000 bearing no interest in substitution for his open account claim.

X Corp. Balance Sheet at Jan. 25, 19X1

Assets:		Liabilities:	
Cash	$2,750	Account Payable	
Office Equipment	200	J. Creditor	$ 0*
		Note Payable	
		J. Creditor	2,000*
		Stockholders' Equity:	
		Preferred Stock:	
		Authorized: 1,000 shares, $5 par; Issued and Outstanding: 10 shares	50
		Common Stock:	
		Authorized: 1,000 shares, $10 par; Issued and Outstanding: 90 shares	900
Total	$2,950	Total	$2,950

The debit and credit for this transaction, classified on the chart at line (8), are:

Jan. 25, 19X1 Dr. Account Payable
 [decrease liability] $2,000
　　　Cr. Note Payable [increase liability]　　$2,000

(9) On January 31, Sam Stockholder exchanges five shares of common stock (which are cancelled) for ten shares of preferred.

X Corp. Balance Sheet at Jan. 31, 19X1

Assets:		Liabilities:	
Cash	$2,750	Note Payable	
Office Equipment	200	J. Creditor	$2,000
		Stockholders' Equity:	
		Preferred Stock:	
		Authorized: 1,000 shares, $5 par; Issued and Outstanding: 20* shares	100*
		Common Stock:	
		Authorized: 1,000 shares, $10 par; Issued and Outstanding: 85* shares	850*
Total	$2,950	Total	$2,950

Note the debit and credit for this transaction, classified on the chart at line (9):

Jan. 31, 19X1   Dr. Common Stock

[decrease equity] $ 50

Cr. Preferred Stock

[increase equity] $ 50

You will have noticed that not only does every occurrence have some offsetting occurrence (which follows from the basic accounting equation), but the two occurrences are always on the opposite sides of accounts, i.e., the debits always equal the credits. Looking again at the chart on page 14 and classifying the events according to our rule that asset accounts show additions on the debit side and decreases on the credit side, while liability and equity accounts behave in the reverse fashion, we may derive the following complete list of all possible types of debits and credits:

Debits	**Credits**
Increase Asset	Decrease Asset
Decrease Liability	Increase Liability
Decrease Equity	Increase Equity

Each of the transaction lines in the chart on page 14 and our nine transactions above involve one entry from each of the columns, a debit and a credit. It is impossible to state a transaction in which both offsetting transactions are in the same column. In every transaction, debits equal credits.

Why does it work this way? It follows from the *balancing* of the balance sheet, and from the brilliant concept that the asset accounts behave in reverse fashion to the liability and equity accounts.

The chart on page 14 will therefore show you that, in order to achieve equal debits and credits, any change on one side of an account must be offset by a change on the opposite side of another account. The second account may be on the same side of the balance sheet, which leaves the total of that side (and the other) unchanged; or the second account may be on the opposite side of the balance sheet, which results in equal changes in the totals of both sides.

This is the fundamental point of the system of double-entry bookkeeping; there is little else to the system except its elaboration. We hammer it home because the law student must grasp it intellectually, for he or she will have little time for the practice drilling of a conventional accounting course.

You may now be tempted to say: "So what? What is the importance of this numbers trick?" The answer is that the full system of double-entry bookkeeping can be thought of as an expansion of the balance sheet in our illustration, and the student will be helped to understand or to record more complicated transactions if he or she keeps this always in mind. The technique will turn out to be a marvelously flexible and inventive system for recording and processing dollar symbols for business transactions, as remarkable in its way as a computer. The analogy is apt for the purpose of describing the relationship of bookkeeping to accounting principles. Just as a computer cannot determine the raw data, but can only process the data—correct or incorrect—which are fed into it, so the bookkeeping system can only record and process the data fed into it. The task of selecting and classifying business events into the raw data for the bookkeeping system and measuring them in numbers is the function of accounting principles, and our perception of the economic world largely depends on these accounting principles.

How far the principles in use are agreed upon, and whether they are correct or at least useful, will be our principal concern after we get past the mechanics of bookkeeping.

D. USE OF THE LEDGER AND JOURNAL

You can now appreciate how cumbersome it is to make up a new balance sheet for each transaction and how it would be virtually impossible to do so for a business with even a few hundred transactions per month. As we have already seen, to make the system work better, and to establish a permanent record of the company's transactions, the items of the balance sheet are recorded in separate accounting records classified by subject matter, each item on a separate sheet or sheets, called an *account*. The collection of accounts, whether kept in a bound book, or in a loose-leaf or card system, or in the memory of a computer, is called the *ledger*. It is one of the two basic accounting records. A simple ledger consists of a book of several pages, each one of which represents a separate account; the changes in that account are recorded on it. For example, the ledger for our X Corp. would have separate pages for each account used: Cash, Office Equipment, Account Payable—J. Creditor, Account Payable—S. Stockholder, Note Payable—J. Creditor, Common Stock, and Preferred Stock.

For convenience in noting increases and decreases in each of these accounts, accountants divide each page in such a way that increases are shown in one column and decreases in another. For example, a ledger page for the Cash account might appear as follows after the January 3, 19X1, contribution of $1,000 for capital:

Cash							Account No. 1
Date	Explanation	Folio	Amount	Date	Explanation	Folio	Amount
1/3/X1	Sale of 100 shares $10 par value Common Stock	1	$1,000				

Several features of this ledger page should be noted:

(1) In this form the page is divided into two sides separated by a double vertical line. The "Folio" columns on the ledger pages are used

to note the number of the journal page on which appears the journal entry from which this entry in the ledger account is made. See the discussion of the journal below.

(2) The January 3, 19X1, increase in Cash appears as a debit.

(3) If Cash or any other asset is decreased, as, for example, by the January 15 payment of $3,000 to James Creditor, supra p. 16, the entry would appear as a credit.

(4) As you know, the convention of showing increases in assets on the left is derived from the fact that the balance sheet itself shows positive balances in assets on the left hand side. Decreases in assets, then, are placed on the right. Conversely, increases in liability and equity accounts are shown by credits and decreases by debits for the same reason—conformity to the balance sheet.

If we were to establish separate ledger pages, the nine transactions of X Corp. during January, 19X1, would appear as shown below. In the following form and in most accounting discussion, the full ledger account form shown above is boiled down to a heading, a divider line separating debits and credits, the amounts, and a date or other symbol identifying the transaction. Because of the horizontal and vertical lines, these short forms are known as "T accounts."

Assets:

Liabilities:

Cash

1/3/X1	$1,000	1/15/X1	$3,000
1/4/X1	5,000	1/16/X1	50
		1/17/X1	200

Account Payable—J. Creditor

| 1/15/X1 | $3,000 | 1/4/X1 | $5,000 |
| 1/25/X1 | 2,000 | | |

Office Equipment

| 1/17/X1 | $ 200 | |

Account Payable—S. Stockholder

| 1/21/X1 | $ 50 | 1/19/X1 | $ 50 |

Note Payable—J. Creditor

| | 1/25/X1 | $2,000 |

Stockholders' Equity:

Common Stock $10 Par

1/16/X1	$ 50	1/3/X1	$1,000
1/19/X1	50		
1/31/X1	50		

Preferred Stock $5 Par

| | 1/21/X1 | $ 50 |
| | 1/31/X1 | 50 |

Make sure you understand why each entry appears where it does. You can check the double aspect of each transaction by finding the two entries for each date. In an actual ledger, the folio reference column would facilitate the identification of companion entries.

If on January 31 you were to total the two columns in each of the above T accounts and "strike a balance" (i.e., net one side against the other and show the net balance), the T accounts would each come to a single figure which would appear on either the right or the left hand side. For example, the Cash account could ultimately look like this:

Cash

1/3/X1	$ 1,000	1/15/X1	$ 3,000
1/4/X1	5,000	1/16/X1	50
		1/17/X1	200
	$ 6,000		
	−3,250		$ 3,250
Balance at			
1/31/X1	$ 2,750		

Note that this balance is the same figure that appeared in the Cash account on the final balance sheet at January 31 above when we were making all entries directly to the balance sheet (p. 19). Note also that the T account, unlike the balance sheet, has the benefit of giving us a complete record of all five Cash transactions.

If the only transactions of an enterprise were those of the kind thus far shown, which were merely items taken from the balance sheet to separate ledger sheets for ease in handling, it would be a simple matter to make up a balance sheet at any time from the balances in the accounts.

However, you will notice that none of these transactions shows the business operating in its chosen activity of selling shoes or ships or sealing wax to make a profit. As we shall see after first discussing the other basic account record, the journal, additional groups of *revenue* and *expense* accounts are needed to record a business's profit-making activities, and these specialized accounts must first be pulled together into a *Profit and Loss Account* to determine their ultimate effect on the Stockholders' Equity account so that a new balance sheet can be made up at the end of an operating period.

In the simple set of accounts on p. 22 of this book, the several pairs of events constituting each transaction can be readily found by matching dates. But in a realistic situation there will be hundreds of accounts in a book or on cards, and thousands of entries, and one could not readily find the offsetting entry of a transaction. Therefore, the bookkeeper must keep, in addition to the ledger, a daily record, or *journal,* in which all aspects of every transaction are first recorded chronologically showing the accounts affected and *from there* transferred to the ledger accounts, with notations on the ledger accounts referring to the journal (or "folio") pages where each whole transaction appears. The nine pairs of debit and credit entries on pages 14 to 20 are journal entries.

To make it easy to make this transfer, the conventional journal entry has a standard form that clearly indicates which account is to be debited and which is to be credited. For example, the January 3, 19X1, opening entry for the receipt of $1,000 cash in return for common stock,

p. 14, supra, requires a debit of $1,000 to the Cash account and a credit of $1,000 to Common Stock, and in the journal the entry will appear:

Journal of X Corp.				Pg. 1
Date	**Account Captions and Explanations**	**Folio**	**Debit**	**Credit**
1/3/X1	Cash		$1,000	
	Common Stock, $10 par			$1,000

For our purposes, journal entries will be depicted as follows, without reproducing the form of the journal page:

Jan. 3, 19X1   Cash $1,000
                   Common Stock, $10 par $1,000

Note that both the caption and the amount for the debit are clearly to the left of the caption and the amount for the credit.

If the nature of the transaction does not clearly appear from the accounts and amounts involved, a brief explanation may be added, e.g.:

"To record the sale of 100 shares of common stock upon incorporation, and the receipt of cash therefor from Mr. Sam Stockholder."

The remaining eight journal entries for X Corp. are:

Jan. 3, 19X1   Cash $5,000
                  Account Payable—J. Creditor $5,000
Jan. 15, 19X1   Account Payable—J. Creditor   3,000
                  Cash   3,000
Jan. 16, 19X1   Common Stock, $10 par   50
                  Cash   50
Jan. 17, 19X1   Office Equipment   200
                  Cash   200
Jan. 19, 19X1   Common Stock, $10 par   50
                  Account Payable—S. Stockholder   50
Jan. 21, 19X1   Account Payable—S. Stockholder   50
                  Preferred Stock, $5 par   50
Jan. 25, 19X1   Account Payable—J. Creditor   2,000
                  Note Payable—J. Creditor   2,000
Jan. 31, 19X1   Common Stock, $10 par   50
                  Preferred Stock, $5 par   50

The process of recording the journal entries in the ledger accounts is called "*posting*". When done, the bookkeeper makes a check (✓) in the "Folio" column to show that the entry has been posted. These nine journal entries, when posted to the ledger accounts, will result in the accounts appearing in the form just illustrated on p. 22.

On the accounts themselves, whether the full ledger pages illustrated on p. 21 or T accounts, the source of the entry into the account is shown by a reference to the journal page (or folio) where the whole transaction appears.

Two words of caution are here necessary for the student:

(1) In rapid conversation, accountants in discussion, or the instructor at the blackboard, will sometimes write entries directly into the T accounts without first having recorded the full transaction in a journal entry (following the practice we followed until we introduced the concept of the journal at p. 23). Or the instructor may analyze a transaction by writing the journal entry, without bothering to post it to the T accounts. But as a matter of theory and real practice, *nothing* reaches the accounts except by first having a journal entry showing all accounting aspects of a transaction in one place, from which the information is posted into the accounts; and *nothing* is recorded in journal entries that does not then get posted into the accounts.

(2) Since this concentrated course for lawyers does not permit the long practice drilling of conventional accounting courses, the law student may think that for the abbreviated problems during the course and on examinations, he or she may omit the meticulous process of journalizing and posting, checking the journal entry to show that posting has occurred, and recording the folio reference on the account to show that source of the information. But even on a dozen transactions, this meticulousness is necessary, and in the long run, orderliness in recording the sources of information will save time, in accounting as in law.

One further word on journalizing and posting. The very simple system just described is used by small firms only. Even modest firms elaborate upon this system to use several sub-journals and sub-ledgers. Larger firms change the form of the journals and ledgers to make the record-keeping more efficient. To take one simple example, every check written represents a credit to the account called Cash. Rather than post each entry to the general journal separately, all checks can be recorded in a "Check Register" and treated as a single credit to Cash. And if a separate bank account is used for all wage payments a "Payroll Journal" might be maintained so that the sum of all checks on that account can also be posted as a single debit to Wages Expense.

Many firms use electronic computers to record and store accounting data. Whatever its form, however, any system can be understood best by first understanding the manual system described above since all the others are modifications of it.

In general, lawyers need not master the techniques of electronic bookkeeping. The introduction to the elements of bookkeeping in this book is sufficient to enable lawyers or others to grasp the complex problems of analysis and meaning of accounting to which this book is principally devoted, and these are indeed problems with which the financial lawyer must grapple. Of course, when lawyers get involved in litigation involving accounting, they may have to learn to understand computer bookkeeping, as they do many other technologies. The complexity and lack of visibility of computer bookkeeping may facilitate frauds and there are special auditing difficulties because of electronic data processing.

One final bit of information may be useful. Novices frequently express anxiety over the problem of what names to give to ledger accounts in making journal and ledger entries for classroom and examination exercises. Although there are conventional names for certain accounts like "Cash", "Accounts Payable" and others, you need not concern yourself about the matter since this is a conceptual course and what counts is an understanding of the concepts, not the proper use of conventional account titles. Indeed, you will find that account titles vary substantially from firm to firm, and some do not even use verbal names but employ numbers or letters instead which are identified by name in a "Chart of Accounts." The important thing is not the name of the account, but knowing whether it is an asset, liability, or equity type account.

To test your understanding of the preceding materials, prepare solutions to the following problems. To aid you in your study, suggested solutions to the numbered problems are reproduced in the Appendix to this chapter. The solutions to the lettered problems are not supplied.

Problem One

The Phillips Flea Powder Co., Inc. was organized February 1, and the transactions below occurred during February. Prepare journal entries, post to T accounts, and prepare a balance sheet as of February 28. You may use the account titles in the following chart:

Assets	Liabilities
Cash	Accounts Payable—Clark
Office Equipment	Accounts Payable—Adams Co.
Notes Receivable—Phillips	Notes Payable—Barkley
Factory Equipment	Notes Payable—Clark
Land	**Equity**
Buildings	Common Stock, $1 par

February 1   The Company received from Mr. Phillips $5,000 cash and issued to him 5,000 shares of its common stock of the par value of $1 per share.

         3   Purchased a desk, typewriter, and chair for $250 on credit from Adams Co.

         7   Purchased land and building for $10,000 from Barkley for use in manufacturing flea powder, paying $1,000 cash, the balance by a promissory note due in ten years, secured by a purchase money mortgage. The estimated value of the land is $2,000 and of the building is $8,000.

      18   Paid Adams Co. $100 on account.

      22   Purchased a packaging machine for $500 on open account from Clark.

      26   Gave Clark a promissory note due in six months to evidence the debt to him.

27   Mr. Phillips, in temporary need of cash, borrowed $100 from the firm and gave his promissory demand note bearing no interest in return.

28   Purchased carpeting, chairs, and filing cabinets for $500 cash.

Problem A

(a) The following transactions are entered into by Celestial Tea and Watercress Co. Please journalize, post, and prepare a balance sheet. (Do not concern yourself with the interest on the notes or depreciation.)

January   1   One thousand shares of the ten thousand authorized shares of $1 par value common stock of the company are issued to Diane for $1,000 cash. This is the first transaction by the newly formed company.

2   The company buys vacant farm land from Debra for $500 cash and gives a $9,500 mortgage and promissory note bearing 8½% interest. Installments of principal of $1,000, except the last, which is $500, plus interest, are due on each anniversary of the documents.

3   It is discovered that an easement exists on the land and Debra agrees to reduce the liability to $9,000 as compensation for the breach of warranty. A new note for $9,000 is substituted with all other terms being identical to the original note.

5   Nicole lends $2,000 to Celestial for an unsecured note bearing interest at 9%, interest and principal payable in six months.

7   Nicole exchanges the note for 500 shares of Celestial common stock plus a new note for $1,500 at the same interest and terms.

(b) Which of the nine types of entries discussed in the text is not illustrated in part (a)? Devise transactions which would illustrate the omitted types and give the journal entries.

Problem B

Please prepare journal entries, post to T accounts, and prepare a balance sheet for the following transactions. Ignore depreciation and interest. Assume that the balance sheet prior to any of the transactions appears as follows:

Balance Sheet of Sal's Smoke Shop at June 30

Cash	$ 5,000	Liabilities:		
Inventory	4,000	Accounts Payable—Natalia	$ 1,500
Plant & Equipment	8,000		
		Proprietorship		15,500
Total	$17,000	Total		$17,000

The business is closed for the month of July but, during that period, the following occurred:

July 2   Sal withdrew $2,000 from proprietorship capital for his personal use.

5   He paid $1,000 cash on account to Natalia.

7   He purchased a new counter for $500 on open account from Alessandra's Outfitters Co.

15   Sal put $500 into the business from his own funds.

20   He withdrew $40 worth of merchandise at cost for personal use for which he paid $40 cash to the business.

26   He gave Natalia a 9% promissory note for the amount owing to her, interest and principal amount due in ten months.

E. REVENUE AND EXPENSE ACCOUNTS: CLOSING PROCESS

Thus far we have shown fairly simple entries to balance sheet accounts. The only transactions that have affected equity have been purchases or redemptions of capital stock. We have not yet considered the results of *operating* the business, producing revenues and expenses, leading to profit or loss.

Revenues of the enterprise will increase the balance in the equity section of the balance sheet and expenses will decrease it. To illustrate, assume that a balance sheet for a sole proprietor appears as follows at February 28, 19X1:

John Baker, Consultant Balance Sheet at Feb. 28, 19X1

Cash	$ 5,000	Notes Payable	$14,000
Office Equipment	1,000		
Building	10,000	Owner's Equity	7,000
Land	5,000		
Total	$21,000	Total	$21,000

If during the next month Baker received $275 as a consulting fee, the balance sheet could be changed as follows:

John Baker, Consultant Balance Sheet at Mar. 31, 19X1

Cash	$ 5,275*	Notes Payable	$14,000
Office Equipment	1,000		
Building	10,000	Owner's Equity	7,275*
Land	5,000		
Total	$21,275*	Total	$21,275*

If he had also paid out $200 in cash for secretarial expense during March, it could appear as follows:

John Baker, Consultant Balance Sheet at Mar. 31, 19X1

Cash	$ 5,075*	Notes Payable	$14,000
Office Equipment	1,000		
Building	10,000	Owner's Equity	7,075*
Land	5,000		
Total	$21,075*	Total	$21,075*

An income statement for Baker could be made up from these data and would look like this:

Income Statement of John Baker for the Month of March, 19X1

Revenue from Consulting Service	$275
Less Expenses:	
Secretarial Expense	200
Net Income	$ 75

How would the T accounts have been affected by these two transactions? Before either transaction, the T accounts appeared as below:

Cash				Note Payable	
Opening Balance	$ 5,000			Opening Balance	$14,000

Office Equipment	
Opening Balance	$ 1,000

Building				Owner's Equity	
Opening Balance	$10,000			Opening Balance	$ 7,000

Land	
Opening Balance	$ 5,000

The journal entries for the two transactions might be:

March 10	Cash	$275	
	Owner's Equity		$275
March 27	Owner's Equity	200	
	Cash		200

Then at March 31, the T accounts would look like this:

Cash					Notes Payable	
Opening Balance	$ 5,000	Secretarial Expense	$	200	Opening Balance	$14,000
Revenue from Consulting Service	275					
	$ 5,075					

Office Equipment

Opening Balance $ 1,000	

Building   **Owner's Equity**

Opening Balance $10,000	Secretarial Expense $ 200	Opening Balance $ 7,000
		Revenue from Consulting Services 275
		$ 7,075

Land

Opening Balance $ 5,000	

This process of accounting for expense and revenue by direct charges or credits to the Owner's Equity account does have the merit of illustrating our earlier point that, in the absence of dividends or capital contributions, net income is the difference in Net Worth between the beginning and end of the period. Yet direct charges or credits to equity for numerous transactions have been found cumbersome.

For this reason, accountants found it convenient to establish separate divisions of the equity account to record expenses and revenue. There theoretically could be a single division of the equity account, recording all changes therein from expenses (debit) and all changes from revenue (credits); but it is more convenient to keep expenses and revenues in separate accounts.

Several accounts could be established. Taking just the expenses, perhaps one expense account could be established for Office Expense, another for Travel Expense, and so on. The degree of detailed information desired will dictate the number and kind of accounts.

If John Baker's accountant used sub-accounts of equity for Secretarial Expense and Revenue from Consulting Services, the journal entries above would be changed to debit the former and credit the latter instead of debiting and crediting Owner's Equity. Then the T accounts would appear:

Cash   **Notes Payable**

Opening Balance $ 5,000	3/27 $ 200	Opening Balance $14,000
3/10 275		

Office Equipment   **Owner's Equity**

Opening Balance $ 1,000	Opening Balance $ 7,000

Building   **Secretarial Expense**

Opening Balance $10,000	3/27 $ 200

Land		Revenue from Consulting Services	
Opening Balance $ 5,000		3/10	$ 275

You should note one important characteristic of the new sub-T-accounts: Note that what was previously shown as a direct increase of (credit to) Owner's Equity is now shown as a credit to a revenue account. What was previously shown as a direct decrease of (debit to) Owner's Equity is now shown as a debit to an expense account. These accounts are essentially parts of the Owner's Equity account and their entries are right-hand or left-hand depending on how they affect Owner's Equity. An expense transaction (a decrease of Owner's Equity) is recorded by a debit to an expense account; and a revenue transaction (an increase of Owner's Equity) is recorded by a credit to a revenue account. Some students are troubled by the fact that an increase in an expense account, a sub-account of equity, is a debit while an increase in the equity account itself is a credit. The explanation is simple: the concept of "expense" is a reduction of Owner's Equity and any increase in expense is manifestly a *decrease* in Owner's Equity.

Our main purpose in setting up separate accounts is to segregate all expenses and revenues from other changes in Owner's Equity (such as an increase due to an additional investment by Baker) so that an income statement can be more easily made up for the accounting period—in this case, the month of March. See the prototype income statement, supra p. 29. Assuming that the end of the accounting period has arrived and this statement has been made up, we could transfer the balances in the expense and revenue accounts to Owner's Equity, achieving the result shown on p. 29. The process of transfers at the end of the accounting period is called "closing" the accounts. Shortly we will see that the closings will make it much more convenient to account for expenses and revenues in the next accounting period, April.[g]

The closing process is made more convenient by collecting within one account all the debits and credits necessary for preparation of the income statement. For this purpose we now transfer all expense and revenue account balances first to an intermediate sub-account of Owner's Equity—the Profit and Loss account.

This is done, in effect, by temporarily reversing our previous decision to have separate accounts for expenses and for revenue, and by moving the entries back into a combined revenue and expense account, which is exactly what our Profit and Loss account is. And we shall

g. In actual practice any closing before year-end is called an "interim closing". The closing is accomplished by making pencil footings in the ledger and transferring the pencil footings to a worksheet. This keeps the revenue and expense accounts cumulative in each book closing. The profit and loss information for the current period is derived by subtracting from the year-to-date figures, the figures from the last interim closing. For simplicity, however, we have treated each interim closing as if it were a final closing.

eventually move the net difference between them back from there into the Owner's Equity account.

We do not violate our rule that no bookkeeping may be done directly on the ledger accounts without recording the complete transaction by journal entries. To preserve the consistency of our bookkeeping system and the useful information that was recorded by segregating expense and revenue accounts, these transfers are not made by crossing out balances in one account and writing them in another. Instead we continue to use the technique of making debit and credit closing journal entries:

(1) March 31 Profit and Loss $200
                    Secretarial Expense $200

This empties the Secretarial Expense account by recording a credit of $200 to balance the debit of $200 for Secretarial Expense on page 30. The other half of the journal entry must be a debit, and, in this case, is to Profit and Loss.

Thus, note that any debit balance in any account may be mechanically transferred to another account by a journal entry. The credit of the journal entry when posted offsets the existing debit and closes the account. This credit is itself balanced in the journal entry by a debit in the same amount to the new account.

The next journal entry is:

(2) March 31 Revenue from Consulting Services $275
                    Profit and Loss $275

This empties the revenue account by a debit which balances out the credit therein. The debit is itself balanced on the journal entry by a credit, which in this case is to Profit and Loss.

Thus, note that any credit entry in any account may be mechanically transferred to another account by a journal entry. The debit of the journal entry closes the credit balance in the account and is itself balanced on the journal entry by a corresponding credit to a different account.

The final journal entry transfers the net excess credit in the Profit and Loss account to Owner's Equity. The entry is:

(3) March 31 Profit and Loss $75
                    Owner's Equity $75

The T accounts will appear:

Revenue from Consulting Services

(2)	$275	$ 275	(From p. 31)

Secretarial Expense

(From p. 30)	$200	$ 200	(1)

Profit and Loss

(1)	$200	$ 275	(2)	
(3)	75	————		

Owner's Equity

	$7,000
	75 (3)
	$7,075

One of the conveniences of the closing process appears at this stage. All the expense and revenue accounts and the Profit and Loss account have been "closed out", i.e., they have zero balances now and the same ledger pages can be used to record transactions for the following accounting period, April.

Another convenience is that we can make up our income statement solely from the Profit and Loss account without the need to turn to separate ledger pages for expense and revenue accounts, and without the danger of missing any. For the simple income statement for this series of transactions, see p. 29. The income statement (or profit and loss statement) is a verbal arrangement of the transactions summarized in the Profit and Loss account, in more or less standardized form, thus making clear the results of operations, i.e., the net effect of all revenue and expense transactions for the period. For a more complex income statement see infra p. 524. That statement is a combination of an income statement and a statement of retained earnings.

In actual practice in a real business, when the closing process begins, the ledger will contain hundreds of accounts, some of which are expense and revenue accounts which will be closed out into the Profit and Loss account. Before he begins the closing process, the bookkeeper determines the net balance in each account. Then he checks for the arithmetical accuracy of his postings and his balances by making a *trial balance*, i.e., a listing and addition of all debit balances and of all credit balances. If the aggregate debits are not equal to the aggregate credits, obviously some mechanical or arithmetical mistake has occurred. A trial balance appears in the first two columns of the table on p. 127.

The same table also shows the next preparatory step for the closing process in a complicated set of books, the sorting out of the items in the trial balance into accounts that go into the income statement (columns 3 and 4) and those that go into the balance sheet (columns 5 and 6). This table is called a "six-column worksheet" or "working trial balance".

In this book we have kept to a minimum the teaching of accountants' techniques like the use of the six-column worksheet and more complicated worksheets. Yet the student should note that our six-column worksheet was prepared by a judge as an aid to the decision of a combined legal and accounting issue.

After the closing process, the Profit and Loss account and all of the individual expense and revenue accounts which were closed into it have zero balances. The net result of operations for the whole period amounted to a net credit in the Profit and Loss account (that is, credits from revenues in excess of debits from expenses), and even this was closed out by a debit to that temporary account, with a credit to Owner's Equity. Thus the whole accounting for operations, from which the income statement is made up, is closed out and ends up as an adjustment to the balance sheet element of Owner's Equity. (That is the reason why, in the absence of dividends and capital contributions, the difference in net worth between the beginning and end of the period equals income less expenses.) The income statement is then made up from accounts that have been closed out on the books, while the balance sheet is made up from the accounts remaining on the books with open balances. The income statement is thus seen as an explanation of the transition from the balance sheet at the beginning to the balance sheet at the end of a period. Thus the structure of accounting is still based on the balance sheet. Yet it is true that the *information* conveyed by the income statement is considered paramount for many purposes of modern financial practice, and a serious question is raised as to the usefulness of the information conveyed by the balance sheet, because of the accounting principles that determine the figures. The significance of this assertion will appear to the reader as he or she reads through this book.

Now that we have introduced the concepts of expense and revenue, let us summarize the rules as to when to debit and when to credit particular accounts. It will be seen that the balance sheet consists of a summary of the accounts for assets, liabilities, and equity (and the latter includes the net effect of expense and revenue transactions). As shown on pp. 14–20 increases (+'s) or decreases (−'s) in these types of accounts will be recorded by debiting or crediting them as indicated below:

Balance Sheet

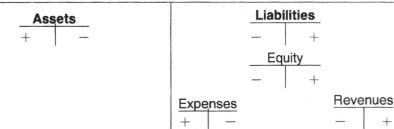

We could construct a chart similar to that on p. 14 adding expenses and revenue on each side, thus creating five items on each side and five times five, or twenty-five, different combinations.[h] But, unlike the nine reasonably realistic transactions set forth on pp. 14–20, illustrating the

h. See R. Amory and C. Hardee, Materials on Accounting 27 (2d ed. 1953).

combinations in the chart on p. 14, many of these twenty-five combinations rarely occur and it takes some unlikely transactions to illustrate them. Realistically, a journal entry building up an expense account will almost always be balanced by a credit to a balance sheet account, for instance:

Dr. Salary Expense

> or

Advertising Expense

> or

Rent Expense

> Cr. Cash [a reduction of an asset account]
>
> > or
>
> Salary Payable [increase of a liability account]
>
> > or
>
> Accounts Payable [increase of a liability account]

A credit to a revenue account is almost always balanced by a debit to a balance sheet account:

Dr. Cash   [increase of an asset account]

> or

Accounts Receivable [increase of an asset account]

> Cr. Revenue—Attorneys Fees
>
> > or
>
> Sales Revenue

In the above journal entries each of these transactions affecting an expense or revenue account has an opposite effect on a balance sheet account. The net credits from profitable operations (i.e., excess of revenue over expenses) will have a counterpart in a net increase of debits on the balance sheet accounts (i.e., increased Cash, Accounts Receivable or other assets); or the Cash may then have been used to pay off (debit) liabilities. The balance sheet accounts are temporarily out of balance and will again balance when the result of operations (i.e., the Net Income credit) is transferred to the Equity account on the balance sheet, thus offsetting the net debit in assets and liabilities. This may be seen in the worksheet on page 127. If expenses had exceeded revenues, the loss would be a net debit to Equity, thereby offsetting the credits consisting of reduced assets and/or increased liabilities.

Thus, we confirm our original proposition that revenue and expense items are convenient subdivisions of the equity section of the balance sheet. Their use avoids having to change the balance sheet directly for each transaction, but at the end of an operating period their net effect must be transferred to the equity section of the balance sheet.

F. ACCOUNTING FOR EQUITY IN A CORPORATION

One more word about the closing process as it relates specifically to a corporation's accounting for equity is necessary. In keeping books of account for a corporation, it has become customary to separate the balance sheet account for Stockholders' Equity into at least two (and more often three or more) different accounts. When a corporation is organized, shares of stock are sold to investors. For example, if 10,000 shares of $10 par value common stock are authorized to be issued, and 1,000 shares are sold by X Corp. for $10,000 cash, the journal entry will be:

    Cash $10,000
        Common Stock, $10 par $10,000

The Stockholders' Equity portion of the balance sheet of X Corp. might then appear:

    Stockholders' Equity:
    Common Stock,
        Authorized: $10 par, 10,000 shares
        Issued and Outstanding: 1,000 shares $10,000

Notice that the balance sheet shows several items of data: the authorized number of shares (i.e., the number of shares which is authorized to be issued in the corporate charter), the par value established in the charter, the fact that only par value, as opposed to no-par value shares are authorized, and that only common stock is authorized. For examples of the information disclosed when more complex capital structures are involved, see the balance sheets on page 526.

For historical reasons (infra pp. 365–369) the par value of stock often bears no relationship to the price paid. Nevertheless the aggregate par value of issued shares has certain legal importance with respect to cash or other distributions to shareholders (infra pp. 370–382) and is kept in a separate account. Any excess of the price paid over par is put in another Stockholders' Equity account, which might be entitled something like Capital Contributed in Excess of Par, or its older names still used in corporation statutes, Capital Surplus or Paid-in Surplus. For example, if X Corp. sold 1,000 shares of $10 par value for $19,000, the entry would be:

    Cash $19,000
        Common Stock $10,000
        Capital Contributed in Excess of Par   9,000

This separation of the two equity accounts is made largely because corporation statutes treat these two aspects of capital differently for dividend purposes. We shall see this more specifically in Chapter VIII.

Incidentally, the last journal entry consisting of three items is known as a "compound" journal entry. It could have been written in a clumsier fashion as follows:

Cash	$10,000	
Common stock		$10,000
Cash	9,000	
Capital Contributed in Excess of Par		9,000

The Stockholders' Equity section of the balance sheet then might appear:

Stockholders' Equity:

Common Stock,

    Authorized: $10 par, 10,000 shares

Issued and Outstanding: 1,000 shares	$10,000
Capital Contributed in Excess of Par	9,000
Total Stockholders' Equity	$19,000

At the end of an accounting period, when the expense and revenue accounts are closed to the Profit and Loss account, that account is then closed to another part of Stockholders' Equity, entitled "Retained Earnings" (at one time commonly called "Earned Surplus" and still so called in corporation statutes). For example, if the Profit and Loss account had a credit balance of $2,373 after closing the expense and revenue accounts, the final closing entry would be:

Profit and Loss	$2,373	
Retained Earnings		$2,373

The Stockholders' Equity section of the balance sheet then might appear:

Stockholders' Equity:

Common Stock,

    Authorized: $10 par, 10,000 shares

Issued and Outstanding: 1,000 shares	$10,000
Capital Contributed in Excess of Par	9,000
Retained Earnings	2,373
Total Stockholders' Equity	$21,373

We shall devote more attention to these equity accounts shortly.

Problem Two

The T accounts of Calypso Catering Co. show balances as follows prior to closing the books for the year. Prepare an income statement for the year and a balance sheet at December 31. Ignore depreciation and interest.

Cash	$70,000
Accounts Payable	22,580
Catering Revenue	122,300
Bonds Payable	50,000
Employees' Wage Expense	22,000
Manager's Salary Expense	15,000
Accounts Receivable	18,900
Rent Expense	2,400
Interest Expense	300
Income Tax Expense	2,200
Land	10,000
Buildings	114,000
Common Stock	
Authorized: 100,000 shares, $1 par	
Issued and Outstanding: 70,000 shares	70,000
Note Payable (due in 6 months)	480
Equipment	10,560

Problem Three

The T accounts of Phillips Flea Powder Co., Inc. at March 1, will have balances as indicated in the balance sheet at February 28, reproduced in the Solution to Problem One appearing in the Appendix. Write the journal entries for each of the following transactions, post to T accounts, and prepare an income statement. This time invent any new account titles you need. Ignore depreciation and income taxes.

March 1 Paid March rent for office space, $200.

      3 Received $400 in cash for services rendered.

      5 Performed services for a political candidate, Al Keseltzer, and billed him $350.

   10 Collected $100 on the Note Receivable.

   12 Paid Adams Co. $150 on account.

   15 Received bill from the telephone company for the first two weeks of March, amounting to $80.

   16 Paid the secretary's salary of $190 for the first half of March.

   21 Issued 1,000 shares of Common Stock for $1,250 in cash.

   25 Paid the March service occupation tax of $5.

   27 Received $400 for services rendered.

   30 Paid the secretary's salary of $190 for the last half of March.

   31 Paid the telephone bill of March 15 and received the bill for the last half of the month, amounting to $82.

Problem C

The balance sheet of Dr. A.C. Doyle, P.C. (Professional Corporation) at March 31, appears as follows:

Balance Sheet of Dr. A.C. Doyle, P.C. at March 31

Cash		$ 4,000	**Accounts Payable:**		
Accounts Receivable:			Moriarty		$ 1,400
Bell	$1,000		**Stockholders' Equity:**		
Holmes	1,500		Capital Stock (Authorized:		
		2,500	1,000 shares, $10 par		
Office Equipment		4,000	Issued and Outstand-		
			ing: 100 shares)	$1,000	
			Capital Contributed in Ex-		
			cess of Par	3,500	
			Retained Earnings	4,600	
			Total Equity		9,100
			Total Liabilities and Stock-		
Total Assets		$10,500	holders' Equity		$10,500

The following transactions occur during April. Please journalize, post, and prepare a balance sheet and income statement for April. Ignore depreciation and any other accruals or deferrals.

April   1   Holmes delivers a check for $1,400 in partial payment of his account.

       3   A patient, Micah, is treated and pays his $40 bill.

       4   The April rent of $250 is paid to the landlord of the office building housing the firm.

       5   Holmes's check is returned, marked "N.S.F." (not sufficient funds). He says that his account was short by $200 but he will send $1,000 by cashier's check and the rest later.

       7   Dr. Doyle purchases a carrying case for $10 for use in making housecalls.

     10   A patient is treated and pays the full $500 bill.

     12   A patient is treated and pays the full $400 bill.

     15   Dr. Doyle pays her assistant $300 for his half month's salary.

     16   Holmes's $1,000 cashier's check is received and deposited.

     17   A patient, Mr. Watson, is treated and pays his $150 bill.

     20   Mrs. Bell pays $500 on account.

     29   The telephone bill for April in the amount of $80 is received and paid.

     30   Dr. Doyle pays her assistant his $300 salary for the remainder of the month.

Problem D

Prepare the May financial statements (balance sheet and income statement only) for Dr. A.C. Doyle, P.C., assuming the following occurrences:

May   1   A fire destroys uninsured office equipment which had cost $200.

3 A patient is treated and pays the $150 bill by giving Dr. Doyle office equipment worth that sum.

5 Holmes pays the remainder of his account.

8 The May rent of $250 is paid.

15 Dr. Doyle's assistant is paid $300 for the first half of May.

18 Mr. Moriarty is paid in full by issuing 140 shares of $10 par value stock to Dr. Doyle for cash and by payment of the cash to Mr. Moriarty.

23 A patient, Mr. Windibank, is treated and billed $700.

31 The assistant is paid $300 for the rest of May.

G. ILLUSTRATED SUMMARY OF THE BOOKKEEPING PROCESS AS EXPLAINED TO THIS POINT

Because the explanation of the bookkeeping process has been piecemeal so far, it may be helpful to proceed from start to finish through the process for a simple set of transactions of a corporation engaged in engineering consulting. Your own experience is the best teacher, and for this reason you should attempt to work out each stage of the problem yourself before reading the solution to it. Your solution should proceed through the following stages:

a. Making original journal entries. (For your convenience, a chart of account titles to be used is set out below.);

b. Posting journal entries to the ledger;

c. Closing expense and revenue accounts to the Profit and Loss account and then to an equity account; and

d. Preparing the income statement and the balance sheet.

Chart of Account Names to be Used [i]

Asset Accounts:

Cash
Accounts Receivable—Patricia Associates
Office Equipment

Liability Accounts:

Account Payable—Acme Office Equipment Co.
Account Payable—Michele Corp.
Note Payable—Acme Office Equipment Co.
Note Payable—First Nat'l Bank

Stockholders' Equity Accounts (including Revenues and Expense)

Common Stock, $1 par
Capital Contributed in Excess of Par
Retained Earnings
Revenue from Consulting Services
Secretarial Expense
Rent Expense
Repairs Expense
Supplies Expense

i. Such a chart, with a detailed description of the content of each account, is typically maintained by the accounting entity.

The Problem. Assume E–Z Corp. is organized and the following events occur in the first month thereafter, January. Prepare a balance sheet at January 31 and an income statement for January. Ignore depreciation and interest.

January 2 Issued 1,000 shares of $1 par value common stock for $9,000 cash paid by Jerry Stockholder. There are 10,000 authorized shares.

3 Borrowed $5,000 from the First National Bank giving in return a 30 day note, without interest.

4 Purchased a desk, typewriter and miscellaneous office equipment for $500 on account from Acme Office Equipment Co.

5 Rendered consulting services to N.B.S. Corp. in January and received $3,000 cash.

8 Paid secretary's salary of $125 in cash for the first week of January to Miss Jones.

11 Paid Acme $300 cash and gave a $200 demand note without interest for the balance.

15 Issued two shares of $1 par value common stock to Acme in satisfaction of the $200 note.

17 Rendered consulting services to Patricia Associates in January and billed it $1,500.

18 Paid rent of $150 cash for January.

23 Received bill from Michele Corp. for repairs to typewriter in amount of $25.

25 Paid $7 cash for office supplies—paper, pencils, erasers, and paper clips. They are expected to last until the end of the month.

30 Received $175 cash for consulting with Calcium Corp. of America in January.

(a) Journal Entries:

January	2	Cash	$9,000	
		Common Stock, $1 par		$1,000
		Capital Contributed in Excess of Par		8,000
	3	Cash	5,000	
		Note Payable—First National Bank		5,000
	4	Office Equipment	500	
		Account Payable—Acme		500
	5	Cash	3,000	
		Revenue from Consulting Services		3,000
	8	Secretarial Expense	125	
		Cash		125

[There ought to be three similar events for the next three weeks, but we have omitted them to shorten the problem.]

	11	Account Payable—Acme	500	
		Cash		300
		Note Payable—Acme		200

Comment: Here note that one liability account was decreased and in addition to a decrease in the asset account, Cash, there was an increase in a liability account, Note Payable—Acme.

January 15 Note Payable—Acme	$200	
Common Stock, $1 par		$2
Capital Contributed in Excess of Par		198

Comment: Discharge of a note payable by issuance of shares of stock is the same (for these purposes) as discharge by a payment of $200 followed immediately by a sale of the shares for $200 cash.

January 17 Account Receivable—		
Patricia Associates	$1,500	
Revenue from Consulting Services		$1,500
18 Rent Expense	150	
Cash		150
23 Repairs Expense	25	
Account Payable—Michele Corp		25
25 Supplies Expense	7	
Cash		7

Comment: You may have preferred to debit an asset account for supplies. However, since the amount is small and the supplies will not last long, the debit should be to expense. We shall shortly study further this intimate relationship between assets and expenses.

January 30 Cash	$175	
Revenue from Consulting Services		$175

(b) Posting:

Cash

1–2	$ 9,000	1–8	$125
1–3	5,000	1–11	300
1–5	3,000	1–18	150
1–30	175	1–25	7
	$17,175		$582
	(582)		
	$16,593		

Accounts Receivable—Patricia Assoc.

1–17	$1,500

Office Equipment

1–4	$500

Account Payable—Acme

1–11	$500	1–4	$500

Account Payable—Michele Corp.

		1–23	$ 25

Note Payable—First Nat'l Bank

		1–3	$5,000

Note Payable—Acme

1–15	$200	1–11	$200

Common Stock—$1 par value

		1–2	$1,000
		1–15	2

Capital Contributed in Excess of Par

		1–2	$8,000
		1–15	198

Retained Earnings

Revenue from Consulting Services

		1–5	$3,000
		1–17	1,500
		1–30	175

Secretarial Expense

1–8	$125

Rent Expense

1–18	$150

Repairs Expense

1–23	$ 25

Supplies Expense

1–25	$ 7

(c) Closing Entries:

To transfer the balances in the four expense and one revenue account to Profit and Loss and then to Retained Earnings, the following entries are necessary:

January 31	Revenue from Consulting Services	$4,675	
	Profit and Loss		$4,675
	Profit and Loss	307	
	Secretarial Expense		125
	Rent Expense		150
	Repairs Expense		25
	Supplies Expense		7

[This could have been written as four separate entries, debiting Profit and Loss, and crediting the four expense accounts respectively, but it is written as a compound entry.]

	Profit and Loss	4,368	
	Retained Earnings		4,368

After posting of these entries to the ledger, the affected T accounts will appear as follows:

Revenue from Consulting Services

1–31	$4,675	1–5	$3,000
		1–15	1,500
		1–30	175

Secretarial Expense

1–8	$125	1–31	$125

Rent Expense

1–18	$150	1–31	$150

Repairs Expense

1–23	$ 25	1–31	$25

Supplies Expense

1–25	$ 7	1–31	$ 7

Profit and Loss

1–31	$ 307	1–31	$4,675
1–31	4,368		

Retained Earnings

		1–31	$4,368

(d) Financial Statements:

Income Statement of E–Z Corp. for the Month of January

Revenue from Consulting Services		$4,675
Less Expenses:		
Secretary	$125	
Rent	150	
Repairs	25	
Supplies	7	
		307
Net income		$4,368

Balance Sheet of E–Z Corp. at Jan. 31

Assets:		Liabilities:		
Cash	$16,593	Accounts Payable	$ 25	
Accounts Receivable	1,500	Notes Payable	5,000	
Office Equipment	500	Total Liabilities		$ 5,025
		Stockholders' Equity:		
		Common Stock,		
		Authorized: $1 par 10,000		
		shares,		
		Issued and Outstanding:		
		1,002 shares	$1,002	
		Capital Contributed in Excess of		
		Par	8,198	
		Retained Earnings	4,368	
		Total Stockholders' Equity		$13,568
		Total Liabilities and Stockholders'		
Total Assets	$18,593	Equity		$18,593

Discussion Problem I

Assume that E–Z Corporation, whose balance sheet at January 31 appears above, has the following transactions in February. Prepare journal entries, post to T accounts, and prepare an income statement for February and a balance sheet at February 28.

February   1   Rent of $150 was paid by check to the lessor of the firm's office.

             2   Jerry Stockholder gave a desk valued at $200 to the corporation for use in its office.

             3   A typewriter was purchased for $300, $150 down and the balance on open account, from Georgia National Corp.

             4   Jerry Stockholder paid $1,000 cash for 3 more shares of stock.

             5   Consulting services were rendered to Heidi Home Teas and an invoice for $280 was sent.

             6   Consulting services for which $1,000 will be charged were nearly completed for the Federated Pacific Life Insurance Co. but no bill has yet been sent, pending completion.

             7   Salaries aggregating $450 were paid by check to secretarial staff for the prior week.

          10   A stock of office supplies was purchased for $20 cash.

          14   Jerry Stockholder picked up a $30 tab for the annual office Valentine's Day party and paid it in cash.

          14   Salaries of $400 cash were paid for the prior week.

          16   Services were rendered to James Corp. which agreed to supply $300 worth of carpeting to E–Z Corp. on demand.

          18   The carpeting was requested and delivered.

          20   The employees collected $10 for Jerry Stockholder's birthday cake and gift, purchased it, and all had a fine time.

          24   A lamp which had cost $20 was broken and a replacement was purchased for $35 cash.

          25   Salaries were paid for the last two weeks of the month in the amount of $575 cash.

26　Patricia Associates paid $500 cash on account.

27　Michele Corp. was paid $25 cash on account.

28　Five thousand dollars cash was paid toward the First National Bank note.

H. ACCOUNTING FOR INCOME TAX EXPENSE

Since the federal government has for many years levied a substantial tax on the net income of business corporations, it is frequently said that Uncle Sam is "a partner" in every business. From the point of view of stockholders, however, the tax is an expense. From the point of view of bondholders, the income tax is an expense that does not arise until the revenues are sufficient to cover their accruing interest; that is why coverage of fixed charges by income is computed before deducting income taxes for purposes of credit analysis. For this reason, to aid analysts, accounting usually shows the liability for income taxes in a separate caption from other accounts payable, and treats the expense a little differently from other expenses on the income statement.

We shall see that, for many reasons of policy, politics and administrative efficiency, tax rules are such that the determination of taxable income almost always differs from financial income determined by accountants. But because these taxes are considered expenses, they must be calculated and charged as expense in the books and in the income statement. One difficulty is that some items are charged as expense or credited as revenue in one period for tax purposes but in a different period for financial accounting purposes. We shall take up the resulting accounting problems in Chapter V.

We shall here go back to the practice problem just completed for E–Z Corporation's January transactions and assume that the income tax is $2,000. The following additional entries would be made:

January	31	Income Tax Expense	$2,000	
		Accrued Taxes Payable		$2,000
	31	Profit and Loss	2,000	
		Income Tax Expense		2,000

This would reduce to $2,368 the remaining credit balance to be closed out from Profit and Loss to Retained Earnings.

The balance sheet will show the new liability for Accrued Income Taxes Payable, and Retained Earnings will be reduced by that amount.

On the income statement, the presentation of Income Tax Expense may be a little different from that of other expenses to assist the credit analyst in making the above-described calculations. The last line of our income statement could be revised to change the caption, and the Income Tax Expense could be shown below it, as follows:

Net Income Before Federal Income Tax	$4,368
Federal Income Tax	2,000
Net Income	$2,368

I. INTRODUCTION TO ACCRUAL AND DEFERRAL AND ADJUSTING ENTRIES

During the Italian Renaissance, when bookkeeping may have been born,[j] it was much simpler than it is today, largely because most accounts at that time were kept for short-term ventures such as financing a trading voyage to India and back. Consider the ease with which you could calculate the net income and net worth of that type of venture in the following illustration:

A group of four business people formed a joint venture to make and sell pennants, trinkets, and buttons for the Nashville World's Fair. They each contributed $25,000 in cash. This and other receipts and disbursements for the ten-month life of the venture (January through October) are listed below:

Jan.	Original cash contri-bution	$100,000	Jan.	Organization costs	$ 10,000
Jan.	Loans	75,000	Jan.	Purchase of small plant	25,000
Jan.–Oct.	Income from sales	400,000	Jan.	Purchase of equip-ment	25,000
Oct.	Receipt from sale of used equip-ment and plant	14,000	Jan.–Oct.	Raw materials	50,000
			Jan.–Oct.	Salaries and wages	45,000
			Jan.–Oct.	Sales commissions	55,000
			Jan.–Oct.	Interest expense	4,000
			Jan.–Oct.	Taxes (other than income taxes)	5,000
			Jan.–Oct.	Miscellaneous ex-penses	50,000
			Oct.	Repayment of loans	75,000
			Oct.	Distribution to own-ers	245,000
		$589,000			$589,000

The net profit of the enterprise ($145,000) is easily determined by calculating the difference between what the entrepreneurs contributed ($100,000) and what they received back ($245,000).[k]

1. AN ACCOUNTING PRINCIPLE

Our illustration is atypical, however, since most businesses have no determinate period of existence and continue for years rather than months. And for those enterprises which continue in existence for

---

j. E. Peragallo, Origin and Evolution of Double Entry Bookkeeping (1938) is a painstaking report of the history of book-keeping which questions some popular myths.

k. Since this venture presumably is a partnership, it will not be liable for federal income taxes and none is shown as an expense.

years, problems which remained latent in the ten-month enterprise become more prominent and demand attention. Although they might have wished to ascertain monthly income for the short-term venture, it really was not too important for the business people to do so. Once the entrepreneurs were committed, by having contributed the $100,000 and purchased the plant, equipment, and supplies, only one of two things could be done to salvage the $100,000 if things went badly—and that was to sell the goods or sell the business. However, in the more typical long-term business venture, the entrepreneur regularly faces many more issues than the question of whether liquidation or continued operation of the business would best conserve his or her wealth. But how can the entrepreneur face the numerous dilemmas unless he or she ascertains profits periodically during the life of the business? This and many other considerations have dictated the conventional practice of determining income and worth periodically—the usual accounting period being one year.[1]

Suppose, to take an exaggerated case, E–Z Corp. on p. 41 has spent $5,000 on pencils and paper clips on January 25 instead of $7. It may appear to the reader that the extra $4,993 of expense would have more than wiped out the monthly profit of $4,368. But is that analysis so clear? We could not have said, as we did on that page, that these supplies are expected to last until the end of the month. Obviously, they will last long beyond that date. And now we meet our first accounting principle,[m] as distinguished from a point in the technology of bookkeeping: Where a cash expenditure (or the incurring of a liability to pay cash) is for an item whose benefit will not all be used up in the present period of operations, we should ordinarily not charge the whole expenditure to expense for this period, but rather use a technique of bookkeeping to *defer* some part of the expense to a later period or periods of operations, which will also benefit from the expenditure.

The foregoing assertion is one aspect of a larger statement as to what accountants are trying to do. They are not merely processing numbers through the bookkeeping technique; they are trying to produce meaningful financial statements, and in many circumstances it would be unrealistic to treat the purchase of a long-term supply of pencils and paper clips as an expense in January just because the cash was paid out in January (or because a liability to pay was incurred in

l. Note that in many of the simplified problems treated in these materials, we often use monthly accounting periods. Most businesses, for management purposes, prepare monthly statements but the year is the basic accounting period. Many firms publish quarterly or semi-annual statements.

m. Accountants have engaged in a long-term debate trying to classify the structure of accounting thought into "postulates," "principles," and "rules" at various levels of generality and specificity.

We need not follow this debate. The FASB calls the rules which it issues by still another name, "standards," and they are issued in numbered "Statements of Financial Accounting Standards." But there are many additional sources of "generally accepted accounting principles." See Chapter II. We shall use the term "accounting principle" to refer to any rule for classifying and measuring in numbers an event in the real world to fit it into the processes of bookkeeping.

January). If accountants were reporting on the total excess of revenues over expenses for a corporation over its whole life, as in our World's Fair venture example, there would not be any difficulty in taking account of the items of expense and revenue whenever cash changed hands. But the needs of management, investors, tax authorities, and others require *periodic* income statements. Thus a chief problem of accounting is to *allocate* items of expense (or costs) and revenues to accounting periods regardless of when the cash expenditures or receipts occur or when obligations to pay or rights to receive cash arise. This process of allocation is called "accrual accounting." It includes both the process of accrual and the process of deferral.

2. THE MECHANICS

Our exaggerated pencils and paper clips case is an example for which deferral is required. Let us reduce the amount to a more realistic figure, say $28. We know that the credit should be to Cash, for $28. What should be the debit? We know that realistically some part of the debit should be to Supplies Expense for this period. If we know in advance just how much of the supplies will be used up in this period, say $6, we could at once write this entry:

Supplies Expense	$ 6	
Deferred Supplies Expense	22	
Cash		$28

The account for Deferred Supplies Expense, despite the word "expense" in its name, is an *asset* account because it is a debit that is not to affect the income accounts (revenues or expenses) for the current period and therefore will appear on the debit side of the balance sheet. Thus, in the second operating period, instead of having to expend cash, the entry to show the expense of using up $8 worth of the pencils and paper clips for that period will be:

Supplies Expense	$ 8	
Deferred Supplies Expense		$ 8

This means that $8 of the expenditure is no longer deferred as Deferred Supplies Expense, but is recognized as Supplies Expense now, leaving $14 still in the account for Deferred Supplies Expense. Similar entries would occur in the following months.

Let us go back to the beginning to note an alternative bookkeeping practice, also followed. At the time of the $28 expenditure we could make this entry:

Deferred Supplies Expense	$28	
Cash		$28

Then at the end of the period we could determine how many supplies had been used up by estimating or counting what is left.

Assume that what is left is estimated at $22. Then at the end of the month we would make an adjusting entry as follows:

| Supplies Expense | $ 6 | |
| Deferred Supplies Expense | | $ 6 |

This leaves us exactly where we were in the first example.

A third possible treatment is also available. We could tentatively assume that all the supplies will be gone this month (as on p. 41) with this entry:

| Supplies Expense | $28 | |
| Cash | | $28 |

Then at the end of the period we check our assumptions and ascertain whether there are any supplies left. If there are, say, $22 worth, we reduce our charge to Supplies Expense by a credit and defer a corresponding amount, by this entry:

| Deferred Supplies Expense | $22 | |
| Supplies Expense | | $22 |

Thus, there are several ways to record the transaction at the beginning of the period, either as an asset, as expense, or part of each. It does not make too much difference which way we do it at first, so long as it is adjusted by an "adjusting entry" to a proper allocation between expense and asset at the end of the period.

We should now note the surprising affinity between expenses and assets. It begins to appear that some assets are just expenses not yet charged to operations but deferred to future periods. Can this be true of such tangible assets as inventory, machinery, and buildings? We shall see that our assertion is largely true even of this kind of asset. The reader can perhaps begin to understand that if many assets are just expenses not yet charged to operations, serious question is now raised as to the meaning of the information in the balance sheet and the basic accounting equation:

$$\text{Assets} - \text{Liabilities} = \text{Net Worth}$$

We have seen an example of deferring an expense. The same principles will sometimes call for deferring revenue. Suppose in the E–Z Corporation problem on p. 41, Calcium Corp. of America paid $350 (instead of $175) on Jan. 30 for *two* months' consulting services, January and February. Accountants agree that it would not be useful to treat all of the $350 (instead of $175) received on Jan. 30 for *two* months' consulting services as revenue for January, leaving nothing for revenue in February to match the expenses which will be incurred in February to serve the Calcium Corp. So we defer part of the revenue by this entry:

Cash	$350	
Revenue from Consulting Services		$175
Deferred Revenue from Consulting Services		175

In February we recognize revenue although no cash has been received in February:

Deferred Revenue from Consulting Services	$175	
Revenue from Consulting Services		$175

We have now seen examples of *deferring* expense and revenue. The characteristic of a deferral is that some event happened during the accounting period of which the accountant takes notice—payment or receipt of cash, or incurring an obligation to pay, or right to receive cash in the future—but he or she pushes off (defers) part of its effect to a future period. In contrast, *accrual* is the accounting process of noting an item of expense or revenue which accounting principle requires to be recognized during the accounting period even though no event in respect to cash or an obligation happened during the period. The event will happen in the future, but its accounting effect is pulled forward (accrued) into the present period. Let us take an example.

Assume that Skylark Corp. derives all of its revenue from consulting services and that its only expenditure is to pay interest on borrowed funds. Also assume that after repaying all its loans in the previous year, it negotiates on January 1, 19X1, a $10,000 loan at 6% per annum interest, both principal and the $600 of interest payable December 31, 19X1. The balance sheet at January 1, 19X1, including the $10,000 obtained on the new loan appears as follows:

Skylark Corp. Balance Sheet at January 1, 19X1

Cash	$10,000	Note Payable	$10,000
Plant & Equipment	5,000	Common Stock	5,000
Total	$15,000	Total	$15,000

Assume further that Skylark has a consistent monthly revenue in 19X1 of $1,000 received in cash and no expenses (other than the interest on the loan).

What would Skylark's income statement show at January 31? For each month until December 31?

If the objective of the income statement is to present fairly the results of operations of the business, it would seem that the income statements for each month of the year should *not* appear as follows:

	Each month, Jan. through Nov.	December
Revenue	$1,000	$1,000
Less Expenses:		
Interest	none	600
Net Income	$1,000	$ 400

December should not bear all of the interest expense just because all of the interest for the year is paid in cash in December, and there is no reason why the other months should fail to bear interest expense just because no interest is paid in cash in those months. A proper income statement for each month in the year, matching expenses and revenue, should show the following, without regard to when the interest is paid or payable:

Revenue	$1,000
Interest Expense	50
Net Income	$ 950

To achieve the purpose which *should* be attained, accountants have adopted the accrual accounting technique of allocating expense to the period in which it was incurred, in their judgment, regardless of when the cash is paid, and of allocating revenue to the period in which it was earned, in their judgment, regardless of when the cash is paid.

For Skylark, the desired effect for January (similarly for each subsequent month through November) can be easily achieved by this simple entry:

January 31	Interest Expense	$50
	Accrued Interest Payable	
	[liability account]	$50

At November 30, the balance sheet would appear as follows:

Skylark Corp. Balance Sheet at November 30, 19X1

Cash	$21,000	Note Payable	$10,000
Plant & Equipment	5,000	Accrued Interest Payable	550
		Common Stock	5,000
		Retained Earnings	10,450
Total	$26,000	Total	$26,000

When the loan and $600 interest is repaid, some of the debits and credits to be made will be obvious:

December 31	Interest Expense	$50	
	Accrued Interest Payable		$50
	Note Payable	10,000	
	?	600	
	Cash		10,600

The "?" must refer to the liability called "Accrued Interest Payable" which is being paid by the payment of cash. Hence the whole year's entries work out very neatly by this simple common sense technique.

This was a case wherein an expense was incurred in periods (January–November) prior to that when the cash was to be paid (December). A similar analysis will lead unerringly to the appropriate bookkeeping entries when *revenue* is earned in one period and the cash is received later. And so too, as we saw earlier with respect to deferrals, when expense is incurred or revenue earned *after* the cash is paid or received the process applies.

Before reading on, try your hand at analyzing the problem of how to account for the situation of the *lender* in our Skylark case where interest *revenue* of $600 is to be received only on December 31, but monthly balance sheets and income statements are to be prepared.

Again the desideratum is to show $50 of interest *revenue* in January and each of the following eleven income statements. Similarly an asset, the accrued right to receive the additional revenue, should be reflected on each balance sheet. To achieve this purpose for January, the entry is:

January 31	Accrued Interest Receivable		
	[an asset account]	$50	
	Interest Revenue		$50

And again on November 30, the balance sheet will be carrying an asset, Accrued Interest Receivable, $550. The December 31 entry is even more obvious than for the expense case just posed:

December 31	Cash	$10,600	
	Note Receivable		$10,000
	Accrued Interest Receivable		550
	Interest Revenue		50

The end-of-the-month journal entries which are designed to accrue (i.e., pull into the current period) revenue or expense as discussed above are termed "adjusting entries," just as are the entries above discussed which are designed to "defer" (push into the next period or periods) revenue or expense items paid in advance.

Again, try your hand at working out the appropriate adjusting entries for the borrower where the interest expense, instead of being paid at the end on December 31, is paid in advance on January 1.

The January 1 entry might be:

January 1	Cash	$9,400	
	Prepaid Interest	600	
	Note Payable		$10,000

The name "Deferred Interest" might also be used for the Prepaid Interest account.

If our aim is again to depict $50 as interest expense each month, the adjusting entry for each month including December will be:

January 31	Interest Expense	$50	
	Prepaid Interest		$50

On each balance sheet the Prepaid Interest will be shown as a gradually decreasing asset until it finally disappears on the balance sheet for December 31.

THE ACCRUAL METHOD

Four Paradigmatic Entries

I. REVENUES

   A. Received, but not yet earned = *Defer* entry:

      Cash

         Deferred Revenue

   B. Earned, but not yet received = *Accrue* entry:

      Account Receivable

         Revenue

II. EXPENSES

   A. Paid, but not yet used = *Prepaid* entry:

      Prepaid Expense (e.g., insurance)

         Cash

   B. Used, but not yet paid = *Accrue* entry:

      Insurance Expense

         Account Payable

Problem E

Rental of $150 per month is due on the first day of each month but is paid in two payments, one of $300 on February 2 and the other of $150 on February 28. Make journal entries for Lessee for the months of January, February, and March, assuming each to be a separate accounting period.

Note on Materiality

Many questions in accounting are eliminated in practice as immaterial because accounting is a practical art. In many of our illustrations in this chapter we followed theory rather than practice in order to explain that theory. But in real life, for example, no bookkeeper or accountant would sweat over the question of whether to capitalize or expense $28 worth of paper clips. The amount is so immaterial to even the smallest business that it doubtless would have been charged to expense to avoid the bother of additional thought.

But what is the criterion of materiality? In the securities law realm two U.S. Supreme Court cases have dealt with this question. TSC Industries, Inc. v. Northway, Inc., 426 U.S. 438 (1976); Basic Inc. v. Levinson, 485 U.S. 224 (1988).

The Court in *Basic*, dealing with the question of when preliminary merger discussions become material so as to make a misrepresentation a material misrepresentation, said at 231–232:

The Court * * * explicitly has defined a standard of materiality under the securities laws, see *TSC Industries, Inc. v. Northway, Inc.*, 426 U.S. 438 (1976), concluding in the proxy-selection context that "[a]n omitted fact is material if there is a substantial likelihood that a reasonable shareholder would consider it important in deciding how to vote." Id. at 449. Acknowledging that certain information concerning corporate developments could well be of "dubious significance," id., at 448, the Court was careful not to set too low a standard of materiality; it was concerned that a minimal standard might bring an overabundance of information within its reach, and lead management "simply to bury the shareholders in an avalanche of trivial information—a result that is hardly conducive to informed decisionmaking." Id., at 448–449. It further explained that to fulfill the materiality requirement "there must be a substantial likelihood that the disclosure of the omitted fact would have been viewed by the reasonable investor as having significantly altered the 'total mix' of information made available." Id. at 449. * * *

The application of this materiality standard to preliminary merger discussions is not self-evident. Where the impact of the corporate development on the target's fortune is certain and clear, the *TSC Industries* materiality definition admits straight-forward application. Where, on the other hand, the event is contingent or speculative in nature, it is difficult to ascertain whether the "reasonable investor" would have considered the omitted information significant at the time.
* * *

Under such circumstances, materiality "will depend at any given time upon a balancing of both the indicated probability that the event will occur and the anticipated magnitude of the event in light of the totality of the company activity." *SEC v. Texas Gulf Sulphur Co.*, 401 F.2d [833 (2d Cir. en banc, 1968] at 849. * * *

Whether merger discussions in any particular case are material therefore depends on the facts. Generally, in order to assess the probability that the event will occur, a factfinder will need to look to indicia of interest in the transaction at the highest corporate levels. Without attempting to catalog all such possible factors, we note by way of example that board resolutions, instructions to investment bankers, and actual negotiations between principals or their intermediaries may serve as indicia of interest. To assess the magnitude of the transaction to the issuer of the securities allegedly manipulated, a factfinder will need to consider such facts as the size of the two corporate entities and of the potential premiums over market value. No particular event or factor short of closing the transaction need be either necessary or sufficient by itself to render merger discussions material.

Consider the starkly contrasting approach that some accountants believe is sanctioned by GAAP whereby a measuring rod is pulled out from the hip pocket and woodenly applied. An administrative law judge, in deciding whether to sanction a major accounting firm for improper conduct in failing to observe professional standards under the Securities and Exchange Commission's Rule 2(e), described the test:

Auditors generally consider amounts that are less than 5 percent of pre-tax income to be immaterial, and anything more than 10 percent of pre-tax income to be clearly material. Auditors must plan the audit to detect errors in the financial statements that individually or in the aggregate are material to the financial statements. They must consider materiality of errors in individual accounts as well as in the aggregate of all the accounts.

In re Ernst & Whinney, [CCH] Fed.Sec.L.Rep. ¶ 84,610 at p. 80,922 (SEC 1990).

It is doubtful whether this formulation would be given legal effect generally. Even auditors would not rely on it in applying GAAS despite the certitude with which the ALJ described it. In the *Ernst & Whinney* case the misstatements were held material under the stated test based on professional standards. Query what the ALJ would have done had the question been whether there was a misrepresentation. Would he have applied the *Basic* test then?

A very prestigious court has intimated that such an accountants' rule of thumb, even if a generally accepted accounting principle, would not be applicable. Cf., United States v. Simon, 425 F.2d 796, 806 (2d Cir.1969):

We do not think the jury was also required to accept the accountants' [expert witnesses'] evaluation whether a given fact was material to overall fair presentation, at least not when the accountants' testimony was not based on specific rules or prohibitions to which they could point, but only on the need for the auditor to make an honest judgment and their conclusion that nothing in the financial statements themselves negated the conclusion that an honest judgment had been made. Such evidence may be highly persuasive, but it is not conclusive, and so the trial judge correctly charged.

J. AN IMPORTANT EXAMPLE OF DEFERRAL—DEPRECIATION ACCOUNTING

Another example of accrual and deferral accounting might give some additional insights and will help you to understand a very significant type of deferred expense—depreciation of fixed assets.

Suppose that on February 15, the Skylark Corp. enters into a lease as lessee of office space at a rental of $200 per month beginning March 1, and pays the March rent in advance. The $200 payment is obviously not an expense in February and so debiting Rent Expense in February would be inappropriate. On analysis it seems that the company has received one asset (a right to office space for a month) for another (cash). Hence an appropriate entry at the time of payment is:

February 15 Prepaid Rent (an asset account) $200

          Cash $200

Then when the books are closed in March, the rent expense incurred and the expiration of the asset (right to office space, or Prepaid Rent) will be evidenced by this adjusting entry:

| March | 31 | Rent Expense | $200 | |
| | | Prepaid Rent | | $200 |

Now suppose instead that the accounting enterprise obtained office space under a five-year lease at a rental of $200 per month, and that the whole five year rental of $12,000 is paid in advance on February 15 for the term beginning March 1. As you know, the appropriate entries are:

February	15	Prepaid Rent	$12,000	
		Cash		$12,000
March	31	Rent Expense	200	
		Prepaid Rent		200

The March 31 entry will then be repeated at the end of each of the next 59 months.

Now, instead of renting an office, let us assume that the enterprise purchases a building for $140,000 and that the building has an estimated useful life of fifty years, after which it will have an estimated salvage value of $20,000. The purchase contract is executed and the price is paid on February 15, but possession is not delivered until March 1. One way to calculate the monthly cost of this building would be, subtract $20,000 from $140,000 to get the net cost for fifty years and divide by the number of months in fifty years (600); thus:

$$\frac{\$140,000 - \$20,000}{600} = \$200$$

Hence the building "costs" $200 per month just like a rented building, and that amount should appear as an expense each month on the income statement.

We could account for this cost by the following entries:

February	15	Prepaid Right to Occupy		
		Building	$140,000	
		Cash		$140,000
March	31	Expense of Occupying		
		Building	200	
		Prepaid Right to Occupy		
		Building		200

and do the same each month thereafter for forty-nine years and eleven months.

Thus each month would have charged to it $200 of expense and the balance sheet asset account would be diminished $200, just as in the example involving the five-year prepaid lease. But suppose that we would like to preserve intact (for financial analysts) the initial cost outlay for the building on our asset account. This is a simple matter. Instead of reducing (crediting) the asset account representing the cost of the building each month, we might record the credits in a sub-account which we could call Expiration of Prepaid Right to Occupy Building.

March 31
[and each   Expense of Occupying Build-
month-end]   ing $200
                         Expiration of Prepaid
                         Right to Occupy Building $200

We might also change the names of our accounts to accord more with customary accounting names, by changing "Prepaid Right to Occupy Building" to "Building"; "Expense of Occupying Building" to "Depreciation Expense"; and "Expiration of Prepaid Right to Occupy Building" to "Accumulated Depreciation" (once called "Reserve for Depreciation"). The entries would then appear:

February 15   Building $140,000
              Cash $140,000

March   31   Depreciation Expense   200
[and each   Accumulated Depreciation   200
month-end]

On the balance sheet of March 31, instead of showing the Building account at $139,800 it would be depicted in this way:

Building $140,000
Less: Accumulated Depreciation   200

Building less Accumulated Depreciation $139,800

The Accumulated Depreciation account is our first example of an offset (or contra) account. In a variety of cases it is desirable, instead of recording the reduction side of an account on the account itself, to record reductions in a separate offset account. This accomplishes two things: (1) it preserves the additions in the main account intact; (2) it increases flexibility by permitting adjustments of the reductions. To take another example, "Accounts Receivable" is a balance sheet account, but it is proper to show on the balance sheet only the net collectible amount, so an offset account for credits entitled "Estimated Uncollectible Accounts" is established. The asset side of the balance sheet may show:

Accounts Receivable $2,000,000
Less Estimated Uncollectible Accounts   20,000

                                           $1,980,000

However, unlike the depreciation case, it is not standard practice to show this information. In fact it is more common to show:

Accounts Receivable (net) $1,980,000

Problem Four

Give the journal entries for each month of the year to account for the purchase and depreciation of a milling machine purchased at January 1 for $24,000 cash. Its expected life is four years and its estimated salvage value is nil.

Discussion Problem II

Prepare journal entries, post them, and prepare an income statement and balance sheet from the following information. Ignore depreciation on all but the building. Ignore taxes.

January 1 One thousand shares of $1 par value common stock of Western Realty Co. are issued for cash as follows:
500 shares to Steven for $5,000;
300 to Gregory for $3,000;
200 to Michael for $2,000.

1 Land and a building are purchased for the firm's own use and conveyed from Katina to the corporation for $35,000, settled by a $5,000 cash payment and a $30,000, 12% note secured by a mortgage. The note is due in six annual installments of $5,000 each at the end of each calendar year, plus accrued interest. The useful life of the building is twenty-five years and estimated salvage value is $5,000. The land is valued at $5,000.

10 A liability insurance policy for the building was purchased at a premium of $365 per annum and the firm was billed this amount.

11 A one year subscription, to begin February 1, for Realty News was purchased for $120 and a check was remitted.

12 A portion of the building was sublet for six months beginning January 15, at a rental of $100 per month. No cash was received.

14 Office equipment was purchased for $500 and installed.

15 Angie, a secretary, was paid $250 for two weeks' work.

16 A salesperson sold a parcel of real estate and the firm received a $4,000 commission, half of which it paid to the salesperson, Mrs. Zoe.

17 Office equipment costing $750 was ordered but not received. $100 was paid in advance.

18 Stationery supplies were purchased from Peter's Equipment Co. for $10 cash.

19 A fire destroyed an empty file cabinet which had cost $60. There was no insurance coverage.

22 The office equipment was received.

22 A lamp which had been purchased for $10 on January 14 was sold to an employee for $30 paid in cash.

28 The secretary was paid $125 of $250 she was owed.

31 A utilities bill for $78 for January was received.

K. ANOTHER IMPORTANT DEFERRAL PROBLEM—ACCOUNTING FOR MERCHANDISE INVENTORY

Periodic Inventory Method. Accounting for merchandise is a special application of accrual accounting. Since cost of the goods which a merchandising business sells is an expense of doing business, like rent or interest expense, accrual techniques serve to indicate the proper bookkeeping treatment for cost of goods. A system could easily be worked out whereby purchases would be charged to an account called Deferred Cost of Goods (an asset account) and then at the end of the month, the appropriate part of this deferral would be credited to that account and charged, just as we did for supplies on p. 48, to an expense account called Cost of Goods Sold. This in fact is the basis for conventional accounting for merchandise. We shall see this in the description of the perpetual inventory method at p. 61, infra. However, customary practice is slightly different from the technique just described. Let us see how the method works.

Putting aside other expenses, profits on sales may be determined by deducting from the amount of sales the cost of all the goods that are sold. The result is often termed "gross profit." How should costs of goods be calculated for income statement purposes? Assuming that cost prices are constant, the cost of the goods sold may be determined by adding the costs of all goods available for sale (i.e., the cost of goods on hand at the beginning of the period and the cost of goods purchased) and deducting therefrom the cost of goods remaining unsold at the end of the period. For example, if Television Sales Company had on hand at March 1, thirty-five television sets which cost $100 each, purchased twenty-two more at the same price, and at March 31 had thirty-nine left, the cost of the sets sold in March would be calculated as follows:

	Inventory (March 1)	$3,500
Plus:	Purchases	2,200
	Cost of Goods Available for Sale	$5,700
Less:	Inventory (March 31)	3,900
	Cost of Goods Sold in March	$1,800

If eighteen sets had been sold at $150 each, gross profit from sales would be $900, calculated as shown on the following income statement:

Television Sales Company
Income Statement for March, 19X1

Sales			$2,700
Less:	Cost of Goods Sold:		
	Inventory at March 1	$3,500	
Plus:	Purchases	2,200	
	Cost of Goods Available for Sale	$5,700	
Less:	Inventory at March 31	3,900	
	Cost of Goods Sold		1,800
	Gross Profit on Sales (Assuming no other expenses)		$ 900
	Net Income		$ 900

The mechanics for collecting these data at the end of the accounting period are fairly simple but, nevertheless, because of the several steps involved, require close attention.

(a) The first figure required, Inventory at March 1, is already shown as a debit balance in the Inventory ledger account left over from the February adjusting entries for the February closing of the books. See the February 28 balance sheet. You will understand how this figure came to be there when we illustrate how the March 31 Inventory figure is derived. The March 1 figure was obtained by going through this same process in February.

(b) As goods are purchased a debit will be made to Purchase Expense account and a credit to Cash, or to Notes Payable or Accounts Payable if the purchase is on credit. For example, if twenty-two television sets are purchased for cash at $100 each, the entry will be:

Purchase Expense	$2,200	
Cash		$2,200

(c)(i) Now, at the end of the month, the bookkeeper sets up a new temporary account, entitled Cost of Goods Sold. It is an expense account. He transfers the debit balance in the Purchase Expense account by closing that account to the new one. The entry is:

Cost of Goods Sold	$2,200	
Purchase Expense		$2,200

(ii) He then also transfers the opening debit balance in the Inventory account to Cost of Goods Sold. If opening Inventory is $3,500, he makes this entry:

Cost of Goods Sold	$3,500	
Inventory		$3,500

The relevant accounts will now appear as follows: [n]

Inventory					Cost of Goods Sold		
Opening balance	$3,500	Mar. 31	$3,500		Mar. 31	$2,200	
					Mar. 31	3,500	

Purchase Expense			
Mar. 10	$2,200	Mar. 31	$2,200

n. Notice how a bookkeeper closes off an account. A *double* line means that debits and credits above it are equal, and need not be further considered in computing the balance in the account. In the Inventory and Purchase Expense accounts, the equality is apparent on inspection, and the double line may be drawn without adding the two sides. But if there are several entries, the bookkeeper will want to find the net difference and draw a double line, to simplify computations thereafter. He or she does this by adding on the smaller side an amount sufficient to balance; the two sides are totalled and the double line drawn; and the amount that has been added on the one side is now shown on the other. Here we have the one exception to the principle (p. 25) that nothing is entered in an account that does not come from a journal entry. This exception is permissible because nothing is really done to the account except to record the same amount on both sides, so arranged that the columns will total to equal amounts and that the balancing double line may be drawn. In lieu of folio references to a journal source, the identical entries are both marked "Bal."

(iii) But we know that this $5,700 total in the Cost of Goods Sold Expense account must be reduced by the amount of goods still on hand and representing cost of goods not yet sold. The bookkeeper will ascertain the physical count of goods on hand and calculate their aggregate cost. Since this $3,900 is the value of goods on hand, not only should it be subtracted from the Cost of Goods Sold account, but it should also be recognized as an asset. Both of these aims are achieved by this entry:

Inventory (at March 31)	$3,900	
Cost of Goods Sold		$3,900

Now the relevant T accounts appear:

Inventory

Opening				
Balance	$3,500	Mar. 31	$3,500	
Closing				
Balance	$3,900			

Purchase Expense

Mar. 10	$2,200	Mar. 31	$2,200

Cost of Goods Sold

Mar. 31	$2,200	Mar. 31	$3,900
Mar. 31	3,500	Bal.	1,800
	$5,700		$5,700
Bal.	$1,800		

We now have available in convenient form for making up our balance sheet the amount of Inventory on hand at the balance sheet date ($3,900) and for making up our income statement, the Cost of Goods Sold ($1,800) showing all three of its components, Opening Inventory ($3,500), Purchases ($2,200), and Closing Inventory ($3,900).

The final step is to close the expense account for Cost of Goods Sold to the Profit and Loss account together with all the other revenue and expense accounts.

Under a variation of this method, the Purchases Expense account is eliminated, and instead Inventory is debited upon each purchase; then in lieu of a debit to Cost of Goods Sold for opening Inventory and a credit thereto for closing Inventory, a credit to Inventory is made in an amount sufficient to bring the balance in Inventory down to the amount of closing Inventory. The balancing debit in the journal entry should be to Cost of Goods Sold (in order to identify that amount) and from there closed out to Profit and Loss. Compare the identical treatment of the Deferred Supplies Expense on p. 48 where that account is first debited.

Perpetual Inventory Method. The perpetual inventory method is another mechanical technique generally less suitable for a company which has many transactions. Under it, a single account (e.g., Merchandise) serves the function of the Inventory and Purchase Expense accounts under the periodic inventory method. Upon a purchase for $100, the entry is:

Merchandise (asset account)	$100	
Cash		$100

On sale of an item (assuming its cost is $10 and sale price is $15), two entries are necessary:

Cash	$ 15	
Sales Revenue		$ 15
Cost of Goods Sold		
(expense account)	10	
Merchandise		10

The Income Statement would show:

Sales Revenue	$ 15
Less: Cost of Goods Sold	10
Gross Profit on Sales	$ 5

On the balance sheet, the assets would include Merchandise of $90.

Because every purchase and sale results in an immediate debit or credit to "Merchandise" account, an inventory count is *always* available, giving rise to the misnomer, "perpetual inventory." Normally, this method is not feasible except for companies which handle large items for which the individual cost is readily available to make possible the last two journal entries shown: e.g., expensive art objects or automobiles.[o]

Problem Five

Calculate the gross profit (Sales Revenue less Cost of Goods Sold) on sales of the Pinchem Shoe Store, Inc. for the month of February, under the following assumptions:

(a) The business was incorporated on January 18, and 2,000 pairs of shoes were purchased for $16,000 on account.

(b) On February 4, 4,000 pairs were purchased for $32,000 cash.

(c) No business was conducted during January. Gross sales of shoes for February were $42,000 and $400 in sales were refunded for returned shoes. The returned shoes were discarded as worthless.

(d) On February 28, 1,000 pairs of shoes were on hand.

(e) Each pair of shoes cost $8.

Problem Six

Prepare journal entries for the following transactions using the periodic inventory method; then post to T accounts; prepare an income state-

---

o. However, computerization now makes perpetual inventory recordkeeping possible for many more businesses. For example, some grocery supermarkets now use computer terminals as cash registers, each coupled with a scanning device that "reads" the computer-coded product designation on the package and triggers an entry to reduce the perpetual record of inventory quantities for the item sold and to cost out the sale according to programmed costs.

ment for the month of March and a balance sheet at March 31, based on the facts set forth below. (Ignore income taxes and reserves and other adjustments not yet discussed.)

Balance Sheet of Television Sales Co. at February 28

Current Assets:			Current Liabilities:	
Cash	$ 45,000		Account Payable	$ 12,000
Accounts Receivable	22,000		Customer Deposit—	
Inventories (110 TV			Pears and Sawbuck,	
sets)	11,000		Inc.	2,000
Total		$ 78,000	Long Term Debt: 10 year	
Prepaid Interest (on			Note Payable, due Dec.	
ten year note)		5,000	31, 19X11, bearing 6%	
Prepaid Rent ($1,200			interest on the unpaid	
paid in advance			balance payable annual-	
Jan. 1, for year.)		1,000	ly in advance on Janua-	
Equipment	$100,000		ry 1	100,000
Less: Accumulated			Stockholders' Equity:	
Depreciation	2,000		Common Shares Autho-	
		98,000	rized: 20,000 shares,	
Land		20,000	$10 par: Issued and	
Buildings	$100,000		Outstanding:	
Less: Accumulated			15,000 shares	150,000
Depreciation	333		Retained Earnings	37,667
		99,667		
		$301,667		$301,667

[Equipment has an estimated useful life of eight years and an estimated salvage value at the end of that time of $4,000. The estimated useful life of the buildings carried in the Buildings account is 50 years, and it is assumed they will have no salvage value, that is, for accounting purposes.]

Assume that the following transactions take place during March:

March 1 Sold a television set for $150 on account to Myers.

2 Purchased ten television sets for $100 each, payable in thirty days to Commodore Television Inc.

4 Myers returned his set in salable condition and his account was cancelled.

5 Cash sales of sets are made in the amount of $1,500.

6 One hundred shares of $10 par value stock are issued for $1,500 cash to Gamble.

7 One set is returned by the company to Commodore Television Inc. as defective and a credit memo reducing the Account Payable in the amount of $100 is received.

11 A parcel of land adjacent to the present premises is purchased from Jones for use as a parking lot. Payment is made by means of a $3,000, 9%, sixty-day promissory note, secured by a mortgage.

12 An additional vacant parcel, immediately adjacent to the one acquired March 11, is acquired for the same purpose for $2,700 cash.

13 Jorgenson is paid $400 by check on his Account Payable.

14 Jacobsen is given a thirty-day note without interest for $500 in payment of his account.

15 Jackson is given ten shares of stock in payment of his $150 account.

16 Jameson takes a television set in payment for his $150 account.

17 An employee receives a television set in lieu of wages of $150.

18 Salaries of $300 for the first half of the month are paid to salaried employees.

19 Wages of $500 are paid for the first half of the month.

20 The president of the company is paid $2,000 for March and April salary.

22 An employee receives ten shares of stock in lieu of $150 wages.

23 $100 erroneously charged to Salary Expense in March is properly to be charged to Wage Expense.

25 A $150 set previously sold for cash in March is returned in salable condition and a credit memo acknowledging a liability in that amount is issued to Harris.

26 Another set sold for $150 cash in March is returned in salable condition and ten shares of stock are issued to the customer.

28 Cash sales of $3,000 are made.

29 Wages of $500 and salaries of $300 for the month are paid.

30 Fifty sets are purchased on account from Azimuth Corp. at $100 each.

31 Ten sets priced at $200 each which had been ordered and paid for in February were shipped to Pears and Sawbuck Co.

31 (A physical inventory is taken and 127 sets costing $100 each are found to be on hand.)

The most orderly procedure to follow in this case is:

(a) Make all journal entries for the above transactions.

(b) Make adjusting journal entries for deferrals and accruals required for any items in the above transactions or for any items appearing on the February 28 balance sheet.

(c) Post all journal entries to T accounts. It is suggested that you group them according to whether they are asset, liability, equity, expense or revenue accounts.

(d)(i) Close all merchandise accounts to Cost of Goods Sold.

(ii) Close Cost of Goods Sold and all other expense accounts and the revenue account to Profit and Loss account.

(iii) Close the Profit and Loss account to Retained Earnings.

(e) Draft the income statement from the items in the Profit and Loss account.

(f) Draft a balance sheet from the balances in all T accounts after closing.

Discussion Problem III

Assuming the March 31 balance sheet developed in the answer to Problem Six dealing with Television Sales Co., as shown in the Appendix on

p. 82, please journalize, post and prepare an income statement and balance sheet for April after the following transactions occur. Ignore taxes.

April   1   A television set is sold for $165 on credit to Winifred.

      2   Five new sets are purchased for $100 each on open account from John's Television, Inc.

      3   An electronic tube tester is ordered at a price of $1,500 from Kristen's Industries, Inc., for use in checking and repairing. Delivery is scheduled for April 15. Payment will be due in May. Useful life is estimated at 2½ years with no salvage value.

      4   Advertising handbills are ordered and received and the $90 cost is paid. The handbills will be distributed by the end of the month.

      6   Three TV sets are sold for $555 to James's Restaurant for $55 down and a $500 note bearing interest at 10% per annum, due in six months.

      7   One set is stolen by an unknown thief. It is not recovered and not insured.

      8   A safe deposit box is rented for a term of one year at a rental of $36.50 for the year paid in advance.

     10   A four-month bank loan is made at an interest rate of 9% per annum in the amount of $3,000 but $90 is deducted in advance, as interest.

     11   Sales of $1,400 on account are made.

     12   Fifteen sets are purchased on open account at $100 each from Mary's TV Inc.

     14   Salaries of $300 are paid for the first half of the month.

     15   Wages of $600 are also paid. The tube tester is received.

     16   The President, Priscilla, receives $1,000 in advance for May salary.

     18   Cash sales of $3,000 are made.

     20   Accounts Payable of $10,000 are paid by check.

     23   Five sets are purchased at $500 cash and received.

     24   A telephone bill is paid for April in the sum of $40.

     26   An automobile is accidentally backed into a TV set in the parking lot, destroying it. The driver, a stranger, pays $50 in settlement on the spot.

     27   An employee who had been dismissed in March is paid $50 for wages which had been negligently overlooked.

     28   Salaries of $600 are paid, half of which is an advance for May.

     29   Wages of $600 are also paid.

     30   A $10 down payment is received from a customer for delivery of a set in the following week at a price of $160.

A physical inventory turns up 114 sets.

WASTE IN INVENTORY

Note that under the periodic inventory method, no effort is made to keep track of the remaining amount of inventory and purchases until the end of the period **p** when it is done by "taking inventory"—i.e.,

---

p. Of course, stock records may be maintained to be sure that stock is available for sale or for use in manufacturing and that new orders can be placed when necessary.

counting to see what is left—rather than by calculating how many items have been sold. There are two reasons for this: (1) the cost of keeping track of small items and parts; (2) some parts of an inventory necessarily disappear otherwise than by sale—e.g., by evaporation, leakage, spoilage, cutting, breakage, grinding operations, etc., and even pilferage. This disappearance is also part of the process of having goods for sale. Thus it is part of the cost of goods sold. The disappearance of inventory from these causes shows up automatically by the process of determining final inventory, without the necessity for any specific entries. Of course, for this reason, if an entry *is* made, say, when a theft is discovered, the accounts will be erroneous.

L. A NOTE ON CONSOLIDATED FINANCIAL STATEMENTS

Most published financial statements you will see are "consolidated statements" meaning the data for a parent and its majority or wholly-owned subsidiaries are treated as if they are those of a single enterprise. See, for example, the statements on pp. 524–529.

In Chapter IX we explain consolidation processes but note here a few items which should be kept in mind.

When one corporation owns shares of stock in another, the separate corporate personalities are usually honored in law. Occasionally the "corporate veil" is "pierced" and the subsidiary's corporate status is ignored so that its legal liabilities become the parent's. Alternatively, the parent's claim as a creditor of the subsidiary is subordinated to the claims of other creditors. Or the assets and liabilities of both firms are aggregated. See, e.g., W. Cary & M. Eisenberg, Cases and Materials on Corporations 151–91 (6th ed. Unabr. 1988).

These legal concepts are quite distinct from the accounting concept of consolidation with which we are here concerned, although some courts have confused them, often by noting the fact that consolidated statements were published as evidence for piercing.

Accountants "consolidate" the financial statements of majority owned subsidiaries and their parent because it is deemed more meaningful to investors to portray them as a single enterprise. SFAS No. 94, *Consolidation of All Majority–Owned Subsidiaries* (1987). (The criterion for consolidation is currently under review by the FASB.)

One might think that it would be easy enough to take the parent's balance sheet assets and add them to the subsidiary's, and do the same with liabilities to get an overall balance sheet. But this is usually not true for balance sheets, nor is it true for income statements. The key point is that the parent's assets shown on its balance sheet include the investment in the capital stock of the subsidiary, which represents assets less liabilities of the subsidiary. One could not sensibly add the two balance sheets without adjustment, because the subsidiary's capital stock shown on the parent's balance sheet, and the subsidiary's own net assets, would duplicate each other and therefore cannot be added together. Thus, the key element in a consolidation of balance sheets is to eliminate the parent's investment in stock of a subsidiary as an asset, substituting therefor the assets and liabilities of the subsidiary; and having eliminated the subsidiary's capital stock as an asset on the left side of the consolidated balance sheet, it and certain related surplus items of the subsidiary are also eliminated from the Stockholders' Equity part of the consolidated balance sheet.

There is nothing in the consolidating problem for the income statement comparable to the foregoing point on the balance sheet. But both the income statement and the balance sheet present problems of elimination of the effect of intercompany transactions. Just as transactions between divisions of the same corporation could not be permitted by accountants to produce corporate revenues or increases in cost-carrying figures for assets, so the theory of the consolidated statements requires elimination of the effect of transactions between companies in the consolidation.

Just as an intercompany loan could not be shown on the consolidated balance sheet as both an asset and a liability of the enterprise, similarly, income of $1 million shown on an income statement for a subsidiary corporation based on sales to its parent corporation could not meaningfully be added to the parent's operations to obtain a sensible picture of the income of the whole enterprise, where the parent had not yet sold the goods to outsiders. Elimination of the sale by the subsidiary against the purchase by the parent in the same amount will also necessitate elimination of the intercompany profit from the goods now in the parent's inventory.

Hence, intercorporate items must be eliminated to avoid duplication and premature recognition. The adjustments can be made only by use of information usually not available in the published statements. For this reason, only a person with access to the company's records can develop a consolidated statement, and so it is usually impossible for the outsider to make up his or her own consolidation from the unconsolidated statements of the companies in the group.

The appropriateness of consolidating the statements, the mechanics of consolidation, the treatment of minority shareholders' interests, the problem of valuation of assets on purchase of a subsidiary for shares of stock of the parent, and other matters will be dealt with in Chapter IX.

But even at this early point a word of caution is necessary. Although consolidated statements are useful for many purposes, they cannot be used reliably for some other purposes, especially for many of the purposes of lawyers, e.g., for determining validity of dividends, in all but a few states, and for analysis of liquidity.[q] The practice of most parent companies in making reports to shareholders is to publish only consolidated statements. For this reason the differences between con-

q. See infra Chapter X.

solidated and unconsolidated statements are not widely recognized, but you must always keep them in mind as a lawyer advising clients.

M.   ACCOUNTING CONVENTIONS

A newcomer to accounting who has supposed that it is a precise system will be surprised at how much is unsettled on questions of how to account for financial events. Great pressures have been brought to bear to narrow the differences in the ways similar transactions are analyzed into accounting terms, and thus to reduce the lack of comparability of the financial statements of different companies. Accounting, like law, is continually being fundamentally re-examined with a view to developing a theoretical underpinning. There is a long way to go. Nevertheless, we can identify certain conventions many of which are being reconsidered in this restudy but which are now being followed.

1.   THE GOING CONCERN CONVENTION

The assets of a company have certain values to the company when used in the normal course in an established business because of the presumed continuity of the business into the future. These values are usually different from the amounts of cash that could be realized in a forced liquidation. For example, a supply of stationery imprinted with the company name would be worthless if the company ceased to do business. Similarly, the amounts regarded as liabilities to a going business are sometimes different from the amounts creditors would claim in a forced liquidation. In addition, the order of priority for liquidation of debts may be different in liquidation from the order in which presented in the balance sheet, i.e., current and long-term, in the case of a going concern. The deferral of costs by debiting assets, the discounting of liabilities, and the arrangement of liabilities by maturity date in the balance sheet must assume that there will be another period or periods in the future to absorb the deferred costs, accrete the interest and pay the debts. The recording of transactions and the preparation of financial statements is conventionally based on the assumption that the business will continue into future periods, and the asset and liability accounts are stated on this basis. In practice, the accountant's test to determine whether the going concern convention is appropriate usually depends on the projected ability of the enterprise to meet its cash flow needs, i.e., pay its debts, for a period of one year.[r]

The going concern convention tells us merely that assets and liabilities are valued and stated on the presumption that the enterprise will continue in business.

r. SAS No. 59 (1988).

SAS No. 59 changes the practice to now require the auditor to investigate going concern status. Previously there was no duty to investigate. See SAS No. 34 (1981); Goldstein & Dixon, New Teeth for the Public's Watchdog: The Expanded Role of the Independent Accountant in Detecting, Preventing and Reporting Financial Fraud, 44 Bus.Law. 439, 464 at n. 144 and 482 (1989).

2. THE PERIODIC REPORT CONVENTION—ACCRUAL AND DEFERRAL

If a business is assumed to have continuity of existence, those interested in its financial well-being cannot await termination of the business to receive reports. Instead, periodic reports are required. The basic period is one year, although it is subdivided for various purposes.

The period of one year, while arbitrary, is a convenient measure of performance for purposes of taxation, splitting up profits and evaluating both management and the direction of the business.

The customary subdivided periods are months or quarters, where a month can be a calendar month (of so many days) or four weeks or perhaps five weeks, and a quarter can be a calendar quarter or three "months" or thirteen or perhaps twelve weeks. Because of the nature of some small businesses, further subdivision may be made to determine weekly, daily or even hourly results. The shorter periods are most generally used only for internal management purposes, although weekly or daily sales, cash receipts, and other data can sometimes be useful to very short-term lenders and some selected short period data may be helpful in spotting trends. With the computerization of our society, accrual basis results are now sometimes reasonably attainable for even very short periods. However, there is ordinarily little usefulness to outsiders for such data covering periods of less than a week.

As we have seen, the need to divide temporally the reports of operations of a business dictates the accrual and deferral of revenue and related expense items. A second category of costs which are not as directly related to revenues recognized in the period but which seem to be somewhat related to that period are also expensed then; an example would be an uninsured fire loss. There is a third category of expenses, including depreciation, interest, and rent, which are systematically spread over the periods to which they contribute to earnings. These last two categories are termed "period costs."

3. CONSISTENCY

Periodic reports are most useful when they are prepared from year to year on a basis consistent with the preceding year. For example, if one particular method of accounting for depreciation has been used in one annual report, a second report will be more easily compared, and therefore more useful, if the same depreciation method is used for it.

From time to time managers seek to alter their methods of accounting for particular items, presumably for the sole purpose of avoiding a showing of profit dips or even losses. In an important pronouncement, the APB provided certain accounting rules and disclosure techniques in an effort to avoid these misleading impressions. See APB Opinion No. 20, *Accounting Changes* (1971), described infra Chapter II.

Appendix to Chapter I

SOLUTIONS TO PROBLEMS NUMBERED ONE TO SIX IN CHAPTER I

Solution to Problem One:

A. Journal entries:

			Dr.	Cr.
Feb.	1	Cash	$5,000	
		Common Stock, $1 par		$5,000
	3	Office Equipment	250	
		Accounts Payable—Adams Co.		250

[Note: Although three different items (the desk, the typewriter and the chair) were purchased, our chart of account titles lists Office Equipment as the only reasonably descriptive title for these items, and it must be presumed that there is no interest in keeping a separate account for each item.]

	7	Land	2,000	
		Buildings	8,000	
		Cash		1,000
		Notes Payable—Barkley		9,000

(Later we shall see that it is desirable to keep separate records for land and buildings, since buildings are depreciable while ordinarily land is not.)

	18	Accounts Payable—Adams Co.	100	
		Cash		100
	22	Factory Equipment	500	
		Accounts Payable—Clark		500
	26	Accounts Payable—Clark	500	
		Notes Payable—Clark		500
	27	Notes Receivable—Phillips	100	
		Cash		100
	28	Office Equipment	500	
		Cash		500

B.　Ledger Accounts:

Cash			
Feb. 1	$5,000	Feb. 7	$1,000
		Feb. 18	100
		Feb. 27	100
		Feb. 28	500

Office Equipment	
Feb. 3	$250
Feb. 28	500

Notes Receivable—Phillips	
Feb. 27	$100

Factory Equipment	
Feb. 22	$500

Land	
Feb. 7	$2,000

Buildings	
Feb. 7	$8,000

Accounts Payable—Clark			
Feb. 26	$500	Feb. 22	$500

Accounts Payable—Adams Co.			
Feb. 18	$100	Feb. 3	$250

Notes Payable—Barkley			
		Feb. 7	$9,000

Notes Payable—Clark			
		Feb. 26	$500

Common Stock, $1 par			
		Feb. 1	$5,000

C.　Balance Sheet:

Phillips Flea Powder Co., Inc.
Balance Sheet at February 28

Assets:			Liabilities:		
Current:			Current:		
Cash	$3,300		Accounts Payable—		
Notes Receivable	100		Adams Co.	$ 150	
Total		$ 3,400	Notes Payable—		
			Clark	500	
Fixed:			Total		$ 650
Land	$2,000		Long Term Debt:		
Buildings	8,000		Notes Payable—Bar-		
Factory Equipment	500		kley		9,000
Office Equipment	750		Total Liabilities		$ 9,650
Total		$11,250	Shareholders' Equity:		
			Common Stock, $1		
			par		5,000
			Total Liabilities and		
Total Assets		$14,650	Shareholders' Equity		$14,650

[This form of balance sheet is termed "classified" because it segregates "current" and "fixed" assets and liabilities.]

Solution to Problem Two:

Income Statement of Calypso Catering Co. for the year ended December 31

Catering Revenue		$122,300
Less: Expenses		
Employees' Wages	$22,000	
Manager's Salary	15,000	
Rent	2,400	
Interest	300	
Income Taxes	2,200	
		41,900
Net Income		$80,400

Balance Sheet of Calypso Catering Co. at December 31

Assets:

Current Assets:		
Cash	$ 70,000	
Accounts Receivable	18,900	
		$ 88,900
Fixed Assets:		
Land	$ 10,000	
Buildings	114,000	
Equipment	10,560	
		134,560
Total Assets		$223,460

Liabilities:

Current Liabilities:		
Accounts Payable	$ 22,580	
Notes Payable	480	
		$ 23,060
Fixed Liabilities:		
Bonds Payable		50,000
Stockholders' Equity:		
Common Stock:		
Authorized: 100,000		
shares, $1 par		
Issued & Outstanding:		
70,000 shares	$ 70,000	
Retained Earnings	80,400	
		150,400
Total Liabilities and Stockholders' Equity		$223,460

Solution to Problem Three:

A. Journal entries (before closing):

March	1	Rent Expense	$200	
		Cash		$200
	3	Cash	400	
		Revenue		400
	5	Account Receivable—Al Keseltzer	350	
		Revenue		350
	10	Cash	100	
		Notes Receivable		100
	12	Accounts Payable—Adams Co.	150	
		Cash		150
	15	Telephone Expense	80	
		Accounts Payable—Tel. Co.		80
	16	Secretarial Expense	190	
		Cash		190

21	Cash	1,250	
	Common Stock		1,000
	Capital Contributed in Excess of Par		250
25	Service Occupation Tax Expense	5	
	Cash		5
27	Cash	400	
	Revenue		400
30	Secretarial Expense	190	
	Cash		190
31	Telephone Expense	82	
	Accounts Payable—Tel. Co.		82
	Accounts Payable—Tel. Co.	80	
	Cash		80

B. Ledger accounts (before closing entries):

Cash

Opening Balance	$3,300	Mar. 1	$ 200
Mar. 3	400	Mar. 12	150
Mar. 10	100	Mar. 16	190
Mar. 21	1,250	Mar. 25	5
Mar. 27	400	Mar. 30	190
		Mar. 31	80

Notes Receivable

Opening Balance	$ 100	Mar. 10	$ 100

Accounts Receivable—Keseltzer

Mar. 5	$ 350	

Land

Opening Balance	$2,000	

Buildings

Opening Balance	$8,000	

Factory Equipment

Opening Balance	$ 500	

Office Equipment

Opening Balance	$ 750	

Accounts Payable—Adams Co.

Mar. 12	$ 150	Opening Balance	$ 150

Accounts Payable—Tel. Co.

Mar. 31	$ 80	Mar. 15	$ 80
		Mar. 31	82

Notes Payable—Clark

	Opening Balance	$ 500

Notes Payable—Barkley

	Opening Balance	$9,000

Common Stock

	Opening Balance	$5,000
	Mar. 21	1,000

Capital Contributed in Excess of Par

	Mar. 21	$ 250

Retained Earnings

Profit and Loss

Secretarial Expense

Mar. 16	$ 190
Mar. 30	190

Rent Expense

Mar. 1	$ 200

Service Occupation Tax Expense

Mar. 25	$ 5

Telephone Expense

Mar. 15	$ 80
Mar. 31	82

Revenue

Mar. 3	$ 400
Mar. 5	350
Mar. 27	400

C. Closing journal entries to be posted:

a	Profit and Loss	$200	
	Rent Expense		$200
b	Profit and Loss	162	
	Telephone Expense		162
c	Profit and Loss	380	
	Secretarial Expense		380
d	Profit and Loss	5	
	Service Occupation Tax Expense		5
e	Revenue	1,150	
	Profit and Loss		1,150
f	Profit and Loss	403	
	Retained Earnings		403

D. The affected T accounts will now appear:

Retained Earnings

	From P & L $ 403

Profit and Loss

Rent	$ 200	Income	$1,150
Telephone	162		
Secretary	380		
Service Tax	5		
Balance to Retained Earnings	403		

Rent Expense

Mar. 1	$ 200	To P & L	$ 200

Telephone Expense

Mar. 15	$ 80	To P & L	$ 162
Mar. 31	82		

Secretarial Expense

Mar. 16	$ 190	To P & L	$ 380
Mar. 30	190		

Service Occupation Tax Expense

Mar. 25	$ 5	To P & L	$ 5

Revenue

To P & L	$1,150	Mar. 3	$ 400
		Mar. 5	350
		Mar. 27	400

E. Financial statements:

Income Statement of Phillips Flea Powder Co. for the month of March

Revenue from Operations		$1,150
Less: Expenses		
Rent	$200	
Telephone	162	
Secretary	380	
Service Tax	5	
		747
Net Income		$ 403

Balance Sheet of Phillips Flea Powder Co. at March 31

Assets:			Liabilities:		
Current Assets:			Current Liabilities:		
Cash	$4,635		Accounts Payable	$ 82	
Accounts Receivable	350		Notes Payable—Clark	500	
		$ 4,985			$ 582
Fixed Assets:			Fixed Liabilities:		
Land	$2,000		Notes Payable—		
Buildings	8,000		Barkley		9,000
Factory Equipment	500		Total Liabilities		$ 9,582
Office Equipment	750		Stockholders' Equity:		
		11,250	Common Stock, $1 par	$6,000	
			Capital Contributed in		
			Excess of Par	250	
			Retained Earnings	403	
			Total Equity		6,653
Total Assets		$16,235	Total		$16,235

Solution to Problem Four:

January	1	Milling Machine	$24,000	
		Cash		$24,000
	31	Depreciation Expense	500	
		Accumulated Depreciation		500

[The same entries for the end of each month thereafter until sold, retired, or completely depreciated.]

Solution to Problem Five:

Calculation of February gross profit:

Sales Revenue (less returns) *		$41,600
Less: The cost of goods sold during February:		
Goods on hand at February 1 (Opening Inventory):	$16,000	
Goods bought during the month (Purchases):	32,000	
	$48,000	
Less: The cost of goods not sold at February 28 (Closing Inventory)	8,000	
Thus yielding the cost of those goods that were sold during February		40,000
Gross Profit		$ 1,600

[* In your calculation, you undoubtedly deducted the $400 at some point to arrive at the $41,600 gross. Customarily, Sales Returns and Allowances are netted against Sales Revenue rather than deducted as a Cost of Goods Sold or another expense. This might be important for such purposes as calculating rent due under a lease calling for a rent of 8% of "Sales Revenue."]

Solution to Problem Six:

A. Journal entries of transactions:

March	1	Account Receivable—Myers	$ 150	
		Sales Revenue		$ 150

2	Purchase Expense	$1,000	
	Account Payable—Commodore		$1,000
4	Sales Returns	150	
	Account Receivable—Myers		150
5	Cash	1,500	
	Sales Revenue		1,500
6	Cash	1,500	
	Common Shares		1,000
	Capital Contributed in Excess of Par		500
7	Account Payable—Commodore	100	
	Purchase Returns		100
11	Land	3,000	
	Note Payable (9%, 60 days)—Jones		3,000
12	Land	2,700	
	Cash		2,700
13	Account Payable—Jorgenson	400	
	Cash		400
14	Account Payable—Jacobsen	500	
	Note Payable (30 days) Jacobsen		500
15	Account Payable—Jackson	150	
	Common Shares		100
	Capital Contributed in Excess of Par		50
16	Account Payable—Jameson	150	
	Sales Revenue		150
17	Wage Expense	150	
	Sales Revenue		150
18	Salary Expense	300	
	Cash		300
19	Wage Expense	500	
	Cash		500
20	Salary—President	2,000	
	Cash		2,000
22	Wage Expense	150	
	Common Shares		100
	Capital Contributed in Excess of Par		50
23	Wage Expense	100	
	Salary Expense		100
25	Sales Returns	150	
	Credit Memo—Harris (Account Payable)		150
26	Sales Returns	150	
	Common Shares		100
	Capital Contributed in Excess of Par		50
28	Cash	3,000	
	Sales Revenue		3,000

29	Wage Expense	$ 500	
	Cash		$ 500
	Salary Expense	300	
	Cash		300
30	Purchase Expense	5,000	
	Account Payable—Azimuth		5,000
31	Customer Deposit—Pears and Saw-		
	buck, Inc.	2,000	
	Sales Revenue		2,000

B.   Adjusting journal entries:

(a)	Interest Expense	$ 500	
	Prepaid Interest (on ten yr. note)		$ 500
(b)	Rent Expense	100	
	Prepaid Rent		100
(c)	Depreciation Expense	1,000	
	Accumulated Depreciation—Equipment		1,000
(d)	Depreciation Expense	167	
	Accumulated Depreciation—Buildings		167

[All figures are rounded out to the nearest dollar.]

(Each of the above is suggested by items on the February 28 balance sheet. The following are adjustments required by the transactions during the month.)

(e)	Interest Expense	$ 15	
	Accrued Interest Payable—Jones		$ 15
(f)	Prepaid Salary—President	1,000	
	Salary—President		1,000
(g)	Cost of Goods Sold	11,000	
	Inventory (March 1)		11,000
(h)	Cost of Goods Sold	6,000	
	Purchase Expense		6,000
	Purchase Returns	100	
	Cost of Goods Sold		100
(i)	Inventory (March 31)	12,700	
	Cost of Goods Sold		12,700

[The Purchase Returns account is an offset account to Purchase Expense, and, as such, you would treat it in reverse to Purchase Expense, by transferring any balance (always a credit balance) to Cost of Goods Sold, as a credit.]

[At this point you should have set up your T accounts, entered opening balances from the February 28 balance sheet and posted the March journal entries (as they are shown at Sections A and B above). To avoid unnecessary duplication of T accounts, they are omitted here. But they would appear as indicated at D below, without the closing entries.]

C.   Closing entries:

(j)	Profit and Loss	$4,200	
	Cost of Goods Sold		$4,200

(k)	Profit and Loss	100	
	Rent Expense		100
(*l*)	Profit and Loss	1,400	
	Wage Expense		1,400
(m)	Profit and Loss	500	
	Salary Expense		500
(n)	Profit and Loss	1,000	
	Salary Expense—President		1,000
(o)	Profit and Loss	515	
	Interest Expense		515
(p)	Profit and Loss	1,167	
	Depreciation Expense		1,167

[At this point, if a tentative compilation showed that the Profit and Loss account had a credit balance, it would be appropriate to make entries for Income Tax Expense as shown in subchapter G, supra. However, in this case there is a debit balance, i.e., a loss, and we will not at this point introduce the accounting complications arising from loss carryovers and carrybacks in tax law. See *APB Op. No. 11*, ¶¶ 42–50 (1967)].

(q)	Sales Revenue	$6,950	
	Profit and Loss		$6,950
(r)	Profit and Loss	450	
	Sales Returns		450
(s)	Retained Earnings (Loss)	2,382	
	Profit and Loss		2,382

[Sales Returns also are an offset account (to Sales Revenue), and any balance (always a debit) should be transferred to Profit and Loss as a debit.]

D. T accounts after adjustment and closing:

(Adjusting and closing entries are lettered, and the transactions during the month are dated.)

Assets and Offsetting Accounts

Cash

Opening				
Balance	$ 45,000	March 12	$ 2,700
March 5	1,500	13	400
6	1,500	18	300
28	3,000	19	500
		20	2,000
		29	500
		29	300

Accounts Receivable *

Opening				
Balance	$ 22,000	March 4	S	150
March 1	150			

Inventories

Opening		(g)		S 11,000
Balance	$ 11,000			
(i)	12,700			

[* For convenience here, all Accounts Receivable have been lumped into one account. They could have been carried in separate T accounts.]

Prepaid Interest

Opening		(a)	$	500
Balance	$ 5,000			

Prepaid Rent

Opening		(b)	S	100
Balance	$ 1,000			

Prepaid Salary—President

(f) $ 1,000	

Buildings

Opening Balance $100,000	

Equipment

Opening Balance $100,000	

Accumulated Depreciation— Buildings

	Opening Balance $ 333
	(d) 167

Accumulated Depreciation— Equipment

	Opening Balance $ 2,000
	(c) 1,000

Land

Opening Balance $ 20,000	
March 11 3,000	
12 2,700	

Liability Accounts

Accounts Payable **

3/ 7 $ 100	Opening	
13 400	Balance	$ 12,000
14 500	3/2	1,000
15 150	30	5,000
16 150	Balance	$ 16,700

Customer Deposit—Pears and Sawbuck, Inc.

	Opening
3/31 $ 2,000	Balance $ 2,000

Long term debt—10 yr. Note

	Opening Balance $100,000

Notes Payable—short term

	3/11 $ 3,000
	14 500

[** All Accounts Payable have been lumped together here for convenience although separate T accounts could have been set up for each.]

Credit Memo—Harris

	3/25 $ 150

Accrued Interest Payable

	(e) $ 15

Stockholders' Equity Accounts Common Shares—$10 Par

	Opening Balance $150,000
	3/ 6 1,000
	15 100
	22 100
	26 100

Capital Contributed in Excess of Par

	3/ 6 $ 500
	15 50
	22 50
	26 50

Retained Earnings

(s)	2,382	Opening Balance	$ 37,667

Salary Expense

3/18	$ 300	3/23	$ 100
29	300	(m)	500

Expense and Income Accounts

Profit and Loss

(j)	$ 4,200	(a)	$ 6,950
(k)	100	(s)	2,382
(l)	1,400		
(m)	500		
(n)	1,000		
(o)	515		
(p)	1,167		
(r)	450		
	$ 9,332		$ 9,332

Salary Expense—President

3/20	$ 2,000	(f)	$ 1,000
		(h)	1,000

Interest Expense

(a)	$ 500	(o)	$ 515
(e)	15		
	$ 515		

Purchase Expense

3/ 2	$ 1,000	(h)	$ 6,000
30	5,000		

Depreciation Expense

(c)	$ 1,000	(p)	$ 1,167
(d)	167		

Purchase Returns

(h)	$ 100	3/7	$ 100

Cost of Goods Sold

(g)	$ 11,000	(h)	$ 100
(h)	6,000	(i)	12,700
		(j)	4,200

Rent Expense

(b)	$ 100	(k)	$ 100

Sales Revenue

(q)	$ 6,950	3/ 1	$ 150
		5	1,500
		16	150
		17	150
		28	3,000
		31	2,000

Wage Expense

3/17	$ 150	(l)	$ 1,400
19	500		
22	150		
23	100		
29	500		

Sales Returns

3/ 4	$ 150	(r)	$ 450
25	150		
26	150		

E.   Income statement for March:

Sales Revenue (less returns)		$ 6,500
Less:		
Cost of Goods Sold:		
Inventory (March 1)	$11,000	
Purchases (less returns)	5,900	
	$16,900	
Inventory (March 31)	12,700	
Cost of Goods Sold		4,200
Gross Profit on Sales		$ 2,300

Less Other Expenses:

Rent	$ 100	
Wages	1,400	
Salaries	500	
Salary—President	1,000	
Interest	515	
Depreciation	1,167	
		4,682
Net Loss from Operations		$ (2,382)

F. Balance sheet at March 31:

Current Assets:			Current Liabilities:		
Cash	$ 44,300		Accounts Payable	$16,700	
Accounts Receivable	22,000		Notes Payable	3,500	
Inventories	12,700		Credit Memo	150	
			Accrued Interest		
Prepaid Interest	4,500		Payable	15	
Prepaid Rent	900		Total		$ 20,365
Prepaid Salaries—					
President	1,000		Long-term debt:		
Total		$ 85,400	ten year Note		100,000
Equipment	$100,000		Total Liabilities		$120,365
Less: Accumulated			Stockholders' Equity:		
Depreciation	3,000		Common Shares:		
		97,000	Authorized:		
			20,000 shares, $10		
			par Issued and Out-		
			standing: 15,130		
			shares		151,300
Land		25,700			
Buildings	$100,000				
Less: Accumulated					
Depreciation	500			151,300	
		99,500	Capital Contributed in		650
			Excess of Par		
			Retained Earnings		35,285
			Total Liabilities and		
Total Assets		$307,600	Stockholders' Equity		$307,600

Chapter II

MAKING AND SELECTING ACCOUNTING PRINCIPLES AND THE ROLE OF THE INDEPENDENT AUDITOR

OBJECTIVES

1. Examine how the Securities and Exchange Commission has delegated to the accounting profession the authority to make generally accepted accounting principles ("GAAP").

2. Determine who, as between management and the auditor, selects among alternative GAAP available to the reporting entity.

3. Consider the distinction between the audit function and accounting.

4. Observe the various forms of auditor's reports and their meaning.

5. Begin a study of internal control and the firm's legal obligations under the accounting and controls provision of the Securities Exchange Act of 1934, § 13(b)(2) (known as "the accounting provisions of the Foreign Corrupt Practices Act").

RELEVANCE FOR LAWYERS

Lawyers deal with questions of disclosure in filings with governmental agencies, published reports, rate-making, legal liability for financial frauds, and other business matters and therefore must understand the sources, applications, and audit of accounting principles as well as the various actors in the process. In addition the accounting and internal controls provisions of the Securities Exchange Act of 1934, § 13(b)(2) require legal oversight.

In Chapter I, we noted a few accounting principles, at least implicitly. For example we saw that ordinary interest and rent are allocated as expenses or revenues over the time period for which the loan or lease extends. Also, we saw that the net cost of tangible assets is depreciated over their useful lives.

Who makes these rules? What are the management's and auditor's respective roles in implementing the rules? Are deviations sanctioned? If so, how? How does a lawyer concerned with questions of compliance locate the rules? Are they "law" or "fact" in litigation?

In this chapter we introduce some preliminary answers to some of these questions, others of which will be further discussed in later chapters.

In addition, the primary responsibility for keeping accounting records and verifying and summarizing them must of course be in the management of a firm. But the divorce of ownership from management in the modern public corporation calls for an independent check, and this is done by outside auditors, independent public accountants who perform the audit task for companies around the world. The auditing task involves two aspects:

(a) verification of the existence of the reported facts; e.g., whether the amount reported as inventory in fact exists as a physical matter; and

(b) determination of the proper application of accounting principles to the facts; e.g., that inventory is valued at lower of cost or market.

In performing these two functions, the auditor employs *auditing* standards, although in the second function he or she also applies *accounting* principles. The guidelines are "generally accepted auditing standards" ("GAAS") and "generally accepted accounting principles" ("GAAP").[a] We also here consider what GAAP and GAAS are and how they are developed.

A. MAKING AND SELECTING ACCOUNTING PRINCIPLES

ARTHUR ANDERSEN & CO. v. SEC

[1976–'77 Transfer Binder] Fed.Sec.L.Rep. (CCH) ¶ 95,720.
U.S.D.C., N.D.Ill., 1976.

[Oral opinion from the bench by Judge Prentice Marshall.]

This is an action brought by the plaintiff, Arthur Andersen & Company against the defendant Securities & Exchange Commission

---

a. Accountants and securities lawyers are fond of acronyms of which there are dozens relevant to accounting and auditing. Although we attempt to note each of them when their referent is first introduced, because of their abundance we also provide a Table of Abbreviations at the beginning of the book for your assistance.

seeking relief under 28 USC Section 2201, and an injunction pendente lite under Rule 65 of the Federal Rules of Civil Procedure.

Defendant's alleged wrong is said to consist of violations of the rule-making provisions of the Administrative Procedure Act, 5 USC Sections 553 and 706, of the SEC's own rule-making regulations which are found in 17 CFR, Section 202.6, and generally of the laws and Constitution of the United States.

The plaintiff, Arthur Andersen & Company, is a general partnership organized and existing under the laws of the State of Illinois with its principal office located in Chicago. It is a firm of independent public accountants. The firm's activities include the examination of and reporting on the financial statements of business enterprises and public bodies. Many of the firm's clients are subject to the jurisdiction of the SEC and are required to include financial statements together with Arthur Andersen's audit reports thereon and filings under the various Acts which are administered and enforced by the SEC. These filings include, but are not limited to, registration statements filed pursuant to the Securities Act of 1933 and annual and periodic reports and proxy statements filed pursuant to the Securities Exchange Act of 1934.

In all of these filings, the plaintiff is required to observe the rules and regulations promulgated by the SEC which govern the form and content of financial statements; in particular, the plaintiff is required to observe the SEC's Regulation SX governing accounting presentations and filings with the SEC. Rule 202(c) of Regulation SX, requires plaintiff to express an opinion relating to the financial statements filed by its clients with the SEC and the accounting principles and practices reflected therein.

The rule does not by itself define or impose any limitations or prerequisites concerning the accounting principles and practices used in preparing the statements; however, the defendant has issued a series of statements known as Accounting Series Releases which are incorporated into * * * Regulation SX by its Rule 1–101(a).

* * *

The plaintiff seeks a preliminary injunction enjoining and restraining the defendant from enforcing or applying two issuances known as ASR 150 and ASR 177, the content and details of which will be touched upon momentarily.

The standards for the issuance of a preliminary injunction are well-known, and the parties and their counsel have addressed them.

The first, in view of the immediacy of the relief which is given, is that the plaintiff demonstrate a likelihood of success on the merits.

* * *

The first item in controversy is defendant's ASR 150, which was issued on December the 20th, 1973. The defendant concedes that the rule-making provisions of the Administrative Procedure Act and the

Commission were not followed prior to the issuance of ASR 150 because as defendant asserts, it is not a rule; rather, it is concerned with defendant's recognition of certain accounting principles enjoying widespread recognition in the accounting profession.

Some history * * * is warranted in appraising the significance, purpose and impact of ASR 150.

On April 25, 1938, prior to the enactment of the Administrative Procedure Act, the defendant issued its ASR 4, which provided in part as follows: "In cases where financial statements filed with this Commission pursuant to its rules and regulations under the Securities Act of 1934 are prepared in accordance with accounting principles for which there is no substantial authoritative support, such financial statements will be presumed to be misleading or inaccurate despite disclosures contained in the certificate of the accountant or in footnotes to the statements provided the matters involved are material.

"In cases where there is a difference of opinion between the Commission and the registrant as to the proper principles of accounting to be followed, disclosure will be accepted in lieu of correction of the financial statements themselves only if the points involved are such that there is substantial authoritative support for the practices followed by the registrant and the position of the Commission has not previously been expressed in rules, regulations or other official releases of the Commission including the published opinions of its chief accountant."

The meaning of the expression "substantial authoritative support" contained in ASR 4 was left to a case-by-case determination. While the Committee on Accounting Procedures of the American Institute of Certified Public Accountants issued [Accounting] [R]esearch [B]ulletins in respect to accounting principles from time to time, and later the Accounting Principles Board of the Institute issued [O]pinions in regard to those principles, there was, as we see it, no single source of authoritative standards. Although the defendant Commission has and has had the power to promulgate its own accounting standards, it has elected historically in deference to and in cooperation with the accounting profession not to do so.

In 1973, conditions within the accounting profession changed. The American Institute of Certified Public Accountants designated the Financial Accounting Standards Board of the Financial Accounting Foundation as the body to establish authoritative accounting principles pursuant to Rule 203 of the American Institute of Certified Public Accountants, which rule was in turn made obligatory upon the members of the AICPA.

It was thereafter that ASR 150 was issued by the SEC. After summarizing the content and import of ASR 4, ASR 150 provides in that respect, as I perceive it, deemed offensive by the plaintiff, as follows: "For the purposes of this policy"—that being the policy previously articulated in ASR 4—"For the purposes of this policy, principles, standards and practices promulgated by the FASB in its statements and interpretations will be considered by the Commission as having substantial authoritative support, and those contrary to such FASB promulgations will be considered to have no such support."

By ASR 150, the defendant SEC has said no more than that it will henceforth, in making its long-standing inquiry into whether a financial statement has been prepared in accord with accepted accounting principles, apply and look to the substantial authoritative support provided by the FASB, will be considered as having substantial authoritative support, while those contrary to the principles approved by the FASB will not be. (sic)

In taking this position, in my judgment, the SEC has done no more than state the obvious. Now that an authoritative profession-accepted collection of accounting principles exists, it will look to them first in making its own judgment on the question of authoritative support.

On the other hand, a principle contrary to the FASB standards will be considered without support. No mention is made for a principle which is neither embraced by nor rejected by the FASB.

ASR 150 emerges, then, as a method by which the SEC will evaluate accounting principles. It does not ordain the result of that evaluation. It does not prescribe per se approval to or rejection of any accounting principle. It merely acknowledges a fact, the existence of an authoritative body of principles, and says that it will credit those principles.

It is not a conditional imperative, which is the characteristic of a substantive rule.

Nor is ASR 150 rendered invalid by the hyperbole that the SEC has delegated impermissibly its rule-making authority to FASB. True, ASR 150 will encompass not only past, but future accounting principles approved by the FASB, but those prospective principles will have no greater force than the present ones do. The SEC will consider them authoritative, which they clearly are and will be, but ASR 150 does not even suggest that the SEC will abdicate its ultimate responsibility to judge the propriety of the accounting principles employed by a registrant.

Accordingly, as to ASR 150, we have concluded preliminarily that the plaintiff has failed to show the requisite likelihood of success on the merits, so as to entitle it to preliminary relief.

[We turn] to ASR 177, which concededly adopted a rule amending Instruction H(f) of Form 10–Q, which is a quarterly financial report which must be filed with the SEC by certain registrants. Plaintiff concedes that the Administrative Procedure Act was followed by the SEC through the comment stage in promulgating H(f). Here plaintiff's complaint is in essence that the SEC arbitrarily rejected the comments which we are told were overwhelmingly adverse to H(f), and alternatively, that H(f) is arbitrary and capricious because it may prove impossible for an accountant's registrant client to comply with it.

As for the first contention, rejection of the comments, our understanding is that the adverse comments originated with the accounting profession. The totality of the record here does not suggest that the SEC is deaf to the opinions of the accounting profession. Indeed, the history of ASR 150 and its forerunner, ASR 4, show precisely the contrary; furthermore, it is not unusual for a group which will be affected by a change in regulations to be opposed to it. The status quo is comfortable, but often not adequate.

It is here on a motion for a preliminary relief that [a] court should give special credence to the expertise of commissions such as the defendant. True, the defendant's decision is subject to review here, but the review should be deliberate and not hasty. Indeed, it is only in the most extraordinary circumstances that the public interest is served by a court peremptorily preempting the legislative judgment of a commission such as the SEC which is charged with protecting the public interest in a given specialized area. No showing of extraordinary circumstances or patent abuse of discretion has been shown here.

Insofar as the impossibility of compliance is concerned, we think that plaintiff and its supporting amicus colleagues read H(f) too severely. It provides this: When a business enterprise changes an accounting principle or practice previously followed, the first Form 10–Q report filed subsequent thereto must include as an exhibit a letter from its independent accountants indicating whether or not the change is to an alternate principle which in his judgment [is preferable under the circumstances. No letter] will be required if the change is made in response to a * * * standard adopted by the FASB which requires the change.

No substantial gloss has been placed upon the phrase "Under the circumstances". But our reading of it at this preliminary stage is that the totality of Amendment H(f) says no more than that the accountant should state why in the particular situation, where a change in practice has been adopted, why that change has been effected. Why "under the circumstances" is the new method preferable to the old? We just do not perceive the impossibility of responding to that inquiry. Some reason must exist for the change. Plaintiff's clients are obliged to state the reasons through their professional spokesmen, the accountants.

Accordingly, in our judgment, plaintiff has again failed to show that degree of likelihood of success on the merits as to warrant a granting of preliminary relief.

* * *

1. WHO MAKES ACCOUNTING PRINCIPLES?

The *Arthur Andersen* case partially answers the question, who makes the accounting principles which the management and auditors apply.

Although the auditing profession in the United States goes back at least to the middle of the Nineteenth Century when absentee English land owners hired Scots to go to the western American territories to check and report on the management of their ranches, there have always been widely varying generally accepted principles applied to similar matters. The mechanics of double-entry bookkeeping had been long-developed, but guidance as to when to recognize an asset or expense, for example, is often a matter of different practices. Indeed until only sixty years ago, at the beginning of the Great Depression, accounting and accountants were ununified, and the concept of "Generally Accepted Accounting Principles" was as yet undeveloped; accounting practice and principles, such as they were, were being formulated within the large public accounting firms, and attempts were being made by leading academics to reduce them to an organized body of principles. The first attempts to authoritatively fix accounting principles were joint efforts of representatives of the American Institute of Certified Public Accountants ("AICPA") and the New York Stock Exchange in 1932. See the six rules adopted by the membership of the AICPA in 1934, five of which were first propounded in a letter to the New York Stock Exchange by an AICPA committee in 1932, reproduced as Chapter 1, Sec. A of *ARB 43* (1953).[b] But after the enactment of the 1933–'34 securities legislation and creation of the Securities and Exchange Commission, leadership passed to the Commission.[c]

Under the federal Securities Act of 1933, any company which seeks to sell securities publicly must file with the SEC a registration statement, and under the Securities Exchange Act of 1934, a company which has securities listed on a stock exchange or which, if not listed, are held by 500 or more shareholders of record when the firm has at least five million dollars in assets, must file a different, although similar, registration statement and annual and quarterly reports. See § 5 of the 1933 Securities Act and §§ 12, 13 and 15(d) of the Securities Exchange Act of 1934 and the regulations thereunder. Those who register under the 1934 Act must also deliver proxy statements at least annually to their shareholders containing information relevant to shareholders' meetings. Among the data mandated for proxy solicitations for annual meetings to elect directors are financial statements and a management analysis of them. Even companies making offerings exempt from 1933 Act registration must comply with certain disclosure requirements of the Commission, as must mutual funds, broker-dealer firms, and other securities professionals. Because financial statements are the heart of SEC disclosure, the Commission has been given power to fix accounting principles with respect to all these disclosure documents.[d]

b. "ARBs" are Accounting Research Bulletins, further explained shortly together with directions for finding their published sources.

c. The history of the development of accounting in the United States and certain other countries is described in S. Zeff, Forging Accounting Principles in Five Countries (1971). See also, B. Yamey and A. Littleton, eds., Studies in the History of Accounting (1956) and J. Carey, The Rise of the Accounting Profession (2 vols.) (1970). The official citation of the 1933 Securities Act is 15 U.S.C. § 77a et seq. We shall use the informal, more well-known citation to each act. E.g., "§ 12 of the 1933 Act."

d. For the very intricate basis for this statement see Fiflis, Current Problems of Accountants' Responsibilities to Third Parties, 28 Vand.L.Rev. 31, 52–62 (1975).

Although these SEC companies are small in number, perhaps 20,000 of the over 10 million business firms in this country, these 20,000 represent virtually all firms whose securities are publicly traded, in terms of value of assets. There are the other 10 million non-SEC companies not legally subject to SEC registration and reporting requirements, although certain aspects of securities laws, such as for example, the anti-fraud rules, are applicable in some of these cases. Nevertheless, you will find that accountants tend to adopt SEC accounting practices even for firms not legally subject to them.

In addition to requiring financial disclosures, the securities laws require that the financial statements prepared by management be given the imprimatur of an independent auditor. There had been in the hearings on the Securities Act of 1933 some proposals that these statements should be audited by government employees, but representatives of the private accounting profession persuaded the Congress otherwise, thus putting the accounting profession in a strategic position the importance of which cannot be overstated. It is hard to think of another circumstance whereby a governmental privilege like access to the public issue and trading markets is conditioned on employment of persons of a particular profession.[e] Unlike accounting principles which are clearly within the authority of the SEC, auditing standards are less clearly so, although they are applied by the Commission in its enforcement proceedings.[f] Despite its power to fix accounting principles, the task is far beyond the Commission's means and has been ceded to the accounting profession in a series of steps described in the *Arthur Andersen* case and in more detail below.

ACCOUNTING SERIES RELEASE NO. 4

Securities and Exchange Commission, 1938.

"ADMINISTRATIVE POLICY ON FINANCIAL STATEMENTS

"The Securities and Exchange Commission today issued the following statement of its administrative policy with respect to financial statements.

"In cases where financial statements filed with this commission pursuant to its rules and regulations under the Securities Act of 1933 or the Securities Exchange Act of 1934 are prepared in accordance with accounting principles for which there is not substantial authoritative support, such financial statements will be presumed to be misleading or inaccurate despite disclosures contained in the certificate of the accountant or in footnotes to the statements provided the matters involved are material. In cases where there is a difference of opinion

---

e. The accounting profession may be divided into two groups: (1) those who do the bookkeeping and accounting for the corporation or other business enterprise as employees or officers, including internal auditing, and (2) independent public accountants (or auditors) who after an audit, render a report on the financial statements of the enterprise prepared by the just-described internal agents of the corporation.

f. Fiflis, supra n. d.

between the Commission and the registrant as to the proper principles of accounting to be followed, disclosure will be accepted in lieu of correction of the financial statements themselves only if the points involved are such that there is substantial authoritative support for the practices followed by the registrant and the position of the Commission has not previously been expressed in rules, regulations or other official releases of the Commission, including the published opinions of its Chief Accountant." [g]

The new agency had the duty to read, review and comment on the documents filed, with the goal of eliciting "full and fair disclosure" of matters that could be deduced from the information filed initially and submitted in response to the staff queries. It is widely accepted that the level and clarity of disclosures in prospectuses and in amended reports was substantially raised as a result of SEC staff involvement in the process. The same result occurred in the caliber and fairness of financial statements included in those filings in which the accounting was altered as a result of staff involvement.

What gave the agency the power to require changes in filed documents? The explanation is simple for new offerings prospectuses. Basically, under the 1933 Act, the intending issuer of securities could not sell the securities until the registration statement was filed and then declared effective by the Commission. At first Commission action was needed to declare a registration statement effective and the Commission required a staff recommendation to do so. It ultimately delegated that power to the staff. This power in the hands of the staff to determine subjectively whether or not an issuer could sell its securities had all the utility of a "lead pipe"; it was an instrument sufficiently effective to enforce the staff demands. It was as simple as this: If you want to sell your securities, then alter your accounting in accordance with our request and we will recommend that the Commission declare your registration statement effective, but if you do not alter your accounting, you cannot sell your securities. Needless to say, nearly every company complied with the staff's requests and every accounting firm involved, upon acquiescence by the client, endorsed the request of the SEC accounting staff by expressing their opinion that the financial statements so prepared were presented fairly in accordance with generally accepted accounting principles. Those companies which did not comply would usually abandon their proposed offerings, lest they become involved in proceedings by the Commission to issue a stop order. This power was not exercised by fiat, but rather under the able oversight of senior members of the accounting staff, nearly all of whom were certified public accountants, and the Commission, nearly all of

---

g. "Reporting" is to be distinguished from "disclosure." The former refers to the numbered columns in the main bodies of the financial statements whereas "disclosure" refers to footnotes and verbal explanations in parenthetic expressions in the body of the financial statements or the auditor's report which appears at the beginning or end of the financials.

whose members over the years have been lawyers. The use of this administrative lead pipe, continued for many years as an effective tool for achieving accounting reform in individual cases in which the SEC staff thought reform was necessary. This administrative device, which was intended by the Congress in the scheme of securities regulation, was used very adroitly and was a principal factor which led to the sterling reputation the SEC has earned over the years.

Accounting developments stemming from the SEC were the result of an interdisciplinary process whereby staff lawyers, financial analysts (quite often these were economists by training) and accountants pooled their ideas into a common approach to each registration statement. The accounting ideas quite often originated with lawyers or financial analysts or sometimes even staff engineers. This interdisciplinary approach added balance to decisions as to what proper accounting should be in each individual case.

After awhile a body of informally decided cases on a particular issue becomes a policy. Thus evolved many of the "unwritten policies" with which practitioners have had to deal in SEC filings. Some of those accounting policies have now been codified in SEC accounting rules, i.e., Regulation S–X, the *Codification of Financial Reporting Policies* and the Staff Accounting Bulletins ("SABs").[h]

Many of the SEC's policies and unwritten requirements for its reporting companies have been adopted by the accounting profession in its formal pronouncements, which also apply to non-SEC companies. For example, much of Accounting Principles Board Opinion 15, *Earnings Per Share*, is merely a codification of by-then-existing common practice fostered by the SEC. In this and in many other pronouncements the enunciators of accounting principles merely followed SEC staff policy in formulating their learned opinions. We shall have more to say about this private sector GAAP-making momentarily.

Any search of the early cases would undoubtedly reveal conflicts. For example, in Litigation Release No. 377 (1946), the Commission went on record, in a successful federal court injunctive action, with a declaration that failure of an oil company, Standard Oil of Kansas, to disclose the "present value" of its proven reserves made the financial statements of that company misleading. Unfortunately, and without any apparent explanation, the SEC did an abrupt reversal causing the staff later to forbid such disclosures on grounds that such disclosure was in the nature of an appraisal or a projection not necessary of fulfillment.

h. The Codification and Reg. S–X incorporate the prior Accounting Series Releases ("ASRs") such as ASR 4, quoted above. Amendments to the Codification of Financial Reporting Policies of the Commission are made through Financial Reporting Releases ("FRRs").

In addition, the Commission's actions enforcing its accounting and auditing requirements are published as Accounting and Auditing Enforcement Releases ("AAERs"). Further, SEC Litigation Releases often indicate positions on accounting issues.

All of these but Litigation Releases, including Reg. S–X, the Codification, and SABs, are compiled in CCH Fed.Sec.L.Rep. The Litigation Releases are indexed there and are published in the SEC Docket.

See Gerstle v. Gamble–Skogmo, Inc., 478 F.2d 1281 (2d Cir.1973), and Foster, *Asset Disclosure for Stockholder Decisions,* Fin.Exec. 32 (July, 1967).

One more factor needs to be mentioned in this background commentary. Because of the expense, inconvenience and embarrassment of publishing and then revising financial statements, the SEC accounting staff is available to discuss with registrants, their independent accountants and attorneys any matter of accounting treatment which might be or has been challenged by the SEC staff in connection with a filing. Ultimately, these conferences are held in the Office of the Chief Accountant of the Commission or the Chief Accountant of the Division of Corporation Finance, who as a practical matter handles many of the conferences. Virtually the entire history of the development of accounting principles during the fifty year history of the Commission has been played out day by day in the form of argument between the SEC staff and registrants, represented by their accountants and attorneys, over what accounting should be acceptable in filings with the Commission.

Publication of the staff's views so expressed might be the way to solve one of the crucially important problems of accounting—how to cope with the imaginativeness of managements who wish to create a favorable accounting picture for their companies, sometimes called "creative accounting," so as to please shareholders and attract new investors. Managers seek thereby to keep up share prices so as to ward off takeover attempts and obtain other perquisites of success. The issue is how to quickly respond to new problems. More accurately, it is how to plug holes in the dike caused by management's inventiveness in creating accounting techniques not clearly outlawed by GAAP. If the staff's views were published quickly and made GAAP for the particular practice, other issuers' financial statements would be bound to follow them.

But sunshine has not yet found its way into the Chief Accountant's office where important precedent-setting decisions are still being made by the regulators behind closed doors. The public sees only the end product of the closed-door meetings and is not given any of the rationale or unpublished facts that enter into the decision. In recent years, a practice has been instituted whereby the staff usually requests a memorandum covering issues to be discussed and the registrant's reasons for its position. Registrants are not told of any memorandum prepared by the staff setting forth the reasons for the staff's position and are not given written reasons for the ultimate decision. How the Chief Accountant's office escaped the movement toward sunshine is not apparent.[i] To resolve such issues, the FASB instead has developed a different technique by appointing an Emerging Issues Task Force

i. For more on the history of the SEC and accounting, see Barr and Koch, Accounting and the SEC, 28 Geo.Wash.L.Rev. 176 (1959); Pines, Securities and Exchange Commission and Accounting Principles, 30 Law and Contemp.Prob. 727 (1965); Sanders, Accounting Aspects of the Securities Act, 4 Law and Contemp.Prob. 191 (1937).

("EITF") whose views are published in the AICPA's monthly Journal of Accountancy.

Although the SEC thus has the authority of the securities law to fix accounting principles, and the "lead pipe" authority of the practicalities of the administrative process, it has, at least in recent years, played more of an overseer's role, allowing the profession to carry the ball in making accounting principles.

After World War II the Commission attempted to announce accounting principles in a revision of Reg. S–X, but both the American Accounting Association ("AAA," a professional organization of academic accountants) and the AICPA objected mightily. See 26 Acctg.Rev. 231 (1951); J. Accountancy A–20 (Nov., 1950). Subsequently, for many years the Commission assumed an essentially, although occasionally interrupted, passive role in the formulation of principles.[j]

The AICPA moved to establish a body of literature that would be accepted as substantial authoritative support by setting up a Committee on Accounting Procedure, which began issuing the ARBs in 1939. ARBs, while quite general in language, followed the trail established by the SEC in cases it handled. Since these recited that their authority rested upon the general acceptability of the opinions so reached, they had an indeterminate status. Further, they were not based on research but were more or less the ad hoc views of the Committee, some members of which viewed their task as serving their client's interests. This unsatisfactory circumstance ultimately led the AICPA to organize the Accounting Principles Board, which issued its first Opinion in 1962. As appears from Appendix A to *APB Op. No. 6*, in 1964, the APB Opinions and the ARBs were given some teeth by a determination of the Council of the AICPA that these pronouncements constituted substantial authoritative support for generally accepted accounting principles and that departure therefrom must be disclosed by AICPA members. Further, the APB was given much more research support.

However, the APB itself soon came under heavy criticism for its slow pace in adopting accounting principles, for the quality of its Opinions and the research behind them, and for what appeared to some to be evidence that some members of the Board, serving without compensation, like the former Committee on Accounting Research,

j. Except for a few noteworthy instances. For example, in ASR 96 (1963), which was subsequently rescinded, the Commission torpedoed an effort of the APB to choose between two methods of accounting for the investment tax credit, by announcing that it would accept either method. In addition, it adopted its own pronouncement on the status of a deferred tax liability as a current liability in ASR 102 (1965), when the APB delayed action.

Professor Chatov has bitterly disapproved this passivity and has argued that the Commission should have taken active control of accounting principles. R. Chatov, Corporate Financial Reporting: Public or Private Control? (1975), especially Chapter 17. Compare Kripke, Book Review, 50 N.Y.U.L.Rev. 47 (1975) expressing some sympathy for the Chatov point of view, but pointing out the Commission's lack of manpower and other difficulties and contending that the overall result could have been better if the Commission had forced the pace of the development of accounting principles in the private sector more strongly.

were representing the desires of their corporate clients in their votes on accounting principles.

Beginning in the 1950s and extending into the late 1960s the SEC appeared to be softening its approach toward accounting matters from its early aggressiveness to a passive acceptance of even remote rationalization offered by the accounting firms in advocating or defending their accounting. The approach seemed to be to try persuasion diligently and if persuasion failed then to accept almost any rationale. In the late 1960s and early 1970s, after barely a decade of this softened approach toward accounting enforcement, large accounting firms were hit with an unprecedented volume of litigation by investors and lenders asserting that they had been misled by audited financial statements, usually statements that had been filed with the SEC. Was there a cause and effect relationship between the SEC's relaxed attitude toward accounting enforcement and the subsequent rash of litigation against accounting firms? Compare the savings and loan debacle which some have blamed on the inadequate supervision of accounting by the regulators.

This history led to the appointment by the AICPA in 1972 of a Committee headed by a lawyer who was a former SEC Commissioner, Francis M. Wheat, which proposed that accounting principles be formed by a new Financial Accounting Standards Board independent of the AICPA, whose members would be paid enough so that they need not and would not engage in any other occupation, and with an elaborate system of funding to keep it in fact independent of the AICPA and other accountants' organizations. The FASB took over from the APB in 1973. It is funded and monitored by the Financial Accounting Foundation, an independent nongovernmental foundation supported by donations from the profession. The SEC formally announced its support of the FASB through *ASR 150* (1973), infra, discussed at length in the *Arthur Andersen* opinion.

ASR 150 declared essentially that the phrase "substantial authoritative support" as used in *ASR 4* would henceforth be construed to mean the official pronouncements of the AICPA's Committee on Accounting Procedure (ARBs), the AICPA's Accounting Principles Board and the Financial Accounting Standards Board. This represented a major statement of policy by the Commission since it was the first time the Commission had identified the pronouncements of any particular organization as constituting substantial authoritative support.

ACCOUNTING SERIES RELEASE NO. 150
Securities and Exchange Commission, 1973.

"STATEMENT OF POLICY ON THE ESTABLISHMENT AND IMPROVEMENT
OF ACCOUNTING PRINCIPLES AND STANDARDS

"Various Acts of Congress administered by the Securities and Exchange Commission clearly state the authority of the Commission to prescribe the methods to be followed in the preparation of accounts and the form and content of financial statements to be filed under the Acts and the responsibility to assure that investors are furnished with information necessary for informed investment decisions. In meeting this statutory responsibility effectively, in recognition of the expertise, energy and resources of the accounting profession, and without abdicating its responsibilities, the Commission has historically looked to the standard-setting bodies designated by the profession to provide leadership in establishing and improving accounting principles. The determinations by these bodies have been regarded by the Commission, with minor exceptions, as being responsive to the needs of investors.

"The body presently designated by the Council of the American Institute of Certified Public Accountants (AICPA) to establish accounting principles is the Financial Accounting Standards Board (FASB). This designation by the AICPA followed the issuance of a report in March 1972 recommending the formation of the FASB, after a study of the matter by a broadly based study group. The recommendations contained in that report were widely endorsed by industry, financial analysts, accounting educators, and practicing accountants. The Commission endorsed the establishment of the FASB in the belief that the Board would provide an institutional framework which will permit prompt and responsible actions flowing from research and consideration of varying viewpoints. The collective experience and expertise of the members of the FASB and the individuals and professional organizations supporting it are substantial. Equally important, the commitment of resources to the FASB is impressive evidence of the willingness and intention of the private sector to support the FASB in accomplishing its task. In view of these considerations, the Commission intends to continue its policy of looking to the private sector for leadership in establishing and improving accounting principles and standards through the FASB with the expectation that the body's conclusions will promote the interests of investors.

"In Accounting Series Release No. 4 (1938) the Commission stated its policy that financial statements prepared in accordance with accounting practices for which there was no substantial authoritative support were presumed to be misleading and that footnote or other disclosure would not avoid this presumption. It also stated that, where there was a difference of opinion between the Commission and a registrant as to the proper accounting to be followed in a particular case, disclosure would be accepted in lieu of correction of the financial statements themselves only if substantial authoritative support existed for the accounting practices followed by the registrant and the position of the Commission had not been expressed in rules, regulations or other official releases. For purposes of this policy, principles, standards and practices promulgated by the FASB in its Statements and Interpretations [1] will be considered by the Commission as having substantial

1. Accounting Research Bulletins of the Committee on Accounting Procedure of the American Institute of Certified Public Ac-countants and effective opinions of the Accounting Principles Board of the Institute should be considered as continuing in force

authoritative support, and those contrary to such FASB promulgations will be considered [2] to have no such support.

"In the exercise of its statutory authority with respect to the form and content of filings under the Acts, the Commission has the responsibility to assure that investors are provided with adequate information. A significant portion of the necessary information is provided by a set of basic financial statements (including the notes thereto) which conform to generally accepted accounting principles. Information in addition to that included in financial statements conforming to generally accepted accounting principles is also necessary. Such additional disclosures are required to be made in various fashions, such as in financial statements and schedules reported on by independent public accountants or as textual statements required by items in the applicable forms and reports filed with the Commission. The Commission will continue to identify areas where investor information needs exist and will determine the appropriate methods of disclosure to meet these needs.

"It must be recognized that in its administration of the Federal Securities Acts and in its review of filings under such Acts, the Commission staff will continue as it has in the past to take such action on a day-to-day basis as may be appropriate to resolve specific problems of accounting and reporting under the particular factual circumstances involved in filings and reports of individual registrants.

"The Commission believes that the foregoing statement of policy provides a sound basis for the Commission and the FASB to make significant contributions to meeting the needs of the registrants and investors.

"By the Commission."

————

The accounting profession has thus through a succession of structural arrangements undertaken to assume control over the permissible GAAP. Although, as we have seen, accounting principles tell us how we can abstract varied human activity into numbers that we can comprehend and compare, and although they would seem therefore to be of the greatest concern to all classes of economic society, the accountants have taken control without any formal recognition that other interested parties who are going to be governed by these principles should have a right to a share in the selection process. It is as if engineers and architects were to insist that only they can determine

with the same degree of authority except to the extent altered, amended, supplemented, revoked or superseded by one or more Statements of Financial Accounting Standards issued by the FASB.

2. It should be noted that Rule 203 of the Rules of Conduct of the Code of Ethics of the AICPA provides that it is necessary to depart from accounting principles promulgated by the body designated by the Council of the AICPA if, due to unusual circumstances, failure to do so would result in misleading financial statements. In such a case, the use of other principles may be accepted or required by the Commission.

what buildings are to be built, without regard to the desires of the customers; or as if only lawyers were permitted to be legislators.

Not all of the Trustees of the Financial Accounting Foundation or the members of the Financial Accounting Standards Advisory Council, which constitute the fund-raising and structural apparatus for the FASB, are accountants. With one exception, members of the FASB have all been accountants.

Despite the SEC's announced support of the FASB in *ASR 150*, some tension has arisen because the SEC has continued with what appears to some to be occasional forays into the formation of accounting principles, as "action on a day-to-day basis" as provided in *ASR 150*. The SEC seeks to distinguish what it is doing, as requirements of disclosure, to be distinguished from reporting. See the fourth paragraph quoted above from *ASR 150*.

But few would doubt that to the extent these disclosure requirements survive, they will ultimately force change directly in the financial statements as well as disclosure outside the financial statements. Thus, the relationship between the SEC and the FASB has been variously characterized by the former as a "coalition" or as "creative tension."

The SEC has also adopted the "moratorium" approach which it uses occasionally and which freezes in place accounting principles on a particular issue and requires that all those companies which have not previously announced their policy of accounting for that issue follow the SEC's desired accounting in the future. For examples of this approach see:

(a) ASR 163, *Capitalization of Interest by Companies Other than Public Utilities* (1974), which precluded companies from subsequently electing to capitalize interest costs. This was followed five years later by SFAS No. 34, *Capitalization of Interest Cost* (1979). *ASR 163* was then rescinded in *ASR 172*.

(b) FRR 3,[k] *Interpretive Release Relating to Accounting for Extinguishment of Debt* (1982), which dealt with the practice of "defeasing" (i.e., for accounting purposes) outstanding debt by depositing with a trustee sufficient securities to provide for all future interest and principal payments. This FRR precluded companies from subsequently recognizing gain on such transactions until the FASB spoke on the matter.

(c) FRR 12, *Accounting for Costs of Internally Developing Computer Software for Sale to Others* (1983), which precluded companies from electing subsequently to capitalize such costs until the FASB spoke on the matter.

Clarence Sampson, formerly the SEC's Chief Accountant and currently one of the seven members of the FASB, has referred to *SFAS No. 34* and stated, " * * * it should be emphasized that the Commission

k. The FRR designation is for Financial Reporting Release noted above.

doesn't insist that the Board adopt exactly the same standard that the Commission would if it [were] dealing with the issue. Rather, it considers whether the adopted standard is within the range of solutions acceptable to the Commission. In this case, without reaching a decision as to whether this was the 'right' answer, the Commission concluded it was acceptable accounting in financial statements filed with the Commission. * * * " [1] That statement suggests rather strongly that the SEC retains a considerable oversight function over the work of the FASB.

Some force for the FASB Standards also comes from Rule 203 of the AICPA's Code of Professional Ethics, adopted in 1973, and referred to above.[m]

Rule 203 reads:

> **Accounting principles.** A member shall not (1) express an opinion or state affirmatively that the financial statements or other financial data of any entity are presented in conformity with generally accepted accounting principles or (2) state that he or she is not aware of any material modifications that should be made to such statements or data in order for them to be in conformity with generally accepted accounting principles, if such statements or data contain any departure from an accounting principle promulgated by bodies designated by Council to establish such principles that has a material effect on the statements or data taken as a whole. If, however, the statements or data contain such a departure and the member can demonstrate that due to unusual circumstances the financial statements or data would otherwise have been misleading, the member can comply with the rule by describing the departure, its approximate effects, if practicable, and the reasons why compliance with the principle would result in a misleading statement.

But this may be a paper tiger; the Ethics Committee of the AICPA is afflicted with a small staff and has proved that it does not relish taking on any of the major accounting firms which are the principal support of the AICPA. See A. Briloff, *More Debits Than Credits,* 350–54, 414 (1976). Thus, the Committee has not found violations of Rule 203 even in the major cases in which the SEC has censured or disciplined accounting firms for approval of questionable accounting.

The real strength behind these industry-developed accounting rules probably is the SEC's authority described above.

In addition to the FASB, there is something called the "GASB," the Governmental Accounting Standards Board, which fixes GAAP for governmental bodies such as states, municipalities, and improvement districts. Of course, just as GAAP for business organizations are not

l. "Statements in Quotes," J. Accountancy, AICPA, August 1983, 45, at p. 54. Adapted from a paper presented by Mr. Sampson at the 1983 Arthur Young Professors' Roundtable at a Columbia University conference.

m. The Council of the AICPA has designated the FASB as the body authorized to state accounting principles. See AICPA, Code of Professional Ethics, App. B. (Mar., 1974 ed.).

exclusively the pronouncements of the FASB (but include AICPA statements, etc.), GAAP for governments are not exclusively GASB pronouncements. GASB is a sister organization to the FASB, both of which operate under the auspices of the Financial Accounting Foundation.

There is still another set of organizations for which other GAAP exist besides business and governments. These are not-for-profit organizations which include universities, churches, hospitals, charities, fraternal societies, etc. Notice that some of these organizations may be governmental organizations whereas others, with a similar purpose, may not. Thus some universities and hospitals are private and others are governmentally sponsored. Some in fact are both.

Although most of the concepts we deal with in this course have application to both governmental and not-for-profit organizations, there are some dramatic differences and we do not purport to deal with them in a comprehensive fashion.

The FASB has jurisdiction over not-for-profit GAAP unless the not-for-profit agency is a governmental organization, in which case GASB has jurisdiction. For more on not-for-profit accounting, see FASB, SFAC No. 4, *Objectives of Financial Reporting by Nonbusiness Organizations* (Dec. 1980). For a current report on the direction of change for non-governmental non-profit organizations, see McLaughlin & Farley, *The Changing Landscape of Not-for-Profit Financial Reporting*, J. Accountancy 77 (April 1989).

There is still another realm—international accounting standards. The profession has established something called the International Accounting Standards Committee ("IASC"), based in London, of which the AICPA is the U.S. representative. Compliance with its pronouncements is currently voluntary although efforts are being made to have various national securities agencies (such as the SEC in the U.S.) adopt IASC standards. See, e.g., 21 Sec.Reg. & L.Rep. 46 (Jan. 6, 1989). So far the effort has not succeeded. If the European Community adopts its own standards, it would seem that the IASC standards would be doomed.

2. WHAT MAKES AN ACCOUNTING PRINCIPLE A GAAP?

AICPA, STATEMENT OF AUDITING STANDARDS NO. 52
(1988).*

"5. Independent auditors agree on the existence of a body of generally accepted accounting principles, and they are experts in those accounting principles and in the determination of their general acceptance. Nevertheless, the determination that a particular accounting principle is generally accepted may be difficult because no single reference source exists for all such principles. The sources of established accounting principles are generally the following:

    a. Accounting principles promulgated by a body designated by the AICPA Council to establish such principles, pursuant to rule 203 (ET section 203.01)[n] of the AICPA *Code of Professional Conduct.*

    b. Pronouncements of bodies composed of expert accountants that follow a due process procedure, including broad distribution of proposed accounting principles for public comment, for the intended purpose of establishing accounting principles or describing existing practices that are generally accepted.

    c. Practices or pronouncements that are widely recognized as being generally accepted because they represent prevalent practice in a particular industry or the knowledgeable application to specific circumstances of pronouncements that are generally accepted.

    d. Other accounting literature.

"6. Category *(a)*, officially established accounting principles, includes Financial Accounting Standards Board (FASB) Statements of Financial Accounting Standards, FASB Interpretations, Accounting Principles Board (APB) Opinions, AICPA Accounting Research Bulletins and, for financial statements of state and local governmental entities, statements and interpretations of the Governmental Accounting Standards Board (GASB). If, for a state or local governmental entity, the accounting treatment of a transaction or event is not specified by a pronouncement of the GASB, applicable pronouncements of the FASB are presumed to apply. Rule 203 * * * provides that an auditor should not express an unqualified opinion if the financial statements contain a material departure from such pronouncements unless, due to unusual circumstances, adherence to the pronouncements would make the statements misleading. Rule 203 * * * implies that application of officially established accounting principles almost always results in the fair presentation of financial position, results of operations, and cash flows, in conformity with generally accepted accounting principles. Interpretation 203-1 * * * of the AICPA *Code of Professional Conduct* states, 'There is a strong presumption that adherence to officially established accounting principles would in nearly all instances result in financial statements that are not misleading.' Nevertheless, rule 203 * * * provides for the possibility that literal application of such a pronouncement might, in unusual circumstances, result in misleading financial statements. When the unusual circumstances contemplated by rule 203 * * * exist and the statements depart from a pronouncement, the auditor's report should present, in a separate paragraph or paragraphs, the information required by rule 203 * * *, including a description of the departure, its approximate effects (if practicable), and the reasons why the departure is necessary to prevent the financial statements from being misleading.

---

    n. The citation to ET section 203.01 is to AICPA, Professional Standards, a two   volume loose leaf service published by Commerce Clearing House, Inc.

In those circumstances, however, unless there are reasons other than the departure to modify his opinion, the auditor should express an unqualified opinion on conformity with generally accepted accounting principles.

"7. If the accounting treatment of a transaction or event is not specified by a pronouncement covered by rule 203 * * *, the auditor should consider whether the accounting treatment is specified by another source of established accounting principles. Categories *(b)* and *(c)* are both sources of established accounting principles. Category *(b)* includes AICPA Industry Audit and Accounting Guides, AICPA Statements of Position, and Technical Bulletins issued by the FASB or GASB; category *(c)* includes AICPA Accounting Interpretations, as well as practices that are widely recognized and prevalent in the industry. If an established accounting principle from one or more sources in category *(b)* or *(c)* is relevant to the circumstances, the auditor should be prepared to justify a conclusion that another treatment is generally accepted. If there is a conflict between sources within those categories, the auditor should consider which treatment better presents the substance of the transaction in the circumstances.

"8. In the absence of a pronouncement covered by rule 203 * * * or another source of established accounting principles, the auditor may consider other accounting literature, depending on its relevance in the circumstances. Other accounting literature includes, for example, APB Statements, AICPA Issues Papers, AcSEC [the Accounting Standards Executive Committee of the AICPA] Practice Bulletins, minutes of the FASB Emerging Issues Task Force, FASB Statements of Financial Accounting Concepts, Concepts Statements of the GASB, International Accounting Standards Committee Statements of International Accounting Standards, pronouncements of other professional associations or regulatory agencies, and accounting textbooks and articles. The appropriateness of other accounting principles depends on its relevance to particular circumstances, the specificity of the guidance, and the general recognition of the issuer or author as an authority. For example, FASB Statements of Financial Accounting Concepts would normally be more influential than accounting textbooks or articles."

3. PUBLISHED SOURCES OF FORMAL GAAP, GAAS AND OTHER PROFESSIONAL STANDARDS

Currently compilations of GAAP issued by the various authoritative bodies (not including the GASB and the IASC) are being published annually by the Financial Accounting Standards Board in two formats and are available from the AICPA. The first is a chronological compilation appearing in two volumes:

> 1989/90 ed., Accounting Standards, Original Pronouncements Issued through June 1973

> 1989/90 ed., Accounting Standards, Original Pronouncements, July 1973–June 1, 1989

The second is a codification by the FASB staff, also in two volumes:

1989/90 ed., Accounting Standards, Current Text as of June 1, 1989, General Standards

1989/90 ed., Accounting Standards, Current Text as of June 1, 1989, Industry Standards

The *Current Text* is based not only on the *Original Pronouncements,* but also on supplemental published interpretations and technical bulletins of the AICPA and FASB.

As between these two, the Original Pronouncements are the ruling authority. As the FASB states in the Current Text, General Standards volume at p. iii, "The authority of the *Current Text* is derived from the underlying pronouncements, which remain in force."

Accounting Research Bulletins were developed from 1939 to 1959 by the Committee on Accounting Procedure of the AICPA.

They were supplanted in 1959 through 1973 by "APBs," Opinions of the Accounting Principles Board of the AICPA, and Accounting Interpretations, issued by the APB.

From 1973 to the present the Financial Accounting Standards Board has issued "SFASs," Statements of Financial Accounting Standards, as well as "SFACs," Statements of Financial Accounting Concepts, FASB Interpretations, and FASB Technical Bulletins as well as other types of releases. "SFAS" is the acronym we use in this text although there is not universal accord on it. Some writers refer to "FASBs," and others to "FASs."

GAAS, on the other hand, are compiled in another two-volume looseleaf format by Commerce Clearing House for the AICPA. These also contain numerous other professional standards and rules, including the AICPA's standards for engagements which are less than full audits ("review services"), Code of Professional Conduct, bylaws, international accounting standards, international auditing standards, standards for management consulting, internal quality controls and tax practice. Amendments to GAAS are published as Statements of Auditing Standards ("SASs") in the Journal of Accountancy, the AICPA's monthly magazine. The two-volume CCH publication is AICPA, Professional Standards.

4. ONCE GAAP ARE MADE, WHO SELECTS AMONG PERMISSIBLE ALTERNATIVES?

Professor Chambers once calculated that in a typical income statement, given all of the possible accounting choices, there were a million possible combinations of results.[o] Although the accountants have been working through the Committee on Accounting Procedure, the APB, and the FASB, to narrow accounting choices, many options remain,

---

o. Chambers, Financial Information and the Securities Market, Abacus 3 (Sept. 1965), reprinted in R. Chambers, Accounting Finance and Management 187–188 (1969).

without any official guides to the individual accountant in the selection thereof. Thus we shall see that pricing of inventories, depreciation of fixed assets, accounting for intangibles and services permit alternatives which are of great disparity. Given these circumstances, who makes the choices?

The official AICPA answer thus far is clearly that the financial statements are those of management, and that management makes the choice among permissible accounting principles. Under APB Op. No. 22, *Disclosure of Accounting Policies* (1972), these must be disclosed in the financials. This is invariably done in the first footnote. See the GE statements at p. 524. The independent auditors expressing their opinions on these statements must approve them as being in accordance with GAAP even though they might prefer a different choice of principles. AU § 110.02. Thus, while the accounting profession operates as a coalition to limit the range of accounting choices, it proclaims that the individual accounting firm cannot control the individual management in the choices left available.

In some instances management has a clear conflict of interest. It is interested in presenting a favorable picture of its stewardship to shareholders, not only to preserve itself in office by election, but to keep stock prices high and hence unattractive to potential takeover bidders. Yet the independent party in the picture, the outside auditor, is not allowed to select GAAP, but the party with a conflicting interest is.

Is this result necessary? Obviously management must be kept responsible for the raw data on transactions recorded in the accounts. But is there any basic reason that the independent public accountant, whose opinion the public relies upon in giving credence to the management's statements, should not be in command in the selection of the accounting principles which transform raw data into conclusory statements as to revenue, expenses, net income and net worth?

As a practical matter, the certifying accountants are not quite as uninfluential as would appear. There are accounting issues where the feasibility of a deal depends on the accountants' willingness to approve management's proposed accounting treatment. When choices as to accounting method arise during the year or during the closing process, management will often anxiously consult the certifying accountants whether they will go along with management's proposed accounting treatment—i.e., whether the accountants will certify the financial statements as being in conformity with GAAP. Management may abandon or modify its own ideas to insure the accountants' certification without qualification, for a qualification raising a question as to compliance with GAAP or any material element of fact may destroy the receptivity of the public to the transaction.

The SEC staff articulated its view in *ASR 173* (1975) as follows:

> [T]he use of accounting principles must be evaluated in the light of their applicability to the facts of the particular case, and * * * professionals must exercise the greatest care and judgment in apprais-

ing their applicability. While management may initially select the principles to be followed, the independent accountant must be satisfied that in his professional judgment the principles selected are those which appropriately describe the business reality within the general framework of the accounting approach to economic measurement.

The SEC has recently gone much further to strengthen the auditor's hand by demanding reports of any disputes between client and auditor, and explanation of the reasons for a change of auditors. Reg. S–X, § 603.02; Form 8K, Item 4. This move is consistent with the Commission's changing perception of the individual auditor's role in the process of selecting among alternative GAAP.

5. CHANGE OF USE OF ONE GAAP TO USE OF A "PREFERABLE" ONE

Entirely apart from the selection of GAAP for a new accounting problem, a firm which has been using one principle may wish to change to another when both are GAAP. For example, it may wish to change from straight-line depreciation of fixed assets to some accelerated depreciation method (which we shall consider in Chapter V).

May a firm change GAAP freely from one year to another depending on management whims (or self-interest)?

ACCOUNTING PRINCIPLES BOARD OPINION NO. 20, ¶¶ 15–17 ACCOUNTING CHANGES
AICPA 1971.*

"Justification for a Change in Accounting Principle

"15. The Board concludes that in the preparation of financial statements there is a presumption that an accounting principle once adopted should not be changed in accounting for events and transactions of a similar type. Consistent use of accounting principles from one accounting period to another enhances the utility of financial statements to users by facilitating analysis and understanding of comparative accounting data.

"16. The presumption that an entity should not change an accounting principle may be overcome only if the enterprise justifies the use of an alternative acceptable accounting principle on the basis that it is preferable. However, a method of accounting that was previously adopted for a type of transaction or event which is being terminated or which was a single, nonrecurring event in the past should not be changed. For example, the method of accounting should not be changed for a tax or tax credit which is being discontinued or for preoperating costs relating to a specific plant. The Board does not intend to imply, however, that a change in the estimated period to be benefited for a deferred cost (if justified by the facts) should not be recognized as a change in accounting estimate. The issuance of an Opinion of the Accounting Principles Board that creates a new accounting principle, that expresses a preference for an accounting principle, or that rejects a specific accounting principle is sufficient support for a change in accounting principle. The burden of justifying other changes rests with the entity proposing the change.

"GENERAL DISCLOSURE—A CHANGE IN ACCOUNTING PRINCIPLE

"17. The nature of and justification for a change in accounting principle and its effect on income should be disclosed in the financial statements of the period in which the change is made. The justification for the change should explain clearly why the newly adopted accounting principle is preferable."

In *ASR 177* which was at the heart of the *Arthur Andersen* case, supra, the SEC applied *APB Op. No. 20* not only to require "preferability" for a change of GAAP in unaudited quarterly financials, but also to implicate the firm's auditors by requiring them to write the "preferability" letter to the SEC even though they have nothing to do with those statements. *ASR 177* contains several SEC specifications regarding preferability. They may be found at (CCH) Fed.Sec.L.Rep. ¶ 74,151 at p. 64,305 et seq.

One commentator stated:

It was evident that the SEC had shifted to the independent accountant a large portion of the responsibility for determining preferability. . . .

Two reasons can be inferred for the SEC's action. First, the SEC was apparently trying to encourage (force?) the accounting profession to delineate explicitly the criteria used in choosing among divergent accounting principles. Second, the SEC intended to make independent accountants the vehicle for achieving more uniform application of these criteria to specific situations and thereby reduce alternatives. . . .

Revsine, *The Preferability Dilemma*, 144 J. Accountancy 80–85 (Sept., 1977).

B. THE INDEPENDENT AUDITOR'S ROLE

1. THE AUDIT FUNCTION

Auditing is a technique of examination of and reporting on the books of account and the underlying data therefor, and of the financial statements of an enterprise. The technique is now controlled by the Auditing Standards Board of the AICPA (ASB), which issues pronouncements known as Statements of Auditing Standards (SASs). *SAS No. 1* (1973) consolidated all prior statements. Several additional SASs have been issued on particular points. The standards so created are formal interpretations of Generally Accepted Auditing Standards and require that members justify departures therefrom. Auditors' reports recite that their examination was made in accordance with GAAS. See the Report of GE's auditors infra p. 566. Does the SEC have primary authority over GAAS? What does the auditing accountant do to determine whether and in what form to issue this report?

FIFLIS, CURRENT PROBLEMS OF ACCOUNTANTS' RESPONSIBILITIES TO THIRD PARTIES

28 Vand.L.Rev. 31, 35–42 (1975).*

" * * * In essence, like most communication tasks, an audit consists of:

(a) Investigation and collection of data;

(b) Drawing of inferences from the findings; and

(c) Presentation of conclusions.[15]

* * *

"Many variations of an 'audit' are possible, ranging from a complete, transaction by transaction reconstruction and investigation of everything done by the client's recordkeepers and other employees, to the opposite extreme of merely reading a statement of accounts receivable. Of necessity, practical limitations and the purpose of the examination will dictate the scope of the audit. * * * [The normal audit of the annual financial statements is what is here described.]

"(I) THE PRELIMINARY SURVEY OF FACTS.

"The first stage undertaken is planning the audit in conformity with the scope of the engagement. When an accountant is employed for a full audit of a client for the first time, usually the partner in charge will make a preliminary survey of the business, gleaning information about the nature of the business, sales trends, manufacturing and marketing techniques, sources of raw materials, conditions in the industry, major customers, products, personnel, budgeting and accounting systems, characteristics of management, affiliations, and the like. In this process, he will collect and review both oral and written data such as organizational charts, annual reports, prior tax returns and financials, accounting manuals, and marketing literature. Either at this point or later, an on-site inspection of major plant and facilities also will be made.

"At this stage he should make an intensive analysis of the prior financial statements, studying ratios and trends to determine unusual variations, sluggish turnover of inventory, manipulations, etc. Also, the basic accounting policies being followed by the client will be ascertained. These policies may be contained in company manuals and minutes or no consistent policies may be followed. The auditor also now must become familiar with the company's accounting procedures—

* Copyright © 1975. Reprinted by permission.

15. Hawkins, Professional Negligence Liability of Public Accountants, 12 Vand.L.

Rev. 797, 803 (1959). The following textual description of the audit process is taken largely from Montgomery's Auditing ch. 4 (8th ed. N. Lenhart & P. Defliese, 1957).

including charts of names of accounts, journals and ledgers used, and the like.

"The reason for this preliminary survey is clear: sound planning of the audit dictates that the auditor understand the nature of the client's business, its operations and organization.

"(II) PLANNING THE 'AUDIT PROGRAM.'

"After this preliminary survey, the next step in the planning stage is development of the 'audit program,' the guide to the audit describing the 'audit procedures': the what, how, and when to do certain things in checking the client's accounting. This task may rest primarily on the senior, who will report to and consult with the manager or partner on some questions.p

"Auditing procedures are designed to establish the reliability and integrity of the client's system of 'internal controls' over its activities. 'Internal control' means the client's *recordkeeping* system and its system of *checking* the operations of the business, for example, the subsystem of matching reports of the receiving department for goods received with vendors' invoices. Audit procedures further include independent checks, such as confirmation of accounts receivable with customers or of bank balances with banks.

"The auditor probably will develop a skeleton audit program based on an opening trial balance of all the ledger accounts, the preliminary survey data including a reading of the documents obtained, and audit procedures common to most audits, such as the confirmation of bank balances, just mentioned. Although he is not an insurer against fraud on the client, he must [design the audit to provide reasonable assurance of detecting not only inadvertent but also intentional irregularities.q] The discovery of such misrepresentations 'is usually more closely associated with the objective of the ordinary examination,' than is the discovery of fraud on the company.

"The skeleton audit program will be re-examined after the auditor reviews and tests the client's internal control system. The better the internal control system the more reliable will be the testing and sampling by the auditor and hence less detailed checking will be required. The internal control system includes not only matters of relevance to the audit, but also administration of all aspects of the business; the auditor need consider only those controls that relate to the safeguarding of assets from loss and the reliability of the financial records. He will make a detailed examination of them in order to determine when he may rely on the client's system and when he must reinforce that system with his own procedures. He will also test the

---

p. The hierarchy of auditors on a job is:

1. Partner in charge,

2. Audit manager,

3. Senior accountant.

q. ASB, SAS No. 53, The Auditor's Responsibility to Detect and Report Errors and Irregularities (1988). The large subject of auditors' responsibilities in dealing with fraud and misrepresentation is the subject of Chapter XIV, infra.

client's system by tracing sample transactions from start to finish to assure that it in fact operates as represented.

"Based on the results of his review and testing of the client's internal control system as well as the results of the study of the preliminary survey, he will prepare a revised audit program, which will consist of specific procedures to test the reliability of the financial statements including, for example, such matters as testing and sampling the books of account for accuracy, reading corporate minutes, contracts and leases (internal evidence), and confirming bank accounts with the bank and receivables with the client's debtors (external evidence).

* * *

"(III) IMPLEMENTATION AND ADJUSTMENT OF THE AUDIT PROGRAM.

* * *

"When the auditor begins the audit program, he will record in working papers his work and findings. Each page will be dated and initialed by all persons who dealt with it. The papers should be indexed and bound and retained for some years. They should also be comprehensible as they are intended for use by others as well as for later use.

"A trial balance is usually the first working paper. Other standard working papers are data from the corporate charter, bylaws, and minutes, and analyses of accounts, prescribed by the audit program. One of the last working papers will be the management's 'letter of representation' executed by the top officers, stating that no relevant post-balance-sheet-date events or other matters make the financial statements misleading, that disclosure of all known shortages has been made, that complete and correct corporate minutes have been supplied, and other matters of like import.

"The working papers not only form the basis for integration of the audit findings with the financial statements but also are the facts that a partner or other reviewer of the field work will check. The SEC has stated that the working papers must support in detail any unusual items as well as all others.[23] They also should establish the adequacy of the audit procedures.

"(IV) THE AUDITOR'S REPORT.

"After completion of the field work and discussions with management of questions raised as to the form of the financial statements, the auditor will 'report' on whether he conducted his examination in accordance with generally accepted auditing standards (GAAS) and whether the statements are presented in accordance with generally accepted accounting principles (GAAP) * * *. The distinction between accounting principles on the one hand and auditing standards and procedures on the other must be kept in mind for much misunder-

23. Interstate Hosiery Mills, Inc., 4 S.E.C. 706, 715–16 (1939).

standing has occurred in judicial opinions and other lawyers' work because of a lack of discrimination between them, even among sophisticated corporate lawyers. This may be because in some cases the two overlap. Nevertheless, by and large they are separate domains.

"Auditing standards address the objectives to be attained by the audit and fix the standard of quality of performance of the audit procedures. GAAS, as established by the AICPA, require the auditor to exercise skill, independence and care, compel adequate planning and supervision of the audit including evaluation of the client's internal controls and independent confirmations, and require the report of compliance with GAAP."

2. WHO MAKES GAAS?

The above article goes on to state:

"After the 1929 crash, the securities industry and the government quickly surmised that investor confidence in business must be restored, and that the best means for doing this was to require fuller financial disclosure. The preliminary drafts of the federal Securities Act of 1933 established the requirement that registration statements be filed (originally with the Federal Trade Commission, and, since 1934, with the then newly established Securities and Exchange Commission) and that a prospectus be delivered to securities purchasers. At first it was not contemplated that financial statements be independently audited unless a special investigation was requested by the FTC. Some consideration was given to audits by government officials but this was rejected after the profession impressed upon the drafting committee the desirability and the greater benefits of private sector audits. * * *

"The following year saw the adoption of the Securities Exchange Act of 1934 with its requirements of company registration, periodic reporting and proxy regulation giving additional impetus to the establishment of the central importance of financial disclosure. Soon after these enactments, a remarkable incident in American business history occurred and caused a great change in the techniques of establishing audit standards and procedures. The AICPA had participated with the Federal Reserve Board as early as 1917 in developing rudimentary audit standards and by 1936 had issued a third version, this time under its own auspices. The Institute by then had come to be spokesman of the profession. As was customary with its pronouncements whenever disagreement occurred, the Institute in the 1936 statement took an ambivalent position on two important auditing problems that divided the profession—the need for independent verification of inventories and external confirmation of receivables with the firm's debtors.

"The equivocal statement enabled one Philip Musica, a twice-convicted confidence man, who rose to the presidency of McKesson & Robbins, Inc., to falsify the statements of that company to the tune of about 20 million dollars, about half being overstated accounts receivable and the rest, fictitious inventories. Musica and his henchmen pretended to order goods from vendors who supposedly retained the goods in storage in their own warehouses for shipment to customers of McKesson & Robbins. Musica then caused checks to be issued in the names of the vendors, intercepted them and used the proceeds to make partial payments to McKesson & Robbins on resales pretended to have been made for the company. About 2.8 million dollars remained glued to the Musica gang's fingers. The result was that inventories as well as receivables were fictitious. The accountants failed to confirm the receivables or take any physical views of the inventories and hence failed to detect the wrongs.

"The enormity of the fraud spurred the accounting profession, through the American Institute Committee on Auditing Procedures, to begin in early 1939 to put its auditing in order by publishing the first of over fifty Statements on Auditing Procedures. The first one required that thereafter inventories be actually observed and that the amount of receivables be confirmed with the debtors.

"The SEC, in the meantime, not happy with its impression of the low standards followed in the McKesson & Robbins audit, conducted an extensive investigation culminating in *Accounting Series Release (ASR) 19*, issued in 1940.

"ASR 19 concluded:

We have carefully considered the desirability of specific rules and regulations governing the auditing steps to be performed by accountants in certifying financial statements to be filed with us. Action has already been taken by the accounting profession adopting certain of the auditing procedures considered in this case. We have no reason to believe at this time that these extensions will not be maintained or that further extensions of auditing procedures along the lines suggested in this report will not be made. Further, the adoption of the specific recommendations made in this report as to the type of disclosure to be made in the accountant's certificate and as to the election of accountants by stockholders should insure that acceptable standards of auditing procedure will be observed, that specific deviations therefrom may be considered in the particular instances in which they arise, and that accountants will be more independent of management. Until experience should prove the contrary, we feel that this program is preferable to its alternative—the detailed prescription of the scope of and procedures to be followed in the audit for the various types of issuers of securities who file statements with us—and will allow for further consideration of varying audit procedures and for the development of different treatment for specific types of issuers.

* * *

"Regardless of whether the seat of power to fix "auditing standards" is in the profession or the SEC, a question deferred for consideration shortly, the bulk of the determinations of auditing standards and procedures, as in the McKesson & Robbins case, has been by the AICPA. At any rate, unlike accounting principles, no one suggests that auditing standards or procedures are to be selected by corporate managements.

"In one major area of auditing standards, however, * * * that of 'independence,' the Commission has not been hesitant to establish its own views.   Occasionally it has fixed other auditing standards.   For example, it has developed detailed audit rules for national securities exchanges, brokers and dealers, and investment companies.   It also has provided standards concerning opening inventories on new audit engagements and review of the work of subordinates of the auditing firm. As in McKesson & Robbins, inventory verification was required in another case on facts arising before the profession adopted its standards but decided thereafter.   In addition, certain requirements for the auditor's report are spelled out in SEC Regulation S–X, Rule 202."

3. THE MEANING OF THE AUDITOR'S OPINION THAT THE FINANCIAL STATEMENTS ARE "PRESENTED FAIRLY IN ACCORDANCE WITH GAAP"

In *Legal Models of Management Structure in the Modern Corporation: Officers, Directors, and Accountants*, 63 Cal.L.Rev. 375, 430–432 (1975), Professor Melvin Eisenberg described an important case which established the legal requirements under the securities laws anti-fraud provisions for an auditor's report.

"The problem in [United States v. Simon, 425 F.2d 796 (2d Cir.1969), popularly known as the *Continental Vending* case] grew out of the use by Harold Roth of two corporations under his control, Continental and Valley, to finance personal stock-market transactions, by causing Continental to loan money to Valley, which in turn lent the money to him. The purpose of making the loans through Valley, rather than directly from Continental to Roth, was to dress up Continental's balance sheet: the loans were shown on Continental's books as an account receivable from Valley rather than from Roth.   At the end of fiscal 1962, Continental's account receivable from Valley arising out of loans destined for Roth exceeded $3.5 million.   Before Continental's financial statements for that year were certified, its accountants learned that the Valley receivable was uncollectible (and therefore could not be shown on Continental's books as an asset) because Roth was unable to repay Valley the amount it had lent him, an amount far exceeding Valley's net worth.   To remedy this, Roth collateralized the Valley receivable, but the collateral consisted principally of stock and convertible debentures in Continental itself.   The accountants, aware of all the relevant facts, nevertheless certified the $3.5 million Valley receivable with only the following qualification, which appeared in a footnote:

The amount receivable from Valley Commercial Corp. (an affiliated company of which Mr. Harold Roth is an officer, director and stockholder) bears interest at 12% a year.   Such amount, less the balance of the notes payable to that company, is secured by the assignment to the Company of *Valley's equity in certain marketable securities*.   As of February 15, 1963, the amount of such equity at current market quotations exceeded the net amount receivable.

"Subsequently the accountants were indicted under the Securities Exchange Act for certifying a false or misleading financial statement.[201] At the trial they called as witnesses eight expert accountants, constituting, in the words of the Second Circuit, 'an impressive array of leaders of the profession,' who testified that the failure to disclose in the footnote the purpose of the loans to Valley and the nature of the collateral was in no way inconsistent with generally acceptable accounting principles. The defendants asked for instructions which, in substance, would have told the jury that 'a defendant could be found guilty only if, *according to generally accepted accounting principles,* the financial statements as a whole did not fairly present the financial condition of Continental at September 30, 1962, and then only if his departure from accepted standards was due to willful disregard of those standards with knowledge of the falsity of the statements and an intent to deceive.' The trial court declined to give this instruction—which would have given the defendants a complete defense in light of the expert testimony—but instead instructed that the critical issue was whether the financial statements *as a whole* fairly presented Continental's financial position and accurately reported its operations. If they did not, the basic issue was whether defendants had acted in good faith. Proof of compliance with generally accepted accounting principles would be 'evidence which may be very persuasive but not necessarily conclusive' on that issue.

"A jury verdict against the accountants was sustained by the Second Circuit in an opinion by Judge Friendly. Thereafter, in a speech to the AICPA, the Chairman of the SEC described the result of the case as follows:

> [T]he court established that it is not enough to merely adhere to rules, even if they are generally accepted principles or standards. Rather a critical test is whether the financial statement, as a whole, fairly presents the position of the company and accurately reports its operation for the period it purports to cover. To meet this test and establish good faith, an accounting report has to reflect pertinent information which those who prepare it have, or in due diligence, should obtain, whether or not the disclosure of that information is required by specific generally accepted principles or standards."

For an analysis of *Simon* and its implications, see Fiflis, *Current Problems of Accountants' Responsibilities to Third Parties,* 28 Vand.L. Rev. 31, 42 et seq. (1975).

201. The indictment was based on (1) the failure of the note to disclose the purpose of the loans to Valley and the nature of the collateral, and (2) the fact that in determining the value of the collateral and the extent to which the Valley receivable was collateralized, the accountants improperly netted Continental's account payable to Valley against its Valley receivable, failed to discover that there was a lien of $1 million against the pledged securities, and failed to disclose that the amount of the receivable had risen by $400,000 between the end of the fiscal year and the date of certification, while the value of the collateral had declined by more than $270,000 between the date of certification and the date the financial statements were mailed. *Id.* at 801, 805–08.

4. NOTE ON THE AUDITOR'S REPORT (OR OPINION) TO THE SHAREHOLDERS (OR TO THE BOARD OF DIRECTORS)

In 1988 the Auditing Standards Board adopted SAS No. 58, *Reports on Audited Financial Statements,* which substantially changes the prior format. The auditor may have a choice of:

(1) An unqualified opinion (i.e., report);

(2) An unqualified opinion including an explanation of an uncertainty or an inconsistency;

(3) A qualified opinion;

(4) An adverse opinion; or

(5) A disclaimer of opinion.

Paragraph 10 explains these:

"*Unqualified opinion.* An unqualified opinion states that the financial statements present fairly, in all material respects, the financial position, results of operations, and cash flows of the entity in conformity with generally accepted accounting principles. This is the opinion expressed in the standard report . . .ʳ

"*Explanatory language added to the auditor's standard report.* Certain circumstances, while not affecting the auditor's unqualified opinion on the financial statements, may require that the auditor add an explanatory paragraph (or other explanatory language) to his report.

"*Qualified opinion.* A qualified opinion states that, except for the effects of the matter(s) to which the qualification relates, the financial statements present fairly, in all material respects, the financial position, results of operations, and cash flows of the entity in conformity with generally accepted accounting principles."

[The bases for qualification include the following:

"a. There is a lack of sufficient competent evidential matter or there are restrictions on the scope of the audit that have led the auditor to conclude that he cannot express an unqualified opinion and he has concluded not to disclaim an opinion.

"b. The auditor believes, on the basis of his audit, that the financial statements contain a departure from generally accepted accounting principles, the effect of which is material, and he has concluded not to express an adverse opinion.]

"*Adverse opinion.* An adverse opinion states that the financial statements do not present fairly the financial position, results of operations, or cash flows of the entity in conformity with generally accepted accounting principles.

"*Disclaimer of opinion.* A disclaimer of opinion states that the auditor does not express an opinion on the financial statements."

According to Roussey, Ten Eyck and Blanco–Best, *Three New SASs: Closing the Communications Gap,* J. Accountancy 44 (Dec. 1988):

The ASB issued SAS no. 58 mainly to better public understanding of the auditor's role. The most visible change brought about by this

r. Typically it reads like the GE Report, infra p. 566. "An unqualified opinion may be important for various purposes, including stock exchange requirements, contractual credit limitations, and the SEC's certification requirements."

SAS is the new auditor's standard report. This SAS requires that report to explicitly address

The responsibilities the auditor assumes.

The work the auditor performs.

The assurance the auditor provides.

In addition, the new SAS mandates two major changes to existing guidance:

1. A new way of reporting on the consistent application of accounting principles.

2. A new way to report on material uncertainties.

THE NEW REPORT FORM

Exhibit 1, below, illustrates the most significant change brought by SAS no. 58: the new and improved auditor's standard report. The new report must be titled, and that title must contain the word "indepen-

EXHIBIT 1

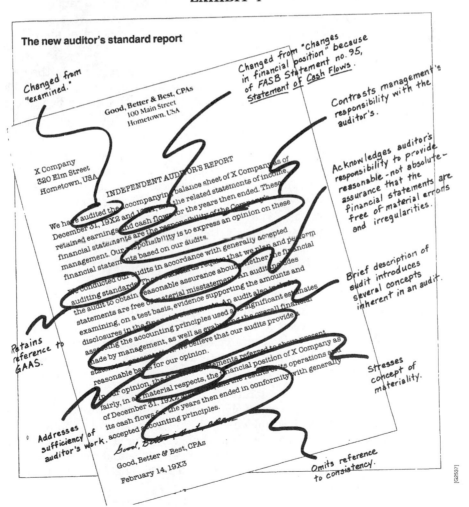

The new auditor's standard report

dent." Moreover, the new report includes three paragraphs: an introductory paragraph, a scope paragraph and an opinion paragraph. The real fundamental changes, however, go beyond these form changes:

Who's responsible for what? The new report explicitly contrasts management's responsibility for the financial statements with the auditor's responsibilities to express an opinion. The introductory paragraph is intended to clear up an often misunderstood concept: The auditor doesn't develop the representations in the financial statements—management does. However, the auditor is responsible for expressing an unbiased opinion on the statements.

Assurance within what limits? The new report describes the auditor's responsibility to plan and perform the audit to obtain *reasonable* assurance, within the context of materiality, that the financial statements contain no material misstatements. While explicitly acknowledging this responsibility for detecting material errors and irregularities, the new report also discusses some of the limitations on that responsibility by introducing the concepts of "reasonable" assurance and materiality. It's intended this be understood in contrast to "absolute" assurance. The words "in all material respects" were added to the opinion paragraph in order to emphasize the concept of materiality.

How does the audit process work? In the scope paragraph, the new report contains a brief explanation of what an audit includes. The idea is to educate users on several factors inherent in the audit process that affect the assurance the auditor provides on the financial statements.

Some guidance was left unchanged by SAS no. 58. For example, although the sample reports shown in the new standard don't include an addressee, the requirement to address the report is still alive and well. Similarly, the Securities and Exchange Commission, in article 2 of regulation S–X, still requires auditors of public companies to indicate the city and state in which the auditor's firm is located.

REPORTING ON INCONSISTENCIES

Another major change initiated by SAS no. 58 is that the auditor's standard report no longer contains a reference to the consistent application of generally accepted accounting principles. Instead, SAS no. 58 requires the auditor to add an explanatory paragraph (after the opinion paragraph) to the report—*but only when accounting principles have not been consistently observed among periods.*

The auditor's responsibility to make sure that all accounting changes are properly accounted for and adequately disclosed in the financial statements has not changed. SAS no. 58 only changes the way an auditor *reports* accounting changes. (For a discussion of the rationale for eliminating the consistency reference and the "subject to" opinion, see "The Auditor's Standard Report: The Last Word or in Need of Change?" JofA, Feb. 87, page 80.)

REPORTING ON UNCERTAINTIES

The third major change brought about by SAS no. 58 is the way the auditor reports on material uncertainties that may affect the financial statements. The new SAS eliminates the "subject to" opinion qualification but retains a "red flag" concept by requiring the auditor to add an explanatory paragraph to the report (after the opinion paragraph) when there's a material uncertainty that may affect the financial statements. This explanatory paragraph should

Describe the uncertainty.

Explain that the outcome is presently unknown.

Refer to the note in the financial statements that describes the uncertainty in greater detail.

SAS no. 58 also identifies factors the auditor should consider in deciding whether to add an explanatory paragraph to the report. Exhibit 2 ⁎ ⁎ ⁎ outlines this guidance.

EXHIBIT 2

Reporting on uncertainties

SAS no. 58 eliminates the "subject to" opinion qualification but retains a 'red flag' concept. Although this new SAS doesn't change the auditor's responsibility to make sure that material uncertainties are properly accounted for and adequately disclosed, it does change the way the auditor *reports* on these uncertainties by requiring the auditor to add an explanatory paragraph to the report because of the material uncertainty.

Probability of material loss

Remote	Reasonably possible	Probable
The auditor will issue a standard unqualified opinion.	The auditor's decision to add an explanatory paragraph (after the opinion paragraph) depends on 1. Whether the probability of unfavorable outcome is closer to remote or to probable. 2. The magnitude of the loss relative to materiality.	The auditor will add an explanatory paragraph (after the opinion paragraph) to the report when the amount of the loss cannot be reasonably estimated.

Additional measures included in an audit are described in more detail in Chapter XIV because they will be more meaningful after you have studied the intervening materials.

C. INTERNAL CONTROLS INCLUDING ACCOUNT-ING RECORDS AND MANAGEMENT'S DUTIES THEREWITH UNDER THE FOREIGN CORRUPT PRACTICES ACT

The auditor operating under GAAS accepts the client's internal controls for what they are worth. The better the client's controls the less demanding will be the auditor's procedures since more reliance may be justifiable. However, the auditor is required to have a thorough understanding of a firm's controls. SAS No. 55, *The Auditor's New Responsibility for Internal Control* (1988) discussed infra, Chapter XIV.

Congress, in the accounting provisions of the Foreign Corrupt Practices Act of 1977, § 13(b)(2) of the 1934 Securities Exchange Act, has introduced a new element by requiring SEC reporting companies to establish "adequate" internal accounting controls—thus establishing a federal minimum standard for this aspect of business operations. (Incidentally, despite the title of the act, § 13(b)(2) is not limited to foreign payments in any way.) Sanctions include criminal penalties and injunctions. Section 13(b)(2) reads:

(2) Every issuer which has a class of securities registered pursuant to section 12 of this title and every issuer which is required to file reports pursuant to section 15(d) of this title shall—

(A) make and keep books, records, and accounts, which, in reasonable detail, accurately and fairly reflect the transactions and dispositions of the assets of the issuer; and

(B) devise and maintain a system of internal accounting controls sufficient to provide reasonable assurances that—

(i) transactions are executed in accordance with management's general or specific authorization;

(ii) transactions are recorded as necessary (I) to permit preparation of financial statements in conformity with generally accepted accounting principles or any other criteria applicable to such statements, and (II) to maintain accountability for assets;

(iii) access to assets is permitted only in accordance with management's general or specific authorization; and

(iv) the recorded accountability for assets is compared with the existing assets at reasonable intervals and appropriate action is taken with respect to any differences.

Because this is a very substantial governmental intrusion into business management, it has aroused the antagonism of business managers.

In any event, the Act has thrust lawyers further into auditing than ever before because the accountants do not purport to pass on "adequacy" under the FCPA of a firm's control system. Although the party line of the bar is that the adequacy of controls is for managers, it is clear that lawyers must explain the legal rules, including what is meant by adequate controls and what are the current practices of the industry in seeking to comply.

The adequacy of controls is probably to be determined by weighing the benefit of any particular control against its cost. Thus, for a company engaged in mining diamonds, a personal search of employees as they leave the premises is probably a necessary measure whereas none should be required for a birdcage manufacturer. In-between cases are a matter of judgment.

One of the most fundamental of controls is the books and records kept by the firm, and the FCPA specifies requirements of reasonable accuracy for them, thus making it management's duty to keep reasonably accurate accounting records as a matter of federal mandate!

The Act requires much more explanation than we can allow here. For conflicting views of an ABA committee and of the SEC, see ABA, Comm. on Corp. Law and Accounting, *A Guide to the New Section 13(b) (2) Accounting Requirements of the Securities Exchange Act of 1934*, 34 Bus.Law. 307 (1978), and Williams, Address to AICPA, adopted as official policy by the SEC, 1934 Act Rel 17,500, 21 SEC Docket 1466 (1981).

The FCPA has had profound effects on the internal controls systems of most publicly held companies.

For example, it is now standard operating procedure for companies to appoint an audit committee of members of the board of directors. Since the committee must have at least a majority of "outside" directors (i.e., non-employees), virtually all public companies now have at least some outside directors. Further, the committee functions as a body to allow the outside auditor to communicate concerns about the management, its system of controls, improper pressures on auditors, etc.

Another effect of the FCPA is for firms to also hire internal auditors who engage full time in administering internal controls. The third important effect is the establishment of written codes of conduct by business firms.

For a description of General Electric Company's audit committee activities and internal auditing, see p. 542 infra. In Chapter XIV infra we further describe SASs No. 55, 60 and 61, all of which concern internal controls.

It has been said by the current chairman of the Accounting Standards Board that "The three most important issues the ASB will be addressing [in the 1990's] are internal control, internal control, and internal control." Collins, The View After the Expectation Gap SASs, J. Accountancy, June, 1989, pp. 111, 112.

D. THE CONCEPTUAL FRAMEWORK VS. GAAP

As has been pointed out elsewhere, despite U.S. v. Simon, supra, financial statements which follow formal pronouncements of the FASB are unlikely to be held misleading. See Fiflis, *Current Problems of Accountants' Responsibilities to Third Parties,* 28 Vand.L.Rev. 31, 71–80 (1975). Thus no overall court-made criterion of fairness is likely to be imposed on SFASs. Since GAAP including SFASs are based in "general acceptance" they are not based in logic. Many SFASs are the product of the political pushes and pulls of various interest groups with the result that many GAAP are inconsistent in principle with each other, as you will find later in this course. Recognizing inconsistencies in present GAAP, the FASB at its very inception launched a Conceptual Framework Study in an effort to locate underlying principles to which its pronouncements might consistently adhere.

That Conceptual Framework Study has resulted in six Concepts Statements ("SFACs") to date:

No. 1, *Objectives of Financial Reporting by Business Enterprises* (Nov. 1978)

No. 2, *Qualitative Characteristics of Accounting Information* (May 1980) (as amended by No. 6)

No. 3, *Elements of Financial Statements of Business Enterprises* (Dec. 1980) (as amended by No. 6)

No. 4, *Objectives of Financial Reporting by Nonbusiness Organizations* (Dec. 1980)

No. 5, *Recognition and Measurement in Financial Statements of Business Enterprises* (Dec. 1984)

No. 6, *Elements of Financial Statements* (Dec. 1985)

Nevertheless as we shall see, in its Statements of Financial Accounting Standards (SFASs) the FASB has issued many which are inconsistent with each other. The most chaotic area of GAAP at present is what is known as "recognition"—the admission of items to the balance sheet and income statement as assets, liabilities, revenues and expenses—the subject of our next chapter.

In this highly practical field, as in law, where theory meets the real world, political accommodation will prevail, although neutral principles will provide the normative guide to provide a check on pragmatic decisions.

Part B

RECOGNITION AND REALIZATION OF REVENUE AND INCOME

Chapter III

RECOGNITION AND REALIZATION OF REVENUE AND INCOME

OBJECTIVES

1. Examine when revenue or income is recognized in the financial accounts, considering which factors are determinative in which circumstances.

2. Consider how accounting terms are interpreted when used in contracts and statutes.

3. Observe the relationship of financial accounting to other types of accounting, notably accounting for tax purposes.

RELEVANCE FOR LAWYERS

Financial determination of an enterprise's revenue and "net income" are regular features of employment contracts, labor agreements, tax statutes, rate regulation provisions, securities disclosure and similar legal settings.

A. INTRODUCTION

Of the two financial statements introduced in Chapter I, the income statement is the one on which more attention is lavished today. It was not always so. Originally lenders placed great reliance on balance sheet data, especially the amounts of current assets—cash, receivables, and inventories—making that data of primary importance. But the focus even for creditors now has shifted on the premise that loans will usually be paid out of the current earnings of an ongoing enterprise rather than from liquidation of receivables and inventory. Investors similarly focus more on a company's past and expected earnings in assessing the attractiveness of a particular investment.

In creating an income statement, two components are obviously at work—revenues and costs. Cost questions generally involve issues of measuring and recognizing an expenditure either in the current period or in some subsequent period. If the latter, it is called an asset until it is time to be expensed, and the cost will be amortized in future periods according to some prescribed methodology. Those matters are, with a few exceptions, deferred to those succeeding chapters that deal directly with the costs involved. The present chapter deals instead with the revenue component for the most part and only occasionally with net income. The principal issue presented is: will the revenue or income (including negative income, or loss) be recognized now or will it be postponed to some future period?

It is not an exaggeration to suggest that the recognition of revenue and income is one of the pivotal questions that financial accounting addresses. A huge percentage of financial scams and investment debacles have exploited or abused the recognition of revenue or income. Likewise, an enormous proportion of enforcement actions undertaken by the Securities and Exchange Commission concern differing resolutions of this problem. Moreover, the contexts in which it can arise are infinite. In Problems C and D of Chapter I, for example, Dr. Doyle treated some patients who paid her on the spot. When was that income earned? Right then, of course. But what if they did not pay her when they were treated? What if their insurance company paid Dr. Doyle in a later accounting period? What if the insurance company paid only 80% of the bill and Dr. Doyle then billed the patient for the remainder? What if Dr. Doyle's corporation owns some vacant land near her office which has increased in value—when is that income recorded? As it appreciates? When sold? What if the sale is for 10% down and the balance in installments? And on and on we go. But the point remains that once we move beyond the simplest scenarios of provision of services with immediate cash-on-delivery, questions of *when* income should be recognized become significant.

But who cares? What difference does it make whether a transaction results in a determination that income has been generated for Year One, or, instead, Year Two, or not at all?

The timing of recognition is dispositive if a company:

(1) is charged with an underpayment of income taxes in Year One;

(2) has a profit-sharing plan with its president who retires at the end of Year One;

(3) is selling its entire business or shares in it by issuing securities soon after the end of Year One.

And so on.

But these prosaic cases are the stuff of our economic life. And in the aggregate they are largely dispositive in shifting wealth among individuals. For example, deferring income taxes on unrealized appreciation of corporate stocks benefits one class of persons, perhaps one or two percent of the population, at the expense of another. See Slawson, *Taxing as Ordinary Income the Appreciation of Publicly Held Stock*, 76 Yale L.J. 623 (1967). Slawson estimated in 1967 that if such appreciation were taxed, other taxes could be cut in half. Cf. ibid. 631–32. Further examples of how accounting shifts wealth are legend. See Zeff, *The Rise of "Economic Consequences,"* J. Accountancy 56 (Dec. 1978). The savings and loan debacle, gauged to cost every man, woman and child in the nation $1,000 to $2,000 each, and worse, likely to prohibit much needed social programs, is viewed by many to have been facilitated by permissive accounting.

In the cases above, the measure of income in Year One is either conclusive or highly relevant to the issue. Oftentimes Year One fits into a pattern of ascendancy or decline over several years and the pattern will be dramatically affected by recognition of a particular item. When the pattern is used to extrapolate into the future, the direction of the extrapolation may be materially affected.

We may also note that these examples illustrate two broad categories of purposes in determining income. Accounting data have both retrospective and prospective uses. For determining, say, income tax liability or an employee's share of profits, the historical facts are clearly the ultimate data relevant to the issue. For prospective purposes such as ascertaining the present value of future income in order to fix the purchase price of the entire business, or the price of shares of stock or the risk level of bonds for that business, historical facts are also relevant. However the great difference is that in this latter case, past profits are merely a factor, not the ultimate datum.

Of course there may also be a difference in what reasonably should be counted as income for these two uses. One of the more obvious cases for differing treatment is an extraordinary event such as the sale of a parcel of unused land. The gain on the sale is clearly a past event, having already occurred and of no future consequence. The income tax authorities will claim a share of the gain as income for the past but an equity or debt investor will not expect income in the future related to this transaction. Whether an employee under a profit-sharing arrangement should share in the gain is entirely dependent on the contract; if the parties had considered the matter in drafting the contract, they might have either excluded or included it, depending on the purpose of their contract. How will a utility rate-making authority consider the matter? Or a manager assessing the performance of a subordinate employee in whose department the asset had been used?

In any event, one question which arises from these examples of different uses of financial data is: should the same formulation of "income" be used for all purposes? We might go on to pose thousands of additional cases of different users and different transactions and then raise the question more expansively: whether income should be determined identically for all of these many uses.

You will not be surprised to hear that the determination of income will not always be identical for these various cases, although there is similar treatment among them by and large—with a certain resultant injustice. Perhaps equally importantly, a single set of accounting records will almost always be the data base for the various determinations. Since GAAP thus are the usual rule in default of a more specific rule tailored to the specific case, GAAP do matter and it behooves the draftsperson or business advisor to understand them.

B. THE ELEMENTS OF REALIZATION

APB *Statement No. 4,* ¶ 159 (1970), states the general rule for recognition of revenue: "Revenue is conventionally recognized at a specific point in the earning process of a business enterprise, usually when assets are sold or services are rendered. This conventional recognition is the basis of the pervasive measurement principal known as realization." Paragraph 150 goes on to state that pervasive principle:

> *Realization.* Revenue is generally recognized when both of the following conditions are met: (1) the earning process is complete or virtually complete, and (2) an exchange has taken place.

The American Accounting Association, the association of the academic branch of the profession, only a few years earlier, had analyzed the realization concept in three parts instead, subdividing the first "condition" stated by the AICPA into the first and third listed below:

> When should realization be considered to have been achieved in a revenue transaction? Three factors have generally been considered significant in answering this question.
>
> (1) The nature of the asset received;
>
> (2) The presence of a market transaction;
>
> (3) The extent to which services have been performed.[a]

We shall use the AAA's trichotomy but alter the order of consideration.

a. AAA, 1964 Concepts and Standards Research Study Committee, The Realization Concept, 40 Acctg.Rev. 312, 314 (1965).

1. THE FIRST FACTOR OF REALIZATION—AN EXCHANGE OR MARKET TRANSACTION

(A) The General Rule

TOOEY v. C.L. PERCIVAL CO.

Supreme Court of Iowa, 1921.
192 Iowa 267, 182 N.W. 403.

DeGraff, J.   This appeal concerns itself with the construction of a written contract of employment between plaintiff and defendant, and involves primarily the legal definition of the term "net profits" as used in said contract.   Plaintiff was engaged as manager of the paper and woodenware department of defendant company and was to receive a salary of $150 per month "and 25 per cent. of the net profits of this department up to December 31, 1916.   Eight per cent. on the amount of capital invested in this department to be deducted before profit division is made.   The division of the profits to be made in January, 1916, and January, 1917."   The contract became effective July 29, 1915.   The stipulated salary was paid and also the net profits on sales made and delivered to defendant's customers "up to December 31, 1916," when the contract was terminated.

Plaintiff's claim is based on the "net profits" on the following items:

* * *

"[1]   The net profits of $8,788.69, being the difference between the total cost price and carrying charges of merchandise purchased for said department during the year 1916, but not delivered to defendant until after December 31, 1916, and the market value of the same merchandise on December 31, 1916."

"[2]   Net profits of $18,781.16, being the difference between the cost price and the market value of merchandise on hand in said department on December 31, 1916."

* * *

I.   We will first apply the principles of bookkeeping to the facts in this case.   These principles are not strictly a legal test, but constitute a valuable first aid in reaching a correct conclusion on the propositions submitted by appellant.

Let us suppose a practical bookkeeper prepared a [worksheet] of the defendant's business at the close of the year 1916.   It would present a general form and appearance as follows:

[The Court's worksheet is omitted and a revision by the editor complying with modern practice appears below.]

WORKSHEET AT DECEMBER 31, 1916

Account	Trial Balance		Income Statement		Balance Statement	
			Expense	Income	Assets	Liabilities
	Dr.	Cr.	Dr.	Cr.	Dr.	Cr.
Cash	6,485.33				6,485.33	
Accounts Receivable	50,000.00				50,000.00	
Accounts Payable		61,830.00				61,830.00
Capital Stock		40,000.00				40,000.00
Sales Revenue		286,981.47		286,981.47		
Opening Inventory (Assumed)	100,000.00		100,000.00			
Purchases	194,567.21		194,567.21			
Closing Inventory				97,052.83	97,052.83	
Miscellaneous Expense	35,000.00		35,000.00			
Freight Expense	1,000.00		1,000.00			
Insurance Expense	250.00		250.00			
Traveling Expense	1,508.93		1,508.93			
Net Profit			51,708.16			51,708.16
	388,811.47	388,811.47	384,034.30	384,034.30	153,538.16	153,538.16

On the assumption of the correctness of the items and the figures used in the preceding [worksheet] plaintiff's percentage of net profits is $12,927.04 for the year ending December 31, 1916, which amount he actually received from the defendant company exclusive of salary.

Let us interpret this [worksheet] in the light of plaintiff's claims.

     *   *   *

     *   *   * It is urged [in the plaintiff's second claim] that at the close of the year 1916 the plaintiff was entitled to 25 per cent. of the difference between the cost price of the merchandise then on hand and the market value of such merchandise at that time. This proposition assumes an actual sale of all merchandise in stock.

Would the annual [Income Statement] show a profit or loss as to merchandise then on hand? Positively no, *   *   *.

The [Purchases and Opening Inventory accounts] would show the value of the merchandise at cost price purchased and received during the year plus the inventory balance of the preceding year. The [Sales Revenue] would show merchandise sales. In the column of the [worksheet] marked ["Assets," opposite "Closing Inventory"] appears the inventory cost value of stock on hand January 1, 1917. The net loss or gain in the merchandise account would be easily determined from these figures.

We are not dealing with a concern in process of liquidation, but with a going concern.

It is also claimed by plaintiff [in his first claim] that the merchandise purchased during the year by the company, but not delivered until after the expiration of his contract, should be taken into consideration, and 25 per cent. of the difference between the total cost price and carrying charges and the market value of the same should be paid to the plaintiff under the terms of his contract. This item would not appear on the balance sheet at the end of the year, nor would it be taken into account by the bookkeeper in determining the net profits of the business. Not until this merchandise was received by the company would [purchases account] be debited and cash, personal accounts payable, or bills payable would then be credited.

To hold otherwise in these particulars, as a matter of practical bookkeeping, the plaintiff would be securing a percentage of the net profits, which we might expect to appear on the [Income Statement] of the company for the [next] year ending 1917. This surely was not within the contemplation of the parties or the terms of the contract.

* * *

II. Let us next apply the test of legal definition. What are the "net profits" in a legal sense?

Plaintiff states that "the phrase 'net profits' and the terms of the contract" are clear and unambiguous. If this were true, this case would not be before us. * * *

* * *

In Jennery v. Olmstead et al., 36 Hun (N.Y.) 536, Peckham, J., speaking for the court, says:

> It does not appear that defendant's counsel treats the method pursued by defendants as showing actual, realized profits, but he terms them *estimated* profits, and argues that the contract meant *estimated* profits, instead of actual, realized profits; for otherwise he claims that every piece of property of the bank would have to be sold annually, in order to determine whether profits were made, which, he very sensibly states, would be absurd. The trouble with this mode of reasoning lies in the confusion of property with profits. * * * The profits are, as I have said, the amount of money received by the bank from its investments, by way of interest, over and above the amount of any money it had received by the sale of property, over and above its costs to the bank. If such a sale had been made, then a profit had arisen; but if not, then no profit had accrued simply from the fact that the property, if sold, would have resulted in a profit.

Profits are not composed of earnings never received or entered upon the books of the corporation. Without receipts or the equivalent in a business, profits do not legally exist.

* * *

III. * * *

Did the parties to the contract in question disclose what they had in mind, and did they interpret the meaning of the term "net profits" by their own acts and conduct? It was the practice of the Percival Company to price all of its annual inventory at cost. This was also true of the Pratt Paper Company for whom plaintiff was general manager for two years preceding his employment by the defendant company. Both companies followed the same method of determining the net profits at the end of each fiscal year.

* * *

Plaintiff was in absolute charge of the matter of making the annual inventory. He was manager of the paper department with full power to buy and sell and with the right to express his own judgment in the matter of the conduct of the business in his department. He acted freely and was untrammeled by any influence on the part of the officers of the defendant company.

In the light of this record, we can find no justification for either the inventory or balance sheet taking a different form upon the termination of the plaintiff's contract. They must remain true to form possessed during the period of his employment when other inventories and balance sheets were prepared and for a like purpose, to wit, to determine the net profits of the business in order to fix the compensation to which plaintiff was entitled under his contract.

Whether we consider this case from the viewpoint of practical bookkeeping, or from a study of the legal definition of net profits, or from the practical construction which the parties themselves put upon the terms of the contract, we reach the same conclusion.

Wherefore the judgment and decree entered by the trial court is affirmed.

Notes

3–1. *Drafter's Dilemma.* It is conceivable that Mr. Tooey intended what he claimed in this suit—that the contract include in the measure of profits the inchoate gain on unsold goods on order or on hand at year end. Since, presumably he did get 25% of the profits on the goods ordered or on hand at the beginning of the year, the result of the case is somewhat perverse—Tooey shared in profits, including appreciation in value of the inventory for which his efforts in acquiring the goods were nil but did not share in unrealized profits for which his efforts were central. Note that Tooey seemed to be engaged in production, not sales. If in sales, the holding would be more in keeping with probable intent.

Clearly the contract drafters could have specified a different result but they did not. Why, in default of that specification, did the court look to GAAP?

In response to these questions, one may generalize that nothing about the law of interpretation of contracts or of statutory construction changes when financial terminology is being used. To the extent that accounting practices are relevant to the drafter's intent or in the judge's opinion illuminate the construction of the contract, they will be given weight. Although there is no magic which gives accountants controlling power over words used in legal contexts simply because they are also used by accountants, accountants have thought out the issues more thoroughly than others, perhaps, thereby meriting greater deference. Of course, if the intent is to incorporate accounting principles, as some contracts clearly state, or if a regulatory agency requires that accepted accounting practices be observed, an accounting determination will be conclusive. Such a determination may involve accounting pronouncements, expert opinions, argumentation, case law, SEC regulations and releases and even the relevance of regulatory policy of other governmental agencies.

But the point remains: know what financial and accounting terms mean, even when used in purely legal contexts. If the standard definitions are acceptable and you wish GAAP to govern as a default rule, fine. If not, define the terms or modify the definition in the contract or statute.

3–2. The Justifications of the Market Transaction Requirement—Conservatism—The Historical Cost Convention—The Constant Dollar Value Assumption. The preceding case showed, among other things, that income ordinarily will not be reported (or "recognized") before it has been "realized" by a market transaction. This "realization" requirement is often criticized as not reflecting the fact of gradual attainment of income over several periods but rather showing all of the gain in the one period in which the asset is sold. A parcel of real estate may be a useful example. When it is purchased in Year One for $60,000 cash, the journal entry is:

| Land | $60,000 | |
| Cash | | $60,000 |

The $60,000 debit is posted to the Land T account and from there to the balance sheet. For Year Two, $60,000 is carried over as the opening balance in the T account. Assuming no sales or additional purchases of land, this account (and the corresponding figure on the balance sheet) stays at $60,000, even if substantial appreciation takes place. If, in Year Ten, the land is sold for $185,000 cash, the entry then is:

Cash	$185,000	
Land		$ 60,000
Gain		125,000

And this Gain figure will appear on the income statement of Year Ten via that Year's Profit and Loss T account. But is Year Ten the period in which the *entire* $125,000 gain was earned? No wonder that Professor Bittker satirizes the realization requirement as "refusing to count your chickens before they are grandparents." [b]

On the other hand, what is the alternative? Increase the debit in the Land T account before it is sold by means of some valuation figure? Such "writing-up" of the value of assets still owned was common in the years before the Great Depression of the 1930's. The Depression forced values down far below their written-up book figures, making those write-ups look misleading. As a result of this experience, accountants generally do not permit recognition of increases in asset values before those assets are disposed of in a market transaction. Indeed, the preference of the SEC for historical cost, unaltered by subsequent write-ups, is even more emphatic. This position requiring realization by a market transaction is often characterized as one of "conservatism," i.e., not leading financial statement readers to believe that the company is wealthier than it really is. It will also be recognized that the requirement of a market transaction before recognizing gain may also be described as the historical cost convention—

b. Bittker, A Comprehensive Tax Base as a Goal of Income Tax Reform, 80 Harv. L.Rev. 925, 968 n. 73 (1967).

carrying assets at cost, not value. Thus realization and the historical cost convention are two sides of the same coin.

To some extent, the realization convention is related to still another basic accounting assumption—that the dollar is constant in value (or perhaps more accurately, fluctuations in the value of the dollar either cancel each other out or are insignificant). Because of this assumption, the cost of a plant purchased in 1933 will be carried at cost in 1933 dollars while a plant purchased in 1970 will be carried at cost in 1970 dollars, both on the same balance sheet, as if the worth of the two types of dollars were identical. With the high rate of inflation of recent decades, this assumption is undergoing a sustained, heavy attack which may force its abandonment.

The constant dollar value assumption, the cost convention and the realization convention are all-pervasive in current accounting practice, and because they are of questionable merit, they raise the most serious questions about current accounting practices. Substantial minority voices are heard on the subject, especially among accountants with academic associations.

Be that as it may, the realization requirement does have some things going for it. First, it seems to conform to many people's intuitive sense of profit. Second, in many cases it will not much matter anyway; note that in *Tooey* although the unrealized appreciation in the year-end inventory was excluded from income, the prior year's appreciation in the beginning-of-the-year inventory (assuming it had been sold) was included, thereby more or less cancelling out the exclusion at year end. Third, it avoids a variety of nasty surprises that subsequent events can produce. For example, in *Tooey* the manager wanted a percentage of the difference between cost and "market value" for any goods on hand at year-end. If he had won and a "market value" was established, how would the company then deal with subsequent mark-downs, special clearance sales, or similar discounts? What if the goods were destroyed by fire or flood and insurance did not cover their full "market value"? Could the company simply take it out of Tooey's pay the next year? Note that Tooey was then no longer employed. Indeed, Tooey was in charge of acquiring the company's merchandise. If these unrealized gains were to be included in his pay computation, would Tooey be tempted to load up at year-end on garbage that might never be sold, especially since he was trying to include goods *on order* as well as goods on hand? The fact that cost has prevailed over six decades suggests that perhaps the safest approach generally is the realization requirement of a market transaction, free of the vagaries that non-sale valuations often engender.

3–3. *Note on the "Trial Balance" and "Worksheets."* The court in Tooey found it helpful to use an accountant's six-column worksheet for its analysis. We may pause to further explain this tool of bookkeeping. Two functions are performed here. The first is the "trial balance" whereby all the debit and credit balances in the ledger (before adjusting and closing entries) are listed and compared. If the totals are not equal, an error is indicated and the bookkeeper must go back and check to find it. If the columns are equal, there may still be an error (e.g., Sales Revenue might have been incorrectly credited instead of Accounts Receivable). The trial balance is merely one check for errors.

The second function of the six-column worksheet is to allow the bookkeeper on a single sheet of paper to allocate the debit and credit balances to either income statement accounts (revenues and expenses) or balance sheet accounts (assets, liabilities, and equity exclusive of the current period's revenues and expenses). Here you will note the relationship between the income statement and balance sheet becomes clear when the bookkeeper adds the two entries to the worksheet which do not yet appear in the ledger in order to cause the debit and credit columns to balance.

(B) Colorable Market Transactions: Shams and Non-sales

A transaction may be a sham or be so tentative as to not satisfy the requirement of being a market exchange transaction.

(1) Shams—"Cooked Books"

UNITED STATES v. STIRLING

United States Court of Appeals for the Second Circuit, 1978.
571 F.2d 708.

MESKILL, CIRCUIT JUDGE:

This is an appeal by David Stirling, Jr., William G. Stirling, Harold M. Yanowitch, Edwin J. Schulz, and Rubel L. Phillips from judgments of conviction entered on March 11, 1977, in the United States District Court for the Southern District of New York, * * * by Marvin E. Frankel, *Judge*, after a six-week jury trial. Appellants were convicted of securities and mail fraud and conspiracy in connection with sales of stock in the Stirling Homex Corporation ("Homex").

* * *

Homex manufactured and assembled prefabricated multi-family modular housing. Its operations consisted of mass-producing individual apartment units, or "modules," using assembly-line production techniques, shipping them to a construction site and installing them in a previously-constructed concrete and steel frame so as to form multi-unit apartment buildings.

* * *

The story is a complicated one, involving land transactions that were not what they were claimed to be, labor relations that were not only inappropriately "cozy" but undisclosed, contracts for module sales based upon guile and trickery rather than agreement, and deceptive bookkeeping practices for which appellants have finally been held accountable. The record shows that appellants engaged collectively in a calculated and multifaceted plan to give the investing public the false impression that Homex was in a sound and steadily improving financial position and at the same time withhold adverse information that was material to an accurate appraisal of the company's prospects. The enterprise began in 1968; in 1970 and 1971 Homex stock was sold to the public for a total of $39 million; in 1972 the company was bankrupt. The jury could permissibly have found the following.

I. THE FOUNDATIONS: INCORPORATION AND GOING PUBLIC

Homex was incorporated as a close corporation in Delaware in 1968; its principal offices and factory were located in Avon, New York, a suburb outside Rochester. The Stirling brothers were its founders, officers and principal owners. Shortly after incorporation, Homex made a private offering, selling 1.6 million shares at $1 each. It thus began as a relatively small concern, doing business primarily with private residential projects developed by the Stirlings. It soon became clear, however, that it would be in the best business interests of Homex to exploit the then-budding public housing market. Accordingly, Homex focused its efforts on sales to public housing authorities in federally-financed housing programs.

In late 1968, the Stirlings decided to explore the possibility of "going public" and approached R.W. Pressprich & Co. as a prospective underwriter. Pressprich agreed to underwrite the public sale of Homex common stock on the condition that Homex's annual net earnings totaled $1 million, as projected by the Stirlings. In January of 1969, when the agreement with Pressprich was reached, Homex was reporting profits at the end of the second quarter of approximately $390,000 from the sale of modules and gross land sales totaling $4.7 million.

By April 30, 1969, however, the end of the third quarter, it became obvious that year-end profits would fall far short of the $1 million required for the underwriting, third quarter gross sales totaling only $900,000. At this point Homex arranged two "sales" of land holdings in order to boost total sales and profits to the amount required for the Pressprich underwriting.

*　　*　　*

Accounting Practices During the 1970–1971 Fiscal Year.

Three incidents during the 1970–1971 fiscal year make it clear that Homex accounting practices during that time were considerably less than straightforward. First, a significant proportion of the modular sales recorded for the first quarter was based upon the assignment of modules to purported sales with housing authorities in Clay, New York, and Southbridge, Massachusetts. These sales were reported as income notwithstanding the fact that there existed neither written contracts nor funding commitments to support the assignments. The unaudited first quarter earnings were supplied to various commercial and investment bankers, eventually leading to an offer to purchase Homex debentures.

Second, beginning in December, 1970, Homex maintained not only a computer file showing assignment of particular modules to construction projects, but also a "special" or "simulation" file. Formally, these files were known respectively as File I and File II; computer room employees, however, called the first file the "real world" file and the second file the "Mickey Mouse" file. Mr. Wilbur Rumley, Scheduling Coordinator for Homex Operations Control, testified at trial that "on File I some apartments were assigned to one project and on File II they were assigned to another." In other words, the Mickey Mouse file was used by Homex to verify to its auditors that certain modules were assigned to certain contracts, thus justifying the inclusion of the price of those modules as income.

Finally, just prior to the filing of Homex's 1971 registration statement, an ambiguous debt confirmation gave Peat Marwick reason to question the inclusion by Homex of $832,000 as an account receivable. Homex had reported the figure as income notwithstanding the fact that it had been spent on the so-called "soft costs" of constructing the Mississippi plant, costs such as architectural and engineering fees and site selection costs. Such costs may be capitalized as costs of construction. Apparently on the theory that Mississippi authorities would one day reimburse it for the expenditures, Homex reported them under accounts receivable. As a result of Peat Marwick's inquiries, Homex shifted the $832,000 from accounts receivable to costs of construction in process.

The 1971 Registration Statement.

On April 21, 1971, Homex filed with the SEC a registration statement intended to cover the sale of 1,025,000 shares of Homex common stock. This was changed by amendment on May 28, 1971, to a new issue of 500,000 shares of Homex cumulative convertible preferred. On July 29, 1971, Merrill Lynch sold and distributed 500,000 shares of Homex preferred stock at $40 per share, netting Homex $19 million.

* * *

Accounting Practices Revisited

Both the draft and final 1971 registration statements represented that Homex recognized the sale of modules "when the units are manufactured and assigned to specific contracts." This prompted the SEC to inquire whether income was being recognized "too far in advance of the date of billing to customers." Homex, through Schulz, responded by letter with the following information:

When the following conditions have been met, the Company records as sales and charges costs with the related costs of modules manufactured.

1. The Company must be designated by the local housing authority, non-profit sponsor or other agencies as the contractor for the project. This designation is supported by a formal commitment from the customer to the Company.

2. The customer must have obtained and submitted evidence to the Company that a commitment of monies to fund the project has been obtained from the appropriate governmental agency under which the project has sponsorship.

3. The numbers and types of modules and the general site plan and improvements must be identified and be the subject of the agreement between the Company and its customers.

4. The Company must assign the manufactured module to a specific project and physically identify the module as being assigned to and reserved exclusively for that specific project and customer. (At the present time this identification is physically attached at the earliest stage of the manufacture of the module.)

5. The module must be completed and be ready for shipment to the customer.

When all these events have occurred, and only when all these events have occurred, does the Company recognize income.

(emphasis added).

Clearly, "all these events" had not "occurred" with regard to the Southbridge, Massachusetts, and Clay, New York, projects. Similarly, they had not occurred with regard to the Mississippi project. The Mickey Mouse file hardly substantiates Homex's claim that it relied solely upon the existence of these events for income reporting. In fact, large scale reassignment of modules to various contracts seems to have taken place whenever it met Homex's needs. Had this practice been disclosed, it would have been clear to Peat Marwick that, as one of its auditors testified at trial,

> Homex was not producing to a specific customer order and exclusively reserving modules for contracts, but rather manufacturing for inventory and therefore instead of having those units in sales, those units would have been in inventory, which would have had a significant effect on the income recognition and the portrayal of the balance sheet.

*   *   *

V. Conclusion

The motion to dismiss the appeal and remand to the district court is denied. Judgments of conviction are affirmed.

A management bent on fraudulent overstatement of revenues must do more than invent numbers because the audit process requires evidential matter to substantiate the numbers—otherwise the auditor will not give a "clean report" that GAAP were observed and that the auditor applied GAAS in making that determination. For this reason several now standard sham devices have been invented. They include such acts as arranging shipments of goods to customers for orders never placed, shipping goods to a company's own warehouse and claiming a sale, selling to nominees of the company who are not making actual purchases, delaying issuance of credits to customers for products returned under such fraudulent sales, delivering to customers under arrangements whereby the customer has no obligation to retain and pay for them, backdating of transactions, and making secret agreements permitting customers to return goods.

In one of the more famous cases, according to The Wall Street Journal (Nov. 15, 1989) at page A3, it was charged that Lincoln Savings and Loan Association had generated $135 million in gains from fifteen real estate transactions "mostly involving empty desert in Arizona." See also Lincoln S&L Ass'n v. Wall, 743 F.Supp. 901 (D.D.C.1990). It was further alleged that the auditing partner who passed on these transactions later was hired by Lincoln at a $900,000 per year salary and when Lincoln's economic viability was questioned by regulators, five United States Senators were induced to urge the regulators to discontinue harassing Lincoln. A former SEC commissioner also allegedly received a favorable $250,000 loan from Lincoln with "unusual payback provisos" including delayed payment of interest. She had volunteered to act as a character witness on behalf of Lincoln's CEO, Charles Keating, before discovery.

Hundreds of other cases exist although involving less prominent characters than Lincoln Savings. Thus, in SEC v. Donald D. Sheelen and Vincent P. Golden, D.C.N.J.Civil Action No. 89–506 (NHP), Feb. 8, 1989, the former chief executive officer and former chief financial officer of Regina Co. settled SEC charges that they caused Regina not to record at least $13 million in product returns; created false invoices and thus fictitious revenues in excess of $5 million; improperly inflated profits by over $3 million by increasing inventories; and recognized at least $6 million in revenue on transactions at the time invoices were sent rather than upon the later shipment of the goods. These actions were allegedly part of a scheme to inflate revenues and profits in order to meet certain targets and to show Regina had steadily increasing sales and earnings popularly known as "income smoothing" or "income management". The two officers also pleaded guilty to criminal charges, were sentenced to one-year and six-month terms, respectively, in a halfway house, and were each placed on five years probation, ordered to perform 500 hours of community service in each of those years and fined $25,000 and $12,500, respectively.

In re Ernest & Whinney and Ferrante, (CCH) Fed.Sec.L.Rep. ¶ 84,610 (SEC, 1990), involved the standard set of devices to cook the books plus others:

    (1) Recognition of revenue on delivery of samples to the firm's own salespeople;

    (2) Excessive allocation of overhead to inventory;

    (3) Capitalization of production costs as tooling costs;

    (4) Capitalization of legal fees as patent costs in litigation based on unfair competition, not involving patents;

    (5) Extension of useful lives of depreciable assets and increase in estimated salvage values.

This case is partially reproduced in Chapter XIV.

We shall have more to say about fraudulent revenue recognition in the next chapter, involving inventory.

(2) The Criteria of a Market Transaction: Non-sales but Non-shams

Transactions between parties may not be shams, but nevertheless may not amount to market transactions because there is no shift of risks of gain or loss on the item being dealt with. In such a case, whether the transaction is a sham need not be considered. If accounted for as a sale, that accounting is not legitimate although the transaction may be what it purports to be, as in the following case. Later, in subpart 2, we shall see another related factor of realization involving the nature of the asset received. There we shall see that a bona fide transaction that does result in a shift of risks still may not be recognized when the asset received in the transaction is not reasonably assured of collection or is otherwise problematical.

IN RE FRANTZ, WARRICK, STRACK AND ASSOCIATES, P.C.

Accounting and Auditing Enforcement Release 86.
Securities and Exchange Commission, 1986.

CBSI's business includes the marketing of business forms used in electronic data processing equipment. During 1981 through 1984, CBSI wholly owned a subsidiary, Craftsman Press, Inc. (Craftsman), which was engaged in the web-offset printing business. There were two aspects to Craftsman's business: (1) the printing operation, and (2) the book binding operation. * * *

During fiscal year 1981, Craftsman had sustained a net loss of $1,887,000 from operations. On a consolidated basis, this loss had caused CBSI to incur a net loss of $334,000, or $.39 per share. * * * The auditor warned CBSI management that continued losses would mandate liquidation of the subsidiary.

Craftsman's losses continued in fiscal year 1983. CBSI's managers concluded that the bindery aspect of Craftsman's operation was losing about $120,000 to $150,000 a month and was causing a greater proportion of the subsidiary's losses than was the printing operation. In March of 1983, Craftsman closed the bindery operation because of its continued operating losses.

In April 1983, a CBSI manager contacted Becker [an accountant] for his opinion concerning the accounting treatment of a hypothetical sale of bindery assets which had an appraised fair market value of $1.8 million. The hypothetical sale price was $2.9 million, payable in cash and a note. In May 1984, Becker reported to the CBSI manager that all of the income from the hypothetical sale would be recognized in the year of the sale. Subsequently, CBSI released its former auditing firm of the past 10 years and engaged Frantz Warrick, where Becker was employed. Frantz Warrick began the CBSI audit just two weeks before the end of CBSI's fiscal year.

On August 26, 1983, two days before the end of CBSI's fiscal year, Craftsman purportedly sold all of its bindery assets to a company founded that same day by a former Executive Vice–President of the subsidiary who had resigned the day before. The sale price was $2.9 million, with $900,000 payable in cash and $2 million payable with a note. The purchasing company borrowed the $900,000 from a third party lender on the basis that the bindery assets, which had an appraised value of $1.4 million to $1.8 million, would secure the loan and that CBSI would guarantee full payment of the purchaser's $900,000 debt in the event of default. The purchasing company also tendered to CBSI a $2 million promissory note bearing interest at the prime rate, which was two to three percent less than the rate at which CBSI could borrow funds. The founder of the purchasing company did not personally guarantee payment or collection of this $2 million note. Moreover, the founder invested an immaterial sum of $20,000, which constituted all of the capital of the purchasing company.

In the financial statements included in its annual report filed with the Commission on Form 10–K for the period ended August 28, 1983, CBSI recognized approximately $1.8 million of a $2.5 million gain from the bindery asset sale.[2] By recognizing this gain, CBSI failed to comply with GAAP * * *.

CBSI should not have recognized any gain from the bindery transaction and should not have treated the transaction as a divestiture of a business operation on August 28, 1983, since the risks and other incidents of ownership had not been transferred to the buyer with sufficient certainty. The bindery asset sale price was approximately $1 million above the appraised fair market value of the assets and represented an unnegotiated premium price based on the bindery successfully operating in the future. Payment of the debt incurred by the purchasing company was to come exclusively from the future successful operations of the bindery. Yet, the bindery had a history of losses and had been closed five months before the transaction because of these losses. Moreover, the purchasing company was newly formed and lacked any operating history. Similarly, there was no significant financial investment in the purchasing company by its founder. The purchasing company also borrowed the down payment for the purchase, and CBSI guaranteed that loan.

There was also a continuing involvement by CBSI in the bindery operation. The founder of the purchasing company continued to manage the remaining printing operations of Craftsman pursuant to a consulting agreement, and he directed the flow of work from the printing operation to the bindery. In fact, the bindery operated alongside of these operations in the same manner as it had before it was closed. CBSI guaranteed payment of the purchasing company's $900,000 loan from a third party lender and subordinated its security interest in the bindery equipment to the third party lender's security

2. The balance of $644,400 reportedly represented an interest rate adjustment based on the difference between the purchaser's note at prime and CBSI's higher costs of borrowing money. This portion of the gain was to be recognized as interest was paid on the promissory note.

interest. Moreover, the purchasing company was dependent on Craftsman for virtually all of its business and income necessary to pay its debts. Finally, payment of principal and interest on the $2 million note was to start 13 months after the transaction, with a balloon payment of $1.3 million not due until the sixth year following the sale. CBSI's continuing involvement in the bindery as well as its risk exposure relating both to the guarantee to the third party lender and to the collection of the $2 million note show that CBSI had not divested itself of the bindery for accounting purposes.

Despite the nondivestiture of the bindery operation and the uncertain collectability of the $2 million note, CBSI recognized $1.8 million of gain from the transaction. Such recognition of gain was a material departure from GAAP. Without the gain, CBSI would have reported a consolidated net loss of $1,164,000 instead of net income of $213,000, which it in fact reported in fiscal 1983.

Note and Problem

3–4. Discounting of Debt Instruments. Footnote 2 of the *Frantz, Warrick* opinion explains that the $2 million promissory note was shown at a value of $644,400 less than $2 million, or $1,355,600, and the related text indicates the gain recognized from the receipt of this note plus $900,000 in cash was approximately $1,800,000. Assuming that figure was precisely accurate, CBSI's journal entry would be:

Cash	$ 900,000	
Note Receivable	2,000,000	
Assets (binding business)		$ 455,600
Gain		1,800,000
Discount on Note Receivable		644,400

On its balance sheet at that time, CBSI would show as an asset:

Notes Receivable	$2,000,000
Less: Discount	644,400
Net	$1,355,600

Note 2 indicates that as interest would be received on the note, the difference between its $2,000,000 face amount and the $1,355,600 net booked, viz. the Discount, amount would be recognized as interest income over the years to maturity.

If the note had a 10–year life, the $644,400 might be amortized on a straight line basis by the following entry:

Note Receivable	$ 64,440	
Interest Revenue		$ 64,440

But how were these numbers derived?

The explanation will be easier if we approach the question first from the point of view of the issuer of the note. We also use this opportunity to dip slightly into some aspects of business finance.

A business may borrow money from a bank or other lender and give a promissory note to repay the amount borrowed with interest at a certain rate. The note is a contract which may range from very simple to very complex. It may or may not be secured (or "collateralized") by a pledge or mortgage of securities or real or personal property. If it is so secured, it may or may not be "with recourse." I.e., a secured note "with recourse" provides that the lender has a right to payment from the issuer of the note regardless of the lender's foreclosure on the property securing the note. There may also be restrictive covenants in the note such as a covenant prohibiting the borrower from paying dividends to shareholders within specified limits. These covenants are often tied to accounting data. For example, a covenant may state that the note shall become immediately due and payable should the "current ratio" (i.e., the ratio of current assets to current liabilities) fall below 0.5. One of the terms of the note, of course, will be the provision for the lender's compensation—the interest.

Interest rates are a function not only of general economic factors but also the specific risks of the borrower. As such rates fluctuate constantly, a borrower may be able to borrow at 9% one day but have to pay 9¼% a day later. Volatility of interest rates has increased greatly in recent years.

If the borrower wishes instead to borrow from insurance companies, pension funds, or other institutional lenders in a private offering, it may again use notes, secured or not, with or without recourse, etc. But it may also modify the notes into multiple fungible units because it may be borrowing from, say, fifty or a hundred different companies. Or it may make a "public offering" to the general public.

In such cases, instead of a single note there will be several standardized notes which are usually called "debentures" if unsecured or "bonds" if secured. Usually they will be in $1,000 denominations with interest payable semi-annually. In the U.S. because of the needs of tax administration they must be "registered" with the issuer—i.e., they must be payable to named payees and not payable to "bearer." Foreign notes, on the other hand, are often bearer instruments.

Debenture and bond offerings are subject to various state and federal securities laws as well, which help to determine the general structure and terms of an issue. Practicalities also enter into fixing the structure.

For example, in the typical debenture or bond offering a trust indenture agreement is entered into between the issuer and a bank or other institution which agrees to act as trustee to administer the debenture holders' or bondholders' rights such as the right to declare a default or to foreclose on a mortgage. This is arranged to avoid the nightmare of having thousands of bondholders variously exercising their rights, etc.

Arranging an offering frequently takes many weeks and raises the same feature noted in footnote 2 of the *Frantz, Warrick* proceeding—a bond issued in a face amount of $1,000, due in ten years, bearing interest on that amount at a rate of 10%, is in fact issued for a price of $980 because the appropriate interest rate is more than 10% on the date of issue. Rather than fine-tune the stated interest rate, the price of the bond is fine-tuned—perhaps as a marketing device, explaining why usually there is a discount rather than a premium. In such a case, the borrower receives $980 and agrees to repay $50 every six months for ten years and then to repay a full $1,000 at maturity. Thus the issuer has the use of $980 for which it pays interest of two types—$50 every six months and $20 more at the end of ten years. The bookkeeping entries will include an amortization of the $20 over ten years. Assuming, for simplicity, only one bond is sold on 1/1/X1 the entries might be:

On issuance on 1/1/X1:

1/1/X1	Cash	$ 980	
	Discount on Bond	20	
	Bond Payable		$1,000

End of Years 1 through 9:

Interest Expense	102	
Cash		100
Amortized Discount on Bond (an offset account to Discount on Bond)		2

Year 10:

Interest Expense	102	
Bond Payable	1,000	
Cash		1,100
Amortized Discount on Bond		2

One may see that in *Frantz, Warrick* the *lender,* CBSI, valued its $2 million note at $1,355,600 and amortized the $644,400 as Interest Income, not as expense.

Similarly the bondholder in our above illustration would show Interest Income of $102 per year, not $100.

In fact our illustration is somewhat misleading because in practice the $20 discount is not amortized on the simple basis we have shown but is done by use of compounding of interest. For our purposes it is unnecessary to delve into the mathematics because even a full explanation of that feature would leave volumes of additional financial calculations unexplained. This is a book for lawyers not financial officers.

In any event, the point is that in *Frantz, Warrick,* the accountants discounted the note by about 33%, to take into account the difference between the nominal, prime, rate of interest and the fair market rate for the borrower.

The FASB is now considering use of present value accounting in a comprehensive manner, including valuation of all assets and liabilities. See FASB, *Discussion Memorandum, An Analysis of Issues Related to Present Value–Based Measurements in Accounting* (1990).

3–5. *Problem.* Should income have been recognized on the following transaction?

USF sold three properties to Burnham Management Corp. for $5,399,000 and recognized profit of $550,000 from the transaction. The letter agreement which covered the sale committed USF to use its best efforts to secure permanent financing to the properties for Burnham and to pay certain underwriting costs upon Burnham's subsequent syndication of the properties. Furthermore, the agreement provided that upon final documentation, which was not prepared and executed, USF was to deliver to Burnham USF's guarantee that Burnham would suffer no loss from operations of the properties. The agreement was also subject to an addendum which provided Burnham with an absolute guarantee against loss from ownership of the properties and a commitment by USF to complete construction of the properties. See *ASR 153* (1974).

(C) Related Party Transactions

If two unrelated parties may engage in a sham transaction, or design it so as to avoid a shift of risk without sham, consider how much easier it is to fabricate a deal when two entities are under common control. The control may take a wide variety of forms: in addition to control through stock ownership by a common owner, parent and subsidiary, or some combination of those two, there may be control by family relatives, contractual arrangements, control of necessary supplies, and so on, *ad infinitum*. See Sommer, *Who's "In Control"?*, 21 Bus.Law. 559 (1966).

Should related parties' transactions be treated like those of unrelated parties?

AICPA, STATEMENT OF AUDITING STANDARDS
NO. 6, ¶ 6
(1975).*

"6. Except for the disclosure requirements of the Securities and Exchange Commission's Regulations S–X and the accounting treatment prescribed by certain Opinions of the Accounting Principles Board when related parties are involved, established accounting principles ordinarily do not require transactions with related parties to be accounted for on a basis different from that which would be appropriate if the parties were not related. Until such time as applicable accounting principles are established by appropriate authoritative bodies, the auditor should view related party transactions within the framework of existing pronouncements, placing primary emphasis on the adequacy of disclosure of the existence of such transactions and their significance in the financial statements of the reporting entity. He should be aware that the substance of a particular transaction could be significantly different from its form."

STATEMENT OF FINANCIAL ACCOUNTING
STANDARDS NO. 57, RELATED PARTY
DISCLOSURES **
FASB, 1982.

"2. Financial statements shall include disclosures of material related party transactions, other than compensation arrangements, expense allowances, and other similar items in the ordinary course of business. However, disclosure of transactions that are eliminated in the preparation of consolidated or combined financial statements is not required in those statements. The disclosures shall include:

a. The nature of the relationship(s) involved

b. A description of the transactions, including transactions to which no amounts or nominal amounts were ascribed, for each of the periods for which income statements are presented, and such other information deemed necessary to an understanding of the effects of the transactions on the financial statements

c. The dollar amounts of transactions for each of the periods for which income statements are presented and the effects of any change in the method of establishing the terms from that used in the preceding period

d. Amounts due from or to related parties as of the date of each balance sheet presented and, if not otherwise apparent, the terms and manner of settlement

"3. Transactions involving related parties cannot be presumed to be carried out on an arm's-length basis, as the requisite conditions of competitive, free-market dealings may not exist. Representations about transactions with related parties, if made, shall not imply that the related party transactions were consummated on terms equivalent to those that prevail in arm's-length transactions unless such representations can be substantiated."

Notes and Problem

3–6. Value in Related Party Transactions. Perhaps the most difficult problem of related party transactions is: what evidence of "value" will be required to substantiate recording of revenue at the price set by the related parties. The authorities all require skepticism as to value. Carmichael, *Arm's Length Transactions in Accounting and Auditing*, J. Accountancy 67 (Dec. 1971); J. Willingham & D. Carmichael, *Auditing Concepts and Methods* 217 (1971); Paton, *Transactions Between Affiliates*, 20 Acctg. Rev. 255 (1945); cf. Johnson, *Non–Arm's Length Transactions: The Auditor's Responsibility*, CPA Journal 39 (Nov. 1974). See the Pennsylvania Railroad's Great Southwest Corporation sale of its "Six Flags" amusement parks in In the Matter of Reports of Great Southwest Corporation [1972–73 Transfer Binder] CCH Fed.Sec.L.Rep. ¶ 79,194 (SEC 1973).

If, as we suggested earlier, the inability to accurately determine value is a major reason for not recognizing income until a sale, does a sale to a related party overcome the difficulty? If auditors nevertheless recognize income in such related party transactions is there any reason remaining for not recognizing income before other sales?

3–7. GAAP: Fact or Law? How did the *Tooey* court and the SEC in *Frantz, Warrick* learn what the "principles of bookkeeping" or GAAP were on which they based their opinions—from evidence or briefs?

Is an accounting principle like a statute or case law, presented by briefs with the tribunal fully entitled to do its own research and make its own conclusions? Or is it a question of fact? Or is it a question of application of law to fact?

Clearly in *Tooey* it was a question of fact. And that fact ordinarily would have to be attested to by an expert in accounting although some judges or administrators would take judicial notice of what they deem to be well known GAAP such as the requirement of a market transaction as in *Tooey*. And the SEC in *Frantz, Warrick* doubtless felt free to apply its own knowledge as administrative agencies often do.

A second question is, what is the source of GAAP; i.e., to what would the expert witness or tribunal refer in determining GAAP? The answer to this question is at least as complex as asking to what would a lawyer look in giving an opinion of law. See the discussion in Chapter II.

3–8. *Problem.* King Resources Company was engaged in oil and gas production as well as the sale of oil and gas interests. In early 1969, it obtained the rights to explore on 22 million acres of Canadian Arctic property merely by agreeing to spend $1 per acre in exploration costs within a certain period. It sold an undivided one-half interest to IOS for $10 million cash plus IOS's assumption of a commitment to spend $11 million, one half of King's original commitment. At the end of 1969, King Resources Company sold the right in 5% of its remaining property interest to "other parties" for $7.5 million and at the start of 1970 purchased the same percentage share from IOS's holdings for an identical price. The "other parties" included John King, the controlling shareholder of King Resources, and some business associates. The result was that King Resources Co. held the same 50% it had held just prior to these last two transactions. (The facts have been simplified and additional data omitted.)

Should King Resources have recognized the $7.5 million as revenue in 1969? What should it have disclosed under *SFAS No. 57?* See The Fund of Funds, Limited v. Arthur Andersen & Co., 545 F.Supp. 1314 (S.D.N.Y.1982).

(D) Exceptions to the Requirement of a Market Transaction

(1) Losses:

Inventories

Inventories must be valued at lower of cost or market value. *ARB No. 43, Ch. 4, St. 5* (1953). Like any other write-down of an asset the result is a charge against income. Hence income, albeit negative income only, is recognized without a market transaction—an exception to the *Tooey* general rule based on the conservatism concept.

Fixed Assets

However, for fixed assets whose value is impaired, there is no settled practice. See FASB, *Discussion Memorandum, An Analysis of Issues Related to Accounting for the Impairment of Long–Lived Assets and Identifiable Intangibles* (1990). Regardless of GAAP, a failure to make a write-down may be fraudulent. SEC v. Bangor Punta Corp., 331 F.Supp. 1154 (S.D.N.Y.1971).

According to an Issues Paper prepared by the Task Force on Impairment of Value of the AICPA Accounting Standards Division, *Accounting for the Inability to Fully Recover the Carrying Amounts on Long Lived Assets* (July 15, 1980), mere temporary declines in fixed assets are not recognized as losses. In fact in practice write-downs are seldom made to fixed assets although formal GAAP require a write-down in certain cases.[c]

If a write-down is made, the debit will be against income and the credit of course will be to the asset account.

The related result of relieving future years of expense or loss charges has not gone unnoticed by business managers. It is believed for example that when managers wish to make a fresh start they are prone to take a "big bath" (i.e., write down assets excessively) so that future years' reported income will cast a favorable reflection on the new management program. Thus a write-down may be abusive and fraudulent.

Because the write-down of an asset is a charge against income, it may be conceptualized either as negative revenue (loss) or as a cost (expense). Partly for this reason, but more importantly because more profitable consideration may be given to write-downs after students have learned more about fixed assets, we defer further consideration to Chapter V.

Marketable Equity Securities—Losses and Recoupments

The recent tender offer surge has resulted in many intercorporate investments among actively traded companies. These securities may be held for investment only, for the long run or temporarily. In some cases, there may be a more-or-less formulated contemplation that the investment may at some future time be increased to a controlling interest. In any case, the securities may be readily marketable or not, or somewhere on the continuum between those extremes. These different characteristics pose differing problems in accounting for securities.

Here we are concerned only with the narrow range of accounting for marketable equity securities in companies not "significantly influenced" by the holder. (The rule of thumb here finds no significance if the investor holds less than 20% of the investee's voting interests.)

c. APB Opinion No. 18, ¶ 19(h) (1971), requires a write-down for "other than temporary" declines in investments accounted for under the "equity" method. This shall be described later in Chapter IX, infra.

APB Opinion No. 30, ¶ 15 (1973), requires a write-down when a segment of a business is committed to be sold or abandoned. And see Chris–Craft Industries, Inc. v. Piper Aircraft Corp., 480 F.2d 341, 367–79 (2d Cir.1973), cert. denied 414 U.S. 910 (1973).

SFAS No. 12, Accounting for Certain Marketable Securities (1975), requires a write-down for a decline in a portfolio to be charged against income if the portfolio is a current asset or if the decline is in a portfolio carried as a fixed asset and the decline is "other than temporary."

SFAS No. 13, ¶ 62, requires a write-down for other than temporary declines in property held under a lease that is in substance a purchase of property.

The accounting prior to *SFAS No. 12* for marketable equity securities not held for control is described in ¶ 1 of that Standard:

> [Some] enterprises are carrying marketable securities at cost, some at market (or variations of market), some at the lower of cost or market, and some are applying more than one of those methods to different classes of securities. During 1973 and 1974, there were substantial declines in market values of many securities. As a result, in many enterprises where securities are carried at cost, the carrying amount is in excess of current market value. In other enterprises where carrying amounts were written down to reflect the market decline, the partial recovery in the market in 1975 has given rise to a situation in which securities are being carried at amounts which are below both original cost and current market value.

The statement then posed these issues in ¶ 3:

> (a) Under what circumstances should marketable equity securities that are carried on a cost basis be written down below cost? (Note that write-up above cost is not contemplated.)

> (b) Should marketable equity securities that have been written down be written back up based on market recoveries or other criteria?

The possibility of write-ups of recoupments suggested in question (b) had never before been contemplated by the FASB or its predecessors; once a write-down occurred, for example, in inventory, the written down value was not raised.

Under *SFAS No. 12*, marketable equity securities held by the investor firm are initially debited at cost, but thereafter appear *on the balance sheet* at the lower of cost or market value on the balance sheet's date, i.e., the end of the period.

Thus if 10 shares of GM Corp. are purchased for $700, Investments initially will be debited $700, and cash or whatever else was used to purchase them will be credited $700. E.g.,

> Investments (10 shares GM) $700
>   Cash $700

If at the close of the year the value is higher, no additional entry is made. If value has dropped to, say $450, the accounting becomes more complex. *SFAS No. 12* requires differing treatment depending on whether the investment is shown as a current asset on a classified balance sheet.

> If a current asset, the entry will be:
>   Loss on Investments Charged to
>   Income $250
>   Valuation   Allowance   for
>   Investments [d] $250

If instead the investment is carried as a non-current asset on a classified balance sheet or if the balance sheet is not classified, the

---

d. An offset (contra) account to the Investments account.

entry, according to *SFAS No. 12* requires a debit directly to equity, not income:

Net Unrealized Loss in Marketable Equity Securities [e] $250

Valuation   Allowance   for
Investments $250

If at the end of the next period the value has increased by any amount, the income or equity account previously debited will be credited up to $250 and the Valuation Allowance for Investment account will be debited. Debiting this account will result in a lesser reduction from the Investments account on the balance sheet.

There are two further wrinkles on all this. First, when two or more securities are involved, they will be aggregated into portfolios of (1) securities carried as current assets, and (2) securities carried as non-current assets or securities of companies not using a classified balance sheet. *SFAS No. 12* then requires determining net values of whole portfolios, not individual companies, and writing them up or down as above.

When a security is sold, the original cost of the security is matched against the sale price in determining gain or loss. *SFAS No. 12* valuations are made at financial statement dates only. Thus, if a price decline on a security carried as a *current* asset has occurred prior to the beginning of the period and has been recognized, the adjustment of the valuation account, which relates only to remaining securities and is made at the end of the period, will automatically "wash out" the prior write down and leave in the income statement, as to this particular security, only a net amount representing the difference between value at the beginning of the period and the selling price.

In the case of investments carried as *non-current* assets, the entire gain or loss on the security for its period of ownership (or period of non-current designation) will remain in the income statement in the period of sale. This is because any prior period recognition of change in value of non-current marketable securities was treated as an equity reduction and not as an income statement adjustment.

Notice that for portfolios carried as current assets, income is charged with decreases (or credited with increases to the extent of the valuation allowance) without realization by sale. Also notice, that because portfolios are aggregates of securities, increases in income may result not only from recoupment in value of a security which had previously dropped in value, but also for increases in value of a security which had not itself previously fallen in value but which offsets present or prior decreases in value of other securities in the same portfolio. These are limited departures from the realization concept going beyond recoupment.

e. SFAS No. 12 requires that this account be shown as a floating debit in the equity section of the balance sheet. See ¶ 11.

Finally, even for investments held in non-current asset portfolios, *SFAS No. 12*, ¶ 22, requires charging income with an "other than temporary" decline (with no subsequent credit to income for recoupments).

(2) Institutional Investors' Portfolio Holdings

Except as changed to the limited extent called for by *SFAS No. 12*, the usual rule against recognizing unrealized appreciation is followed by accountants in most cases in the valuation of securities, whether the securities are temporary or permanent holdings, marketable or not. However, it is common practice to show market value parenthetically in the balance sheet.

By convention, in accordance with the general rule, increase or decrease in value of securities assets is recognized in the income statement on the date of sale or other disposition.[f] Thus, the existence of a portfolio of marketable securities having a value in excess of cost provides a convenient opportunity to "manage" earnings to the extent of that excess by simply rolling over the investments into new securities.[g]

A principal exception to this is the investment company. An investment company is a company meeting the legal definition in Section 3 of the Investment Company Act of 1940 (the "1940 Act"). Most of these are companies whose assets consist almost solely of marketable securities and are popularly known as "mutual funds." For regulatory purposes, investment companies are divided into two categories. Open-end companies are those whose capital varies from day to day, or from moment to moment, by the issuance and redemption of capital stock, i.e., open-end mutual funds. Outstanding shares of open-end companies are not normally traded among shareholders because § 22(d) of the 1940 Act inhibits such trading. (For the intricacies of mutual fund share trading, see United States v. National Association of Securities Dealers, Inc., 422 U.S. 694 (1975)).

The SEC, exercising its authority under the 1940 Act, has for many years required open-end investment companies to state their assets at value, showing cost parenthetically. The principal reason for this accounting requirement is to provide an orderly and consistent basis to determine the price at which the open-end company may sell and

---

f. In the case of depreciable assets, debiting depreciation based on cost recognizes appreciation indirectly over the life of the asset by failure to base that depreciation charge on fair value. But this recognition is in the income statement only and not in the balance sheet.

g. Current ordinary income, and not an extraordinary item or retained earnings, is credited, since the rules distinguishing "extraordinary items" from ordinary items of income do not treat security gains as extraordinary. See infra pp.

210–211 on by-passing the income statement. However, in 1983 after the SEC blocked Aetna Life & Casualty from claiming income from certain anticipated tax-loss benefits, [See Loomis, Behind the Profits Glow at Aetna, Fortune Magazine 54, (Nov. 15, 1982)] and the insurer announced that it would sell some of its portfolio securities to make up for that amount [Fortune p. 6 (Mar. 7, 1983)] the SEC reportedly compelled separate disclosure of the portfolio gain.

redeem its shares and to prevent abuses such as the "managed" earnings referred to in the second preceding paragraph.

Closed-end companies are those whose capital is fixed, like commercial and industrial companies, and whose outstanding shares are sold in the market place or privately between shareholders. A few of these companies, i.e., those whose assets consist almost solely of marketable securities, are called closed-end mutual funds. For many years, closed-end investment companies were given their choice of carrying their investments either (a) at cost, showing value parenthetically, or (b) at value, showing cost parenthetically. The reason for this dispensation appears to be that many of the closed-end companies hold substantial assets, other than readily tradeable securities for which there is no immediate liquidity or ready market. Also, the need for reliable value determination is not as intense as in an open-end fund where a redemption of shares at too high a price or a sale of new shares at too low a price would have an adverse effect on other shareholders in terms of assets available for future investment. This condition does not exist in a closed-end company, except in the rare situation where a closed-end company will buy or sell its own shares. Another unstated reason was that closed-end company shares usually trade at a substantial discount (e.g., 20%) below market value of the portfolio.

Nevertheless, in 1973, the AICPA promulgated an Industry Audit Guide, Audits of Investment Companies, which requires that assets of all investment companies be carried at value. SEC accounting rules, (Articles 6, 6A, 6B, and 6C of Regulation S–X), have now been modified to accommodate this AICPA pronouncement.

(3) Regulatory Accounting and the S&L Debacle; Deja Vu for the Bank Crisis

The thrift institutions (savings and loan associations and certain other specialized lenders) were in deep trouble by the early 1980s because they were forced by competition to pay interest rates of 15% or more to their depositors although they had previously made still-outstanding thirty-year loans, some at low rates of 6% or less, causing negative yield ratios.

The value of their mortgages had fallen to from 50 to 60% of face value in many cases and the thrifts had to suffer substantial losses when attempting to improve the yield ratio by selling low interest mortgages and reinvesting in higher interest, high risk mortgages. The anticipated losses were so severe that many thrifts might show negative net worth and there was speculation that the Federal Savings and Loan Insurance Corporation (FSLIC) would not be able to handle all the expected failures with its limited funds available. In short, the sky was falling.

It was assumed that the thrifts needed time to restructure their balance sheets to match interest rates and maturities in receivables with interest rates and maturities on deposits and other payables.

With the passage of time—no one knew how long—interest rates would decline, some loans would mature or be paid off and available funds could be reinvested at interest rates commensurate with rates being paid. What was needed was an *accounting bridge* over this undefined period of time that would give the thrifts time to restructure their balance sheets without throwing depositors into a panic.

The regulators, most importantly the Federal Home Loan Bank, sought accounting gimmicks to camouflage the impending disaster. They adopted a provision that required thrifts, in regulatory reports, to defer any loss on mortgages sold and amortize those losses over the life of the mortgages sold. See 12 C.F.R. § 563, c. 14 (1982); Mills, *Accounting Alchemy*, Barron's Mag. p. 29 (May 31, 1982).

This would permit a thrift to sell $10,000,000 face value of mortgages yielding $800,000, an average of 8%, for, say, $7,000,000, and amortize the $3,000,000 loss over the composite life of the mortgages sold, say twenty years. The $7,000,000 proceeds could then be reinvested in mortgages paying 15% or $1,050,000 per year. In addition, federal income tax loss carrybacks gave the thrifts substantial additional funds to invest at current rates. The effect of all this was to produce a positive yield ratio of interest on receivables compared to interest on payables and without any reduction in reported net worth.

The "accounting bridge" seemed to work at first. Interest rates had come down somewhat, many thrifts had sold off their low yielding mortgages, deferred the losses and reinvested at shorter maturities and higher rates. All of this was accomplished with only minimal reduction in net worth shown in regulatory reports and the FSLIC was able to handle the surprisingly few failures declared (by regulatory authorities) during this period.

However, the whole scheme was dependent on the higher yielding, high risk new investments being good. They were not. Indeed many were outright frauds with hundreds of millions of dollars being loaned on near worthless security. Huge shopping centers and hotels were built in deserted areas with the contractors receiving full payment and the thrifts holding the bag. The rest is history as taxpayers are now bailing out an estimated half trillion dollar loss.

One of the accounting practices of thrifts as well as banks and other financial institutions involves the notes held by the institution and not resold. In the simple case where the appropriate interest rate has risen from, say, 8% when a note was made to, say, 12%, the present value of the note clearly has fallen. See the Appendix to this book. If the institution believes it has the requisite ability and intent to hold for the long-term, no write-down is made to market. If it is planned to resell the note currently, a write-down is made.

But the issue is not always so easily resolved. To illustrate, suppose a S&L has loaned $100 million to Needy Corp. at 8% due in ten years secured by a real estate mortgage and the deal goes sour in the first year so that the S&L takes over the property with the hope of reselling it to another operator. Should the note be carried at market if lower?

Human nature being what it is, a desperate bank or S&L, worried about being closed down by regulators or about losing deposits should word get out, will make every effort to avoid finding that the note is not held for the long-term. This type of problem, dependent on institutional intent to a great degree, prompted an SEC staff member to quip, "Psychoanalytic accounting is not practicable or useful." The result is that regulators and depositors may be misled. This is one more of the causes of the S&L debacle.

The Chairman of the SEC in 1990 began to press for reporting investments of institutional lenders at lower of cost or market. The Commission, the AICPA, and the FASB thereupon began to study the proposal. In the meantime, the SEC now will require enhanced footnote disclosure.

Nevertheless, officials of the Federal Reserve Board, the Comptroller of the Currency and the Federal Deposit Insurance Corporation have all voiced opposition to changing GAAP.

Alan Greenspan, Chairman of the Federal Reserve Board, in a letter to the Chairman of the SEC questioned the value of requiring lower of cost or market accounting. "To mark an asset to a market price intended to reflect the value of a loan were it liquidated immediately is interesting, but not a relevant measure of the success of commercial banking," he told the SEC Chairman. Banks already adjust for changes in their portfolio's value through such devices as loan loss reserves, he added.

The Fed chairman further challenged the practicality of using market-based accounting for financial institutions. He said that only about one-third of bank assets on average have ready market values. Forcing banks and other institutions to adopt market value accounting for a portion of their investment securities, but not for all balance sheet and off-balance sheet items, could result in volatility in reported earnings and capital that is not indicative of the bank's true financial condition. He added that banking organizations already are required to disclose the market value of their investment securities in financial statements and regulatory financial reports, although the valuations are not reflected in reported earnings. Further, adoption of market value accounting also could affect the amount of securities that banks are willing to hold. Greenspan speculated that many institutions would likely reduce their holdings of marketable instruments, thereby reducing the liquidity of banking organizations. "This effect would work against one of the important objectives of the international risk-based capital framework," he asserted.

"Unless reasonably specific standards are developed, reported market values may not be consistent across institutions, and opportunities may exist for the overstatement of reported market values of assets, earnings, and capital," Greenspan wrote. "Furthermore, auditors would have little basis for evaluating, and when necessary, challenging, market value estimates. Examiners would face similar verification problems."

In addition, the Fed chairman warned his SEC counterpart that market value accounting would involve considerable cost and reporting burdens, especially for smaller institutions. What did Mr. Greenspan learn from the S&L scandal?

The SEC's initiative is just the opening salvo. The Chairman has stated that in his view, fair value accounting should be used for all the assets of financial institutions.

(4) The "Equity" Method

Assume that under the governing dividend statute Parent Corporation is permitted to pay dividends out of its own "net assets in excess of capital stock at par value." On January 1, Parent Corp. acquires 100% of the shares of Sub–Corp. whose net assets are carried on Sub–Corp.'s books at $2,560,000. A year later Sub–Corp.'s net assets are carried on its books at $3,000,000 because of profits having been earned in the amount of $440,000. Assuming "net assets" under the statute means book carrying value, may Parent under the statute increase the carrying value of its investment account for Sub–Corp. by the amount of the increase in net assets of Sub–Corp.?

APB Opinion 18, *The Equity Method of Accounting for Investments in Common Stock* (1971), prescribes that, subject to certain limitations, this should be done in *consolidated financial statements,* or in *parent company financial statements* prepared for issuance to stockholders as the financial statements of the primary reporting entity. *APB Op. No. 18* does not otherwise deal with the question of whether the resulting increase or decrease in net assets should be posted to the parent company's accounts, except by analogy. A court could go either way on the dividend issue. This accounting is referred to as the equity method and, as a rule of thumb, applies where the parent owns at least 20% of the equity of the subsidiary.

We shall further consider the equity method of accounting for subsidiary corporations in Chapter IX infra. We mention it here as another exception to the requirement of realization, or at least a special case.

(5) Agricultural and Mining Products—Recognition Upon Completion of Production Before Sale

As Rule 1 of *ARB No. 43, Ch. 1,* states, for certain agricultural and precious metals businesses, income is often recognized before sale.

One practice abandons the cost convention and switches to value—at resale value (less cost of disposal). This results in recognition of profits before sale of goods—before realization—contrary to *Tooey* and Rule 1. In fact, however, few mining companies follow the practice of recognizing revenue before sale. H. Barden, *The Accounting Basis of*

Inventories 134 (AICPA Acctg. Research Study No. 13, 1973). Agribusiness accounting also is evidenced by varying practices. See H. Jaenicke, *Survey of Present Practices in Recognizing Revenues, Expenses, Gains and Losses* 72–75 (FASB Research Report, 1981), which is based on AICPA Issues Paper, *Accounting for Agricultural Cooperatives, Agricultural Producers, and Hedging Transactions by Agricultural Cooperatives and Producers* (The Agribusiness Comm. of the Auditing Standards Div., AICPA, Aug. 1, 1980). In 1982 AICPA Proposed Statement of Position, *Accounting by Agricultural Producers and Agricultural Cooperatives,* (September 10, 1982), recommended that growing crops of agricultural producers be reported at the lower of cost or market and that inventories of harvested crops and livestock held for sale also be reported at the lower of cost or market unless certain conditions are met. It recommends that an agricultural producer be permitted to report harvested crops and livestock held for sale at market less estimated costs of disposal, only if (a) the product has a reliable market price that is readily available, (b) the product has relatively insignificant and predictable costs of disposal, and (c) the product is available for immediate delivery.

Would an income statement of a timber grower, vintner, or distiller be meaningful if it failed to take into account increase from natural processes? Whatever your own answer to this question is, accountants have generally been very hesitant to recognize the increase as income solely on this ground, although there is some support for it in the authorities. See W. Paton & A. Littleton, *An Introduction to Corporate Accounting Standards* 52 (AAA Monograph No. 3, 1940); W. Paton & W. Paton, Jr., *Asset Accounting: An Intermediate Course* 458 (1952); H. Finney and H. Miller, *Principles of Accounting, Intermediate* 149–50 (6th ed., 1965), R. Wixon, *Accountants' Handbook* 15.11–12 (5th ed., 1970); H. Hatfield, *Surplus and Dividends* 30–39 (1943); Rowbury, *Timber Depletion,* 22 Acctg.Rev. 137 (1947). For a comment, see H. Jaenicke, supra 79–80.

Where a company owning timberlands engages in reforestation, it is asserted that the practice of writing up assets to show accretion has become acceptable (Finney and Miller, supra 325–327) but the credit is not to income. However, current financial statements in the annual reports of large owners of timberland do not show any recognition of natural increase, not even to counterbalance a depletion charge for cutting. Thus their forest lands are seriously understated. The practice of not reflecting such increase has caused Georgia–Pacific and Weyerhauser, both large holders of timberlands, to embark on a sustained massive advertising program to make the public generally aware that trees grow!

Would it be more helpful to investors (holders and sellers of securities as well as buyers) to have natural increase estimated and disclosed on financial statements with the protection of independent audits, rather than omitted from the financial statements under present practices?

(6) Personal Balance Sheets

During the 1964 Democratic Presidential nomination campaign President Lyndon Johnson, who had never made an adequate living in private employment, was reputed to have made many millions through his political power. Yet his wealth was stated at a mere $3.5 million in accordance with GAAP as certified by a major accounting firm. The chairman of the Republican National Committee quipped that following GAAP in this case was the equivalent of carrying Manhattan Island at the original cost of $24. The campaign office of Johnson's major Democratic contender, Senator Hubert Humphrey, published a report of Humphrey's personal wealth prepared by Touche, Ross, stating:

> Because of the nature and purpose of this presentation, the statement of value of household goods and of financial condition of the principal has been prepared on the basis of present market value of their assets, which basis of reporting we believe to be appropriate in the circumstances.

Senator Humphrey lost the nomination to President Johnson.

Almost two decades later the AICPA, reversing its prior position, required use of current value rather than historical cost for personal financial statements of political candidates as well as applicants for bank loans, etc. AICPA, Acctg.Stan.Div. SOP No. 82–1, *Accounting and Financial Reporting for Personal Financial Statements* (Oct. 1, 1982) J. Accountancy 135 (Dec. 1982); AICPA, ASB, *Personal Financial Statements—Compilation, Review and Audit* (1983). These statements typically are balance sheets only and present no question of recognizing unrealized gains as income. The Vietnam War began and escalated during Johnson's term. Did GAAP have its most stunning effect on our civilization?

2. THE SECOND FACTOR OF REALIZATION—NATURE OF ASSET RECEIVED

Chapter 1A of *ARB No. 43*, ¶ 1, ("Rule One") states that "Profit is deemed to be realized when a sale in the ordinary course of business is effected, unless the circumstances are such that the collection of the sale price is not reasonably assured." An important application of the qualification in this GAAP is illustrated below for one type of leveraged buyout ("LBO").

GAIN RECOGNITION ON THE SALE OF A BUSINESS OR OPERATING ASSETS TO A HIGHLY LEVERAGED ENTITY

SAB 81, CCH Fed.Sec.L.Rep. ¶ 74,141 Topic 5, Ch. U.
Securities and Exchange Commission, 1989.

Facts: A registrant has sold a subsidiary, division or operating assets to a newly formed, thinly capitalized, highly leveraged entity

(NEWCO) for cash or a combination of cash and securities, which may include subordinated debt, preferred stock, warrants, options or other instruments issued by NEWCO. In some of these transactions, registrants may guarantee debt or enter into other agreements (sometimes referred to as make-well agreements) that may require the registrant to infuse cash into NEWCO under certain circumstances. Securities received in the transaction are not actively traded and are subordinate to substantially all of NEWCO's other debt. The value of the consideration received appears to exceed the cost basis of the net assets sold.

Question: Assuming the transaction may be properly accounted for as a divestiture,[1] does the staff believe it is appropriate for the registrant to recognize a gain?

Interpretive Response: The staff believes there often exist significant uncertainties about the seller's ability to realize non-cash proceeds received in transactions in which the purchaser is a thinly capitalized, highly leveraged entity, particularly when its assets consist principally of those purchased from the seller. The staff believes that such uncertainties raise doubt as to whether immediate gain recognition is appropriate. Factors that may lead the staff to question gain recognition in such transactions include:

(1) situations in which the assets or operations sold have historically not produced cash flows from operations that will be sufficient to fund future debt service and full dividend requirements on a current basis. Often the servicing of debt and preferred dividend requirements is dependent upon future events that cannot be assured, such as sales of assets or improvements in earnings.

(2) the lack of any substantial amount of equity capital in NEWCO other than that provided by the registrant; and/or

(3) the existence of contingent liabilities of the registrant, such as debt guarantees or agreements that require the registrant to infuse cash into NEWCO under certain circumstances.

The staff also believes that even where the registrant receives solely cash proceeds, the recognition of any gain would be impacted by

---

1. Transactions such as these require careful evaluation to determine whether, in substance, a divestiture has occurred. Staff Accounting Bulletin Topic No. 5–E provides the staff's views on circumstances that may exist that would lead the staff to conclude that the risks of the business have not been transferred to the new owners and that a divestiture has not occurred. Topic 5–E indicates that factors to consider in determining whether a transaction should be accounted for as a divestiture include:

• continuing involvement by the seller in the business;

• absence of significant financial investment in the business by the buyer;

• repayment of debt, which constitutes the principal consideration in the transaction, is dependent on future successful operations; or

• the continued necessity for debt or contract performance guarantees on behalf of the business by the seller.

Ed's. note. See In re Frantz, Warrick at p. 137 for a case where a divestiture was held not to have occurred.

Accounting for LBOs is far more complex than SAB 81 suggests. E.g., see Gorman, LBO Frontiers in the 1990s: Can Accounting Keep Pace?, J. Accountancy 100 (June, 1990).

the existence of any guarantees or other agreements that may require the registrant to infuse cash into NEWCO, particularly when the first two factors listed above exist.

———

When the exception in Rule 1 supra, becomes applicable, SFAS No. 5, *Accounting for Contingencies* ¶ 23 (1975) states:

> Inability to make a reasonable estimate of the amount of loss from uncollectible receivables * * * precludes accrual [of the Bad Debt Expense] and may, if there is significant uncertainty as to collection, suggest that the installment method, the cost recovery method, or some other method of revenue recognition be used * * * [See *APB Opinion No. 10,* ¶ 12 following].

ACCOUNTING PRINCIPLES BOARD OPINION NO. 10, ¶ 12 *

AICPA, 1966.

Installment Method of Accounting

"12.   Chapter 1A of ARB No. 43, paragraph 1, states that 'Profit is deemed to be realized when a sale in the ordinary course of business is effected, unless the circumstances are such that the collection of the sale price is not reasonably assured.' The Board reaffirms * * * that revenues should ordinarily be accounted for at the time a transaction is completed, with appropriate provision for uncollectible accounts. Accordingly, it concludes that, in the absence of the circumstances[8] referred to above, the installment method of recognizing revenue is not acceptable."

———

In one context, "retail land sales," it became abundantly clear that the guidance of GAAP just described was inadequate.

The FASB in SFAS No. 66, *Accounting for Sales of Real Estate* (1982), ¶ 100, has defined "retail land sales" as:

> * * * sales, on a volume basis, of lots that are subdivisions of large tracts of land. They are characterized by down payments so small that local banks and savings and loan institutions would not loan money on the property at market rates or purchase the buyer's note against the buyer's general credit. If the buyer cancels the contract within an established cancellation period, its money is refunded. Defaults by the

---

8.   The Board recognizes that there are exceptional cases where receivables are collectible over an extended period of time, and, because of the terms of the transactions or other conditions, there is no reasonable basis for estimating the degree of collectibility. When such circumstances exist, and as long as they exist either the installment method or the cost recovery method of accounting may be used. (Under the cost recovery method, equal amounts of revenue and expense are recognized as collections are made until all costs have been recovered, postponing any recognition of profit until that time.)

(Ed's. note.   Under the installment method each cash payment is apportioned between cost recovered and profit in the same ratio as total cost and total profit.)

buyer after the cancellation period result in recovery of the land by the seller and forfeiture of at least some principal payments made by the buyer.

The FASB has totally rejected the so-called "cost-recovery" method for retail land sales but permits one of four other methods of accounting depending on whether certain conditions have been met ranging from non-recognition of the sale (so that the property continues to be treated as the seller's, with a debit to cash for any deposit received and a credit to a liability account for the deposit liability) to full recognition of the accrued profit as on the ordinary sale of goods. See *SFAS No. 66,* ¶¶ 45–48.

Receipt of a Non-liquid, Measurable Asset—Exchanges of Property in Non-monetary Transactions

But what if the seller receives non-liquid property in exchange; say an owner of a parcel of real estate trades it for another parcel, or a baseball club trades players, or an airline trades transportation of a group of television performers for two minutes of televised advertising? These barter transactions have become increasingly common and demand accounting answers.

Accountants have expressed the view that here measurability rather than liquidity should control recognition of Revenue. AAA, 1964 Concepts and Standards Research Study Committee, *The Realization Concept,* 40 Acctg.Rev. 312, 318 (1965). *Opinion No. 29* (1973) below now subscribes to that view.

The result is that income is recognized just as if a liquid asset were received, provided that the other realization factors are satisfied.

Note

3–9.　The Cash Receipts Method. Although it is now well-settled that receipt of even a non-liquid asset will not prevent recognition, may the accounting entity choose to say that it nevertheless will not recognize revenue (or expense) at any point short of receipt or disbursement of cash— i.e., may it select "the cash method" of recognizing revenue and expense? Many entities, particularly professional partnerships and corporations and non-profit organizations, in unaudited statements reflect expenses in the period when paid in cash and revenues in the period when cash is received and no effort is made to match expenses with related revenues. This method is also permitted for tax purposes when inventories are not involved. Treas.Regs. 1.446–1(c). In many cases, particularly where credit purchases are involved, this "cash method" yields meaningless results. It also permits evasive control of results: e.g., the professional who asks the client to mail a check on December 31, so that the client can deduct the expense in the old year while the professional, reporting on the cash basis, will not receive and recognize the revenue for tax purposes until the next year.

Is the "cash basis" a legitimate method of accounting which will enable the auditor to give a "clean opinion" that the accounting comports with

GAAP? Seemingly not, where accruals and inventories would be appropriate and are significant because those accruals and inventories would not be included in the resulting presentation of financial position and results of operations. *SAS No. 1,* § 620.05–§ 620.06 (1973); Devore, *Reporting on Cash–Basis Statements,* J. Accountancy 58 (May, 1959). But in accounting for professionals and service organizations without inventories and without meaningful accruals, the position is not as clear.

See Carson, *Cash Movement: The Heart of Income Measurement,* 40 Acctg.Rev. 334 (1965), for a suggestion that accrual accounting is nothing more than an expedient adjustment to cash basis accounting. One may add that the convenience of a clear signal for entry of debits and credits by receipts and issuance of checks must be relevant. Moreover, many professionals provide unpaid services or follow a policy of not enforcing collection against unwilling clients including those who are financially capable of paying, thus making the cash method more realistic than the accrual method which would call for the bookkeeper to ascertain whether payment is expected.

The cash method otherwise has no status in theory or accepted practice. The view of accountants is stated by the AAA, 1964 Concepts and Standards Research Study Committee, *The Realization Concept,* 40 Acctg. Rev. 312, 314 (1965): "[I]t is difficult to explain the persistence of the 'cash method of recognizing revenue' by doctors, lawyers and accountants except in terms of income tax advantage and an unwillingness to maintain separate income tax and financial reporting records."

3. THE THIRD FACTOR OF REALIZATION—COMPLETION OF THE EARNING PROCESS

The preceding topic, exchanges of property, brings us to the most intractable of the elements of realization—completion of the earning process. Clearly this factor contains more than a trace of circularity— it states that income is earned when the earning process is complete. It may best be grasped by addressing a few concrete cases to ascertain what is meant.

(A) The General Rule

(1) Delivery and Passage of Title

For ordinary sales of product, as in *Tooey v. C.L. Percival Co.,* completion of the earning process is generally deemed to occur approximately when title to the goods passes to the buyer or, as a practical surrogate therefor, when delivery is made.

Notice that this implies not only that a market transaction, a sale, must occur before revenue will be recognized, but that in addition the revenue earning process must have been completed by production and delivery of the goods. That this is so is further evidenced by generally accepted practices concerning executory contracts and receipt of prepayments on sales. Thus when two parties contract for the sale of goods or services, no bookkeeping entry is made to recognize the parties' revenues or expenses or anything else. Even if the buyer pays a cash advance to the seller, no revenue or expense is recognized by either party although the cash transaction is recognized:

Buyer's Entry:

Prepaid Deposit	$ X	
Cash		$ X

Seller's Entry:

Cash	$ X	
Deferred Revenue		$ X

The reason for deferring revenue recognition until completion of the earning process rather than recognizing it earlier and also accruing estimated related expenses is suggested by the facts in Beacon Publishing Co. v. Commissioner, 218 F.2d 697, 699 (10th Cir.1955), an income tax case which held that cash received in advance for newspaper subscriptions to be delivered later was not taxable revenue when received. There the court pointed out that, "[a]n important feature of the accrual system is that income shall be reported at such a time that it will, so far as possible, be offset by expenditures incident to earning it, rather than expenditures related to earning other income." This is so largely for the reason that the related expenditures may be difficult to ascertain until they are incurred.

Note the comments of Mr. Grady, infra p. 220, to the effect that passage of title ordinarily controls the realization of income on sale of goods but stating that invoicing plus delivery is often used and implying that any convenient procedure for booking revenue from day to day may be used. In connection with this, one should consider Pacific Grape Products Co. v. Commissioner of Internal Revenue, 219 F.2d 862 (9th Cir. 1955). There the Commissioner determined deficiencies in the taxpayer's returns for the years 1940–1944, holding that it had improperly taken sales into income in the years 1939 through 1941, and that some of the income of each year should be deferred to later years. The taxpayer was a canner which each year contracted for the sale of its current pack. Ordinarily the goods were sold during the calendar year, but on occasion the seller withheld shipment at the buyer's request. The contracts provided in that case that the unshipped goods would be billed and paid for on December 31. The taxpayer therefore treated, as completed, sales of the goods still on hand subject to these orders on December 31 and reported income correspondingly. The Commissioner and the Tax Court held that this method of reporting income did not properly reflect the taxpayer's income, on the ground that title to the goods had not passed because they had not been identified to the contract. The Court of Appeals rejected this because the Uniform Sales Act, then applicable, recognized a sale of fungible unseparated goods, and this clearly conformed to the intention of the parties. The Court of Appeals also reversed the refusal of the lower courts to give effect to custom or usage supporting recognition of revenue even if title did not pass.

HERZFELD v. LAVENTHOL, KREKSTEIN, HORWATH & HORWATH

United States Court of Appeals for the Second Circuit, 1976.
540 F.2d 27.

Laventhol, Krekstein, Horwath & Horwath, a firm of certified public accountants ("Laventhol"), appeals from an amended judgment for the amount of $153,000, entered against it and in favor of plaintiff, Gerald L. Herzfeld ("Herzfeld") after a trial to the Court. * * *

Originally, Herzfeld had sued Laventhol and eleven other defendants primarily to recover $510,000 which he claimed that he had paid for certain securities of Firestone Group, Ltd. ("FGL"), namely, two FGL units, each unit consisting of a $250,000 FGL note and 5000 shares of FGL stock at $1 a share, a total of $255,000 per unit. The substance of Herzfeld's charges was that the representations made to him by the defendants in connection with the purchase were materially misleading and that there were omissions of material facts, all of which were inducing factors, and on which he relied, in making his purchase and in not exercising his right of rescission. Herzfeld predicated his suit upon alleged violations of the securities laws of the United States, Section 352–c of the New York General Business Law and common law fraud.

* * *

FGL was a California company engaged principally in the business of purchasing real estate and thereafter syndicating or reselling it. In November 1969, FGL planned to raise $7,500,000 by the private placement through Allen and Company, Incorporated, of the aforementioned units. Lee Meyer, a defendant, was an Allen vice-president and also a FGL director.

Through friends, Herzfeld became interested in the venture. A purchase agreement, entitled "Note and Stock Purchase Agreement", dated November 10, 1969, was delivered to Herzfeld by FGL with an accompanying letter which advised him that the closing date for the sale of the notes would be December 16, 1969, "to permit the preparation of audited financial statements, as at and for the eleven months ended November 30, 1969, copies of which will be delivered to you." The letter added that these "audited statements will serve as the basis for confirming the unaudited Projected Financial Statements annexed to the Note and Stock Purchase Agreement as Exhibit B."

Exhibit B was a balance sheet and income statement. It portrayed FGL as a strikingly profitable corporation with over $20 million in assets, a net worth of close to a million dollars, sales of over $17 million, deferred income of $2.7 million and an after-tax income of $315,000. FGL warranted that it fairly presented its financial condition as at November 30, 1969.

Herzfeld read the entire income statement and the balance sheet and noted that it represented FGL as being very profitable, with earnings of approximately $2 a share for the period ending November 30, 1969. He then signed the agreement to purchase two units thereunder.

To prepare the promised audit (to be as of November 30, 1969), FGL retained Laventhol as the accountants for the task. The Herzfeld–Laventhol lawsuit and this appeal therefrom involve only the deeds and alleged misdeeds of Laventhol in making its audit which was submitted to FGL and thereafter to the security purchasers, including Herzfeld.

* * *

The spotlight of Herzfeld's claim of a materially misleading audit, knowingly made with admitted awareness of the facts, focuses upon Laventhol's accounting treatment of two real estate transactions in which FGL allegedly engaged in late November 1969, referred to herein as the FGL–Monterey purchase and the FGL–Continental sale. Purporting to reflect these transactions are two agreements. Each agreement is on an identical printed form entitled "AGREEMENT FOR SALE OF REAL ESTATE" and certain typewritten provisions have been inserted therein. The first is dated November 22, 1969 and is between Monterey Nursing Inns, Inc. ("Monterey") as seller and FGL as buyer. The transaction was subject to two conditions: (1) the buyer's approval of a preliminary title report and CC&R's [covenants, conditions and restrictions] of Record on each property (there is no evidence that any such documents were ever prepared, delivered or approved); and (2) execution of a * * * lease per terms of "Exhibit D attached hereto" (no such exhibit appears to have been attached). Twenty-three (23) nursing homes were the subject of the sale "as per Exhibit 'A' attached hereto" (no such exhibit appears to have been attached). The purchase price is stated as $13,362,500, $5,000 of which was payable before November 30, 1969 (i.e., upon the signing of the contract).

On an identical printed form with almost identical typewritten inserts is an agreement by FGL as seller to sell to Continental Recreation Company, Ltd. ("Continental") as buyer. Again, there is no Exhibit A listing the properties. The purchase price is stated as $15,393,000 with $25,000 as a down payment, other payments to be made in 1970 and thereafter.

This purchase and sale of nursing homes, if ever consummated, would have been the largest single transaction in the history of FGL. Placing these two purported agreements side by side, if the obligations therein were ever fulfilled in the future, FGL would have bought Monterey for $13,362,500 and sold it for $15,393,000, thus producing a profit, when, as and if the transactions were consummated, of $2,030,500, no part of which was even contemplated as having been received prior to November 30, 1969, and only payments of $5000 by FGL to Monterey and $25,000 from Continental to FGL may have been made.

A comparison of the financial condition of FGL with and without these transactions demonstrates the importance of them to FGL:

	Monterey Included	Monterey Excluded
Sales	$22,132,607	$6,739,607
Total Current Assets	6,290,987	1,300,737
Net Income	66,000	[169,000]
Deferred Profit	1,795,000	–0–
Earnings/Share	$0.10	[0.25]

Thus, the accounting treatment of these transactions determined the health of FGL's financial picture. Laventhol knew this was so. By this treatment, namely, immediate recognition of a so-called profit, Laventhol notes, dated November 30, 1969, reveal the conversion of estimated $772,108 losses into a $1,257,892 gain by the addition of the $2,030,500 "profit". These work papers contain the following entries:

"Estimated loss 4 months ended 4/30/69	200,000
Estimated loss 7 months ended 11/30/69	572,108
Loss before sale to Continental Recreation	772,108
Profit on sale to Continental Recreation	2,030,000 [sic]
Profit before income taxes	1,257,892" [sic]

Little wonder that when at the outset a Laventhol partner was discussing the situation from an accounting standpoint, he referred to it as a "fictitious or proposed or artificial transaction." Appendix ("App.") p. 887. But Laventhol undertook the task, albeit it had to engage in considerable soul-searching during it. Laventhol also learned that Monterey transactions were nowhere recorded in the FGL books and that there were no corporate minutes or resolutions approving or even adverting to the transactions. The absence was remedied by Laventhol, who prepared adjusting entries and ordered the FGL controller to enter them in the FGL books. Illustrative is the letter from Laventhol's audit manager to FGL's controller enclosing "the journal entries which *we generated* for the financial statements at November 30" (emphasis added). These very entries were prepared by Laventhol as if the transaction had been consummated: yet the agreements on their face showed that no profits could result therefrom until long after November 30.

Under date of November 30, 1969, appears as a general journal entry (Journal No. 9) an item "Profit on sale $2,030,500" and also a credit of $3,995,000 "to record purchase and sale of various hospitals from Monterey . . .". A further Laventhol paper, dated December 6, 1969, reverses a tax liability entry on the Continental sale which reads that Laventhol "will not record as sale since not enough deposit was given to Firestone".

The November 22 and 26 contracts came to Laventhol's attention on or about December 1st through its partners, Chazen and Lipkin, and Schwabb, the audit manager. Schwabb sought Lipkin's advice about the proper way to report the transactions in the audit. Lipkin sought to gather the pertinent information by meeting with Scott, a FGL vice-president, and Firestone. Scott told him that FGL was busy acquiring the necessary documentation. Firestone said that the agreements were legitimate and described Continental's principal, Max Ruderian, as an experienced real estate operator and a wealthy individual. Laventhol learned that Continental had a net worth of $100,000 and that its assets consisted of "miniature golf courses plus other assets". Ruderian's business practice was to "buy and resell prior to final payment on his sales contracts".

Lipkin also examined the sales contracts. He was an attorney but had only practiced one year. He concluded that the contracts were legally enforcible. He consulted another Laventhol partner who assured him that there need be no concern about Ruderian. Ruderian's references concurred in the appraisal.

Lipkin also consulted over the telephone with a Los Angeles attorney. The attorney did not see the contracts, nor were the contracts in their entirety read to him, despite the fact that his offices were only one-half hour away by cab. Nevertheless, the attorney gave a telephone opinion that they were valid and enforcible.

The first tangible results of Laventhol's accounting efforts appear in its audit enclosed in its letter to FGL, dated December 6, 1969. In the consolidated balance sheet as of November 30, 1969, the amount of $1,795,500 was recorded "as unrealized gross profit". The same characterization was given to this assumed profit in the income statement with a reference to an explanatory Note 4. This Note only explained the $1,795,500 by stating that "because of the circumstances and nature of the transactions, $1,795,500 of the gross profit thereon will be considered realized when the January 30, 1970 payment is received." The $1,795,500 was apparently arrived at by first adding the $25,000 paid upon execution of the Continental agreement, the $25,000 not yet due (until January 2, 1970) and $185,000—a liquidated damage figure for non-performance. These amounts totalled $235,000. They were apparently considered as received and were deducted from the then fictitious profit of $2,030,500, resulting in the figure of $1,795,500. This first December 6, 1969 report is marked "Withdrawn & Superseded".

The reason for the withdrawal is found in the testimony that FGL wanted the audit to reflect the entire amount of $2,030,500 as pre-November 30, 1969, income resulting from a sale by FGL to Continental. On December 4, 1969, Chazen and Lipkin met with FGL officers. Firestone objected to the tentative accounting treatment of the Monterey transactions, and FGL threatened to withdraw its account and sue Laventhol if the private financing did not go through.

A second report (also dated December 6, 1969) was then submitted by Laventhol. In the income statement "unrealized gross profits (Note 4)" was changed to "Deferred gross profit (Note 4)" and Note 4, itself to read:

"Of the total gross profit of $2,030,500, $235,000 is included in the Consolidated Income Statement and the balance $1,795,500 will be considered realized when the January 30, 1970 payment is received. The latter amount is included in deferred income in the consolidated balance sheet."

It was this second report which was distributed to the investors, including Herzfeld.

Unlike the initial report, the opinion letter accompanying this second and final report was qualified. It stated:

"In our opinion, subject to collectibility of the balance receivable on the contract of sale (see Note 4 of Notes to Financial Statements) the accompanying consolidated balance sheet and related consolidated statements of income and retained earnings present fairly the financial position of [FGL] . . .."

Recognizing the difference between the financial statements (Exhibit B to the purchase agreement of November 10, 1969) and the Laventhol audit (December 6, 1969) submitted to Herzfeld and others, on December 16, 1969, FGL attempted to explain by a letter of that date the shift of $1,795,500 from a current to a deferred basis. The financial statements and the qualified opinion letter accompanied the FGL letter which purported to "explain" the distinctions between unaudited projections originally contained in the Agreement and Laventhol's report. No claim is made that Laventhol in any way participated in, or was responsible for, this FGL letter.

The FGL letter reads:

"One transaction which is reflected in the November 30 audited financial statements has been treated as producing deferred gross profit rather than current gross profit. While the combination of current and deferred income is actually higher than projected ($1,411,557 as compared with $1,360,000 projected) the shift of $1,795,500 of gross profit on this transaction from a current basis to deferred basis by the auditors has reduced current net income below that originally projected. . . .

Deferred income shown on the audited balance sheet has been increased to $2,834,133 as against $1,421,000 projected. A breakdown of the components of the deferred income account is shown in the audited financial statements. . . .

If for any reason you find that the changes reflected in the audited financial statements are of a nature which would have resulted in a change in your investment decision, we will arrange to promptly refund to you your subscription payment. . . .

Allen & Company will undertake to replace any cancelled subscriptions with others on the same terms and conditions so that in any event the Firestone Group, Ltd. will have available to it the proceeds from the sale of at least 25 units.

Herzfeld read this letter outlining the differences, the "Consolidated Statement of Income and Retained Earnings" and noted the deferred gross profit item of $1,795,500. He did not read the Laventhol opinion letter or Note 4. Apparently, relying on what he had seen, he was satisfied with his investment and did not take advantage of the rescission offer.

Neither the Monterey nor the Continental transactions were consummated and somewhat over a year later FGL filed a petition under Chapter XI of the Bankruptcy Act. * * *

The Trial Court first considered Herzfeld's claim under § 10(b) of the Securities Exchange Act of 1934, and Rule 10b–5 thereunder. 15 U.S.C. § 78j(b); 17 C.F.R. § 240.10b–5.[5] The Court found that "Laventhol knew that its audited report was required for the FGL private placement and that investors would be relying on the financial statements"; that Laventhol had access to information concerning FGL which was not available to investors. As to Laventhol's legal duty, the Court held that it was the policy of the securities laws that investors be provided "with all the facts needed to make intelligent investment decisions [which] can only be accomplished if financial statements fully and fairly portray the actual financial condition of the company." 378 F.Supp. at 122.

After analyzing the facts, the Court concluded that "the Laventhol report was materially misleading." Id. at p. 124. The Court found that Note 4, claimed by Laventhol to be fully explanatory, was misleading: (1) in not disclosing that Continental, obligated to pay almost $5,000,000, had assets of only some $100,000; (2) in affirmatively stating that FGL had "acquired" the nursing homes (when it had not); (3) in reporting that $1,795,500 was deferred income; and (4) in stating that there was a lease back (when apparently no such lease existed). The Court's conclusion was that "the inclusion of the Monterey transaction in sales and income was misleading without a full disclosure by Laventhol of all the material facts about the transactions." Id. at p. 125.

Examining the report as a whole, the Court also found ten materially misleading omissions in Laventhol's failure to disclose (1) Continental's net worth; (2) the printed form language which suggested that they were mere options; (3) the absence of Ruderian's personal liability; (4) Ruderian's practice of reselling property before he paid for it; (5) the absence of any records of the Monterey transactions in FGL books; (6) the relative importance of the contracts; (7) the loss FGL would suffer

5. "§ 240.10b–5 Employment of manipulative and deceptive devices.

It shall be unlawful for any person, directly or indirectly, by the use of any means or instrumentality of interstate commerce, or of the mails or of any facility of any national securities exchange,

(a) To employ any device, scheme, or artifice to defraud,

(b) To make any untrue statement of a material fact or to omit to state a material fact necessary in order to make the statements made, in the light of the circumstances under which they were made, not misleading, or

(c) To engage in any act, practice, or course of business which operates or would operate as a fraud or deceit upon any person, in connection with the purchase or sale of any security."

if the sales fell through; (8) the absence of any title search; (9) that FGL had not acquired title; and (10) that the attorney ventured his opinion about the enforcibility of the contract without having examined the printed forms.

The Court held that Laventhol had the necessary *scienter* (merely the Latin adverb for "knowingly"), namely, "knowledge of the fact that the figures created a false picture . . .", and in addition, that Laventhol "had actual knowledge of the omitted facts which render[ed] its report misleading." Id. at p. 127. In light of Laventhol's concession that it was actually aware of the facts which the Trial Court correctly determined made Laventhol's affirmations misleading, we need not dwell upon the particular evidentiary items which the Court invoked to supplement its rationale.

The Laventhol report, if not the original inducing factor for the purchase, was read by Herzfeld. The Court therefore concluded that "The report's false picture of FGL's financial condition was, thus, a substantial, even crucial, factor in convincing Herzfeld that his investment decision to purchase the securities was right," Id. at p. 129, and that Herzfeld had shown sufficient reliance thereon. Characterizing the case as one of affirmative misrepresentations, the Court held that the correct test was whether the misrepresentations were a substantial factor in Herzfeld's decision to go through with his purchase of the FGL securities and determined that the Laventhol material was such a factor.

Laventhol contends that the Court erred and would have us attribute Herzfeld's purchase of the securities to his own enthusiasm, his acquaintance's touting, the FGL letter which accompanied the Laventhol report—in short, to everything but the Laventhol material. As to the Laventhol material, Laventhol argues that Herzfeld ignored it and emphasizes that Herzfeld read neither the opinion letter nor footnote 4 to which both the opinion letter and the income statement referred. This, to Laventhol, is fatal because it contends, *inter alia,* that the only statement made by an auditor upon which an investor is entitled to rely is the auditor's opinion letter. We agree with none of these arguments.

The Trial Court invoked the appropriate reliance test. Generally speaking, a plaintiff in a Rule 10b–5 damage action must prove that the misrepresentation was a "substantial factor" in his securities activities.

* * *

The Trial Court correctly applied the "substantial factor" test. Even assuming that persons other than Laventhol first aroused Herzfeld's interest in FGL, or that the FGL cover letter which accompanied the Laventhol material may have influenced Herzfeld somewhat, these considerations do not defeat Herzfeld's claim. Herzfeld was not required to prove that the Laventhol material was the sole and exclusive cause of his action, he must only show that it was "substantial", *i.e.,* a significant contributing cause.

The Laventhol material was clearly a substantial factor. Looking at the transaction as a whole, it becomes clear that the investment decision was predicated upon confirmation of the Agreement's financial presentation by the Laventhol audit. The FGL letter explicitly informed the tentative investors of this fact and the Agreement itself conditioned its financial data on the auditor's confirmation. Herzfeld examined the Agreement and its income statement which suggested that FGL was a "very profitable company". When the Laventhol material was distributed he checked its income statement which provided the crucial corroboration of the Agreement's picture of corporate health. As the Trial Court observed "He paid particular attention to the earnings indicated and was very impressed by the deferred gross profit of $1,795,000. [sic] The latter figure, he understood, meant 'that this is a profit that the company had made and was going to pick up in a subsequent accounting period.'" In reliance upon this corroborative Laventhol financial statement, Herzfeld completed his investment in FGL securities.

In view of our imposition of liability on the ground that the Laventhol audit was materially and knowingly misleading and that Herzfeld relied thereon, we need not pass upon the questions whether there was a violation of New York State statutory or common law.

The issue here is not one of negligence, but of the "materially misleading" treatment of facts known to Laventhol in its submitted audit.

The function of an accountant is not merely to verify the correctness of the addition and subtraction of the company's bookkeepers. Nor does it take a fiscal wizard to appreciate the elemental and universal accounting principle that revenue should not be recognized until the "earning process is complete or virtually complete", and "an exchange has taken place." Insofar as FGL's interest in the Monterey transactions is concerned, the earning process had hardly commenced, let alone neared completion. As of November 30, 1969, FGL had paid only $5,000 cash out of $13.2 million dollar purchase price and accepted a $25,000 "deposit" under a $15.3 million contract. Conditions for closing were unsatisfied. There remained the consummation of its purchase from Monterey, the furnishing to Continental of current title reports, and the delivery of the CC & R's and a copy of a lease. By the close of November 30, 1969, title had not passed. Nor was this the exceptional instance of a conditional sale or a long-term lease with purchase option, where the retention of title does not vitiate the economic reality of a consummated exchange.

Reference to the SEC's Accounting Series Release No. 95, 28 F.R. 276, 5 CCH Fed. Securities Rep. ¶ 72,117, p. 62,272 ("ASR # 95") points toward the same conclusion. That release lists several factors whose presence, according to the SEC, singly or in combination, raises a question of the propriety of current recognition of profit in real estate transactions. Not less than three of these factors inhere in the Monterey transaction including (1) evidence of financial weakness of the purchaser (Continental's insignificant net worth relative to the resale property price); (2) substantial uncertainty as to amount of proceeds to be realized because of form of consideration—*e.g.*, non-recourse notes; (3) small or no down payment. Because the FGL offer was a private placement, ASR # 95 was not directly applicable to Laventhol's audit. But since ASR # 95 merely codifies basic principles of accrual accounting theory, we do not reject its corroboration of our own independent conclusions.

If the hoped-for profit of $2,030,500 were ever to be realized, it could only come after the transactions had been consummated—and consummation was never even contemplated before the audit date, November 30, 1969. FGL's profit till for this transaction as of that date was as bare of profits as Mother Hubbard's cupboard, bare of bones.

An accountant should not represent on an audited statement that income and profit exist unless underlying facts justify that conclusion. Here, the underlying facts known to Laventhol dictated precisely the contrary course, namely, that income should not have been recognized for the accounting period ending November 30, 1969. And were it not for Laventhol's disregard of Statements on Accounting Procedure No. 33, Ch. 2, p. 16 (1963) ("SAP 33") it would have confronted additional evidence pointing in the same direction. SAP 33 states:

> "Sufficient competent evidential matter is to be obtained through inspection, observation, inquiries and confirmations to affirm a reasonable basis for an opinion regarding the financial statements under examination".

Laventhol knew that the issuance of FGL securities depended upon a correct ascertainment of that condition. It is undisputed that, without the Monterey–Continental transactions, for the eleven months preceding November 30, FGL had sustained a loss of $772,108. Query: by what accounting legerdemain was this figure converted into a substantial profit? The Monterey purchase added nothing to the FGL till. To the contrary, it reduced it by $5,000 (if the check was honored). The Continental sale produced a down payment of $25,000 (if made) but no profit. In fact, if the hoped-for profit of $2,030,500 were ever to be realized, it could only come after the transactions had been consummated—and consummation was never even contemplated before the audit date, November 30, 1969.

Laventhol points to the Trial Court's finding that the Monterey–Continental transactions were not "phony". This finding, however, only implies that there were signed agreements between the parties. By no stretch of the imagination does it imply that profits of $2,030,500 were realized therefrom before November 30, 1969, or would be at any time until consummation. In fact, both agreements showed on their face that the principal payments were to be made in 1970.

In such circumstances, the recognition of Monterey transactions was a materially misleading statement which, once included at the top of the income statement as a sale, resulted in, or necessitated, compensating adjustments which distorted all the financial figures which followed. A reasonable man in Herzfeld's position might well have acted otherwise than to purchase the FGL securities, had the truth been told and the Monterey transactions not been misleadingly represented as a consummated purchase and sale. * * *

This misleading impression was aggravated by Laventhol's labelling of the $1,795,500 as "deferred" as opposed to "unrealized" gross profit. Such nomenclature conveyed the erroneous impression that all that profit was so much cash in hand and would be recognized periodically *in futuro* just as if it were prepaid interest or management fees. But as Laventhol well knew, net cash had increased only $20,000, and the transaction was still in doubt.

Having engendered its own quandary, it ill behooves Laventhol to seek the solace of SAP 33, which concerns the rendition of a qualified auditing opinion. But even assuming the propriety of allowing Laventhol [to] extricate itself by the simple expedient of disclaiming or qualifying its opinion of the very financial statements which it concocted, Laventhol did not follow the route proscribed by SAP 33. At Chapter 10, page 58, SAP 33 provides, *inter alia:*

> "When a qualification is so material as to negative an expression of opinion as to the fairness of the financial statement as a whole, either a disclaimer of opinion or an adverse opinion is required."

> * * *

> "When a qualified opinion is intended by the independent auditor, the opinion paragraph of the standard short-form report should be modified in a way that makes clear the nature of the qualification. It should refer specifically to the subject of the qualification and should give a *clear explanation of the reasons for the qualification* and of the effect on financial position and results of operations, if reasonably determinable." (emphasis added)

But Laventhol did not provide a *clear explanation of the reasons for the qualification.* A simple note would have sufficed saying in substance:

> "Agreements for the purchase of Monterey Nursing Inns, Inc. for $13,362,500 and the sale thereof to Continental Recreation, Inc. for $15,393,000, have been executed. When, as and if these transactions are consummated, FGL expects to realize a profit of $2,030,500."

Instead, Laventhol chose to delete from its first so-called explanatory Note 4, the sentence "Because of the circumstances and nature of the transaction, $1,795,500 of the gross profit therein will be considered realized when the January 30, 1970 payment is received" and substituted therefor the sentence "Of the total gross profit of $2,030,500, $235,000 is included in the Consolidated Income Statement and the balance, $1,795,500 will be considered realized when the January 30, 1970 payment is received." The substituted note also changed "unrealized gross profit" to "deferred income". Even in the first Note, there is no explanation of what were the circumstances and nature of the transaction or, in the second Note, how or why $235,000 could qualify as gross profit or income as of November 30, 1969.

From the very outset of the audit, the danger signals were flashing.

(1) Even if Laventhol accepted the agreements as not "phony", on the face of the Monterey agreement were two conditions to be performed, *i.e.*, approval by FGL of a title search and a lease back. There was no proof that they were performed or that Laventhol made any effort to verify these facts.

(2) Normally on transactions of such magnitude and vital importance, corporate minutes, resolutions and other corporate papers authenticating the transaction would be examined. No proof of such examination was presented.

(3) Laventhol demonstrated an awareness that the legality of the agreement with Continental might be important. However, a telephone call to an attorney who did not even see or read the agreement and who only heard such excerpts as Laventhol's partner chose to read to him, scarcely qualifies as a legal opinion as to enforcibility.

(4) As for Continental, Laventhol knew that it had contractually committed itself to pay $15,300,000 to FGL and that Continental had assets of only some $100,000, consisting mostly of miniature golf courses. Laventhol was aware that Max Ruderian was a well-known, successful, and wealthy real estate operator and had signed the Continental agreement but there is no document which evidences that Ruderian's wealth was in any way committed to the Continental purchase.

(5) The absence of entries of the transactions on FGL's books and the necessity for Laventhol to create journal entries thereof.

(6) Laventhol, whose duty it was to reveal the truth rather than be subservient to the dictates of its clients, FGL, should have taken warning from FGL's pressurizing tactics to change "unrealized profits" to "deferred".

In sum, we affirm the result reached by the Trial Court in holding that the Laventhol report contained materially misleading omissions and misrepresentations. The term "result" is used advisedly. Although we agree with the facts as found by the Trial Court, we do not accept its opinion that all of the ten items specified therein were required to be included in Laventhol's report. The vice of the report was its representation that the Monterey transactions were consummated and the concomitant statement that current and deferred profit had been realized. This would have been remedied by simply not recognizing the sales as completed transactions for the accounting period ending November 30, 1969. A specific listing of the facts which dictated that treatment would have been unnecessary.

There remains for consideration the effect, if any, of the Supreme Court's recent decision in *Ernst & Ernst v. Hochfelder*, 425 U.S. 785 (1976). In that case, a firm of accountants petitioned the Court to review a decision of the Seventh Circuit. The Court of Appeals had reversed a decision of a trial court granting summary judgment in favor of the accountants and against securities purchasers in an action based upon an alleged negligent audit by Ernst & Ernst. The gist of the charge was that the accountants "failed to utilize 'appropriate auditing procedures' in its audits of First Securities, thereby failing to discover internal practices of the firm said to prevent an effective audit." *Hochfelder, supra,* 96 S.Ct. at 1379.

The Supreme Court clearly defined the scope of its decision as "whether a private cause of action for damages will lie under § 10(b) and Rule 10b–5 in the absence of any allegation of 'scienter'—intent to deceive, manipulate, or defraud. [footnote omitted]" Id. at 1381. There is no question here that Herzfeld's amended complaint against Laventhol adequately alleged scienter in that Laventhol

> "(a) employed a device, scheme or artifice to defraud plaintiff; (b) made untrue statements of material facts or omissions to state material facts necessary in order to make the statements made, in light of the circumstances under which they were made, not misleading; and (c) engaged in transactions, practices and a course of business which operated as a fraud and deceit on plaintiff." App. p. 112a

The difference, therefore, between the factual situation before the Supreme Court in *Hochfelder,* where "[T]hroughout the lengthy history of this case respondents have proceeded on a theory of liability premised on negligence, specifically disclaiming that Ernst & Ernst had engaged in fraud or intentional misconduct. [footnote omitted]" Id. at 1391 and the case before us involving affirmative acts by Laventhol which were materially misleading, is clear. The accountants here are not being cast in damages for negligent nonfeasance or misfeasance, but because of their active participation in the preparation and issuance of false and materially misleading accounting reports upon which Herzfeld relied to his damage.

Nor does Herzfeld's failure to read the opinion letter or "explanatory" footnote vitiate his reliance upon the figures in the financial statement which he did examine. The opinion letter and "explanatory" footnote were as misleading as the figures in the financial statement. None of these discrete portions of the Laventhol audit adequately disclosed the serious question marks surrounding the Monterey transaction.[h]

* * *

Note and Problem

3–10. *GAAP for Sales of Real Estate.* SFAS No. 66, *Accounting for Sales of Real Estate* (1982), deals with the fact that sales contracts for real

---

h. Laventhol, the nation's seventh largest auditing firm, went into bankruptcy in late 1990, claiming that the cause was the large number of liability claims being asserted against it. This was the first bankruptcy of a major accounting firm in the U.S. Others may follow from the S&L mess and bank troubles.

estate take a wide variety of forms, making it difficult to apply the general standards of receipt of a measurable asset and completion of services. *SFAS No. 66* fixes GAAP for these variations.

3–11. *Problem.* Suppose West Publishing Co. sells 100 volumes of a book to the Student Book Store granting a right to return within six months for a full refund any volumes the store is unable to sell. At what point should revenue be recognized? See SFAS No. 48, *Revenue Recognition When Right of Return Exists* (1981).

(2) In–Kind Exchanges Other Than in Culmination of the Earning Process

ACCOUNTING PRINCIPLES BOARD OPINION NO. 29
ACCOUNTING FOR NONMONETARY
TRANSACTIONS *

AICPA, 1973.

* * *

"Definitions

"3.   The meanings of certain terms used in this Opinion are:

(a) *Monetary assets and liabilities* are assets and liabilities whose amounts are fixed in terms of units of currency by contract or otherwise. Examples are cash, short- or long-term accounts and notes receivable in cash, and short- or long-term accounts and notes payable in cash.

(b) *Nonmonetary assets and liabilities* are assets and liabilities other than monetary ones. Examples are inventories; investments in common stocks; property, plant and equipment; and liabilities for rent collected in advance.

* * *

(e) *Productive assets* are assets held for or used in the production of goods or services by the enterprise. Productive assets include an investment in another entity if the investment is accounted for by the equity method but exclude an investment not accounted for by that method. *Similar productive assets* are productive assets that are of the same general type, that perform the same function or that are employed in the same line of business.

* * *

"7. *Nonmonetary Exchanges.*   Many nonmonetary transactions are exchanges of nonmonetary assets or services with another entity. Examples include (a) exchange of product held for sale in the ordinary course of business (inventory) for dissimilar property as a means of selling the product to a customer (b) exchange of product held for sale in the ordinary course of business (inventory) for similar product as an accommodation—that is, at least one party to the exchange reduces transportation costs, meets immediate inventory needs, or otherwise reduces costs or facilitates ultimate sale of the product—and not as a means of selling the product to a customer, and (c) exchange of productive assets—assets employed in production rather than held for sale in the ordinary course of business—for similar productive assets or for an equivalent interest in similar productive assets. Examples of exchanges in category (c) include the trade of player contracts by professional sports organizations, exchange of leases on mineral properties, exchange of one form of interest in an oil producing property for another form of interest, exchange of real estate for real estate.

* * *

OPINION

"Basic Principle

"18. The Board concludes that in general accounting for non-monetary transactions should be based on the fair values of the assets (or services) involved which is the same basis as that used in monetary transactions. * * *

"21. *Exchanges.* If the exchange is not essentially the culmination of an earning process, accounting for an exchange of a nonmonetary asset between an enterprise and another entity should be based on the recorded amount (after reduction, if appropriate, for an indicated impairment of value) of the nonmonetary asset relinquished. The Board believes that the following two types of nonmonetary exchange transactions do not culminate an earning process:

a. An exchange of a product or property held for sale in the ordinary course of business for a product or property to be sold in the same line of business to facilitate sales to customers other than the parties to the exchange and

b. An exchange of a productive asset not held for sale in the ordinary course of business for a similar productive asset or an equivalent interest in the same or similar productive asset (similar productive asset is defined in paragraph 3 and examples are given in paragraph 7)".[6]

---

(3) Seller's Obligations Not Completed Even After Delivery

Substantial question arises as to the timing of accounting recognition of sales where the seller remains obligated for partial performance even after delivery. In 1962 the SEC discussed this issue in *Accounting Series Release No. 95,* a part of which is reprinted below. This release dealt with real estate companies and, although rescinded, its principal provisions have subsequently been included in *SFAS No. 66* (1982).

---

6. The fact that an exchange of productive assets is not a taxable transaction for tax purposes may be evidence that the assets exchanged are similar for purposes of applying this Opinion.

ACCOUNTING SERIES RELEASE NO. 95

Securities and Exchange Commission, 1962.

"A number of recent cases have come to the attention of the Commission in which the gross profits on certain real estate transactions were taken into income under circumstances which indicate that they were not realized in the period in which the transactions were recorded. * * *

"Circumstances such as the following tend to raise a question as to the propriety of current recognition of profit:

* * *

2. Substantial uncertainty as to amount of costs and expenses to be incurred.

* * *

In the following illustrative cases, taken from recent filings, the Commission deemed it inappropriate to recognize gross profit as recorded as having been realized at the time of sale.

Case No. 1

"On the last day of its fiscal year a registrant engaged principally in the development of real estate sold a block of 1,000 lots to a non-affiliated construction company for $1,100,000, receiving a cash payment of $100,000 and a non-recourse note of $1,000,000 due in one year, secured only by the lots transferred. Interest was limited to 6% for one year or $120 per house. A profit of $500,000 before taxes was recorded on the transaction.

"The transaction was subject to, among others, the following conditions and arrangements:

a. Each lot was to be released upon payment of $1,000 plus interest at the time of closing the sale of a house and lot.

b. The registrant was to make the determination of when the houses were to be constructed and to arrange the construction loans.

c. The registrant was to be exclusive sales agent for the construction company, arrange financing and conduct closings with the home buyers.

d. The construction company was to be paid a maximum of $500 profit and an additional $100 to cover overhead expenses on each house sold. Profits to be received by the construction company were to be applied against the note owed to the registrant."

Problem

3–12. Problem. TV Sales Co. sells television sets under warranties providing for replacement of defective parts discovered within one year of sale. Experience indicates the company spends about 2% of the sale price for each set in servicing the warranty. If a set is sold for $400 cash what should be the accounting?

(B) Exceptions to Requirement of Completion of the Earning Process

(1) Accounting for Rent and for Interest

When tangible property is leased by one party to another, the lease may be essentially a sale of the entire property on credit, or it may be merely a transfer of the temporary use and enjoyment of only part of the bundle of rights constituting the property. If the former, it should be treated as a credit sale with appropriate recognition of revenues and expenses or gains and losses. If the latter, the general rule is that revenue (for the lessor) or expense (for the lessee) should be recognized as time passes, rather than on termination of the lease. Thus if the rental is $60 per month, payable currently, the lessor will recognize $60 revenue each month and the lessee, $60 expense.

The same treatment is given for interest on a loan, the "rent" for capital. The matter of accounting for more complicated leases is a difficult and complex one and is covered in Chapter XI.

(2) The Percentage of Completion Method

A method for accelerating recognition prior to completion, known as the "percentage of completion method," permits recognition of a portion of the profit on a long-term contract before full completion.

This method has wide application for large construction projects not only involving real estate but also ships and airplanes. It comports more closely to the gradual accretion of value than does the *Tooey v. Percival* realization rule.

An examination of the bookkeeping techniques used for long-term construction type contracts casts further light on the pragmatic character of the factor of completion of the earning process. In addition, this is an area significant in amount of transactions and is of frequent concern for lawyers because of its widespread use in defense spending, a large segment of the gross national product.

ACCOUNTING RESEARCH BULLETIN NO. 45
LONG–TERM CONSTRUCTION–TYPE CONTRACTS *
AICPA, Committee on Accounting Procedure, 1955.

"1.   This bulletin is directed to the accounting problems in relation to construction-type contracts in the case of commercial organizations engaged wholly or partly in the contracting business.   *   *   *

* Copyright © 1955 by the American Institute of Certified Public Accountants, Inc.

"Generally Accepted Methods

"3. Two accounting methods commonly followed by contractors are the percentage-of-completion method and the completed-contract method.

"4. The percentage-of-completion method recognizes income as work on a contract progresses. The committee recommends that the recognized income be that percentage of estimated total income, either:

(a) that incurred costs to date bear to estimated total costs after giving effect to estimates of costs to complete based upon most recent information, or

(b) that may be indicated by such other measure of progress toward completion as may be appropriate having due regard to work performed.

Costs as here used might exclude, especially during the early stages of a contract, all or a portion of the cost of such items as materials and subcontracts if it appears that such an exclusion would result in a more meaningful periodic allocation of income.

"5. Under this method current assets may include costs and recognized income not yet billed, with respect to certain contracts; and liabilities, in most cases current liabilities, may include billings in excess of costs and recognized income with respect to other contracts.

"6. When the current estimate of total contract costs indicates a loss, in most circumstances provision should be made for the loss on the entire contract. If there is a close relationship between profitable and unprofitable contracts, such as in the case of contracts which are parts of the same project, the group may be treated as a unit in determining the necessity for a provision for loss.

"7. The principal advantages of the percentage-of-completion method are periodic recognition of income currently rather than irregularly as contracts are completed, and the reflection of the status of the uncompleted contracts provided through the current estimates of costs to complete or of progress toward completion.

"8. The principal disadvantage of the percentage-of-completion method is that it is necessarily dependent upon estimates of ultimate costs and consequently of currently accruing income, which are subject to the uncertainties frequently inherent in long-term contracts.

"9. The completed-contract method recognizes income only when the contract is completed, or substantially so. Accordingly, costs of contracts in process and current billings are accumulated but there are no interim charges or credits to income other than provisions for losses. A contract may be regarded as substantially completed if remaining costs are not significant in amount.

"10. When the completed-contract method is used, it may be appropriate to allocate general and administrative expenses to contract costs rather than to periodic income. This may result in a better matching of costs and revenues than would result from treating such expenses as period costs, particularly in years when no contracts were completed. It is not so important, however, when the contractor is engaged in numerous projects and in such circumstances it may be preferable to charge those expenses as incurred to periodic income. In any case there should be no excessive deferring of overhead costs, such as might occur if total overhead were assigned to abnormally few or abnormally small contracts in process.

"11. Although the completed-contract method does not permit the recording of any income prior to completion, provisions should be made for expected losses in accordance with the well established practice of making provision for foreseeable losses. If there is a close relationship between profitable and unprofitable contracts, such as in the case of contracts which are parts of the same project, the group may be treated as a unit in determining the necessity for a provision for losses.

"12. When the completed-contract method is used, an excess of accumulated costs over related billings should be shown in the balance sheet as a current asset, and an excess of accumulated billings over related costs should be shown among the liabilities, in most cases as current liability. If costs exceed billing on some contracts, and billings exceed costs on others, the contracts should ordinarily be segregated so that the figures on the asset side include only those contracts on which costs exceed billings, and those on the liability side include only those on which billings exceed costs. It is suggested that the asset item be described as 'costs of uncompleted contracts in excess of related billings' rather than as 'inventory' or 'work in process,' and that the item on the liability side be described as 'billings on uncompleted contracts in excess of related costs.'

"13. The principal advantage of the completed-contract method is that it is based on results as finally determined, rather than on estimates for unperformed work which may involve unforeseen costs and possible losses.

"14. The principal disadvantage of the completed-contract method is that it does not reflect current performance when the period of any contract extends into more than one accounting period and under such circumstances it may result in irregular recognition of income.

"Selection of Method

"15. The committee believes that in general when estimates of costs to complete and extent of progress toward completion of long-term contracts are reasonably dependable, the percentage-of-completion method is preferable. When lack of dependable estimates or inherent hazards cause forecasts to be doubtful, the completed-contract method is preferable. Disclosure of the method followed should be made."

Assume that Western Builders, Inc. on January 1, 19X1, enters into a contract to erect a large building for a fixed price of $10 million. (The problem would be the same if the contract were for a large item of personal property like a ship.) It is estimated that Western's costs will be $9 million and the construction work will last 3 years from January 1, 19X1. The contract provides that 25% of the price will be paid when ⅓ of the job is completed (as determined by the incurrence of ⅓ of the total estimated cost); 25% will be paid when the second third is completed; and the balance on final completion.

On December 31, 19X1, ⅓ of the work is completed and $2.5 million in cash is received. Costs for the ⅓ were $3 million paid by Western in cash. In the second year the second third is completed at a cost of $3 million paid in cash, and $2.5 million cash is received from the buyer. And at the end of the third year, the building is completed at an additional cost of $3 million and $5 million cash is received from the buyer.

(a) Completed Contract Method

Assume the balance sheet of Western appears as follows at January 1, 19X1.

Balance Sheet
Western Builders, Inc. at January 1, 19X1

Assets:		Liabilities:	
Cash	$3,000,000	Notes Payable (non-interest bearing)	$2,000,000
		Capital Stock	1,000,000
	$3,000,000		$3,000,000

Assume all expenditures, invoicing, and receipts occur on the last day of each year and that there are no other transactions or expenses or income.

If we treat the sale of this building like the sale of ordinary goods, no income should be recognized until the job is completed, in 19X3. But it would be disastrous to treat as expenses the $3,000,000 paid out in each of 19X1 and 19X2 when there was no income. Therefore, the matching concept requires that no costs should be recognized, but instead they should be deferred in the income statement until 19X3. If we defer the costs in 19X1 and 19X2, we end up with income statements for 19X1 and 19X2 which reflect no revenues or expenses and no gain or loss from this transaction, and an income statement for 19X3 showing revenues of $10 million, expenses of $9 million and net profit of $1 million.

The journal entries, T accounts, and financial statements for each of the three years on this "completed contract" basis would be as follows:

19X1

(a) Journal entries:

Dec. 31, 19X1 (1) Cash $2,500,000

                Deferred Billings $2,500,000

                (The account name, "Deferred Billings," is used more commonly than "Deferred Income" or "Prepaid Income" by long-term contractors.)

                (2) Deferred Costs   3,000,000

                Cash   3,000,000

                (The account name, "Deferred Costs," is used more commonly than "Deferred Expenses" or "Prepaid Expenses" by long-term contractors.)

(b) T accounts at end of 19X1:

Cash				Notes Payable	
Opening		$3,000,000 (2)			Opening
Balance $3,000,000					Balance $2,000,000
(1) $2,500,000					

Deferred Costs			Capital Stock	
(2) $3,000,000				Opening
				Balance $1,000,000

Deferred Billings	
	$2,500,000 (1)

(c) Financial Statements

(i) Income statement—none shown since there is neither income nor expense in current year from this transaction.

(ii) Balance sheet—the foregoing accounts would produce this balance sheet:

Balance Sheet of Western Builders, Inc. at December 31, 19X1

Cash	$2,500,000	Notes Payable	$2,000,000
Deferred Costs	3,000,000	Deferred Billings	2,500,000
		Capital Stock	1,000,000
	$5,500,000		$5,500,000

But it is not customary to show the balance sheet in this form. Some argue that the balance sheet is "padded" unless the two deferred items are netted against each other. See *ARB No. 45*, and Herwitz, *Accounting for Long–Term Construction Contracts: A Lawyer's Ap-*

proach, 70 Harv.L.Rev. 449 (1957), for the proliferation of problems of disclosure if in one contract Deferred Costs exceed Deferred Billings, and in another contract Deferred Billings exceed Deferred Costs. And see *ASR 164* (1974).

We show below the customary form of balance sheet for 19X1 in which the two items are netted:

Balance Sheet of Western Builders, Inc. at December 31, 19X1

Cash	$2,500,000	Notes Payable	$2,000,000
Costs of Uncompleted Contracts in Excess of Billings	500,000	Capital Stock	1,000,000
	$3,000,000		$3,000,000

The item "Cost of Uncompleted Contracts in Excess of Billings" may be thought of as an Account Receivable for work done, although not contractually due, or as an Inventory of Work in Progress. If the net result had been a credit (entitled "Billings on Uncompleted Contracts in Excess of Costs") it might be thought of as a liability like a Customer's Deposit for goods sold but not yet delivered.

For 19X2, the journal entries for 19X1 are repeated; no income statement is required and the balance sheet at December 31, 19X2 will show a netted figure of $1,000,000 representing the cumulative costs incurred in this contract, $6,000,000, less cumulative billings in the contract, $5,000,000.

Upon completion of the contract in 19X3, the revenue and expense are recognized in the income statement for the year ended December 31, 19X3 as follows:

Revenues from contracts	$10,000,000
Costs incurred on contracts	9,000,000
Gross profit	$ 1,000,000

The balance sheet at December 31, 19X3, after repayment of monies borrowed to finance the contract, would be as follows:

Balance Sheet of Western Builders, Inc. at December 31, 19X3

Cash	$4,000,000	Notes Payable	$2,000,000
		Capital Stock	1,000,000
		Retained Earnings	1,000,000
	$4,000,000		$4,000,000

This method of accounting for long-term construction type contracts is called the "completed-contract" method. Its obvious drawback is that the entire net profit is reflected only in the year of completion, thereby giving a distorted picture of the operating performance of the company for the three years.

This method seems to show a picture of performance that is unacceptable. For this reason, many firms use a different technique which has the purpose and effect of reflecting a portion of the estimated profit in each year depending on some measure of progress toward completion, usually the costs incurred that year.

(b) Percentage-of-Completion Method

This second method is designated the "percentage-of-completion" method. Based on the same example, the journal entries, T accounts, and financial statements using the percentage-of-completion method would appear as follows:

19X1

(a) Journal entries:

(1)	Cash	$2,500,000	
	Deferred Billings		$2,500,000
(2)	Deferred Costs	3,000,000	
	Cash		3,000,000
(2a)	Accrued Profit	333,333	
	Income		333,333

(Then close Income to Retained Earnings):

(2b)	Income	333,333	
	Retained Earnings		333,333

The "Accrued Profit" account may be thought of as an additional Account Receivable for work done, although not yet contractually due. It is a fraction of the expected total profit in proportion to the costs incurred to date to the total anticipated costs.

(b) T accounts:

Cash

Opening			
Balance	$3,000,000	$3,000,000	(2)
(1)	$2,500,000		

Notes Payable

	Opening	
	Balance	$2,000,000

Deferred Costs

(2)	$3,000,000	

Capital Stock

	Opening	
	Balance	$1,000,000

Accrued Profit

(2a)	$ 333,333	

Deferred Billings

	$2,500,000	(1)

Income

(2b)	$333,333	$333,333	(2a)

Retained Earnings

	$333,333	(2b)

(c) Financial Statements:

(i) Income statement for 19X1 (will contain one line as follows): Income on Uncompleted Contract $333,333

(ii) Balance sheet shown in "netted" form only. Note the expanded caption for the deferred item.

Western Builders, Inc.
Balance Sheet at December 31, 19X1

Cash	$2,500,000	Notes Payable	$2,000,000
Cost of Uncompleted Contracts and Accrued Profit in Excess of Billings	833,333	Capital Stock	1,000,000
		Retained Earnings	333,333
	$3,333,333		$3,333,333

19X2

(a) Journal entries—entries (3), (4), (4a) and (4b) are identical with entries (1), (2), (2a) and (2b) for 19X1 above.

(b) The accounts at end of 19X2 will be supplemented by posting entries (3), (4), (4a) and (4b).

(c) Financial Statements:

(i) Income statement 19X2 will contain the same one line item as in 19X1: Income on Uncompleted Contract $333,333

(ii) Balance sheet December 31, 19X2:

Balance Sheet of Western Builders, Inc. at December 31, 19X2

Cash	$2,000,000	Notes Payable	$2,000,000
Cost of Uncompleted Contracts and Accrued Profit in Excess of Billings	1,666,666	Capital Stock	1,000,000
		Retained Earnings	666,666
	$3,666,666		$3,666,666

19X3

(a) Journal entries:

(5)	Cash	$5,000,000	
	Deferred Billings		$5,000,000
(6)	Deferred Costs	3,000,000	
	Cash		3,000,000
(6a)	Accrued Profit	333,333	
	Income		333,333
(6b)	Income	333,333	
	Retained Earnings		333,333

(b) At this point certain T accounts read as follows:

Deferred Costs			Deferred Billings	
(2)	$3,000,000		$ 2,500,000	(1)
(4)	3,000,000		2,500,000	(3)
(6)	3,000,000		5,000,000	(5)
	$9,000,000		$10,000,000	

	Income	
(2b)	$ 333,333	$ 333,333	(2a)
(4b)	333,333	333,333	(4a)
(6b)	333,333	333,333	(6a)

Accrued Profit			Retained Earnings	
(2a)	$ 333,333		$ 333,333	(2b)
(4a)	333,333		333,333	(4b)
(6a)	333,333		333,333	(6b)
	$1,000,000		$ 1,000,000	

Since all of the income from the job has already been recognized and is now realized by completion under any theory, we may close out the deferral and accrual accounts as follows:

(12)	Deferred Billings	$10,000,000	
	Deferred Costs		$9,000,000
	Accrued Profit		1,000,000

Try your hand at making up the 19X3 income statement and balance sheet.

Notes

3–13. Percentage of Completion Method "Preferable." *SFAS No. 56,* ¶ 6, issued in 1982 by the FASB states:

> 6. The percentage-of-completion and completed-contract methods are not intended to be free choice alternatives for the same circumstances under either ARB 45 or SOP 81–1. ARB 45 states that "when estimates of costs to complete and extent of progress toward completion of long-term contracts are reasonably dependable, the percentage-of-completion method is preferable" and "when lack of dependable estimates or inherent hazards cause forecasts to be doubtful, the completed-contract method is preferable." SOP 81–1 states that the two methods "should not be acceptable alternatives for the same circumstances" and specifies criteria for choice of method similar to those in ARB 45. In applying either ARB 45 or SOP 81–1, a contractor should evaluate the facts and circumstances pertaining to contract work performed and decide which of the two methods is appropriate.

3–14. Sources of Interpretive Problems in ARB No. 45. Numerous difficulties may arise in interpreting *ARB No. 45.* See Herwitz, *Accounting for Long–Term Construction Contracts: A Lawyer's Approach,* 70 Harv.L.Rev. 449 (1957). See also, Jennings & McCosh, *Construction in Progress—A Different Approach,* 42 Acctg.Rev. 598 (1967).

3–15. *Losses Under the Percentage of Completion Method.* In our Western Builders example, how much of an estimated loss of $1 million (on a revised estimate in the first year that cost will amount to $11 million) should be recognized each year under each method? See Cornell v. Seddinger, 237 Pa. 389, 85 A. 446 (1912); In re Touche Ross & Co., SEC Rel. AAER No. 16, [Current Vol.] Fed.Sec.L.Rep. (CCH) ¶ 73,416 (1983). Is there any reason for treatment of losses differently from gains?

(3) Program Costs—An Inapt Analogy

There are two additional problems which on the surface appear to be similar to that of accounting for costs and profits on a long-term construction contract. Here we ignore revenue recognition and go to the other element—costs. One of the problems is the case of investment in special purpose inventory in excess of current needs in order to reduce unit costs in the expectation of future orders. The other is the investment in development and physical facilities in the expectation of future orders. These cases differ vastly from those heretofore considered because there is no contract; thus there is lacking not only the completion of services, but also a market transaction and receipt of an asset in exchange. Consider a case like the Ford Motor Company's famous Edsel, but using wholly arbitrary figures. Assume that the tools, jigs and dies for production cost $300,000,000. How much of this should be charged as cost of goods sold on each Edsel sold? Obviously there is no answer unless one first makes an assumption as to how many Edsels will be sold. Assume alternatively, (1) that the factory estimates that 1,000,000 cars per year will be sold in each of three years; (2) the estimate is for 500,000 cars per year in each of three years; or (3) that in fact only 100,000 are sold in each of the first two years under either of the prior assumptions and that the product is discontinued at the end of the second year.

POLIN v. CONDUCTRON CORP.

United States Court of Appeals for the Eighth Circuit, 1977.
552 F.2d 797.

It is the claim of the plaintiff that the January, 1966 proxy statement, the 1965 Annual Report, as well as the First 1966 Annual Report, the Second 1966 Annual Report, the 1967 Annual Report, the Press Release of May 3, 1968, and the 1968 Annual Report, all contained false and misleading statements, "particularly with reference to Conductron's aircraft simulator business * * *."

In order to analyze properly the frauds allegedly practiced almost throughout Conductron's entire corporate life, it is necessary to acquire some perspective as to the simulator business, its origins, its prospects, and its costs, since all are comprehended, in one form or another, in fraud charges covering the years in question.

The simulator, as the name implies, simulates something else. With respect to aircraft, the simulator duplicates ("simulates") the cockpit of the plane. Through an intricate system of wiring and programming, and with the aid of computers, aircraft operating characteristics may be simulated for various situations, both routine and of serious nature. The entire plane performance is duplicated, from take-off, through systems performance, radio navigation and communication, descent, approach and ground operations. The savings accomplished through the use of a simulator are of substantial magnitude. The airplane being simulated, costing from $5,000,000 to $25,000,000 is released for other operations by a simulator costing from $1,000,000 to $2,000,000. Moreover, there is no danger during training to the fledgling pilot or his airplane. The training, in fact, is so detailed that after the simulator work is completed, only "one final flight in the airplane [is required] before they [the pilots] had to fly passengers * * *."

But the problems involved in simulator manufacture parallel in complexity the operations of the machine itself, since the design, engineering, and manufacture require from two to five years. Since the simulator must match exactly the airplane it is intended to simulate, plane changes require simulator changes, and even between planes of the same general design, such as the Boeing 737, to simulate one is not to simulate all. In addition, different airlines flying the same plane may order different cockpit configurations, as changes are made in equipment, causing unanticipated and substantial losses, arising not only from production design costs but also from changes in the hardware that goes into the simulator cockpit.

The simulator engineers with the Electronic Equipment Division (EED) of MDC did not come to Conductron as novices. As Mr. Toole, then an employee of EED put it, "My feelings were that we had a technical break-through in simulation, one that was worth pursuing as a new line of business. One that had a great deal of potential with the airlines and with the military." The new line of business was anticipated to be profitable, not only because of a large upswing in the purchases of aircraft, but because EED's advanced technology made the competition "rather minimal, in that no large companies who you might say had huge resources behind them were involved." But the roseate future envisioned did not materialize. In fact, the operation foundered.

MDC, through the EED division, obtained contracts for one 737 simulator from Boeing in September, 1965 and for two more 737 simulators from United Airlines the following month. "Everybody was pretty pleased," testified Mr. McDonnell, Chairman of the MDC Board, in his deposition. In January of 1966 Conductron acquired EED. The contracts for the three 737 simulators were transferred from EED to Conductron, MDC promised Conductron continued business, paid $5,000,000 as part of the agreement, and promised substantial grants for research. It is significant that all parties here recognized the need for additional funds for this purpose.

Increased aircraft purchases were made by the airlines in September of 1966. Conductron felt that its technology would be of great interest to the lines "and it was apparent to us that we would make a lot of sales." But Conductron anticipated achieving a substantial "commonality" among the same aircraft. This did not result. The aircraft (Boeing 737) was itself changed, cockpits were altered, each airline in effect wanted its own simulator with the result that substantial losses were suffered by Conductron. In addition, "competitions were quite vicious," with the result that prices were steadily driven down. Other factors contributed, and in substance, the aircraft market dried up. In addition, special problems developed with the C–5A military aircraft simulator which Conductron was building for Lockheed.

We turn to the matter of costs and the reporting thereof. Obviously, the research and development costs could not be borne by the first model produced. The cost assigned to any unit depended upon the competitive market, cost estimates, and the number of the model to be produced. It is clear that at this point an accounting and disclosure problem is presented.

Conductron made its agreement with MDC for acquisition of EED on January 7, 1966. It is with respect to the representations made, and omitted, in the proxy statement issued in connection therewith that plaintiff's initial charges of misrepresentation arise. The plaintiff's principal challenge is that the proxy statement did not disclose the anticipated losses in the simulator business. The short answer, on the record, is that defendants anticipated substantial profits, not losses. It is true that defendants' roseate economic anticipations were doomed, but economic prognostication, though faulty, does not, without more, amount to fraud. Moreover, the proxy statement gave fair warning that the development and other start-up costs would depend for recovery upon future contracts. The information disclosed with reference thereto stated:

> The Division recently received contract awards from the Boeing Company and United Air Lines to design and build three 737 aircraft transport pilot training simulators for a total of $2,760,966. Expected additional contracts for the Boeing 737 simulator will be necessary to recover development and other start up costs.

It could not reasonably be said that an investor of plaintiff Polin's experience was unaware of the significance of this statement.

But beyond the minutiae of the various charges made and behind them as justification therefor, running through the entire series of reports, lies a fundamental accounting problem, namely, when and how Conductron should have written off the design and development costs of the simulator program. These costs were large and could not be charged in their entirety against the first simulators from a competitive standpoint. An amortization over the entire contract life was utilized.[27] If a sufficient number of simulators are sold, amortization presents no problem. If not, due to economic conditions, lack of acceptance of the plane, or other cause, the manufacturer will suffer a loss. The point to be observed here is the fact that a disparity between expenditures and selling price of an early simulator does not result in a "loss." The Conductron Corporation followed a system of accounting employed under these circumstances by its accountants, Ernst & Ernst, under which initial non-recurring costs were allocated pro-rata over the life of the program, rather than being charged off in their entirety at the beginning of the program.

Plaintiff's complaints about the annual reports all revolve around the dates of the reporting of what plaintiff terms "anticipated simulator losses" and the accuracy of the accounting judgments made. As to the latter, these are matters of judgment, a judgment clearly dependent upon constantly changing factors. It was in recognition by Ernst & Ernst of such variables present in the operation being conducted that no provision for losses was made until the Second 1966 Annual Report, covering the period July 1—December 31, 1966. The Ernst & Ernst Report approving the financial statements in the Second 1966 Annual Report was dated March 17, 1967. Mr. Anderson, the Ernst & Ernst partner in charge of the Conductron auditing, testified that "I would think that there was significantly more information available in March of 1967 than there was in July of 1966," this latter being the date of the Ernst & Ernst Report approving the financial statements in the First Annual Report for 1966. Such information required the recognition of certain losses at that time, but Ernst & Ernst cautioned the corporation about the difficulties inherent in making such judgments, stating, in part:

> [It] should be recognized that the estimates of losses referred to herein are subject to considerable revision as the contracts progress, based upon the demonstrated experiences to date.

27. Direct Examination of Mr. Toole, Project Manager for Trainers and Simulators at Conductron:

Mr. MANNINO: * * * I think it is important to determine at this point whether or not an amortization procedure as opposed to an instant write-off procedure was used on the simulators * * *.

* * *

THE WITNESS: Well, I was not in the financial side of our company, and I don't know exactly how this was handled from a financial standpoint, but my understanding was that we would spread the development cost over a quantity of simulators. The quantity was predicted based primarily on the number of aircraft that would be purchased. The airlines had a policy of buying one simulator for about every twenty airplanes they bought, and we could look at the aircraft market itself and predict the requirement for simulators at the various airlines.

* * *

Q Now, can you explain what Conductron did in order to recover development costs in its prices, if it did anything?

A This was what we were amortizing over the predicted market.

The financial reports we examine were certified by Ernst & Ernst to be fair and accurate after substantial investigative research. The Court found, moreover:

> [W]e have carefully reviewed each of these reports, as well as the earnings statements and the press releases, in light of plaintiff's complaints and find that none of them are fraudulently misleading either by omissions or by affirmative statements. It is true, of course, that each report painted a gloomier picture of the extent of the losses incurred and anticipated than the preceding one, but there is no substantial basis for the contention that any of the reports withheld material information or fraudulently minimized losses which should have been anticipated.

Under our review of this lengthy record we find no clear error of fact or misapplication of applicable law. There is no sustainable claim for damages or rescission. What we had were, possibly, too-sanguine hopes for the future, as well as differences of opinion between accountants as to the complex problems of financial reporting of the new device, but the elements of fraud, the deceptions, the duplicities and the distortions normally concomitants of false and misleading statements, are completely missing.

* * *

Incidentally, although the court in *Polin* referred to these costs as "research and development," they are not to be confused with what the FASB means by that term. In SFAS No. 2, *Accounting for Research and Development Costs,* ¶¶ 8–10 (1974), there is an effort to distinguish "research" ("aimed at discovery of new knowledge") and "development" ("translation of research findings or other knowledge into a plan or design for a new product or process or for a significant improvement to an existing product or process") from other activities. The distinction of *Polin* is crucial as we shall see that *SFAS No. 2* requires expensing all research and development costs, contrary to the treatment of program costs.

ASR 173 discussed the program method of accounting for products requiring extensive research and make-ready under which substantial initial costs are incurred for a product although sales are not firmly committed but are nevertheless deemed highly probable. The program method of Talley Industries was described:

> In 1969 Talley accounted for its cost of sales on a program basis ("program method") for fixed price U.S. Government contracts at its Mesa, Arizona operations. Similar products were grouped into a program. At fiscal year end (March 31, 1969) a gross profit ratio based on estimates was established and was used in the following manner; actual sales for the fiscal year were added to projected sales for the following year as determined by known backlog and projection by Talley's management of anticipated contracts and actual costs for the year's production were added to costs estimated by Talley's manage-

ment to complete the sales projected for the following year; a gross profit ratio based on total estimated costs was established and applied to the dollar amount of actual sales made in the audit year to determine the cost of sales for the year. Any costs incurred in the audit year in excess of the amount recognized as cost of sales in that year by this computation was carried forward as part of inventory. The gross profit ratio so determined, adjusted for actual manufacturing overhead, was used by Talley throughout the following fiscal year to compute cost of sales for unaudited interim periods.

Is the analogy to the percentage-of-completion method apt? What standards should govern use of this method? Talley's then accountants were disciplined by the SEC for approving the program method after it became apparent that the projected sales could not be achieved. See *ASR 173* (1975).

In *ASR 164* (1974), the SEC established additional disclosure requirements for long-term contract and program method accounting in "certain critical areas of long-term contract activity, particularly with respect to the nature of costs accumulated in inventories, the effect of cost accumulation policies on cost of sales, and the effect of revenue recognition practices on receivables and inventories. * * * Registrants and their independent public accountants must make the determination as to what information regarding such matters is required to constitute satisfactory financial statement disclosure under generally accepted accounting principles."

4. RECOGNITION FOR SERVICE TRANSACTIONS
BOISE CASCADE CORP. v. UNITED STATES
United States Court of Claims, 1976.
530 F.2d 1367, cert. denied 429 U.S. 867 (1976).

OPINION

PER CURIAM:

These are consolidated cases, in which plaintiffs seek the recovery of nearly $2,400,000 in income taxes plus interest thereon, paid for the years 1955 through 1961. * * *

Trial Judge Fletcher's opinion, as modified by the court, follows:

* * *

In its business, Ebasco Services enters into contracts to perform engineering and similar services. Under the various terms of these contracts, Ebasco is entitled to bill fixed sums either in monthly, quarterly, or other periodic installments, plus such additional amounts as may be provided for in a particular contract. Depending on the terms of the different contracts, payments may in some cases be due prior to the annual period in which such services are to be performed, and in some cases subsequent thereto.

For a number of years prior to 1959 and continuing to the time of trial, Ebasco included in its income for both book and tax purposes amounts attributable to services which it performed during the taxable year, a procedure accepted by the Internal Revenue Service on prior audits. Ebasco determined the amounts so earned by dividing the estimated number of service hours or days required to complete the particular contract into the contract price. The resulting quotient represents an hourly or daily rate which is then multiplied by the number of hours or days actually worked on the contract during the taxable year. As the contract is performed, the rate is adjusted to reflect revised estimates of the work required to complete the contract.

Where Ebasco billed for services prior to the tax year in which they were performed, it credited such amounts to a balance sheet account called "Unearned Income". Where the services were performed in a subsequent period, the "Unearned Income" account was debited, and such amounts were included in an income account called "Service Revenues." The amount recorded in the latter account was included in income for both book and tax purposes. In determining the amount which was to be included in the "Unearned Income" account, the costs of obtaining the contract were not taken into account;[1] and, with the exception of prepaid insurance and similar items, all such amounts were expensed in the tax year during which they were incurred. The amounts in the "Unearned Income" account were treated as liabilities and were excluded from gross income for each tax year consistently in Ebasco's books, records, and shareholder reports, as well as in its tax returns. All of the amounts included in the account during one tax year were earned through the performance of services during the following year and were included in income for such following tax year. When the amounts credited to the "Unearned Income" account were collected, Ebasco had an unrestricted right to the use of such funds.

During the three tax years in issue, an average of over 94 percent of the amounts included in the "Unearned Income" account was received by Ebasco under contracts which obligated it to perform engineering services in connection with the design and construction of electric generating plants. These contracts either required that services be performed by a specified date or required that Ebasco should perform those services "with all reasonable dispatch and diligence," as "expeditiously as possible," or some comparable requirement. The small remaining amounts in the account were received either under contracts which required Ebasco to perform specific services in connection with a specific project of a client, or required Ebasco to provide consultation and advice on an annual basis for an annual fee.

In addition to its "Unearned" account, Ebasco maintained an "Unbilled Charges" account computed in the same manner as the "Unearned Income" account. The balance in such account represented amounts earned through the rendering of services, or on partially completed contracts, or earned prior to contracting under all of which

---

1. These amounts included the cost of preparing bids, proposals, and estimates, overhead, advertising, and selling expenses.

payment was not then due by the terms of a contract or was not billable and due prior to execution of a future contract. Stated another way, the amounts included in this account were those which Ebasco was not entitled to bill or receive until a year subsequent to the year in which the services were actually rendered. Such amounts were recorded in "Service Revenues" and included in income for tax as well as book purposes in the taxable year in which the services were rendered. Likewise, the costs attributable to the rendering of services which produced the year-end balance in the "Unbilled Charges" account were deducted from gross income in the year such services were rendered. In 1959, 1960, and 1961 there were approximately $405,000, ($56,000), and $179,000 of such net amounts, respectively, carried in the "Unbilled Charges" account.

Plaintiffs' consolidated income tax returns for 1959 through 1961 were audited by the Government, and the amounts in the "Unearned Income" account were included in taxable income for Federal tax purposes. These adjustments were made pursuant to section 446(b) of the 1954 Code under which the Commissioner determined that plaintiffs' deferral method of accounting did not clearly reflect income. During the same examination for the same tax years, no adjustments were made to the "Unbilled Charges" or the "Service Revenues" accounts.

At trial Ebasco presented expert testimony related solely to the accounting practices described above. The sole witness was a qualified certified public accountant and a partner in a major accounting firm. Based on his broad experience with comparable service companies and his personal familiarity with the accounting practices of Ebasco, he expressed his expert opinion with respect to the accounts in issue and the changes made by the Commissioner.

He testified that the method of accounting used by Ebasco which employs both an "Unearned Income" account and an "Unbilled Charges" account and is based on accruing amounts as income at the time the related services are performed is in accordance with recognized and generally accepted accounting principles and clearly reflects Ebasco's income. He indicated that this method properly matched revenues with costs of producing such revenues and is particularly appropriate in this case because almost all of Ebasco's income is derived from the performance of services by its own personnel. He further testified that this method of accounting was widely used by companies engaged in rendering engineering and similar services, and that such method clearly reflected the income of Ebasco.

With respect to costs incurred in obtaining contracts, such as bid preparation, overhead, advertising, and other selling expenses, the witness considered them to be properly deducted in the year incurred as continuing costs of doing and developing business.[2] He explained

2. The witness distinguished such costs from commissions which in some instances may properly be amortized where they relate directly to the contract involved and thus reduce the amount realizable under such contract.

that these costs should not properly be amortizable over the life of any particular contract since they were costs connected with new business development and were unrelated to performance of the contract.

The accounting method proposed by the Commissioner requires Ebasco to accrue as income the amounts included in the "Unearned Income" account and also requires the accrual, consistent with plaintiffs' accounting method, of amounts in the "Unbilled Charges" account. In the opinion of plaintiffs' expert, this method of accounting was not in accordance with generally accepted accounting principles and did not clearly reflect Ebasco's income. To him, the Commissioner's method was erroneous in that it required the inclusion in income of amounts billed but not yet earned on contracts in one accounting period without at the same time acknowledging the obligations and costs to be incurred by Ebasco in the future performance of such contractual commitments. He termed such method as "hybrid" in that while it recognized the accrual method with respect to unbilled charges which were earned but not yet billable, it had the effect of imposing a cash basis method as to the billed but unearned charges in the "Unearned Income" account.

Finally, the witness testified that if Ebasco were to use a method of accounting under which amounts in the "Unearned Income" account would be accrued as income and amounts in the "Unbilled Charges" account would *not* be accrued as income, such method would more clearly reflect the income of Ebasco than the method of accounting proposed by the Commissioner. He stated that, while such method was not technically in accordance with generally accepted accounting principles, it was a more logical and consistent approach to use in determining the income of Ebasco than the Commissioner's method.

The remaining issues involved in this case thus concern the accounting method employed by one of the plaintiffs, Ebasco Services (referred to below as "Ebasco"). Plaintiffs maintain that the method of deferral accounting employed by Ebasco (as described above) clearly reflects income and, therefore, is entirely proper for Federal income tax purposes. Alternatively, they contend that if Ebasco is required to accrue as income amounts in its deferred "Unearned Income" account, then in order clearly to reflect income, it should not accrue as income the amounts included in its "Unbilled Charges" account (also described above). With regard to the first of these contentions, the Government responds that the method of deferral accounting employed by Ebasco did not in fact clearly reflect income for tax purposes. As to the alternative contention, the Government agrees with Ebasco's original accounting treatment and insists that amounts in the "Unbilled Charges" account were properly accrued. The Government adds that acceptance of Ebasco's alternative contention would necessarily mean a change of accounting method for which plaintiffs admittedly have failed to obtain the consent of the Secretary or his delegate as required by section 446(e) of the 1954 Code.

These issues present but another facet in the continuing controversy over the proper timing for Federal income tax purposes of various income and expense items incurred by an accrual basis taxpayer. Based on expert accounting testimony presented by Ebasco at trial, it can hardly be disputed that Ebasco's system for deferral of unearned income is in full accord with generally accepted accounting principles as that phrase is used in financial or commercial accounting. But such a showing alone is not determinative for income tax purposes. The taxpayer must also show that its method clearly reflects income for the purposes of the Internal Revenue Code. Thus, while generally accepted methods of accounting are of probative value and are treated with respect by Treas.Reg. § 1.446–1(a)(2), they are not necessarily synonymous with the proper tax accounting to be afforded an accrual item in a given situation. * * *

This variance is especially noticeable in cases where the taxpayer's accounting method results in the deferment of income. The taxpayer in such a situation is generally relying on well-known accounting principles which essentially focus on a conservative matching of income and expenses to the end that an item of income will be related to its correlative expenditure. Tax accounting, on the other hand, starts from the premise of a need for certainty in the collection of revenues and focuses on the concept of ability to pay. Thus, under this theory, where an item of income has been received even though as yet unearned, it should be subject to taxation because the taxpayer has in hand (or otherwise available) the funds necessary to pay the tax due. * * *

[I]t can readily be seen that, under Ebasco's system, all amounts reported as income were determined with reference to the related services performed within the annual accounting period. The record clearly establishes that such system is a generally accepted accounting method for a business such as Ebasco's. Does it clearly reflect income as required by section 446 of the Code? [3]

Defendant stoutly responds to that question in the negative. It relies heavily on the decisions of the Supreme Court in *American Automobile Ass'n v. United States,* 367 U.S. 687, 81 S.Ct. 1727, 6 L.Ed. 2d 1109 (1961) and *Schlude v. Commissioner of Internal Revenue,* 372 U.S. 128, 83 S.Ct. 601, 9 L.Ed.2d 633 (1963), which cases defendant contends have firmly established the rule that, in the absence of a specific statutory exception, a taxpayer has no right to defer recogni-

---

3. In pertinent part, section 446 reads:

"SEC. 446. *General rule for methods of accounting.*

"(a) *General rule.*—Taxable income shall be computed under the method of accounting on the basis of which the taxpayer regularly computes his income in keeping his books.

"(b) *Exceptions.*—If no method of accounting has been regularly used by the taxpayer *or if the method used does not clearly reflect income,* the computation of taxable income shall be made under such method as, in the opinion of the Secretary or his delegate, does clearly reflect income." [Emphasis supplied.]

tion of income received or accrued under a contract for the performance of services.

Counsel for Ebasco respond with equal vigor that Ebasco's accounting system does, in fact, clearly reflect income. To them, the Supreme Court in the above-cited decisions only held that the Commissioner of Internal Revenue did not abuse his discretion under section 446 by rejecting what the Court referred to as a "purely artificial" accounting method. Ebasco's counsel are astonished that defendant could in this case interpret *American Automobile* and *Schlude* as preventing any income deferral when, as recently as 1971, the Commissioner, in Rev. Proc. 71–21, 1971–2 C.B. 549 has held that taxpayers may defer the inclusion in income of payments received in one taxable year for services to be performed in the next succeeding year.

Although one can hardly speak with complete confidence in this troublesome and confusing area of tax law as affected by modern accounting methods, I think it fair to conclude that, on balance, Ebasco's position in this litigation is the reasonable one of the conflicting viewpoints.

The starting point, of course, must involve a close look at the trilogy of Supreme Court decisions dealing with the problem of income deferral. Those cases are *Automobile Club of Michigan v. Commissioner of Internal Revenue,* 353 U.S. 180, 77 S.Ct. 707, 1 L.Ed.2d 746 (1957); *American Automobile Ass'n v. United States, supra,* and *Schlude v. Commissioner, supra.*

In *Michigan,* the Court sustained the action of the Commissioner of Internal Revenue in rejecting the taxpayer's method of deferral accounting pursuant to the authority of section 41 of the 1939 Code, the predecessor of 1954 Code section 446(b), *supra.* The taxpayer was engaged in performing various services to the automotive industry including the rendition of services to members of the club but only upon their specific request. Under its method of accounting, the club deferred taking into income the full amount of annual membership dues which the club required to be paid in advance, irrespective of whether the dues-paying member might call upon the club for any services during the 12–month period. Upon collection, these prepaid amounts were deposited in the club's regular bank account and used for general corporate purposes. In its books, the club entered these prepaid amounts into a liability account titled "Unearned Membership Dues," and thereafter for each of the 12 months of membership, one-twelfth of the amounts so paid was credited to an account called "Membership Income." In sustaining the Commissioner's rejection of this accounting method as not clearly reflecting income, the Court held:

> The pro rata allocation of the membership dues in monthly amounts is *purely artificial and bears no relation to the services which petitioner may in fact be called upon to render for the member.* Section 41 vests the Commissioner with discretion to determine whether the petitioner's method of accounting clearly reflects income. We cannot

say, in the circumstances here, that the discretionary action of the Commissioner, sustained by both the Tax Court and the Court of Appeals, exceeded permissible limits * * * 353 U.S. 189, 77 S.Ct. 712. [Emphasis supplied.]

Four years later, the issue returned to the Court in the *American Automobile* case. While the facts were essentially similar to those in *Michigan,* it was contended in *American Automobile* that the earlier case did not control because the Court had before it at last a full record containing expert accounting testimony that the system used was in accord with generally accepted accounting principles, that proof of membership service cost was detailed, and that the correlation between such cost and the period of time over which the dues were credited as income was shown and justified by proof of experience.

The Court, however, was unimpressed. Unable to perceive any significant difference between the methods of operation and accounting employed by the two automobile clubs, the Court held that, just as in *Michigan,* the American Automobile Association's system of accounting was "purely artificial" because "substantially all services are performed only upon a member's demand and the taxpayer's performance was not related to fixed dates after the tax year." 367 U.S. 691, 81 S.Ct. 1729. The Court explained at 692, 81 S.Ct. at 1729:

> It may be true that to the accountant the actual incidence of cost in serving an individual member in exchange for his individual dues is inconsequential, or, from the viewpoint of commercial accounting, unessential to determination and disclosure of the overall financial condition of the Association. That "irregularity," however, is highly relevant to the clarity of an accounting system which defers receipt, as earned income, of dues to a taxable period *in which no, some, or all of the services paid for by those dues may or may not be rendered.* The Code exacts its revenue from the individual member's dues which, no one disputes, constitute income. When their receipt as earned income is recognized ratably over two calendar years, *without regard to correspondingly fixed individual expense or performance justification,* but consistently with overall experience, their accounting doubtless presents a rather accurate image of the total financial structure, but fails to respect the criteria of annual tax accounting and may be rejected by the Commissioner. [Emphasis supplied.]

The third of this trilogy of cases is *Schlude v. Commissioner, supra,* where the Court again rejected an attempt by an accrual basis taxpayer to defer prepaid amounts for future services. The taxpayers there operated a dance studio and offered dancing lessons under contracts which required the students to pay their tuition in advance with no right to refund, *i.e.,* the studio was entitled to receive the advance payments under the contracts irrespective of whether the studio was ever called upon to render any teaching services.[5] At the end of each

---

5. No dates for dancing lessons were fixed but simply left to a mutually agreeable arrangement between student and teacher. Significant amounts of income flowed from cancellations resulting in no performance of services.

fiscal period, the total number of actually taught hours were multiplied by the applicable hourly rate. The resulting sum was then deducted from the deferred income account and reported as earned income on taxpayers' financial statements and income tax returns.

The Court held that the case was "squarely controlled by *American Automobile Association,*" (372 U.S. 134, 83 S.Ct. 604) and sustained the Commissioner's rejection of Schlude's accounting method. Said the Court at 135–136, 83 S.Ct. at 605:

> The *American Automobile Association* case rested upon an additional ground which is also controlling here. Relying upon *Automobile Club of Michigan v. Commissioner,* 353 U.S. 180, 77 S.Ct. 707, 1 L.Ed.2d 746, the Court rejected the taxpayer's system as *artificial since the advance payments related to services which were to be performed only upon customers' demands without relation to fixed dates in the future. The system employed here suffers from that very same vice,* for the studio sought to defer its cash receipts on the basis of contracts which did not provide for lessons on fixed dates after the taxable year, but left such dates to be arranged from time to time by the instructor and his student. Under the contracts, the student could arrange for some or all of the additional lessons or could simply allow their rights under the contracts to lapse. But even though the student did not demand the remaining lessons, the contracts permitted the studio to insist upon payment in accordance with the obligations undertaken and to retain whatever prepayments were made without restriction as to use and without obligation of refund. At the end of each period, while the number of lessons taught had been meticulously reflected, the studio was uncertain whether none, some or all of the remaining lessons would be rendered. *Clearly, services were rendered solely on demand in the fashion of the American Automobile Association and Automobile Club of Michigan cases.* [Emphasis supplied.]

It seems clear to me that, despite defendant's vigorous contention to the contrary, this trilogy of Supreme Court decisions cannot be said to have established an unvarying rule of law that, absent a specific statutory exception, a taxpayer may never defer recognition of income received or accrued under a contract for the performance of future services, no matter whether such deferral clearly reflects income.

Defendant persuasively argues, however, that its interpretation of the cases is justified by the Court's additional ground for decision in both *American Automobile* and *Schlude.* In both cases, it is true, the Court's majority and minority opinions gave close consideration to the legislative history of sections 452 and 462 of the 1954 Code. These sections contained the first explicit legislative sanctions of deferral of income (§ 452) and deduction of future estimated expenses (§ 462). In the next year, however, both sections were retroactively repealed. Ch. 143, 69 Stat. 134. To the majority in *American Automobile,* this repealer action constituted "clearly a mandate from the Congress that petitioner's system was not acceptable for tax purposes." 367 U.S. 695,

81 S.Ct. 1731. The dissent, of course, viewed the legislative history in different perspective.[7]

To me, the dilemma and its likely solution, have been gracefully and accurately stated by the able and comprehensive opinion of the Fifth Circuit Court of Appeals in *Mooney Aircraft, Inc. v. United States,* 420 F.2d 400, 408–409 (5th Cir., 1969) where the court observed:

> This alternative ground, based on legislative intent, would seem to dispose of the entire question: *all* deferrals and accruals are bad unless specifically authorized by Congress. But the Court was careful to discuss the legislative history as dictum and restricted its holding to a finding that the Commissioner did not abuse his discretion in rejecting the *AAA's* accounting system. It specifically refrained from overruling *Beacon Publishing Co. v. Commissioner of Internal Revenue,* 218 F.2d 697 (10th Cir.1955) (deferral of prepaid subscriptions) and *Schuessler v. Commissioner of Internal Revenue,* 230 F.2d 722 (5th Cir.1956) (accrual of expenses of 5–year service period), distinguishing them on the ground that future performance was certain. *AAA, supra,* 367 U.S. at 692, n. 4, 81 S.Ct. 1727. It seems, then, that the Court is for the present taking a middle ground pending Congressional reform and clarification in this extremely confused area of the law: While the repeal of §§ 452 and 462 does not absolutely preclude deferrals and accruals, it indicates that the Commissioner should have very broad discretion to disallow such accounting techniques when there is any reasonable basis for his action.

The *Mooney Aircraft* approach was foreshadowed by the Seventh Circuit's decision in *Artnell Company v. Commissioner of Internal Revenue,* 400 F.2d 981 (7th Cir., 1968). There, Chicago White Sox, Inc. had received and accrued in a deferred unearned income account amounts attributable to advance ticket sales and revenues for other services related to baseball games to be played thereafter during the 1962 season. Prior to such performance, however, Artnell acquired Chicago White Sox, Inc., liquidated it, and continued operation of the team. In the final short-year return filed as transferee by Artnell in behalf of White Sox, Inc., Artnell excluded the deferred unearned income previously received by White Sox. The Commissioner required such amounts to be accrued as income to White Sox on receipt, and the Tax Court sustained him. In reversing and remanding, the Seventh Circuit analyzed the Supreme Court's trilogy, *supra,* and said at 400 F.2d 984–985:

---

7. For example, in his *Schlude* dissent, Mr. Justice Stewart observed at 372 U.S. 139–140, 83 S.Ct. 607:

"For the reasons I have elsewhere stated at some length, to rely on the repeal of §§ 452 and 462 as indicating congressional disapproval of accrual accounting principles is conspicuously to disregard clear evidence of legislative intent. The Secretary of the Treasury, who proposed the repeal of these sections, made explic-itly clear that no inference of disapproval of accrual accounting principles was to be drawn from the repeal of the sections. So did the Senate Report. The repeal of these sections was occasioned solely by the fear of temporary revenue losses which would result from the taking of 'double deductions' during the year of transition by taxpayers who had not previously maintained their books on an accrual basis." [Footnotes omitted.]

Has the Supreme Court left an opening for a decision that, under the facts of a particular case, the extent and time of future performance are so certain, and related items properly accounted for with such clarity, that a system of accounting involving deferral of prepaid income is found clearly to reflect income, and the commissioner's rejection deemed an abuse of discretion? Or has it decided that the commissioner has complete and unreviewable discretion to reject deferral of prepaid income where Congress has made no provision? The tax court apparently adopted the latter view, for it concluded "that the Supreme Court would reach the same decision regardless of the method used by the taxpayer for deferring prepaid income."

It is our best judgment that, although the policy of deferring, where possible, to congressional procedures in the tax field will cause the Supreme Court to accord the widest possible latitude to the commissioner's discretion, there must be situations where the deferral technique will so clearly reflect income that the Court will find an abuse of discretion if the commissioner rejects it.

Prior to 1955 the commissioner permitted accrual basis publishers to defer unearned income from magazine subscriptions if they had consistently done so in the past. He refused to allow others to adopt the method. In 1955 his refusal was held, by the tenth circuit, in *Beacon*, to be an abuse of discretion. In *Automobile Club of Michigan*, the Supreme Court distinguished *Beacon*, on its facts, because "performance of the subscription, in most instances, was, in part, necessarily deferred until the publication dates after the tax year." The Court, however, expressed no opinion upon the correctness of *Beacon*. In 1958, Congress dealt specifically with the *Beacon* problem. It is at least arguable that the deferral as income of prepaid admissions to events which will take place on a fixed schedule in a different taxable year is so similar to deferral of prepaid subscriptions that it would be an abuse of discretion to reject similar accounting treatment.

In any event the prepaid admission situation approaches much closer to certainty than the situations considered in *Automobile Club of Michigan, American Automobile Association*, or *Schlude*. [Footnotes omitted.]

Judicial reaction to *Artnell* has been mixed. * * *

Defendant's reaction, of course, is simply that "*Artnell* was wrongly decided." * * *

Out of this melange, one must choose a path. To use one of Justice Holmes' favorite expressions, I "can't help" but conclude that what Ebasco is pleased to call its "balanced and symmetrical" method of accounting does in fact clearly reflect its income. It achieves the desideratum of accurately matching costs and revenues by reason of the fact that the costs of earning such revenues are incurred at the time the services are performed. *See, Mooney Aircraft, supra*, 420 F.2d at 403. Entirely unlike the factual situations before the Supreme Court in the automobile club and dance studio cases, Ebasco's contractual obligations were fixed and definite. In no sense was Ebasco's performance of services dependent solely upon the demand or request of its clientele.

Based upon the foregoing considerations, it is necessary to conclude that Ebasco's method of accounting under which income is accrued as the related services are performed clearly reflects its income, and, accordingly, the Commissioner is not authorized by § 446(b) to impose another method of accounting. Therefore, the amounts accrued in Ebasco's "Unearned Income" account are not taxable until the year in which Ebasco performs the services which earn that income.

(A) *Financial Accounting for Service Transactions*

An ever-increasing portion of our gross national product consists of services, including providing customers with the use of both monetary (financing) and non-monetary resources (e.g., leasing, technology transfers, automobile club memberships, health spa memberships) as well as such personal services as legal, accounting, advertising, public relations, and technical consulting and servicing. Evidencing this trend is the fact that in its June, 1983 issue, Fortune Magazine initiated the "Fortune Service 500"—listing and providing data on the 500 largest service companies—similarly to its much older sibling—the 500 largest industrial companies listing. Yet, except for the most straightforward financing and leasing transactions, the accounting has been anarchistic and highly discretionary. Only recently has the profession begun to address the problems of proper recognition for service transactions. It is far from reaching adequate solutions because thus far the development of GAAP has been on an ad hoc basis.

At the outset of this chapter, we pointed out that the FASB's criterion of sound accounting from the point of view of the primary users, investors and creditors, is whether the accounting helps these users in their task of determining their own expectable cash flow. But we may suggest that in fact what accounting provides may be something less—perhaps just a set of convenient rules to provide auditors with guidelines to follow—a cookbook. Accounting for service transactions illustrates this possible characterization even more clearly than does accounting for sales of products.

It seems simple enough in the abstract to outline desirable accounting for services, keeping in mind the gradual accretion of income from performance of the earning process as in the *Boise Cascade* case. In 1978 the FASB issued an Invitation to Comment on an AICPA-proposed Statement of Position, Accounting for Service Transactions. That Draft sought to bring all service industries under the same accounting umbrella, notwithstanding the substantial economic differences among industries and the fact that many of the industries have no relation to each other. [Incidentally, here we see that revenues and expenses are both considered together. It is even more difficult to separate the two for service transactions than for sales of products—hence this subpart makes no pretext of doing so.]

AICPA, DRAFT STATEMENT OF POSITION, ACCOUNTING FOR SERVICE TRANSACTIONS FASB, INVITATION TO COMMENT, ACCOUNTING FOR CERTAIN SERVICE TRANSACTIONS
FASB, 1978.*

* * *

"8. A service transaction may involve a tangible product that is sold or consumed as an incidental part of the transaction or is clearly identifiable as secondary or subordinate to the rendering of the service. The following guidelines apply to transactions in which both services and products are provided:

(a) If the seller offers both a service and a product in a single transaction and if any product involved is not separately stated in such a manner that the total transaction price would vary as a result of the inclusion or exclusion of the product, the product is incidental to the rendering of the service and the transaction is a service transaction that should be accounted for in accordance with the recommendations in this statement of position. For example, equipment maintenance contracts that include parts in their fixed price are service transactions, even though there may be individual contracts in which the value provided under the contract in the form of a tangible product is ultimately greater than the value provided in the form of services.

(b) If the seller of a product offers a related service to purchasers of the product but separately states the service and product elements in such a manner that the total transaction price would vary as a result of the inclusion or exclusion of the service, the transaction consists of two components: a product transaction that should be accounted for separately as such and a service transaction that should be accounted for in accordance with the recommendations in this statement of position.

* * *

"10. Revenue from service transactions should be recognized based on performance, because performance determines the extent to which the earnings process is complete or virtually complete. Performance is the execution of a defined act or acts or occurs with the passage of time. Accordingly, revenue from service transactions should be recognized as follows:

(a) *Specific performance method* —Performance consists of the execution of a single act and revenue should be recognized when the act takes place. For example, a real estate broker should record sales commissions as revenue upon the consummation of a real estate transaction (also see paragraph 17).

(b) *Proportional performance method*—Performance consists of the execution of more than one act and revenue should be recognized based on the proportionate performance of each act. * * *

(c) *Completed performance method*—If services are performed in more than a single act, the proportion of services to be performed in the final act may be so significant in relation to the service transaction taken as a whole that performance cannot be deemed to have taken place until execution of that act. For example, a transportation company which agrees to transport freight between two locations, may perform many acts such as packing, loading, and actual transportation of the goods. However, the final act of delivering the freight to its destination is so significant that the company should recognize revenue upon delivery. If services are to be provided in an indeterminate number of acts over an indeterminate period of time, there may be no basis for estimating the degree to which performance has taken place. In these situations, revenue should be recognized when performance is completed (also see paragraph 17).

(d) *Collection method*—If there is a significant degree of uncertainty surrounding realization of service revenue (for example, many personal services), revenue should not be recognized until collection.

"Applying the Proportional Performance Method

"11. If a service transaction involves a specified number of identical or similar acts (for example, the processing of monthly mortgage payments by a mortgage banker), an equal amount of revenue should be recognized for each act. Based on experience, some companies may be able to estimate the number of acts provided for in the service arrangements. If the amounts related to the acts a company does not expect to perform are nonrefundable and do not escheat, total service revenues should be recognized equally over the number of acts the company reasonably expects to perform.

"12. If a service transaction involves a specified number of defined but not identical or similar acts (for example, a correspondence school that provides evaluation, lessons, examinations and grading, and so forth), the following guides for revenue recognition should be used:

(a) Revenue recognized for each act should be based on the ratio of the seller's direct costs to perform each act expected to be performed to the total estimated direct costs of the transaction, if such costs can be reasonably determined.

(b) If the measurements suggested in (a) are impractical or are not objectively determinable, revenue should be recognized on a systematic and rational basis over the estimated period during which the acts will be performed; the method selected should reasonably relate revenue recognition to performance. For example, the sales value of each act may be objectively determinable. Revenue should be recognized based on the ratio of the sales value of each of those acts to the total of such individual sales values. The straightline method should be used to recognize revenue if no other systematic and rational basis is more representative of the pattern in which proportional performance takes place.

"13.   If a service transaction involves an unspecified number of identical or similar acts with a fixed period of performance (for example, a maintenance contract on office equipment), revenue should be recognized on the straightline method over the specified period during which the acts will be performed, unless evidence shows that some other method is more representative of the pattern in which performance takes place.   Normal seasonality of service or prior experience as to the incidence of performance may constitute such evidence.   If the seller agrees to provide facilities for a fixed period and the costs incurred by the seller are substantially the costs of holding a facility available for use, only the straightline method should be used to recognize revenue.   Such performance is more closely related to the passage of time than to the incidence of use of the facility by the purchaser.

"Cost Recognition

"14.   The principles set forth in the professional literature (see, for example, paragraph 155 of APB Statement 4) for recognizing costs state, in general, that costs should be charged to expense in the period in which the revenue with which they are associated is recognized as earned.   Costs are not deferred, however, unless they are expected to be recoverable from future revenues.   Because of the wide range of service transactions and the variety of revenue recognition methods that may be appropriate depending on the circumstances, the division believes that more specific guidance is needed to implement those general principles.   The following paragraphs are intended to provide that guidance.

"Definitions

"15.   The following definitions related to costs have been adopted for purposes of this statement of position:

(a) *Initial direct costs* are costs incurred that are directly associated with negotiating and consummating service agreements.   *   *   *

(b) *Direct costs* are costs that have a clearly identifiable beneficial or causal relationship (i) to the services performed or (ii) to the level of services performed for a group of customers, for example, servicemen's labor and repair parts included as part of a service agreement.

(c) *Indirect costs* are all costs other than initial direct costs and direct costs.   They include provisions for uncollectible accounts, general and administrative expenses, advertising expenses, and general selling expenses.   *   *   *

"Indirect Costs

"16.   Indirect costs should be charged to expense as incurred.

"Initial Direct Costs and Direct Costs

"17. *Cost recognition under the specific performance and completed performance methods*—If revenues are recognized on a service transaction under the specific performance or completed performance methods as described in paragraphs 10(a) and 10(c), all initial direct costs and direct costs should be charged to expense at the time revenues are recognized. * * *

"18. *Cost recognition under the proportional performance method*—Initial direct costs should be charged to expense at the time revenues are recognized. Thus, initial direct costs should be deferred and allocated over the term of service performance in proportion to the recognition of service revenue. * * *

"19. The division believes that generally there is a close correlation between the amount of direct costs incurred and the extent of performance achieved. Since revenues are recognized in a manner related to performance achieved, direct costs, other than initial direct costs, should be charged to expense as incurred. * * *

"20. *Cost recognition under the collection method*—If the degree of uncertainty surrounding realization of service revenue is so significant that revenues are recognized only when collected, initial direct costs and direct costs should be charged to expense as incurred. * * *

"Initiation and Installation Fees

"23. A service transaction may involve the charge of a nonrefundable initiation fee with subsequent periodic payments for future services or a nonrefundable fee for installation of equipment essential to providing the future services with subsequent periodic payments for the services. Initiation and installation fees may in substance be wholly or partly an advance charge for future services, such as discussed below:

(a) *Initiation fees*—If there is an objectively determinable value of the franchise or privilege granted by the initiation fee itself, that value (not in excess of the initiation fee charged) should be considered revenue, and the related direct costs should be charged to expense at the initiation date. If the value of the initiation fee cannot be determined objectively, the fee should be considered an integral part of the service transaction including the future services. * * *

(b) *Inseparable installations*—If the equipment and its installation costs are essential for the service to be provided and are not normally offered for separate sale, the installation fee should be considered an advance charge for future services. The installation fee should be recognized as revenue over the estimated period future services are to be provided. Costs of installation and installed equipment, except for net amounts recoverable on removal of the equipment, should be deferred and amortized over the period the installation is expected to provide revenue.

Fiflis, Acctg, 4th Ed. ACB—9

(c) *Separable installations* —If the customer is able to and frequently does separately purchase the installation or the future services, the installation fee is not a service transaction (see paragraph 8(b))."

————

The FASB has adopted a series of pronouncements regulating a few service industries, which basically call for recognition of income in proportion to performance but which are not wholly consistent with the above SOP or among themselves.

In contrast to the relatively simple *Boise Cascade* situation, a few cases in point will illustrate the difficulties and the arbitrariness of the present GAAP for services.

Accounting for the simplest forms of use of monetary resources calls for recognizing income over the period of use. Hence, if the First National Bank lends $1,000 to a customer at 10% simple interest for five years, interest payable annually, the bank will recognize $100 revenue each year for the five years (diminished along with its other loans to some extent by a charge to Bad Debt Expense).

The same is true for simple conventional leases. Thus if a storekeeper leases a cash register for six months for $600, the lessor will accrue rental income on a straightline basis (i.e., equally each day) and the storekeeper will similarly accrue rental expense. Thus if the first two months of the term fall in year 1, rental revenue and expense, respectively, for year 1, are $200.

But there are other much more complex service transactions including more complex lease and monetary use transactions.

For example life insurance companies on sales of ordinary life insurance policies receive cash which they invest for their own benefit in return for undertaking and administering the pooling of the risks of mortality of policyholders. Typically the salesperson who sells the policy receives his or her commission at the time of the sale, the premiums are paid in a level amount for a period of time and the policy proceeds are paid on death.

Does the proposed SOP set forth supra tell us how to account for these events? Concerning accounting for the premium revenues, is "performance" the payment of the proceeds at death or is it the standing ready to pay throughout the existence of the policy? Or if both, is the payment of proceeds so significant that recognition of premium revenue should be deferred until then?

As to the cost, should the salesperson's commission be charged to expense when paid, amortized over some period or deferred until the policy proceeds are paid? Should the proceeds be deducted when paid or should they be anticipated by establishing a reserve throughout the life of the policy, or during its later years? In fact SFAS No. 60, *Accounting and Reporting by Insurance Enterprises* (1982), spreads the premium income and expenses over a period of years and the policy proceeds are expensed when incurred, all in accordance with a set of complex formulae which we need not consider here. The above-quoted draft SOP does not comport with this accounting for ordinary life companies except in the roughest sense—revenue and expense are recognized over the period of performance of the contract.

Similarly, other SFAS's provide specific guidance for a few industries under guidelines which deviate in varying degrees from the draft SOP. See, e.g., SFAS No. 45, *Accounting for Franchise Fee Revenue* (1981); No. 50, *Financial Reporting in the Record Music Industry* (1981); No. 51, *Financial Reporting by Cable Television Companies* (1981); No. 53, *Financial Reporting by Producers and Distributors of Motion Picture Films* (1981); No. 61, *Accounting for Title Plant* (1982); No. 63, *Financial Reporting by Broadcasters* (1982); No. 65, *Accounting for Certain Mortgage Banking Activities* (1982).

According to H.R. Jaenicke, *Survey of Present Practices in Recognizing Revenues, Expenses, Gains and Losses* (FASB, 1981):

> [S]everal alternative recognition methods are used for services. Some of those methods are inconsistent or conflict with recognition principles for analogous events . . . For example, recognition of initial franchise fee revenue must be delayed until performance is substantially complete, despite the widespread use of a proportional performance (percentage-of-completion) basis for many other service transactions and many long-term construction contracts.

> The relationship between revenue recognition and recognition of initial costs directly associated with negotiating and consummating service agreements varies widely. In some cases (for example, franchisor accounting), both revenue and directly related costs are deferred until it is deemed appropriate to recognize revenue. In other cases (for example, cable television accounting), those direct costs are recognized as expenses when incurred, and an equal amount of revenue is simultaneously recognized. A third alternative (for example, the proposed SOP on service transactions' discussion of the proportional performance method) assigns revenues to periods ratably as direct costs are incurred.

(B) Note Contrasting Financial Accounting With Tax Accounting as to the Realization Test for Services Rendered

As is apparent from *Boise Cascade*, income tax law resembles financial accounting in its use of concepts like income, expense, accrual and deferral. On audit of a taxpayer's income tax return, the starting point is the books of account, reflecting the thousands of normal accounting choices and judgments for the year involved. The mechanical techniques of calculating inventory, depreciation (when the Accelerated Cost Recovery System does not apply), bad debts, etc. for tax purposes follow those used for financial accounting purposes. Moreover, IRC § 446(a) states a general rule that taxable income shall be computed under the method of accounting on the basis of which the taxpayer regularly computes his income in keeping his books.

But *Boise Cascade* fails to illustrate that § 446(a) has been applied in practice merely to require the use of *an* accrual method of tax accounting when an accrual method of financial accounting is employed or *a* cash method for both tax and financial accounting. It has not been construed to require *identical* accounting for the details of transactions on both the tax return and the books. See Sobeloff, *New Prepaid Income Rules: IRS Reversal of Position Will Aid Many Taxpayers,* 33 J. Taxation 194, 199 at n. 25 (1970). There has been one long-extant exception, for LIFO inventory reporting, requiring a taxpayer to use LIFO reporting for financial reporting in order to be able to use it for tax reporting. IRC § 472. This is commonly referred to by tax practitioners as a "booking" requirement. For many years, the Internal Revenue Service has required "booking" in other situations as well. Raby & Richter, *Conformity of Tax and Financial Accounting,* J. Accountancy 42 (Mar., 1975).

Nevertheless, financial accounting and "tax accounting" required by the Internal Revenue Service frequently diverge, for the aim of the latter is to obtain tax payments (or often to encourage capital expenditures or to achieve other non-revenue purposes by special tax advantages). In the final analysis, therefore, the taxpayer and GAAP cannot decide on accounting for tax purposes, and IRC § 446(b) provides that if the method of accounting used by the taxpayer does not "clearly reflect income," the computation of taxable income shall be made under such method as in the opinion of the Commissioner of Internal Revenue does clearly reflect income. Thus, the IRS (or a court reviewing its determinations) ultimately decides what the principles of tax accounting will be. Important divergences therefore exist between permissible financial accounting and permissible tax accounting, and these divergences are themselves sources of difficult financial accounting problems. Tax authorities have expressed the hope that many of the divergences of tax accounting from financial accounting may be eliminated but the differences continue.[i]

For a brief period (1987–89) the Internal Revenue Code §§ 56(f) and (g) imposed a tax based on the difference between taxable income and financial income raising much concern that tax income would thus dictate GAAP. Presumably that is precisely what would have happened had these provisions extended beyond 1989.

5. SOME MISCELLANEOUS REVENUE TRANSACTIONS

(A) Non-reciprocal Transfers to the Accounting Entity

Suppose a majority shareholder or some nonshareholder for that matter (e.g., a municipality seeking to encourage local industry) makes a donation of cash or property to a corporation but receives nothing

---

i. See IRS News Release No. 1125 (Apr. 14, 1971), 1971 CCH Fed.Tax.Rep. ¶ 6608; former Commissioner of Internal Revenue Sheldon S. Cohen ably demonstrated why the differences probably will continue in Cohen, Accounting for Taxes, Finance and Regulatory Purposes—Are Variances Necessary? 44 Taxes 780 (1960).

tangible in return. How should this be accounted for by the corporation? APB Opinion No. 29, *Accounting for Nonmonetary Transactions,* ¶ 18 (1973), indicates that the transaction must be recorded by a debit to the asset (cash or property in the cases posited) at its value. Whether the credit is to a capital account ("Contributed Capital" or, to lawyers, "Capital Surplus") or income is not stated in this Opinion but it is generally credited to a capital account since it is a transaction for capital, not a transaction for profit.

For grants from governments, such as were once commonly made to attract industries to particular locales, there are variant practices. In addition to crediting capital or income, the choices include a credit to a deferred income account for amortization over some future period. Apparently another practice is to reduce the carrying value of any related asset. Thus if a local government donates land to a railroad to build an overpass, the value of the land may be credited to income, deferred income, capital, or the asset account for track.

If the grant is forfeitable on a failure to fulfill conditions, such as the railroad's failure to construct the overpass within two years, the credit, of course, must be to a liability or deposit account at least until the construction is substantially completed. See H. Jaenicke, supra at 124–25.

(B) Early Extinguishment of Debt

If a company on January 1, 19X1, had issued a bond payable for $1,000 at 10% interest, due in twenty years, and had received $1,000 cash, the bond would be shown as a liability at $1,000 on the balance sheet. If ten years later the same firm was able to issue a new ten year bond but at 20% interest, what would be the then present value of the first bond? It is certainly less than the second bond's value since the anticipated stream of cash flow (out from the debtor) for the next ten years aggregates $2,000 for the first bond and $3,000 for the second (interest plus return of principal).

See Appendix A of this book which indicates the present value of the first bond to the creditor, assuming 20% as the appropriate discount rate for all cash receipts, is $581 (the present value of a $100 annuity each year for ten years plus a $1,000 lump sum at the end of the tenth year). Thus, presumably, the debtor could buy back this first bond in the market place at $581. If it does so, the $419 difference from face value is credited to income as an extraordinary item at the time of repurchase and the 20% interest on the new debt is charged to income as paid. See SFAS No. 26, *Early Extinguishment of Debt* (1972). This is the accounting even if instead of repurchasing the first bond it is "refunded" by redeeming the old with new bonds, having face values of $581 and bearing 20% interest. Ibid. [SFAS No. 4, *Reporting Gains and Losses from Extinguishment of Debt* (1975), amended ¶ 20 of Opinion No. 26 to require such income to be separately shown as an extraordinary item on the income statement.]

On the subject of refunding generally, see Healy, *Treatment of Debt Discount and Premiums Upon Refunding*, 73 J. Accountancy 199 (1942).

(C) *"In Substance Defeasance"*

In mid–1982, Exxon Corp. reported a $130 million "profit" from *buying* for cash a sufficient amount of U.S. government bonds to generate cash to service the interest and principal on an old bond issue paying a lower-than-current market rate. Instead of refunding the old bonds, Exxon placed the government securities in trust, not showing them as an asset, but crediting cash for the purchase price, debiting the old bonds in their face amount, and crediting the difference as income. It was as if, using our prior illustration, the debtor corporation had retained the old bonds with the present value of $581, purchased government securities with a present value of $581 and made the following journal entry:

Bond (old)	$1,000	
Cash		$581
Income		419

Is this appropriate?

While not mentioning Exxon by name, the SEC stated, in Release No. 33–6421, 6 Fed.Sec.L.Rep. (CCH) ¶ 72,403 (1982) that such a transaction does not result:

> in any actual transfer or satisfaction of the debtor corporation's legal liability. The debtholders continue to look to the debtor corporation for repayment, and the debtholders may not even be aware of the transaction. Accordingly, in the "trust" arrangement, the debtor faces the risk of additional liability equal to the difference between the face value of the debt and the then market value of the collateral securities in the event the debt becomes immediately due because of a breach of debt covenants by either the debtor or the trustee. In case of bankruptcy, it is also unclear whether the dedicated assets are legally insulated from other creditors.

The FASB issued an "Action Alert" dated August 11, 1982, announcing its tentative conclusion that this debt should not be considered extinguished. According to The Wall St. Journal, Aug. 13, 1982, p. 4, col. 4:

> An Exxon spokesman said, "We feel the action we took was in accordance with generally accepted accounting principles that now exist, and our auditors have agreed." He added that the FASB proposal isn't final and is subject "to much review and comment."

Are accounting principles thus to be construed like a criminal code?

Now see SFAS No. 76, *Extinguishment of Debt and the Offsetting of Restricted Assets Against Related Debt* (1983), evidencing capitulation by the FASB, acquiescing in the Exxon technique. Did principle or power prevail here?

Presumably Exxon's reason for doing this was that, as a part-owner of Aramco (the Arabian American Oil Company—i.e., the Saudi family's oil marketing firm), it was being stuck with costs for oil in excess of rates for oil sold by other nations to other oil companies, thus its anticipated profit-showing for 1982 was inferior to other oil firms. The effect of the $130 million profit infusion just described would enhance the income statement that year. Is it not even more clear that the SEC's original action was correct?

Why did not Exxon merely repurchase its old bonds? Here keep in mind that the tax system is another important constraint on business decisions.

SFAS No. 76, *Extinguishment of Debt and the Offsetting of Restricted Assets Against Related Debt* (1983), prescribes standards for extinguishment of debt. Essentially, where a debtor company acquires U.S. government securities, or securities "guaranteed" or "backed" by the U.S. government, in an amount sufficient, with the interest, to meet scheduled interest and principal payments of an outstanding debt issue and places them in an irrevocable trust (undefined), SFAS No. 76 states that the "debtor shall consider the debt to be extinguished for financial reporting purposes." See Paragraphs 3 and 4. The SEC promptly issued FRR 15, *Interpretive Release Relating to Accounting for Extinguishment of Debt*, which established the following additional "requirements" a public company must meet in order to avail itself of the SFAS No. 76 extinguishment accounting:

(a) Only certain types of U.S. government backed securities will qualify for deposit to the trust. Specifically, the backing must run to the *timing* of the payment as well as ultimate collection. Very few U.S. government guaranteed or backed securities meet this requirement.

(b) The trustee must be independent, and trustees that meet the eligibility requirements of §§ 310(a)(1) and 310(a)(2) of the Trust Indenture Act of 1939 will be presumed to be appropriate trustees. FRR 15 is silent about trustees that do not meet those requirements.

(c) There must be an assessment of the "likelihood" of acceleration of the debt maturities, such as those due to violation of a covenant or due to cross-default provision involving a violation of a covenant of another debt issue. No standards are given for assessing the likelihood of acceleration, which may leave the matter to future determination by the courts.

(d) Irrevocable is defined: "The trust must be designed so that neither the corporation nor its creditors or others can rescind or revoke it, or obtain access to the assets."

(D) Troubled Debt Restructuring

Suppose a bank has loaned $1,000 to a debtor at 20% interest payable annually in arrears for a period of five years and, in the second year, the debtor fails to pay interest, and the loan is renegotiated to extend the due date for five more years and reduce interest to 3% from the end of the first year. Has the bank incurred an accounting loss in year two?

As a matter of economics, comparing present values, it has. If 20% is the going rate, and the debt and interest were collectible, the present value of the original loan at the end of year one, would be $1,000; whereas, the 3% loan has a present value of $315 and the bank has traded an asset carried on its books at $1,000 for one worth $315.

But if a large bank instead of having lent $1,000 in our hypothetical case, had lent, say $3 billion, to a borrower in Mexico at 20% for five years and then had renegotiated the loan to a ten year one at 3%, the loss of present value would be over $2.7 billion and could be a cause for some irritation on the part of the bank's depositors (or U.S. taxpayers who may be called upon to underwrite these loans) if they were so informed.[j] To avoid this discomfort, SFAS No. 15, *Accounting for Debtors and Creditors for Troubled Debt Restructuring* (1977), sweeps the facts under the rug and permits the debt to be carried at the original amount although receipts will be considered returns of capital until the face amount is recouped. *SFAS No. 15* does not require disclosure of the fair value of the new note.

Is this accounting that serves the interests of the society and of investors in banks?

In fairness to the accounting profession it should be said that it did attempt to have the loss recognized on the books of the banks, but the pressures from bankers were overpowering. For a description of the contest during the thick of it (when the troubled debts were on private real estate developments) see T. Fiflis & H. Kripke, *Accounting for Business Lawyers* 309 (2d ed. 1977) where we also then predicted the current, much larger, problem of defaults by third-world nations. Nevertheless the banks, unlike the S&L's, were able to buy enough time with this device to enable them to gradually write off their third world debt without precipitating a panic.

C. "BY–PASSING" THE INCOME STATEMENT

The expression, "the bottom-line," has become part of the American language, connoting the perceived ultimate hard reality about any matter under discussion. It is derived from the simplistic notion that the bottom-line of the income statement—net earnings—contains the quintessential information desired by readers of the financial statements who use it to compare with prior years' earnings of the same firm and with earnings of other firms.

In fact, the typical income statement displays much more than the simple difference between operating revenues and expenses on the

---

j. At the end of 1982 the top ten U.S. banks had made 10% of their loans outstanding (amounting to 170% of their equi- ty) to third-world nations. Bank of America had 60% of its equity exposed in Mexican debt, and Citicorp, 58%.

bottom line. Further, as already noted, there is a good deal of supplementary disclosure in footnotes (or parenthetic expressions within the body of the statements) of executory contracts (e.g., leases), or inflation data.

But there is another aspect of the isolated earnings figure which is troublesome. Should it include or should it exclude a material amount paid on a judgment for a defective product manufactured and sold in some prior period? Or a large gain or loss on the sale of a plant in the current period?

The argument for exclusion of these items as "prior period adjustments" or "extraordinary items" of the current period would be that, to the extent they cannot be expected to be regularly recurring, they make reported income of the period useless as a datum for predicting future income. See APB Opinion No. 9, *Reporting the Results of Operations* ¶¶ 10–12 (1966), for the arguments, favoring exclusion, known as the "current operating performance" view.

On the other hand, the subjectivity of determining probable recurrence may tempt some managements to include gains in earnings while omitting losses. In any event, disparate judgments may be expected, making difficult a comparison among different companies or among different periods for the same company. The arguments for inclusion (the "all-inclusive" view) are set forth in *APB Op. No. 9.*

Although the market may not be fooled by these different reporting methods, some think it is, and accounting has struggled long and hard over this question which has come to be labelled, "by-passing the income statement."

Accounting for the time being has resolved the problem by requiring inclusion in income of virtually all prior period adjustments and extraordinary items but requiring some of them to be shown on the income statement under a separate caption such as "Extraordinary Items" (with related tax effects) after the figure for income from ordinary operations.

D. FORMAT OF THE INCOME STATEMENT— NON-RECURRING ITEMS

More specifically, all "extraordinary items" and matters which were once considered "prior period adjustments" (with the exception of (1) corrections of errors in prior income statements, (2) recognition of certain tax benefits realized from the purchase of subsidiary companies, (3) changes resulting from certain changes of GAAP used in the financials and (4) certain changes in interim financials which are to be credited or debited to retained earnings) are to be included in the figure of net income in the income statement. However, the extraordinary items must be separately shown before net income, as follows:

Income before extraordinary items	$X
Extraordinary items (less applicable income tax)	$Y
Net income	$Z

The criteria for extraordinary items are severely restrictive, limiting them substantially. See APB Opinion No. 30, *Reporting the Results of Operations,* ¶¶ 19–24 (1973). The four prior period adjustments noted above are established in SFAS No. 16, *Prior Period Adjustments,* ¶ 11 (1977) and its predecessors cited therein.

Incidentally, no matter how the particular item is displayed on the income statement, if it is included in income, the journal entry will include a debit to expense (or loss) or a credit to revenue (or gain). To by-pass instead requires a debit or credit to a balance sheet equity account, usually retained earnings.

Two other non-recurrent income items are treated separately like extraordinary items and for the same reason. One is income during the period from discontinued operations, as when a business segment has been sold or closed down. The other is the effect on income from changes in accounting principles; e.g., a change from straight-line to some accelerated depreciation method. The GE Statement of Earnings, infra, p. 524, illustrates the treatment of an extraordinary item and two changes in accounting principles.

The GE statement illustrates the three standard divisions of an income statement required by GAAP:

Income from ordinary (recurring) operations after taxes	$X
Income from non-recurring items (extraordinary items, discontinued operations and accounting changes)	$Y
Earnings per share	$Z

Part C

COST ALLOCATION

Chapter IV

ACCOUNTING FOR INVENTORIES

OBJECTIVES

1. Understand the wide range of measurements of inventory costs under GAAP which impact, dollar for dollar, income, current assets and net assets.

2. Observe the widespread abuses in inventory accounting due to the practical difficulties of auditing inventories and illustrate the responsibilities of auditors.

RELEVANCE FOR LAWYERS

Inventories are difficult to audit; in addition GAAP permit widespread differences in the carrying value of inventory, and, consequently, variations in charges against income for the cost of goods sold. Because private credit agreements, indentures for preferred stock and publicly held debt, tax laws and other legal regulations depend on inventory accounting, business lawyers must be familiar with GAAP and GAAS for inventories and their abuses in order to draft, administer and litigate these regulations. Moreover, costs of manufactured inventories are highly relevant in investment analysis and very often of great consequence to lawyers in measuring damages in business litigation, considering antitrust issues, and interpreting government contracts.

A. INTRODUCTION

We have already described the mechanics of bookkeeping for Inventory and Cost of Goods Sold Expense in Chapter I, and the two techniques used, the "periodic inventory" and "perpetual inventory" methods, which you may wish to review for study of this chapter.

In order to determine income for a firm engaged in buying, or manufacturing, and selling tangible goods, the costs incurred for purchase or manufacture of the goods which have been sold are matched against related revenue from those sales. *ARB No. 43, Chapter 4, Statement 2,* § 4 (1953). To accomplish this matching, the costs must be allocated between goods which have been sold and inventory—goods which have not yet been sold. For this reason, the same criteria must be applied to the two questions: (1) When are goods deemed sold so as to result in recognition of Sales Revenue? (2) When are goods deemed sold so as to result in recognition of Cost of Goods Sold Expense?

As to those goods not deemed sold, they are deferred costs, shown as an asset, closing Inventory. From this it is readily seen that for each dollar allocated to closing Inventory, and therefore *not* charged to Cost of Goods Sold Expense, operating income of the current period is increased by a dollar. In addition, gross profit margin (sales less cost of goods sold, reduced to a common denominator as a percentage of sales) is similarly affected. Operating income is material in many contexts, and gross profit margin is a very important datum to creditors, investors, and tax auditors who compare margins of other companies and of the same firm for other periods to detect variations in performance. To illustrate, see the following simple income statements based on different assumptions as to the amount of closing Inventory.

Income Statement for X Corp. for the Year 19X1

		(Assuming closing Inventory of $600)		(Assuming closing Inventory of $700)
Revenues		$1,500		$1,500
Less Cost of Goods Sold:				
Opening Inventory	$ 700		$ 700	
Plus Purchases	400		400	
	$1,100		$1,100	
Minus closing Inventory	**600**		**700**	
Cost of Goods Sold		500		400
Gross Profit		**$1,000**		**$1,100**
Less other expenses		300		300
Net Profit		**$ 700**		**$ 800**

Also creditors attach great significance to current assets, one of the more important of which for manufacturing and merchandising companies, is closing Inventories, because of their liquidity. Because of one or another of these impacts of inventory accounting, many managers cannot resist the temptation to stretch or violate GAAP.

Problem

4–1. *Problem.* Suppose you represent the stockholders in a class action brought against officers, directors and the firm's auditors for negligence in failing to detect and stop embezzlement through "skimming" by the president of a merchandising firm. Her technique was to cause about ten percent of sales, and corresponding cash receipts, to not be recorded, and to pocket the cash. For several years the company's gross profit margin varied from 48% to 52% but in the three years in which the embezzlements occurred, the margins were 44%, 40% and 38%. Should these facts be admissible as evidence in the suit? For what purpose?

See Chapter XIV infra p. 682, discussing SAS No. 56 on "analytical techniques".

BOWMAN & BOURDON, INC. v. ROHR

United States District Court, D. Massachusetts, 1969.
296 F.Supp. 847, affirmed per curiam 417 F.2d 780 (1st Cir.1969).

FORD, DISTRICT JUDGE. Plaintiff's principal claim in this action is for rescission or damages based on defendants' alleged misrepresentation and failure to state material facts in connection with a sale of the stock of C. Drew and Company, Incorporated (Drew).

* * *

In January, 1966 plaintiff Bowman visited the Drew plant and met with Rohr to discuss the possibility of Bowman's making an investment in Drew. * * * Rohr showed Bowman financial statements covering the operations of the company for the year 1965 and for the six-month period ending on June 30, 1966. These statements indicated that Drew had shown an operating profit of $16,595.84 for 1965, and an operating loss of $1,020.71 for the following six-month period. Rohr told Bowman this loss had been due to difficulties encountered in connection with a government contract, that the situation was under control, and that the company had "turned the corner" and was now operating profitably.

Bowman requested substantiation of the claim that the company was operating profitably. It was agreed that an inventory would be taken as of October 31, 1966.

Bowman was present on the first of several days spent in making the physical count, but then left. After the count was completed, the items were priced by [defendant] Rohr and his clerical employees.

Items of completed products or work in process were shown on the Drew inventory at a cost figure composed of the elements of material cost, direct labor costs, and an allocation of overhead expenses. The cost elements were determined by Rohr. Material cost he calculated on the basis of steel prices and his determination, based on his experience in the business, of the amount of steel used in each tool. Labor unit costs were based on a system which Rohr had instituted of maintaining production records showing how many of a particular tool were put through a particular process by a particular worker in a week, and on Rohr's knowledge of the wage rates of each such worker.

After completion of the pricing Rohr communicated the total inventory figure to the accountants who prepared the requested financial statements. These showed an operating profit of $2,862.80 for the four-month period ending October 31, 1966. Bowman received a copy of these statements, but at this time neither he nor the accountants were given any information about the inventory other than the total figure.

Negotiations between Bowman and Rohr were resumed, and resulted in an oral agreement in December and a written contract in January under which Rohr sold all his stock in Drew to Bowman's corporation, the corporate plaintiff here. On January 26, 1967, Bowman assumed control of Drew. Bowman shortly after taking over Drew loaned $31,675 to Drew. * * *

When financial statements were prepared for Drew for the fiscal year ending June 30, 1967, these statements showed an operating loss for the year of $77,000. Bowman then hired an accountant to review the financial data. In connection with this review he asked for and received for the first time the original inventory sheets of the October, 1966 inventory.

Comparison of the unit costs of items listed on the October, 1966 inventory with the unit costs shown for the same items on the June 30, 1966 inventory showed many changes in the unit material and labor costs from June to October. There were both increases and decreases in these cost figures but the net result was an increase. * * *

    * * *

The accountant's revised financial statements as of October 30, 1966, adjusted by using for the October inventory the unit prices shown on the June inventory, indicated an operating loss for Drew for the four-month period of approximately $13,500, instead of a $2800 profit.

    * * *

Rohr in his testimony conceded that he had made many changes in unit prices. While he disagreed in part with the figures of Shaller, the accountant, he conceded that his increases in unit prices had added at least $3000 to the total of the October inventory and that without these increases the financial statements would have shown an operating loss for the four-month period.

    * * *

Plaintiffs based their claim for recovery on the provisions of § 12 and § 17 of the Securities Act of 1933, 15 U.S.C. § 77*l* and § 77q and particularly on § 10(b) of the Securities Exchange Act of 1934, 15 U.S.C. § 78j(b), and Rule 10b–5 promulgated thereunder, 17 C.F.R. § 240.10b–5, which impose liability, *inter alia,* for misrepresentations of material facts in connection with the sale of securities.

* * * The real issue is whether Rohr by his conduct has made any untrue statement of a material fact or omitted to state a material fact so as to make him liable under Rule 10b–5(2).

* * * This question of profitable operation was clearly a material fact, affecting the value of the Drew stock. So also was the size of the inventory. As was obvious to both parties, the October inventory would be a factor in the accountant's preparation of the financial statements which would confirm or disprove Rohr's statement as to profitable operation. It is also clear that Bowman was relying on Rohr to produce a correct inventory figure.

As Rohr has admitted, the changes in unit prices were substantial enough to determine whether the financial statement would show a profit or loss for the four-month period. Of course, if Rohr deliberately fixed unit costs at an inflated figure, that would constitute misrepresentation of a material fact. But even assuming that Rohr's increases in unit labor cost figures were made in good faith, based on the best information available to him, and reflected as accurately as could be done the true cost of the tools, a question still remains. The net result of these changes was to increase the total of the October inventory, and ultimately to produce on the financial statement a profit figure which did not represent a true profit on operations but merely a bookkeeping profit reflecting the change in the basis for pricing the tools in inventory. The resulting financial statements, therefore, did not reflect the true picture of the profitability of Drew's operations. In the absence of any knowledge of the changes in unit labor costs, these statements were clearly deceptive. Consequently, Rohr's failure to reveal to Bowman the fact that he had made these changes was an omission to state a material fact necessary in order to make the statements made, in the light of the circumstances under which they were made, not misleading.

* * *

The October financial statements of Drew do not show any real operating profit, but only an apparent profit due to Rohr's price adjustment. The actual result of Drew's business for the four-month period was an operating loss. Drew had been losing money before the four-month period. It has been losing money ever since. Rohr's statement in August, 1966, that the company had turned the corner and was operating profitably was an untrue statement of a material fact.

Rohr, of course, knowingly made the changes in unit costs. While not an accountant by profession, he is a Chartered Life Underwriter, and has had training in accounting. He certainly knew that the increases he was making would eventually result in an apparent increase in operating profit on the financial statements, a profit figure which would be misleading in the absence of any knowledge of the unit price changes.

Plaintiff seeks rescission of the contract for the sale of the stock, tendering the stock to Rohr and seeking return of the $89,000 paid. Rescission is a normal remedy in such cases and is appropriate here.

*   *   *

Judgment will be entered for plaintiffs in accordance herewith.

Note

4–2. *Inventory Fraud.* Note that in *Bowman & Bourdon,* there was fraud whether or not the closing Inventory valuation was correct because of the effect on reported income for the period of the change. Brief consideration of the possibility that the new valuation was correct suggests that it probably was. Practitioners quickly learn that closely held businesses often *understate* Inventory in order to understate income for tax purposes and doctor their books to avoid discovery on an income tax audit. When some of these firms later "go public" or make an exempt offering requiring disclosure of financial data under the securities laws, or otherwise sell an interest in the business, if fraud liability is to be avoided, the valuations must be corrected and any contingent tax or other liability resulting from the understatement must be disclosed. Frequently the managers choose instead to forego sale or the financing and the hoped-for benefits.

Once a firm is publicly held, the temptation is the opposite—to overstate Inventory valuations so as to inflate income to bring glory to the managers or add to their incentive compensation. One such case in which a company which had so practiced to deceive, then continued its tangled web to weave, is Cenco, Inc. v. Seidman & Seidman, 686 F.2d 449 (7th Cir. 1982).

In *Cenco,* the management first inflated the Inventory and hence income for the purpose of selling its stock at inflated prices, often by issuing the stock in a takeover of another firm. After so gorging, the management later decided to cover up the fraud by pretending that inventory was being destroyed by fires and other disasters and, with a gall reminiscent of the parenticide who threw himself on the mercy of the court because he was an orphan, sought still another benefit by making false claims to insurers for losses from the phony destruction.

Some of the details are described in a related case, SEC v. Cenco, Inc., 436 F.Supp. 193 (N.D. Ill.1977), at pp. 195–96:

> [A]ccording to the [SEC], [this] was [not] simply a paper caper, but it also involved journeys by several individual defendants to warehouses around the country where they prepared documents and arranged for some portions of inventory to be shipped to a central site or to a public warehouse, from which they were later returned to company facilities. Another alleged aspect of inventory manipulation concerned shipment of some products to the defendant packaging company where they were repacked in new cartons with labels reflecting a larger content number than actually existed.

For the second stage of the fraud, the SEC complaint further alleged (436 F.Supp. at 195):

. . . that in order to conceal the previous inventory inflation some of the individual defendants launched an elaborate plan of simulated inventory destruction to adjust Cenco's financial status and reports. This plan during 1974 and 1975 allegedly involved manipulation of computer listings utilized in checks on inventory and preparation of false computer information to support the claims of destruction, submission of altered documents to the auditors, presentation of inaccurate information to the Board of Directors in an effort to provide economic justification for reducing inventory levels by destruction rather than a less drastic method, and the filing of falsified reports to the SEC.

For a history of the extensive civil and criminal litigation in this matter, see In re Cenco Inc. Securities Litigation, 529 F.Supp. 411 (N.D. Ill.1982), and Cenco, Inc. v. Seidman & Seidman, 686 F.2d 449 (7th Cir. 1982).

Inventory fraud has always been a favorite sport. See in addition to the above and others too numerous to cite, the classic case, In re McKesson & Robbins, 8 SEC 853 (1941), and a more recent case, Bernstein v. Crazy Eddie, Inc., 702 F.Supp. 962 (E.D.N.Y.1988). "Eddie" is currently a fugitive from justice.

B. WHAT SHOULD BE COUNTED AS INVENTORY?

At the close of the period, when inventory of a widget business is counted, would it be wrong simply to have the stock clerk count up the widgets on hand in the stockroom and on the shelves and use that count to calculate the dollar value of the widgets inventory? This count would fail to include goods which have been ordered from suppliers and even paid for, or those shipped out by the business and, in either case, en route C.O.D., F.O.B. shipping point, on consignment, on approval, or on condition. And it would include goods sold but not yet shipped. Would such a count be correct? What criteria are to be considered in resolving this question of what to include in inventory given the importance of inventory to both the income statement and balance sheet? See the following excerpt.

P. GRADY, ARS NO. 7, INVENTORY OF GENERALLY ACCEPTED ACCOUNTING PRINCIPLES FOR BUSINESS ENTERPRISES, 242–243

AICPA (1965).*

"Consideration of title. Legal title to inventories, and to other assets on the balance sheet, may be the line of demarcation followed in determining the inclusion of specific items. This rule should not be followed blindly; it has its limitations as a satisfactory basis for settling doubtful cases and, under certain circumstances, may be disregarded. Customarily, purchases in transit are included in inventory and sales in transit are excluded, regardless of the status of title, although purchases in transit shipped F.O.B. the purchaser's plant may properly be excluded from inventory. For accounting purposes, the treatment should be consistent between periods.

"Following are examples of items that should be included in inventories, following the rule of legal title:

Goods in transit (shipped F.O.B. the vendor's shipping point on or prior to the balance-sheet date) should be in the purchaser's inventory.

Consignments out (in the hands of the consignee) should be in the consignor's inventory.

Bailments (in the hands of the bailee) should be in the bailor's inventory.

Goods out on approval (in the hands of the prospective customer) should be in the seller's inventory.

Protective title to C.O.D. and certain types of export shipments remains with the seller until payment is made; the seller of goods on the installment basis may also retain protective title. Shipments under these arrangements are customarily accounted for as sales by the seller before payment is made and title passes. The important consideration is not one of title, but whether the receivable is collectible."

Two other accountants, in describing this practice, have intimated that deviation from legal title is somehow a questionable practice, stating: "There are a number of limitations to the legal rule *as a practical solution* to inventory questions, and *where there is no legal controversy, present or imminent,* other more practical criteria are often employed." *Accountants' Handbook* 12.21 (Wixon & Kell, eds., 4th ed., 1956). This deference of these accountants for some imagined "legal rule" is clearly incorrect. No legal rule states that inventory accounting depends on title. Legal title fixes GAAP only if the accountants say so. If accounting custom is otherwise, that custom is GAAP. For an illustration of the correct view, see Pacific Grape Products Co. v. Commissioner of Internal Revenue, 219 F.2d 862, 869 at n. 10 (9th Cir. 1955), quoting Judge Opper dissenting in the Tax Court opinion below (17 T.C. at 1110): "Methods of keeping records do not spring in glittering perfection from some unchangeable natural law but are devised to aid businessmen in maintaining sometimes intricate accounts."

In fact, it now seems clear that considerations other than title often do apply: most importantly, whether the related revenue from the sale of goods is to be recognized. For example we have it from Mr. Grady that when protective title to already-shipped goods is retained by the seller, the goods nevertheless are excludable from the seller's inventory if the receivable is collectable. Moreover, we have seen in Chapter III on revenue recognition that under SFAS No. 48, *Revenue Recognition When Right of Return Exists* (1981), revenue from goods sold on approval is to be recognized not according to whether title has passed but based on other specified criteria. If the revenue is recognized, in order properly to match cost of goods sold, the inventory will be diminished, whereas if revenue is not recognized, the goods must be included in inventory. Since the criteria of *SFAS No. 48* are basically independent of legal title, legal title does not dictate whether to include or exclude the item in inventory.

Nevertheless to the extent it continues to regulate *revenue recognition* on sale of goods, legal title of necessity regulates inventory accounting, but only by virtue of the *matching* logic.

Consistency between periods is the other important consideration as Grady makes clear. Once the criteria for inclusion or exclusion from inventory are fixed, the entity must classify goods into includable and excludable categories and calculate the number of units to be included by a physical count unless it is on a "perpetual inventory" method, although even then a physical count is used to verify the records and take into account losses by errors, theft, leakage, spoilage and the like.

Notes

4–3. *Auditors' Responsibility for Inventory Errors.* If inventory is based on a physical count or on records, what is to prevent an unscrupulous management from overstating profits each year by the simple expedient of reporting the count at a figure higher than the actual count? What is the auditor's duty? See In the Matter of McKesson & Robbins, Inc., 8 SEC 853 (1941), summarized in *ASR 19* (1940); *SAS No. 1*, §§ 331, 542 (1973); *ASR 90* (1962).

For the *Cenco* inventory fraud, previously noted, in *ASR 196,* 1934 Act Release No. 12,752, 10 SEC Dkt. 9, [1937–82 Transfer Binder for Accounting Series Releases] Fed.Sec.L.Rep. (CCH) ¶ 72,218 (1977), the Securities and Exchange Commission staff painstakingly described the audit failures. A small fraction of the SEC's report (pp. 62,521–62,523) gives the flavor of a faulty audit:

> As a part of the observation of the physical count of inventory, Seidman & Seidman auditors checked the accuracy of the CMH [a Cenco subsidiary] counting procedures by test counting the results recorded by CMH personnel. Seidman & Seidman recorded certain of these test counts on schedules which were included in the observation workpapers. The purpose of recording these test counts was to provide evidential matter upon which the auditors could reach a conclusion on the reliability of the CMH representations of the quantities reflected in the computer listings.
>
> * * *
>
> The comparison of recorded test counts to the computer listings in the nine warehouse locations in which the inventory count was observed indicated error rates ranging from .9% to 38.8% of the test counts, with error rates in excess of 10% in several locations.

* * *

Seidman & Seidman did attempt to ascertain the reasons for the differences in [one location's] comparisons, following discovery that the bulk of the differences were uniformly an increase by a multiple of ten. A similar pattern also appeared in another comparison. The auditors first demanded an explanation from Cenco management and were informed by the former director of CMH operations that the pattern of differences was attributable to errors made by a key-punch operator. The auditors then asked to see the inventory tags, but the same CMH official stated that the tags had been destroyed. Seidman & Seidman did not ascertain the extent to which such "key-punch errors" might have affected the untested portion of the inventory listing. The Seidman & Seidman workpapers do not contain any reference to this investigation. Without attempting any further procedures, the auditors apparently accepted management's explanation and concluded that no adjustments to the bulk of the . . . inventory were required.

Seidman & Seidman undertook alternative procedures in another audit area which was in part related to the CMH quantity representations. The Seidman & Seidman auditor who performed the price testing of the CMH inventory determined that, as in previous years, in numerous instances CMH was unable to produce sufficient vendor invoices to support the purchase by CMH of the quantities being price tested. This was true even though Seidman & Seidman ultimately accepted vendor invoices reflecting the purchase of the item by any CMH branch, regardless of the location of the inventory actually being price tested. The alternative procedure utilized in this instance suggested that even if CMH had sold none of the inventory items during the preceding year, CMH could not account for the increase in quantity between April 30, 1972 and April 30, 1973. While Seidman & Seidman's records indicate that substantial time was devoted to the CMH inventory, the auditors did not, as we believe they should have, further extend their procedures in view of these results.

* * *

Although Seidman & Seidman was aware of a significant overstock problem, it did not, as its audit program required, perform any documented analysis of the rate of turnover of the CMH inventory and did no other similar testing. Based on the results of the physical inventory the staff has calculated that the rate of inventory turnover was significantly below industry standards. Although we recognize that the function of an independent auditor is not to review the appropriateness of management business decisions, we believe that an analysis of the rate of inventory turnover as well as appropriate comparison of the rate to industry standards and other suitable tests are important audit procedures which generate significant evidential matter regarding the salability of goods on hand.

Seidman & Seidman prepared a schedule which set forth the comparative inventory balances at April 30, 1972 and April 30, 1973 for a number of the CMH branches. This schedule reflected significant increases from the prior year. A CMH financial officer wrote on this schedule management's explanations for the increases in inventory amounts. Seidman & Seidman did not attempt to determine the reasonableness or credibility of these explanations. It is our opinion that Seidman & Seidman unduly relied on these explanations and did not take those steps necessary under the circumstances to verify their reasonableness. This is particularly so in light of the fact that the amount of increase in inventory was substantially greater than the corresponding increase in sales.

* * *

4–4. *Fraud Against, and Fraud for; By Management and By Others.* Since it was the audited firm's own management which was the primary wrongdoer in *Cenco,* an interesting question arises if the audited firm is held liable to investors, whether the auditor is liable to the firm for negligent failure to detect the fraud of the managers. Does the resolution depend on whether the fraud was *against* the audited firm (e.g., embezzlement) or *on behalf of* the audited firm and against outsiders (as in *Cenco*)? Or on whether the wrongdoers are upper echelon or lower echelon employees? Judge Posner in Cenco, Inc. v. Seidman & Seidman, 686 F.2d 449 (7th Cir.1982), thought both factors highly relevant and held that the corporation could recover where top managers falsified the records for the purpose of benefitting the corporation.

Cenco was held not applicable in cases where the corporation is insolvent and the action is for the ultimate benefit of creditors although the claim is that of the corporation. E.g., Schact v. Brown, 711 F.2d 1343, 1348 (7th Cir.1983). To the same effect is Bonhiver v. Graff, 311 Minn. 111, 248 N.W.2d 291 (1976) (a case preceding *Cenco*).

4–5. *Purchase Commitments.* Assume Tofu Corp. orders $30,000 worth of soybeans to be used in making its product for sale, paying nothing down. At the time of the order, what journal entry will be made on its books? None. See *Tooey v. Percival,* supra Chapter III. If $10,000 cash is paid with the order, what entry will be made? Obviously, the Cash account must be credited in the amount of $10,000; the balancing debit is made to an account which may be entitled "Deposits on Orders," "Purchase Commitments," or the like. Is that an asset or an expense account?

C. ACCOUNTING FOR INVENTORIES OF MANUFACTURING CONCERNS; COST ACCOUNTING

Cost accounting for manufactured goods affects not only the income statement and balance sheet but is also determinative in many pricing decisions. Since many legal disputes center in pricing questions, cost accounting questions are met frequently in a legal practice. For example, damages in actions on contracts for the delivery of goods may depend on cost accounting concepts. See Vitex Manufacturing Corp. v. Caribtex Corp., 377 F.2d 795 (3d Cir.1967) (seller of goods entitled to recover sale price less direct costs saved on buyer's breach by non-acceptance, thereby granting seller the contribution of the broken contract toward direct costs). Cases involving charges of antitrust violations under the Robinson–Patman Act for charging prices below cost obviously involve cost accounting. In fact any case in which value of a product or service supplied is in issue involves cost accounting concepts. Thus where the Bureau of Land Management sued to recover the cost of quelling a forest fire negligently started by the defendant, allocation of the BLM's overhead was allowed in addition to direct costs. See the unreported case, United States v. Denver & Rio Grande Railroad Co., C–74–145 (D.Utah 1975) (cited in United States v. Reserve Mining Co., 423 F.Supp. 759 (D.Minn.1976) (overhead costs of Corps of Engineers recoverable in suit to recover for environmental clean-up). Perhaps of more current importance, cost accounting concepts will apply in "Superfund" and other clean-up cases which involve huge sums. See also Annot., *Construction of "Cost–Plus" Contracts,* 2 ALR 126 (1919), 27 ALR 48 (1923); Annot., *Overhead Expense as Recoverable Element of Damages,* 3 ALR 3d 689 (1965); see Moyle, *Accounting Techniques for Establishing a Cost Differential Defense Under the Robinson–Patman Act,* 39 Notre Dame L.Rev. 1 (1963); Taylor, *Cost Accounting Under the Robinson–Patman Act,* 3 Antitrust Bull. 188 (Mar.—Apr. 1958); Sawyer, *Accounting and Statistical Proof in Price Discrimination Cases,* 36 Iowa L.Rev. 244 (1951). In general, see Simon, *Cost Accounting and the Law,* 39 Acctg.Rev. 884 (1964).

Lawyers on either side of such cases should be aware of the arbitrary, conventional nature of cost accounting. For the techniques of cost accounting, see the Appendix to this chapter.

Another fact which may be of practical importance may be noted. Defense contracts are based on costs to a very great extent. (Even if few of them are priced at "cost plus" a percentage of cost, the pricing is usually agreed to be based on "reasonableness.") From 1970 to 1980 the federal government had in force a "Cost Accounting Standards Board" which fixed cost accounting standards for these contracts. But as part of the deregulatory efforts of the period, it was abolished in 1980. After a decade of scandal in defense contracting, however, with overcharges estimated by one observer at $50 billion annually, it was reinstated in early 1989. A similar organization is now established as an independent body in the Office of Federal Procurement Policy. Its task covers all government procurement contracts in excess of $500,000. See J. Accountancy 16–17 (Jan. 1989).

D. VALUATION OF INVENTORY

The second major problem of inventory accounting for both merchandisers and manufacturers (the first being what to count in inventory) is how to value the goods which are included in closing inventory after determining their quantity. There are two modes of valuation used in varying circumstances: (1) cost or market, whichever is lower; and (2) net realizable value.

1. COST

(A) What Is Included in Cost?

ARB NO. 43, CHAPTER 4, STATEMENT 3
AICPA, 1953.*

"The primary basis of accounting for inventories is cost which has been defined generally as the price paid or consideration given to acquire an asset. As applied to inventories, cost means in principle the sum of the applicable expenditures and charges directly or indirectly incurred in bringing an article to its existing condition and location.

"Discussion

" * * * The definition of cost as applied to inventories is understood to mean acquisition and production cost.[2] * * * "

Problem and Note

4–6. Problem. Are the following items (all received and paid for by X Corp. and all relating to merchandise held for sale by X Corp.) to be included in inventory or excluded under Statement 3?

(a) Freight charges on merchandise purchased.

(b) Insurance premiums for insurance against loss while merchandise was in transit to X Corp.

(c) Storage costs after merchandise is received.

(d) Storage costs for Swiss cheese for 60 days after received by X Corp. (Assume the cheese must be aged the 60 days to make it suitable for sale.)

(e) Salaries and overhead of merchandise purchasing department.

(f) Quantity discount on merchandise purchased.

(g) Cash discount for prompt payment on merchandise purchased.

See *Technical Issues Feature,* J. Accountancy 80–81 (Oct. 1987).

4–7. *Interest Cost in Financing Inventory.* Most dealers in automobiles, appliances, and equipment do not pay cash for their inventory, but finance the purchase on a "floor plan" arrangement, and may pay interest for several months before the goods are sold and the debt paid. Is this interest a current interest expense or should it be added to the cost of the related inventory? See SFAS No. 34, *Capitalization of Interest Cost,* ¶ 38 (1979):

> Some believe that interest should be capitalized as a cost of holding assets, but, in general in the present accounting model, costs are not added to assets subsequent to their readiness for use. Consideration of that proposal would require a comprehensive reexamination of a fundamental principle underlying present practice. One of the

2. In the case of goods which have been written down below cost at the close of a fiscal period, such reduced amount is to be considered the cost for subsequent accounting purposes.

consequences of restricting the focus to acquisition cost was that capitalization of interest as a holding cost was rejected. Thus, earning assets and nonearning assets not undergoing the activities necessary to get them ready for use do not qualify for interest capitalization under this Statement.

SFAS No. 34, ¶ 10 states:

* * * [I]nterest cost shall not be capitalized for inventories that are routinely manufactured or otherwise produced in large quantities on a repetitive basis because, in the Board's judgment, the informational benefit does not justify the cost of so doing.

Should interest on the cost of the Swiss cheese in 4–5(d) above (or aging of whiskey) be capitalized?

(B) Flow of Cost Assumptions

Even if it is clearly understood what elements of cost are to be included in inventory cost, because costs change, another problem arises—what flow of costs should be assumed? To illustrate the question, assume three widgets had been purchased at costs of $2, $3 and $5, respectively, and all are on hand when a customer buys one. What is the cost of goods sold? You will find that GAAP contemplate alternative answers of $2, $3, $5, and $3.33 even for this simplest of cases.

ARB NO. 43, CHAPTER 4, STATEMENT 4
AICPA, 1953.*

"Cost for inventory purposes may be determined under any one of several assumptions as to the flow of cost factors (such as first-in first-out, average, and last-in first-out); the major objective in selecting a method should be to choose the one which, under the circumstances, most clearly reflects periodic income.

"Discussion

"6. The cost to be matched against revenue from a sale may not be the identified cost of the specific item which is sold, especially in cases in which similar goods are purchased at different times and at different prices. While in some lines of business specific lots are clearly identified from the time of purchase through the time of sale and are costed on this basis, ordinarily the identity of goods is lost between the time of acquisition and the time of sale. In any event, if the materials purchased in various lots are identical and interchangeable, the use of the identified cost of the various lots may not produce the most useful financial statements. This fact has resulted in the development of general acceptance of several assumptions with respect to the flow of cost factors (such as *first-in first-out, average,* and *last-in first-out*) to provide practical bases for the measurement of period income.[3] In some situations a reversed mark-up procedure of inventory

---

* Copyright © 1953 by the American Institutes of Certified Public Accountants, Inc.

3. Standard costs are acceptable if adjusted at reasonable intervals to reflect current conditions so that at the balance-

pricing, such as the retail inventory method, may be both practical and appropriate. The business operations in some cases may be such as to make it desirable to apply one of the acceptable methods of determining cost of one portion of the inventory or components thereof and another of the acceptable methods to other portions of the inventory.

"7. Although selection of the method should be made on the basis of the individual circumstances, it is obvious that financial statements will be more useful if uniform methods of inventory pricing are adopted by all companies within a given industry."

The above excerpt from *Statement 4* mentions the standard cost, first-in first-out (FIFO), average cost, last-in first-out (LIFO), identified cost and retail inventory methods. The meaning of these terms will be briefly described.

Standard Cost. Standard costs, referred to in footnote 3, are predetermined or estimated prior to production. Standard material costs are usually computed from actual usage information or from bills of materials. Standard labor costs are obtained from production records or from time studies. Standard overhead costs are derived from estimated and actual overhead expenses applied to operations at normal capacity. All of these standard costs are usually based on prices and wages current when the standards are established. During the production period, differences between actual costs and standard costs are usually accumulated in separate variance accounts.

For valuing inventories, standard costs may be converted to actual costs by adding or deducting the applicable variances. Variances should be carefully evaluated to ascertain the percentages to be used to adjust the standard costs. The standard costs may be properly adjusted for variances attributed to the period in which the inventory was produced or it may be preferable to adjust standard costs for variances developed over a more extended period. Analysis of the variances may indicate that a portion of unfavorable variances from standard costs reflect inefficiencies or abnormalities that should be charged to expense rather than added to inventory. Favorable variations from standard costs (the excess of standard cost over actual cost), if material, should be applied as a reduction of the standard cost of inventory.

The proper use of standard costing is considered to be a progressive and desirable method of determining cost for inventory purposes. It exemplifies the concept of bringing forward only the useful cost of inventory and may be helpful in determination of reproduction cost.

------

sheet date standard costs reasonably approximate costs computed under one of the recognized bases. In such cases descriptive language should be used which will express this relationship, as, for instance "approxi-mate costs determined on the first-in first-out basis, or if it is desired to mention standard costs, "at standard costs, approximating average costs."

An example will best serve to explain each of the other methods mentioned. Assume that X Corporation buys widgets and sells them at an approximate 50% markup from current costs. Opening inventory and purchases for the year are as follows:

	Quantity	Cost per Widget	Total Cost
Opening Inventory	100	$1.00	$ 100
Feb. 1, Purchase	200	1.10	220
Apr. 1, Purchase	100	1.20	120
Jun. 1, Purchase	300	1.30	390
Aug. 1, Purchase	400	1.40	560
Oct. 1, Purchase	100	1.50	150
Dec. 1, Purchase	200	1.60	320
Total	1,400	X	$1,860
Ending Inventory	300	X	X

(1) First-in, First-out (FIFO)

This method is based on the assumption that the oldest goods will be sold first and that the cost of the remaining goods should be determined at the cost of those goods last purchased.

From our example, it would appear that the inventory of 300 widgets, priced on the FIFO basis would amount to $470—the cost of the last 300 widgets.

(2) Average Cost

There are several different possible average costs depending on what figures go into the computation. A simple average of the costs in our example above would be the total of the individual figures listed under Cost per Widget divided by seven or $1.30 per widget for a total of $390. A weighted average cost per widget could be calculated by dividing the $1,860 total of the Total Cost column of the table by the 1,400 total of the Quantity column, resulting in a weighted average cost of $1.33 per widget.

The total inventory valuation would then be:

$$300 \times \$1.33 = \$399$$

Other averages could include an average based on purchases for only the last six months, etc.

(3) Last-in, First-out (LIFO)

The basic underlying theory for this method is that operations require maintenance of a certain minimum quantity of inventory at all times and that increases in the value of this basic inventory represent unrealized profit that should not be included in income. This method also is compatible with the assumption that current purchases are used for current sales and therefore the most recent purchases should be charged against the most recent sales even though the physical movement of goods is different.

The basic inventory is carried at its original cost of acquisition with the practical effect during a period of rising prices of eliminating from inventory and including as a reduction of income the approximate increase in the value of those inventories obtainable under most of the other methods of determining inventory cost. Under these circumstances, the use of the LIFO method will result in reduction of income and, since it will also be used for income tax purposes, taxes payable will be reduced, thereby enhancing cash flow and liquidity of the business.

In the example, the LIFO inventory valuation would be $320, the cost of the first 300 units.

(4) Identified Cost

Under this method each item purchased would be marked or otherwise specifically identified with its cost. At inventory-taking time, the inventory valuation would be determined by adding up the specific cost of the 300 items on hand. This technique is cumbersome when many units are involved in purchases and inventories.

(5) Retail Inventory Method

Basically this method uses the retail price of the items in the inventory because it is too difficult to trace the cost of numerous items, and reduces them by the gross profit margin. Thus if the gross profit margin on items in one category of goods sold by a drugstore is 20%, the inventory cost can be ascertained by multiplying the aggregate retail price of all goods in the inventory by 80%. There are numerous technicalities applied in actual practice, but the system is basically as just stated.

(6) Other Techniques (Including Base Stock)

There are other techniques in use for pricing inventories, but those mentioned above are the more common ones. The base stock method has a good deal to commend it although it has fallen into disuse. It is mentioned here because it is found in the cases and also because it is often said to be the forerunner of the LIFO method. The base stock method assumes that the business must have a minimum base stock always on hand to keep the production and/or sales processes moving. That being so, the base stock is like any other fixed asset that remains in the business. Hence, it is unimportant how it is priced so long as the price is constant, and an arbitrary value is often chosen; in this way current cost of goods sold will be charged with those costs currently being incurred. Any inventory on hand in excess of the base stock is priced on FIFO, LIFO, average cost or any other basis. Thus in the example if the base stock were 100 widgets, valued at 50 cents, the opening inventory would have been $50 and the closing inventory, valued on the base stock plus FIFO method would be $50 (for the first 100 units) plus $320 (for the last 200) or $370 *in toto*.

Problem and Note

4–8. Problem. Are profits greatly affected by the inventory method chosen? Assume that Peripatetic Shoe Corp. has been using a FIFO method of inventory valuation but wishes to consider the effects of changing to some other method. If its profit for the year under the FIFO method is $20,000, its FIFO opening inventory is $12,000, and closing inventory is $15,000, what would its profit be if the opening and closing inventories under the other methods were as follows? (Assume in each case sales revenues of $40,000, purchases of $18,000, and other expenses of $5,000.)

	Opening	Closing
Weighted Average	$12,500	$14,500
LIFO	9,000	10,000
Identified Cost	10,000	14,000

4–9. Frequency of Use for Different Costing Methods. The AICPA's publication *Accounting Trends & Techniques* includes an annual survey of accounting practices followed in stockholders' reports. The 1989 edition of that publication indicated that inventory cost determination methods used by surveyed companies were as follows:

INVENTORY COST DETERMINATION

	Number of Companies			
	1988	1987	1986	1985
Methods				
First-in first-out (fifo)	396	392	383	381
Last-in first-out (lifo)	379	393	393	402
Average cost	213	216	223	223
Other	50	49	53	48
Use of LIFO				
All inventories	20	18	23	26
50% or more of inventories	207	221	229	231
Less than 50% of inventories	90	86	74	83
Not determinable	62	68	67	62
Companies Using LIFO	**379**	**393**	**393**	**402**

2. A CRITIQUE OF LIFO

For many years LIFO was a prime example of the tax tail wagging the dog. The LIFO inventory technique was little used before it became permissible for federal income tax purposes.[a] Since that time (1938) it has become one of the three most popular inventory pricing methods, probably because (a) unlike accelerated depreciation, LIFO is usable for tax purposes only if it is also used for financial reporting

a. For the history of the development of LIFO, see Dein, Inventory Costs, in Modern Accounting Theory 158, 177 (M. Backer, ed. 1966).

purposes, and (b) in a period of rising prices it results in the matching of revenue with the highest available inventory costs and thus shows low income and low tax liability.[b] Thus the "booking" requirement means that the low income for tax purposes must also be reported for financial purposes.

Some managements would rather give up the tax postponement or reduction in order to report larger earnings on financial statements for various reasons: e.g., a desire to obtain larger payments under management incentive compensation plans tied to GAAP income, avoid "takeovers," make stock options more valuable, pay larger dividends or keep shareholder confidence. For example, Allegheny Ludlum Steel Corp. announced that it would seek to change from LIFO to FIFO despite the fact that a $6 million tax bill would be incurred for the year of the change. The Wall Street Journal commented that despite the tax bite, the change "would be attractive, * * * having the effect * * * of boosting earnings during a period when operations are turning slack for most steelmakers." It might have added " * * * thus exposing them to takeover efforts by suitors wooing unhappy shareholders." But several empirical studies have indicated that the market is not fooled by the difference between income reported on a LIFO and income reported on a FIFO basis, and, indeed, the market may tend to put a lower value on companies which seem to be unnecessarily disbursing cash for taxes by trying to show higher reported income through retention of FIFO.

Is LIFO a desirable method of accounting for the flow of inventory costs? There are conflicting views.

INVENTORIES IN HANDBOOK OF MODERN ACCOUNTING 1420–1423

Second Edition (S. Davidson and R. Weil 1977).*

"The acceptance of conventional accounting procedures which recognize cost, or the lower of cost or market, in stating inventories appears to have been a natural consequence of the thought that the principal financial statement is the balance sheet. In reflecting the financial position of a business, it is logical to determine the shareholders' equity by deducting the total of the liabilities from the valuation of the assets.

"The development and acceptance of the lifo * * * inventory method resulted from increasing emphasis being placed upon the income statement. Under currently accepted accounting concepts, the statement of financial position is conceived of as reflecting amounts for the assets (other than cash, receivables, and sundry assets from which the maximum cash realization is fixed) that merely represent the unabsorbed portion of expenditures incurred in the past but applicable to the future and to be charged against the gross revenue of some

---

b. IRC § 472(c).

* Copyright © 1977 by McGraw–Hill Book Company. Reprinted by permission.

future period. From this viewpoint, it was logical to develop an accounting convention relative to inventories designed to result in a more appropriate charge being made against current sales for the cost of goods sold. The basic principle of lifo is that current income is better determined by deducting from the sales of the accounting period the cost of replacing the merchandise used in making the sales; in view of the difficulty of computing the cost for each sale, however, the desired end result is approximated by stating the inventory on a lifo basis.

"The physical quantity of goods may remain constant from year to year, but the number of dollars invested in that inventory may increase or decrease solely as a result of changes in prices. So long as a businessman relies upon continuous turnover of inventory to produce income, it is important that the effects of mere changes in prices be distinguished from profits attributable to the sale of merchandise.

"If there is on hand at the beginning and end of any year the same physical quantity of goods, but solely as a result of changes in prices, the dollar amount attributed to those goods for inventory purposes has increased 10 percent, this 10 percent increase in the dollar amount represents an unrealized inventory profit. This profit cannot be used to pay taxes or wages or dividends but must be retained in the business in order to permit its very continuation by replacing the goods which have been sold. If these unrealized inventory profits continue, the business can be forced to secure additional capital to finance the higher-cost purchases, even though there has been no actual growth.

"It is equally significant that a decline in the value of an inventory can, under the fifo inventory method, depress the operating results; the lifo method similarly attempts to distinguish this type of charge against income from the normal results of current business operations."

INVENTORY PRICING AND CHANGES IN
PRICE LEVELS

American Accounting Association Committee on Concepts and Standards
Underlying Corporate Financial Statements, 1953.

"The so-called FIFO method of inventory valuation possesses three attractive characteristics: First, in the great majority of cases it so nearly approximates the physical movement of goods that the actual differences in flow can be ignored; second, it eliminates all possibility of influencing profits through selection of individual items from a homogeneous inventory or through the mere expansion or contraction of inventory quantities; third, the method produces a balance-sheet quantum which is, in general, a reasonable reflection of the current market.

"The principal objection to FIFO is its failure to compensate for changes in the price level. It is observed that in those cases where inventories are a material factor in the determination of annual earnings the costs charged against the year's revenues may, when prices change, produce an effect upon profits which appears erratic. Thus, low costs may be matched against relatively high selling prices and vice versa. The effect produced during periods of steeply rising prices is often described as one of 'fictitious inventory profits.'

"With respect to this point, it should first be noted that, in the absence of changes in the *general* level of prices, the so-called inventory profits are as real as are the profits under any conceivable set of circumstances. Clearly such profits may not be disbursable as dividends if the business is to maintain its level of physical stock. The fact, however, that a portion of the profits must be retained in the business because of higher costs of inventory in no way denies the validity of the profits as such. *To argue otherwise is to confuse profit determination on the one hand with financial management on the other.*

"When, on the other hand, the general price level has undergone change it is evident that historical FIFO has distinct limitations. Significantly, however, the defect is not implicit in the FIFO assumption but rather in the adherence to historical dollar symbols.

"In an appraisal of LIFO certain points are especially to be noted:

(1) To the extent that price changes of the goods under consideration match changes in the general level of prices, the resulting profit figures are theoretically superior to those attained by realistic flow assumptions unadjusted for price-level changes. To the extent, however, that the price changes do not so move in parallel fashion, the *artificial LIFO* method may easily exaggerate, conceal, or even show in reverse, real gains and losses.

(2) The inventory valuation which results for *artificial LIFO* may become so far out of date as to be seriously misleading ∗ ∗ ∗.

(3) The LIFO method is peculiarly open to the charge that through its use the periodic profits can be influenced to a substantial extent by the expedient of contracting or expanding the inventory quantities. Otherwise stated, it is literally true that up to the end of the year, management, under LIFO, has considerable leeway in deciding what the cost-of-goods-sold figure for the year shall be. In an extreme case, at the very end of the year, a quantity of goods equal to the entire quantity sold during the year could be acquired and such last-minute purchases would, under this artificial flow assumption, be treated as if they were the goods actually sold during the past twelve months. In reverse, the inventories are subject to intentional depletion for the purpose of influencing the profit figure.

(4) Given temporary involuntary depletion of LIFO inventories, reported net income for the period or periods of depletion receives the full impact of all previously unrecognized price gains or losses pertinent to the inventory reduction and may, as a result, be grossly misleading as an index of current performance."

Regardless of the merits, LIFO swept the field during the recession of 1974 and 1975, when companies desperate for cash could no longer afford the luxury of paying unnecessary taxes in order to maintain or bolster reported earnings. Reported earnings were thereby reduced by about $4 billion.

A complexity in changing from FIFO to LIFO or, in fact, any other accounting change, is ¶ 17 of *APB Op. No. 20* which you will recall requires that the change be to a method deemed to be "preferable." The SEC construed this, in *ASR 177* (1975) relating to interim statements, to mean that the auditor must be persuaded of preferability and must so state in a communication to the Commission. It would indeed be easy for both management and the auditors to conclude that LIFO is preferable because it saves taxes by reducing income, but the FASB holds that the improvement to justify a change must be in financial reporting, not the income tax effect alone. See FASB, Interpretation No. 1, *Accounting Changes Related to the Cost of Inventory* (1974), an interpretation of *APB Op. No. 20*.

But a non-tax justification was also at hand. The SEC and many others had warned of the danger of showing "inventory profits," which they thought were illusory when arising simply from increases in price levels while inventory was held. See ASR 151, *Disclosure of Inventory Profits Reflected in Income in Periods of Rising Prices* (1974).

See *Note, An Examination of Some Considerations Relating to the Adoption and Use of the Last-in, First-out (LIFO) Inventory Accounting Method,* 28 Vand.L.Rev. 521 (1975).

Problems in Liquidation of LIFO Inventory

4–10. *Problem.* What will be the effect on gross profits of a reduction in the number of units in closing LIFO inventory below the number of units in opening inventory referred to in item (3) of the preceding excerpt? Assume the following facts in making your calculations.

Opening inventory (LIFO): 100 units valued at $10 each

Closing inventory: 50 units

Purchases: 100 units at $40 each

Sales: 150 units at $50 each

Calculate the gross profit if instead 150 units had been purchased at $40 each.

4–11. *Problem.* How much income *should* the income statement reflect? Would it make any difference to you whether the inventory reduction was due to:

(a) a shortage of supply of the goods?

(b) an intentional failure by management to replace inventory for the sole purpose of showing a larger profit than would have been shown if inventory levels were kept normal?

(c) an accidental failure to replace inventory?

(d) a shrinkage in volume of operations causing prudent management to decrease inventory levels?

Should the gain from liquidation of the LIFO inventory be treated as an extraordinary item? See *FASB Interpretation 30, ¶ 11 (1979).*

APB Opinion No. 28, *Interim Financial Reporting*, as amended, provides in ¶ 14b that:

> Companies that use the LIFO method may encounter a liquidation of base period inventories at an interim date that is expected to be replaced by the end of the annual period. In such cases the inventory at the interim reporting date should not give effect to the LIFO liquidation, and cost of sales for the interim reporting period should include the expected cost of replacement of the liquidated LIFO base.

As of a fiscal year end, however, the creation of a reserve for replacement of liquidated LIFO inventories is not usually permitted for accounting purposes. When such liquidations have taken place, SEC Staff Accounting Bulletin Topic 11F requires disclosure, either on the face of the income statement or in a footnote, of the amount of income realized as a result of the inventory liquidation. The creation of reserves for replacement of liquidated LIFO inventories was authorized for tax purposes where the shortage was due to war. IRC § 1321.

When there has been an involuntary conversion of LIFO inventory at an interim date within a year for which replacement is intended by year end but which is not made and the taxpayer does not recognize gain for income tax reporting purposes, it is not necessary to recognize the gain from liquidation for accounting purposes. *FASB Interpretation 30,* ¶ 11.

4–12. *Problem.* What would be the effect of a large *purchase* of inventory items near the end of the year when prices are rising rapidly?

3. LIFO "RESERVES" OR "REVALUATIONS"

Note 15 to the GE financial statements in its 1989 annual report reads:

Note 15 GE Inventories

December 31 (In millions)	1989	1988
Raw materials and work in process	$5,492	$5,603
Finished goods	3,103	2,863
Unbilled shipments	249	246
	8,844	8,712
Less revaluation to LIFO	(2,189)	(2,226)
LIFO value of inventories	$6,655	$6,486

LIFO revaluations decreased $37 million in 1989 compared with an increase of $150 million in 1988.

What is the meaning and purpose of all this data?

From the preceding subpart you know that the LIFO value of Inventory will be different from the FIFO value—usually lower when prices are rising, the most common case.

But how is an analyst to compare incomes of two companies in the same industry, one of which uses FIFO and the other LIFO, since only the company knows the difference?

The solution is for the LIFO company to disclose the difference. It is often referred to as the LIFO "reserve" or in the GE statements, "revaluation." Thus GE's 1989 LIFO Inventory valuation on its books is $6,655,000,000. If it had used FIFO, Inventory would have had a value of $8,844,000,000. Its LIFO "reserve" was $2,189,000,000, or it was "revalued" downward by that amount.

The analyst would then know that the cumulative impact (for prior years as well) on retained earnings from using LIFO was $2,189,000,000 less than if FIFO had been used.

But this data would not indicate how much different the current year's income would have been had FIFO been used. Why not? Because one would not know how much of the difference occurred in the current year. For this data, one would ascertain the LIFO reserve at the end of the prior year, compare it with the end of the current year and if the reserve increased (the usual case), one would conclude that income for the current year would have been that much *more* for the current year. On the other hand, if the reserve decreased, income would have been that much *less*.

But notice that these differences are in pre-tax income. Why? Because the difference was not taxed. In fact the very purpose of using LIFO was probably to get the tax advantage.

Note 15 to GE's financial statements thus would indicate, contrary to the usual case, that GE's pre-tax income would have been $37,000,000 less in 1989. However it would have been $150,000,000 more in 1988 had it used FIFO.

4. COST OR MARKET, WHICHEVER IS LOWER

(A) Should a Writedown to Market Be Made?

Instead of using cost, should we reduce the inventory carrying amount to "market," if lower? As noted earlier, any deviation from carrying assets at historical cost on the books, whether the deviation is up or down, entails recognition of unrealized gain or loss. (However, writing up the book basis of assets is unusual.) Of course, recognition of loss occurs when inventory is written down.

ARB NO. 43, CHAPTER 4, STATEMENT 5
AICPA, 1953.*

"A departure from the cost basis of pricing the inventory is required when the utility of the goods is no longer as great as its cost. Where there is evidence that the utility of goods, in their disposal in the ordinary course of business, will be less than cost, whether due to physical deterioration, obsolescence, changes in price levels, or other causes, the difference should be recognized as a loss of the current period. This is generally accomplished by stating such goods at a lower level commonly designated as *market*.

"Discussion

"8. Although the cost basis ordinarily achieves the objective of a proper matching of costs and revenues, under certain circumstances cost may not be the amount properly chargeable against the revenues of future periods. A departure from cost is required in these circumstances because cost is satisfactory only if the utility of the goods has not diminished since their acquisition; a loss of utility is to be reflected as a charge against the revenues of the period in which it occurs. Thus, in accounting for inventories, a loss should be recognized whenever the utility of goods is impaired by damage, deterioration, obsolescence, changes in price levels, or other causes. The measurement of such losses is accomplished by applying the rule of pricing inventories at *cost or market, whichever is lower.* This provides a practical means of measuring utility and thereby determining the amount of the loss to be recognized and accounted for in the current period."

ARB NO. 43, CHAPTER 4, STATEMENT 10
AICPA, 1953.*

"Accrued net losses on firm purchase commitments for goods for inventory, measured in the same way as are inventory losses, should, if material, be recognized in the accounts and the amounts thereof separately disclosed in the income statement.

"Discussion

"17. The recognition in a current period of losses arising from the decline in the utility of cost expenditures is equally applicable to similar losses which are expected to arise from firm, uncancellable, and unhedged commitments for the future purchase of inventory items. The net loss on such commitments should be measured in the same way as are inventory losses and, if material, should be recognized in the accounts and separately disclosed in the income statement. The utility of such commitments is not impaired, and hence there is no loss, when the amounts to be realized from the disposition of the future inventory items are adequately protected by firm sales contracts or when there are other circumstances which reasonably assure continuing sales without price decline."

BRANCH v. KAISER

Supreme Court of Pennsylvania, 1928.
291 Pa. 543, 140 A. 498.

JUSTICE FRAZER.

Defendants appealed from a decree entered by the court below on a bill in equity, filed by a trustee in bankruptcy, to compel repayment by respondents of moneys paid out as dividends alleged to have been wrongfully declared by the directors of the bankrupt corporation.

*   *   *

The corporation in question, known as the Girard Grocery Company, was incorporated in 1908 under the laws of this Commonwealth, for the purpose of carrying on a wholesale business principally in groceries and food products. *   *   * The original capital was $175,000, later increased to $1,000,000, divided into 10,000 shares of $100 each, of which there was issued and outstanding at the time of the bankrupt proceedings, stock to the aggregate value of $441,800. The business was prosperous from the start and by the year 1920 the corporation had accumulated a surplus of assets over liabilities of approximately $171,000, and for a number of years, up to 1920, had declared and paid dividends. In that year, however, it met with financial disaster, suffering a loss of $1,000,000, due, as claimed by respondents and admitted by the trustee, not to mismanagement, neglect or wrongful practices on the part of the directors, but to a condition in the market for certain commodities, chiefly sugar and food products, which, to supply the demands of customers, it had bought outright and contracted for future deliveries, at the then prevalent high prices, but these suddenly enormously slumped, particularly sugar, large quantities of which the company had bargained for, in addition to immediate purchases, at prices ranging from 26 to 28 cents a pound, and which suddenly dropped to as low as 5½ cents a pound, entailing in this one item, a loss of $500,000. A similar amount was lost on purchases of food products. This occurrence culminated during the fiscal year of the company between July 1, 1920, and June 30, 1921. It was a post-war condition in the market which the directors could neither foresee nor prevent.

*   *   *

It is averred in the bill of complaint, and not denied in the answer of defendants, that as a result of the $1,000,000 loss in 1920 the corporation became in fact insolvent and the capital wholly or in part impaired and dissipated. *   *   * At this point respondents, who had the active management and control of the business, committed error disastrous to them in every respect. Instead of acquainting the stockholders with the actual unstable financial condition of the corporation, for which they were blameless, facing the publicity of the unquestioned insolvency, of which they certainly had knowledge, and setting about for a legal adjustment of affairs, they deliberately adopted and put into practice a bold and reprehensible system of deception, designed to conceal the insolvency from the stockholders and the public with the expectation of recouping, by means of future business, the loss of the $1,000,000 and thereby again place the company upon a sound financial standing. * * *

Respondents exercised a practically exclusive supervision over and management of the company's business and financial transactions and in this situation appear to have experienced no difficulty in putting into effect their plans for an effective concealment of the loss of 1920 and to enable the company, as they hoped, to emerge financially rehabilitated from its troubles. These plans included false over-valuation of assets, refraining from notice of the $1,000,000 loss in their reports, a presentation of false annual statements, and a diversion into dividends of profits that should have been applied to lessening the capital's impairment. A summary of these practices will show the extent and method of their operations. Beginning with the close of the fiscal year of 1921, they made no record in the company's books of the $1,000,000 loss, gave no notice of it in their annual report and merely noted in that report a deficit of $22,756.87. In addition, they presented inflated inventory sheets, giving to the actual merchandise the company had on hand a cost valuation, when in fact the value had enormously decreased. The same methods of concealment, misrepresentation and fictitious inventories were continued during the years down to and including 1925.

These methods and practices, as set forth in detail in the bill, are frankly admitted in respondents' answer, with the explanation, or excuse, that "the increase in the item of inventory was made with the intent and purpose of carrying on the business of the said Girard Grocery Company for the benefit of its stockholders."

* * *

In our opinion, we need not enter further into this discussion. It is undisputed that respondents by illegal methods made and continued concealment, from both the stockholders of the company and the public, of the precarious financial standing of the corporation, repeatedly inflating inventories of goods on hand, thus presenting a fraudulent over-valuation of assets, and, lastly, declared dividends, at the time the corporation was insolvent and its capital seriously depleted and impaired, out of profits that should have been used for its stabilization. The court below found the disbursements were illegal, under the Act of May 23, 1913, P.L. 336, and that the directors are personally liable for the dividends so declared. We concur in that judgment.

* * *

In fact, as Professor Horngren states:

A full-blown lower-of-cost-or-market method is rarely encountered in practice. Why? Because it is expensive to get the correct replacement costs of hundreds or thousands of different products in inventory. Still, auditors definitely feel that the costs of inventories should be fully recoverable from future revenues. Therefore auditors inevitably make market-price tests of a representative sample of the ending inventories.

In particular, auditors want to write down the subclasses of inventory that are obsolete, shopworn, or otherwise of only nominal value.

C. Horngren, Introduction to Financial Accounting 183 (2d ed. 1984).

Questions

4–13. Question. What are the entries to write down inventory to recognize a loss when market is less than cost under the periodic and perpetual inventory methods?

4–14. Question. Does writing down inventory to market when it is lower than cost adequately disclose on the income statement the nature of the loss? Would you suggest separating on the income statement the loss due to decline in market from gain or loss from operations? Paragraph 14 of *ARB No. 43, Chapter 4* states: "When substantial and unusual losses result from the application of this rule it will frequently be desirable to disclose the amount of the loss in the income statement as a charge separately identified from the consumed inventory costs described as *cost of goods sold.*"

4–15. Question. IRC § 472 and Regs. § 1.472–2 prohibit use of lower of cost or market if LIFO is used, and instead require the use of cost. What is the rational basis for this prohibition? It is not based on sound accounting practice as may be seen from Mr. Wellington's dissent to *ARB No. 43, Chapter 4*, indicating that lower of cost or market is used under LIFO.

(B) What Is "Market"?

ARB NO. 43, CHAPTER 4, STATEMENT 6
AICPA, 1953.*

"As used in the phrase *lower of cost or market* the term *market* means current replacement cost (by purchase or by reproduction, as the case may be) except that:

(1) Market should not exceed the net realizable value (i.e., estimated selling price in the ordinary course of business less reasonably predictable costs of completion and disposal); and

(2) Market should not be less than net realizable value reduced by an allowance for an approximately normal profit margin.

"Discussion

"9. The rule of *cost or market, whichever is lower* is intended to provide a means of measuring the residual usefulness of an inventory expenditure. The term *market* is therefore to be interpreted as indicating utility on the inventory date and may be thought of in terms of the equivalent expenditure which would have to be made in the ordinary course at that date to procure corresponding utility. As a general guide, utility is indicated primarily by the current cost of replacement of the goods as they would be obtained by purchase or reproduction. In applying the rule, however, judgment must always be exercised and no loss should be recognized unless the evidence indicates clearly that a loss has been sustained. There are therefore exceptions to such a standard. Replacement or reproduction prices would not be appropriate as a measure of utility when the estimated sales value, reduced by the costs of completion and disposal, is lower, in which case the realizable value so determined more appropriately measures utility. Furthermore, where the evidence indicated that cost will be recovered with an approximately normal profit upon sale in the ordinary course of business, no loss should be recognized even though replacement or reproduction costs are lower. This might be true, for example, in the case of production under firm sales contracts at fixed prices, or when a reasonable volume of future orders is assured at stable selling prices.

"10. Because of the many variations of circumstances encountered in the inventory pricing, Statement 6 is intended as a guide rather than a literal rule. It should be applied realistically in the light of the objectives expressed in this chapter and with due regard to the form, content, and composition of the inventory. The committee considers, for example, that the retail inventory method, if adequate markdowns are currently taken, accomplishes the objectives described herein. It also recognizes that, if a business is expected to lose money for a sustained period, the inventory should not be written down to offset a loss inherent in the subsequent operations."

Putting *Statement 6* another way, "market value," as used in valuing inventory under the "lower of cost or market" technique, means the median of the figures for "replacement value," "net realizable value" (NRV), and "net realizable value minus normal profit margin" (NRV–NPM). Let us assume an inventory whose net realizable value is $4, and the normal profit on that inventory is $2 so that net realizable value minus normal profit margin is $2. Then assume three different replacement values of $5, $3 and $1. From the following chart, you will see that where replacement value is $5, "market" is $4; where replacement value is $3, "market" is also $3; and where replacement value is $1, "market" is $2; as we have noted, in each case, "market" is the median figure.

	Case # 1 Assumed Replacement Value of $5	Case # 2 Assumed Replacement Value of $3	Case # 3 Assumed Replacement Value of $1
Replacement Value, Case # 1	$5		
NRV, all 3 cases	$4	$4	$4
Replacement Value, Case # 2		$3	
NRV–NPM, all 3 cases	$2	$2	$2
Replacement Value, Case # 3			$1

5. VALUATION OF INVENTORY IN SOME INDUSTRIES AT NET REALIZABLE VALUE

ARB NO. 43, CHAPTER 4, STATEMENT 9
AICPA, 1953.*

"Only in exceptional cases may inventories properly be stated above cost. For example, precious metals having a fixed monetary value with no substantial cost of marketing may be stated at such monetary value; any other exceptions must be justifiable by inability to determine appropriate approximate costs, immediate marketability at quoted market price, and the characteristic of unit interchangeability. Where goods are stated above cost this fact should be fully disclosed.

"Discussion

"16. It is generally recognized that income accrues only at the time of sale, and that gains may not be anticipated by reflecting assets at their current sales prices. For certain articles, however, exceptions are permissible. Inventories of gold and silver, when there is an effective government-controlled market at a fixed monetary value, are ordinarily reflected at selling prices. A similar treatment is not uncommon for inventories representing agricultural, mineral, and other products, units of which are interchangeable and have an immediate marketability at quoted prices and for which appropriate costs may be difficult to obtain. Where such inventories are stated at sales prices, they should of course be reduced by expenditures to be incurred in disposal, and the use of such basis should be fully disclosed in the financial statements."

E. CONSISTENCY

The fraud in *Bowman & Bourdon* supra was the result of inconsistency in valuing opening and closing inventories.

ARB NO. 43, CHAPTER 4, STATEMENT 8
AICPA, 1953.*

"The basis of stating inventories must be consistently applied and should be disclosed in the financial statements; whenever a significant change is made therein, there should be disclosure of the nature of the change and, if material, the effect on income.

"Discussion

"15. While the basis of stating inventories does not affect the over-all gain or loss on the ultimate disposition of inventory items, any inconsistency in the selection or employment of a basis may improperly affect the periodic amounts of income or loss. Because of the common use and importance of periodic statements, a procedure adopted for the

* Copyright © 1953 by the American Institute of Certified Public Accountants, Inc.

treatment of inventory items should be consistently applied in order that the results reported may be fairly allocated as between years. A change of such basis may have an important effect upon the interpretation of the financial statements both before and after that change, and hence, in the event of a change, a full disclosure of its nature and of its effect, if material, upon income should be made."

F. SHOULD VALUE ALWAYS BE USED IN LIEU OF COST?—A SUGGESTION FOR REFORM

R. SPROUSE & M. MOONITZ, ARS NO. 3, A TENTATIVE SET OF BROAD ACCOUNTING PRINCIPLES FOR BUSINESS ENTERPRISES 27–32
AICPA, (1962).*

"*Inventories.* Inventories are destined for sale to customers in one turnover period, a period which for many commodities is relatively short. As a consequence, whenever the ultimate proceeds from sale can be established, the data should be recorded in the accounts. As a specific case in point, inventories which are readily salable at known prices with negligible costs of disposal, or with known or readily predictable costs of disposal, should be measured at net realizable value (i.e., anticipated sales proceeds less costs of completion and disposal). These conditions are most likely to exist in the cases of certain agricultural products and the products of certain extractive industries. Cotton, wheat, corn, oats, rye, soy beans, barley, raw sugar, coffee beans, gold, silver, copper, and crude oil are but a few of the products which are already accounted for in this manner. By-products of all types are also commonly measured and accounted for at net realizable value.[4]

"This procedure will have the result of assigning most if not all of the change in resources and the related profit or loss to the period of production (or other activity) when the actual effort was made. While it leads to the same result, it differs in attitude from the one expressed in Chapter 4 (Inventory Pricing) of *Accounting Research Bulletin No. 43*. That source recognizes the acceptability of stating inventories above cost 'only in exceptional cases,' specifically, 'precious metals having a fixed monetary value with no substantial cost of marketing' and 'other exceptions' which can be justified by 'inability to determine

4. For convenience throughout the discussion of inventories, a perpetual-inventory system is assumed, so that "cost of goods sold" is merely the result of a transfer from the inventory account to expense, and not the result of a separate calculation of a residual, as under the periodic-inventory method of calculation. The discussion could be restated in terms of a periodic-inventory system. The results, however, are the same under either procedure.

appropriate costs, immediate marketability at quoted market price, and the characteristic of unit interchangeability.'

"Instead of classifying this procedure as 'exceptional' we find it to be in keeping with the major objectives of accounting. Measurement of inventories at net realizable value is the preferred method whenever the measurement is objectively determinable. Historical cost is far from a satisfactory basis for pricing inventories because it rarely reflects either present utility or future benefits. Its alleged major advantage in the case of inventories is its definiteness. But where a more useful measure (e.g., net realizable value or current replacement cost) is available and is also capable of close estimate and prediction, it should take precedence over historical cost. In centering their attention on 'verification,' accountants frequently select less useful instead of more useful procedures. Verifiability (definiteness, objectivity) is a necessary condition. Other attributes need to be considered and a choice made from the array of all procedures which meet the test of objectivity.

"In many cases, however, inventories cannot satisfactorily be priced at net realizable value (a future exchange price). Even where selling prices are determinable, the amount which can readily be sold, the length of time required in order to accomplish the sales and the selling and disposal costs are apt to be uncertain and incapable of adequate verification. Under these circumstances, the treatment of inventories as though they were receivables is not justified. Instead, they are still in the category of 'costs awaiting disposition.' The choice, therefore, lies between a past and a present exchange price.

"The consistent use of acquisition cost (a past exchange price) as a valuation basis results in the deferral of any gain or loss that may be accruing until the item is sold or otherwise disposed of. As a consequence, inventory valuations are out of date and relate not to the present or to the future but to the past. Furthermore, as soon as two or more items in the inventory are acquired at different dates, the acquisition costs do not even relate to the same point of time.

"Since the use of a future exchange price is ruled out as inapplicable in these cases, and a past exchange price as defective, we are left logically with the possibility of using a current exchange price, or replacement cost. The use of current (replacement) cost as the basis for inventory measurement eliminates the need for any assumption as to the flow of actual costs incurred. The current cost of inventories is the same whether the related underlying records and tax returns are based on an assumption of a last-in, first-out flow of actual costs incurred, a first-in, first-out flow, a weighted average, or specific identification. Measurement of inventories at current cost means that goods sold (expense) should also be measured at current cost, thereby accomplishing the avowed purpose of the last-in, first-out method. It also means that inventory on hand will be measured at a figure which is at least as useful, if not more useful, than the one derived by the use of first-in, first-out.

"The relevance of current (replacement) cost to a going concern is underlined whenever the enterprise continues to manufacture or purchase the items contained in its inventory. This behavior creates a forceful presumption that current (replacement) costs represent at least the minimum economic value of those items to the enterprise.

"The use of current (replacement) cost has the further advantage of introducing a clean-cut distinction in the accounts between profit from holding an item through a price rise or fall, and profit from 'operating margins,' that is, the difference between sales price and current (replacement) cost of the goods sold. To record 'holding' gains or losses completely would require the adjustment of each item of finished goods to current cost at the moment of sale, and of unsold items of all inventory classes (finished goods, work in process, materials and supplies) at the end of each accounting period. In this manner, the transfer from finished goods to cost of goods sold would always be at the most current cost, and the unsold items would also appear at the most current cost in the balance sheet. This procedure can be simplified in most cases, however, by adjusting the finished goods account to current cost periodically at the end of each month or calendar quarter, and not at the moment of sale. This adjusted figure would then be used during the succeeding month or quarter to cost out all goods sold during that period. The resultant inaccuracy in the separation of 'holding' and 'operating' gains or losses would not be significant unless costs were changing rapidly and substantially.

"This holding gain or loss should be included as an integral part of the profit calculation, classified along with the related gain or loss on goods sold, for the following reasons:

1. The changes in prices have occurred, they are objectively determined, and the accounting entity is clearly affected. Furthermore, ultimate realization is reasonably assured because current cost is below current selling price by a normal profit margin. As a result, no useful purpose is served by delaying recognition of the changes.

2. The separate disclosure of holding and operating gains (losses) is of significance in analyzing and interpreting the results of operations. This disclosure is most readily accomplished by inclusion of the data in the formal records and financial statements.

3. The amount of the unrealized element is of significance in connection with income taxes and may be with respect to the legal aspects of dividend policy. The disclosure of this amount is readily accomplished by reporting the extent and the effect of the adjustment made to beginning and ending inventories.

"*Comparison with current procedures.*   *   *   *

"By contrast with the emphasis in Chapter 4 of *Accounting Research Bulletin No. 43* on acquisition cost and on the lower of acquisition cost or market, we extend the use of current (replacement) cost to the cases where it exceeds acquisition cost. The rationale for our position is identical with that cited in support of the use of replacement cost when it is lower than actual cost, namely, that 'as a general guide, utility is indicated primarily by the current cost of replacement of the goods as they would be obtained by purchase or reproduction.'

"The cost or market, whichever is lower, rule has been defended on the grounds that (1) it results in the recognition of 'a loss of utility' in the period during which that loss takes place, and (2) it prevents the measurement of inventory items at amounts which are in excess of the amount which can be recovered in the future when the inventory items are used or sold. The rule has long been criticized, primarily on the basis of its inherent inconsistency. If current replacement cost is objective, definite, verifiable and more useful when it is lower than acquisition cost, it also possesses those attributes when it is greater. By the use of current replacement cost, a change in 'utility' is recognized in the period when the change takes place. And inventory items would still be measured at amounts which are below current selling prices by the amount of the operating margin (gross profit).

"Some have argued that the recognition of gains in a manner similar to that for losses is not acceptable because of (1) the need for conservatism (i.e., the need to recognize losses but not to anticipate gains), and (2) the absence of realization. Conservatism of this type is, however, short-lived. The recognition of a loss this period and the accompanying reduction in reported profit inevitably means an offsetting increase in some future period. More serious, however, is the incompatibility of this type of conservatism with consistency, and the inherent lack of fairness in its application to inventories. The recognition of 'unrealized losses' accompanied by the nonrecognition of 'unrealized gain' produces information which discriminates in favor of those acquiring as opposed to those disposing of equities. Assuming that the market value of an enterprise's securities are affected to some extent by its financial position and the results of its operations as reported in its financial statements, consider the effect on an enterprise of a substantial 'unrealized loss' on marketable securities (recognized by application of the rule of cost or market, whichever is lower) and an unrealized but unrecognized gain of the same amount on inventories.

"The absence of realization is no bar to the use of current (replacement) costs for inventories. The 'cost or market' rule has served a useful purpose in this regard. It has trained accountants to detect, measure, and evaluate current (replacement) costs so that an extension of their use becomes both practical and natural."

Appendix to Chapter IV

COST ACCOUNTING FOR MANUFACTURED GOODS

A manufacturer of goods will incur costs for raw materials used and labor applied in producing the goods, plus factory overhead costs such as depreciation on plant and equipment, electric power, insurance and the like.

Although cost accounting for manufactured goods initially may seem to be complicated, the basic concepts should be comprehensible.

Assume a beginning balance sheet as follows:

X Corp. Balance Sheet at 1/1/X1

Cash	$5,000,000	Liabilities	$–0–
Inventories:		Equity:	8,000,000
Raw Materials	200,000		
Work in Process	400,000		
Finished Goods	800,000		
Plant	1,600,000		
Total	$8,000,000	Total	$8,000,000

To begin, we will talk about the three general ledger inventory control accounts used by many businesses and the movement of various costs into and out of these accounts. For purposes of this explanation, we have shown these separately in the above balance sheet.

(1) In order to produce a product, the company must acquire the needed raw materials such as purchased parts, wire, metal stampings, lumber, etc. When these items are purchased the related costs are added (debited) to the Raw Materials Inventory account and the purchase costs are added (credited) to Accounts Payable or Cash. E.g., assume a purchase of raw materials for $1 million:

Raw Materials Inventory	$1,000,000	
Cash		$1,000,000

(2) When the materials are withdrawn from the plant stockroom or storage, usually on the basis of a materials requisition, the assigned

dollar value is added (debited) to Work in Process Inventory and deducted from (credited to) the Raw Materials Inventory Account. Assume the transfer of raw materials valued at $900,000 from the warehouse to the production line:

Work in Process Inventory	$900,000	
Raw Materials Inventory		$900,000

(3) During the production process, direct labor costs are incurred which (a) are added (debited) to a Labor Expense account. Assume cash of $600,000 is paid for manufacturing labor:

Labor Expense	$600,000	
Cash		$600,000

Then (b), that labor cost is transferred to Work in Process Inventory:

Work in Process Inventory	$600,000	
Labor Expense		$600,000

(4) Similarly, overhead costs such as for electricity, depreciation on machinery, etc. incurred in production for the period (a) are added (debited) to appropriate accounts, e.g., Utility Expenses.

Utilities Expense	$200,000	
Depreciation Expense	150,000	
Miscellaneous Expenses	250,000	
Accumulated Depreciation		$150,000
Cash		450,000

(b) Then for the portion (say $400,000) of above attributable to manufacturing:

Manufacturing Overhead Expense	$400,000	
Utilities Expense		$150,000
Depreciation Expense		100,000
Miscellaneous Expenses		150,000

(c) In turn, this amount is transferred to Work in Process Inventory:

Work in Process Inventory	$400,000	
Manufacturing Overhead Expense		$400,000

(d) Finally, as to the unallocated portions, these are transferred to P & L account:

P & L	$200,000	
Utilities Expense		$50,000
Depreciation Expense		50,000
Miscellaneous Expenses		100,000

(5) As of the end of each period, the costs of materials, labor and overhead for finished production are removed from (credited to) the Work in Process Inventory account and added (debited) to the Finished Goods Inventory account. Assume transfer from Work in Process to Finished Goods Inventory for completed goods:

Finished Goods Inventory	$1,800,000	
Work in Process Inventory		$1,800,000

(6) At the end of each accounting period, it is necessary to remove from (credit) the Finished Goods Inventory account the costs associated with the finished goods sold and to add (debit) such costs to the Cost of Goods Sold account. The adjusting entry is:

Cost of Goods Sold	$1,700,000	
Finished Goods Inventory		$1,700,000

(7) At least once annually a complete physical inventory is taken of raw materials, work in process and finished goods, and necessary adjustments are made between the accounts for these items and the Cost of Goods Sold Account. For this purpose, it is necessary to determine the cost value to be assigned to the materials in each category of inventory, the labor cost content and the amount of overhead properly allocable to work in process and finished goods inventory. Assume the result is a correction of inventory and Cost of Goods Sold to reflect physical inventories showing Raw Materials Inventory to be $290,000 instead of $300,000; Work in Process Inventory to be $515,000 instead of $500,000; and Finished Goods Inventory to be $880,000 instead of $900,000:

Cost of Goods Sold	$15,000	
Work in Process Inventory	15,000	
Raw Materials Inventory		$10,000
Finished Goods Inventory		20,000

When posted to the ledger, the balances appear as follows:

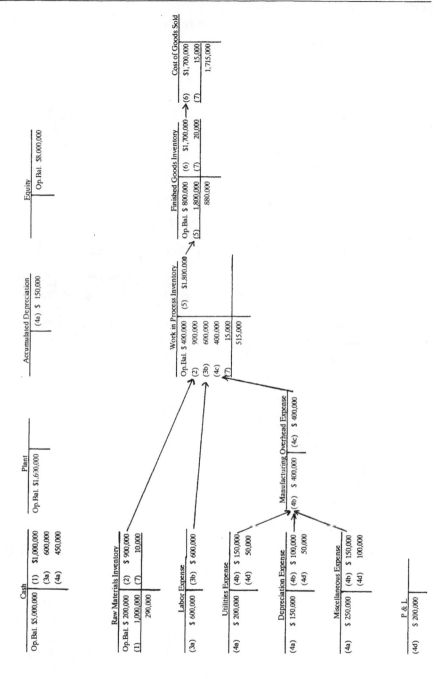

To recapitulate, portions of the foregoing relevant to Cost of Goods Sold may be depicted as follows:

	Raw Materials	Work in Process	Finished Goods	Cost of Goods Sold
Inventories at beginning of the period	$ 200,000	$ 400,000	$ 800,000	
Add raw materials purchased	1,000,000			
Transfer raw materials to Work in Process	(900,000)	900,000		
Add cost of production labor		600,000		
Add manufacturing overhead		400,000		
Sub-totals	$ 300,000	$2,300,000	$ 800,000	
Transfer to Finished Goods from Work in Process		(1,800,000)	1,800,000	
Transfer Finished Goods to Cost of Goods Sold			(1,700,000)	$1,700,000
Sub-totals	$ 300,000	$ 500,000	$ 900,000	$1,700,000
Reflect physical inventory adjustments	(10,000)	15,000	(20,000)	15,000
Inventories at end of period	$ 290,000	$ 515,000	$ 880,000	
Adjusted Cost of Goods Sold				$1,715,000

The raw material and labor costs are often referred to as "prime" or "direct" costs. The overhead costs, sometimes referred to as "indirect" costs or "burden," encompass a variety of costs associated with the production process.

In this process certain types of general overhead such as the president's salary and advertising costs are not included as they are not more than remotely related to *manufacturing* costs. Interest costs are also specifically excluded. See SFAS No. 34, *Capitalization of Interest Cost,* ¶ 10 (1979).

Considerable variations in the application of these overhead costs to inventories are found in practice. Irrespective of the cost accounting systems used, many businesses utilize standard rates of overhead which are periodically revised. These rates may be applied to direct labor dollars or hours, machine hours or on some other acceptable basis, and they are usually based on normal operations of the plant.

In applying overhead costs to inventories under an actual cost system, studies should be made to identify abnormal or unusual items, as well as those that do not relate to production, and to establish the relationship of operations of the inventory production period to the normal level of operations. For example, abnormal scrap, unusually large repairs or production at low percentages of capacity would usually require adjustment in applying overhead costs to inventories.

Usually the determination of material costs and labor costs per unit of production at each stage of production is not unduly difficult.

With respect to overhead costs, many companies—irrespective of the cost accounting system used—utilize standard rates of overhead which are periodically revised to reflect the company's actual experience. Such standard rates usually are preferable to frequent redeterminations of actual rates which, over short periods of time, may fluctuate radically and abnormally. If too much overhead cost has been applied to production of the period, the excess should be applied ratably as a reduction of Work in Process and Finished Goods Inventories and Cost of Goods Sold. When too little overhead cost has been applied to production of the period, the deficiency is usually charged to Cost of Goods Sold unless there is a good reason for adding the amount to inventories.

Critics suggest that cost-accounting has become increasingly unreliable because the easy-to-determine labor component in recent years has become proportionately less than the difficult-to-determine overhead component including depreciation, interest, and research and development costs. Another difficulty is in allocating overhead among two or more products. If the allocation is in proportion, say, to direct labor costs, yet one product requires more labor in proportion to overhead, the costing will be misleading. See Worthy, *Accounting Bores You? Wake Up,* Fortune, p. 43 (Oct. 12, 1987). (That ought to do it!)

For a particularly thorough description of abuses in valuing manufactured inventories, see In re Hope, SEC AAER No. 109A, Fed.Sec.L. Rep. (CCH) ¶ 73,509A (1986), a companion case to *Ernst & Whinney,* infra p. 624.

PHOTO–SONICS, INC. v. COMMISSIONER

United States Court of Appeals, Ninth Circuit, 1966.
357 F.2d 656.

ELY, CIRCUIT JUDGE:

We face a petition for review of a Tax Court decision upholding the assessment of a deficiency in the payment of income taxes.   *   *   *

The controversy stems from taxpayer's method of accounting for its inventory of goods which it manufactured. Under the method, generally described as "prime costing" or "prime cost", only the cost of direct labor and materials were allocated to inventory value. No portion of factory-overhead expense, variable or fixed, was included.

The key to validity of an accounting method is, in accounting terms, a matching of costs and revenues and, in terms of the taxing statute, a clear reflection of income. Int.Rev.Code of 1954, §§ 446, 471. The Government urges that, just as labor and materials cannot be expensed in the year in which such expenses are incurred without giving due regard to whether the manufactured product remains on hand, factory-overhead expenses which constitute a portion of the cost of unsold manufactured products cannot be expensed as they are incurred but rather should be allocated to the manufactured products and deducted, as a cost of sale, when the goods are sold. It contends that proper allocation of factory-overhead expenses, both fixed and variable, to the inventory is the only manner by which the taxpayer's income for a given period may be clearly reflected.

It may be that "direct costing", the allocation to inventory of labor, materials, and variable factory overhead, is an accurate method by which to account for inventory. If consistently applied, it would not seem to be less satisfactory than the method advanced by the Government, *i.e.*, the "absorption costing" method under which labor, material, and both fixed and variable factory overhead are allocated. Both methods are accepted, although "absorption costing" seems now to be preferred by most American accountants.[1] The Tax Court arrived at its determination "without attempting to lay down any broad principles applicable to inventories." 42 T.C. at 936. We, exercising similar restraint, are concerned with a particular accounting method only as it relates to the particular facts which are before us.

Here, the taxpayer allocated no portion of its factory-overhead expense to inventory. The regulations clearly specify that such be done. Treas.Reg. § 1.471–3(c) (1964). A method which excludes all factory-overhead costs is not an acceptable accounting practice. See American Institute of Certified Public Accountants, Accounting Research Bull. No. 43. The significance of failure to allocate any of such costs to inventory is emphasized by looking in this case, as an example, to one of the items of unallocated factory overhead, shop and tool expense. This expense represented items purchased during the year which were either too inexpensive to depreciate or were consumed during the year. The Tax Court found that it amounted to $8,215.34 in 1958, $40,397.22 in 1959, and $103,896.18 in 1960. Thus, in an expanding business in which some of the products manufactured in one fiscal period are sold in a subsequent fiscal period, the expenses which are attributable to the cost of sales in a subsequent year are matched against the lower sales revenues of a prior year. The effect of such a practice, if allowed, would obviously permit taxpayer to report less income than the amount which was truly earned. It would not be an "accounting practice * * * clearly reflecting the income" as required by section 471.

* * *

We are not persuaded that the Commissioner's determination was arbitrary. It follows that the Tax Court's decision, not clearly erroneous, must be Affirmed.

---

1. The statute and regulations should not be interpreted so as to permit the taxing authority arbitrarily to impose its own preferred system of accounting upon taxpayers. If a taxpayer employs a method which is acceptable under accounting standards, even though some might say that it does not conform "as nearly as may be to the best accounting practice" (Int.Rev.Code of 1954, § 471), the taxpayer's choice of method should not be disturbed if it clearly reflects income. This is particularly so when a taxpayer has consistently applied his method, without the Commissioner's challenge, for a reasonable period of time.

Chapter V

ALLOCATION OF LONG-TERM COSTS OF TANGIBLE ASSETS; DEPRECIATION AND DEPLETION

OBJECTIVES

1.   Comprehend the nature of depreciation as being another measurement and cost allocation exercise, just as with inventories.

2.   Understand the concept of measuring cost for constructed fixed assets and the various GAAP options for cost allocation.

3.   Note the differences in tax and financial accounting for fixed assets and the problem of financial accounting for income tax expense which this poses.

RELEVANCE FOR LAWYERS

Depreciation costs enter into making public policy for taxation, development and preservation of the infrastructure as well as in microeconomic matters, in all of which lawyers are involved.

A. INTRODUCTION

Long-lived assets may be tangible, like buildings, land, equipment or natural resources, or intangible, like patents, goodwill or organizational costs. Accountants divide them into three categories:

(a) Natural resources,

(b) Tangible or "fixed" assets, and

(c) Intangibles.

Intangibles are the subject of the next chapter and include things like patents and goodwill.

For all three, the basic accounting issues are:

(a) What is the measure of the initial cost of the asset? (E.g., what part of the attorney's fees, research costs or overhead are to be capitalized as the "cost" of a patent and what part are simply expenses of the period in which incurred?)

(b) How shall the capitalized cost be allocated to the accounting periods during which it is used? Here there are several sub-issues:

　(i) Shall useful life be based on time or on units of operation of the asset?

　(ii) What is the estimated useful life?

　(iii) What is the estimated salvage value at the end of that useful life?

　(iv) Shall the cost be allocated on a level basis each year, or shall some accelerated method be used? (When natural resources are involved, this allocation process is referred to as "depletion." For fixed assets the corresponding term is "depreciation" and for intangibles, "amortization.")

(c) What shall be the accounting when any of the estimates or practices in (b) are changed after the first accounting period?

(d) How shall gain or loss be determined on sale or other disposition?

At the outset, we may note that these questions may be answered differently for different items within the same firm and may be changed from one year to the next—within limits. We should also note that the questions usually will be answered differently for financial accounting than for income tax reporting purposes, unlike LIFO inventory accounting.

The treatment of long-term costs affects income significantly, but amounts charged rest to a great extent on discretionary judgments of management. For example, an estimate of useful life of a building may be forty years but an estimate of thirty or fifty years, changing depreciation expense by over 20%, probably would be equally defensible.

There are many dramatic illustrations. One of the games managers play with depreciation was described, apparently without concern, in *The New York Times* for Feb. 10, 1988 at p. 29:

The General Motors Corporation reported today that its fourth-quarter earnings more than doubled, while its earnings for all of 1987 rose 21 percent.

The quarterly and yearly profits were increased by a change in accounting standards, adopted in the third quarter, to provide longer depreciation periods for the company's plants and equipment.

The financial results were approximately in line with expectations of financial analysts.

G.M. said it earned $835.8 million, or $2.36 a share, in the fourth quarter, compared with $382.3 million, or 97 cents a share, a year earlier. The whole year's earnings were $3.6 billion, or $10.06 a share, up from 1986's $2.9 billion, or $8.21 a share.

The change in accounting standards increased 1987 earnings by $800 million, or $2.55 a share, the company said. Without the change, earnings for the year would have declined 3 percent, to $2.8 billion, or $7.51 a share.

Thus a 3% decline was converted to a 21% gain for the year by a change in estimated useful lives of fixed assets. Who is fooled by all this doublespeak? Why would the managers of a faltering company act in this way?

The answer probably lies in the fact that, regardless of whether investors are deceived, this change in reported income under GAAP is likely to effect wealth transfers under profit-sharing, wage and salary contracts, as well as through taxation, dividends, etc. In addition, it may be that, as long as no one reveals the emperor's invisible cloak, things will go smoothly. Nevertheless, real people are seriously affected in substantial ways.

B. THE NATURE OF DEPRECIATION

The GAAP concept of depreciation is described in the following paragraph of AICPA, *Accounting Terminology Bulletin No. 1* (1953):

54. * * * Depreciation accounting may take one of a number of different forms. The term is broadly descriptive of a type of process, not of an individual process, and only the characteristics which are common to all processes of the type can properly be reflected in a definition thereof. These common characteristics are that a cost or other basic value is allocated to accounting periods by a rational and systematic method and that this method does not attempt to determine the sum allocated to an accounting period solely by relation to occurrences within that period which affect either the length of life or the monetary value of the property. Definitions are unacceptable which imply that *depreciation for the year* is a measurement, expressed in monetary terms, of the physical deterioration within the year, or of the decline in monetary value within the year, or, indeed, of anything that

actually occurs within the year. True, an occurrence within the year may justify or require a revision of prior estimates as to the length of useful life, but the annual charge remains an allocation to the year of a proportionate part of a total cost or loss estimated with reference to a longer period.

In Commissioner v. Idaho Power Co., 418 U.S. 1, at 10–12 (1974), the Supreme Court described its view of the nature of depreciation for tax purposes:

> The Court of Appeals opined that the purpose of the depreciation allowance under the Code was to provide a means of cost recovery, Knoxville v. Knoxville Water Co., 212 U.S. 1, 13–14 (1909), and that this Court's decisions, e.g., Detroit Edison Co. v. Commissioner of Internal Revenue, 319 U.S. 98, 101 (1943), endorse a theory of replacement through "a fund to restore the property." 477 F.2d, at 691. Although tax-free replacement of a depreciating investment is one purpose of depreciation accounting, it alone does not require the result claimed by the taxpayer here. Only last Term, in United States v. Chicago, Burlington & Quincy Railroad Co., 412 U.S. 401 (1973), we rejected replacement as the strict and sole purpose of depreciation:
>
> > Whatever may be the desirability of creating a depreciation reserve under these circumstances, as a matter of good business and accounting practice, the answer is * * * "[d]epreciation reflects the cost of an existing capital asset, not the cost of a potential replacement." Id., at 415.

Contrast an academic's proposal:

> * * * If a depreciation method is to be helpful, it must show economic reality in live and current terms—and in particular how much of the firm's wealth is consumed in a period and how much remains at the end. The wealth in question is the asset's stock of potential services. The method must try to appraise them in a sensitive way. But this is precisely what is done by the market for worn assets. So a plausible starting point is that a good depreciation method should simulate what goes on in the minds of buyers and sellers of worn assets. These people presumably make some estimate of how many units of input (time or use, according to the kind of asset) an asset can still give; and they then try to assess what the units are worth, having regard to prices of alternatives and to the pattern of pending repair outlays, etc. A good method should reflect much the same considerations. * * *

W. Baxter, *Depreciation* 31 (1971).

Would General Motors' 1987 ploy have worked under Professor Baxter's proposal?

If the purpose of GAAP is primarily to inform public investors to facilitate their investment decisions, it would seem that a concept of income and its complement, capital, should be one that facilitates comparisons among competing investments, including not only other publicly held firms but governmental debt securities, various private credit instruments, real estate, art, books, etc. Presumably only universal concepts of capital as being net worth at fair value and income as the change in net worth for the period would do. Professor Baxter's proposal seems based on these concepts.

On the other hand, given the long life of depreciable assets, the value of which will vary based on changing technology, scarcity of the asset, etc., and also given the changing value of money through inflation and deflation, could it be said that there can be *no* rational underlying concept of capital and income for the GAAP and tax concept?

One is tempted to suggest that depreciation accounting, like certain laws ("mala prohibita"), often sets forth a rule only because without it there would be a vacuum permitting anarchy.

C. MEASURING COST; TO "CAPITALIZE" OR TO "EXPENSE"?

When a cost is incurred, under existing GAAP the bookkeeper must decide whether to debit an expense or an asset account. Sometimes this is an easy matter. When a building is purchased, he or she will debit an asset account, and for the cost of a pencil, will debit an expense account. But what criteria determine how to treat the cost of installing air conditioning in an old building? Replacing a defective door? Putting an additional ton of gravel on the tar and gravel roof? How much does a new building cost if the bricks, mortar, labor, etc. amount to $X and interest on the construction loan is $Y?

1. REPAIRS OR REPLACEMENTS

The cost of an item of repair will be expensed if the expenditure will have a useful life not extending beyond the accounting period, but the obverse is not always true. Almost every expenditure to repair an item will last into at least the next accounting period, and most last much longer. Yet accountants and the courts hold that many of these may be expensed.

No satisfactory test for determining when to capitalize and when to expense has been formulated. Some of the factors usually considered, in addition to whether the term of usefulness of the cost incurred is less than one accounting period, are: the materiality of the amount involved, whether the cost will contribute to revenue in subsequent periods, whether it is incurred for a separable unit or is for enhancement of some existing unit, whether it restores an asset to its original condition or creates a severable asset, and whether the cost is a recurring one.

For example, in a tax case, equally applicable to financial accounting, Kansas City Southern Railway Co. v. United States, 125 Ct.Cl. 287, 112 F.Supp. 164 (1953), a court upheld the railroad's current repairs expense deduction for the cost of driving poles into its roadbed to correct defects caused by "water pockets," saying, "The fact that the replacements, once made, would be good for many years, would not seem to be significant. When a building or a machine is repaired, it is not unusual that the repaired portion is better than and will outlast the parts that have not yet needed repairs."

Why is not the long useful life determinative in favor of capitalizing the cost? Is there a relationship between repairs and depreciation? Consider the usual case of depreciation of a building composed of many parts, such as a roof, walls, heating units, doors, etc., all having varying useful lives, some of which are quite short in comparison with the expected useful life of the building as a whole. For example, the floor covering may have an estimated life of only a few years. Nevertheless the entire initial cost of the building including the covering is depreciated as if all components will last until the building as a whole is no longer useful. However, replacement of the floor coverings will be expensed. The effect of charging repairs to expense is to cause an increasing amount of costs to be charged to expense as the asset ages—perhaps a reasonable pattern of cost allocation. Or perhaps it is simply an arbitrary practice.

2. DIRECT COSTS AND OVERHEAD DURING CONSTRUCTION

Issues of whether to capitalize interest and other costs incurred during construction of a fixed asset also are of great moment. The costs principally at issue are normally divided into (a) direct costs of the construction, (b) interest during construction, and (c) other overhead.

(A) Direct Costs

There has never been any doubt that direct costs, i.e., the materials and labor incorporated in the project, are to be included in the cost of the constructed asset. See, e.g., Commissioner v. Idaho Power Co., 418 U.S. 1, 13 (1974).

However, it is not always easy to determine to what asset a cost is applicable. For an illustration of the difficulties in allocating production costs between inventory and tooling, see part (3) of *In re Ernst & Whinney,* (CCH) Fed.Sec.L.Rep. ¶ 84,610 (SEC 1990), partially excerpted in Chapter XIV.

(B) Interest During Construction

STATEMENT OF FINANCIAL ACCOUNTING STANDARDS NO. 34, CAPITALIZATION OF INTEREST COST

FASB, 1979.*

"SUMMARY

"This Statement establishes standards for capitalizing interest cost as part of the historical cost of acquiring certain assets. To qualify for interest capitalization, assets must require a period of time to get them ready for their intended use. Examples are assets that an enterprise constructs for its own use (such as facilities) and assets intended for sale or lease that are constructed as discrete projects (such as ships or real estate projects). Interest capitalization is required for those assets if its effect, compared with the effect of expensing interest, is material. If the net effect is not material, interest capitalization is not required.

* * *

"10. * * * [I]nterest cost shall not be capitalized for inventories that are routinely manufactured or otherwise produced in large quantities on a repetitive basis because, in the Board's judgment, the informational benefit does not justify the cost of so doing. In addition, interest shall not be capitalized for the following types of assets:

a. Assets that are in use or ready for their intended use in the earning activities of the enterprise.

b. Assets that are not being used in the earning activities of the enterprise and that are not undergoing the activities necessary to get them ready for use.

* * *

"12. The amount of interest cost to be capitalized for qualifying assets is intended to be that portion of the interest cost incurred during the assets' acquisition periods that theoretically could have been avoided (for example, by avoiding additional borrowings or by using the funds expended for the assets to repay existing borrowings) if expenditures for the assets had not been made."

Notes on Implicit Interest

5–1. *Implicit Interest—Implicit Revenue.* Note that *SFAS No. 34* is limited to actual interest on borrowings. Nevertheless it has become customary for certain regulatory and rate-making purposes to capitalize interest on the money invested in the construction, whether the money was actually borrowed ("explicit interest"), as under *SFAS No. 34,* or supplied by the common stock investment of the equity shareholders ("implicit interest").

The debit to the asset when the interest is explicit is balanced by a credit to Cash or a payable; when the interest is implicit, however, the debit is balanced by a credit to revenue. How astonishing! No cash receipt accompanies this "revenue." However, the reason for capitalization of implicit interest is that the investors in regulated companies in most jurisdictions get no return on their money on borrowed funds during the construction because, under traditional principles of utility rate-making, the rate base includes only plant-in-use. Yet investors (1) have committed their own funds, forgoing earnings they could have obtained otherwise during the construction period; or (2) have agreed to pay interest on borrowed funds, which must come from their investment funds. Capitalization will result in an increased rate base, in turn requiring greater allowed return in future periods, thereby compensating the investors.

Where, contrary to the tradition, the rate base includes construction-in-progress, as is currently allowed by many rate-making bodies, this reason for capitalizing interest (implicit or explicit) disappears.

5–2. *Probability of the Revenue.* *SFAS No. 71,* ¶ 15 (1982) as modified by *SFAS No. 90,* ¶ 8 (1986), expressly makes this regulatory accounting into GAAP also for regulated firms. Hence not only are rates based on this accounting, so, too, are published financial statements.

SFAS No. 90, ¶¶ 8 and 9, does require as a condition to capitalization of implicit interest on equity that it be "probable" that it be included as an allowable cost in future rate-making. Because development of nuclear power generating capacity was a major public policy priority in the 1970's and 1980's, and these plants not only cost billions but, in some cases, have yet to be placed in operation, this qualification has become increasingly significant. For example, Public Service Co. of New Hampshire, the owner of the infamous Seabrook nuclear plant, in several years of the 1980's reported substantial earnings when, but for its implicit interest revenue, it would have reported losses. The company recently became the first large public utility to go into bankruptcy and others have followed. The implicit interest "revenue" for this company is in never-never land. Who gained and who lost?

Many investors are ignorant about this kind of reported revenue, and it could cause misleading impressions especially in today's changed environment in which bankruptcies of public utilities are more likely. Several lawsuits have been brought alleging fraud in financial statements reporting such revenue. E.g., see the consent order in Independent Investor Protective League v. Teleprompter Corp., summarized at BNA Sec.Reg.L.Rep. # 262 at p. A–22 (July 24, 1974).

Nevertheless when, in 1984, the FASB considered changing *SFAS No. 71,* the change was averted, largely because it was believed that the reduction of reported earnings would result in alteration of important financial ratios (e.g. the ratio of interest costs to earnings) which would adversely affect bond ratings and payment of dividends. This in turn would raise the costs of capital, requiring increased consumer rates for electricity, gas, etc.

This is one more illustration of how the form of portrayal of data may affect the distribution of wealth.

5–3. *Coordination of GAAP and Regulatory Accounting.* GAAP for regulated industries may vary from GAAP for nonregulated industries for many items other than implicit interest described above. Several SFAS's in addition to No. 71 may apply to regulated enterprises, the most important of which in the current period of deregulation is SFAS No. 101, *Regulated Enterprises—Accounting for the Discontinuation of Application of FASB Statement No. 71* (1988).

5–4. *The Rationale.* Paton analyzes the problem of implicit interest for nonregulated firms by asking whether the accounting statements are to be prepared from the point of view of the equity owners or of all investors, including lenders. Adopting the point of view of the equity owners, he reasons that the equity owners would not be helped by "accruing in the accounts any element of estimated return to the stockholder in advance of the process of production . . ." and that therefore implicit interest on equity should not be capitalized. W.A. Paton & W.A. Paton, Jr., *Asset Accounting* 474–78 (1952).

How should dividends on preferred stock, sold to fund construction, be treated?

(C) Other Costs During Construction

If a firm is engaged in constructing a plant for its own use, the cost of the plant will include not only interest during construction but also depreciation on fixed assets such as trucks used in the construction. See Commissioner v. Idaho Power Co., 418 U.S. 1, 10–12 (1974).

Other items of costs which are identifiable to a fixed asset and clearly measurable may be allocated to the project. Examples would include such items as electric power cost measured by a special meter installed for the purpose, and payroll taxes and fringe benefits applicable to labor hours identified to the construction job. In the past, there have been instances of allocating general corporate overhead or items of administrative expense to such projects. Such a practice is no longer acceptable.

D. ACCOUNTING FOR LONG–TERM ASSETS IN THE EXTRACTIVE INDUSTRIES; MEASURING THE COST AND AMORTIZING IT (DEPLETION)

A special problem of accounting for tangible and intangible costs exists in the extractive industries. Assume that an oil and gas firm strikes oil or gas once in ten tries. Should it charge to an asset account the costs of exploration and drilling the dry holes? Should it charge to expense exploration, drilling, and development costs prior to production by producing wells? Or should some or all of these costs be capitalized? Practices vary. The two polar extremes are termed "full-costing" and "successful efforts." See T. Fiflis, H. Kripke & P. Foster, Accounting for Business Lawyers 232–40 (3d ed. 1984) for a description of oil and gas accounting.

In any event, the capitalized costs must be amortized, usually according to units of production. The term applied to this allocation process is "depletion."

E. USEFUL LIFE AND SALVAGE VALUE

As we have noted in subpart B, the cost of a fixed asset less salvage value is spread over its useful life and that is to be done in some "rational and systematic" fashion. Thus, after determining the amount to be capitalized as the cost of the fixed asset, the next factors to be determined are useful life and salvage value. The Supreme Court discussed the problem of what is the useful life and why salvage value must be deducted from cost. The case is not currently of great relevance to tax accounting but it correctly explains GAAP for financial reporting.

MASSEY MOTORS, INC. v. UNITED STATES

Supreme Court of the United States, 1960.
364 U.S. 92.

MR. JUSTICE CLARK delivered the opinion of the Court.

These consolidated cases involve the depreciation allowance for automobiles used in rental and allied service * * *. The Courts of Appeals have divided on the method of depreciation which is permissible in relation to such assets, and we therefore, granted certiorari to resolve this conflict. 361 U.S. 810, 812. We have concluded that the reasonable allowance for depreciation of the property in question used in the taxpayer's business is to be calculated over the estimated useful life of the asset while actually employed by the taxpayer, applying a depreciation base of the cost of the property to the taxpayer less its resale value at the estimated time of disposal.

[T]he taxpayers are husband and wife. In 1950 and 1951, the husband, Robley Evans, was engaged in the business of leasing new automobiles to Evans U–Drive, Inc., at the rate of $45 per car per month. U–Drive in turn leased from 30% to 40% of the cars to its customers for long terms ranging from 18 to 36 months, while the remainder were rented to the public on a call basis for shorter periods. Robley Evans normally kept in stock a supply of new cars with which to service U–Drive and which he purchased at factory price from local automobile dealers. The latest model cars were required because of the demands of the rental business for a fleet of modern automobiles.

When the U–Drive service had an oversupply of cars that were used on short-term rental, it would return them to the taxpayer and he would sell them, disposing of the oldest and least desirable ones first. Normally the ones so disposed of had been used about 15 months and had been driven an average of 15,000 to 20,000 miles. They were ordinarily in first-class condition. It was likewise customary for the taxpayer to sell the long-term rental cars at the termination of their leases, ordinarily after about 50,000 miles of use. They also were usually in good condition. The taxpayer could have used the cars for a longer period, but customer demand for the latest model cars rendered the older styles of little value to the rental business. Because of this, taxpayer found it more profitable to sell the older cars to used car dealers, jobbers or brokers at current wholesale prices. Taxpayer sold 140 such cars in 1950 and 147 in 1951. On all cars leased to U–Drive taxpayer claimed on his tax returns depreciation calculated on the basis of an estimated useful life of four years with no residual salvage value. The return for 1950, for example, indicated that each car's cost to taxpayer was around $1,650; after some 15 months' use he sold it for

$1,380; he charged depreciation of $515 based on a useful life of four years, without salvage value, which left him a net gain of $245, on which he calculated a capital gains tax. In 1951 the net gain based on the same method of calculation was approximately $350 per car, on which capital gains were computed. The Commissioner denied the depreciation claims, however, on the theory that useful life was not the total economic life of the automobile (i.e., the four years claimed), but only the period it was actually used by the taxpayer in his business; and that salvage value was not junk value but the resale value at the time of disposal. On this basis he estimated the useful life of each car at 17 months and salvage value at $1,325; depreciation was permitted only on the difference between this value and the original cost. The Tax Court accepted the Commissioner's theory but made separate findings. The Court of Appeals reversed, holding that useful life was the total physical or economic life of the automobiles—not the period while useful in the taxpayer's business. 264 F.2d 502.

First, it may be well to orient ourselves. The Commissioner admits that the automobiles involved here are, for tax purposes, depreciable assets rather than ordinary stock in trade. Such assets, employed from day to day in business, generally decrease in utility and value as they are used. It was the design of the Congress to permit the taxpayer to recover, tax free, the total cost to him of such capital assets; hence it recognized that this decrease in value—depreciation—was a legitimate tax deduction as business expense. It was the purpose of § 23(1) and the regulations to make a meaningful allocation of this cost to the tax periods benefited by the use of the asset. In practical life, however, business concerns do not usually know how long an asset will be of profitable use to them or how long it may be utilized until no longer capable of functioning. But, for the most part, such assets are used for their entire economic life, and the depreciation base in such cases has long been recognized as the number of years the asset is expected to function profitably in use. The asset being of no further use at the end of such period, its salvage value, if anything, is only as scrap.

Some assets, however, are not acquired with intent to be employed in the business for their full economic life. It is this type of asset, where the experience of the taxpayers clearly indicates a utilization of the asset for a substantially shorter period than its full economic life, that we are concerned with in these cases. Admittedly, the automobiles are not retained by the taxpayers for their full economic life and, concededly, they do have substantial salvage, resale or second-hand value. Moreover, the application of the full-economic-life formula to taxpayers' businesses here results in the receipt of substantial "profits" from the resale or "salvage" of the automobiles, which contradicts the usual application of the full-economic-life concept. There, the salvage value, if anything, is ordinarily nominal.

* * * Congress intended by the depreciation allowance not to make taxpayers a profit thereby, but merely to protect them from a

loss. The concept is, as taxpayers say, but an accounting one and, we add, should not be exchangeable in the market place. Accuracy in accounting requires that correct tabulations, not artificial ones, be used. Certainly it is neither accurate nor correct to carry in the depreciation equation a value of nothing as salvage on the resale of the automobiles, when the taxpayers actually received substantial sums therefor. On balance, therefore, it appears clear that the weight of both fairness and argument is with the Commissioner.

Our conclusion as to this interpretation of the regulations is buttressed, we think, by a publication issued by the Commissioner in 1942, the same year as Regulations 111, and long before this controversy arose. It is known as Bulletin "F." * * * Again on page 2, Bulletin "F," in discussing depreciation, emphasizes that it is based on "the useful life of the property in the business." What is more significant is the simple clarity with which, on page 7, it defines salvage value to be "the amount realizable from the sale * * * when property has become no longer useful in the taxpayer's business and is demolished, dismantled, or retired from service."

       * * *

Finally, it is the primary purpose of depreciation accounting to further the integrity of periodic income statements by making a meaningful allocation of the cost entailed in the use (excluding maintenance expense) of the asset to the periods to which it contributes. This accounting system has had the approval of this Court since United States v. Ludey, 1927, 274 U.S. 295, 301, 47 S.Ct. 608, 610, 71 L.Ed. 1054, when Mr. Justice Brandeis said, "The theory underlying this allowance for depreciation is that by using up the plant, a gradual sale is made of it." The analogy applies equally to automobiles. Likewise in Detroit Edison Co. v. Commissioner, 1943, 319 U.S. 98, 101, 63 S.Ct. 902, 904, 87 L.Ed. 1286, this Court said:

> "The end and purpose of it all [depreciation accounting] is to approximate and reflect the financial consequences to the taxpayer of the subtle effects of time and use on the value of his capital assets. For this purpose it is sound accounting practice annually to accrue * * * an amount which at the time it is retired will with its salvage value replace the original investment therein."

Obviously a meaningful annual accrual requires an accurate estimation of how much the depreciation will total. The failure to take into account a known estimate of salvage value prevents this, since it will result in an understatement of income during the years the asset is employed and an overstatement in the year of its disposition. The practice has therefore grown up of subtracting salvage value from the purchase price to determine the depreciation base. On the other hand, to calculate arbitrarily the expected total expense entailed by the asset on the false assumption that the asset will be held until it has no value is to invite an erroneous depreciation base and depreciation rate, which may result in either an over- or an under-depreciation during the period of use. * * * The alternative is to estimate the period the asset will be held in the business and the price that will be received for it on retirement. Of course, there is a risk of error in such projections, but prediction is the very essence of depreciation accounting. * * *

Accounting for financial management and accounting for federal income tax purposes both focus on the need for an accurate determination of the net income from operations of a given business for a fiscal period. The approach taken by the Commissioner computes depreciation expense in a manner which is far more likely to reflect correctly the actual cost over the years in which the asset is employed in the business.[7]

We therefore conclude that the Congress intended that the taxpayer should, under the allowance for depreciation, recover only the cost of the asset less the estimated salvage, resale or second-hand value. This requires that the useful life of the asset be related to the period for which it may reasonably be expected to be employed in the taxpayer's business. Likewise salvage value must include estimated resale or second-hand value. * * *

Note

5–5. *The Battle of the Experts*. *Massey* contains a buried lesson in the facts of life. Footnote 7 of the Court's opinion contains a sampling of written authorities which seem unanimously to support the *Massey* result. Yet the taxpayer was able to obtain several expert accountants to testify that useful life means economic useful life. See the Court of Appeals

---

7. Several writers in the accounting field have addressed themselves, without reference to the income tax laws, to the problem of giving content to the terms "useful life" and "salvage value" and their conclusions support what has been said.

Grant and Norton, Depreciation (1949), 145–146:

"[Assets such as passenger automobiles] may be expected to have substantial positive salvage values. Average salvage values must therefore be estimated before straight-line depreciation rates can be established. Salvage values will depend on average lives which may in turn depend on the owner's policy with regard to disposal of such assets. For example, if it is company policy to trade in passenger automobiles after three years, the estimation of average salvage value is simply the estimation of the average trade-in value of a 3–year–old passenger automobile."

Kohler, A Dictionary for Accountants (1952), 371, defines salvage value as:

"Actual or prospective selling price, as second-hand material, or as junk or

scrap, of fixed assets retired, or of product or merchandise unsalable through usual channels, less any cost, actual or estimated, of disposition; * * *"

Useful life is defined, id., at 440–441, as follows:

"Normal operating life in terms of utility to the owner; said of a fixed asset or a fixed-asset group; the period may be more or less than physical life or any commonly recognized economic life; service life."

Saliers, Depreciation Principles (1939), 72:

"Salvage is the value an article possesses for some use other than that to which it has been devoted. When it can be so used it is said to possess another cycle of life. Junk or scrap value is that which an article is worth if broken up. In making allowance for depreciation the basis to be used is cost less whatever it is estimated that the salvage or scrap will amount to."

opinion sub nom. Evans v. Commissioner, 264 F.2d 502, 511–12 (9th Cir. 1959), reversed in the opinion reprinted above.

F. CHANGES IN ESTIMATES

After a depreciable asset has been held for a few years, it may become apparent that the original estimates of useful life or salvage value, or both, were incorrect. The depreciation rate may thus be too high or too low. Suppose that a milling machine cost $10,000 at January 1, 19X1, with an estimated salvage value of $2,000 and useful life of 4 years. After 2 years, at the beginning of 19X3, it is found to have a probable useful life of 8 years and the same salvage value. How should it be accounted for? *APB Op. No. 20,* ¶ 31 (1971) provides:

> 31. The Board concludes that the effect of a change in accounting estimate should be accounted for in (a) the period of change if the change affects that period only or (b) the period of change and future periods if the change affects both. A change in an estimate should not be accounted for by restating amounts reported in financial statements of prior periods or by reporting pro forma amounts for prior periods.

Try your hand at the journal entries for acquisition and depreciation and any other related entries for 19X1 through 19X8.

A change in estimated useful life or salvage value is not a change in GAAP requiring a "preferability" determination under *APB Op. No. 20. In re Ernst & Whinney,* (CCH) Fed.Sec.L.Rep. ¶ 84,610 at p. 80,933 (SEC, 1990). Is this desirable given the potential for abuse illustrated by the General Motors story described at the beginning of this chapter?

G. DEPRECIATION METHODS

ATB No. 1, ¶ 54 calls for a "rational and systematic method" for allocating fixed asset costs to accounting periods. See also *APB Statement No. 4,* ¶ 159 (1970).

1. STRAIGHT–LINE METHOD

In Chapter I we saw an illustration of depreciation computed on a straight-line basis (i.e., cost less salvage value is allocated equally each year over the period of useful life of the asset).

2. UNITS OF OPERATING TIME AND PRODUCTION METHODS

It is equally rational and systematic to measure on the basis of operating time or of units of output. For example, a bottling machine may be depreciated over its estimated useful life consisting of 4,000 hours of operation. In this case, each accounting period will be charged with $\frac{1}{4,000}$ of the cost less salvage multiplied by the number of hours the machine is operated in the period. Or if the machine is estimated to be capable of filling 500,000 bottles before becoming useless to the business, each period will be charged with 1/500,000 of the cost less salvage, multiplied by the number of bottles turned out.

Would it be suitable for an automobile company to use either of these methods in depreciating its body stamping dies for 19X1? (Assume that it turned out 1,000,000 automobiles in 19X1 and had 1,000 stamping dies each of which could be used 5,000 times before becoming unusable.) Further assume that the dies cannot be used for models other than 19X1 vintage.

3. INVENTORY (OR APPRAISAL) METHOD

For small tools which often disappear and therefore result in a cost which involves this loss as well as depreciation in the ordinary sense, a method of accounting is used which is sometimes called either the inventory or appraisal method. The period charge to depreciation expense is calculated in much the same way cost of goods sold is calculated, but with the additional element of writing down the closing inventory of tools by an amount to account for depreciation in the sense used by accountants.

4. ACCELERATED METHODS

Immediately after World War II, the requirement for new productive assets, rising costs and high federal income tax rates all combined to cause a reconsideration of depreciation methods. The straight-line method then in general use failed to satisfy certain demands. This reconsideration continues. The concept of holding gains and losses has its most substantial effects on depreciation of fixed assets. Insofar as the issue concerns depreciation (by any method) on appreciated values rather than cost, it is discussed infra page 287.

The discussion did lead first the Treasury by Regulations in 1946, and then Congress in § 167 of the Internal Revenue Code of 1954, to sanction larger charges to depreciation (and thereby lower taxable profits) through accelerated depreciation methods. This gave accelerated depreciation unprecedented popularity even for non-tax, financial accounting purposes. Those methods, i.e., double declining balance and sum-of-the-years'-digits, were based on the concept of spreading the cost over the useful economic life of the asset and they found credence in generally accepted accounting principles.

NATIONAL ASSOCIATION OF RAILROAD AND UTILITIES COMMISSIONERS, REPORT OF COMMITTEE ON DEPRECIATION pp. 70–71

(1943).

"Fixed-percent-of-declining-balance Method

"This method is a plan under which a uniform per cent is applied to the remaining net book cost (cost less depreciation reserve) of plant throughout its estimated service life. The formula by which the uniform rate is determined is:

$$R = 1 - \sqrt[E]{\frac{s}{c}}$$

Where

    R = depreciation rate
    s = net salvage
    c = cost of plant
    E = service life

[22-2]

"If the plant has no net salvage, it is necessary in applying the formula to assume a nominal salvage because, in strict theory, it would be impossible to reduce the plant cost to zero by applying a uniform per cent to a diminishing balance.

"Applying the formula in an assumed example of a unit of plant with a 10–year life, cost of $1,000, and net salvage of $50, a rate of approximately 26 per cent is indicated. This rate would apply to $1,000 in the first year, giving depreciation expense of $260. The second year the depreciation expense would be 26 per cent of $1,000 minus $260, or $193. The third year 26 per cent of ($1,000–$260–$193) or $142, and so on to the tenth year when the charge would be $17.

"A significant characteristic of this method is that it loads the early years of service life with the major portion of the cost to be depreciated. Since maintenance expenses are generally higher when property is old, this characteristic results in leveling somewhat the combined depreciation and maintenance expenses, and the rapid accumulation of depreciation reserve may be considered as resulting in conservatism in financial statements. Nevertheless, it has not been used to a great extent and is not likely to be generally accepted in utility accounting. The principal reasons for this view are that it cannot be satisfactorily applied on a group or average basis.

"Sum-of-the-years'-digits Method

"This method is a plan in which the successive years of service life are numbered in reverse order and the depreciation rate to be applied in a particular year is equal to the fraction of which the numerator is the number assigned to that year and the denominator is the sum of all the digits by which the years are respectively numbered. Thus, in the case of a service life of 10 years, the sum of the years' digits from 1 to 10, respectively, is 55 and the respective annual depreciation rates are $10/55$, $9/55$, etc., to the 10th year when the rate would be $1/55$.

"This method loads the depreciation heavily on the early years of service life and is subject to the same comments made in connection with the fixed-percent-of-declining-balance method."

———

Contrast the NARUC formula above for the declining balance method with the IRC concept of the declining balance method in Treas. Reg. § 1.167(b):

DECLINING BALANCE METHOD

(a) Application of method.—The declining balance rate may be determined without resort to formula. Such rate determined under section 167(b)(2) shall not exceed twice the appropriate straight line rate computed without adjustment for salvage. While salvage is not taken into account in determining the annual allowances under this method, in no event shall an asset (or an account) be depreciated below a reasonable salvage value.

Hertz Corp. v. United States, 364 U.S. 122 (1960), rejected the view that because the Treasury regulation applies the declining balance method for pre–1981 acquisitions to cost without deducting salvage, and produced a mathematical residue at the end of useful life which "represents salvage value," actual salvage value may be disregarded in determining the extent of allowable depreciation. *Hertz* was codified in the last sentence of Regs. § 1.167(b) quoted above. The NARUC formula for the declining balance method would not present this issue. How do the statements of this method by NARUC and by the IRS differ?

Promptly after the IRC permitted accelerated depreciation, the predecessor of the APB approved these tax methods of depreciation as GAAP, thus illustrating another way in which GAAP are sometimes affected by tax accounting. *ARB No. 44* (1954) and *ARB No. 44 (Revised)* (1958).

These ARBs define "declining balance" depreciation to include accelerated depreciation methods such as the "sum-of-the-years'-digits" and the declining balance methods of the tax law as GAAP. In fact the tax declining balance method is more often used in financial accounting than is the formula described in the NARUC excerpt. The sum-of-the-years'-digits method is seldom used for either tax or financial accounting.

Question

5–6. *Question.* Is a change from a straight-line method to an accelerated method a change in accounting principles so as to require "preferability," or is it merely a change in an estimate? See *APB Opinion No. 20,* ¶ 32 (1971).

5. TAX ACCOUNTING VS. GAAP FOR FIXED ASSETS

We have already indicated that, unlike LIFO accounting for inventories, there is no tax law "booking" requirement for depreciation. In fact the overwhelming majority of firms use a straight-line method for financial reporting and various accelerated methods for tax purposes.

Because fixed assets often have lives extending for decades, and because of periodic revisions of the Internal Revenue Code, there are four extant regimes of accounting for fixed assets for income tax purposes, depending on when particular assets were placed in service. These regimes cover assets placed in service in each of five periods:

(a) Pre–1946;

(b) 1946 through 1971;

(c) 1972 through 1980;

(d) 1981 through 1986;

(e) 1987 to the present.

Since many long-lived assets may still be subject to tax depreciation even under the pre–1946 law and tax years of many years ago may still be subject to litigation for many future years, it is necessary to be aware of the old law as well as the present law.

(a) Pre–1946

In the simple days before 1946, the straight-line method was used for most tax purposes.

(b) 1946 through 1971

The rapid inflation of World War II stimulated industry to seek and obtain accelerated depreciation, first, under IRS regulations in 1946, and then by statute in the Internal Revenue Code of 1954.

As we have noted, straight-line, double declining balance and sum-of-the-years'-digits methods plus any method resulting in lesser depreciation charges were permitted for tax purposes after 1946. For the most part those included the methods previously described as GAAP including the units of operating time method, the inventory method, etc.

To provide guidance for Internal Revenue Service auditors and taxpayers, the Bulletin F guideline lives mentioned in *Massey Motors* were adopted in 1942. They provided an elaborate list of fixed assets and recommended periods of useful life to which, after 1946, either the straight-line or accelerated methods might be applied. The IRS and taxpayers were once said thus to be subject to "a scientific method [for fixing useful lives] known as horse trading." B. Bittker & L. Lokken, *Federal Taxation of Income, Estates and Gifts* 23–69 (2d ed. 1988).[a]

To further diminish the pressure from taxpayers seeking to maximize annual deductions, in 1962, Bulletin F was withdrawn and guideline lives were established which were 30–40% shorter. In 1962 Congress also allowed a substantial leeway for estimates of salvage value— permitting a deviation of as much as 10% of original cost. Thus, for a $100 asset with a five-year useful life and reasonable salvage value of $15, the taxpayer could estimate it at as low as $5 without being subject to liability. As will appear, this was the beginning of an erosion and ultimate disappearance of the concept of salvage value for tax purposes.

(c) 1972–1980—the Asset Depreciation Range ("ADR") System

For property placed in service in this period, further liberalization of constraints on useful lives were implemented by permitting taxpayers to elect a useful life from 80% to 120% of a complex of industry-wide class lives established by the ADR system.

---

a. This note is largely based on Bittker & Lokken's chapter 23.

Although salvage value was not used to determine net cost, depreciation deductions ceased when all but salvage value had been deducted.

To further alleviate taxpayer stress, a generous repair deduction allowance was established, which minimized disputes. Moreover, up to $10,000 of costs could be expensed each year for businesses purchasing depreciable assets costing less than $210,000 in any year.

The ADR system was optional for taxpayers who alternatively could employ one of the old depreciation methods using reasonable useful lives and salvage values. However, the guideline lives of the pre–1971 regime were not to be used.

(d) 1981–1986—Accelerated Cost Recovery System ("ACRS")

For tangible assets placed in service in 1981 and thereafter until 1986, a radically different system applied under IRC § 168. Here useful life and salvage value disappear as relevant concepts. Instead, there are statutorily prescribed recovery periods which are far shorter than any reasonable estimate of useful lives. The purpose of ACRS was to grant larger depreciation deductions for the announced purpose of stimulating the economy.

Most tangible property placed in service after 1981 and before 1987 is deductible only under ACRS. (Intangibles were outside ACRS.)

The ACRS established a very small number of class lives, made them very short relative to actual useful lives and eliminated salvage value as a limitation on deductibility. Most personal property was recoverable over two and one-half to five years, and at first most realty over fifteen years, although the latter was later changed first to eighteen years and then to nineteen years.

The ACRS used tables to designate the recovery periods rather than depreciation methods such as the straight-line or one of the accelerated methods, although the tables basically allowed about 150% of the declining balance method for personalty and 175% for realty over the shortened recovery periods. Taxpayers also could elect to slow down depreciation if that appeared to serve their interests.

(e) 1987 to Present; Modified ACRS

For tangible property placed in service after 1986, the prior ACRS was replaced with another comprehensive set of rules which Congress perversely also designated as ACRS, presumably to disguise its substantial reduction of business taxpayers' benefits. The principal difference is longer recovery periods and a return to use of depreciation methods rather than prescribed tables.

For tangible personal property, six classes of from three to twenty years and for real property two classes of twenty-seven and a half and thirty-one and a half years were established. The old ACRS 1981–86 tables do not apply but rules requiring one of the depreciation methods do—for realty straight-line only, but for personalty up to 200% declining balance (except for the fifteen- and twenty-year classes which are limited to 150% declining balance) with a zero salvage value in all cases. However, a switch is made to straight-line as soon as the switch increases the year's allowance. Also, an election may be made to use straight-line for personal property depreciation with longer lives instead of ACRS. For property depreciable on other than a useful life basis, § 168(f) excludes it from the modified ACRS.

H. DEFERRED TAXES

The determination of the amount of taxable income (i.e., income tax accounting) is not congruent with the determination of financial income (i.e., income as shown on the income statement), not only because of different cost recovery methods for fixed assets, but also because of many other differences between tax and financial accounting.

There are two categories of differences. Some financial accounting revenues and expenses are simply not revenues or expenses for income tax purposes. E.g., tax free interest on municipal bonds and the non-deductible amortization of goodwill do not affect taxable income but do affect financial income. These are often termed "intraperiod" differences. The other category is termed "interperiod" differences. For example, we have noted that under tax law, some items of prepaid income (cash received in advance of delivery of goods) may be taxed in the year the cash is received or due but be deferred in the financial income statement until realized by delivery. Also we have seen that the depreciation expense for financial accounting will differ from the deduction for income tax purposes under ACRS or otherwise.

This second category of intertemporal differences presents a complex accounting problem which can be most easily illustrated by making some simplified assumptions for an illustration. Assume a machine which costs $600, has no salvage value and a useful life of three years, is depreciated on the straight-line basis for financial purposes but for the calculation of taxable income is deductible $300 in Year 1, $200 in Year 2 and $100 in Year 3. Assume a 50% tax rate. See the following table.

Table I

	Year 1		Year 2		Year 3	
	Tax Return	Financial Income Statement	Tax Return	Financial Income Statement	Tax Return	Financial Income Statement
Gross Income	$1,000	$1,000	$1,000	$1,000	$1,000	$1,000
Other Expenses	400	400	400	400	400	400
Income before Depreciation and Taxes	$ 600	$ 600	$ 600	$ 600	$ 600	$ 600
Depreciation	300	200	200	200	100	200
Net Income before Taxes	$ 300	$ 400	$ 400	$ 400	$ 500	$ 400
Tax Payable Currently	$ 150	$ 150	$ 200	$ 200	$ 250	$ 250
Net Income after Tax		$ 250		$ 200		$ 150

Note that the amount on the line labelled Tax Payable Currently is the same within each year for both the "Financial Income Statement" column and the "Tax Return" column. This means simply that the current portion of the tax for financial purposes as well as the tax due for tax purposes is the amount determined by the tax return, even though for Years 1 and 3 it is disproportionate with the amount shown as Net Income before Taxes on the financial income statement. I.e., for Year 1 the tax is 15/40 or 37½% of income and for Year 3 it is 25/40 or 62½%, although the tax rate is consistently 50% by our hypothesis. It is characteristic of accelerated depreciation methods that because the amount of depreciation taken is accelerated in early years, the permissible depreciation is less than a straight-line amount in later years. This results in retribution consisting of a higher tax liability in the later years because of the tax saving from the accelerated depreciation deduction in the earlier years.

At present GAAP permit as one remedy for this perceived incongruity, "normalizing" the amount of tax expense shown on the financial income statement—making it what it normally would have been had the tax depreciation amount been the same as the financial statement amount. The journal entries would be:

Year 1	Tax Expense	$200	
	Deferred Tax Liability		$ 50
	Cash		150
Year 2	Tax Expense	200	
	Cash		200
Year 3	Tax Expense	200	
	Deferred Tax Liability	50	
	Cash		250

It should be noted that the Deferred Tax Liability is shown on the right side of the balance sheet between liabilities and stockholders' equity at the end of Year 1 but it is not a liability in any legal sense. The Internal Revenue Service is not claiming that the taxpayer owes any further amount. There is no legal liability for that amount. When and if the taxpayer does reach Year 3 under the conditions herein indicated for Year 3, the tax rate may be different and the taxpayer may have offsetting factors which will preclude the extra liability. But the question for accounting has been considered to be not whether there is in fact a legal liability, but whether the showing of a Deferred Tax Liability on the balance sheet and the Tax Expense on the income statement best promotes informative reporting.

Under *SFAS No. 96* (1987) this conceptualization of the Deferred Tax Liability has been changed, although *SFAS No. 96* is optional at the present and it is generally expected that *SFAS No. 96* will be modified if not rescinded. The deferred tax accounting described in our example of the three-year, $600 machine is crystallized in APB Opinion No. 11, *Accounting for Income Taxes* (1967), and continues to be permitted. By 1990 about 20% of 1,600 firms surveyed had changed to the new method of *SFAS No. 96* (e.g., see the GE financials, p. 544)—the others were awaiting the outcome of proposals to change *SFAS No. 96*.

One reason some firms have eagerly adopted the accounting of *SFAS No. 96* is that to convert from *APB Op. No. 11* to *SFAS No. 96,* much of the deferred credit on many firms' books must be reduced by debits to that account balanced by corresponding credits to income—thereby increasing reported net income. See the GE income statement, infra p. 544, showing $577,000,000 additional income in 1987.

Regardless of whether *SFAS No. 96* in its present form or some altered state will become GAAP, there are substantial effects of *APB Op. No. 11* since it was the rule until 1987 and continues in use for most firms. Further it is necessary background to understanding *SFAS No. 96* and battles over its implementation. Hence, a few words about this present GAAP are in order here.

Despite its obvious merit in our example, and the neatness with which deferred tax accounting is available to normalize the taxes and the income in the three years, there are extremely bitter opponents of the requirement. The argument of the opponents of normalization, somewhat sparsely summarized in ¶ 28 of *APB Op. No. 11,* has its roots in the contention that the deferred taxes in many situations will never really be payable, and therefore that the credit is part of stockholders' equity.

The proponents of the normalization method rely on the matching concept for their argument that the tax expense should be recognized in the same year as the revenue which will give rise to it. See *Opinion No. 11,* ¶¶ 29–31.

The opponents would not quarrel with our three-year example on the $600 machine shown supra. They would admit that in the context of the single machine, the situation is sure to reverse itself and a tax saving in the earlier years will become an excessive tax liability in later years, and provision should be made therefor. See *APB Op. No. 11,* ¶¶ 26–27. Their contention, rather, is that no single machine may be viewed in isolation, and the impact of the discrepancy between accelerated tax depreciation and straight-line depreciation for financial purposes can only be viewed in the context of a whole company. The argument is that American industry in general is continuously expanding; that there is always accelerated depreciation on new facilities to even out the less-than-straight-line depreciation on machines that are approaching the end of their service life.

An illustration is necessary to explain this point. Extra depreciation taken in the early years on a particular asset must be balanced by lesser depreciation on that asset in later years because the aggregate cannot exceed the cost of the asset. Perhaps counter-intuitively, it does not follow that therefore extra depreciation on the aggregate of assets acquired from time to time will balance with the lesser depreciation on that aggregate *in a way which will result in net after-tax income being identical with what it would have been if straight-line depreciation had been taken.* There is a factor of the cumulative effect of accelerated depreciation. Let us examine an illustration to determine this cumulative effect.

Referring again to our $600 machine with a three-year useful life and no salvage value, we ignore the interest earned on the $50 deferred until the tax is paid in the third year, and also ignore the possibility that the general tax rate will change or the taxpayer's tax bracket may change before the tax is paid for the third year. Still ignoring these matters, will the early years' tax saving be paid if several asset items are purchased and the total plant investment increases from year to year or remains level after a few years? The answer is, no, under these assumptions, as can be seen by working through the comparative depreciation schedules below. The first schedule shows depreciation on an accelerated basis, and the second shows it on a straight line basis.

Table II
Tax Return Annual Depreciation—Accelerated Basis

	Yr. 1	Yr. 2	Yr. 3	Yr. 4	Yr. 5
Machine # 1 (Purchased in Yr. 1)	$300	$200	$100		
Machine # 2 (Purchased in Yr. 2)		300	200	$100	
Machine # 3 (Purchased in Yr. 3)			300	200	$100
Machine # 4 (Purchased in Yr. 4)				300	200
Machine # 5 (Purchased in Yr. 5)					300
Total Annual Depreciation	$300	$500	$600	$600	$600

Financial Statement Annual Depreciation—Straight Line Basis

	Yr. 1	Yr. 2	Yr. 3	Yr. 4	Yr. 5
Machine # 1 (Purchased in Yr. 1)	$200	$200	$200		
Machine # 2 (Purchased in Yr. 2)		200	200	$200	
Machine # 3 (Purchased in Yr. 3)			200	200	$200
Machine # 4 (Purchased in Yr. 4)				200	200
Machine # 5 (Purchased in Yr. 5)					200
Total Annual Depreciation	$200	$400	$600	$600	$600

From this illustration it appears that in the first two years $200 more tax depreciation is taken and a consequent $100 tax saving (assuming a 50% tax rate) over the straight line method is obtained. And as long as a new machine is purchased each year, at a cost of at least $600, this $100 tax will never fall due because, as is shown, in the following years, tax depreciation exceeds or equals financial income depreciation contrary to the case of the single machine for Year 3 in Table I. Given inflation and the normal tendency of business to expand, plus the fact that if the business declines, the applicable tax rate may also decline, there is a substantial chance that even more taxes will be saved.[b]

b. Davidson, Accelerated Depreciation and the Allocation of Income Taxes, 33 Acctg.Rev. 173, 175–76 (1958), illustrates this point in more detail.

It must also be noted that sometimes financial income is temporarily *less* than taxable income, the opposite of our above illustration. Thus for certain prepayments, GAAP require deferral while tax law requires recognition. In such cases initially, under the normalization technique of *APB Op. No. 11,* there will be a debit to an asset account instead of a credit to a liability. And, of course, in the later years even in our example it is possible that, as in the case of Year 3 for our single asset illustration, debits to liabilities will exceed credits.

Therefore a basic question is whether, for all firms in the aggregate, the credits do in fact generally exceed the debits to the deferred tax account. Price Waterhouse published a study contending that an examination of 100 leading companies showed that only a minute fraction of the deferred tax liability set up over the twelve years from 1954 to 1965 was actually needed for cases where the tax liability reversed.[c] One may doubt how persuasive this is, because a twelve-year period within which there was no really deep depression and stoppage of investment in industrial plant is probably insufficient for a real test. A more recent study of 2,637 firms for the years 1954–73 concludes that about half of the firms each year experienced a decrease while the rest experienced a build-up, but the methodology and accuracy of conclusions of this study have been thrown into doubt.[d] Another leading accounting firm, Lybrand, Ross Brothers & Montgomery, issued a public statement in opposition to the Price Waterhouse position.[e]

More recently an update of still another study was made, taking into account the criticism that prior studies did not include years in which a recession occurred. In Davidson, Rasch & Weil, *Professional Notes,* J. Accountancy 138 (Oct. 1984), the authors reported on their findings for 1973–82:

> Of the 22,559 cases in which there was a change in the [liability] account balance, 17,220 (76.3%) were increases and 5,339 (23.7%) were decreases. This is a slightly lower percentage of increases than in the preceding 20 years, but increases still overwhelm decreases. The dollar amount of the increases is more than eight times as great as the amount of the decreases, a higher ratio than before.
>
> The conclusion reached by a Price Waterhouse study in 1967 and by the 1977 study—that the deferred tax credit account is seldom decreased by tax payments arising from the reversals of depreciation timing differences—continues to hold true when the data are extended

c. Price Waterhouse & Co., Is Generally Accepted Accounting for Income Taxes Possibly Misleading Investors? A Statement of Position on Income Tax Allocation (July, 1967).

d. Herring & Jacobs, The Expected Behavior of Deferred Tax Credits, J. Accountancy 52 (Aug., 1976). Professional Notes, J. Accountancy 53 (April, 1977). See Standard Oil Company (New Jersey) Prospectus of February 16, 1970, at p. 24 with accountants' opinion by Price Waterhouse & Co.

e. News Release dated July 28, 1967. Other studies include Voss, Accelerated Depreciation and Deferred Tax Allocation, 6 J. Acctg. Res. 262 (1968), and Livingstone, Accelerated Depreciation and Deferred Taxes: An Empirical Study of Fluctuating Asset Expenditures, Empirical Research in Accounting, Selected Studies (Supp. to J. Acctg. Res.) 93 (1967).

to include the financial reports through 1982. The amount of the credit balances continues to grow at a substantial rate, and the rate of growth can be expected to accelerate as the accelerated cost recovery system is applied to new plant asset acquisitions.

Another study extended the Davidson, Rasch and Weil study and confirmed it. See Skekel & Fazzi, *The Deferred Tax Liability: Do Capital Intensive Companies Pay It?* J. Accountancy 142 (Oct. 1984).

These and other studies, establishing the preponderance of credits for deferred taxes, were an important motivating force behind adoption of *SFAS No. 96.* See Beresford, Best & Weber, *Accounting for Income Taxes: Change Is Coming,* J. Accountancy 72 (Jan. 1984).

We will not burden you with an explanation of *SFAS No. 96,* not because it is one of the more arcane accounting standards, but because it is generally expected at press time that it will be substantially altered if not rescinded shortly.

However we may describe its conceptual basis briefly.

We have shown that the basic concept of *APB Op. No. 11,* just described, is that income should reflect not only income taxes payable for the year but also the taxes that would have been payable for that year had financial income included items which will in later years reduce or increase income taxes without affecting financial income; i.e., the so-called normalization of income tax expense.

This concept, emphasizing the income statement effects, is rejected by *SFAS No. 96* in favor of a concept that calls for emphasizing the balance sheet instead. The idea is that the unpaid income taxes (from, say, accelerated depreciation) should be shown as a liability. Then any increases or decreases in this liability from year to year will increase or decrease income tax expense in the future. This concept gives a name to the *SFAS No. 96* method, known as the "liability method."

However, once we get beyond this basic concept, to its implementation, *SFAS No. 96* makes so many arbitrary compromises that we may safely say that the basic concept is nearly abandoned. Most importantly, nothing is done to address the problem just described (also present under *SFAS No. 96*) which results in most firms using accelerated depreciation for tax purposes never paying the deferred tax—a strange "liability." Moreover, even for those who do pay, many years later, nothing is done in *SFAS No. 96* to discount the liability to present value. See the following note concerning discounting.

It all goes downhill from here.

For an excellent informed and clear explanation of the very complex technicalities of the present version of *SFAS No. 96,* see L. Nikolai & J. Bayley, *Intermediate Accounting,* Ch. 22 (4th ed. 1988).

Notes

5–7. *Discounting of Tax Liability.* Recall that a payment not due for some period of time has a present value lower than the face amount due. See the Appendix to this book. The illustration in the text ignored this discount factor, in accordance with *APB Op. No. 10,* ¶ 6, reaffirmed in *APB Op. No. 21,* n. 3. If the deferred tax is not likely to be paid in the near future, application of principles of present value would bring the liability down close to zero since the deferred tax account represents, in effect, an interest-free loan from the U.S. Government. Should there be a discount of the deferred tax liability? For an affirmative answer, see Davidson, *Accelerated Depreciation and the Allocation of Income Taxes,* 33 Acctg. Rev. 173, 177 (1958). Discounting continues as an issue after *SFAS No. 96.* See id. ¶ 6. And see Stepp, *Deferred Taxes: The Discounting Controversy,* J. Accountancy 98 (Nov. 1985). Discounting, of course, is a concept relevant to valuation of all costs and liabilities which will involve cash payments at some future date. Accounting has been slow to adopt it but in 1989 the FASB appointed a Task Force to study the concept under the title, "Interest Methods."

5–8. *"Normalization" and "Flow-through."* As indicated in Table I, above, comprehensive interperiod tax allocation methods are also known as normalization. The nonallocation methods are referred to as "flow-through" techniques. The term normalization is derived from the fact that the tax expense is shown as it normally would be on the income reported as subject to tax. "Flow-through" means that the tax reduction is flowed through the income statement to net income.

I. LEASE ACCOUNTING—A PREVIEW

We shall consider lease accounting in detail in Chapter XI because of the vast economic significance of leasing in today's economy brought on by tax and financial considerations. Leasing is expected to increase even more in the future. For example automobile manufacturers, advised by their economic consultants that consumers will soon be unable to afford to purchase autos, have launched educational advertising campaigns to make leasing more acceptable. Here we shall present a brief conceptual overview because many leases are accounted for as purchased fixed assets which are therefore depreciated.

You already know that the lessor under an ordinary lease carries the leased asset in its balance sheet, deducts depreciation and recognizes rental income on a straight-line basis regardless of how payments are received. And the lessee merely debits rent expense on a straight-line basis and credits cash or a payable.

It is common ground that a lease may not be a true lease but may be a thinly disguised sale of the asset; e.g., a lease of an automobile for five years with an option in the lessee to purchase it at the end of the term for $1. If the lease is in fact a sale, should accounting bury its head in the sand and treat it like an ordinary lease?

GAAP say no. An ordinary lease is termed an "operating lease" in SFAS No. 13, *Accounting for Leases* (1976). But when the "lease" is in fact a purchase, it is termed a "capital lease."

The *lessee's* accounting for capital leases calls for debiting an asset and crediting a liability at inception for the present value of the lease payments to be made, and then taking depreciation expense periodically on that amount and dividing the debits for payments made between interest expense and amortization of the liability.

Accounting for a *lessor's* capital lease is slightly more complex because the lessor may be the "seller" of the leased item (a "sales-type" lease) or instead may be a third party financier, such as a bank (in which case the lease is termed a "direct financing" lease). For a sales-type lease, the lessor's accounting usually correlates with the lessee's— the lessor treats the asset as sold and recognizes income on the sale immediately. Thereafter it takes no depreciation, and a portion of the receipts is treated as periodic interest income on the receivable and the balance as receipt of principal.

When the lease is a "direct-financing" lease, the bank or other lender of course recognizes no profit on the sale of the asset at the time of the lease, but recognizes its income as interest on a straight-line basis over the term of the lease.

The complexities of lease accounting are in measuring these components and in determining whether a capital lease or an operating lease is involved. There are some other intricacies for sales and leasebacks, "leveraged-leases" and related party leases.

J. SALES OF FIXED ASSETS: HEREIN OF THE "UNIT" AND "GROUP" METHODS OF DEPRECIATION

The composition of the unit to be depreciated will affect amounts charged to repairs, capitalized assets, and depreciation expense. For example, if an entire factory is the unit, replacement of one of a hundred lathes might be charged to expense, while if the unit is the lathe, it will be capitalized.

Another problem is how to account for a disposition of the asset.

When a fixed asset is sold, the price will only coincidentally be equal to cost less accumulated depreciation. Where the price does vary from net book value, is it appropriate to reflect the difference in income as gain or loss? Or in the Retained Earnings account? Or in neither?

Suppose that a factory is sold for $75,000 cash. It had cost $100,000, for which Accumulated Depreciation was $70,000. On sale, the entry is:

Cash	$75,000	
Accumulated Depreciation	70,000	
Plant		$100,000
Gain from Sale of Plant		45,000

If the asset sold instead was one of seventy-five milling machines some of which were sold and replaced every year, would any entry affecting income be appropriate? For enterprises owning many fixed assets a technique has been developed whereby some of the inaccuracies may be averaged out, because it is recognized that any gain or loss on sale is strictly a function of the accuracy of the depreciation method selected years before and of the estimates of useful life and salvage value.

To illustrate, assume that Ajax Corp. owns five milling machines for which it has paid $1,200 each and the useful lives are estimated to be five years, after which the salvage value is estimated to be $200.

Using a straight line rate of 20% for the charge to depreciation, the credit to Accumulated Depreciation each year will be $200 per machine. At the end of the third year, the machines would be carried on the balance sheet as follows:

Milling Machines	$6,000
Less: Accumulated Depreciation	3,000
Net	$3,000

If one of the machines is sold for $800 at the end of the third year, our prior technique of accounting for the sale would call for the following entry:

Cash	$800	
Accumulated Depreciation	600	
Milling Machine		$1,200
Gain on Sale of Machine		200

This method of handling depreciation questions on an individual basis is known as the "unit method."

But has a true gain been earned on the sale of this machine? Or did we err in our five year estimate of useful life? Or our estimate of salvage value? And if we did, have other errors in the opposite direction for the other machines occurred?

Because of these questions and for other reasons, the "group method" of accounting for fixed assets has been developed. Under this method, in effect, the entire cost of a unit retired is charged to Accumulated Depreciation, and the entire consideration on resale is credited to that account. The net entry for the above transaction would be:

Cash	$800	
Accumulated Depreciation	400	
Milling Machine		$1,200

It will be seen that this entry is the same as the previous one, except that the gain is treated as an adjustment to Accumulated Depreciation.

Thus no gain or loss is recognized, and the entire adjustment is in the Accumulated Depreciation account. In this way it is thought that the income statement will not be charged or credited with as many gains or losses caused largely by wrong estimates as would occur under the unit method. It is likely that the gains on some machines will be offset by losses on others, and the accumulated depreciation for the group will work out to be just about right, if the estimates of useful life and salvage value were accurate as averages.

Note and Problem

5–9. *Errors in Assumptions Under the Group Method.* In United States v. New York Telephone Co., 326 U.S. 638 (1946), the Court correctly detected an error in application of the group method in that the average useful life of the group was mistakenly made too long, with the result that net plant was overstated. The following is a simplified version of the problem:

Assume that the assets of a regulated public utility company were acquired from a related person for $100 and debited to Plant. Then assume the FCC determines that the price to the buyer was $20 in excess of original cost when first devoted to the public service. Under settled law, the FCC could order a write-down to $80 so that the rate base would be enhanced by these assets only to the extent of $80.

But in *New York Telephone* when, instead of immediately determining the need for a write-down, the FCC waited until after the plant was retired, it was argued that it was too late to order the rate base to be reduced by $20. But that argument was rejected.

The assets had a remaining useful life at time of purchase of four years but were put into a group with a useful life of ten years. After the fourth year when they were retired and $100 was debited to Accumulated Depreciation in accordance with the group method and credited to Plant, there was still $60 attributable to these assets which was carried in the rate base. The entries were these:

On Acquisition:		
Plant	$100	
Cash		$100
Aggregate of Debits and Credits for Years 1 through 4:		
Depreciation Expense	40	
Accumulated Depreciation		40
On Retirement in Year 5:		
Accumulated Depreciation	100	
Plant		100

After these entries, Accumulated Depreciation for the group had been wrongfully reduced by $60, leaving net Plant for that group overstated by $60 thus permitting the $20 write-down.

Could this situation have arisen if the unit method had been followed?

Another question suggested is why did the case ever come to court, let alone go all the way to the Supreme Court? It is hard to explain on any basis other than that the accounting issues were sufficiently obscure to allow some lawyers (a) never to have grasped the issues; or (b) to believe that some opposing lawyer or the courts might not grasp them.

5–10. *Problem.* A building is carried at cost ($90,000) less Accumulated Depreciation ($80,000) but is insured for fair market value of $175,000. It is totally destroyed by fire and the full insurance amount is received. This is treated as a disposition with a resultant gain of $165,000. But what should be the accounting if the $175,000 is used to rebuild an identical facility? See FASB Interpretation No. 30, *Accounting for Involuntary Conversions of Nonmonetary Assets to Monetary Assets* (1979), weighing the contrasting arguments:

(a) An involuntary conversion of an asset not held for sale should be treated as an in-kind exchange under *APB Op. No. 29,* ¶ 21 (see part K below), when insurance proceeds are used to replace the destroyed asset;

(b) The receipt of insurance proceeds is like any other voluntary sale.

K. TRADE–INS

The accounting for trade-ins of productive assets for similar ones is prescribed by APB Opinion No. 29, *Accounting for Nonmonetary Transactions,* ¶¶ 18, 21 and 22 (1973), which calls for no recognition of gain:

18. * * * The fair value of the asset received should be used to measure the cost if it is more clearly evident than the fair value of the asset surrendered. * * *

21. *Exchanges.* If the exchange is not essentially the culmination of an earning process, accounting for an exchange of a nonmonetary asset between an enterprise and another entity should be based on the recorded amount (after reduction, if appropriate, for an indicated impairment of value) of the nonmonetary asset relinquished. The Board believes that the following [does] not culminate an earning process:

* * *

b. An exchange of a productive asset not held for sale in the ordinary course of business for a similar productive asset or an equivalent interest in the same or similar productive asset (similar productive asset is defined in paragraph 3 and examples are given in paragraph 7).[6]

Since losses are recognized (as stated in ¶ 21 for impairments of value) but gains are not, the entries depend on whether there is a gain or loss, which in turn depends on the valuation of either the old or the new asset (whichever one is used, per ¶ 18 above, for measurement).

To illustrate, assume that an old machine has a book value of $700 (original cost, $1,200, less $500 of Accumulated Depreciation) and together with $400 cash is traded for a similar new machine. Even if

---

6. The fact that an exchange of productive assets is not a taxable transaction for tax purposes may be evidence that the assets exchanged are similar for purposes of applying this Opinion.

the value of the new asset is $1,200, and the old is $800, the gain is not recognized no matter which value is used:

(a) New Machine	$1,100	
Accumulated Depreciation	500	
Old Machine		$1,200
Cash		400

On the other hand, if the value of the new machine is $1,000 and the old is $600, no matter which value is "more clearly evident," the entry is:

(b) New Machine	$1,000	
Accumulated Depreciation	500	
Loss	100	
Old Machine		$1,200
Cash		400

If the "more clearly evident" value would result in a gain, no gain is recognized as in (a) whereas if it shows a loss, the loss is recognized as in (b).

But suppose the old machine is sold for its $800 value to a third party and that $800 plus another $400 cash is used to purchase the new machine. Viewing the two transactions as separate, and using the unit method, the entries would be:

Cash	$800	
Accumulated Depreciation	500	
Old Machine		$1,200
Gain		100
New Machine	$1,200	
Cash		1,200

This results in $100 more income than does the trade-in although the only difference is that three parties instead of two are involved. This explains why many firms no longer trade in used vehicles, etc., but sell them.

Is this a case of accounting dictating business practice? Or is it a gimmick allowing managers to manipulate income? Does it help explain why so many accountants (and lawyers) are so well paid for their expertise in this arcane subject? Would it make even a traditionalist wonder if the Critical Legal Studies movement is justified? Should *APB Op. No. 29* be amended to cover this situation?

L. THE RIGHT SIDE FOR ACCUMULATED DEPRECIATION

The credit side of the balance sheet cannot be broken down into a sharp dichotomy between liabilities and stockholders' equity. There are some very indeterminate credits. See Sprouse, *Accounting for What–You–May–Call–Its*, J. Accountancy 45 (Oct. 1966). Thus, instead of only liabilities and stockholders' equity, it may be that the right side of the balance sheet can best be seen as a source of funds.

The Accumulated Depreciation account has a credit balance, and is treated as a contra account to the related asset. Hence it is displayed on the balance sheet as follows:

Buildings, at Cost	$104,000
Less: Accumulated Depreciation	62,000
	$ 42,000

The SEC so requires in Reg. S–X, Rule 3–11. See *APB Op. No. 12*, ¶¶ 2–5 (1967), reaffirming this position.

There was a time when this account, ambiguously labelled "reserve for depreciation," appeared with other "reserves," on the right side of the balance sheet. A justification for its appearance on the right side is the argument that the right side shows sources of the corporate funds—creditors, stockholders, and in this case depreciation. See H. Ross, *The Elusive Art of Accounting* 151 (1966); Simon, *The Right Side for Accumulated Depreciation,* 34 Acctg.Rev. 97, 100–01 (1959).

M. WRITE–DOWNS ON IMPAIRMENT OF VALUE—THE "BIG BATH"

In the words of Walter Schuetze, a leading accountant, "in the absence of a decision to abandon or dispose of assets at a loss, the timing and amount of any write-down are largely discretionary." Schuetze, *Disclosure and the Impairment Question,* J. Accountancy 26, 28 (Dec. 1987). An FASB research study is the basis for this assertion. See H. Jaenicke, *Survey of Present Practices in Recognizing Revenues, Expenses, Gains and Losses* 147–56 (1981). In that study, Professor Jaenicke points out the increasing urgency of the problem because of accelerating technological and economic changes and lists the difficulties which have made clear guidance impossible:

How does one know when the cost of an asset is sufficiently impaired to necessitate a write-down?

Should the write-down be mandatory if there is a chance that the asset will regain its stature or only when impairment is permanent?

How does one distinguish with confidence temporary and permanent impairments?

How does one disaggregate impaired individual assets from other elements in an operating unit?

Should write-ups be permissible for recoupment in assets that had been written down?

Under what circumstances, if any, would a shortened amortization period or an accelerated depreciation method coupled with a reduction in residual value be more appropriate than a write-down (for example, a change from units-of-production depreciation to an accelerated depreciation method for facilities operating significantly below normal levels)?

How should write-downs to recognize impairments be measured?

Even if a write-down is made, the last question is answered variously in practice as Schuetze points out:

> There are some hard data on inconsistencies in practice. The Financial Executives Institute (FEI) surveyed a number of companies reporting unusual charges in 1985. Of 24 companies reporting write-downs of fixed assets retained by the business (either idle or still in use), 60% of the decisions to write down the asset were based on a probability test similar to that in FASB Statement No. 5, *Accounting for Contingencies,* and 36% of the decisions were based on the permanent decline test. Thirteen of the write-downs (46%) were measured by net realizable value, 5 (18%) by undiscounted expected future cash flows, 4 (14%) by the net present value of future cash flows, and 3 (11%) by some combination of the former methods. The remaining three write-downs were based on current replacement cost, percentage of historical cost based on expected long-term capacity, and historical cost reduced by the cost of holding a building that could not be sold.

On this question, a major abuse is the "big bath" write-off. The concern of the SEC has been with excessive write-downs which would have the effect of improperly increasing future reported profits because of lower depreciation charges in the future years. As a result, as noted previously, the Commission's accounting staff places a maximum limit on the write-down to the discounted expected net cash flow. The minimum write-down the Commission believes should be to *un*discounted expected net cash flow. This is a very broad range for any long-lived asset.

The FASB staff is currently working on these issues. See FASB, Discussion Memorandum, An Analysis of Issues Related to Accounting for the Impairment of Long–Lived Assets and Identifiable Intangibles (1990).

N. THE DEPRECIATION BASE—COST OR VALUE

The 1930s were marked by a sharp deflation of values, thus discrediting the financial and accounting practices of the 1920s which led to the Great Depression. Pursuant to these practices securities had been sold and financial empires built on the basis of appraisals of companies and assets which were used to justify upward revisions of the carrying values of these assets. It was therefore easy when modern accounting came to be formulated in the 1930s and early 1940s, largely under the leadership of the SEC, for accountants and the SEC to set their faces firmly against write-ups, and to require assets to be carried at historical cost. See *ARB No. 43, Chapters 9A and 9B* (1953), and the revision of Chapter 9B in *APB Op. No. 6,* ¶ 17 (1965), and see also APB Statement No. 4, *Basic Concepts and Accounting Principles Underlying Financial Statements of Business Enterprises,* ¶ 145 (1970).

But after World War II, there began an inflation which has continued with few interruptions until the present time.

The owners of fixed assets have reacted to this in various ways. One way, urged by many shortly after World War II, was to contend that the inflated prices of those days were temporary, because a depression had always followed a war. Therefore, it was argued that the prices then being paid for fixed assets were excessive and the assets would not be worth that amount in the subsequent depression. Accordingly, it was argued that an immediate charge to expense was justified to write the asset down to an amount comparable to prewar amounts for similar assets. See The Guaranty Survey (Guaranty Trust Company of New York) September 24, 1947; E.I. DuPont deNemours & Company Annual Report, 1948. All attempts to have these special charges made tax-deductible failed, and the public accountants also refused to sanction them even for financial reporting purposes. See *ARB No. 43, Chapter 9A,* ¶ 9 (1953). Since the expected depression did not materialize, this contention has long since passed into oblivion.

The more substantial argument was based on the fact that with replacement costs constantly going up, depreciation based on ancient prewar historical costs would not provide funds sufficient for the replacement of the plants and machinery when they wore out, and that an extra charge to depreciation and credit to a replacement cost reserve was appropriate. See United States Steel Corporation Annual Reports in the 1940s and 1950s. Pittsburgh Plate Glass Company said in its Annual Report for 1948: "Net income actually was not as large as it is stated because conventional (and we think archaic) accounting principles and internal revenue regulations do not permit the Company to include in operating costs sufficient amounts (Depreciation) to replace worn out plant and equipment." General Electric Company is particularly interesting because, having argued in its Annual Report for 1948 that it would continue to base depreciation on original cost, it said in its Annual Report for 1957 that the income tax laws did not recognize the inflation situation and that taxes had to be paid on capital lost through inflation, since excessive earnings were being reported because of depreciation required to be based on cost.

The heart of the matter appears in the United States Steel Corporation Annual Report for 1954 where, referring to the accelerated amortization authorized by the Internal Revenue Code for wartime emergency facilities, it was said: "During World War II and the Korean conflict, inflation undermined the buying power of depreciation dollars. * * *" One may ask, "What are depreciation dollars?" The answer is that United States Steel is referring to the dollars of revenue recovered in cash and not subject to taxation because of the depreciation expense deduction.

This kind of reasoning assumes that the purpose of depreciation is to provide funds with which to replace plant. Obviously, however, even if operations are on a profitable or break-even basis so that the amount of depreciation is initially recovered in cash, the cash by no means remains reserved for reinvestment over the period of a plant's life. It may be reinvested in new inventory, in receivables, or even in additional plants. There is no assurance that depreciation and the profitable operations will provide the funds for a replacement plant when the time comes.

Moreover, it is by no means certain that the plant will be replaced. A company may choose to abandon that line of business. It may build a larger or smaller plant in a different location and under different conditions. It may replace the present plant with a plant using a new technology costing more or less. Thus, the old blast furnaces in the steel industry are being replaced with basic oxygen furnaces.

Therefore a staff study of the AICPA, *ARS No. 6* (1963), condemned this kind of argument for enhanced depreciation allowances and said that the function of depreciation was not to produce cash or to provide for replacement. But there is another basis for depreciation in excess of cost. Professor Bonbright strongly supported the concept that there is no income unless capital efficiency remains unimpaired. He describes this as a fourth concept of income complementing three previously described by him.

J.C. BONBRIGHT, THE VALUATION OF PROPERTY
Vol. II, 906–907 (1937).*

"[The Fourth Concept of Unimpaired Capital Efficiency we use] * * * to denote that interpretation of income under which the income from any property is construed to mean the gross receipts yielded by this property after reservation of a sufficient amount of these receipts to continue operations and also to replace the property, when it must be retired, with an equally efficient substitute. The peculiar characteristic of this concept is that it required the perpetual maintenance of an intact capital *capacity*—not of an intact capital *value*. Its most obvious departure from what we have called the accounting concept lies in its implications as to the proper annual deductions for depreciation. Traditional accountancy requires the building up of a reserve sufficient to amortize the historical cost of the depreciable fixed assets on a retirement date. On the other hand, the present interpretation of income requires the establishment of a reserve sufficient to replace the discarded assets with other assets of substantially similar efficiency. It calls for what has been called replacement accounting as distinguished from retirement accounting."

A leading legal writer on accounting is also greatly concerned by this problem of maintaining capital efficiency unimpaired, as is seen from the following.

HACKNEY, ACCOUNTING PRINCIPLES IN CORPORATION LAW

30 Law and Contemp.Prob. 791, 803, 810–812 (1965).*

"Accounting Valuation Principles

"In the first decades of this century, accounting concepts of income and the objectives of the dividend statutes appeared to be generally in accord with each other and with the view that a balance sheet was intended to show the worth-value of assets compared with liabilities and that all increase in such net worth was deemed 'profits.'

"During the 1920s—a period of considerable price inflation, following a long period with no serious over-all deflation—revaluations of fixed assets became frequent, justified largely on the grounds (1) that under then current conditions balance-sheet assets stated at invested cost were so undervalued that they could no longer fairly present the company's financial position and (2) that new values were needed in order to provide a basis for computing depreciation expense and amortization necessary for competitive pricing decisions. The desire of the utility industry to recover replacement costs from rates charged to customers, the perhaps gratuitous interpretation of the sixteenth amendment as allowing all pre–1913 unrealized appreciation in value to escape taxation as pre–1913 'income,' and the economic 'going-concern' theory that basic productive capacity must be maintained before any income could be shown all combined to allow current 'worth' valuation of assets to be reflected in balance sheets for accounting purposes.

"The great depression resulted in a violent reaction against admitting to the balance sheet any valuations in excess of historical cost. More and more the accounting notion of income came to insist that periodic income consists of excess of receipts earned or accrued over an allocable portion of costs spent or accrued, so that income has come to represent accrued receipts less allocable costs, rather than an increase in net worth.

* * *

"Accountability for Original Values

"The historic cost principle, as previously indicated, is one of the most widely accepted of accounting principles, yet is frequently misinterpreted and actually seems to be a misnomer for the principle it represents.[55] Actually, accounting theory maintains that original costs

---

* Reprinted with permission from a symposium, Uniformity in Financial Accounting appearing in Law and Contemporary Problems (Vol. 30, No. 4, Autumn, 1965), published by the Duke University School of Law, Durham, North Carolina. Copyright, 1965, 1966, by Duke University.

55. The principle, more accurately stated, is that *original value* is the basis of accountability to the enterprise; cost is merely the best evidence of such value in the great majority of instances. See Research Study No. 3, at 25–27; Research Bull. No. 48, at 24. "Cost" is not simply a matter of proper and accurate recording of facts, but requires difficult and judgmatic decisions as to what costs are the relevant costs (e.g., allocable overhead and interest

(or values) are not always and without exception to be adhered to, but that new values may properly be entered when historic costs 'are no longer significant measurements of the accountability of the corporation for those assets.' In practice, however, historical acquisition costs remain the only valuation basis used.[57]

"It would, of course, be possible for exhaustion charges always to be based on current values without doing violence to the realization postulate prohibiting the recognition of increases in value for income purposes. The real question is whether the ultimate objective in the determination of reported income is to be primarily one of *maintenance of economic capital*—testing the income-producing ability of management by charging it with full provision for the fair value of the amount of consumption of its income-producing tools—or one of *stewardship*—testing the achievement of management in terms of accomplishment with what was historically entrusted to it. Economic theory would urge that basic enterprise productive capacity be maintained before any net receipts or increase in values could be deemed to constitute income, with the result that exhaustion charges would equal the current value of the actual physical loss occasioned by wear, tear, obsolesence, and so forth, which would have to be made good before there could be any net income. There has been in the official pronouncements of the SEC and the professional accounting associations an astonishing lack of agreement on or even discussion of the nature of income to serve as a guide in the choice of accounting practices or principles; but the entire preceding discussion of the development of accounting principles as they exist today indicates that accountancy has in practice chosen the stewardship approach of accountability for historic costs; in other words, the fundamental principle involved is that income is properly conceived of as a matter of *accountability for money values of assets originally entrusted to management or committed to the enterprise.*[59]

"Accountancy justifies its approach by arguing that it is primarily concerned with historical description and that accounting is not a process of constant revaluation but a matter of taking original values and deciding what subsequent historic events will be recognized for accounting purposes. In accountancy the events to be reported—the

during period of construction). See Research Study No. 7, at 254–55; Study Group on Business Income, Changing Concepts of Business Income 28–33; William A. Paton & William A. Paton, Jr., Asset Accounting chs. IX, X (1952); George O. May, Financial Accounting ch. VI (1943).

57. * * * Grady states that fixed assets should be carried at "cost of acquisition or construction in the historical accounts, unless such cost is no longer meaningful," but the only example he gives is a write-down, not a write-up. Research Study No. 7, at 252–53. * * *

59. * * * The difference in approach is exemplified by Blough's assertion that the accounting concept of depreciation has nothing to do with financing the replacement of assets or maintaining the productive capacity of plant and equipment (J. Accountancy, July 1958, pp. 78–79), while Spacek argues that there can be no income until original capital has been returned in terms of today's purchasing power. Spacek, Can We Define Generally Accepted Accounting Principles?, J. Accountancy, Dec.1958, p. 40, at 44.

raw materials of accounting—consist essentially of exchange transactions. Substantially all charges (both expenses and assets) are therefore to be based on actual past transactions, while all credits to profit and loss are to await realization and be based on a consummated sale following delivery or performance of service.

"The surprising thing is that the stewardship approach to the determination of income is recognized to be better suited to reflect profitability for an original owner than for a recent investor, and to be comparatively inapt as a means of projecting future profits (and therefore present value); [62] yet the prime objective of public accounting today is to serve the recent investor and the potential investor in the large publicly held companies having listed or widely traded securities and in the company making a public offering of its securities.

"There has, nevertheless, been dissatisfaction within accounting circles with the limitations of the stewardship concept, resulting in increasing attempts to recognize current values in recording revenues and to charge current receipts with costs adjusted for changes in the price level or else with the best possible approximation of current values; [63] but so long as total charges are limited to aggregate historic cost totals, it is obvious that the more costs that are charged off currently to income, the fewer are the costs that remain to be carried forward as assets to be charged against income of future years." [f]

The official accounting pronouncements have never departed from the principle that fixed assets and depreciation thereon are based on historical cost. *ARB No. 43, Chapters 9A and 9B; APB Op. No. 6, ¶ 17 (1965).*

The agitation still continues for depreciation allowances based on fair value or replacement cost, rather than on historical cost. Decades ago the AICPA's staff condemned all of the arguments of this nature on

62. See, e.g., George O. May, Financial Accounting 19 (1943): "No one has a right to interpret a report of stewardship as though it were an invitation to invest."

63. The much-criticized Research Study No. 3, for example, states that "accounting data are based on prices generated by past, present, or future exchanges which have actually taken place *or are expected to* " [id. at 6 (emphasis added)], and concludes that "current market price is * * * superior to past market price (acquisition cost) as a measure of the 'foregoing' or 'sacrifice' involved in the use or other disposition of the asset." Id. at 27.

f. Throughout his writings Mr. Hackney makes clear that he is doing more than pointing out the distinction between the concepts of "stewardship" and "maintenance of economic capital." He favors the latter. Later in the foregoing article (p. 818) he asks: "Will the law in a period of rapidly rising prices accept as sufficient exhaustion charges based on historical cost? Or might a court hold that recovery and maintenance of economic capital are necessary before income may be reported and distributed to shareholders?" But in a portion of the same article excerpted infra, p. 391, Mr. Hackney summarizes a long discussion by saying: "It is believed that the difficulties to a court of law in abandoning the accounting approach to asset valuations are enormous and little recognized."

the ground that they were motivated by the effort to acquire a tax benefit. *ARS No. 6*, p. 2 (1963). Certainly it seems idle to hope to get a tax benefit unless the accountants show that they are serious about the theory by increasing the depreciation charges for financial reporting purposes. However, it should now be pointed out that some of the proposed systems for fair value or replacement cost accounting would recognize the appreciation as "holding gain," so labelled in the income account, where it might offset any increased depreciation deduction. Other systems would offset the unrealized appreciation of the asset not by a credit to an income account but by a credit directly to an equity account. See the dissent to ARB No. 43, Chapter 9A, *Depreciation and High Costs.*

This is not just a dry accounting issue. The view of most of the writers is fairly close to that of Mr. Hackney. But some eminent accounting teachers have attacked this view on the ground that it is simply playing into the hands of those who want a tax deduction of depreciation on appreciated values. They argue that this would necessarily be at the expense of middle class taxpayers, wage earners, and small businessmen, whose taxes have constantly increased as the increased nominal amounts of income move into higher tax brackets without increased purchasing power. There is no powerful lobby clamoring for tax relief for them to match the corporate lobby.

The mechanics of depreciation based on current value may take any of several forms. One technique was required by the SEC under a temporary requirement of supplementary disclosure of replacement cost before the adoption of *SFAS No. 33*, now repealed. For a short period the SEC required supplementary disclosure of replacement cost under *ASR 190* (1976) and in one of its *Staff Accounting Bulletins, No. 7* (1976), it gave an illustration of how to make the necessary computations:

"C. EXAMPLE OF DEPRECIATION COMPUTATIONS

"*Facts:*

Assume the following:

	Year		
	1	2	3
Replacement cost of new asset having three year life:			
Beginning of year	$100	$140	$160
End of year	140	160	200
Average for the year	120	150	180

"*Question:*

"What are replacement cost depreciation expense and accumulated depreciation for each of the three years?

"*Interpretive Response:*

"The amounts are as follows:

	Year		
	1	**2**	**3**
Depreciation expense * * * (computed as ⅓ of average replacement cost for the year)	$40	$50	$60
Accumulated depreciation (computed as proportion of end of year replacement cost which has expired i.e., ⅓, ⅔, ⅔)	47	107	200
Depreciated replacement cost * * * (end of year replacement cost less accumulated depreciation)	93	53	–0–

"It should be noted that in the example given depreciation expense does not total to accumulated depreciation; in year 1 there is a $7 difference and in years 2 and 3 there is a cumulative difference of $17 and $50, respectively. These amounts, frequently referred to as 'backlog depreciation,' are not includable in replacement cost depreciation expense * * *."

Chapter VI

ACCOUNTING FOR INTANGIBLE COSTS (HEREIN PRINCIPALLY OF GOODWILL)

OBJECTIVES

1. Further explore the process of making GAAP by noting the economics and politics of GAAP-making for Goodwill arising from mergers and acquisitions.

2. Understand the current GAAP for Goodwill and other intangible costs, concerning:

    (a) measurement;

    (b) whether to "capitalize" intangible costs as assets or to expense them; and

    (c) if capitalized, whether and how they are to be amortized or written down.

3. Consider the conceptual bases for that accounting for intangibles and the qualifications on the financial statements implicit in that accounting.

4. Understand "purchase" vs. "pooling of interests" in mergers and acquisitions.

5. Consider normative guides to improve GAAP for intangibles.

RELEVANCE FOR LAWYERS

Lawyers advise on tax, corporate, and securities law and the financial aspects of mergers and acquisitions, on contracts involving the concept of income or profit such as retirement or other compensation plans, "cost-plus" supply contracts, or loan agreements. This chapter provides the framework for the lawyer to gain the necessary understanding of accounting for intangible costs which arise in these contexts.

A. THE ACCOUNTING ISSUES

The basic quest of business is to increase the net economic well-being of the firm; i.e., to make a profit by incurring costs to generate revenues in excess of those costs. But periodically measuring that profit poses various difficulties, one of which is allocation of revenues and costs to appropriate periods.

We began to consider how to allocate revenues under the realization convention in Chapter III on revenue recognition and pursued that issue in the next two chapters on inventory and depreciation costs. We have seen that revenues and their matchable costs such as the costs of goods sold are to be recognized in the same period or periods and that the best period for this matching is when all the events for the incurrence of the cost have occurred and therefore are fairly certain.

But not all costs are so easily matchable as those for goods sold. The continuum of costs has been divided into three parts:

(a) Those costs which are directly related to specific revenues, e.g., the cost of goods sold;

(b) Costs essential to the activities of the business but only generally related to revenues and therefore not easily matchable with particular revenues, e.g., depreciation on plant and equipment; and

(c) Costs incurred in the business but even less closely related to particular revenue-raising activity, e.g., a fire loss, research and development costs, start-up costs and "goodwill."

Those listed in (b) and (c) are sometimes termed "period costs." See APB Statement No. 4, *Basic Concepts and Accounting Principles Underlying Financial Statements of Business Enterprises,* ¶¶ 156–60 (1970).

Suppose that Chromo–Zoan Corp. has developed a gene-splicing technique for treating AIDS but is prohibited from marketing it in the U.S. without governmental approval. This is its only product. Assume:

(a) In year one it spends a million dollars in legal fees in a successful effort to obtain that approval;

(b) In year two another two million dollars is spent in successfully seeking approval in the European Community;

(c) In year three, three million dollars is spent in an unsuccessful effort to defeat an effort by the U.S. agency to rescind its original proposal. The U.S. operation is discontinued.

Should any or all of the costs be charged as expense in the year paid, or should they be deferred to future years by capitalizing them, i.e., by debiting an asset account? If capitalized, in which future years, if any, should the costs be expensed (amortized or "killed off")? You will see that these questions, for intangible costs, are like the questions for depreciation of tangible assets; but the answers are not only more difficult but also less generally agreed upon, in some cases leading to arbitrary rules. Moreover, conservatism is even more powerful in accountants' thinking about intangibles so that there is a bias toward immediate expensing. Further, the income tax laws are more stingily administered for intangibles so that some intangibles are simply never deductible for tax purposes but must be permanently capitalized even though GAAP call for amortization.

B. FORMAL GAAP CONCERNING INTANGIBLES—HEREIN OF GOODWILL AND "PURCHASE" OR "POOLING OF INTERESTS"

We have pointed out that in today's complex economy, intangibles are becoming an increasingly larger part of business costs, rivaling depreciation and, for manufacturing and merchandising businesses, cost of goods sold. This is due in part to the relative increase in services transactions, the costs for which are likely to be intangibles in the hands of both the supplier and consumer, e.g., advertising or legal services. In addition, the ever-increasing high technology is itself largely composed of intangible costs as are the costs of training personnel to administer it. The merger movement also has enhanced the amount of intangible costs being carried on balance sheets. For example, Time–Warner has over $9 billion in Goodwill on its balance sheet— about a quarter of its entire value—arising from the merger of Time, Inc. and Warner Communications.

Intangibles may be acquired in connection with the purchase of tangible assets or sometimes without a purchase of tangible assets. For instance, an inventory can be acquired together with the trade names used in its marketing and the benefits from a recent campaign advertising that trade name. Or one can acquire patents or trademarks without any related inventory or other tangible assets. Other intangibles can be self-developed, e.g., start-up expenditures believed to have continuing value.

Prior to 1970 the only formal GAAP for intangibles concerned purchased intangibles and required their capitalization. Those with determinate lives then were to be amortized ratably over those lives but, when they were deemed to have become worthless, were to be "written off" (that is, charged to expense). As to self-developed intangibles there was anarchy as to whether and when they were to be capitalized and if so, when expense would be charged. But they, too, if capitalized, were to be written off in any event when they were deemed to have become worthless. See *ARB No. 43, Chapter 5* (1953); *APB Op. No. 9,* ¶ 24 (1966).

1. WHAT IS "GOODWILL"?

As we have seen, any particular firm, accounting for its assets and liabilities at historical cost, is likely to be worth more or less than its net asset book carrying value, because values of assets and liabilities change from their original cost, while original cost remains the book carrying value generally. But more than this, the result of conventional accounting is to leave much else that is never reflected in the balance sheet accounts as assets or liabilities. For example the cost of training personnel is charged to expense as incurred, yet no one would deny that a purchaser and seller of the business would consider a trained staff a valuable resource of the business. Moreover, the staff's value may vary widely from the training costs incurred, depending on many factors for which funds are not expended. Thus when an entire firm is sold, the purchase price will almost always be different from net assets shown on the balance sheet and the difference is caused by at least two distinct factors:

(a) the change in value of items from historical costs carried in the accounts; and

(b) other valuable features not on the books.

To illustrate, suppose that Acquiring Corp. pays $30,000 in cash and assumes Target Corp.'s booked liabilities of $12,000, a total price of $42,000, in return for all the assets and business of Target Corp. carried on Target's books at $35,000. Assume Target's balance sheet at the transaction date appears as follows:

Target Corp. Balance Sheet at Date of Sale

Accounts Receivable		$ 5,000	Accounts Payable	$12,000
Inventory		10,000	Common Stock, $1 par	5,000
Plant	$22,000		Capital Contributed in Excess of Par	8,000
Less Accumulated Depreciation	2,000			
Net Plant		20,000	Retained Earnings	10,000
Total		$35,000	Total	$35,000

Further assume that Target's plant is deemed to have a value of $24,000 instead of its depreciated historical cost of $20,000, while all the other booked assets and liabilities have a fair value equal to their book value. Also assume that there are no other identifiable tangible or intangible assets. This still leaves $3,000 of the price unaccounted for. Presumably the buyer did not simply make a gift to Target of this amount but believed that although the tangible assets were worth only $39,000 (book plus the $4,000 in excess of book for the plant), the entire business was worth the $42,000 paid.

Accepting all this for the moment, what will be the purchaser's journal entry? In part it must be:

Accounts Receivable	$ 5,000	
Inventory	10,000	
Plant	24,000	
?	3,000	
Accounts Payable		$12,000
Cash		30,000 [a]

The custom is to term the $3,000 item, "Goodwill." Notice that the value exists before as well as after the transaction although it does not appear on Target's books before that event.[b]

What is this thing called "Goodwill"? Is the following effort to explain it satisfactory?

FASB DISCUSSION MEMORANDUM, ACCOUNTING FOR BUSINESS COMBINATIONS AND PURCHASED INTANGIBLES, pp. 47–51

(1976).[*]

"Determining the nature of goodwill has long been controversial and continues to be perplexing.

"Goodwill has not been defined precisely. Most writers generally agree, however, about certain characteristics.

    1. Goodwill relates to a business as a whole and, accordingly, is incapable of separate existence and of being sold apart from the identifiable assets of the business.

    2. Individual factors that may contribute to goodwill are not susceptible to independent valuation by any method or formula. Their values can be determined only as an aggregate in relation to a business as a whole.

    3. The future benefits of goodwill recognized in a combination may have no relationship to the costs incurred in the development of that goodwill. Goodwill may exist in the absence of specific costs to develop it.

"Accounting literature is replete with divergent opinions about the nature of goodwill. A brief statement of the two broad views that embrace most of those opinions is followed by discussion of each view:

    1. Goodwill represents expected earnings in excess of anticipated normal earnings.

a. Target's journal entries will be:

Cash	$30,000	
Accounts Payable	12,000	
Accumulated Depreciation	2,000	
Accounts Receivable		$ 5,000
Inventory		10,000
Plant		22,000
Gain		7,000

b. The form of this transaction is a purchase and sale of assets and assumption of liabilities. However, the net results on the purchaser's financial statements would be identical if Target's stock were purchased for the same consideration and either Target were dissolved or, if retained as a subsidiary, its financial statements were consolidated with Acquiring Corp.'s statements.

    [*] Copyright by Financial Accounting Standards Board, 401 Merritt 7, P.O. Box 5116, Norwalk, Connecticut 06856–5116. Reprinted with permission. Copies of the complete document are available from the FASB.

2. Goodwill represents intangible resources attributable to a company's above-average strength in areas such as technical skill and knowledge, management, and marketing research and promotion that cannot be separately identified and valued.

"View 1: Goodwill represents excess future earnings potential

"According to this view, a combinor's primary motivation in entering into a combination is to obtain additional future earnings. The aggregate cost reflects an evaluation of the combinee's earning power. Where the aggregate cost exceeds the current value of the combinee's net identifiable assets, the excess must relate to expected additional earning power. Were it not for the expectation of additional future earnings, no amount would be paid for goodwill. Even where goodwill is not evident from past earnings performance, as in companies in bankruptcy or in the development stage, goodwill may exist in terms of expectations about future earnings.

"This earning power concept of goodwill is consistent with U.S. Treasury Department, Internal Revenue Service *Revenue Ruling 59–60*, which defines goodwill as an expectation of earnings in excess of a fair return on the capital invested in tangibles or other means of production. One of the techniques most widely used by IRS agents and many appraisers for valuing goodwill directly is the capitalization of earnings formula. * * *

"Catlett and Olson concluded in *Accounting Research Study No. 10* that the earning power concept of goodwill is the most relevant one for accounting purposes. They contended that goodwill differs from other elements contributing to the value of a business because (a) it is not a separable resource or property right apart from the business as a whole and (b) its determination generally involves evaluating the business as a whole. They further contended that the estimated current value of goodwill to be recognized in a combination is determined by an investor (the combinor) based primarily on its evaluation of the estimated earnings of the business and the relationship of those earnings to the desired level of return on investment.

"View 2: Goodwill represents certain intangible resources

"According to this view, if aggregate cost for a combinee exceeds the current value of the net identifiable assets acquired, the combinee presumably possesses some other resources that have value to the combinor. Some have indicated that this view is simply an extension of the earning power concept because even those who emphasize earning power acknowledge that advantageous factors and conditions contribute to that earning power. For example, Catlett and Olson indicated that possible advantageous factors and conditions of a company contributing to its earning power include:

1. Superior management team

2. Outstanding sales manager or organization

3. Weakness in the management of a competitor

4. Effective advertising

5. Secret manufacturing process

6. Good labor relations

7. Outstanding credit rating resulting from an established reputation for integrity (thereby providing a company extra equity 'leverage' through more than ordinary borrowings at favorable interest rates)

8. Top-flight training program for employees

9. High standing in a community through contributions to charitable activities and participation in civic activities by a company's officers

10. Unfavorable developments in operations of a competitor

11. Favorable association with another company

12. Strategic location

13. Discovery of talents or resources

14. Favorable tax conditions

15. Favorable government regulation

"IRS *Revenue Ruling 59–60*, which indicates that goodwill, in the final analysis, is based on earning capacity and its value, suggests that other factors may contribute to intangible value, such as prolonged successful operations over a long period of ownership and prestige and renown of the business. * * * "

2. MEASURING GOODWILL

We asked you to accept the buyer's $3,000 valuation of Goodwill in our illustration. But how would the buyer or others determine that value?

KIMBALL LAUNDRY CO. v. UNITED STATES

Supreme Court of the United States, 1949.
338 U.S. 1.

JUSTICE FRANKFURTER * * *

On November 21, 1942, the United States filed a petition in the United States District Court for the District of Nebraska, to condemn the plant of the Kimball Laundry Company in Omaha, Nebraska, for use by the Army for a term initially expiring June 30, 1943, and to be extended from year to year at the election of the Secretary of War. The District Court granted the United States immediate possession of the facilities of the company, except delivery equipment, for the requested period. The term was subsequently extended several times. The last year's extension was to end on June 30, 1946, but the property was finally returned on March 23, 1946.

The Kimball Laundry Company is a family corporation the principal stockholders of which are three brothers who are also its officers.

The Laundry's business has been established for many years; its plant is large and well equipped with modern machinery. After the Army took over the plant, the Quartermaster Corps ran it as a laundry for personnel in the Seventh Service Command. Most of the Laundry's 180 employees were retained, and one of the brothers stayed on as operating manager. Having no other means of serving its customers, the Laundry suspended business for the duration of the Army's occupancy.

On November 19, 1943, a board of appraisers appointed by the District Court, in accordance with Nebraska law, reported that "the just compensation for the value of the use of the premises taken by the United States of America is the sum of $74,940.00 per annum. . . ." The appraisers made no award of damages for the loss of patrons, which they recognized to be probable, because at that time the amount of the loss could not be appraised. The Government and the Laundry both appealed the appraisers' award, and the question of just compensation was tried to a jury in March of 1946. The jury awarded an annual rental of $70,000—a total of $252,000 for the whole term—and $45,776.03 for damage to the plant and machinery beyond ordinary wear and tear. The rental award was intended to cover taxes, insurance, normal depreciation, and a return on the value of the Laundry's physical assets. Interest at the rate of 6 per cent was added from November 22, 1942, the day on which the Army took possession, on the amount due for the period between that date and June 30, 1943, and on the rental for each year thereafter from the beginning of the year until paid. Interest on the sum awarded for damage to the plant and machinery was adjudged to run from the date of the verdict, since the plant had not then been returned.

The Laundry appealed to the Court of Appeals for the Eighth Circuit, assigning numerous errors in the admission and exclusion of testimony and in the instructions to the jury. The Court of Appeals affirmed the District Court, 166 F.2d 856, and we granted the Laundry's petition for certiorari, 335 U.S. 807, because it raised novel and serious questions in determining what is "just compensation" under the Fifth Amendment.

These questions are not resolved by the familiar formulas available for the conventional situations which gave occasion for their adoption. As Mr. Justice Brandeis observed, "Value is a word of many meanings." *Southwestern Bell Telephone Co. v. Public Service Comm'n*, 262 U.S. 276, 310. For purposes of the compensation due under the Fifth Amendment, of course, only that "value" need be considered which is attached to "property,"[2] but that only approaches by one step the problem of definition. The value of property springs from subjective needs and attitudes; its value to the owner may therefore differ widely from its value to the taker. Most things, however, have a general

2. U.S. Const. Amend. V: ". . . nor shall private property be taken for public use, without just compensation."

demand which gives them a value transferable from one owner to another. As opposed to such personal and variant standards as value to the particular owner whose property has been taken, this transferable value has an external validity which makes it a fair measure of public obligation to compensate the loss incurred by an owner as a result of the taking of his property for public use. In view, however, of the liability of all property to condemnation for the common good, loss to the owner of nontransferable values deriving from his unique need for property or idiosyncratic attachment to it, like loss due to an exercise of the police power, is properly treated as part of the burden of common citizenship. See *Omnia Commercial Co. v. United States,* 261 U.S. 502, 508–09. Because gain to the taker, on the other hand, may be wholly unrelated to the deprivation imposed upon the owner, it must also be rejected as a measure of public obligation to requite for that deprivation. *McGovern v. New York,* 229 U.S. 363; *United States ex rel. T.V.A. v. Powelson,* 319 U.S. 266.

The value compensable under the Fifth Amendment, therefore, is only that value which is capable of transfer from owner to owner and thus of exchange for some equivalent. Its measure is the amount of that equivalent. But since a transfer brought about by eminent domain is not a voluntary exchange, this amount can be determined only by a guess, as well informed as possible, as to what the equivalent would probably have been had a voluntary exchange taken place. If exchanges of similar property have been frequent, the inference is strong that the equivalent arrived at by the haggling of the market would probably have been offered and accepted, and it is thus that the "market price" becomes so important a standard of reference. But when the property is of a kind seldom exchanged, it has no "market price," and then recourse must be had to other means of ascertaining value, including even value to the owner as indicative of value to other potential owners enjoying the same rights. Cf. *Old South Association v. Boston,* 212 Mass. 299, 99 N.E. 235. These considerations have special relevance where "property" is "taken" not in fee but for an indeterminate period.

* * *

At the core of petitioner's claim that it has been denied just compensation is the contention that there should have been included in the award to it some allowance for diminution in the value of its business due to the destruction of its "trade routes." The term "trade routes" serves as a general designation both for the lists of customers built up by solicitation over the years and for the continued hold of the Laundry upon their patronage.

At the trial petitioner offered to prove the value of the trade routes by testimony of an expert witness based on the gross receipts attributable to each class of customers, and the testimony of one of its officers was offered to show that this value had wholly disappeared during the three and one-half years of the Army's use of the plant. It further offered to show the cost of building up the customer lists, which had not been capitalized but charged to expense, and losses which would be incurred after the resumption of operations while they were being rebuilt. The petitioner also attempted to introduce evidence of its gross and net income for the eighteen years preceding the taking, the amount of dividends paid, and the ratio of officers' salaries to capital stock and surplus, on the theory that this evidence would shed additional light on the value of the Laundry as a going business. The trial court rejected these offers as not bearing upon the "fair market value or fair use value of the property taken" and instructed the jury that it should not consider diminution in the value of the business. The Court of Appeals affirmed because, in its opinion, whatever may have been the loss in value of the business or the trade routes brought about by the taking, "The Government did not take or intend to take, and obviously could not use, the Company's business, trade routes or customers." 166 F.2d at 860.

Tne market value of land as a business site tends to be as high as the reasonably probable earnings of a business there situated would justify, and the value of specially adapted plant and machinery exceeds its value as scrap only on the assumption that it is income-producing. And income, in the case of a service industry, presupposes patronage. Since petitioner has been fully compensated for the value of its physical property, any separate value that its trade routes may have must therefore result from the contribution to the earning capacity of the business of greater skill in management and more effective solicitation of patronage than are commonly given to such a combination of land, plant, and equipment. The product of such contributions is an intangible which may be compendiously designated as "going-concern value," but this is a portmanteau phrase that needs unpacking.

Though compounded of many factors in addition to relations with customers, that element of going-concern value which is contributed by superior management may be transferable to the extent that it has a momentum likely to be felt even after a new owner and new management have succeeded to the business property. But because this momentum can be maintained only by the application of continued energy and skill, it would gradually spend itself if the effort and skill of the new management were not in its turn expended. See Paton, Advanced Accounting 427, 435 (1941). Only that exercise of managerial efficiency, however, which has contributed to the future profitability of the business will have a transferable momentum that may give it value to a potential purchaser; that which has had only the effect of increasing current income or reducing expenses of operation has spent itself from year to year. The value contributed by the expenditure of money in soliciting patronage, although likewise of limited duration, differs from managerial efficiency in that it derives not merely from the contribution of personal qualities but from original investment or the plowing back of income. As such it may sometimes be more readily recognized as an asset of the business. It is clear, at any rate, that the value of both these elements, in combination, must be regarded as identical with the value alleged to inhere in the trade routes.

Assuming, then, that petitioner's business may have going-concern value as defined above, the question arises whether the intangible character of such value alone precludes compensation for it. The answer is not far to seek. The value of all property, as we have already observed, is dependent upon and inseparable from individual needs and attitudes, and these, obviously, are intangible. As fixed by the market, value is no more than a summary expression of forecasts that the needs and attitudes which made up demand in the past will have their counterparts in the future. See *Ithaca Trust Co. v. United States*, 279 U.S. 151, 155; cf. 1 Bonbright, The Valuation of Property 222 (1937). The only distinction to be made, therefore, between the attitudes which generate going-concern value and those of which tangible property is compounded is as to the tenacity of the past's hold upon the future: in the case of the latter a forecast of future demand can usually be made with greater certainty, for it is more probable on the whole that people will continue to want particular goods or services than that they will continue to look to a particular supplier of them. It is more likely, in other words, that people will persist in wanting to have their laundry done than that they will keep on sending it to a particular laundry. But as the probability of continued patronage gains strength, this distinction becomes obliterated, and the intangible acquires a value to a potential purchaser no different from the value of the business' physical property. Since the Fifth Amendment requires compensation for the latter, the former, if shown to be present and to have been "taken," should also be compensable. As Mr. Justice Brandeis observed for the Court in *Galveston Elec. Co. v. Galveston*, 258 U.S. 388, 396, "In determining the value of a business as between buyer and seller, the goodwill and earning power due to effective organization are often more important elements than tangible property. Where the public acquires the business, compensation must be made for these, at least under some circumstances." *   *   *

What, then, are the circumstances under which the Fifth Amendment requires compensation for such an intangible? Not, indeed, those of the usual taking of fee title to business property, but the denial of compensation in such circumstances rests on a very concrete justification: the going-concern value has not been taken. Such are all the cases, most of them decided by State courts under constitutions with provisions comparable to the Fifth Amendment, in which only the physical property has been condemned, leaving the owner free to move his business to a new location. *   *   *

The situation is otherwise, however, when the Government has condemned business property with the intention of carrying on the business, as where public-utility property has been taken over for continued operation by a governmental authority. If, in such a case, the taker acquires going-concern value, it must pay for it.

We conclude, therefore, that since the Government for the period of its occupancy of petitioner's plant has for all practical purposes pre-empted the trade routes, it must pay compensation for whatever transferable value their temporary use may have had. The case must accordingly be remanded to the District Court to determine what that value, if any, was. In making that determination, the Court should consider any evidence which would have been likely to convince a potential purchaser as to the presence and amount of petitioner's going-concern value, for this, as we have pointed out, must be considered identical with the value alleged to inhere in the trade routes. Though we do not mean to foreclose the consideration of other types of evidence or the application of other techniques of appraisal, it may shed some light on the problem to indicate as briefly as possible the relevance of the evidence rejected at the trial to the determination of the presence and amount of this value.

One index of going-concern value offered by petitioner is the record of its past earnings. If they should be found to have been unusually high in proportion to investment in its physical property, that might have been a persuasive indication to an informed purchaser of the business that more than tangible factors were at work.[7] Such a purchaser might well have measured the value thus contributed by capitalizing, at a rate taking into account the element of risk [8] and the number of years during which these factors would probably have effect, the excess of the probable future return upon investment in the business over a return which would be adequate compensation for the risk of investment in it.[9] If the figure chosen as representing invest-

---

7. The Government argues that if petitioner's testimony as to the value of its physical property were accepted, it could have no going-concern value because its average net earnings for the five years preceding the taking were too low to establish any excess return. The alleged value was about $650,000, and the average annual earnings $39,375.39, a return on that value of about 6%. On the other hand, the Government's own expert witnesses respectively valued the physical property, after allowing depreciation, at $455,000 and $433,500, and on that basis the rate of return would be about 9%. It is not for us, at any rate, to assume that 6% rather than 5% or some lower figure is the lowest that would compensate investment in the physical property.

8. The importance of varying in accordance with varying risks the percentage at which income is capitalized to obtain business value has been emphasized by the Securities and Exchange Commission in computing value for purposes of § 77B reorganizations. See Note, 55 Harv.L.Rev. 125, 133 (1941). See also Fisher, The Nature of Capital and Income, c. 16, "The

Risk Element" (1906); Angell, Valuation Problems 14 (Practicing Law Institute, 1945).

9. See Yang, Goodwill and Other Intangibles, cc. 5, 6 (1927); Simpson, *Goodwill* in 6 Encyc.Soc.Sci. 698, 699 (1931). For a systematic discussion of the steps involved in making such an estimate, see Accountants' Handbook 869 *et seq.* (Paton ed., 1944). It would be theoretically possible, of course, to arrive at the total value of the business not by adding going-concern value obtained by capitalization of excess income to a valuation of the physical property obtained in some other way, but by capitalization of all income. See 1 Bonbright, The Valuation of Property, cc. 11, 12 (1937); 1 Dewing, Financial Policy of Corporations, Bk. II, c. 1 (4th ed., 1941); cf. *Consolidated Rock Products Co. v. Du Bois,* 312 U.S. 510, 525–26; *Institutional Investors v. Chicago, M., St. P. & P. R. Co.,* 318 U.S. 523, 540–42. But a forecast of future earnings is subject to inaccuracy resulting both from the difficulty of discounting the nonrecurrent circumstances which entered into the record of past earnings upon which the forecast is based (even if no

ment were cost, however, the possibility would probably have been recognized that the capitalized value of the excess income might involve duplication of value already reflected in the valuation of the site.

In addition to or as a substitute for net income as an index of going-concern value, a purchaser might have been influenced by such evidence of expenditure upon building up the business as petitioner's records of payments to deliverymen for the solicitation of new customers. Instead of beginning with excess earnings resulting in part from expenditure on solicitation and then capitalizing them to reach going-concern value, such expenditure can be regarded as a direct contribution, in proportion to the amount of its long-term effectiveness, to the capital assets of the business. But the legitimacy of the inference that expenditures for the purpose of soliciting business have resulted in a value which will continue to contribute to the earning capacity of the business in later years and which is therefore a value that a purchaser might pay for, necessarily depends on the character of the business and the experience of those who are familiar with it.[11] This, at any rate, is a matter which is open to proof.

Though not capitalized and carried on the books, it is obvious that such an asset may be present even in a business losing money or at any rate not making enough to have any "excess" income. A relevant measure of its value, however, would be the gross income of the business, as is recognized by the method of estimating going-concern value that has been employed in cases dealing with the excess-profits tax base of laundry businesses. See *Metropolitan Laundry Co.,* 2 B.T.A. 1062; *Pioneer Laundry Co.,* 5 B.T.A. 821. Petitioner offered proof of the value of its trade routes based on just such a method and further

projection of future earnings is expressly made, past earnings can be used as a basis of capitalization only on the assumption that they will continue) and the hazards of any prediction of future conditions of business. See May, *A Footnote on Value,* 72 J. of Accountancy 225 (1941); Orgel, Valuation under The Law of Eminent Domain § 216 (1936). The consequences of inaccuracy are reduced by confining the capitalization to excess income, but of course it is a question of fact whether future excess income can be predicted with certainty sufficient to persuade a purchaser of the business to pay for its capitalized value.

* * *

11. In the case of a business like the laundry business which must entice patrons from already established competitors in an area confined by the range of delivery service, it may be that expenditure upon solicitation is regarded as a capital expenditure for part of a combination of income-producing assets quite as much as

investment in the land and building. Compare *Houston Natural Gas Corp. v. Commissioner,* 90 F.2d 814 (C.A.4th Cir.), holding the salaries and expenses of solicitors of new customers for a public utility to be a capital expenditure nondeductible from current income because contributing to income in future years. The Tax Court, its predecessor, the Board of Tax Appeals, and the Courts of Appeals have frequently held such analogous expenditures as those made to increase the circulation of newspapers and for certain forms of advertising to be capital expenditures. For collections of such cases, see 4 Mertens, Law of Federal Income Taxation § 25.18 and § 25.27 (1942). See also Dodd and Baker, Cases and Materials on Business Associations 1125–26 (1940). Compare the materials on valuation of goodwill as part of a decedent's gross estate collected in 2 Paul, Federal Estate and Gift Taxation § 18.16 (1942), and Paul, Federal Estate and Gift Taxation § 18.16 (1946 Supplement).

offered to show that it was a method generally used in the laundry business. If so, it would also be relevant.[12]

But even though evidence in one or more of these categories may tend to establish the value of petitioner's trade routes, the consequence of its inadequacy may require complete denial of compensation where that would not be the result in the case of its tangible property. The reason is this: evidence which is needed only to fix the amount of the value of the tangible property is required to establish the very existence of an intangible value as well as its amount. Since land and buildings are assumed to have some transferable value, when a claimant for just compensation for their taking proves that he was their owner, that proof is *ipso facto* proof that he is entitled to some compensation. The claimant of compensation for an intangible, on the other hand, who cannot demonstrate a value that a purchaser would pay for has failed to sustain his burden of proving that he is entitled to any compensation whatever. This is a burden, moreover, which must be sustained by solid evidence; only thus can the probability of future demand be shown to approximate that for tangible property. Particularly is this true where these issues are to be left for jury determination, for juries should not be given sophistical and abstruse formulas as the basis for their findings nor be left to apply even sensible formulas to factors that are too elusive.

If the District Court, bearing in mind these cautions, should find petitioner's evidence adequate to submit to the jury for a finding as to the presence and amount of the value of the trade routes, it will then be necessary also to instruct it as to computation of the compensation due. Consistently with an approach which seeks, with the aid of all relevant data, to find an amount representing value to any normally situated owner or purchaser of the interests taken, no value greater than the value of their temporary control would be compensable. Since, as we have noted, value of this sort can have only a limited duration, the value of the trade routes for the period of the Army's occupancy of the physical property might be estimated by computing the discounted value as of the beginning of the period of the net contribution likely to have been made to the business during that period had it been carried on; its value for each year would be the net contribution for that year. But here, as hitherto, we mean only to illustrate and not to prescribe the course which may be taken upon remand of the case.

Petitioner also protests against the basis chosen by the lower courts for the award of interest. It argues that the Government, having taken the whole property on November 21, 1942, should pay interest from

12. Proceeding from the assumption that laundry businesses are a class having uniform characteristics, this method presupposes informed opinion both as to the normal ratio of a given volume of expenditure on solicitation to a given volume of gross income and as to the normal duration of the contribution to gross of a given amount of such expenditure. The Board of Tax Appeals cases cited as well as petitioner's offer of proof involved the further refinement that the ratios chosen varied with the gross income attributable to each class of customers.

that day on the total amount of the award. We have already rejected, however, the only possible theory upon which this claim could rest— that the proper method of computing the award is to determine the difference between the value of the business on the date of taking and its value on the date of return. It follows from our holding that the proper measure of compensation was an annual rental which came due only at the beginning of each renewal of the Army's occupancy, that interest should be payable on each installment of rental only from that date.

For proceedings not inconsistent with this opinion, the case is

Reversed and remanded.

MR. JUSTICE RUTLEDGE, concurring.

As I understand the opinion of the Court, its effect is simply to recognize that short-term takings of property entail considerations not present where complete title has been taken. Rules developed for the simple situation in which all the owner's interests in the property have been irrevocably severed should not be forced to fit the more complex consequences of a piecemeal taking of successive short-term interests. Such takings may involve compensable elements that in the nature of things are not present where the whole is taken.

With this much I agree. But having recognized the possible compensability of intangible interests, I would not subscribe to a formulation of theoretical rules defining their nature or prescribing their measurement. What seems theoretically sound may prove unworkable for judicial administration. But I do not understand the opinion of the Court to do more than indicate possible approaches to the compensation of such interests. Since remand of the case will permit the empirical testing of these approaches, I join in the Court's opinion.

*   *   *

MORRISSEY, INTANGIBLE COSTS, IN MODERN ACCOUNTING THEORY
198–201 (M. Backer, ed. 1966).*

"Valuation—Direct Method.

"A sophisticated application of the direct method of valuing goodwill would require the following information:

1. A normal rate of return for representative firms in the industry.

2. The fair value of tangible assets and any identifiable [intangible] assets other than goodwill.

3. The estimated future earnings of the firm.

4. The probable duration of any 'excess' earnings attributable to goodwill.

5. A discount rate to apply to [the excess earnings].

"By applying the normal rate of return to the fair value of the * * * assets (including any intangible assets other than goodwill), the normal or typical earnings are determined. The difference between these normal earnings and the firm's estimated future earnings is designated as the 'excess' earnings. These 'excess' earnings are then valued by discounting them over their probable duration.

"Because of obvious weaknesses in the formal analysis described above, a buyer and seller frequently value goodwill by using a less complex application of the direct method. For example, no attempt may be made to distinguish between normal and excess earnings. A price is determined by adding to the agreed fair value of the net tangible assets an amount equivalent to the seller's total earnings for a short period, perhaps one to three years. Tangible assets may be relatively immaterial in a service-oriented business or in a professional practice, such as public accounting or law. In these cases the total purchase price, which may be viewed as a payment almost entirely for goodwill, often consists of the aggregate earnings, either past or anticipated, for a period of years.

"Even though the courts 'in countless cases' [32] have employed the formal method described, or some variation of it, to determine a value for goodwill, and even though this method is often described in accounting literature (thus perhaps explaining its widespread use by the courts), many accountants find this method of valuation unsatisfactory.

* * *

"In spite of such reservations, an understanding of this general method is desirable for several reasons. First, it provides a framework within which the effect of various assumptions (for rates of return, estimated future earnings, and duration of goodwill) can be systematically examined. Second, the method is actually used in practice. Third, an understanding of a formal, direct method of valuing goodwill provides a useful background to a consideration of other methods."

———

Morrissey's "direct method", also described by Justice Frankfurter in *Kimball Laundry,* is in frequent use by courts in valuing businesses involved in insolvency reorganizations and recapitalizations where there is no actual sale. It is also applied in measuring damages where a business has been diminished or destroyed, as well as in pre-deal deliberations for takeovers where a market transaction later occurs.

Since GAAP now recognize Goodwill on the books of account only when an acquisition has occurred, a post hac method of measuring

32. "Court Decisions Concerning Goodwill," Accounting Review, April 1956, p. 274.

Goodwill, as described in APB Opinion No. 16, *Business Combinations,* ¶ 87 (1970), may be used:

> 87. An acquiring corporation should allocate the cost of an acquired company to the assets acquired and liabilities assumed. . . .
>
>> First, all identifiable assets acquired, either individually or by type, and liabilities assumed in a business combination, whether or not shown in the financial statements of the acquired company, should be assigned a portion of the cost of the acquired company, normally equal to their fair values at date of acquisition.
>>
>> Second, the excess of the cost of the acquired company over the sum of the amounts assigned to identifiable assets acquired less liabilities assumed should be recorded as goodwill. . . .
>
> Independent appraisals may be used as an aid in determining the fair values of some assets and liabilities. Subsequent sales of assets may also provide evidence of values. . . .

Presumably you recognize that this is precisely the method we used in our illustration involving Acquiring Corp. and Target Corp.

At this point the alert lawyer may do his client a real service. Since Goodwill is not deductible on the tax return in either a lump sum or by amortization, it is important to allocate as much as possible of a purchase price to depreciable or amortizable assets, rather than to Goodwill. The following will illustrate this point and also provide some further insights to other intangibles.

HEATH, PROPERTY VALUATION PROBLEMS AND THE ACCOUNTANT

J. Accountancy 54, 57–58 (Jan., 1964).*

"The entire outstanding stock of a company was purchased for approximately $5 million. * * * An initial cost approach study indicated that the cost of reproduction less depreciation from all causes of the land, buildings and equipment, amounted to about $1,200,000. After adding cash and receivables in the amount of $1,500,000, the total of $2,700,000 clearly indicated that something was out of balance with the purchase price of $5 million, and that possibly there were other assets contributing to this difference.

"A study of past and prospective earnings of the company as compared to other concerns in the industry, capitalized at an appropriate risk factor, indicated an amount close to purchase price. This conclusion further supported the initial observation that there was something other than plant, property and equipment and working capital contributing to the earnings. While the company had a good reputation, most of its work was with governmental agencies, and it did not seem logical to assume that the difference between the purchase price of some $5 million and the sum of the value of the land, buildings, equipment and allowances for working capital was all good will. It was learned upon further probing that the acquired concern owned several patents and licensing agreements. These were valued by determining the present worth of the amount of the potential profits, after taxes, generated by this protection and discounted at a suitable risk factor over the remaining life of the agreements. Since this protection had a terminable life, it was considered amortizable.

"Another item not originally considered but subsequently valued was engineering time, draftsmen time, and overhead applicable to production drawings. This valuation process gave the cost of reproduction of the drawings and, by relating the various drawings to the respective products and future life, it was possible to ascertain present value. This also was considered amortizable.

"It was learned that the acquired company was about to market new models. Without such new models, it would place the acquiring company in a position of having nothing new to market and it might take three to five years to design, test and prepare for sale a line of products similar to present models, with only a minimum of sales during this development period. These 'product model rights' were valued by capitalizing the difference in potential profits with and without such product model rights. This required a study of projected sales and profits under both circumstances with consideration given to return on the investment in working capital and plant assets during the unproductive time. Although the life of a given model of a product is not determinable with precise accuracy, it was found that with specific reference to this company's products, about three years after the introduction of an item, modifications of the model by the originating company or its competitors usually obsoletes the original model. Therefore, it was possible to determine, on the average, by classes of products, what might be the life and the period over which the value assigned should be amortized.

"An additional intangible factor was disclosed in this company's unique engineering staff. Over the years, an engineering staff had been assembled which was unique in that collectively it was specifically suited and trained in the phases of electronics in which this company was engaged. Studies indicated that the company had expended significant amounts in recruiting and assembling this staff. It was possible to determine what it might cost to replace such personnel. It was also found out that in this industry—due to concentrated pirating of personnel by all concerns—most staffs turned over approximately every seven years. Again here is a situation where it appears that there is a wasting of assets, with a life that could be determined with reasonable accuracy, and thus they should be considered amortizable.

"A trademark was also disclosed and valued. Although this did not have a determinable life, the amount allocated could be treated as a loss if and when the trademark was ever abandoned.

"After giving consideration to the values placed on the foregoing intangibles there was still a gap as compared to the purchase price. * * * Investigation established that the quality of the company's products, its established customer relations, and its other intangible elements contributed to a profit potential in excess of a normal return on assets already valued. This profit potential was measured and capitalized to determine the amount applicable to the nebulous 'goodwill' element.

"Summarizing this case, it is pointed out that had the study stopped with the valuation of normal plant property and equipment, the taxpayer might have been left with a finding of $2,300,000 (difference between $5 million purchase price and $2,700,000 appraised cost of reproduction new less depreciation value of plant, property and equipment and working capital) as a nondepreciable good-will item. By further study it was possible to identify, value, and ascertain a terminable life for several significant assets which were not included with conventional plant, property and equipment nor in working capital. The nominal good-will figure which was established after these further studies was justified on the basis of the excess return on investment over a norm for the industry."

3. ACCOUNTING FOR ACQUIRED GOODWILL

After purchased Goodwill is measured and capitalized, what happens? For many years accounting gave a most unsatisfactory answer. This was, in substance, that one could do anything with the Goodwill, except charge it off immediately to retained earnings or other equity. See *ARB No. 43, Chapter 5* (1953); *APB Op. No. 9*, ¶ 21 (1966).

But practice was made not only by the old ARB, but also by the fact that financial analysts and notably the SEC looked askance at Goodwill as a balance sheet asset, and brought pressure for its amortization. Conservative corporations acquiesced, thus creating a heavy income charge. Financial analysts would tend to deduct it as an asset and from net worth insofar as they gave heed to the balance sheet. But there were corporations which recorded Goodwill and for long periods kept it on the balance sheet unamortized, avoiding an income charge, with recitals in the footnotes to the balance sheet that it was deemed to be of continuing value. This freedom was altered in 1970 by *APB Op. No. 17* although pre-existing Goodwill continues on many balance sheets.

ACCOUNTING PRINCIPLES BOARD OPINION NO. 17
AICPA, 1970.*

INTANGIBLE ASSETS

Summary

"Problem

"1. An enterprise may acquire intangible assets from others or may develop them itself. Many kinds of intangible assets may be identified and given reasonably descriptive names, for example, patents, franchises, trademarks, and the like. Other types of intangible assets lack specific identifiability. Both identifiable and unidentifiable assets may be developed internally. Identifiable intangible assets may be acquired singly, as a part of a group of assets, or as part of an entire enterprise, but unidentifiable assets cannot be acquired singly. The excess of the cost of an acquired company over the sum of identifiable net assets, usually called goodwill, is the most common unidentifiable intangible asset.

"2. Accounting for an intangible asset involves the same kinds of problems as accounting for other long-lived assets, namely, determining an initial carrying amount, accounting for that amount after acquisition under normal business conditions (amortization), and accounting for that amount if the value declines substantially and permanently. Solving the problems is complicated by the characteristics of an intangible asset: its lack of physical qualities makes evidence of its existence elusive, its value is often difficult to estimate, and its useful life may be indeterminable.

*   *   *

"Scope and Effect of Opinion

*   *   *

"5. This Opinion covers the accounting for both identifiable and unidentifiable intangible assets that a company acquires, including those acquired in business combinations. 'Company' in this Opinion refers to both incorporated and unincorporated enterprises. The conclusions of the Opinion apply to intangible assets recorded, if any, on the acquisition of some or all of the stock held by minority stockholders of a subsidiary company. This Opinion also covers accounting for costs of developing goodwill and other unidentifiable intangible assets with indeterminate lives.

"6. The provisions of this Opinion apply to costs of developing identifiable intangible assets that a company defers and records as assets. Some companies defer costs incurred to develop identifiable intangible assets while others record the costs as expenses as incurred. Certain costs, for example, research and development costs and pre-operating costs, present problems which need to be studied separately.

The question of deferral of those costs is beyond the scope of this Opinion.

*   *   *

"Conclusions

"9. The Board concludes that a company should record as assets the costs of intangible assets acquired from others, including goodwill acquired in a business combination. A company should record as expenses the costs to develop intangible assets which are not specifically identifiable. The Board also concludes that the cost of each type of intangible asset should be amortized by systematic charges to income over the period estimated to be benefited. The period of amortization should not, however, exceed forty years.

*   *   *

"*Amortization of Intangible Assets*

"27. The Board believes that the value of intangible assets at any one date eventually disappears and that the recorded costs of intangible assets should be amortized by systematic charges to income over the periods estimated to be benefited. Factors which should be considered in estimating the useful lives of intangible assets include:

a. Legal, regulatory, or contractual provisions may limit the maximum useful life.

b. Provisions for renewal or extension may alter a specified limit on useful life.

c. Effects of obsolescence, demand, competition, and other economic factors may reduce a useful life.

d. A useful life may parallel the service life expectancies of individuals or groups of employees.

e. Expected actions of competitors and others may restrict present competitive advantages.

f. An apparently unlimited useful life may in fact be indefinite and benefits cannot be reasonably projected.

g. An intangible asset may be a composite of many individual factors with varying effective lives.

The period of amortization of intangible assets should be determined from the pertinent factors.

"28. The cost of each type of intangible asset should be amortized on the basis of the estimated life of that specific asset and should not be written off in the period of acquisition. Analysis of all factors should result in a reasonable estimate of the useful life of most intangible assets. A reasonable estimate of the useful life may often be based on upper and lower limits even though a fixed existence is not determinable.

"29. The period of amortization should not, however, exceed forty years. Analysis at the time of acquisition may indicate that the indeterminate lives of some intangible assets are likely to exceed forty years and the cost of those assets should be amortized over the maximum period of forty years, not an arbitrary shorter period.

"30. *Method of amortization.* The Board concludes that the straight-line method of amortization—equal annual amounts—should be applied unless a company demonstrates that another systematic method is more appropriate. The financial statements should disclose the method and period of amortization. Amortization of acquired goodwill and of other acquired intangible assets not deductible in computing income taxes payable does not create a timing difference, and allocation of income taxes is inappropriate."

Note on the Scope of APB Opinion No. 17

It will be seen that with respect to the first issue of whether to capitalize or to expense, *APB Op. No. 17,* ¶ 9, as to *acquired* intangibles, requires capitalization whether they are separately identifiable or not, and whether they are of determinate or indeterminate lives. This is basically identical to what *ARB No. 43, Chapter 5,* had required.

Opinion No. 17, ¶ 9, may have gone slightly beyond *ARB No. 43* for other matters. Concerning *self-developed* intangibles which are *not identifiable,* it requires immediate expensing. With regard to others, *APB Op. No. 17* does not specify either expensing or capitalization.

On the second issue of how to account for any intangible costs which are in fact capitalized including self-developed identifiable intangibles, *APB Op. No. 17* requires amortization over the periods to be benefited but not in excess of 40 years whereas *ARB No. 43, Chapter 5,* had not required amortization for intangibles with indeterminate lives. The Opinion seems to do little else. See the following interpretation by the AICPA staff.

AICPA, ACCOUNTING INTERPRETATIONS
J.Acctg., April, 1971, pp. 70, 74.

"*Question*—APB Opinion No. 17 requires that intangible assets acquired after October 31, 1970 be amortized over a period not exceeding 40 years. Does this Opinion encourage the capitalization of identifiable internally developed intangible assets which have been generally charged to expense in the past?

"*Interpretation*—APB Opinion No. 17 does not change present accounting practice for intangible assets in any way except to require that intangible assets acquired after October 31, 1970 be amortized. Paragraph 6 notes that the costs of some identifiable intangible assets are now capitalized as deferred assets by some companies while other companies record the costs as expenses when incurred. This paragraph also specifies that the question of whether the costs of identifiable internally developed intangible assets are to be capitalized or charged to expense is not covered by the Opinion. Therefore, the Opinion does not encourage capitalizing the costs of a large initial advertising campaign for a new product or capitalizing the costs of training new employees."

Note

6-1. *Goodwill in the Savings and Loan Scandal.* The savings and loan (or "thrift") crisis began in the late 1970s as hundreds of thrifts failed because they had extended long-term loans of up to thirty years' duration at rates which were lower than subsequent rates which the thrifts were forced by competition to pay their depositors and other creditors. At that time one standard procedure for the Federal Savings and Loan Insurance Corporation, which guaranteed their deposits, was to arrange a merger of the failed thrift with a more successful one. These mergers tested *APB Op. No. 17* and it was found wanting. It was amended by SFAS No. 72, *Accounting for Certain Acquisitions of Banking or Thrift Institutions* (1983).

The problem was explained at ¶ 22 of *SFAS No. 72:*

22. When banking or thrift institutions are acquired in periods of high interest rates, application of the purchase method [i.e., the method described above] and subsequent amortization of acquired intangibles over an extended period of time may produce a significant effect on the subsequent reported results of operations of the combined enterprise. In such periods, if low-rate interest-bearing assets are discounted to their fair values using current interest rates, the fair value of liabilities assumed may exceed by a substantial amount the fair value of tangible and identifiable intangible assets acquired. That excess often has been reported as goodwill in applying the purchase method * * *. The discount on the interest-bearing assets is amortized to income [i.e., credited] over the remaining lives of those assets using the interest method. If the goodwill is amortized straight-line over a period that exceeds the period the discount is amortized to income, the subsequent reported earnings for the combined enterprise may show a dramatic increase compared with the sum of the separate results of those enterprises absent the combination.

The strong-arm solution is in the second sentence of ¶ 5 following:

If, in such a combination, the fair value of liabilities assumed exceeds the fair value of tangible and identified intangible assets acquired, that excess constitutes an identifiable intangible asset. That asset shall be amortized to expense over a period no greater than the estimated remaining life of the long-term interest-bearing assets acquired.

To illustrate in plain English, assume that Failed Thrift twenty years ago had made a $1,000 mortgage loan for thirty years at 6% interest with interest due at the end of each year and principal due at maturity, ten years from now. Further assume that the thrift had just now sold a $1,000 bond payable, also due in ten years, bearing interest at 9%, the now current market rate for such bonds. Thus its cash receipts each year for the remaining ten years before maturity of the mortgage loan would be $60 and its cash disbursements for its bond would be $90, not a good thing. But if Successful Thrift acquires Failed Thrift's assets and liabilities, and the current rate for mortgage loans made by it to homeowners is, say 15%, Successful Thrift would discount the $1,000 mortgage loan receivable to $550.80 (see Appendix), and amortize the discount as income over ten years, then debit Goodwill $449.20 and, but for *SFAS No. 72*, amortize it as expense over forty years. In the years until maturity Successful Thrift would recognize positive net income as follows:

	Cash interest received	$ 60.00
Plus:	Amortized discount on mortgage loan (over 10 years)	44.92
	Subtotal	$104.92
Less:	Cash bond interest paid	(90.00)
	Amortized goodwill (over forty years)	(11.23)
	Net Income	$ 3.69
	Net Cash Flow	(30.00)

Since in fact the cash *loss* each year is $30, the pre-*SFAS No. 72* treatment seems abusive and perhaps is one reason for the several years' delay in addressing the crisis. (Other accounting devices described elsewhere in this book also served this same end. If any of these devices were done without the blessings of the accounting profession, the regulators, industry and Congress, they would have been called fraud.) Multiplying these numbers by several billions gives a more accurate picture of the concerns.

One, of course, should ask why Successful Thrift would take a $550.80 asset in return for assuming a $1,000 liability in connection with it. The answer in part lay in the above accounting, which gives a false picture of prosperity. But appearances have achieved an exalted status in today's world. It also may be that there are indeed other unbooked assets such as the benefits of obtaining additional borrowers and depositors who in the future may supply other business to the thrift or bank (e.g., such depositors and borrowers may be captive prospects for the thrift's lucrative credit card business). Or it may be that all an unscrupulous management needs is a little time to milk the thrift of a few millions before it fails. Other considerations are further discussed in the text of *SFAS No. 72*.

This is just one lesson in how GAAP, like bad law, are often made on hard cases.

4. NEGATIVE GOODWILL

We have just seen that Goodwill is recognized as an asset, or debit, when the credits, i.e., consideration paid for assets in cash or stock, exceed the debits to be recorded for specific assets. What happens when the deal is different, when the individual asset values exceed the consideration, as in this journal entry?

Individual Assets (aggregating)	$10,000	
Cash		$9,000
?		1,000

Prior to 1970 many firms had treated this as a deferred credit, yielding a credit to revenue for future periods, i.e., a highly questionable boost to net income. But it was sharply attacked in Sprouse, *Accounting for What–You–May–Call–Its*, J. Accountancy 45 (Oct. 1966).

Paragraph 88 of *APB Op. No. 16* now requires that fair value be allocated to assets and liabilities acquired in a business combination accounted for as a purchase. If the amount so allocated exceeds cost of the acquired company, "the excess over cost should be allocated to reduce proportionately the values assigned to noncurrent assets (except long-term investments in marketable equity securities) in determining their fair values * * *. [Only if] the allocation reduces the noncurrent assets to zero value, the remainder of the excess over cost should be classified as a deferred credit and should be amortized systematically to income over the period estimated to be benefited but not in excess of forty years."

5. PURCHASE ACCOUNTING AND POOLING OF INTERESTS—THE BROADER CONTEXT OF THE GOODWILL ISSUE

The accounting we have been describing is known as "purchase" accounting.

There is another form of accounting available under specified conditions where Acquiring Corporation uses not cash but its own capital stock in order to acquire either the capital stock or the business of Target. In this case, since the shareholders of both firms continue as owners, the items on the two balance sheets are added together without any Goodwill arising or revaluation of the assets of Target to current values, in what is known as a "pooling of interests." The accountants carefully avoid the terms "acquisition" or "purchase" as applied to a pooling of interests, because they consider that if an acquisition is involved, there must be purchase accounting. They emphasize that the word "pooling" implies a coming together of two groups of assets and ownerships into a pooled enterprise.

For a detailed explanation of purchase and pooling accounting, see Chapter IX, pp. 458–449 infra.

Interestingly in the later stages of the takeover craze in the 1980s, acquisitions of companies in leveraged buyouts,[c] which are accounted for as "purchases", resulted in enormous amounts of Goodwill appearing on balance sheets, which when amortized, were projected to result

---

c. A leveraged buyout (or "LBO"), once known as a "bootstrap" acquisition, may occur in several forms. One form may be briefly illustrated:

Condor Corp., with few assets, induces a group of lenders to loan it $5 billion at a very high interest rate, evidenced by what came to be known as high risk or "junk" bonds, for the purpose of making a tender offer to shareholders of Quarry Corp. (Their high risk results from the fact that there is little equity capital in the corporation.) After the successful completion of the tender offer, and a second-stage merger of the two corporations whereby any non-tendering shareholders of Quarry are bought out for cash, the post-merger corporation now owes the $5 billion on the bonds, which are secured by the former Quarry Corp.'s assets. "Pooling" accounting of course is not available because of the discontinuity of interest of shareholdings. Goodwill therefore is likely to result.

in low reported earnings or even losses for many years. Thus when Time Inc. combined with Warner Communications to form Time–Warner, $9 billion in Goodwill was debited (Paramount Communications, Inc. v. Time Inc., 571 A.2d 1140 (Del.1990) (text following n. 11)), assuring Time of virtually zero reported earnings for many years to come. See opinion below (In re Time Inc. Shareholder Lit., [1989 Tr. Bin.] Fed.Sec.L.Rep. (CCH) ¶ 94,514 (Del.Ch.1989) (text following n. 11)). Nevertheless this impact on reported earnings has become of much less concern to investors who now focus on cash flow—having learned much about accounting from such transactions. Moreover in many buyouts (not including Time–Warner) the shares are privately held so reported earnings are of less consequence.

C. ACCOUNTING FOR RESEARCH AND DEVELOPMENT COSTS AND FOR COMPUTER SOFTWARE DEVELOPERS—A NEW CONCEPTUAL BASIS OF ACCOUNTING?

One is continually struck by the rapidity of technological change and by such statements as that the sales of a genetic engineering company arise from products that were not in existence ten years ago. Financial analysts look on large expenditures for research and development (R & D) as a sign that the company is lively and likely to grow, and conversely look askance at low expenditure of this kind.

Are these expenditures current expenses like self-developed Goodwill, or should they be treated as deferred costs (assets) until the resulting revenues are realized? But when will the revenues be realized, and is there any assurance that they will be realized? If a long-term research project is under way and has not yet reached a conclusion by the end of an accounting period, do we know whether there ever will be a salable product from the expenditures being undertaken? Even if we think that there will be such a product, what happens if we gauge the public taste wrongly or if a competitor comes out simultaneously with a new product that appeals to the public more than ours?

Because of such circumstances, financial analysts looked skeptically at deferrals of large amounts of R & D. On the other hand, much R & D that is charged off to expense undoubtedly produces successful products and will produce revenues in the future. Thus, an immediate charge-off policy is likely to support future net income at the expense of current income and is looked upon favorably by financial analysts.

The Boeing Company, for instance, took several years to develop its first commercial jet planes, the 707 and 720, and again went through another cycle to develop its three-engine jet planes, the 727s. One market letter pointed, as a favorable market indication, to the fact that Boeing charged off its R & D for each of these planes to current expense, thus penalizing current income, and protecting future revenue of these planes from R & D costs when the plane revenues would begin to flow.

The general question of whether or not to capitalize acquired intangibles has presented problems, but the intractable problem whether to capitalize self-developed intangibles such as R & D surpasses those presented by acquired intangibles. *ARB No. 43* did not attempt to deal with this question for self-developed intangibles of any sort and *APB Op. No. 17,* as we have seen, was interpreted to not change prior practices for self-developed identifiable intangibles, although it required expensing of self-developed non-identifiable intangibles.

Among intangibles expressly left unregulated by the APB (*Opinion No. 17,* ¶ 6) were research and development costs. The FASB tackled this problem as one of its earliest projects.

STATEMENT OF FINANCIAL ACCOUNTING STANDARDS NO. 2 ACCOUNTING FOR RESEARCH AND DEVELOPMENT COSTS

FASB, 1974.*

*   *   *

"8. For purposes of this Statement,

(a) *Research* is planned search or critical investigation aimed at discovery of new knowledge with the hope that such knowledge will be useful in developing a new product or service (hereinafter 'product') or a new process or technique (hereinafter 'process') or in bringing about a significant improvement to an existing product or process.

(b) *Development* is the translation of research findings or other knowledge into a plan or design for a new product or process or for a significant improvement to an existing product or process whether intended for sale or use. It includes the conceptual formulation, design, and testing of product alternatives, construction of prototypes, and operation of pilot plants. It does not include routine or periodic alterations to existing products, production lines, manufacturing processes, and other on-going operations even though those alterations may represent improvements and it does not include market research or market testing activities.

*   *   *

"Accounting for Research and Development Costs

"12. All research and development costs encompassed by this Statement shall be charged to expense when incurred.

"Disclosure

"13. Disclosure shall be made in the financial statements of the total research and development costs charged to expense in each period for which an income statement is presented.

* * *

"Basis for Conclusions

* * *

"37. The Board considered four alternative methods of accounting at the time research and development costs are incurred:

(a) Charge all costs to expense when incurred.

(b) Capitalize all costs when incurred.

(c) Capitalize costs when incurred if specified conditions are fulfilled and charge all other costs to expense.

(d) Accumulate all costs in a special category until the existence of future benefits can be determined.

"38. In concluding that all research and development costs be charged to expense when incurred (see paragraph 12), Board members considered the factors discussed in paragraphs 39–59. Individual Board members gave greater weight to some factors than to others."

The factors referred to in ¶¶ 39–59 were:

— the high degree of uncertainty of the future benefits of R & D;

— the lack of a demonstrable causal relationship between R & D expenditures and future benefits;

— inability to measure the future benefit to enable it to be booked as an asset;

— the absence of usefulness to investors in assessing cash flow potential from the capitalization of R & D.

The last factor, innocuous as it sounds, is portentous.

In the 1977 edition of this book, we pointed out that this deference to investors' own cash flow and risk analyses was revolutionary thinking, never before given effect in the official pronouncements on intangibles, and the natural question to ask was: Would these criteria be applied to the other self-developed intangibles not now covered by official pronouncements of the APB and FASB? And the next question was: Would the FASB apply these criteria to acquired intangibles and self-developed intangibles which *are* covered by *APB Op. No. 17?* We should have added the third logical question: Would the FASB apply these criteria to all of accounting?

Thereafter in its Statement of Financial Accounting Concepts No. 1, *Objectives of Financial Reporting by Business Enterprises* (1978), the FASB further explained the ideas expressed in ¶¶ 39–59 of *SFAS No. 2.* Aside from these conceptual generalizations, the answer to all three of our questions so far is that relevant GAAP are inconsistent. Only in some cases are investors supplied with information which will enable them to make their own future cash flow estimates. In fact the FASB failed to follow the outlined approach in SFAS No. 69, *Disclosures about Oil and Gas Producing Activities* (1982), although it did extend *SFAS No. 2* to computer software in *SFAS No. 86* (1985). This SFAS holds portents for high technology industry accounting in the near future.

It is often difficult in high technology businesses to ascertain just when R & D stops and production begins. Moreover, there is still disagreement in the FASB as to whether the "economic income" or the "informational perspective" prevails. See the dissent by Mr. Mosso to the following.

STATEMENT OF FINANCIAL ACCOUNTING STANDARDS NO. 86 ACCOUNTING FOR THE COSTS OF COMPUTER SOFTWARE TO BE SOLD, LEASED, OR OTHERWISE MARKETED

FASB, 1985.*

*   *   *

"SCOPE

"2. This Statement establishes standards of financial accounting and reporting for the costs of computer software to be sold, leased, or otherwise marketed as a separate product or as part of a product or process, whether internally developed and produced or purchased. It identifies the costs incurred in the process of creating a software product that are research and development costs and those that are production costs to be capitalized, and it specifies amortization, disclosure, and other requirements. As used in this Statement, the terms *computer software product, software product,* and *product* encompass a computer software program, a group of programs, and a product enhancement. This Statement does not address the accounting and reporting of costs incurred for computer software created for internal use or for others under a contractual arrangement.

"Research and Development Costs of Computer Software

"3. All costs incurred to establish the technological feasibility of a computer software product to be sold, leased, or otherwise marketed are research and development costs. Those costs shall be charged to expense when incurred as required by FASB Statement No. 2, *Accounting for Research and Development Costs.*

"4. For purposes of this Statement, the technological feasibility of a computer software product is established when the enterprise has completed all planning, designing, coding, and testing activities that are necessary to establish that the product can be produced to meet its design specifications including functions, features, and technical performance requirements. * * *

"Production Costs of Computer Software

"5. Costs of producing product masters incurred subsequent to establishing technological feasibility shall be capitalized. Those costs include coding and testing performed subsequent to establishing technological feasibility. Software production costs for computer software that is to be used as an integral part of a product or process shall not be capitalized until both (a) technological feasibility has been established for the software and (b) all research and development activities for the other components of the product or process have been completed.

"6. Capitalization of computer software costs shall cease when the product is available for general release to customers. Costs of maintenance and customer support shall be charged to expense when related revenue is recognized or when those costs are incurred, whichever occurs first.

"Purchased Computer Software

"7. The cost of purchased computer software to be sold, leased, or otherwise marketed that has no alternative future use shall be accounted for the same as the costs incurred to develop such software internally, as specified in paragraphs 3–6. If that purchased software has an alternative future use, the cost shall be capitalized when the software is acquired and accounted for in accordance with its use.

"Amortization of Capitalized Software Costs

"8. Capitalized software costs shall be amortized on a product-by-product basis. The annual amortization shall be the greater of the amount computed using (a) the ratio that current gross revenues for a product bear to the total of current and anticipated future gross revenues for that product or (b) the straight-line method over the remaining estimated economic life of the product including the period being reported on. Amortization shall start when the product is available for general release to customers.

"Inventory Costs

"9. The costs incurred for duplicating the computer software, documentation, and training materials from the product masters and for physically packaging the product for distribution shall be capitalized as inventory on a unit-specific basis and charged to cost of sales when revenue from the sale of those units is recognized.

    * * *

"This Statement was adopted by the affirmative votes of five members of the Financial Accounting Standards Board. Messrs. Kirk and Mosso dissented.

"Mr. Kirk and Mr. Mosso dissent * * *

"This Statement sets the stage for extending the reach of Statement 2, with its mandatory expensing requirement, to a broad sweep of routine production activities because it assigns the bulk of computer programming activities (detail program design, coding, and testing) to the classification of research and development. Certainly, much research and development-type activity does take place in the computer software industry. However, most detail program design and coding activities are not discovery- or design-oriented in the sense of Statement 2; they are just the meticulous execution of a plan—skilled craftsmen applying proven methods as in any production process.

*   *   *

"Mr. Mosso's dissent is based on the view that computer software is a key element in the ongoing shift of emphasis in the U.S. economy from tangible outputs and physical processes to intangible outputs and creative processes. Changes of that nature are evident in both emerging and old-line industries. In his view, accounting should accommodate this transition by reporting the results of creative processes on the balance sheet when those results comprise reasonably probable future economic benefits. Otherwise, financial statements will lose relevance as creative activities proliferate."

Notes

6–2. *GAAP Effects on Public Policy.* Mr. Mosso's dissent may be of concern to accountants, who might be put out of work if his fears eventuate. But more likely, as the author's experience shows, accounting will be highly relevant, and indeed, highly affective (even if destructively) on our society. For example, in the latest takeover era, R & D costs had a double significance. A firm which had been doing much R & D reported lower earnings and, of course, paid out cash for these costs. A corporate raider with a short-term profit horizon found great benefit in cutting R & D expenses thereby increasing both reported earnings (and the value of the acquired shares) as well as cash flow.

Some believe that the U.S. economy was thus substantially impacted because potential target companies tended to minimize R & D in order to eliminate this accounting and cash flow plum from the eyes of raiders. This in turn diminished long-term American production and the general standard of living as well as our competitive status with certain foreign nations.

6–3. *Note on Off–Balance Sheet, Off–Income Statement Accounting for R & D.* Because *SFAS No. 2* requires concurrent expensing of R & D costs, many publicly held firms, especially high technology companies, had sought by various means to alter this effect. One such attempt was to set up a separate entity such as a limited partnership, with the publicly held company or its subsidiary as a general partner to manage the R & D activities and to supply the partnership with the results of any preliminary work already performed. In fact the public firm may perform all the R & D work as a contractor with the partnership—which is largely a paper entity. To assure that any successful results of the additional R & D accrue to the public firm, an option or other contractual right may be given to acquire that product.

If the economic substance of the arrangement does not result in a transfer of the risks and rewards to the other investors in the partnership, it would seem that the form should be ignored and the R & D costs should be expensed by the publicly held company under *SFAS No. 2.*

If instead those risks are transferred it would seem appropriate for the public corporation to account on the basis that it has a contract to perform services for the partnership.

SFAS No. 68, *Research and Development Arrangements* (1982), adopts these two treatments as GAAP.

D. WHETHER TO CAPITALIZE OR EXPENSE SPECIFIC TYPES OF INTANGIBLES— EXISTING PRACTICE

Little progress has been made in altering the old hodgepodge of practices in the years since *APB Op. No. 17.* Instead much formal hodgepodging has occurred. Several SFAS's have been published dealing with companies engaged in records and music, cable television, motion pictures, insurance, and broadcasting. Only in very broad outlines is there consistency among these. In this section we describe the practices concerning several of the more common intangibles.

1. PRE–OPERATING COSTS

In 1953 taxpayer bought out a competing applicant for a television station, and paid that applicant $25,799.19 for expenses which the rival had expended in 1948–52 and had capitalized for the training of personnel to operate the station. Taxpayer also later reimbursed the rival for $27,330 expended by the latter from 1953 until the commencement of operations in 1956 for additional training expenses. Taxpayer amortized the total amount of $53,129.19 and charged it to expense over the years 1952 through 1956, which were years before it received any of the revenues from television broadcasting. Richmond Television Corp. v. United States, 345 F.2d 901 (4th Cir.1965), vacated 382 U.S. 68 (1965). Should the deductions be allowed for corporate financial reporting in the year 1953, in 1952–56 as claimed, in 1955 when a construction permit for the station was granted, or in 1956 when the taxpayer received a three year license to commence broadcasting, or in 1956–58, the term of the license? Or for some other period such as one equal to the average term of employment, say eight years. Note that in 1965 non-renewals of FCC licenses for the prior twenty-five years had been under ¹/₁₀ of 1%. See Richmond Television Corp. v. United States, 354 F.2d 410 (4th Cir. 1965), and 345 F.2d 901 (4th Cir. 1965).

Was the $27,330 item an "acquired" intangible? Was either item a "pre-operating" item, and therefore outside the ambit of *APB Op. No. 17?* (See ¶ 6.)

In connection with this problem, see also *Fed. Power Commission Order No. 486,* Util.L.Rep. (CCH), Fed. ¶ 5503 (1973), establishing uniform accounting procedures for the costs of training employees to operate and maintain nuclear power and other new types of generating plants. The order states: "It appears to us that those training costs associated with new or nonconventional facilities are in the nature of a pre-operating cost, and are therefore properly capitalizable as an integral cost of the facility (includable in rate base)" and thus depreciable over the life of the plant. It went on to state: "Obviously, newly-trained personnel are subject to the same attrition factors as all employees. However, we think that the benefits of the original training in operation and maintenance of the facility provide an input that lasts throughout the life of the project. * * * This concept incorporates the cost of replacement training being charged to current operations."

2. START–UP COSTS

Many businesses experience losses after they open new stores or new branches. These are not pre-operating costs. It takes time before a store or branch pays for itself, i.e., until the staff is assembled and trained, working efficiently, and producing a volume of business sufficient to pass the break-even point. Moreover, in the case of financial enterprises like finance companies or banks, even though the volume of business being done month-by-month has reached a suitable level, the branch will not be profitable until the cumulative outstanding amount of loans built up over several months reaches the point where the interest return covers the expenses of the enterprise.

Many companies adopt the practice of avoiding the reduction of income which would otherwise result from charging to income the start-up cost of new branches by treating it as a deferred cost which is then charged against income over the first few years of profitable operation. This practice is based on the determination that the costs will ultimately be recovered. For a description of the use of this technique, see Green v. Jonhop, Inc., 358 F.Supp. 413 (D.Or.1973).

What happens if the branch never reaches the break-even point? Obviously, the losses of the past cannot be treated indefinitely as an asset, but must be sent through the income account. See, e.g., Note G to 1974 financial statements of Western Union Corporation, described in J. Cox, *Financial Information, Accounting and the Law* 403 (1980). To prevent avoiding the recognition of losses indefinitely, usual practice is that deferral of start-up costs will not extend beyond a limited period of time, say one year, from the opening of the branch.

Questions

6–4. *Question.* Does *APB Op. No. 17* deal with the issue of whether to capitalize or expense these start-up costs? The dissent of Mr. Schuetze to *SFAS No. 7* gives a negative answer to this question.

6–5. *Question.* At the same time that the FASB began consideration of R & D, it initiated study of start-up and relocation costs, but these efforts were not then carried through to a Standard, and only R & D was covered in the final *SFAS No. 2*. If the criteria of that Standard were applied to start-up costs, what would their treatment be?

3. ORGANIZATION COSTS

Organization costs include attorneys' and official fees in procuring a corporate charter and other costs of starting the enterprise. They theoretically have utility for the life of the firm, and under the continuity assumption should therefore be permanently capitalized, or at least capitalized subject to being reduced in part only on a permanent shrinkage in the business. See W.A. Paton & W.A. Paton, Jr., *Asset Accounting* 472–73 (1952). Nevertheless, most accountants have written off these costs either when incurred or within a few years thereafter. The sixty-month amortization rule of IRC § 248 for income tax purposes has caused a general practice to develop whereby these costs are amortized over five years. *APB Op. No. 17* appears not to determine whether these costs should be capitalized.

Question

6–6.   *Question.* What would *SFAS No. 2* require if its rationalia were extended to organization costs?

4. HUMAN RESOURCES—TRAINING COSTS IN ESTABLISHED ENTERPRISES

Salaries and wages paid to new employees are not the same as payments to trained personnel. Even the least skilled trades require at least a few moments of training which does not result in concurrent production, and some require years.

How are training costs for existing firms accounted for under *APB Op. No. 17?* These are usually expensed and nothing appears on the balance sheet for the value of a trained team or a smoothly operating plant, and *APB Op. No. 17,* ¶ 24 seems to prohibit any different treatment. Is this meaningful accounting? [d]

d. R.G. Barry Corp.'s 1969 Annual Report describes an experimental effort to value this human resource element of the corporation. On pro forma financial statements (i.e., statements prepared "as if" assumed facts occurred) supplementing its regular statements, an asset, "Net Investments in Human Resources," is carried at $986,094. According to The Wall St. Journal, April 3, 1970, at 9, col. 2:

The figure covers Barry's estimate of its investments in about 150 managerial jobs from first level supervisors to the company president, and attempts to reflect hiring and training costs, as well as an estimated replacement cost for persons already on the payroll when the system began.

Such spending is treated like a capital item if it is expected to show a return beyond the current accounting period, and as an expense if the benefit of the expenditure is expected immediately. A salary, for example, is a current expense. But the expense of training a computer operator might be amortized over several years. If a new computer system comes along, the cost of training for the old system is written off, and, if the operator quits, the company's total investment in him is written off.

*   *   *

Barry, which has a total of 1,700 employees, says its lowest investment in the kinds of jobs it has analyzed so far is about $3,000. It figures a first-line su-

5. ADVERTISING AND PROMOTIONAL COSTS

Problems

6–7. *Problem.* Rev.Rul. 68–561, 1968–2 Cum.Bull. 117 reads:

* * * The taxpayer is a public utility engaged in the sale and distribution of natural gas and manufactured gas. As a part of its general campaign to increase the consumption of gas, the taxpayer instituted incentive programs, the primary feature of which is the award of cash allowances to builders, contractors, and owners of buildings for either the construction of "all gas" homes or the conversion of heating, hot water, or other systems to gas. Other expenditures incurred in connection with the taxpayer's campaign were (1) salaries paid to its representatives, (2) allowances paid directly to builders and apartment house owners who advertise homes or apartments making reference to gas, and (3) direct advertising costs of the sales campaign.

Cash allowances made to builders, contractors, and homeowners to construct all gas homes or to convert heating, hot water, or other systems to gas, secure benefits to the taxpayer that can reasonably be expected to have value extending beyond the years in which they were paid or incurred. Such benefit is the increased sales of gas as a result of obtaining new customers. * * * Therefore, these payments are capital in nature and are recoverable through depreciation deductions under section 167 of the Code. The period over which the benefits secured will extend and, hence, the period over which the expenditures are depreciable is a question of fact.

The other expenditures (salaries and advertising) are less directly and significantly productive of intangible assets having a value extending beyond the taxable years in which they were paid or incurred.

pervisor represents a $4,000 investment; a middle manager, $16,000; and a top level manager, $34,500. "If we had to replace a president it would cost considerably higher than $35,000", Mr. Woodruff said. "We've never had to do that."

The human resource investment shows up on Barry's balance sheet on the liabilities and equity side as $493,047 for an appropriation for human resources, and an equal amount of deferred tax credit.

On the pro-forma statement of income, Barry defers $173,569 of "human resource expenses applicable to future periods." This has the effect of increasing net income by about $87,000. The expenses will be amortized in future periods.

The system, said Mr. Woodruff, eventually should aid decision making, especially for companies with operations in widespread locations. "Conventional profit and loss figures don't tell you what a manager has done with the human resources at his plant," he said.

Mr. Woodruff noted, for instance, that a manager can show good profit results "while driving people and actually depleting his human resources. Under conventional terms such a manager will get promoted, and the poor guy that follows him has to rebuild the organization. We're going to try to avoid rewarding the guy who does that." The new system, for example, will quickly indicate the costs of losing personnel and the additional expense of recruiting and training new people.

The R.G. Barry experiment is described in Pyle, Human Resource Accounting, Fin. Anal.J. 69 (Sept.–Oct., 1970).

See McRae, Human Resource Accounting as a Management Tool, J. Accountancy 32 (Aug., 1974). A bibliographical study is E. Caplan & S. Landekich, Human Resource Accounting: Past, Present, and Future (1974).

Such expenditures may, therefore, be treated as ordinary and necessary business expenses deductible under section 162 of the Code.

What does *APB Op. No. 17* require for these costs? Is the distinction made between the cash allowances, on the one hand, and salaries and advertising, on the other, persuasive?

Does it matter whether the physical embodiment of the advertising is short-lived or long-lived? E.g., compare broadcast commercials, billboards leased for a term, and signs given free to retailers. See Alabama Coca–Cola Bottling Co., 28 CCH Tax Ct. Mem. 635 (1969).

6–8. *Problem.* For an interesting treatment of advertising expense, see L.P. Larson, Jr., Co. v. William Wrigley, Jr., Co., 20 F.2d 830 (7th Cir. 1927).

6–9. *Problem.* If *SFAS No. 2* were extended to these costs, what would be the result?

6. PATENTS AND COPYRIGHTS

Certain assets such as patents and copyrights have fixed durations, i.e., a patent has a legally protected life of seventeen years. The question of the useful life, however, immediately presents a factual question of judgment. The patent might be useful for its full term. On the other hand, the owner might know from the nature of the patent that the product is only a fad and will no longer be useful after, say, five years, or that experience with the type of gadget in question indicates that it will have a useful life of not more than five or eight years. In such cases, the amortization period should be the expected useful life. Conceivably, instead of determining life on a time basis, the owner could estimate how many units of production would embody the patent and he could amortize cost in proportion to the number of units sold.

Suppose that a patent was developed by its current owner and that he spent $100,000 trying to perfect a desired process and all of these efforts turned out to be false leads. Finally, on the expenditure of another $10,000 he achieved a breakthrough and invented a gadget which he patented. What is the cost of the invention—$10,000 or $110,000? How much was fruitless effort and should be immediately charged off to expense because it will produce no revenue in the future, and how much of it should be "capitalized," i.e., treated as a deferred cost of the asset and amortized?

If R & D must be expensed immediately, how can any value be attributed to an asset account for a self-developed patent? *SFAS No. 2* would seem to leave little room logically for capitalization of patent development costs.[e] Very careful analysis will be necessary and one would intuit that the difficulties of definition and classification plus the practicalities would cause variations in practice. If you are interested

e. Although there is some room. For example, ¶ 10 expressly states that "legal work in connection with patent applica- tion" is excluded from the definition of R & D.

in seeing the sophistry necessitated here, see FASB Interpretation No. 6, *Applicability of FASB Statement No. 2 to Computer Software* (1975), which preceded *SFAS No. 86* considered in Part C supra.

E.   "BIG BATH" WRITE–OFFS

Start up costs, Goodwill, and other capitalized intangibles and fixed assets have sometimes been written off together with other capitalized costs in "big bath" write-offs occasioned by a loss or a necessity to write-down or write-off other assets that have lost value. See the discussion of big baths in Chapter V.

F.   NOTE ON LAW AND THE GAAP GAP

Accounting's inability to develop formal GAAP with respect to many intangibles means that the courts may feel more free to determine appropriate accounting and disclosure requirements than they would have, had formal GAAP existed. For example, in Republic Technology Fund, Inc. v. The Lionel Corp., 483 F.2d 540, 546 (2d Cir. 1973), a Second Circuit panel held that Goodwill carried at $998,000 should have been written down on six-month interim financial statements where the company had experienced a $189,000 loss for the period—despite an expert accountant's testimony to the contrary. The Court stated:

> We commence with the $998,000 item for good will of Anton–Imco Electronics Corp., as to which the interim statement of earnings reflected no discount even though this subsidiary had sustained a loss of $188,842 as of June 30. Mr. Easton, Lionel's auditor, acknowledged that the operating loss of Anton–Imco was a "factor to be considered" in deciding whether there was a diminution of the good will. He felt, however, that this single factor was outweighed by the fact that Anton–Imco was only in its first year of operation as a Lionel subsidiary and in his words was "engaged in the development of a new machine—I believe it was a money sensor, a money changing device— and based on all the information that was available at that time the prospects for success seemed very reasonable." Thus, in the opinion of Mr. Easton, credited by the district court, despite Anton–Imco's losses there was no "diminution in value" of its good will.
>
> We cannot accept Mr. Easton's evaluation as a matter of law. The notes to the consolidated interim statements of income contain the following statement:
>
>> This company recently designed and developed a currency recognizing device, several prototype models of which have been built up to this time. The device has not yet been marketed and there is no assurance at this time as to whether it will be a profitable item.
>
> Nowhere do the notes in any way indicate that Anton–Imco had shown a $189,000 loss as of June 30 or that the retention of $998,000 as its good will was based upon the prospects of success of this currency

Fiflis, Acctg, 4th Ed. ACB—13

recognizing device which had not yet been marketed. Cf. Petersen Engine Co., Inc., 2 S.E.C. 893, 906 (1937); Lewis American Airways, Inc., 1 S.E.C. 330, 342 (1936) (misleading to designate "patent applications" as "patent rights" or "patents" under intangible assets heading in a balance sheet). Indeed, since the interim statements do not include a balance sheet but only consolidated statements of income they contained no reference at all to the good will item. This makes them in our view, all the more misleading. The person viewing the statements would have no reason to suspect that the consolidated earnings were at least subject to question since despite a loss on the part of a major division for the first half-year, its good will was still being carried at a full initial valuation equivalent to about 8 per cent of the Lionel total book value. Cf. R. Mautz, Financial Reporting by Diversified Companies 157–58 (1968) quoted in T. Fiflis & H. Kripke, Accounting for Business Lawyers 556–57 (1971) (investor needs to know "relative importance" of several industries comprising a diversified corporation accurately to forecast future prospects).

For explication of the intuitively correct proposition that the courts are more prone to fix accounting principles when there are no formal GAAP in FASB pronouncements or the like, see Fiflis, *Current Problems of Accountants' Responsibilities to Third Parties,* 28 Vand.L.Rev. 31, 73–80 (1975).

Chapter VII

ACCOUNTING FOR CONTINGENT EXPENSES

OBJECTIVES

1. Understand GAAP concerning whether and when to recognize expenses which are not certain to occur but which are contingent on future events, especially matters in litigation.

2. Understand the lawyer's role in accounting and securities law disclosure of uncertainties.

RELEVANCE FOR LAWYERS

The existence of uncertainties more often than not involve legal questions since they arise from contracts, torts or property obligations which frequently depend on complex legal analysis. If an uncertainty exists, Securities and Exchange Commission regulations and GAAP, where applicable, require disclosure at least. The lawyer is implicated in both areas. We shall see the regularly recurring auditing routine whereby auditors query a firm's legal counsel concerning uncertainties and the intricate treaty between the two professions choreographing the steps for resolving the resultant tensions. In addition accounting treatment of uncertainties may give rise to legal disputes as to the appropriateness of that treatment in tax, rate-making, securities fraud, and other proceedings.

In the last three chapters we explored costs which were relatively certain and the problems revolved around measurement and allocation as expense in the period the cost occurred or in some later period or periods, or both. In each case the transaction required a debit to an expense or a deferred expense account. The corresponding credit was then to another asset account or to a liability account. In this chapter, the first question is whether there should be any entry at all. We shall see that when no bookkeeping entry is made, there nevertheless remains a question of whether disclosure, by footnotes to the financial statements or within the text of the financials, must be made.

We shall begin our inquiry with the simplest accounting issue—one where the lawyer is generally not involved except for litigation based on misrepresentation due to failure to follow GAAP.

A. ACCOUNTING FOR BAD DEBTS ON RECEIVABLES

As we have seen, accounts receivable are not recognized on the books until the revenue giving rise to the receivable is recognized, which usually means when it is realized. At that time, the entry is:

Account Receivable—Jones	$1,000	
Sales Revenue		$1,000

We also have seen that in accordance with ¶ 23 of SFAS No. 5, *Accounting for Contingencies* (1975), where there is "significant uncertainty as to collection," there is no full recognition immediately, and the installment method, the cost recovery method, or some other method of revenue recognition should be used. See note 8 to ¶ 12 of *APB Op. No. 10.*

Note

7–1. *Non-use of Present Value of Receivables.* Should receivables be recognized at face amount or at present value when they are payable at a distant date and bear little or no interest? The AAA Committee on Concepts and Standards Underlying Corporate Financial Statements said, in *Accounting and Reporting Standards for Corporate Financial Statements, 1957 Revision,* 32 Acctg.Rev. 536, 538 (1957): "Under conditions of exchange involving a substantial time lag between purchase or sale and ultimate payment, the effective exchange price may be defined as the amount of the expected payment discounted to its present worth at an appropriate rate of interest." But *APB Op. No. 21,* ¶ 3(a) (1971), which fixed GAAP, excludes ordinary receivables due within one year from its scope. The reasons for this overstatement of value may include the immateriality of amount, a cost-benefit analysis, or the view that users of financial statements may readily make their own approximations. For long-term receivables (and payables) *APB Op. No. 21* does require use of present values.

But what should be the accounting when the specific account is not uncertain of collection, but there is a statistical probability that some accounts will not be good?

STATEMENT OF FINANCIAL ACCOUNTING STANDARDS NO. 5 ACCOUNTING FOR CONTINGENCIES

FASB, 1975.*

* * *

"3. When a loss contingency exists, the likelihood that the future event or events will confirm the loss or impairment of an asset or the incurrence of a liability can range from probable to remote. This Statement uses the terms *probable, reasonably possible,* and *remote* to identify three areas within that range, as follows:

(a) *Probable.* The future event or events are likely to occur.

(b) *Reasonably possible.* The chance of the future event or events occurring is more than remote but less than likely.

(c) *Remote.* The chance of the future event or events occurring is slight.

"4. Examples of loss contingencies include:

(a) Collectibility of receivables.

* * *

"8. An estimated loss from a loss contingency (as defined in paragraph 1) shall be accrued by a charge to income if *both* of the following conditions are met:

(a) Information available prior to issuance of the financial statements indicates that it is probable that an asset had been impaired or a liability had been incurred at the date of the financial statements. It is implicit in this condition that it must be probable that one or more future events will occur confirming the fact of the loss.

(b) The amount of loss can be reasonably estimated.

* * *

"22. The assets of an enterprise may include receivables that arose from credit sales, loans, or other transactions. The conditions under which receivables exist usually involve some degree of uncertainty about their collectibility, in which case a contingency exists * * *. Losses from uncollectible receivables shall be accrued when both conditions in paragraph 8 are met. Those conditions may be considered in relation to individual receivables or in relation to groups of similar types of receivables. If the conditions are met, accrual shall be made even though the particular receivables that are uncollectible may not be identifiable.

"23. If, based on available information, it is probable that the enterprise will be unable to collect all amounts due and, therefore, that at the date of its financial statements the net realizable value of the receivables through collection in the ordinary course of business is less than the total amount receivable, the condition in paragraph 8(a) is met because it is probable that an asset has been impaired. Whether the amount of loss can be reasonably estimated (the condition in paragraph 8(b)) will normally depend on, among other things, the experience of the enterprise, information about the ability of individual debtors to pay, and appraisal of the receivables in light of the current economic environment. In the case of an enterprise that has no experience of its own, reference to the experience of other enterprises in the same business may be appropriate."

———

Even if no particular account receivable is known to be uncollectible, it is known that for most businesses with any large number of credit sales, some of the accounts will in fact become uncollectible. To account for this probability, the accountant does recognize the gross sales income and does debit Accounts Receivable in the same amount, but periodically he or she partially offsets these entries by a debit to a Bad Debt Expense account and a credit to an Estimated Bad Debt Loss account. The entries might be:

Accounts Receivable	$10,000	
Sales Income		$10,000
Bad Debt Expenses	100	
Estimated Bad Debt Losses [a]		100

This Estimated Bad Debt Losses account is unlikely to be shown as a liability on the balance sheet. Instead it will probably be shown as an offset to Accounts Receivable, just as an Accumulated Depreciation account is generally shown as an offset to the related asset account. Thus the balance sheet might depict on the asset side:

Accounts Receivable	$10,000
Less: Estimated Bad Debt Losses	100
Net	$9,900

The following excerpt explains the techniques in use. Finney and Miller use the term, "Allowance for Doubtful Accounts," for what we have termed, "Estimated Bad Debt Losses." Both terms, and variations, are found in practice.

H. FINNEY AND H. MILLER, PRINCIPLES OF ACCOUNTING, INTERMEDIATE
176–179 (6th Ed. 1965).*

"Allowance for doubtful accounts. The creation of an allowance for doubtful accounts is intended to accomplish two results, namely:

---

a. Formerly this account was called "Reserve for Bad Debts".

To charge the loss by the sale of goods to customers whose accounts prove to be uncollectible against the period that caused the loss.

To show the estimated realizable value of the customer's accounts.

"It is not always possible, however, to accomplish both of these results, as will be shown in the following discussion of methods of estimating the amounts to be credited to the allowance account.

"The three customary procedures for computing the periodical credits to the allowance account are indicated below:

(1) Adjusting the allowance account to the amount of loss estimated by aging the accounts receivable and considering supplementary data.

(2) Adjusting the allowance account to a percentage of the accounts open at the end of the period.

(3) Increasing the allowance account by a percentage of the sales for the period.

"The per cents used in the second and third methods are usually determined from the loss experience of prior periods. However, full consideration should be given to changes in economic conditions or in the credit policy of the company, because such changes may cause the losses to differ materially from those of the past.

"Aging accounts. When this method is used, a list of all accounts may be made on working papers, with columns with various headings such as 'Not due,' '1 to 30 days past due,' '31 to 60 days past due,' and so forth. All accounts in the subsidiary ledger are then listed, and the component elements of the balances are classified in the proper columns.

"An accounts receivable aging schedule, summarizing the data assembled in the working papers, is illustrated [below]:

Age of Accounts Receivable
December 31, 1965 and 1964

	December 31, 1965		December 31, 1964	
	Amount	Per Cent of Total	Amount	Per Cent of Total
Not due	$15,000	30.93%	$20,000	41.67%
1 to 30 days past due	12,000	24.74	16,000	33.33
31 to 60 days past due	8,000	16.50	5,000	10.42
61 to 90 days past due	6,000	12.37	4,500	9.38
91 to 120 days past due	4,000	8.25	1,000	2.08
More than 120 days past due	2,000	4.12	1,000	2.08
Bankrupt or with attorneys	1,500	3.09	500	1.04
Total	$48,500	100.00%	$48,000	100.00%

"The amount of the allowance account is then determined on the basis of the age of the past-due accounts. Supplementary information must also be considered, because it may be known that some accounts not past due are doubtful, whereas others long past due may be collectible. In this connection, the credit terms must, of course, be taken into consideration, for the terms will determine when an account is past due.

"This method has the advantage of accomplishing the second of the two objectives stated above, because it results in a fairly accurate valuation of the accounts on the books. However, it may easily result in a failure to distribute losses to the periods during which they were caused. Bad debt losses are caused by making sales to customers who do not pay their accounts. Theoretically, therefore, provision for the loss should be made in the period in which the sales were made. But, if the aging method is used, accounts may not appear to be uncollectible until a date subsequent to the period of sale; in that case the loss, or the provision therefor, will not be charged to income until a period subsequent to that of the sale. Thus, one period will get the credit for the income and a later period will get the charge for the loss.

"Percentage of open accounts. If a company's experience indicates that a certain per cent of the accounts open at any date will ultimately prove uncollectible, the total allowance requirement at any date can be estimated by multiplying the open account balances by the loss experience per cent. The allowance account is then credited with an amount sufficient to increase the existing balance to the estimated required balance. The theory of this method is the same as the theory of the preceding method; the difference lies in the procedure of estimating the total allowance requirement. It is not a method to be recommended; it is subject to the disadvantage pointed out in connection with the aging method, and it is difficult to obtain experience data from which to make a reliable estimate of the per cent to be applied.

"Percentage of sales. The best matching of revenues and expenses (or losses) for a period is usually made by crediting the allowance account at the end of the period with a percentage of the sales of the period. The rate is computed on the basis of the statistics of sales and bad debt losses of the past periods. Theoretically, the rate should be computed by dividing the losses of past periods by the charge sales of past periods, not by the total sales. The rate thus ascertained should be applied to the charge sales for the current period. But, practically, it makes very little difference whether or not this distinction is made. By using the total sales to compute the rate, a per cent is obtained lower than that which results from dividing losses by credit sales. This lower rate is then applied to the total sales for the period instead of to the credit sales.

"If statements are prepared monthly, it is important that allowance provisions be made monthly rather than annually; otherwise, the monthly balance sheets may show very inaccurate net valuations of the receivables. Assume that balance sheets are prepared monthly, but no provision for losses on the year's sales is made until the end of the year. Obviously, in all balance sheets prepared before the close of the year, the receivables will be shown without provision for losses on receivables which arose from sales during the year—presumably, the major portion of the receivables. On the other hand, if an adequate allowance account exists throughout the year by reason of provisions in prior years, the year-end provision based on the total sales for the year will produce an excessive allowance account.

"When the credit to the allowance account is computed as a percentage of sales, there is some danger that the account balance may become excessive or may prove to be inadequate, regardless of whether provisions are made monthly or annually. For this reason, the accounts receivable should be reviewed from time to time for the purpose of estimating probable losses, the amount of which can be compared with the existing allowance account balance. If it is excessive or inadequate, the per cent applied to sales should be revised accordingly.

"Recoveries. If a collection is made on an account once charged off as uncollectible, the customer's account should be recharged with the amount collected, and possibly with the entire amount previously written off if it is now expected that collection will be received in full. The collection should then be credited to the customer's account. These entries are made in the customer's account so that it will show that the debtor has attempted to re-establish his credit by the payment.

"What account should be credited when the customer's account is recharged? From the standpoint of theory, the following may be said:

It is conservative to credit recoveries to the allowance account if the credits to it were determined by multiplying the sales by a per cent representing the relation of net bad debt losses (losses less recoveries) to sales. It is not correct if the per cent used in computing the provision represents the relation of gross write-offs to sales; in this case, recoveries should be credited to an income account.

"If the allowance account was credited on a valuation basis (by aging the accounts or using a per cent representing the relation of losses to account balances), it makes no difference, from a theoretical standpoint, whether recoveries are credited to the allowance account, to the Bad Debts expense account, or to an income account, as the allowance account balance and likewise the net income will be the same in any case. For, if a recovery is credited to the allowance account, the amount to be charged to expense at the end of the period to raise the allowance account to its required balance will be reduced by the amount of the recovery; if the recovery is credited to the Bad Debts expense account or to an income account, the charge for the current provision will be correspondingly increased; the net income will be the same by either method.

"From a practical standpoint, the choice of methods is usually of no serious consequence, because the loss reserve and the net operating charge for bad debts are usually matters of estimate; the theoretical considerations, therefore, seem to be of no great practical importance unless recoveries are of abnormally large amounts."

An illustration of the mechanics may help better to understand the Finney and Miller excerpt. (For this purpose we gratefully accept the merciful option stated in the last paragraph of the excerpt.)

Assume that we have determined that the amount to be set up in accordance with one of the methods mentioned in the excerpt is $500. The entry is:

Bad Debt Expense	$500	
Estimated Bad Debt Losses		$500

When in fact a particular account becomes uncollectible, the entry is:

Estimated Bad Debt Losses	$75	
Account Receivable—X Corp.		$75

If X Corp. thereafter pays the account, the entries are:

(a) Account Receivable—X Corp.	$75	
Estimated Bad Debt Losses		$75
(b) Cash	$75	
Account Receivable—X Corp.		$75

Although a single entry debiting Cash and crediting Estimated Bad Debt Losses would have the same net effect (since the debit and credit to Account Receivable—X Corp. cancel each other out), it is preferable to use both entries (a) and (b) so as to have the X Corp. account reflect the true credit status of X Corp. (i.e., its debt-paying history).

B. UNCERTAINTIES AND CONTINGENCIES GENERALLY

Estimated bad debts are but one type of contingent loss or expense commonly incurred. We also have seen another type—estimated liabilities for product warranties. But there are many others.

Uncertainties of a very material nature have arisen in recent years because of major readjustments in the economy. For example, the volatility in fuel costs and interest rates; capital outlays required for compliance with environmental controls; and liability for failure to comply with laws concerning securities, voting rights, and sex and race discrimination. Also consider loan losses of financial institutions, marketable securities, and situations where a company is engaged in a small number of projects with dominant effect on results of operations.

Perhaps this concern for uncertainties muddied the waters sufficiently to cause many firms in the '60's to resume a generally discredited practice of establishing reserves for merely anticipated (but not yet actual) casualties by charges to income.[b] There is no longer support in

---

b. The term "reserve" is falling into disuse, precisely because it has so many different meanings and has led to confusion. Accounting Terminology Bulletin No. 1, ¶¶ 57–64 (1953). But the term is still employed, albeit to mean several different things:

    (a) It was a term applied to credits which were valuation accounts for assets—e.g., reserve for depreciation, now

GAAP for this view (*SFAS No. 5*, ¶ 14, infra), although many casualty insurers defended this "smoothing" of income from period to period through established reserves for the anticipated catastrophe losses. But *SFAS No. 5* now prohibits even the insurance practice.

However, there are many other types of loss contingencies ranging between the extremes of bad debt losses and merely anticipated casualties. Depending on application of the standards of *SFAS No. 5*, these items will either be accrued (by a debit to expense, referred to in *SFAS No. 5* infra as a "charge to income", and a credit to a liability or contra asset account), merely disclosed, or neither. Where should the lines be drawn?

STATEMENT OF FINANCIAL ACCOUNTING STANDARDS NO. 5, ACCOUNTING FOR CONTINGENCIES

FASB, 1975.*

"4. Examples of loss contingencies include:

(a) Collectibility of receivables.

(b) Obligations related to product warranties and product defects.

(c) Risk of loss or damage of enterprise property by fire, explosion, or other hazards.

(d) Threat of expropriation of assets.

(e) Pending or threatened litigation.

(f) Actual or possible claims and assessments.

(g) Risk of loss from catastrophes assumed by property and casualty insurance companies including reinsurance companies.

(h) Guarantees of indebtedness of others.

(i) Obligations of commercial banks under 'standby letters of credit.'

(j) Agreements to repurchase receivables (or to repurchase the related property) that have been sold.

* * *

accumulated depreciation; and reserve for bad debts, now estimated bad debt losses.

(b) Some reserves were liability accounts based on estimates—e.g., reserve for service warranty liability, now estimated service warranty liability.

(c) Some reserves were mere segregations of surplus—e.g., reserve for construction of new plant, or reserve for possible unknown contingencies. It is only in this context that the term "re-serve" continues in favor. ATB No. 1, ¶ 60.

One can see that when these varied types of credit accounts were all lumped together on the right side of the balance sheet under the caption, "Reserves," they did not contribute to understanding.

"Accrual of Loss Contingencies

"8. An estimated loss from a loss contingency (as defined in paragraph 1) shall be accrued by a charge to income if *both* of the following conditions are met:

(a) Information available prior to issuance of the financial statements indicates that it is probable that an asset had been impaired or a liability had been incurred at the date of the financial statements. It is implicit in this condition that it must be probable that one or more future events will occur confirming the fact of the loss.

(b) The amount of loss can be reasonably estimated.

"Disclosure of Loss Contingencies

* * *

"10. If no accrual is made for a loss contingency because one or both of the conditions in paragraph 8 are not met, or if an exposure to loss exists in excess of the amount accrued pursuant to the provisions of paragraph 8, disclosure of the contingency shall be made when there is at least a reasonable possibility that a loss or an additional loss may have been incurred.[6] The disclosure shall indicate the nature of the contingency and shall give an estimate of the possible loss or range of loss or state that such an estimate cannot be made. Disclosure is not required of a loss contingency involving an unasserted claim or assessment when there has been no manifestation by a potential claimant of an awareness of a possible claim or assessment unless it is considered probable that a claim will be asserted and there is a reasonable possibility that the outcome will be unfavorable.

* * *

"12. Certain loss contingencies are presently being disclosed in financial statements even though the possibility of loss may be remote. The common characteristic of those contingencies is a guarantee, normally with a right to proceed against an outside party in the event that the guarantor is called upon to satisfy the guarantee. Examples include (a) guarantees of indebtedness of others, (b) obligations of commercial banks under 'standby letters of credit,' and (c) guarantees to repurchase receivables (or, in some cases, to repurchase the related property) that have been sold or otherwise assigned. The Board concludes that disclosure of those loss contingencies, and others that in substance have the same characteristic, shall be continued. The disclosure shall include the nature and amount of the guarantee. Consideration should be given to disclosing, if estimable, the value of any

---

6. For example, disclosure shall be made of any loss contingency that meets the condition in paragraph 8(a) but that is not accrued because the amount of loss cannot be reasonably estimated (paragraph 8(b)). Disclosure is also required of some loss contingencies that do not meet the condition in paragraph 8(a)—namely, those contingencies for which there is a *reasonable possibility* that a loss may have been incurred even though information may not indicate that it is *probable* that an asset had been impaired or a liability had been incurred at the date of the financial statements.

recovery that could be expected to result, such as from the guarantor's right to proceed against an outside party.

*   *   *

"Appropriation of Retained Earnings

"15. Some enterprises have classified a portion of retained earnings as 'appropriated' for loss contingencies. In some cases, the appropriation has been shown outside the stockholders' equity section of the balance sheet. Appropriation of retained earnings is not prohibited by this Statement provided that it is shown within the stockholders' equity section of the balance sheet and is clearly identified as an appropriation of retained earnings. Costs or losses shall not be charged to an appropriation of retained earnings, and no part of the appropriation shall be transferred to income.

*   *   *

"Gain Contingencies

(a) Contingencies that might result in gains usually are not reflected in the accounts since to do so might be to recognize revenue prior to its realization.

(b) Adequate disclosure shall be made of contingencies that might result in gains, but care shall be exercised to avoid misleading implications as to the likelihood of realization.

*   *   *"

It is often difficult to distinguish an existing but unspecified loss or liability (such as bad debt expense) from a non-existing but merely anticipated obligation. The majority and dissenting opinions in the following income tax case held different views on this point.

UNITED STATES v. GENERAL DYNAMICS CORP.

Supreme Court of the United States, 1987.
481 U.S. 239.

The issue in this case is whether an accrual basis taxpayer providing medical benefits to its employees may deduct at the close of the taxable year an estimate of its obligation to pay for medical care obtained by employees or their qualified dependents during the final quarter of the year, claims for which have not been reported to the employer.

*   *   * From 1962 until October 1, 1972, General Dynamics purchased group medical insurance for its employees and their qualified dependents from two private insurance carriers. Beginning in October, 1972, General Dynamics became a self-insurer with regard to its medical care plans. Instead of continuing to purchase insurance from outside carriers, it undertook to pay medical claims out of its own funds, while continuing to employ private carriers to administer the medical care plans.

To receive reimbursement of expenses for covered medical services, respondent's employees submit claims forms to employee benefits personnel, who verify that the treated persons were eligible under the applicable plan as of the time of treatment. Eligible claims are then forwarded to the plan's administrators. Claims processors review the claims and approve for payment those expenses that are covered under the plan.

Because the processing of claims takes time, and because employees do not always file their claims immediately, there is a delay between the provision of medical services and payment by General Dynamics. To account for this time lag, General Dynamics established reserve accounts to reflect its liability for medical care received, but still not paid for, as of December 31, 1972. It estimated the amount of those reserves with the assistance of its former insurance carriers.

We think that this case, like *Brown*, [v. Helvering, 291 U.S. 193 (1934)] involves a mere estimate of liability based on events that had not occurred before the close of the taxable year, and therefore the proposed deduction does not pass the "all events" test. We disagree with the legal conclusion of the courts below that the last event necessary to fix the taxpayer's liability was the receipt of medical care by covered individuals. A person covered by a plan could only obtain payment for medical services by filling out and submitting a health expense benefits claim form. Employees were informed that submission of satisfactory proof of the charges claimed would be necessary to obtain payment under the plans. General Dynamics was thus liable to pay for covered medical services *only* if properly documented claims forms were filed. Some covered individuals, through oversight, procrastination, confusion over the coverage provided, or fear of disclosure to the employer of the extent or nature of the services received, might not file claims for reimbursement to which they are plainly entitled. Such filing is not a mere technicality. It is crucial to the establishment of liability on the part of the taxpayer. ✳ ✳ ✳

That these estimated claims were not intended to fall within the "all events" test is further demonstrated by the fact that the Internal Revenue Code specifically permits insurance companies to deduct additions to reserves for such "incurred but not reported" (IBNR) claims. *See* 26 U.S.C. § 832(b)(5) (providing that an insurance company may treat as losses incurred "all unpaid losses outstanding at the end of the taxable year"); § 832(c)(4) (permitting deduction of losses incurred as defined in § 832(b)(5)). If the "all events" test permitted the deduction of an estimated reserve representing claims that were actuarially likely but not yet reported, Congress would not have needed to maintain an explicit provision that insurance companies could deduct such reserves.[c]

c. Ed's. note. Is this the only possible inference?

[Justice O'Connor, dissenting, stated:]

In my view, the circumstances of this case differ little from those in *Hughes Properties.* [United States v. Hughes Properties, Inc., 476 U.S. 593 (1986) (holding that casino operator may deduct amounts guaranteed for payment on "progressive" slot machines but not yet won by any playing patrons).] The taxpayer here is seeking to deduct the amounts reserved to pay for medical services that are determined to have been provided to employees in the taxable year, whether or not the employees' claims for benefits have been received. The taxpayer's various medical benefits plans provided schedules for the medical and hospital benefits, and created a contractual obligation by the taxpayer to pay for the covered services upon presentation of a claim. The courts below found that the obligation to pay became fixed once the covered medical services were received by the employee. Once the medical services were rendered to an employee while the relevant benefit plan was in effect, General Dynamics could not avoid liability by terminating the plan prior to the filing of a claim. Neither could General Dynamics extinguish its liability by firing an employee before the employee filed a claim for benefits.

The holding of the Court today unnecessarily burdens taxpayers by further expanding the difference between tax and business accounting methods without a compelling reason to do so.

Notes

7–2. *Financial Accounting for "IBNR" Claims.* The practice for "incurred but not reported" (IBNR) claims referred to by the Court for casualty insurance companies is viewed by the SEC as being squarely within *SFAS No. 5.* See SEC, *SAB No. 87* (1989), adding Topic 5–W to SEC, Staff Accounting Bull. Series, 6 Fed.Sec.L.Rep. (CCH) ¶ 74,087 and ¶ 74,141. Hence it would seem that General Dynamics should accrue the expense for financial reporting purposes, despite its disallowance in tax accounting, as Justice O'Connor stated.

7–3. *Liabilities Based on Anticipated Legislation.* In the first quarter of 1975, just after the promulgation of *SFAS No. 5,* Exxon Corp. reportedly established a reserve estimated by outside analysts at $400 million for possible increases in federal income taxes then being considered by Congress and potential Mideast oil price rises then under negotiation and which could apply retroactively. Is this in accordance with *SFAS No. 5?* See Koppel v. Middle States Petroleum Corporation, 197 Misc. 479, 96 N.Y.S.2d 38 (1950), predating *SFAS No. 5,* allowing accrual of a similar charge as against preferred shareholders claiming a dividend right.

One might ask what motivated Exxon to make this charge reducing income. Perhaps the answer is that Exxon's action served to reduce an embarrassing multibillion dollar profit after a period of rapidly rising gasoline and oil prices.

7–4. *Guarantees, Including Guarantees of Municipal Bonds.* Guarantees of indebtedness of others and certain other matters such as standby letters of credit are special cases under ¶ 12 of *SFAS No. 5* which are to be *disclosed* even if the liability is deemed remote.

Of course, *SFAS No. 5* may require *reporting* of a guarantee liability if loss is probable and measurable. See SEC, *SAB No. 60* (1985).

In recent years high interest rates have caused municipalities and firms which issue large amounts of long-term debt to seek guarantees of their debt because they find that this reduces interest rates demanded by investors by thus reducing risk. The aggregate liabilities of banks and insurance companies alone for these guarantees was estimated at $437 billion and growing in 1984. SEC, *SAB No. 60,* n. 1 (1985). Further, the increase in competition among banks and insurance companies has caused them to seek even greater revenues from issuing such guarantees, providing further impetus. The result is that hundreds of billions of dollars now are subject to guarantees, running as long as thirty years and almost none of which is reported on balance sheets.

This particular problem provides us with another illustration of how accounting issues affect our society. Because mere disclosure without booking of a guarantee results in "off balance sheet" debt (i.e., no liability is reported in the liabilities section), regulators of financial institutions such as banks and insurance companies must be concerned with the stability of such firms which become heavily involved in the guarantee business. At the same time, non-regulated firms may obtain a competitive advantage over such regulated firms if they can write unlimited amounts of guarantees. This puts pressure in turn on regulators to loosen restrictions. Similar pressure was part of the cause of the thrift industry crisis.

7–5. *The Poloron Products Case.* Poloron Products, Inc. manufactured and sold 50 million hand grenade bodies to the U.S. Army for $1.00 each under express warranties that they were free from defects. Eight million were claimed by the Army to be defective. Poloron's general counsel, without investigation, gave an opinion to its auditors that the warranty claim was groundless and would not cause a material impact on Poloron's financial position. In addition, much false information was supplied to the auditors who thereupon disclosed the existence of the claim without accruing an expense or stating the range of liability. The SEC filed a complaint for an injunction against the Chief Executive and Chief Financial Officers of Poloron. SEC, AAER 223, Fed.Sec.L.Rep. (CCH) ¶ 73,692 (1989).

7–6. *Frequent Flyer Liabilities.* The major airlines provide frequent flyer bonuses to passengers by providing free or discounted trips after passengers accumulate a certain amount of paid mileage. For recent years the value of these free trips for all lines has been estimated at about $1 billion, although the anticipated out-of-pocket costs were estimated to be less because otherwise unfilled seats often are used to satisfy these obligations. Should this liability be accrued under *SFAS No. 5?* Should the amounts be based on normal rates for flights, on one of the special rates established by the line, on out-of-pocket costs, or on some other basis? See AICPA, Proposed SOP, *Accounting for Frequent Travel Award Programs* (1989).

7–7. *Liabilities for Non-pension Post-employment Benefits.* General Dynamics' liability for medical benefits is small potatoes compared to liabilities for unfunded post-employment benefits for health care and life insurance, or tuition assistance or legal advisory services.

It has been said by the ABA Committee on Law & Accounting in its August, 1990 Report, that reporting these liabilities "would have a greater effect on financial statements than any other FASB pronouncement has ever had. Total liabilities on all corporate balance sheets have been estimated to be as high as $2 trillion or higher; it has been stated that in 1988, over one-fourth of the 500 largest industrial companies would have reported losses as a result of the change."

SFAS No. 81, *Disclosure of Post-retirement Health Care and Life Insurance Benefits* (1984) has mandated disclosure for several years now. For an illustration see n. 6 to the GE statements in Chapter X. Recognition in the accounts was the subject of several years of study by the FASB and at the end of 1990 the FASB issued SFAS No. 106, *Employers' Accounting for Post-retirement Benefits Other Than Pensions.* The accounting for pension benefits is established in SFAS No. 87, *Employers' Accounting for Pensions* (1985), and No. 88, *Employers' Accounting for Settlements and Curtailments of Defined Benefit Pension Plans and for Termination Benefits* (1985). See Chapter XII infra.

The issues were described in Scott & Upton, FASB, *Highlights of Financial Reporting Issues* (Dec. 1988): *

"Consider, for a moment, the perhaps unusual but not unrealistic case of a 65–year–old recently retired employee with a 45–year–old spouse. The retired employee is eligible for employer-provided post-retirement health care benefits and can be expected to live for 15 years. (The spouse can be expected to live another 20 years beyond that.) If the employer's postretirement health care plan includes dependents, the employer has accepted an obligation to provide health care insurance, at whatever cost, to one or both individuals for an estimated 35 years. That is a significant obligation typically not accrued in financial statements today.

"The Board has tentatively concluded that postretirement benefits, like pensions, are a form of deferred compensation. That view is the key to the conclusions found in the exposure draft. Like other forms of deferred compensation, the Board believes that postretirement benefits should be recognized in a company's financial statements as they are earned by employees.

"What Is the FASB Trying to Accomplish?

"The Board's principal mission is to work toward improvements in financial reporting. Having reached the conclusion that the rendering of employees' service pursuant to a postretirement benefit plan creates a significant obligation and that the cost of promised postretirement benefits should be recognized in financial statements during the working lives of covered employees, the Board's exposure draft has the following objectives:

To have reported income reflect the cost of postretirement benefits over the period they are earned by employees

To make the balance sheet more informative and more complete by including a measure of the obligation to provide postretirement benefits

To make reported amounts more comparable and understandable by mandating a single method for measuring the obligation and cost

To enhance disclosure of the extent and effects of an employer's promise to provide postretirement benefits

"What Is Wrong with Current Accounting for Postretirement Benefits?

"Most companies today account for postretirement benefits on a 'pay as you go' basis. The problems with that accounting are twofold: First, the cost of the benefits is recognized in the period it is paid, not in the period the company receives the employee's service and the employee earns the benefits. Accrual accounting is designed to record income and expenses in the periods in which they are earned or incurred. Second, the obligation to provide benefits in the future is not included on the balance sheet with the company's other liabilities. As a result, financial statement users may reach erroneous conclusions about a company's financial condition. A company with significant unrecorded obligations, for example, may appear healthier than a competitor that has a much smaller obligation.

"Is the Cost Really Measurable? Isn't This Information Too Soft to Be Meaningful?

"Unquestionably, measuring the obligation for postretirement benefits requires estimates of uncertain future events. That is unavoidable because, typically, the cost of fulfilling the promises made under the plans is not fixed. The promised benefits may be more or less expensive depending on future events like technological advances or changes in how medical care is provided. The Board realizes that those estimates may have a larger margin of error than some other estimates used in financial reporting.

"How Would the Proposed Accounting Work?

"The proposed accounting is generally similar to the accounting for pensions specified in FASB Statement No. 87, 'Employers' Accounting for Pensions.' The Board concluded that the obligation to provide postretirement benefits is essentially the same as an obligation to provide pensions. As a result, differences between the proposed accounting and pension accounting are limited to those areas in which there are fundamental differences in the nature of the employer's promise to provide the benefits.

Like a pension, the current year's cost of a postretirement benefit is the product of a complex computation with several variables. To begin with, any accounting for postretirement benefits that recognizes the cost before payments are made must deal with two questions: First, how much will the benefits cost? Second, how should the cost of the benefits be assigned to individual years of an employee's career?"

Disclosure by Reserves Out of Surplus

One mechanic for disclosure without accrual of the loss as a charge against income is simply to add a footnote to the financial statements explaining the contingency. Another device is to "segregate surplus" by removing an amount from Retained Earnings and placing it in a restricted account. E.g.:

Retained Earnings	$X
Restricted Retained Earnings	$X

Aside from disclosure, this technique serves no additional useful purpose since it does not result in any real effect; e.g., there is no segregation of cash or other assets. At one time, it was envisioned as a way of inhibiting payment of dividends but this is clearly not assured; even if a dividend statute limits dividends to Unrestricted Retained Earnings, the company can reverse the journal entry above at any time it desires so as to unrestrict the Retained Earnings. The company has little need for this eccentric device to remind it of the possible undesirability of the dividend.

Professor Herwitz points out that the device is unlikely to be used for a specific claim for fear it will prejudice the company in the litigation either by disclosing a willingness to settle for the amount shown or as an admission against interest. D. Herwitz, *Accounting for Lawyers* 365 (1980).

See *SFAS No. 5*, ¶ 15 supra for accounting limitations on such restricted retained earnings.

C. AN AUDITING PROBLEM FOR ACCOUNTANTS AND LAWYERS—ATTORNEYS' RESPONSES TO AUDITORS' REQUESTS FOR INFORMATION

1. THE PROBLEM

We have just considered whether under GAAP certain contingent liabilities must be accrued or disclosed. But contingencies, unlike, say, the purchase or sale of goods, are not routine entries in a set of books. They are most likely known only to a few individuals in the firm, if at all, and are often quite ephemeral. As such, it takes effort to ferret them out and then to assess them. Furthermore, there is likely to be disagreement as to the probability or possibility of occurrence and as to the measurement of these items under *SFAS No. 5*, ¶¶ 8 and 10. Attorneys are heavily involved in determining their existence, probability of loss and measurement.

What are the auditor's duties in this regard and what must management and company counsel reveal to the auditors when pressed? The answers to these questions are long and complex.

GAAS require auditors to verify management information insofar as reasonably possible. Prior to 1975 an auditor faced with the need to verify whether the financial statements showed all contingent liabilities required by antecedents of *SFAS No. 5* would do the most logical thing and ask the reporting firm's counsel if he or she was aware of any such contingencies and to assess them. At first counsel treated such queries cavalierly, usually stating that none were likely to succeed against the firm.

However, at about this same time the SEC was exerting great efforts to draft attorneys and auditors as policemen to enforce the securities laws by imposing substantive liability and professional sanctions under SEC Rule 2(e) permitting the disbarring of professionals from SEC practice. See, e.g., L. Loss, *Fundamentals of Securities Regulation* Ch. 11 (1988); R. Jennings & H. Marsh, *Securities Regulation* 1181–1240 (6th ed. 1987). Further, plaintiffs' lawyers increasingly named both auditors and counsel as principal defendants or aiders and abettors under the all-encompassing Rule 10b–5, also then at its apex of application. E.g., Fiflis, *Current Problems of Accountants' Responsibilities to Third Parties,* 28 Vand.L.Rev. 31 (1975); *Advisors to Management: Responsibilities and Liabilities of Lawyers and Accountants,* 30 Bus.Law. 227 (1975).

In an effort to protect themselves and their clients, auditors began to expand the scope of their requests to include all possible claims which might be asserted against the client. See Deer, *Lawyers' Responses to Auditors' Requests for Information,* 28 Bus.Law. 947 (1973). At the same time, lawyers, for the same reason, became more circumspect in rendering opinions, thus causing an impasse. Further, with respect to claims which had not yet been asserted, managers and counsel were concerned that if they disclosed these to auditors, the auditors might publish some of the claims under *SFAS No. 5,* and the injured parties would then assert their claims. Additionally, this raised issues of the attorney-client privilege and the client's willingness to seek advice of counsel. It was also feared that disclosures and assessments might result in admissions against interest. On the other hand, when the lawyer failed or refused to reveal all, the auditor felt constrained to qualify his opinion, and the client was made unhappy because of the perceived effects on security prices [d] and because "qualified reports" (see Chapter II) were not acceptable in SEC filings. In a case where the secret involved illegality, if counsel was not consulted, the result might be to forego the opportunity for counsel to advise the client to comply with the law. On the other hand, prospective investors have always had a keen interest in knowing of potential losses and these are the principal users of audited financial statements.

---

d. But see Alderman, The Role of Uncertainty Qualifications: Evidence to Support the Tentative Conclusions of the Cohen Commission, 144 J.Acct. 97 (Nov. 1977) (finding no effect on securities prices from qualified opinions). The Alderman study has been questioned. See J. Cox, Financial Information, Accounting and the Law, 416 n. 34 (1980).

A host of additional questions were raised by these problems and resulted in a remarkable bit of lawmaking by the American Bar Association and the AICPA. Portions of *SFAS No. 5* reproduced below were the first leg of a three-legged stool. The other two were put in place with the nearly concurrent publication by the ABA of its *Statement of Policy Regarding Lawyers' Responses to Auditors' Requests for Information*, 31 Bus.Law. 1709 (1976), and by the AICPA of SAS No. 12, *Inquiry of Client's Lawyer Concerning Litigation, Claims and Assessments* (1976). A detailed commentary (31 Bus.Law. 1715) and introductory analysis (31 Bus.Law. 1737) accompanied the policy statement. And see *Second Report of Comm. on Audit Inquiry Responses Regarding Initial Implementation*, 32 Bus.Law. 177 (1976). Collectively, these items are often referred to as the "Treaty" between the professions. By all accounts it has operated with remarkable success and without problems. See Hinsey, *Communications Among Attorneys, Management and Auditors*, 36 Bus.Law. 727 (1981); Fuld, *Lawyers' Responses to Auditors—Some Practical Aspects*, 44 Bus.Law. 159 (1988). Let us take a brief overview of the resolution of these problems.

2. THE RESOLUTION

STATEMENT OF FINANCIAL ACCOUNTING STANDARDS NO. 5 ACCOUNTING FOR CONTINGENCIES

FASB, 1975.*

"Litigation, Claims, and Assessments

"33. The following factors, among others, must be considered in determining whether accrual and/or disclosure is required with respect to pending or threatened litigation and actual or possible claims and assessments:

(a) The period in which the underlying cause (i.e., the cause for action) of the pending or threatened litigation or of the actual or possible claim or assessment occurred.

(b) The degree of probability of an unfavorable outcome.

(c) The ability to make a reasonable estimate of the amount of loss.

"36. If the underlying cause of the litigation, claim, or assessment is an event occurring before the date of an enterprise's financial statements, the probability of an outcome unfavorable to the enterprise must be assessed to determine whether the condition in paragraph 8(a) is met. * * * The fact that legal counsel is unable to express an opinion that the outcome will be favorable to the enterprise should not necessarily be interpreted to mean that the condition for accrual of a loss in paragraph 8(a) is met.

"37.   *   *   * If an unfavorable outcome is determined to be reasonably possible but not probable, or if the amount of loss cannot be reasonably estimated, accrual would be inappropriate, but disclosure would be required by paragraph 10 of this Statement.

"38.   With respect to unasserted claims and assessments, an enterprise must determine the degree of probability that a suit may be filed or a claim or assessment may be asserted and the possibility of an unfavorable outcome. For example, a catastrophe, accident, or other similar physical occurrence predictably engenders claims for redress, and in such circumstances their assertion may be probable; similarly, an investigation of an enterprise by a governmental agency, if enforcement proceedings have been or are likely to be instituted, is often followed by private claims for redress, and the probability of their assertion and the possibility of loss should be considered in each case. By way of further example, an enterprise may believe there is a possibility that it has infringed on another enterprise's patent rights, but the enterprise owning the patent rights has not indicated an intention to take any action and has not even indicated an awareness of the possible infringement. In that case, a judgment must first be made as to whether the assertion of a claim is probable. If the judgment is that assertion is not probable, no accrual or disclosure would be required. On the other hand, if the judgment is that assertion is probable, then a second judgment must be made as to the degree of probability of an unfavorable outcome."

———

In describing the treaty resolving this problem, it will be easier to understand if we separate the topics of pending or threatened claims, on the one hand, from unasserted claims, on the other.

(A) *Unasserted Claims*

If a firm owns a factory building but it encroaches onto neighboring land by fifty feet, although no one but the president and the firm's attorney are aware of this fact, and the statute of limitations for ejectment has seven more years to run, must disclosure or accrual be made on financial statements under *SFAS No. 5?* Must the management or counsel reveal this data to the auditors if asked to reveal all potential claims? Must or may the auditors ask that question? If not, what will the auditors ask under GAAS? If the auditors follow GAAS, what will be the duties of management and counsel?

From the universe of all possible claims, a category of unasserted claims that are not probable of assertion clearly need not be disclosed under *SFAS No. 5.* This is so because, if not probable of assertion, the claim will not satisfy the conditions of ¶ 8 for accrual ((a) "probable that an asset had been impaired or a liability had been incurred" and (b) "the amount of loss can be reasonably estimated") or ¶ 10 for disclosure ("a reasonable possibility that a loss . . . may have been incurred"). Thus, if the factory encroachment is deemed not probable of assertion,

SFAS No. 5 does not require disclosure.   Nor is disclosure required even if assertion is probable but there is no reasonable possibility that the outcome will be unfavorable (see *SFAS No. 5*, ¶ 10, last sentence) or be material.   AU 337.12.

The problem, of course, is who should make the judgments concerning assertion, outcome, and materiality?   The reasonable alternatives include:

     (a) management,

     (b) counsel,

     (c) auditor, and

     (d) any combination of these.

Immediately it becomes apparent that if the auditor participates, any attorney-client privilege is lost, even if the ultimate resolution is that the item need not be disclosed in the financial statements.[e]

In addition, there is no reason to believe that the auditor is better qualified than management and counsel to determine these questions. Moreover, the auditor in these circumstances does not desire to undertake an additional responsibility.

As to the lawyer, it is believed that the prime concern is in maintaining client confidences and the attorney-client privilege, thereby encouraging clients to consult counsel.

For these reasons, *SAS No. 12* places the responsibility on the management who must assure the auditor that it has disclosed all unasserted claims that the lawyer has advised must be disclosed under *SFAS No. 5*.   If management and counsel concur in concluding that the claim is not required to be disclosed, the auditor is not told about it.   If counsel disagrees with management's determination of improbability, and management fails to disclose to the auditor, counsel must consider his or her obligation to withdraw or do otherwise under applicable law. But counsel is not licensed to disclose the uncertainty.   Cf. In re Carter and Johnson, Rel. 34–17597 (SEC 1981).

However, it is unlikely that, contrary to management's determination, counsel will determine that an unasserted claim must be disclosed because the ABA's Statement of Policy takes a very hard line here.   It states:

> That judgment will infrequently be one within the professional competence of lawyers and therefore the lawyer should not undertake such assessment except where such judgment may become meaningful because of the presence of special circumstances, such as catastrophes, investigations and previous public disclosure [as in *SAS No. 12*, ¶ 38],

e.   E.g., In re Fisher, 51 F.2d 424 (S.D. N.Y. 1931) (even where the attorney and the accountant are the same person, communications to him qua accountant are not privileged as attorney-client communications.   There is no accountant-client privilege at common law but several states have enacted a statutory privilege.   See generally, R.J. Gormley, The Law of Accountants and Auditors, ¶ 3.03(3) (1981), for a very fine discussion.

or similar extrinsic evidence relevant to such assessment. Moreover, it is unlikely, absent relevant extrinsic evidence, that the client or anyone else will be in a position to make an informed judgment that assertion of a possible claim is "probable" as opposed to "reasonably possible" (in which event disclosure is not required). In light of the legitimate concern that the public interest would not be well served by resolving uncertainties in a way that invites the assertion of claims or otherwise causes unnecessary harm to the client and its stockholders, a decision to treat an unasserted claim as "probable" of assertion should be based only upon compelling judgment.

Then to make clear that the lawyer also is not endorsing the client's view that some unasserted claims are not probable, the Statement goes on to say:

> Consistent with these limitations believed appropriate for the lawyer, he should not represent to the auditor, nor should any inference from his response be drawn, that the unasserted possible claims identified by the client (as contemplated by Paragraph 5(c) of the Statement of Policy) represent all such claims of which the lawyer may be aware or that he necessarily concurs in his client's determination of which unasserted possible claims warrant specification by the client; within proper limits, this determination is one which the client is entitled to make—and should make—and it would be inconsistent with his professional obligations for the lawyer to volunteer information arising from his confidential relationship with his client.

The mechanism established by *SAS No. 12* for dealing with all of this is to have the management send a letter to counsel who has been named by the management as having devoted substantive attention to a particular matter or matters as to which management believes disclosure is required. The relevant facts about any such matter are therein repeated. The letter asks counsel to "Please furnish our auditors such explanation, if any, that you consider necessary to supplement the foregoing information, including an explanation of those matters as to which your views may differ from those stated."

Thus, if management does not deem the matter one that must be disclosed, counsel is not asked about it and the auditor is not told.

However, a partial safeguard against management's incorrect determination that an unasserted matter need not be disclosed is a requirement that if counsel is named by management as having been engaged or given substantive attention on some disclosed matter, counsel must acknowledge an undertaking indicated in the following statement in management's letter to counsel:

> We understand that whenever, in the course of performing legal services for us with respect to a matter recognized to involve an unasserted possible claim or assessment that may call for financial statement disclosure, if you have formed a professional conclusion that we should disclose or consider disclosure concerning such possible claim or assessment, as a matter of professional responsibility to us, you will so advise us and will consult with us concerning the question

of such disclosure and the applicable requirements of Statement of Financial Accounting Standards No. 5. Please specifically confirm to our auditors that our understanding is correct.

Please specifically identify the nature of and reasons for any limitation on your response.

———

To recapitulate, the auditor under *SAS No. 12* must:

(a) obtain assurance from management that it has disclosed all unasserted claims that the lawyer has advised are probable of assertion and must be disclosed under *SFAS No. 5* (*SAS No. 12,* ¶ 5d);

(b) have management send a letter to counsel (¶ 6) containing a list describing and evaluating unasserted claims deemed probable of assertion and having a reasonable possibility of an unfavorable outcome, but only those for which the lawyer has been engaged and to which he or she has devoted substantive attention (¶ 9c);

(c) request counsel to state to the auditor any views different from management's (¶ 9e).

(d) However, a condition to this process being satisfactory to the auditor is that counsel must specifically acknowledge an undertaking that when "the lawyer has formed a professional conclusion that the client should disclose or consider disclosure" of such a claim, the lawyer will so advise the client (¶ 9f and g).

If counsel refuses to answer the request in (c) above, that may call for a qualified report. ¶ 13. The ABA Statement states, in ¶ 5, that the client should consider assertion probable only if it is reasonably certain. Also, the ABA Statement iterates that an inquiry to the lawyer would be improper if it requested information as to other than "probable" assertions of a claim as to which the outcome is possibly unfavorable.

Independently of the lawyer's response to the auditor, the lawyer may have obligations under legal or ethical rules when the client improperly fails to disclose. The ABA Statement of Policy says:

In any event, where in the lawyer's view it is clear that (i) the matter is of material importance and seriousness, and (ii) there can be no reasonable doubt that its non-disclosure in the client's financial statements would be a violation of law giving rise to material claims, rejection by the client of his advice to call the matter to the attention of the auditor would almost certainly require the lawyer's withdrawal from employment in accordance with the Code of Professional Responsibility. (See, e.g., Disciplinary Rule 7–102(A)(3) and (7), and Disciplinary Rule 2–110(B)(2).) Withdrawal under such circumstances is obviously undesirable and might present serious problems for the client. Accordingly, in the context of financial accounting and reporting for loss contingencies arising from unasserted claims, the standards for which are contained in FAS 5, clients should be urged to disclose to the auditor information concerning an unasserted possible claim or assessment (not otherwise specifically identified by the client) where in the course of the services performed for the client it has become clear to the lawyer that (i) the client has no reasonable basis to conclude that assertion of the claim is not probable (employing the concepts hereby enunciated) and (ii) given the probability of assertion, disclosure of the loss contingency in the client's financial statements is beyond reasonable dispute required.

(B) Pending or Threatened Claims

As to other claims, *SAS No. 12* requires that the auditor:

(a) obtain from management a description and evaluation of such claims and assurance that management has disclosed all items required to be disclosed by *SFAS No. 5* (*SAS No. 12,* ¶ 5b);

(b) request management to send a letter to counsel (id. ¶ 6) containing a list of such claims as to which counsel has been engaged and has devoted substantive attention (¶ 9b);

(c) which letter requests counsel to evaluate the likelihood of an unfavorable outcome and estimate the potential loss and to note omissions from the list. (¶ 9d)

The ABA has stated that "[i]n view of the inherent uncertainties, the lawyer should normally refrain from expressing judgments as to outcome except in those relatively few clear cases where it appears to the lawyer that an unfavorable outcome is either 'probable' or 'remote.'" The ABA has also stated that "the amount or range of potential loss will normally be as inherently impossible to ascertain." ABA, *Statement of Policy Regarding Lawyers' Responses to Auditors' Requests for Information,* ¶ 5 (1975), below.

When the attorney responds that he or she is unable to evaluate the outcome or estimate the potential loss, the company may be able to represent in the notes to the financial statements that "in the opinion of *management,* the litigation will not have a material adverse effect on the Company." If company management has discussed the matter with its attorney including its responsibility for disclosure, the auditor may thus have a basis for an "unqualified opinion." If the attorney concludes that there is no reasonable basis for the opinion expressed by management—and that the client is thus misrepresenting facts—the attorney is probably obligated to resign his engagement as counsel and the auditor may thus be put on inquiry notice. *SAS No. 12,* ¶ 11.

In its 1980 Annual Report, Johns–Manville Corporation included the following note to its financials:

Note 5—Contingencies

The Company is a defendant or co-defendant in a substantial number of lawsuits brought by present or former insulation workers, shipyard workers, factory workers and other persons alleging damage to their health from exposure to dust from asbestos fiber or asbestos-containing products manufactured or sold by the Company and, in most cases, by certain other defendants. The majority of these claims allege that the Company and other defendants failed in their duty to warn of the hazards of inhalation of asbestos fiber and dust originating from asbestos-containing products. In the opinion of Management, the Company has substantial defenses to these legal actions, resulting in part from prompt warnings of the possible hazards of exposure to asbestos fiber emitted from asbestos-containing insulation products following the 1964 publication of scientific studies linking pulmonary disease in insulation workers to asbestos exposure.

Also included in these legal actions are a number of cases brought by some of the Company's own employees and by employees of other manufacturing companies which use asbestos fiber in their operations. These suits typically allege that the Company and other defendants failed to warn of the hazards associated with the use of such fiber. In the opinion of Management, the Company has substantial defenses to these legal actions including the fact that, with respect to employees of other manufacturing companies, it had no special knowledge not in the possession of the plaintiffs' employers which would give rise to a special duty on the part of the Company, and, with respect to the employees of the Company, that applicable workers' compensation statutes provide appropriate defenses to most such claims.

It is the Company's belief that the claims and lawsuits pending and which may arise in the future relate to events and conditions existing in prior years. More specifically, it is the Company's belief, based on the following factors and assumptions, that since at least prior to the period covered by these financial statements, no significant new potential liabilities have been created for the Company with respect to diseases known to be related to asbestos and arising from asbestos fiber and/or asbestos-containing products manufactured or sold by the Company:

That since the mid–1970's, the Company has sold asbestos fiber in the United States only in pressure pack, block form or other similar condition and not in a loose form;

That by 1973, the Company had ceased domestic manufacture of thermal insulation products containing asbestos which are the products principally involved in disease claims made against the Company;

That the Occupational Safety and Health Administration (OSHA) established a maximum exposure standard for asbestos fiber of five fibers per cubic centimeter in 1972 and lowered that standard to two fibers per cubic centimeter in 1976. It is assumed that compliance with such standards in the work place was achieved within a reasonable time following such promulgation and is continuing to date; and

With respect to any use not complying with the OSHA asbestos standards, the Company's defensive posture with respect to claims arising out of such environments will be significantly enhanced.

As of December 31, 1980, the Company was a defendant or co-defendant in 5,087 asbestos/health suits brought by approximately 9,300 individual plaintiffs. This represents a substantial increase from the December 31, 1979 level of 2,707 cases (brought by approximately

4,100 plaintiffs) and the December 31, 1978 level of 1,181 cases (brought by approximately 1,500 plaintiffs). During 1979, the Company was named as a defendant in an average of 141 cases per month (brought by an average of 196 plaintiffs) as compared with an average of 65 cases per month (brought by an average of 83 plaintiffs) in 1978. During the first three quarters of 1980, the Company was named as a defendant in an average of 194 cases per month (brought by an average of 382 plaintiffs); this rate increased to an average of 304 cases per month (brought by an average of 403 plaintiffs) in the fourth quarter of 1980. During 1980, the Company disposed of 402 claims at an average disposition cost (excluding legal expenses) of $23,300, substantially all of which was paid by applicable insurance. This level of disposition cost represents a significant growth from the pre–1980 level of approximately $13,000 per claim. The growth in these two areas has significantly increased the uncertainties as to the future number of similar claims which the Company may receive, and the future disposition costs of the pending and future claims. Also during 1980, to resolve uncertainties as to the correct interpretation of a number of provisions in the various policies of insurance maintained by the Company and applicable to these claims, it was necessary for the Company to bring a declaratory judgment action to have such issues resolved by a court of law. While it continues to be the Company's opinion that its position with respect to these issues is sound and in accord with the weight of judicial precedents, any litigation involves uncertainties to some degree.

Because of the uncertainties associated with the asbestos/health litigation, and in spite of the substantial defenses the Company believes it has with respect to these claims, the eventual outcome of the asbestos/health litigation cannot be predicted at this time and the ultimate liability of the Company after application of available insurance cannot be estimated with any degree of reliability. No reasonable estimate of loss can be made and no liability has been recorded in the financial statements. Liabilities, if any, relating to asbestos/health litigation will be recorded in accordance with generally accepted accounting principles when such amounts can be reasonably estimated. Depending on how and when these uncertainties are resolved, the cost to the Company could be substantial.

———

The company soon thereafter was bankrupted by these liabilities.

Problem

7–8. *Problem.* Congress adopted the Comprehensive Environmental Response, Compensation and Liability Act of 1980 as amended ("CERCLA"), 42 U.S.C. §§ 9601–75 (West 1983 & Supp. 1989), in response to debacles such as the poisonings of Love Canal, New York, and Times Beach, Missouri, requiring certain persons to pay the costs of clean-up of environmentally dangerous sites. Generally all present or former owners or operators of the site and any persons who generated hazardous substances at the site or transported them there are potentially responsible persons

("PRP's") who may be held liable jointly and severally for clean-up costs. The Environmental Protection Agency ("EPA") is empowered to obtain assistance from the PRP's in investigating the liability and may then order a clean-up or contract for it and recover the costs from the PRP, including the EPA's own overhead costs. Liability is not quite absolute but statutory defenses are very limited, including acts of God, acts of war and acts or omissions of third parties if the PRP exercised due care to avoid the hazard. In addition, the corporate veil is only a limited protection of shareholders and parent corporations. It has been said that the average site clean-up cost is $30 million.

In Financial Reporting Release 36, (CCH) Fed.Sec.L.Rep. ¶ 72,436 (1989), the SEC posed this problem:

> FACTS: A registrant has been correctly designated a PRP by the EPA with respect to cleanup of hazardous waste at three sites. No statutory defenses are available. The registrant is in the process of preliminary investigations of the sites to determine the nature of its potential liability and the amount of remedial costs necessary to clean up the sites. Other PRPs also have been designated, but the ability to obtain contribution is unclear, as is the extent of insurance coverage, if any. Management is unable to determine that a material effect on future financial condition or results of operations is not reasonably likely to occur.

(a) What are the duties of the auditors, management and counsel retained to advise on the CERCLA liability?

(b) Entirely apart from GAAP, the SEC set forth this example of a case in which the company must disclose these facts in its Management Discussion and Analysis ("MD & A") section of its quarterly reports to the SEC and its shareholders' annual report, stating:

> Based upon the facts of this hypothetical case, MD & A disclosure of the effects of the PRP status, quantified to the extent reasonably practicable, would be required.[30] For MD & A purposes, aggregate potential cleanup costs must be considered in light of the joint and several liability to which a PRP is subject. Facts regarding whether insurance coverage may be contested, and whether and to what extent potential sources of contribution or indemnification constitute reliable sources of recovery may be factored into the determination of whether a material future effect is not reasonably likely to occur.

---

30. Designation as a PRP does not in and of itself trigger disclosure under Item 103 of Regulation S–K and Instruction 5 thereto, 17 C.F.R. 299.103, regarding "Legal Proceedings," because PRP status alone does not provide knowledge that a governmental agency is contemplating a proceeding. Nonetheless, a registrant's particular circumstances, when coupled with PRP status, may provide that knowledge. While there are many ways a PRP can become subject to potential monetary sanctions, including triggering the stipulated penalty clause in a remedial agreement, the costs anticipated agreement entered into in the normal course of negotiation with the EPA, generally are not "sanctions" within either Instruction 5(b) or (c) to Item 103. Such remedial costs normally would constitute charges to income or in some cases capital expenditures.

*

Part D

STOCKHOLDERS' EQUITY

Chapter VIII

REGULATION OF DISTRIBUTIONS TO STOCKHOLDERS

OBJECTIVES

1. Comprehend the revolution in the law regulating corporate share issuances and distributions by way of dividends or share repurchases in this modern era of highly leveraged companies.

2. Relate the law to accounting concepts and GAAP to facilitate statutory interpretation.

3. Understand the requirements for quasi-reorganizations of troubled companies.

RELEVANCE FOR LAWYERS

For many decades until recently lawyers have been relatively free of serious concerns about the validity of dividends and the structuring of quasi-reorganizations of troubled companies. Nevertheless a great deal of expensive legal work was necessitated by arcane rules placing hurdles and hoops in the way of share issuances and repurchases and dividends. Now following the revolution in the law of corporate distributions in many of the commercially important states (but not Delaware) and the proliferation of highly leveraged firms resulting from leveraged buyouts and recapitalizations, both of those features are reversed. Many firms formerly safe from insolvency are faced with difficult issues concerning distributions to shareholders. However, under the new legislation being adopted by an increasing number of the states, much of the make-work will disappear. This chapter provides a modern basis for dealing with the issues given present day GAAP and the new statutes. It also deals with the older law extant in about thirty-five states.

A. INTRODUCTION

To this point our principal concern has been to describe accounting as a financial disclosure device for serving the needs of creditors and equity investors. We now change our focus to the law of corporate share issuances and distributions which has undergone a revolutionary change in the past decade as several of the commercially more important states adopted the Revised Model Business Corporation Act financial provisions. In this process we also shall sketch the outlines of GAAP for corporate equity.[a]

It may be predicted that with the wave of leveraged buyouts and large number of recapitalizations in defense against takeovers, state law limitations on dividends will again become important in corporate law practice. This is likely because many firms have wiped out surpluses and have incurred huge amounts of debt, making insolvency a much greater risk than it had been for six decades. Yet at the same time lawyers have had far less exposure to these problems than those who faced the issues in the 1930s and 1940s. This chapter serves as a survey of this area of the law.

It is here that there is the greatest interplay of law and accounting. At the early part of this century accountants, groping for guiding principles, found that the courts had fashioned certain rules for dividend and tax law purposes. As a result early accounting treatises referred to legal requirements as bases for various rules of accounting. Lawyers, for their part, also sought legitimacy in accounting practices for their legal determinations having realized that accountants are the experts in this area. See, for example, Tooey v. Percival, supra Chapter III. Despite these revealing deferential tendencies, both disciplines now recognize that different policies may be pertinent in law and in accounting for particular events.

1. THE LEGAL ENTITY

For some purposes it is necessary to deal with financial data for legal entities which are often different from the economic entity;

---

a. Accounting for corporate equity is a very large field and we shall not attempt to describe it entirely. APB Opinion No. 29 (1973) provides guidance for many problems of accounting for corporate equity such as accounting for dividends in kind, spinoffs and other reorganizations. The purchase or pooling problem for corporate combinations, discussed in Chapter VI, and more extensively described in Chapter IX, is the subject of many accounting pronouncements, some of which are only briefly described in those chapters. See also ARB 43, Chapter 1A, ¶ 2 (capital surplus not to be used to relieve income account of charges); id. ¶ 6 (re donated stock); and APB Opinion No. 14 (1969) (accounting for warrants and convertible debt). For a comprehensive study, see B. Melcher, Stockholders' Equity (AICPA Accounting Research Study No. 15) (1973). On accounting and legal problems on initial issuance of shares generally, see Manne, Accounting for Share Issues Under Modern Corporation Laws, 54 Nw.U.L.Rev. 285 (1959) (an early call for elimination of the concept of par which also explains the accounting for several matters which we do not cover here, including issuance of two different classes of securities for a lump sum, subscription contracts, issuance and exercise of privileges for convertible shares, rights, warrants, options and convertible bonds).

consolidated financial statements are usually considered meaningless in determining surplus available for dividends and share repurchases.[b] In this chapter, we shall deal with financial accounting of the corporate legal entity only.

2. THE POLICY BASES FOR A LAW LIMITING CORPORATE DISTRIBUTIONS

The corporation, with its legal hierarchy of shareholders who elect directors who, in turn, name officers to operate the business, is much more complex than appears at first blush. Any generalizations, including the following, about how it functions are likely to be overly simplistic.

Shareholders have an interest in receiving corporate distributions which ordinarily are necessary to provide incentive for investment and for the prudent conduct of the business. But because the legal system holds that the corporate entity has separate legal status, ordinarily its creditors cannot recover from shareholders if the corporation does not pay the creditor's claim. Thus creditors have an interest in avoiding the corporation's impairing its ability to pay by distributing its assets to shareholders. Since dividends are declared by the board of directors, which is elected by shareholders, the interests of creditors may require protection if they are to be adequately served. Similarly, when there are two or more classes of shareholders, say common stockholders and preferred stockholders,[c] with the common typically controlling the election of directors, those directors could favor the common unless limited somehow.

As a result, legislatures, observing the potential for unfairness to creditors or senior equity holders and the interest in limited distributions to shareholders, adopted various restrictions on corporate distributions.

Legal advisors to creditors long ago realized that these statutory limitations were so filled with loopholes as to be useless, and as a result came to rely on contractual limitations on distributions by their corporate debtors. Creditors therefore lost interest in statutory reform. Nevertheless to take full advantage of the loopholes and to avoid traps for unwary corporate managers required a good deal of very expensive legal guidance. Only when the rapier-like pen of Bayless Manning (a former Dean of Stanford Law School and corporation law professor become Wall Street lawyer) was put to battle did the bar respond. In

b. Kern v. Chicago & Eastern Ill. R. Co., 6 Ill.App.3d 247, 285 N.E.2d 501 (1972). California has altered this result to require use of consolidated equity in determining validity of dividends. See Cal.Corp.Code § 114 (West 1977 and Supp.1983).

The rule may not be as clearly settled as we indicate. Kern relied on only one case as "analogous authority," Cintas v. American Car & Foundry Co., 131 N.J.Eq. 419, 25 A.2d 418, 1942, affirmed per curiam 132 N.J.Eq. 460, 28 A.2d 531 (1942). See the more complete discussion at T. Fiflis & H. Kripke, Accounting for Business Lawyers 533–45 (1971).

c. For a description of preferred stock see N. Lattin on Corporations § 129 et seq. (2d ed. 1971). Preferred stock typically carries no voting right except after a default.

his book, now in a third edition, B. Manning & J. Hanks, *Legal Capital* (3d ed. 1990), he succeeded in laying bare the utter futility of then current law. This motivated reform of the Model Business Corporation Act, the revised version of which has been adopted by about fifteen states in the past five years. It will be referred to as the Revised MBCA and the former act as the MBCA. We shall consider these revolutionary changes but of necessity must also review the archaic law of the other two-thirds of the states. This will have the advantage of making Manning's proposals and the Revised Model Business Corporation Act very clearly the only reasonable path to follow.

B. LIMITATIONS ON THE ISSUANCE OF SHARES

1. THE BASIC RULES

In the nineteenth century, when the law in this area developed and which still reigns in Delaware and most other states, corporations which sought funds from investors traditionally issued shares of stock having a designated "par value" in the amount per share sought to be received therefor. For example, investors might be offered shares for a price of $100 having a par value of $100 per share stated on the stock certificate. It may have been necessary to have the price marked on the stock certificate as a psychological suggestion to the purchaser that he or she was getting money's worth, or par value may have been a device to assure investors that all were making equivalent contributions for equivalent shares. Whether par was a selling gimmick, or was designed to assure equal contributions, need not concern us here. What is worth noting is that, in time, corporation law came to require that, whatever the par value, that amount, as a minimum, was required to be paid in to the corporation for each share issued.[d] The theory was either that there was a statutory obligation to pay in par or that a failure to do so was a misrepresentation to creditors.[e]

d. E.g., the Model Business Corporation Act ("MBCA") § 18 states: "Shares having a par value may be issued for such consideration expressed in dollars, not less than the par value thereof, as shall be fixed from time to time by the board of directors.

"Shares without par value may be issued for such consideration expressed in dollars as may be fixed from time to time by the board of directors unless the articles of incorporation reserve to the shareholders the right to fix the consideration. In the event that such right be reserved as to any shares, the shareholders shall, prior to the issuance of such shares, fix the consideration to be received for such shares, by a vote of the holders of a majority of all shares entitled to vote thereon * * *."

In 1984 the MBCA was substantially revised. Both versions will be referred to from time to time, the earlier one as the MBCA and the later as Revised MBCA.

e. W. Cary & M. Eisenberg, Cases and Materials on Corporations 1422, (6th ed. unabr. 1988) states:

[This] liability—that imposed upon those who subscribe to par-value shares under an arrangement by which the shares are to be treated as paid-up shares, although the subscriber has not paid or even agreed to pay the full par value in money or money's worth—is not based upon any fiduciary duty and is not limited to those subscribers who are also promoters. In the majority of jurisdictions, the courts have based the liability on the

Par is fixed by the articles of incorporation, drafted by the incorporators, and amendable from time to time, typically by majority votes of both directors and shareholders as provided in the governing corporation statute.[f] There is no legal regulation stating what amount the par value of common stock must be. Hence it is an arbitrary figure. However, since value at least equal to par must be paid in under the statutes, it is not without significance because the law permits the obligation to be enforced in some circumstances by creditors, shareholders, or the corporation.[g] Shares that are not fully paid up to par value are said to be "bonus," "discount" or "watered shares,"[h] and oftentimes "watered shares" or "watered stock" is the expression used for all three types. The term is a pun derived from the practice of certain ranchers or traders who watered their livestock before weighing at sale points.

Because the obligation to pay par value is legally enforceable in some circumstances, in a successful effort to eliminate this liability, two alternative practices developed. Under one of these practices the par value of shares is fixed at a very low figure relative to the amount paid in, so as to remove all doubt as to whether an amount at least equal to par value has been paid in. For this reason it is common to see $1 or $.01 or even $.001 par value stock sold for a substantially higher price. Since par long ago lost any relationship to money's worth, low par is used even when cash is paid in to the corporation for the stock because there are other advantages to low par, having to do with subsequent

theory of a misrepresentation to creditors, as stated in Hospes v. Northwestern Mfg. & Car Co., [48 Minn. 174, 50 N.W. 1117 (1892)]. In other jurisdictions, it is based on the statutory obligation theory as stated in Easton National Bank v. American Brick & Tile Co., [70 N.J.Eq. 732, 64 A. 917 (Ct.Err. & App.1906)]. Under either theory the liability is measured not by the amount of the subscriber's profits, but by the difference between the par value of the shares taken and the amount he has in fact given therefor, in money paid or value of property transferred or services rendered. Under the misrepresentation theory, the liability is a liability to creditors alone, and to certain creditors only; it cannot be asserted by the corporation. * * * [T]he statutory obligation theory permits enforcement by a receiver or trustee in bankruptcy, and there is some authority permitting the corporation to enforce it.

f. E.g., MBCA § 54(d) states: "The articles of incorporation shall set forth the aggregate number of shares which the corporation shall have authority to issue; if such shares are to consist of one class only, the par value of each of such shares, or a statement that all of such shares are without par value; or, if such shares are to be divided into classes, the number of shares

of each class, and a statement of the par value of the shares of each such class or that such shares are to be without par value."

g. See W. Cary & M. Eisenberg, Cases and Materials on Corporations, 1422–34 (6th ed. unabr. 1988).

h. The terms used describe three situations:

(a) "Bonus" shares are shares issued without payment of any amount, perhaps as a "bonus" for the purchase of another class of security. GAAP usually require accounting for such at fair value with a charge to income.

(b) "Discount" shares are shares issued for an amount less than par; e.g., $10 par stock issued for a $7 cash payment.

(c) "Watered shares" or "watered stock" are shares issued for non-liquid property which is worth less than par although asserted to be worth at least par.

GAAP require accounting at the fair value of the property received or at transferor's cost, if less, in the case of transfer from a controlling person or a member of a controlling group.

issuances and distributions.[i] One may note from the General Electric Company financials at p. 559 that GE's shares have a par value of 63¢.

The less used alternative practice which developed is the issuance of "no-par" stock; i.e., shares with no-par value, but, as now required by statutes, with a "stated value" fixed by the directors at time of issuance.[j] Under applicable statutes, stated value is often treated like par value—it must be paid in or else someone may have a right to enforce the payment. However, depending on the statute, it may be that the stated value of no-par stock, unlike par, does not mark the upper limit of liability. See Israels, *Problems of Par and No Par Shares: A Reappraisal*, 47 Colum.L.Rev. 1279 (1947); Denny & Howell, *Some Problems Raised By Issuing Stock for Overvalued Property and Services in Texas*, 40 Tex.L.Rev. 377 (1962). For this reason, many practitioners believe it may be wiser to use low par rather than no-par with a low stated value.

The aggregate of the issue amounts of both par and stated value are sometimes referred to as "stated capital" as in the Delaware statute quoted in the prior footnote or as "legal capital" although under some

i. For example, if the first sale of the stock were for $10 and par were $10, it would be troublesome if the market price of the security later fell to $7 and the company wished to sell additional shares. Although judicial doctrine has fashioned an exception to the rule that par must be paid in this circumstance [see Handley v. Stutz, 139 U.S. 417 (1891)], the issuers and its lawyers would clearly prefer to avoid the question, whether Handley v. Stutz applies in the particular jurisdiction, by fixing par at, say, $1, enabling sale at $10 initially and $7 subsequently, without any formal difficulty.

j. For example, Delaware Corp. Code § 154 requires at least an amount equal to par, for par value shares, or some of the consideration received for no-par shares to be allocated to legal capital. See Del.Corp. Code § 154, which reads:

Any corporation may, by resolution of its board of directors, determine that only a part of the consideration which shall be received by the corporation for any of the shares of its capital stock which it shall issue from time to time shall be capital; but, in case any of the shares issued shall be shares having a par value, the amount of the part of such consideration so determined to be capital shall be in excess of the aggregate par value of the shares issued for such consideration having a par value, unless all the shares issued shall be shares having a par value, in which case the amount of the part of such consideration so determined to be capital need be only equal to the aggregate par value of such shares. In each such case the board of directors shall specify in dollars the part of such consideration which shall be capital. If the board of directors shall not have determined (1) at the time of issue of any shares of the capital stock of the corporation issued for cash or (2) within 60 days after the issue of any shares of the capital stock of the corporation issued for property other than cash what part of the consideration for such shares shall be capital, the capital of the corporation in respect of such shares shall be an amount equal to the aggregate par value of such shares having a par value, plus the amount of the consideration for such shares without par value. The amount of the consideration so determined to be capital in respect of any shares without par value shall be the stated capital of such shares. The capital of the corporation may be increased from time to time by resolution of the board of directors directing that a portion of the net assets of the corporation in excess of the amount so determined to be capital be transferred to the capital account. The board of directors may direct that the portion of such net assets so transferred shall be treated as capital in respect of any shares of the corporation of any designated class or classes. * * *

statutes "legal capital" includes capital contributed in excess of par or other capital surplus.

The practical elimination of liability for watered, bonus, or discount stock is desirable from the point of view of the managers of the corporation, not only because it removes the liability (which in actuality is not a major concern since potential plaintiffs are likely to be hindered by numerous stumbling blocks making such suits extremely difficult [k]), but also because it enables corporate attorneys to supply the frequently-requested opinions of counsel to the effect that the stock is or, upon issuance as planned, will be fully-paid and non-assessable.[l] As noted, and as will be further discussed later, it also permits flexibility in making subsequent share issuances and distributions to shareholders.

Hence it seems that the concepts of discount, bonus and watered stock are of everyday relevance to attorneys, both at the time of issuance of shares and when an opinion of counsel is required, although the attorney's job is routine.

One who is puzzled by the law's failure to prevent the low par or low stated value "abuse" here should realize that better solutions to the problem have long since been devised. First, state and federal securities laws require that on initial issuance of shares full disclosure of material facts must be made, including disclosure of the value of consideration to be received for shares, the intended use of the proceeds of the issuance, and the dilution of the value of the new investors' shares. (E.g., if they pay in $100 but receive shares of only $40 in book value, this fact must be disclosed to them in advance.) Second, state law of fiduciary obligations and state and federal antifraud laws also protect investors to some extent perhaps by giving existing shareholders preemptive rights to purchase and establishing rights to require fair prices for subsequent issues. Given these safeguards, it is difficult to find any prejudice to creditors or shareholders—at least for the problems at the time of issuance of shares. With respect to *distributions*, discussed later, disclosure and fiduciary obligations to other equity holders may not be enough since distributions may prejudice existing creditors and investors. However here the laws of creditors' rights provide some protection to creditors as do most of the dividend statutes which prohibit distributions on insolvency.

Should a suit be brought for failure to pay in the par or stated value, many nice questions favored by legal technicians may arise. For example, if the market value of the shares issued by an already existing corporation is less than par and only that market value is paid in, will this case be considered an exception to the rule against watered stock; [m] will the usual rule prevail, that the directors' good faith valuation of

---

k. See B. Manning, Legal Capital p. 52 (2d ed. 1981).

l. Such opinions of counsel are commonly required on stock acquisitions and by underwriters on the offering of securities by the issuer or a selling shareholder.

m. See Handley v. Stutz, 139 U.S. 417 (1891).

property will be accepted by the courts; [n] or will the courts make their own determination of value?

These questions need not detain us here. [o] Suffice it to say they are almost always avoidable by the use of no-par or low par and the careful use of standard routines by practitioners.

Of course, careless lawyers may still cause watered stock problems. See, e.g., Bing Crosby Minute Maid Corp. v. Eaton, 46 Cal.2d 484, 297 P.2d 5 (1956) (overvaluation of a going business resulted in issuance of stock for less than par); Elward v. Peabody Coal Co., 8 Ill.App.2d 234, 132 N.E.2d 549 (1956) (stock option price below par). If a watered stock problem arises, the lawyer can then learn the esoterica about liability. Here we have suggested what customary practice dictates—the use of low par or no-par with low stated value, preferably the former, to avoid the need for the further lesson in liability.

In 1980 the financial provisions of the old Model Business Corporation Act (MBCA) were amended and ultimately resulted in the Revised MBCA. [p] The basis for the change, eliminating the notion of par value was based on the obvious facts, just noted, that regardless of the theory of requiring contribution of par value;

(1) the par value system did not work,

(2) it caused a good deal of useless expense, and

(3) it often was misleading.

Section 6.21 of the Revised MBCA eliminates the requirement that shares be issued with par or stated value and that the consideration received for initial issuance be other than "adequate."

The result of these changes undoes all the basic rules stated above as the official commentary notes:

Since shares need not have a par value, under section 6.21 there is no minimum price at which specific shares must be issued and therefore there can be no "watered stock" liability for issuing shares below an arbitrarily fixed price. The price at which shares are issued is primarily a matter of concern to other shareholders whose interests may be diluted if shares are issued at unreasonably low prices or for overvalued property. This problem of equality of treatment essentially involves honest and fair judgments by directors and cannot be effectively addressed by an arbitrary doctrine establishing a minimum price for shares such as "par value" provided under older statutes. [q]

n. See W. Cary & M. Eisenberg, Cases and Materials on Corporations 1434–36 (6th ed. unabr. 1988).

o. See ibid. For an outline of the procedural and substantive questions of liability for watered, bonus, and discount shares, see B. Manning, Legal Capital 46–56 (2d ed. 1981).

p. Changes in the Model Business Corporation Act—Amendments to Financial Provisions, 34 Bus.Law. 1867 (1979), approved, 35 Bus.Law. 1365 (1980). In 1984 they were incorporated in the Revised Model Business Corporation Act and modified in 1986. Changes in the Model Business Corporation Act—Amendments Pertaining to Distributions, 42 Bus.Law. 259 (1986), approved, 42 Bus.Law. 1207 (1987).

q. See ABA Comm. on Corp. Laws of Sec. of Corporation, Banking and Business Law, Official Text of Revised Model Bus. Corp. Act 102 (1985).

2. ACCOUNTING FOR THE INITIAL ISSUANCE OF SHARES

Under the older statutes in effect in about thirty-five states, accountants have felt it necessary to designate legal capital as a separate item on the balance sheet. Interestingly, the accounting practice is uniform regardless of the particular governing state's law.[r] For example, if ten shares of $1 par stock are issued for $95, the journal entry will be:

Cash	$95	
Capital Stock (10 shares common stock, $1 par)		$10
Capital Contributed in Excess of Par		85

Here we encounter a sharp split between legal thinking and accounting thinking. Although "legal" capital is $10, the accountants' view is that the capital is the amount contributed by the stockholders; and they therefore consider that capital stock ($10 above) plus capital surplus ($85 above) are both capital. See *ATB No. 1,* ¶¶ 65–70 (1953). They consider that capital surplus and earned surplus are conceptually different, and they therefore reject both of these traditional legal terms as confusing, and use other account captions such as, "Capital Contributed in Excess of Par (or Stated) Value" and "Retained Earnings." But the old terms are still used in all but a few states like California and we shall use them in this chapter.

On the other hand, under the Revised MBCA, the accounting for issuance of shares could be quite as simple as accounting for a sole proprietorship with all debits and credits to a single account which might be called Capital. Since accountants lag behind the law (as lawyers lag behind accounting) no settled practice can yet be reported. However, if past practice is a guide, accountants may well continue to use the same old reporting mode whether or not the Revised MBCA governs.

C. LIMITATIONS ON DISTRIBUTIONS

1. THE CONCEPT OF LEGAL CAPITAL APPLIED TO DISTRIBUTIONS

Whatever the policy grounds for the rule that par or stated value must be paid in to the corporation on issuance of its shares, we have seen that it virtually has been eliminated as a safeguard to creditors.

An equally useless corollary to that requirement is the typical statutory provision or case law holding that dividends or other voluntary distributions[s] should not be paid to shareholders if the result would

---

r. In the United States, dividend law is regulated by the law of the state of incorporation generally. But some states also regulate foreign corporations' dividends. See e.g., N.Y.Corp. Code §§ 103, 510.

s. Many types of informal dividends may be paid to shareholders, especially in close corporations; e.g., payment of shareholders' personal expenses, such as for an automobile or pleasure trip, excessive salaries, etc. For a collection of early cases,

be to reduce the corporation's net assets below the aggregate par or stated value of issued shares. This rule had its genesis in Wood v. Dummer,[t] where Mr. Justice Story said that the capital of a corporation was a "trust fund" for creditors. Until the Revised MBCA the basic concept of Wood v. Dummer had survived to some extent in the law of every state—namely, that the capital of a corporation is to be preserved for the benefit of creditors. See Comment, 49 Yale L.J. 492 (1940). Without such a restriction on distributions a brand new corporation could issue, say, one share of $10 par stock for a consideration of $10 in cash, and then turn around and declare and pay a $10 dividend, thus nullifying the rule requiring par or stated value to be paid in.

If one can perceive a policy of protecting creditors in this rule against distribution of legal capital, one might also perceive an embryonic policy of protecting preferred shareholders, or other senior equity security holders when there is more than one class of stock outstanding. Preferred stockholders may feel some small comfort from knowing that the "cushion" of legal capital exists to prevent distributions which would diminish the corporation's net assets below that amount.

Although the latter rule was useless, the two rules at least were consistent (and equally useless). Two points may be made. First, a prospective creditor who inspects the balance sheet of a corporation and finds a low par or stated capital and most of the net worth embodied in capital surplus should know what we have indicated, that most corporation laws to some extent permit the distribution of capital surplus as well as earned surplus to stockholders, giving creditors no protection beyond the legal capital consisting of par or stated capital.[u] In the fifteen or so states adopting the Revised MBCA this charade was abandoned.

Not equally well-known is the fact that just as lawyers minimized the effect of the rule that the legal capital must be paid in to the corporation, by use of low par or low stated value no-par stock, so too they minimized the effect of the rule limiting distributions out of legal capital and pushed it even farther by various techniques permitting reduction of legal capital without creditors' approval. The conclusion is that such a corporation law provides creditors with very little actual protection, despite Wood v. Dummer. See B. Manning, *A Concise Textbook on Legal Capital* p. 52 (2d ed. 1981).

see E. Dodd & R. Baker, Cases and Materials on Corporations 1177–80 (2d ed. 1951), incidentally stating that the courts frequently fail to note the applicability of dividend restrictions in those situations.

t. 30 Fed.Cas. 435 (C.C.D.Me.1824).

u. But note the concept of "watered surplus" and potential liability therefor. This concept holds that where property worth, say, $70 is contributed to a corporation for capital stock of a par or stated value of, say, $10, even if capital stock is credited $10, if capital surplus is credited in any amount greater than $60 the excess is "watered surplus" for which liability may lie. See G. Loewus & Co. v. Highland Queen Packing Co., 125 N.J.Eq. 534, 6 A.2d 545 (Ch. 1939); Israels, Problems of Par and No Par Shares: A Reappraisal, 47 Colum.L.Rev. 1279, 1289–91 (1947).

These inadequacies, instead of causing legislative abandonment of this futile effort, led legislatures to seek various means to improve the protection of creditors against improvident shareholder distributions which centered on the distinction between capital and income and on the concept of insolvency. Here is where the trouble began. Although economists and accountants spend their careers in dealing with these concepts, lawyers in statutes treated them as if they were understood when in fact they were not. We shall see the resultant chaos in subpart 2, next.

For now suffice it to say that as a result creditors today do not rely upon statutory protection against shareholder distributions. Trade creditors rely instead on security interests or careful monitoring of their receivables while commercial lenders require disclosure of financial data, security interests, and contractual limitations on distributions. It is in the areas of disclosure and statutory and contractual limitations that the practitioner must understand the accounting in order to serve his clients properly. We shall first consider the statutes and then describe the contractual limitations on distribution.

2. STATUTORY RESTRICTIONS ON PAYMENT OF DIVIDENDS

Corporation codes and more general creditors' rights laws restrict corporate distributions by way of dividends or share redemptions.[v] Since reacquired shares obviously are of no value to the corporation or its creditors,[w] any payment by the corporation for them, from the point of view of the corporation or creditors, is a diminution of economic capital, and logically is akin to a dividend. Nevertheless, in this subpart, we consider only dividends because redemptions present some unique considerations which shall be separately considered.

All dividend statutes employ one or some combination of the following types of schemes:

(a) a test based on the effects on a balance sheet and having legal capital as a basic term (e.g., a statute prohibiting a distribution if net assets remaining would be less than legal capital);

v. The term "redemption" is ambiguous; it is used to denote a purchase pursuant to contractual option of either the shareholder (an option to put) or the corporation (an option to call). The option is part of the terms of the stock usually contained in the corporate charter. [In many states directors are given authority, if so provided in the corporate charter, to fix the terms of stock by directors' resolution without need to include the terms in the charter. This is sometimes referred to as a "blank stock" provision. Its greater current relevance is in authorizing poison pills as takeover defenses.]

w. If a corporation holds a share in itself there is no more value for creditors to reach than there would be for an individual's creditors when that individual promises to pay himself a sum of money. However, most corporation statutes do designate such shares as "treasury stock" and consider them to be part of the legal capital thereby restricting distributions. Treasury shares are said to be "issued but not outstanding shares." We shall see, infra, the fantastically complicated accounting for treasury shares and the modern trend toward elimination of this strange legal construct as in the Revised MBCA § 6.31(a) which makes reacquired shares into unissued shares.

(b) a "nimble dividends" concept (i.e., permitting dividends out of recent earnings);

(c) an income statement test (e.g., prohibiting distribution except out of accumulated earnings);

(d) prohibition of distributions while insolvent or which would result in insolvency.

Most of these, including the Revised MBCA, use accounting terminology. The Revised MBCA uses only the insolvency type of scheme.

(A) Balance Sheet Test Statutes

Delaware Corporations Code § 170, in part, reads:

(a) The directors of every corporation, subject to any restrictions contained in its certificate of incorporation, may declare and pay dividends upon the shares of its capital stock * * * out of its surplus, * * *.

§ 154 defines "surplus":

The excess, if any, at any given time, of the net assets of the corporation over the amount [of legal] capital shall be surplus. Net assets means the amount by which total assets exceed total liabilities. Capital and surplus are not liabilities for this purpose.

The net effect of this part of the Delaware statute is that dividends may be paid out of net assets in excess of legal capital. Thus, we can see that a Delaware corporation's surplus is determined as follows:

	Assets
Less:	Liabilities (exclusive of equity)
Equals:	Net Assets
	Net Assets
Less:	Legal Capital
Equals:	Surplus available for dividends.

The Delaware statute and others like it are often referred to as "balance sheet test" dividend statutes because of their use of balance sheet concepts. In fact the truly distinctive feature of this first type of statute is its dependence on legal capital to define the dividend pool. In the Delaware statute we find legal capital exalted to its highest level and all the criticisms about its arbitrariness and unreality apply.

Although one element of the Delaware dividend pool, legal capital, is unambiguous, the terms "assets" and "liabilities" are undefined. Because accounting terminology is used, the question is raised whether GAAP will control the meanings of the terms. For example, difficult questions arise such as whether: unrealized appreciation should be included in the measure of "assets"; deferred charges of various sorts are "assets"; deferred credits, such as those resulting from income tax allocations, are "liabilities"; goodwill is to be counted; research and development is to be expensed.

We shall explore this question later as it is crucial in all four types of statute.

(B) "Nimble Dividends" Statutes

Delaware § 170, alternatively, provides for payment of dividends out of the current or the prior year's earnings, stating, "in case there shall be no * * * surplus, [dividends may be paid] out of * * * net profits for the fiscal year in which the dividend is declared and/or the preceding fiscal year." This is described as a "nimble dividends" statute since directors must be nimble enough to act in a timely fashion in order not to lose the opportunity. It is apparent that a nimble dividends statute negates any real interest in protection of creditors. This is not surprising in a state like Delaware which has no specific insolvency limitation in its corporation code and which also employs the traditional legal capital concept merely giving lip service to creditor protection.

The Delaware provision is explained in B. Manning, *A Concise Textbook on Legal Capital* 76–77 (2d ed. 1981) *:

> The law of stated capital and dividend restriction is the product of a continuing conflict between an urge to protect creditors by a simplistic mechanical rule, on the one hand, and, on the other, the pressures of business reality. Business reality won a big round in the development of the concept of so-called "nimble dividends".

> As a practical business matter, a corporation that has accumulated large deficits and has a heavy burden of unpaid debt has no prospect of obtaining further credit unless new equity capital can be attracted to the enterprise. In turn, there is no hope of attracting additional equity capital unless there is some prospect that dividends will be paid. The old deficits must not, therefore, be allowed to block future dividends. The obvious—perhaps the only—way out is to arrange matters so that dividends can be paid if the enterprise earns a current profit from its operations, even though the deficits piled up in previous years have not yet been eliminated. The Delaware corporation statute in 1927 took the lead in authorizing that result. * * *

> * * * Under the Delaware act, dividends—aptly called "nimble dividends"—may be paid out in any fiscal year in which, or in the year following a year in which, there are earnings, in spite of the presence of a deficit and without the Model Act requirement that the deficit first be written off against available capital surplus. The Delaware act makes it possible for a deficit company, deeply under water, to distribute its earnings to equity holders with respect to a fiscal year in which they are earned and thereby to continue indefinitely the deficit condition of the balance sheet. The statutory authorization of nimble dividends makes overt and explicit the usually unadmitted reality—the abandonment of all effort to protect creditors through stated capital machinery. The Delaware provision does, however, nod in the direction of protecting the preferred shareholder by forbidding distribution of current earnings to common shareholders if the value of the corpora-

tion's net assets is not at least equal to the stated capital of the outstanding preferred shares.

It is apparent that under this form of statute, also, as already stated, the question of whether GAAP control is sharply raised—is "net profits" computed by GAAP, or otherwise?

(C) Earned Surplus [or Income Statement] Statutes

California Corporation Code § 500(a) reads, in part:

> Neither a corporation nor any of its subsidiaries shall make any distribution to the corporation's shareholders * * * unless:
>
> > * * * The amount of the retained earnings of the corporation immediately prior thereto equals or exceeds the amount of the proposed distribution; * * *

This statute adopts the modern accounting term, "retained earnings," for earned surplus.

Notice that the rationale of a restriction on distributions except out of earned surplus extends the protection of creditors and shareholders. Where dividends cannot be paid except from earned surplus the purpose is to prevent distribution of shareholder contributed capital, not merely legal capital. The concept is that shareholders invest in a business and do not wish to receive back part of their capital investment as dividends or to have any other class of shareholders receive it—at least without notice, or, under more restrictive statutes, without a shareholders' vote.

The "old" Model Business Corporation Act dividend provisions are often described as being based upon an income statement test, but there are so many exceptions to them that the old act approaches being a balance sheet test statute. The basic provisions are old MBCA § 45(a)[x] which expressly permits dividends out of earned surplus, defined in § 2(1) as "net profits, income, gains and losses," and § 46 permitting dividends out of "capital surplus" if authorized by the articles of incorporation or a shareholder vote and requiring notification that the dividend is from capital surplus. Since § 2(m) of the statute defines "capital surplus" as the difference between "surplus" and "earned surplus," the sum of earned surplus and capital surplus equals surplus, and since the statute further defines surplus to mean net assets in excess of stated capital,[y] it permits dividends out of net assets in excess of stated capital, but, if any part of the dividend is from capital surplus, only if the charter or a shareholder vote so provides and only with notice to shareholders.

x. The old statute is found in 1 Model Bus.Corp.Act Ann. 2d §§ 45, 46 (1971).

y. Old MBCA § 2(k) states: "Surplus means the excess of the net assets of a corporation over its stated capital."

The structure of the statutory terms is shown by the following chart, which also reveals that the key terms, "assets" and "liabilities" and therefore, "surplus," are undefined:

Col. (1) Statutory Terms	Col. (2) Old MBCA § number of item in col. (1)	Col. (3) Description of items in col. (1)
Assets		
Less: Liabilities		
leaves Net Assets		
Less: Stated Capital	§ 2(j)	Par value of par value shares plus consideration for no-par shares (except any part allocated to capital surplus under § 21)
leaves Surplus	§ 2(k)	
Less: Earned Surplus	§ 2(*l*)	Net profits, income, gains, and losses, less distributions
leaves Capital Surplus	§ 2(m)	

The New York Business Corporation Law § 510(b), permitting distribution from "surplus" does not require a charter provision or shareholder vote for distributions out of capital surplus, but merely requires notice (§ 510(c)).

It is clear that the question of whether GAAP define assets, liabilities and earned surplus arises under this type statute also.

HACKNEY, THE FINANCIAL PROVISIONS OF THE MODEL BUSINESS CORPORATION ACT

70 Harv.L.Rev. 1357, 1366 (1957).*

"It might be argued that net profits, income, gains, and losses for any period of years are not limited to what appears in all the income statements, but rather include the entire increase in net assets over the period as determined by a comparison of balance sheets at the opening and closing of the period. However, if earned surplus is not to mean all surplus, paid-in and other capital surplus should be excluded. Therefore, the net effect of interpreting the definition of earned surplus as a balance-sheet change in net assets is to define it to mean all surplus less capital surplus, whereas the Model Act approach is to define earned surplus and then provide that capital surplus shall be the remainder. The difference in approach is illustrated by the comment to the Model Act definition of 'earned surplus,' stating that 'earned surplus, at any time, includes current profits and is not necessarily a year-end figure.' This seems to make it clear that the income or profit-and-loss account of a corporation is the vital figure and not the figure reflected by the change from year to year in the excess of assets over liabilities. In this light, it seems that the Model Act is not a balance-sheet type of statute; earned surplus is a figure to be determined by adding together all net profits, income, gains and losses over the period of time provided for in the Model Act definition."

———

Incidentally, Hackney also points out elsewhere that mere use of terms like "profits" or "surplus profits" traditionally has not been sufficient to make a statute an "income statement" type statute. Indeed he forcefully shows that these are usually deemed balance sheet tests. Hackney, *Corporate Law Aspects of Some Recent Developments in Accounting*, 3 J. of Law and Commerce 1, 24 (1983).

3. APPRAISAL OF THESE FIRST THREE TYPES OF DIVIDEND STATUTES

"Historically, the principal objective of dividend law has * * * been the preservation of a minimum of assets as a safeguard in assuring the payment of creditors' claims * * *." [z] Do the just-described dividend statutes in fact perform this function? In his book, Dean Manning appraises them.

B. MANNING, A CONCISE TEXTBOOK ON LEGAL CAPITAL
pp. 84–90, 108 (2d ed. 1981).[*]

"First, the legal capital machinery makes only the most marginal effort to protect groups or classes of shareholders from each other despite their often conflicting interests.

"As for creditors, the system makes no attempt to ward off two of their main worries—incurrence by the corporation of additional debt liabilities and creation of secured or senior debt claims. The system does purport to guarantee that shareholders have put something into the corporate pot and that they will not redistribute corporate assets to themselves without first protecting the corporate creditors. Does it work at all?

"We have no systematic empiric studies. It is a safe generalization, however, that the statutory legal capital machinery provides little or no significant protection to creditors of corporations, and that they, knowing this, do not rely upon it. They instead seek to achieve their protection through [contractual means]. * * * The legal capital schemes embedded in the nation's corporation acts are inherently doomed to a low level of effectiveness (perhaps even zero). Some of the reasons are:

z. D. Kehl, Corporate Dividends (1941). Accord, B. Manning, Legal Capital 59 (2d ed. 1981).

* Copyright © 1981. The Foundation Press, Inc. This book is now in its third edition with a new co-author, B. Manning & J. Hanks, Legal Capital (3d ed. 1990).

1. The system is analytically incomplete in the same sense that a protective encircling wall is useless if not closed throughout its perimeter. A balance sheet surplus figure, and even an earned surplus figure, is the product of dozens of judgmental accounting decisions. If one were seriously interested in using surplus accounts as an on-off switch for certain transactions, he would inevitably find himself involved in full scale regulation of corporate accounting systems, just as state utility commissions have found that pursuit of the goal of fair rate regulation has inexorably transformed them into legislatures of accountancy and tribunals of bookkeeping. * * *

2. Given that the original purpose of the legal capital scheme was to protect creditors from transactions that benefit shareholders but prejudice creditors, it is at least odd that the statutes should hand over all the control switches and levers to the shareholders and those whom the shareholders elect, the board of directors. The statutes are detailed and explicit about the procedures and steps to be taken in order to effect changes in the capital structure of a corporation, but the decision-making power is always vested in the board or the shareholders, or the two together; * * *.

3. A corporation's 'legal capital' is a wholly arbitrary number, unrelated in any way to any economic facts that are relevant to a creditor. No one who is considering whether to lend money today to General Motors Corporation is interested in knowing what, or whether, a shareholder paid for his shares 50 years ago, or what was the par value that was stamped on the stock certificate that he received at that time. Given the existence of the legal capital system, the creditor would prefer to see a high stated capital figure rather than a low one, but from his standpoint the stated capital is simply a fortuitously derived number that could as well have been taken from a telephone directory as from a series of unconnected and irrelevant historical events.

4. Similar to the next preceding point is the fact that the entire system has no fundamental 'why' to it. There is no reason why a reasonable man would take the number called stated capital and use it as a measure for limiting distributions to equity investors. At the same time, the kinds of things the creditor is interested to know and does want to police * * * are left unasked and unattended by the legal capital system.

5. The statutory legal system is inherently deficient for want of a time dimension. Ancient, present and future economic events are all scrambled together without regard to their differing current economic significance. In computing the availability of 'surplus', a debt due in twenty years is treated no differently from a debt due next week; to a lender it makes a lot of difference. For purposes of the statute, cash and other quick assets are treated exactly the same as assets that would take years to liquidate for purposes of paying debts; a prospective creditor sees it differently. It is assumed by the statute that creditors

of today and tomorrow care about sales of stock made years before. They don't. And so forth.

6. Efforts to apply the system in context of sophisticated modern corporate finance produce appalling, even revolting, conceptualistic debate. In the manner of medieval theologians at their worst, lawyers and accountants hold up (and are forced to hold up) sensible economic transactions while they wrangle over the appropriate stated capital treatment for stock subscriptions, agreements to purchase stock, mergers, treasury share cancellation, retirement conversions, stock warrant purchases, option exercises, stock discounts, liquidation preferences, allocation of 'capital' among classes, series, and individual shares, etc., etc., endlessly. No one is to be faulted for this pointless expenditure of the energies of intelligent men and women; it is the inevitable, and unresolvable, by-product of the primitiveness and essential irrelevance of the legal capital system.

7. Whether one views it as a blessing or a deficiency of the existing statutory systems, it is at least a fact that the corporation acts do not pursue the implementation of their own scheme with any real seriousness.

—Statutes that provide for nimble dividends admit overtly that companies with heavily impaired legal capital may still make payments to shareholders. The Model Corporation Act goes almost as far when it permits deficits to be written off against capital surplus.

—Where dividend payments may be made to shareholders and charged to paid-in surplus, the statute offers a direct invitation to the lawyer architect to design a capital structure using low par stock and creating large paid-in surplus accounts—an invitation that is usually accepted.

—Many of the statutes permit payments to shareholders to be charged against reduction surplus, a form of surplus that is usually easy for the board to generate. The Model Act through its provisions allowing shareholder distributions to be charged against capital surplus explicitly directs attention to this device.

—The statutes leave an open trap door for corporate assets to go out to shareholders to buy in their stock.

* * *

—The statutes display no interest in providing serious remedies and they are a procedural wasteland. Almost no instances can be found where liability was in fact imposed either on directors or on shareholders for violations of the stated capital scheme.

—When a certificate of dissolution is filed with respect to a corporation, the entire stated capital machinery is instantaneously suspended. Of course it is true that the corporation acts call for payment of creditors during the process of corporate liquidation and impose liability on the directors if that mandate is disregarded. But once the dissolution certificate has been filed, following a dissolution vote by shareholders under the local procedure, asset distributions may be made to the corporation's shareholders with no further regard for the statutory stated capital provisions. It is at least peculiar that a system designed to create a protective cushion to protect creditors against distributions to shareholders should automatically cut out of operation in precisely the situation where massive distributions to shareholders are most likely to occur—in precisely the situation, indeed, of *Wood v. Dummer,* the progenitor of the entire system.

—The most persuasive evidence of the quintessential triviality of the system, however, lies in the fact that any corporation lawyer of moderate skill can nearly always arrange things (perhaps at some expense and after some procedural dance figures) so as to make a lawful shareholder distribution so long as insolvency is not the immediate consequence. Advance planning and precautionary steps by the lawyer can also go very far to prevent the legal capital question from ever arising for his corporate client.

8. It may be, though difficult to prove, that the legal capital system has some unfortunate side effects. It can operate as a trap. Many lawyers are not sufficiently familiar with the arcana of legal capital to recognize a related problem when it does arise, and warn their client accordingly. Other practitioners, more sensitized but without the experience or ingenuity to design around the system, sometimes feel compelled to advise their clients that a transaction that is economically sensible cannot be lawfully consummated even though no genuine economic risk to creditors exists. In particular, the legal capital system may operate to prevent the performance of stock buy-out agreements in close corporations when one of the partners of the enterprise has died or withdrawn; in such cases the economic consequences upon the estate, upon the surviving widow, upon the withdrawing partner, and upon those remaining in the enterprise can be severe. Finally, while class-voting has its merits, it is also true that a skillful corporate lawyer representing a special stock class in a multiclass corporation can use the legal capital class voting requirement as a stick-up gun at the head of the board of directors and majority holders who are seeking to restructure the corporation's capital accounts to the advantage of the enterprise, its creditors and its community. Stated capital procedures should not facilitate extortion of one class of shares by another but they can.

"It now seems fair to ask:

(i) Does the present day statutory legal capital machinery made up of par value, stated capital, and related noneconomic concepts—controlled as it is by the shareholders, directors and their lawyers and accountants—effectively perform any significant relevant function in protecting creditors of corporations?

(ii) If the statutory machinery does perform a significant function, is it sufficiently great to warrant the aggregate investment of time, energy and dollars that is now required of thousands of lawyers, accountants, law teachers, law students, and an occasional judge?

(iii) Given the institutional and contractual protections that are available to creditors of corporations today, do they have a real need for special statutory protection?

(iv) If so, is anything more needed than the Massachusetts provision forbidding a distribution to shareholders if the company is insolvent or if it would be rendered insolvent by the distribution?"

In fact, many extant corporation codes do prohibit dividends on insolvency; however, in all but about fifteen states these prohibitions are a supplement to one or more of the just-described types of statutes.[aa] In some states, Delaware notably, there is no such provision. But even in such states as Delaware the provisions of the Uniform Fraudulent Conveyances Act [bb] or common law rules against giving away property when insolvent, or when insolvency results, may apply.[cc] And the federal Bankruptcy Reform Act of 1978, § 548,[dd] with provisions similar to the UFCA, may apply. Where the dividend law has a specific provision on insolvency, the question may arise whether it preempts any of these other, more general, state rules based on insolvency.[ee]

It should also be noted that the remedies for violation of one of these insolvency acts or rules may differ substantially from those for another. Typically, violations of dividend statutes cause a primary liability to arise for directors whereas the other acts may result in liabilities of the shareholders.[ff]

The concepts of insolvency used in these acts vary between two poles: insolvency in the equity sense and insolvency in the bankruptcy sense.

Insolvency in the equity sense is usually described as the inability to pay debts as they fall due in the usual course of business. The bankruptcy sense is an excess of liabilities (defined variously) over assets (also defined variously).

aa. E.g., California Corporation Code § 501; N.Y.Bus.Corp.L. §§ 102(1)(8); 510(a); MBCA § 45 infra. See Mass.Bus. Corp.L. Ch. 156B, § 61 for the Massachusetts provision. Massachusetts case law, in fact, has imposed additional common law restrictions akin to some of the statutes in other states. See E. Dodd & R. Baker, Cases and Materials on Corporations 945 et seq. (2d ed. 1951).

bb. Unif. Fraudulent Conveyance Act § 4, 7A U.L.A. 164, 205 (1971).

cc. D. Kehl, Corporation Dividends 36 (1941). For an earlier collection of cases where the statutes are not the primary basis for the decision, see E. Dodd & R. Baker, Cases and Materials on Corporations 945–69 (2d ed. 1951).

dd. Bankruptcy Reform Act of 1978, 11 U.S.C. § 548 (1982).

ee. See W. Cary & M. Eisenberg, Cases and Materials on Corporations 1299 and n. 2 (6th ed. unabr. 1988).

ff. See W. Cary & M. Eisenberg, Cases and Materials on Corporations 1357–61 (6th ed. unabr. 1988).

4. INSOLVENCY TEST STATUTES AND THE REVISED MODEL BUSINESS CORPORATION ACT

The drafters of the Revised Model Business Corporation Act considered and endorsed Dean Manning's criticism, rejecting all the other three types of dividend statutes in favor of an insolvency statute exclusively, using *both* tests of insolvency as the threshold for payment of dividends.

Revised MBCA §§ 6.40(c) and (d) read:

(c) No distribution may be made if, after giving it effect:

(1) the corporation would not be able to pay its debts as they become due in the usual course of business; or

(2) the corporation's total assets would be less than the sum of its total liabilities plus (unless the articles of incorporation permit otherwise) the amount that would be needed, if the corporation were to be dissolved at the time of the distribution, to satisfy the preferential rights upon dissolution of shareholders whose preferential rights are superior to those receiving the distribution.

(d) The board of directors may base a determination that a distribution is not prohibited under subsection (c) either on financial statements prepared on the basis of accounting practices and principles that are reasonable in the circumstances or on a fair valuation or other method that is reasonable in the circumstances.

Does Revised MBCA § 6.40(d) meet Dean Manning's objections numbered 1 and 5? Does it not continue to require an accounting system to define and measure assets and liabilities? Notice that § 6.40(d) as adopted in 1979, seems to eliminate an absolute safe harbor defense to directors who accept financial statements prepared in accordance with GAAP because it specifically requires that the accounting principles must be "reasonable in the circumstances." See Hackney, *Corporate Law Aspects of Some Recent Developments in Accounting*, 3 J. of Law and Commerce 1, n. 55 at 15 (1983). However, it would seem that financial statements prepared in accordance with GAAP would ordinarily be deemed "reasonable in the circumstances." See part D following.

D. THE RELATIONSHIP OF GAAP TO THE LAW OF THE STOCKHOLDERS' EQUITY SECTION OF THE BALANCE SHEET

Let us now turn to the interpretive question as to the source of the meanings of accounting terms like "assets," "liabilities," "profits," etc. found in all four types of statutes. Should courts attempt to develop their own definitions of "assets" and "liabilities," and of "earned surplus," and "income" in interpreting dividend statutes, or should they instead adopt an approach like that of the Revised MBCA or otherwise defer to GAAP?

COX v. LEAHY

Supreme Court of New York, Appellate Division, Third Department, 1924.
209 App.Div. 313, 204 N.Y.S. 741.

VAN KIRK, J. The plaintiff is the trustee in bankruptcy of Kingsbury–Leahy Company. There were three causes of action stated in the complaint, but of these the cause of action tried and decided was the action under section 28 of the Stock Corporation Law, to recover the loss sustained by the corporation or its creditors by the declaration and payment of a 50 per cent. dividend. The trustee in bankruptcy of the corporation may maintain such an action. * * * Section 28 of the Stock Corporation Law, so far as material, is as follows:

> "*Liability of Directors for Making Unauthorized Dividends.*—The directors of a stock corporation shall not make dividends, except from the surplus profits arising from the business of such corporation, nor divide, withdraw or in any way pay to the stockholders or any of them, any part of the capital of such corporation, or reduce its capital stock, except as authorized by law. In case of any violation of the provisions of this section, the directors under whose administration the same may have happened, except those who may have caused their dissent therefrom to be entered at large upon the minutes of such directors at the time, or were not present when the same happened, shall jointly and severally be liable to such corporation and to the creditors thereof to the full amount of any loss sustained by such corporation or its creditors respectively by reason of such withdrawal, division or reduction."

The words "capital of such corporation" means property capital, and property accumulated by the corporation in excess of its capital stock at par constitutes the surplus profits, and may be so regarded in the declaration of dividends. Equitable Life Assur. Soc. of United States v. Union Pacific R.R. Co., 162 App.Div. 81, 147 N.Y.Supp. 382, affirmed 212 N.Y. 360, 106 N.E. 92, L.R.A. 1915D, 1052.

The amount of the directors' liability under this section of the statute is confined to the loss sustained by the corporation or its creditors by the wrongful payment of the dividend; that is, to the amount that the dividend paid exceeded the surplus profits of the corporation at the time. * * * The directors of a corporation may declare and pay a dividend, when the corporation has surplus profits equal to or greater than the amount of the dividend paid. The fact that the corporation has not the ready funds sufficient to pay the dividend and therefore borrows money with which to pay the dividend, does not render the declaration and payment illegal. * * *

On April 8, 1912, the Kingsbury–Leahy Company was incorporated under the Stock Corporation Law of New York, with an authorized capital of $40,000, divided into 400 shares, of the par value of $100 each. The purpose of the corporation was to deal in, sell, operate, and let for hire automobiles and other vehicles, and to buy, sell, and deal in goods and merchandise incidental to the operation, building, repair, and equipment of such vehicles. * * *

The corporation did a considerable, and generally improving, business, but no dividend was declared until October 18, 1916, * * *. [T]he dispute is confined to a few of the items in the statement of assets and liabilities. * * *

* * *

Third item—prepaid insurance and taxes: The prepaid insurance, we think, was an asset. It had an actual value belonging to the company. Not only in law is it an asset, but in practice prepaid insurance is uniformly entered as an asset in making the balance sheet of a business. The asset account should be increased by the amount of the unearned premiums, $590.04. We think prepaid taxes rest on a different basis. They are in no wise available for a refund, and are paid for past expenses of government as well as future.

Note on Legal Capital as Financial Capital, Not Physical Capital

"Capital" and "income" are basic concepts which we use throughout this book. We must be concerned with them because financial disclosure perceives one of its tasks to be the disclosure of "income" of an enterprise and that process requires distinguishing income from capital under a well-accepted description of income as that which may be consumed during a period while leaving the owner "as well off" at the end of the period as he was at the beginning.[gg] To leave one "as well off" means to preserve capital. Dividend law is related in the sense that dividends are considered appropriate only if either out of income or not out of its complement, capital.

But what is capital?

Part of the question has been settled—the concept of capital is to be a "financial" concept not a "physical" concept—although the determination is being seriously challenged. The financial concept measures capital of a corporation by the monetary value of the contributions of shareholders. If this amount is maintained, the rest is income. A physical capital concept would require assets aggregating the initial productive capacity of the business to remain unimpaired.

Any change in the difference between net assets and one or the other concept of capital would be income under that concept (positive or negative) for the period of change. To illustrate: if a firm acquired $40,000 from stockholders in exchange for issuance of stock to them, then purchased a plant for that amount, and later sold the plant for $70,000 which it promptly reinvested in another identical plant, under a financial capital concept, $30,000 would be considered income where-

gg. H. Simons, Personal Income Taxation 49 (1938).

as under a physical capital concept there is no income—the utility of the firm's plant remains as it was.

From this illustration it may be seen that a major difference between the financial capital and physical capital concepts is that realized holding gains and losses on physical capital are income under the financial capital concept but remain capital under the physical capital concept. The realized holding gain in the illustration is the $30,000 increment in value of the plant upon sale.[hh] It is important to note that under the physical capital concept even *realized* holding gains on productive assets are not income available for distribution to owners.

By the time of Cox v. Leahy, the question had been settled for purposes of American dividend law. As Cox v. Leahy illustrates, the choice was in favor of a financial concept, "capital stock at par," although the statutory language used in § 28 of the Stock Corporation Law there in question and the court's explanation was the most confusing possible. Close reading, however, will reveal that the court would permit a dividend to the extent of net assets in excess of the aggregate par value of its capital stock. This aggregate par value is a "financial capital" concept since it is measured by the money value invested by share owners, not the physical capital.

The Court in *Cox* noted that "capital" as used in the statute meant "property capital," i.e., physical capital. However, the statute did *not* prohibit distribution of physical capital but *expressly permitted it, to the extent of "surplus profits,"* which it defined as "property * * * in excess of its capital stock at par," thus rejecting any notion of preserving the physical capital and opting for the financial concept of capital.

In fact the issue of whether capital was to mean physical or financial capital had been previously decided in New York in Equitable Life Assurance Society v. Union Pacific Railroad Co., cited and followed in *Cox*. In that case, Equitable, a preferred stockholder, sued the Union Pacific to enjoin payment by it of an $80,000,000 dividend to the

---

hh. Realized holding gains would include not only the excess of sale price, on the one hand, over cost minus accumulated depreciation on the other, but also would include *previously* realized holding gains accruing as the plant was being used up. Thus, if the plant was purchased in year one for $40,000, and $30,000 was attributed to depreciable buildings (with no salvage value) and $10,000 to land, and straight line depreciation was charged to expense at 10%, or $3,000 per year, a holding gain of $200 for the year would have been realized if the replacement cost of a new identical plant increased to, say, $32,000 by year end (or $28,800 after deducting 10% of the $32,000 replacement cost for one year's use). The benefit to the user was $3,200 whereas only $3,000 was actually charged to depreciation expense. Hence, $200 of the $2,000 increase in value was "realized" in this year (along with $3,000 of the original cost) and will appear as part of the year's net income since that amount was *not* deducted as an expense. This is a realized holding gain. The remaining $1,800 increase in value to $28,800 above the $27,000 depreciated cost for the year is unrealized holding gain. If the land had increased in value, since it is not depreciable, no holding gain would be realized until sale. Prior thereto any increase would be "unrealized" holding gains. The physical capital concept would call for nondistribution of both the $200 realized holding gain and the $1,800 unrealized holding gain. The financial capital concept is ambivalent regarding this question. Current accounting practice would consider the $200 realized holding gain to be income, but not the $1,800 unrealized holding gain.

common stockholders. Equitable claimed that the dividend was paid out of "capital" and therefore was illegal, based on the following circumstances. Union Pacific had issued its stock and invested the proceeds in another railroad company's shares. Over the years these had increased in value and were sold for cash whereby a $58,000,000 profit was realized. The proceeds were reinvested in still another railroad company and a portion of these latter shares was paid as the contested dividend in kind, together with cash aggregating to $80,000,000. The Union Pacific company had other surplus also available which when added to the $58,000,000 mentioned, exceeded the $80,000,000 dividend.

The court held that the appreciation realized on sale of the investment in the first railroad was available for dividends, saying this was not capital, making clear its view that capital was the financial capital—the money value amount paid in for the stock of the Union Pacific by its shareholders and not the then current value of the railroad asset originally acquired.

Which concept is correct? Or more accurately, which concept better serves the needs of society?

The proponents of the physical capital concept urge their view on the ground that a financial capital concept permits ultimate liquidation and distribution of the business given the fact that inflation is constant over the long run. This is apparent from our prior illustration whereby 30/70 of the productive assets of the business would be allowed to be distributed under the financial capital concept.

Opponents suggest that corporate managements have a duty to keep the concern a going one, and will not be misled into liquidation and distribution by a naive misunderstanding of financial capital. Nor, say the opponents, will management be prevented from doing so by a physical capital concept.[ii]

We must hasten to add that both the physical and the financial concepts of capital are here only generally outlined. Buried in this illustration are a myriad of issues, both as to the financial capital and the physical capital concepts. For example, financial capital could be either the aggregate par or stated value of issued stock, or it could also include capital paid in in excess of par or stated value. Similarly, financial or physical capital also could be stated in terms of constant dollars (units of purchasing power) or historical dollars.

Under the financial capital concept, over the lifetime of the enterprise, whichever of these valuation attributes is used, the "income" will

---

ii. For a more detailed explanation of the arguments, see FASB, Discussion Memorandum, and Analysis of Issues Related to Conceptual Framework for Financial Accounting and Reporting: Elements of Financial Statements and Their Measurement, ¶¶ 298–312 (1976). And see FASB, Exposure Draft, Proposed Statement of Financial Accounting Concepts, Reporting Income, Cash Flows, and Financial Position of Business Enterprises, ¶¶ 90–105 (Nov. 16, 1981).

be the excess of net receipts over the initial financial capital (i.e., cash value paid in) stated in either historical or constant dollars.

Constant or historical dollars also may be used when the capital concept is physical capital, but the measure of that physical capital (unlike the measure of financial capital), of course, will change as the value of the physical capital changes by holding gains and losses.

But physical capital has further ambiguities. Is it the value of the particular assets invested in, or is it the value of a plant with the power to produce the same *volume* of output? Or the same *value* of output?

For the time being, the financial capital concept prevails for both GAAP and dividend law and realized holding gains are considered income. However, the shortcomings of the financial capital concept are becoming apparent even to the naive in a period of rapidly changing prices and technology.

RANDALL v. BAILEY

Supreme Court of New York, New York County, 1940.
23 N.Y.S.2d 173, affirmed 288 N.Y. 280, 43 N.E.2d 43 (1942).

WALTER, JUSTICE. A trustee of Bush Terminal Company, appointed in a proceeding under section 77B of the Bankruptcy Act, 11 U.S.C.A. § 207, here sues former directors of that company to recover on its behalf the amount of dividends declared and paid between November 22, 1928, and May 2, 1932, aggregating $3,639,058.06. At the times of the declarations and payments, the company's books concededly showed a surplus which ranged from not less than $4,378,554.83 on December 31, 1927, down to not less than $2,199,486.77 on April 30, 1932. The plaintiff claims, however, that in fact there was no surplus, that the capital was actually impaired to an amount greater than the amount of the dividends, and that the directors consequently are personally liable to the corporation for the amount thereof under Section 58 of the Stock Corporation Law. Defendants claim that there was no impairment of capital and that the surplus was actually greater than the amount which plaintiff concedes as the amount shown by the books.

The claims of the plaintiff, although branching out to a multitude of items, are basically reducible to four [of which two are here omitted]:

1. It was improper to "write-up" the land values above cost and thereby take unrealized appreciation into account.

2. It was improper not to "write-down" to actual value the cost of investments in and advances to subsidiaries and thereby fail to take unrealized depreciation into account.

     *   *   *

Until 1915 the company's land was carried upon its books at cost. In 1915 the land was written up to 80% of the amount at which it was then assessed for taxation, and in 1918 it was written up to the exact amount at which it was then so assessed. Those two write-ups totalled $7,211,791.72, and the result was that during the period here in question the land was carried on the books at $8,737,949.02, whereas its actual cost was $1,526,157.30. Plaintiff claims that the entire $7,211,791.72 should be eliminated because it represents merely unrealized appreciation, and dividends cannot be declared or paid on the basis of mere unrealized appreciation in fixed assets irrespective of how sound the estimate thereof may be. That obviously and concededly is another way of saying that for dividend purposes fixed assets must be computed at cost, not value, and plaintiff here plants himself upon that position, even to the point of contending that evidence of value is immaterial and not admissible. If that contention be sound, the company indisputably had a deficit at all the times here involved in an amount exceeding the dividends here in question. The importance of the question so presented, both to this case and to corporations and corporate directors in general, is thus apparent, and it is, I think, surprising that upon a question so important to and so often occurring in the realm of business there is, not only no decision which can be said to be directly in point, but, also, no discussion in text-book or law magazine which does much more than pose the question without answering it. * * *

* * *

The words of the statute, as it existed during the period here involved, are: "No stock corporation shall declare or pay any dividend which shall impair its capital or capital stock, nor while its capital or capital stock is impaired, nor shall any such corporation declare or pay any dividend or make any distribution of assets to any of its stockholders, whether upon a reduction of the number of its shares or of its capital or capital stock, unless the value of its assets remaining after the payment of such dividend, or after such distribution of assets, as the case may be, shall be at least equal to the aggregate amount of its debts and liabilities including capital or capital stock as the case may be." Stock Corporation Law, § 58, as enacted by Laws 1923, c. 787.

If the part of the statute containing the words "unless the value of its assets" etc. is to be read as relating back to the beginning of the section, the lack of merit in plaintiff's contention is apparent, for the statute would then read: "No stock corporation shall declare or pay any dividend * * * unless the value of its assets remaining after the payment of such dividend * * * shall be at least equal to the aggregate amount of its debts and liabilities including capital or capital stock as the case may be." I think there is much to be said in support of the view that that is what was intended, but nevertheless the structure of the statute is such as to make that reading grammatically impossible, and I hence prefer to base my decision upon the assumption that the controlling words of the statute are merely these: "No stock corporation shall declare or pay any dividend which shall impair its capital or capital stock, nor while its capital or capital stock is impaired."

[The court considered cases which decided that the financial capital concept had been adopted in New York, concluding] [t]hose statements by our highest court seem to me to make it entirely plain that the terms capital and capital stock in these statutes mean an amount, i.e., a value, of property up to the limit of the number of dollars specified as the par value of paid-up issued shares (or as the stated value of no-par shares), and that when the amount, i.e. the value, of the company's property exceeds that number of dollars the excess, whether "contributed by the stockholders or otherwise obtained" is surplus or surplus profits and may be distributed as dividends until the point is reached where such dividends "deplete the assets," i.e. the value of the assets, "below the sum," i.e. below the number of dollars, specified as the par or stated value of the paid-up issued shares. In other words, the capital or capital stock referred to in these statutes is the sum of the liability to stockholders, and any value which the corporation's property has in addition to that sum is surplus. And I cannot doubt that the words "otherwise obtained" and "accumulated," as used by the court in the cases just mentioned, include an appreciation in the value of property purchased whether realized or unrealized.

*   *   *

*   *   * [In] an article on "Dividends from Unrealized Capital Appreciation" in 6 New York Law Review, 155 (1928), which the plaintiff has thought worthy of citation, it is admitted that the courts of New York invariably have held that "the excess of assets over capital and other liabilities constitutes the surplus available for dividends".

In Cox v. Leahy, 209 App.Div. 313, 204 N.Y.S. 741, unrealized appreciation in land values actually was taken into account in determining whether or not dividends had been improperly paid. See page 316 of 209 App.Div., 204 N.Y.S. 741. *   *   * [T]here is also the high authority of Mr. Justice Brandeis for the statement that surplus may consist of increases resulting from a revaluation of fixed assets. Edwards v. Douglas, 269 U.S. 204, 214, 46 S.Ct. 85, 70 L.Ed. 235.

*   *   *

*   *   * I am of the opinion that the same reasons which show that unrealized appreciation must be considered are equally cogent in showing that unrealized depreciation likewise must be considered. In other words, the test being whether or not the value of the assets exceeds the debts and the liability to stockholders, all assets must be taken at their actual value.

I see no cause for alarm over the fact that this view requires directors to make a determination of the value of the assets at each dividend declaration. On the contrary, I think that is exactly what the law always has contemplated that directors should do. That does not mean that the books themselves necessarily must be altered by write-ups or write-downs at each dividend period, or that formal appraisals must be obtained from professional appraisers or even made by the directors themselves. That is obviously impossible in the case of corporations of any considerable size. But it is not impossible nor unfeasible for directors to consider whether the cost of assets continues over a long period of years to reflect their fair value and the law does require that directors should really direct in the very important matter of really determining at each dividend declaration whether or not the value of the assets is such as to justify a dividend, rather than do what one director here testified that he did, viz. "accept the company's figures." The directors are the ones who should determine the figures by carefully considering values, and it was for the very purpose of compelling them to perform that duty that the statute imposes upon them a personal responsibility for declaring and paying dividends when the value of the assets is not sufficient to justify them. What directors must do is to exercise an informed judgment of their own, and the amount of information which they should obtain, and the sources from which they should obtain it, will of course depend upon the circumstances of each particular case. * * * If directors have blindly or complacently accepted either cost or any other arbitrary figures as indicative of value, they have not exercised either discretion or judgment and no court is required to act as if they had. When directors have in fact exercised an informed judgment with respect to the value of the company's assets, the courts obviously will be exceedingly slow to override that judgment, and clear and convincing evidence will be required to justify a finding that such judgment was not in accordance with the facts. In the last analysis, however, the issue, in any case in which it is claimed that dividends have been paid out of capital, is the value of the assets and the amount of the liabilities to creditors and stockholders at the times the dividends were declared and paid.

     * * *

Notes and Problem

8–1. *Cases Involving Unrealized Appreciation or Depreciation.* There is remarkably little solid case law on the question of dividends or distributions out of unrealized holding gains.

In Mountain States Steel Foundries, Inc. v. Commissioner of Internal Revenue, 284 F.2d 737 (4th Cir. 1960), a federal tax case, the Commissioner assessed tax deficiencies based on the disallowance of deductions for interest on notes given in part payment of the purchase price of the stock of dissenting stockholders, on the grounds that the stock purchase agreement impaired the capital of the corporation and was invalid under state law. The court held that impairment of capital was to be determined on the basis of the values of the assets, even though not recorded on the books.

Titus v. Piggly Wiggly Corp., 2 Tenn.App. 184 (1925), held that unrealized appreciation could overcome surplus deficits, thus permitting dividends out of realized profits. But in Morris v. Standard Gas & Electric Co., 31 Del.Ch. 20, 63 A.2d 577 (1949), in determining whether a dividend could be paid in view of a proviso prohibiting a payment thereof which would reduce the capital below the liquidation preference of preferred stock, the court assumed that assets should be valued by taking into account unrealized holding losses and held that even then the proviso had not been activated.

Berks Broadcasting Co. v. Craumer, 356 Pa. 620, 52 A.2d 571 (1947), held that unrealized appreciation was not a source of dividends, but this conclusion was mandated by the then Pennsylvania statute. Kingston v. Home Life Insurance Co., 11 Del.Ch. 258, 101 A. 898 (1917), has a dictum to the same effect, which seems questionable since the then Delaware statute authorized dividends "out of surplus or net profits arising from the business." Did both of these tests (surplus and net profits) embody the accounting concept of realization?

George E. Warren Co. v. United States, 76 F.Supp. 587 (D.Mass.1948), held that under the law of Maine unrealized diminution in value of an asset or assets must be taken into account in determining the legality of dividends and hence the question whether the corporation was subject to a tax for failure to distribute profits.

Vogtman v. Merchants' Mortgage & Credit Co., 20 Del.Ch. 364, 178 A. 99 (1935), held that unrealized diminution in value of mortgages must be taken into account in determining the legality of dividends out of net assets in excess of stated capital.

Note that most of these cases involved unrealized appreciation or depreciation in securities or mortgages, not tangible assets.

8–2. *Unrealized–Unliquid.* There is a practical reason for not paying dividends from unrealized holding gains even if legally permissible. Unrealized appreciation is exactly that, unrealized. It does not make the corporation any more liquid. Randall v. Bailey itself illustrates the point beautifully. The land was written up on the books from $1.5 million to $8.7 million without any realization that would produce cash, and the company paid $3.6 million in dividends. The fact that the company ended up in reorganization in the bankruptcy courts should make one pause to reflect.

8–3. *Problem.* Would the prepaid taxes in Cox v. Leahy or unrealized appreciation in Randall v. Bailey be included in "assets" under Revised MBCA § 6.40?

HACKNEY, ACCOUNTING PRINCIPLES IN CORPORATION LAW *

30 Law and Contemp.Prob. 791, 813–823 (1965).

*   *   *

"Historically, it is said, the courts have adopted and followed accounting principles in the valuation of assets for dividend purposes. Whether the one adopted and followed the other or the two just happened to coincide, it does appear that until three or four decades ago accounting and legal concepts of income and dividend regulation were generally in accord with the increase-in-net-worth concept of

* Reprinted with permission from a symposium, Uniformity in Financial Accounting appearing in Law and Contemporary Problems (Vol. 30, No. 4, Autumn, 1965), published by the Duke University School of Law, Durham, North Carolina. Copyright, 1965, 1966, by Duke University.

income. In view of the fundamental shift of accounting emphasis in recent years from the balance sheet to the income statement and the accompanying radical changes in principles of accounting for assets, the question may be restated as follows: to what extent will corporation laws, historically oriented in a 'worth' concept of valuation, look to and follow accounting principles that are income-oriented and do not purport to render book valuations of any significance in a 'worth' context?

"At first glance, it might appear doubtful whether the law has changed its approach so as to keep pace with accounting developments. There is nothing explicit in the Model Business Corporation Act or any recent legislation to indicate that the law *consciously intended* to make the radical change from the historic legal concept of income as increase in balance-sheet surplus of worth-value to the modern accounting concept of income as an excess of realized money receipts over expired historic money costs.

"The pattern of both old and recent corporation law statutes has been not to attempt to prescribe a theory of value or a detailed method of initially valuing acquired assets on the acquiring corporation's books. The Model Business Corporation Act is representative. It says nothing concerning carrying values for assets acquired for a consideration other than stock. It provides that shares are to be issued for a 'consideration expressed in dollars' (section 17) without attempting to prescribe the principle of valuation. Section 18 deals with what constitutes *proper* consideration but not with how it is to be valued, and then provides that, in the absence of fraud, the judgment of the board of directors or the shareholders 'as to the *value* of the consideration received' shall be conclusive. Again the statute does not specifically prescribe the concept of valuation intended. In the determination of the amount of stated capital and surplus arising upon the issue of shares, section 19 speaks only in terms of the 'consideration received.' *Surplus* is defined in section 2 to mean 'the excess of the net assets of a corporation over its stated capital,' while *net assets* is defined to mean 'the amount by which total assets' exceed total debts.

"Here it is important to remember the distinction * * * among three different purposes the law has for valuing acquired assets and, consequently among three possibly varying approaches to the problem of valuing the same assets:

First, the law prescribes that the value of assets acquired for stock must be determined in order to decide such matters as whether the stock is validly issued, fully paid, and nonassessable and whether previously existing shareholders of the issuing corporation have any complaint as to an inadequate value of assets received for securities given in exchange.

Second, the value of assets to be entered on the books (whether acquired for stock or some other consideration) must be fixed in order to compute the amount of surplus or excess of net assets over capital of the issuing corporation under the applicable statutes relating to dividends and distributions.

Third, the assets must be entered at some dollar figure on a corporation's books in order to determine future exhaustion charges—for example, (1) the base upon which depreciation of fixed assets or amortization of intangibles will in the future be taken and (2) the 'cost' of inventories that will be utilized in the cost-of-goods-sold formula. Such valuation determines the expected quantum of assets that will be 'generated' or returned to the enterprise and that may not be paid out as dividends but will be returned tax-free from future revenues, and likewise determines in large part the amount of the expenses and deductions charged to revenue before computing the net income of the company.

"Whether the valuation of assets for these three different purposes must be identical is a difficult question that is seldom discussed. It should be recognized that the first two valuation requirements are aimed at purely legal questions—watered stock, fairness of issue price vis-à-vis existing shareholders, and surplus available for distribution—while the third is formulated essentially in accounting terms relating to the computation of income.

"The import of such provisions as section 18 of the Model Act may throw some doubt upon the possibility of initially valuing assets for any of the three purposes at other than fair value to the corporation. That section is aimed principally at watered stock and the question of whether shares are fully paid and nonassessable; the objectives of the law seem clearly to require that the concept of worth-value be utilized for this purpose. However, since the conclusiveness of the valuation by the shareholders or directors under section 18 may be only for the purpose of fixing the extent of the outstanding obligation of the shareholders with respect thereto, this section may not *necessarily* mean that in fixing stated capital and computing surplus and future exhaustion charges, the book value of corporate assets must be the same worth-value so ascertained.

"There does seem to be a direct and close relationship between valuation for stock-assessability purposes and valuation for dividend purposes under an impairment-of-capital test: it is logical that if shares are fully paid and nonassessable under section 18, then net assets on the books should at least equal stated capital, and the next dollar earned should yield surplus (net assets in excess of capital) available for dividend purposes. If shares were issued at a discount then the deficit surplus (which the law would require to be made up out of earnings before a positive earned surplus could arise) should logically be the same dollar amount as the discount based upon fair value. Furthermore, in order for the shares not to become 'watered' over the course of time by inadequate depreciation and amortization charges, it would seem that such charges should be based upon no less than the same values that determined the prior question of assessability and initially watered stock. To the extent that other classes of shareholders and security holders have a right to insist upon the receipt of a certain amount of consideration (fairly valued) upon the issue of stock, they may have an equal right to demand that exhaustion charges used in the determination of future income be sufficient to maintain the cushion represented as originally obtained.

*   *   *

"Traditional principles of law, in requiring that assets *purchased* be entered initially on the books at their fair value, and the recent amendments and enactments attempting to accommodate the law to pooling-of-interests accounting, are in accord with 'g. a. a. p.' as to the valuation of assets. The law likewise appears to be in accord with such principles when it comes to valuing inventories that have appreciated in value because of unrealized appreciation or because of changes in the price level: the law, just as rigorously as accounting principles, has asserted the requirement of realization before recognition in the computation of income. Similarly, it would appear that the law is in accord with 'g. a. a. p.' when it requires depreciation to be taken and when it follows 'g. a. a. p.' of inventory valuation, particularly the requirement that inventories be written down to current values.

"Do these areas of accord between specific legal requirements and 'g. a. a. p.' mean that the law will follow all other accounting principles of valuation? Depreciation, for example, has been shown above to be in accounting a process of cost allocation, not valuation. But suppose an old building the cost of which has been completely depreciated on a company's books has continuing economic usefulness because of changed circumstances: is it to be valued at zero for dividend purposes? Or suppose a building has physically depreciated to half its original condition and one-half its cost has been depreciated to date but that changed neighborhood conditions—or a changed price level—give it a market or rental value equal in dollars to its original cost: what value is to be used for dividend purposes? Deferred charges were shown above to be properly carried forward as assets, in the discussion of the going-concern postulate; but will the law allow without question the existence of unamortized debt discount and expense to be included in ascertaining the existence of 'surplus profits' for dividends? May work in process be valued in excess of immediately realizable market value in accordance with accounting principles? Is it legally proper to enter and value a receivable at the amount of the anticipated future cash receipts when the present realizable value of such receivable may be lower because of expected delay in payment and there may be some legal aspect of the transaction that presently bars the right to sue and obtain immediate judgment?

"Will the law in a period of rapidly rising prices accept as sufficient exhaustion charges based on historical cost? Or might a court hold that recovery and maintenance of economic capital are necessary before income may be reported and distributed to shareholders?

"A famous New York case has held that under a statute prohibiting any distribution by a corporation 'unless the *value of its assets* remaining after the payment' thereof shall be equal to its liabilities including capital, assets may be computed upon the basis of present values. Under a statute or common law restriction speaking solely in terms of surplus, net assets in excess of capital, net profits, earned surplus, or surplus profits, or some such term, may unrealized appreciation be taken into account? Would it make any difference whether the unrealized appreciation were of inventories held for sale, or of supplies held for consumption, or of fixed assets held for productive use, or of investments of surplus funds, or of self-developed goodwill?

"It is commonly stated that an increase in asset values must be 'realized' before it can be utilized in the computation of funds available for dividends, at least under statutory tests phrased in terms of profits or impairment of capital. On the other hand, many dicta and a few holdings indicate that whenever 'value' is a factor to be considered in application of the legal test, some form of current worth-value is acceptable.

"It is believed that the difficulties to a court of law in abandoning the accounting approach to asset valuation are enormous and little recognized. It will be seen, for example, that it is not simply a question of taking the accountants' balance sheet and adding unrealized appreciation; as has been amply illustrated above, virtually all accounting valuation principles lead to book values having no certain or rational relationship to current worth-values, and some accounting 'assets' might not be deemed an asset at all under a legal rule based upon realizable values. Any dividend or other legal rule of valuation that purports to be based on current worth-values must today recognize that no concept of valuation is so far removed from the objective sought as the concept found in 'g. a. a. p.' and that therefore virtually every single book entry going to make up the entire balance sheet would be subject to challenge and adjustment. The accounting balance sheet hardly seems even a likely place to start the process of worth-valuation.

"If it is up to a court or to a company's officers or attorney, then, to determine the current fair worth-value of a corporation's net assets, how is such valuation to be accomplished, and what concept of value is to be used? A few of the many difficult questions arising are as follows:

(a) Are the assets to be valued on a piecemeal basis (or by classes), or is the over-all enterprise to be valued?

(b) If the enterprise is to be valued on an over-all basis—(i) How can this be done without reference to earnings and dividends? If they are considered, how are earnings to be computed, and how is the legality of dividends to be judged without reference to the revaluation being made? (ii) Is the aggregate market value of issued securities (if actively traded) the best evidence of over-all value (with appropriate discount for blockage, and so on)? If so, again, how can the reciprocal effect of earnings (and dividends) upon such market value of securities be eliminated? (iii) May self-developed goodwill be included as an asset? If not, how can such value be eliminated from the market price of securities or from the price a willing buyer would pay for the business as a whole? For dividend purposes, why distinguish between self-developed and purchased goodwill? (iv) How would such a new over-all valuation be distributed among the tangible assets of the corporation? Again, what of the excess, which can be allocated to nothing but self-developed goodwill?

(c) If the assets of the enterprise are to be separately revalued—(i) What concept of value is to be used—replacement value, or market value, or economic value (the present discounted value of future returns attributable to the asset), or appraisal value, or forced sale value, or historical cost adjusted for price-level variation? (ii) Should different concepts of value be used for such assets as inventories, which are held for sale in the ordinary course of business; investments, some marketable and some unmarketable, some having a definite business purpose and others being income-producing uses of excess cash; and fixed assets, which presumably could not be sold unless the enterprise were liquidated? [83] How would you value deferred charges or capitalized advertising and promotion expense, which may well have considerable value-in-use or earnings potential but might yield nothing to a foreclosing creditor?

(d) Under any method of valuation—(i) What relationship would the new values have to future depreciation charges, cost-of-goods-sold, and other income determination factors? Might the overall valuation method be used to determine surplus available for dividends while the piecemeal valuation method might be used for exhaustion charges? Would dividends then no longer be a function of income? Or would income simply be the annual difference between aggregate net asset values? (ii) What statements would be given to shareholders? Would a third set of books have to be kept (in addition to federal income tax returns and the audited financial statements)? (iii) How often would the revaluation have to be made? Every few years? Every year? Every dividend declaration date?

"The subjective nature of revaluation—as attested by the range of experts' testimony as to estimated market values or appraised values possible—is widely asserted. The expense and difficulty involved for every corporation, of whatever size, constantly to revalue its assets argues against such a legal approach. The availability of funds for

---

83. Gibson, Surplus, So What?, 17 Bus. Law. 476, 488–489 (1962):

Within the realm of economic fact, the governing question must be in some such terms as whether a fixed asset, designed and useful for a specific function, really embodies value in any traditional or disposable sense, apart from its successful exploitation in that function. Put the other way, the question is whether the fixed asset is not irretrievably committed to the specific enterprise and accordingly is, apart from earnings potential, rather a collection of liabilities than an accumulation of values.

It has become a truism that value is a word of many meanings. The present suggestion is that, for the philosophy of corporate "surplus," it may have no meaning at all.

dividends under any such legal rule would no longer be a legal question capable of answer by the corporation's attorney, but simply a matter of business judgment or for determination by a valuation expert.

"An increasing number of states have provisions similar to section 43 [jj] of the Model Act, authorizing reliance by the board of directors upon financial statements certified by the corporation's officers or independent public accountants. Such statutes argue strongly that valuation in accordance with modern 'g. a. a. p.' was intended. Persuasive also is the absence in the statutes of any guidance as to how the questions as to valuation raised above are to be answered; the myriad latent problems involved in abandoning accounting principles of valuation make it likely that courts would feel it necessary to defer to accounting principles. Especially is this true under the increasingly common 'earned surplus' statutes recently enacted; it seems implicit in the term 'earned surplus' that accumulated earnings (rather than surplus of worth-values) are intended to be the fundamental basis for dividends. It is, therefore, difficult to dispute the argument that accounting principles of asset valuation—having as their objective [a fair] computation of income—come closest to yielding that legal 'earned surplus' or 'surplus (other than capital surplus)' that is the basic source for dividends under most statutes.

"It is not surprising to conclude that accounting principles can govern the legal issues of funds available for dividends, purchase of treasury stock, and other questions, except for the limited areas where there is a specific statute or other governing legal principle. * * * Professor Ralph J. Baker, one of the most discerning of legal commentators, some years ago forecast judicial reaction to the problems of valuation for dividend purposes as follows:

> The suggestive factor is that, whether we like it or not and whether we are wholly aware of it or not, the accountants may be making our law. * * * If the case is well tried, with submission of accounting literature as evidence and accounting testimony or depositions, what accountants of standing do and say may make the decision. * * * [G]ood accounting practice may be enough even though it falls short of being *uniform* accounting practice.

"If the above conclusion is accepted, it means that today principles of valuation for state corporation law purposes, fundamentally based upon cost (or useful cost), are to be interpreted as aimed not at fixing anything resembling actual present worth but rather at setting up the flow of cost factors so as most accurately to reflect current income in accordance with generally accepted principles of accounting. This conclusion is most obviously true under statutory dividend rules laid down in terms of profits or net income; but in addition it also means that a statutory balance-sheet-surplus test that may appear to be based upon fair net worth of assets has instead, through the principles of valuation followed, been turned into a retained-earnings test based

jj. Ed's. note. Now MBCA § 35.

essentially upon accumulated income as [determined] in accordance with generally accepted accounting principles.

"If the conclusion is sound, it also suggests that lawyers must be diligent to examine, analyze, publicly criticize, and otherwise contribute to the formulation of accounting principles."

Note

8–4. *Dividend Law and Changing GAAP.* The Hackney article deals with the question whether dividend law should follow GAAP, based on the GAAP at that time emphasizing realization of income. Does his conclusion that GAAP should control dividend law hold for the many recent changes in GAAP calling for recognition of income when there has been no realization in the conventional sense? E.g., for recoupment of value following a drop from cost for marketable equity securities carried as current assets pursuant to *SFAS No. 12?* For the increase in equity of investees accounted for under the equity method of *APB Opinion No. 18?* For the special equity adjustment for foreign exchange transactions under *SFAS No. 52?* For another perceptive article exploring these issues, see Hackney, *Corporate Law Aspects of Some Recent Developments in Accounting,* 35 J. of Law and Commerce 1 (1983). And see the following.

CURRENT ISSUES ON THE LEGALITY OF DIVIDENDS FROM A LAW AND ACCOUNTING PERSPECTIVE: A TASK FORCE REPORT.*

39 Bus.Law. 289–303 (1983).**

"When a corporation declares dividends the governing limitations usually arise from the application of provisions in loan agreements, indentures, or charter provisions. In the drafting of these provisions, questions arising under accounting conventions or business practices can be dealt with explicitly or, in the case of banks or other private lenders, can be the subject of negotiations.

"Although they do not arise so often in practice, the limitations in state corporation laws can also present questions as to the legality of corporate dividends. At this level there is considerably less flexibility in dealing with such questions.

*   *   *

"The first issue considered is how a number of developments in generally accepted accounting principles (GAAP) would be treated under these state laws regulating payment of dividends to stockholders. These developments include:

* John C. Jaqua, New York, chairman. Members: Byron F. Egan, Dallas; Ted J. Fiflis, Boulder; Eugene J.T. Flanagan, New York; Samuel P. Gunther, New York; William P. Hackney, Pittsburgh; Howard L. Meyers, Philadelphia; Larry P. Scriggins, Baltimore.

(1) Statement of Financial Accounting Standards (SFAS) No. 52 (specifying accounting and reporting requirements for translation of foreign currency transactions and foreign currency financial statements into U.S. dollars or another currency used in reporting financial statements): Recording in a separate component of stockholders' equity the effect of translation of foreign financial statements into U.S. dollars or another reporting currency.[kk]

(2) Accounting Principles Board (APB) Opinion No. 18 (the equity method of accounting for investments in common stock): The adjustment of net income of a parent or investor for changes in the investment (asset) from cost to reflect the share of subsequent earnings or losses of unconsolidated subsidiaries, corporate joint ventures, and certain investee companies.

(3) SFAS No. 12 (accounting and reporting for marketable securities): The adjustment of net income in the case of current assets and a separate equity account in the case of noncurrent assets to reflect changes in market value of marketable equity securities, cost being a ceiling.

(4) APB Opinion No. 11 (accounting for income taxes): The application of interperiod tax allocation procedures arising out of timing differences in the payment and accrual of income taxes resulting in deferred credits when GAAP accrual precedes tax payment and deferred charges when GAAP accrual follows tax payment.

"The second issue discussed is whether state laws should provide a safe harbor for directors based on the essentially procedural test of declaring dividends in good faith reliance on financial statements prepared in conformity with generally accepted accounting principles, or whether directors must also determine whether the accounting principles used (GAAP or other) are reasonable or appropriate in the circumstances.

* * *

"TREATMENT OF ACCOUNTING DEVELOPMENTS UNDER
DIVIDEND STATUTES

"The following are the principal questions considered regarding the prospective treatment by courts of the above accounting principles under distribution statutes:

(1) Would the direct recording in equity required by SFAS No. 52 and (for noncurrent assets) by SFAS No. 12 be recognized in a balance sheet test permitting payment out of surplus or payment that does not impair capital?

kk.   Ed's. note. Both SFAS No. 52 and APB Opinion No. 18 mentioned in item (2) following are explained infra at Chapters XIII and IX, respectively. SFAS No. 12 (item 3) is described in Chapter III and APB Op. No. 11 (item 4) in Chapter V.

(2) Where payment must be out of earned surplus or the kind of surplus must be identified, would the amounts in (1) be earned surplus, capital surplus, or neither?

(3) Would the direct recording in equity under SFAS No. 12 and SFAS No. 52 without reference to the income statement be recognized as an exclusion from the net profits calculation under the nimble dividend statutes?

(4) Would the recognition in net income of the parent or investor to reflect asset adjustment occasioned by subsequent earnings or losses of unconsolidated subsidiaries or investees under APB Op. No. 18, or the recognition in net income of changes in market value of equity securities carried as current assets as required by SFAS No. 12 (not to exceed cost) be given effect under the statutes referred to in (1), (2), and (3) above? Stated another way, would the changes in surplus to reflect asset carrying value be recognized?

(5) Would deferred credits and deferred charges arising out of interperiod allocation of timing differences between GAAP accounting and tax requirements be given effect under the statutes referred to in (1), (2), and (3) above? Should such deferred credits be available for dividends? Could the recording of a deferred tax charge (asset) be said improperly to increase the amount available for dividends under nimble dividend statutes since the tax payment expense has been postponed for accounting purposes?

(6) Would increases in the carrying value of assets arising out of foreign exchange translation (SFAS No. 52), increases in investments (APB Op. No. 18), or increases in market value of equity securities not carried as current assets (SFAS No. 12) be recognized as generally available for dividends under statutes which restrict the distribution of surplus arising from unrealized appreciation or revaluation of assets?

"Initially, determination must be made as to what accounting principles would be applied by directors and courts in assessing these and other questions under financial statement tests of state dividend statutes. It is the argument of this paper that generally accepted accounting principles (GAAP) represent the most practical answer, in the vast majority of cases will be consistent with present statutes, and should provide directors with a necessary safe harbor in authorizing distributions under accounting tests.

"GAAP AS A LEGAL STANDARD

"Under the statutes, the accounting principles to be applied in determining net assets and liabilities are generally unspecified. What, then, are the accounting principles to be applied under these statutes prescribing a financial statement test? GAAP is by far the most practical standard for the courts.

"First, with the exception of some closely regulated industries, GAAP accounting is required by the Securities and Exchange Commission [14] for publicly held companies and is effectively required by the American Institute of Certified Public Accountants (AICPA) for both public and private companies.[15] These requirements have resulted in a single set of accounting principles for most publicly traded and larger private companies. Thus lenders, trade creditors, and, especially important for our purposes, equity investors receive GAAP statements for such companies.

"Second, the objectives of the financial accounting standards for general purpose external financial reporting, as set forth in the FASB's summary of its Statement of Financial Accounting Concepts No. 1,[16] include:

§ 1210.34: Financial reporting should provide information that is useful to present and potential investors and creditors and other users in making rational investment, credit, and similar decisions. The information should be comprehensible to those who have a reasonable understanding of business and economic activities and are willing to study the information with reasonable diligence.

§ 1210.37: Financial reporting should provide information to help present and potential investors and creditors and other users in assessing the amounts, timing, and uncertainty of prospective cash receipts from dividends or interest and the proceeds from the sale, redemption, or maturity of securities or loans. Since investors' and creditors' cash flows are related to enterprise cash flows, financial reporting should provide information to help investors, creditors, and others assess the amounts, timing, and uncertainty of prospective net cash inflows to the related enterprise.

§ 1210.40: Financial reporting should provide information about the economic resources of an enterprise, the claims to those resources (obligations of the enterprise to transfer resources to other entities and owners' equity), and the effects of transactions, events, and circumstances that change resources and claims to those resources.[17]

"These objectives have not been and may never be fully achieved, but they demonstrate that GAAP financial statements are designed, in part, to show the ability of a corporation that is a going concern to pay cash dividends. Such objectives are consistent in a realistic way with the purposes of the dividend statutes: the protection of creditors, shareholders, and the relationships among the shareholders. For a going concern, a basic assumption of GAAP, these objectives come far closer to carrying out these protective functions than the fair valuation

14. Codification of Financial Reporting Policies, 5 Fed.Sec.L.Rep. (CCH) ¶ 72,401, § 101 (1982).

15. Code of Professional Ethics Rules, 203, 204 (AICPA 1980), *reprinted in* 2 AICPA Professional Standards ET §§ 203, 204 (1981).

16. Objectives of Financial Reporting by Business Enterprises, FASB Statement of Fin. Acc't Concepts No. 1, viii (1978), *reprinted in* Accounting, 3 AICPA Professional Standards AC § 1210 (1981).

17. *Id.*

standard of the Bankruptcy Law,[18] the fair salable value standard of the Uniform Fraudulent Conveyance Act,[19] referred to *infra,* or the continuing process of valuation and revaluation such as that contemplated by *Randall v. Bailey.*[20] For a going concern considering the declaration of dividends, it seems inappropriate to require a valuation of assets on the basis of theoretical current realization when such assets are not going to be the subject of current realization. (See discussion of statutory financial statement *infra.*)

"Third, the courts are quite unequipped to choose among and revise accounting principles. It is not a question of accepting, rejecting, or revising a particular item: instead an interrelated set of principles that focus on agreed objectives must be devised. Beneath the concepts of assets, liabilities, net income, and surplus is a complex network of definitions, assumptions, and judgments which are often individually, and always collectively, complex.[21]

"Fourth, some jurisdictions implicitly recognize GAAP as the standard for accounting determinations through statutes permitting directors to rely on financial statements prepared by public accountants.[22] Several states expressly permit the use of generally accepted accounting principles.[23]

"CONSIDERATION OF ABOVE SIX QUESTIONS

"Assuming GAAP is the legal standard, it produces reasonable answers under the statutory financial measurement tests when applied to the six questions above.

"(1) The direct recording in a separate equity account of translation gains and losses and changes in market values of equity securities carried as noncurrent assets should not present legal problems under balance sheet tests permitting payment out of surplus or payment without impairing capital. This equity account would not ordinarily be thought of as capital, because it has not been contributed by stockholders,[24] or as liability as discussed more fully below. Hence this equity account appears to be surplus (positive or negative) under the common statutory balance sheet test definitions. Also, it is called a component of equity in the accounting standards.

"(2) Assuming the answer to (1) above is that these amounts are surplus or net assets in excess of capital, are they earned surplus? There is an obvious inconsistency in including as earned surplus or

---

18. 2 Collier on Bankruptcy § 101(26)[4] (15th ed. 1982).

19. Uniform Fraudulent Conveyance Act § 2 (1918).

20. 288 N.Y. 280, 43 N.E.2d 43 (1942).

21. Conceptual Framework for Financial Accounting and Reporting: Elements of Financial Statements and Their Measurement (FASB Discussion Memorandum 1976); Jaenicke, Survey of Present Practices in Recognizing Revenues, Expenses, Gains, and Losses (FASB Research Report 1981).

22. Del.Code.Ann. tit. 8, §§ 141(e), 172 (1975); N.Y.Bus.Corp.Law § 717 (McKinney 1963 & Supp. 1982–83).

23. Md.Corps. & Ass'ns Code Ann. § 1–402 (1982); N.C.Gen.Stat. § 55–49 (1982); Cal.Corp.Code § 114 (West 1977 & Supp. 1982).

24. Montgomery, Auditing 611 (9th ed. 1975).

retained earnings an item which under SFAS No. 12 and SFAS No. 52 expressly did not and cannot go through the income statement. In addition, such amounts do not appear to fit into commonly used definitions of earned surplus or retained earnings. For instance, Montgomery recites the following definition of retained earnings: 'The balance of net profits, income, gains and losses of a corporation from the date of incorporation (or from the latest date when a deficit was eliminated in a quasi-reorganization) after deducting distributions therefrom to shareholders and transfers therefrom to capital stock or capital surplus accounts.' [25] This definition, as well as statutory definitions,[26] does not appear to contemplate that the separate equity accounts referred to above would be earned surplus or retained earnings. Hence, we believe the equity account referred to in SFAS No. 12 and SFAS No. 52 does not constitute earned surplus or retained earnings.

"(3) Similarly, if GAAP is the standard, an item stated by SFAS No. 12 and SFAS No. 52 to be excluded from the income account, whether positive or negative, would not appear to affect net profits for purposes of the nimble dividend statutes.

"(4) Under the equity method of accounting of APB Op. No. 18 an adjustment to the investment (asset) on the parent balance sheet would be made to reflect earnings and losses, and is included in determining the parent's net income in the case of investments in subsidiaries, corporate joint ventures, and common stock where the investor has the ability to exercise significant influence over the operating and financial policies of the investee.

"Initially, there are two special problems in applying APB Op. No. 18. First, APB Op. No. 18[27] is stated to apply to parent company financials only when they 'are prepared for issuance to stockholders as the financial statements of the primary reporting entity'[28] (a concept arising, we understand, from state franchise tax considerations). Because, where there are consolidated subsidiaries, consolidated financials are practically always the primary reporting medium, APB Op. No. 18 is not by its terms required to be applied to the parent company financial statements assumed by practically all state laws as the basis for dividend tests applicable to the parent, although it is clearly a permissible accounting practice under GAAP. (Consolidated statements are expressly required in California[29].) This apparently leaves companies the option of using the equity method for parent-only statements for the purpose of declaring dividends. At a minimum it would seem that the courts should under these circumstances accept equity

---

25. *Id.* at 625 (quoting from Accounting Terminology Bulletin No. 1, para. 34).

26. *See, e.g.,* N.Y.Bus.Corp.Law § 102(a)(6) (McKinney 1963), Ohio Rev.Code Ann. § 1701.32(A) (Baldwin 1979).

27. APB Op. No. 18, *supra* note 11, *reprinted in* Accounting, 3 AICPA Professional Standards AC § 5131 (1981).

28. *Id.* at AC § 1531.01.

29. Cal.Corp.Code § 114 (West 1977 & Supp. 1982).

accounting as a permissible method for such parent company statements and not require the use of the alternate cost method.[31]

"Second, the accounting called for by APB Op. No. 18 would be subject to state laws prohibiting equity accounting under dividend tests. Where there is an express statutory command to the contrary (for example, in Ohio[32]), equity accounting would not be available. When there is no such statute and, based in part on our conclusion under (6) as to the inapplicability of the general prohibitions against revaluation, the adjustments contemplated by APB Op. No. 18 would appear to be properly includable under the statutes referred to in questions (1), (2), and (3) as surplus, earned surplus, or net profits.

"Both APB Op. No. 18 and SFAS No. 12 (for current assets) call for recognition in the determination of net income before a 'realization' in the sense of an exchange transaction (e.g., receipt of a dividend or sale) has occurred. In fact there are a number of other situations where realization is not required for recognition of revenue under generally accepted accounting principles.[33] The task force sees no reason why courts should insist on realization through receipt of a dividend (ABP Op. No. 18) or sale of securities (SFAS No. 12) for recognition of changes in asset carrying value. (See (6) below for discussion of whether statutes and cases on unrealized appreciation of assets apply to the accounting principles under discussion.)

"(5) The subject of deferred taxes is, of course, extremely complex. However, it appears that deferred charges or deferred credits created under APB No. 11 by timing differences in the tax payment and GAAP accrual requirements should be recognized by courts under the statutes referred to in (1), (2), and (3). (For an early case holding that prepaid taxes are not a proper asset for dividend calculations under a balance sheet test, see *Cox v. Leahy*.[34])

"A deferred tax charge represents, from the financial accounting point of view, a prepayment of taxes. The prepayment arises because taxes are paid on revenue or credits in a period prior to the recognition of such revenue or credits for financial accounting purposes or because expenses or debits are deducted for tax purposes in a period after their accrual for financial accounting purposes. As noted above, one question under the financial statement statutes is whether the courts would recognize the creation of an asset (deferred charge) as contrasted with

---

31. This question is sometimes raised in different terms: Must the corporate joint venture or an investee actually declare dividends for its earnings to be included in the investor's income. The fact that the subsidiary's earnings have not been paid up as a dividend should no more as a legal matter affect the dividend-paying ability of the parent than would a capital contribution by the parent of cash to the subsidiary. In our view the amounts recorded by the investor representing changes in the inves-

tee's or venture's earnings and losses are adjustments to the carrying value of the asset (the investment) on the investor's books—an asset measurement—and no declaration is necessary.

32. Ohio Rev.Code Ann. § 1701.32(A) (Baldwin 1979).

33. *See generally* Jaenicke, *supra* note 21.

34. 209 A.D. 313, 204 N.Y.S. 741 (1924).

the immediate recording of the tax expense which would occasion a reduction in surplus. A similar question under the nimble dividend statutes is whether the postponement of the expense will be given effect. Present GAAP prescribes the deferred method based on the matching concept under which the tax effects of timing differences are deferred currently and allocated to income tax expense of future periods when the timing differences reverse.[35] Statement of Financial Accounting Concepts No. 3,[36] however, states that while this deferred method of allocation does not fit its definitions of assets and liabilities, either of two other methods, the liability method or the net-of-tax method, would meet the definitions.[37] Furthermore, the definitions of assets and liabilities are based on the assumption that a balance sheet may carry debit balances that are not necessarily assets (as defined) and credit balances that are not necessarily liabilities (as defined).[38] Hence, it is apparent that continuation in financial accounting of interperiod income tax accounting is still very much a possibility. For the present, of course, APB Op. No. 11 and the deferred method are required by GAAP. Without here getting into the differences among the three methods for interperiod income tax accounting, it would seem that courts ought to accept the principle and leave to the evolution of GAAP the particular method to be followed.

"A deferred tax credit is created when financial accounting recognition of revenue or credits precedes the period of tax payment thereon or when expenses or debits are deducted for income tax purposes in a period prior to their accrual for financial accounting purposes. The analysis is similar to that noted above for the deferred tax charge, but with the additional question of where the deferred tax credit fits into a balance sheet test, i.e., is it a liability, a surplus, or something else?

"At one time, a number of public utility companies apparently carried a deferred credit tax account as a segregated component of retained earnings, which method of accounting was accepted by the SEC and various state regulatory commissions. However, the AICPA subsequently explicitly rejected this approach, and the SEC ultimately concurred in principle.[39]

"Although APB Op. No. 11 states that a deferred credit does not represent a payable in the usual sense,[40] it provides explicitly that a deferred credit should be excluded from any account in the stockholder's equity section of the balance sheet.[41] Furthermore, under today's accounting, liabilities on a balance sheet include, in addition to econom-

35. APB Op. No. 11, *supra* note 13, *reprinted in* Accounting, 3 AICPA Professional Standards AC § 4091, at §§ 4091.16 to .18 (1981).

36. Elements of Financial Statements of Business Enterprises FASB Statement of Fin. Acc't Concepts No. 3 (1980), *reprinted in* Accounting, 3 AICPA Professional Standards AC § 1230 (1981).

37. *Id.* at AC §§ 1230.163–165.

38. *Id.* at AC § 1230.153.

39. For the story of the battle between a group of electric utility companies on the one hand and the AICPA on the other, see Fiflis and Kripke, *Accounting for Business Lawyers,* 531–35 (2d ed. 1977).

40. APB Op. No. 11, *reprinted in* AC § 4091, *supra* note 35, at § 4091.56.

41. *Id.* at § 4091.58.

ic obligations, 'certain deferred credits that are not obligations but that are recognized and measured in conformity with generally accepted accounting principles.'[42]

"Prior to promulgation of APB Op. No. 11, two other basic methods of interperiod allocation of income taxes had been utilized in practice. Under the liability method of allocation, the deferred tax credit would be shown as an account payable or other obligation payable in future years, clearly a liability.[43] Under the net-of-tax allocation method, a deferred tax credit requires reduction of the carrying value of the related asset, and no credit is made to any liability or net worth account.[44] Thus regardless of the tax allocation method followed for accounting purposes, the deferred tax credit account should not be deemed to be a credit to surplus under those statutes which define surplus as net assets after deducting liabilities and capital.

"For the general reasons given above, we believe a court should follow GAAP where there is no statutory impediment and should do so in a situation like deferred taxes where the accounting profession is still seeking clarification of a very difficult problem. Any other result—that dividends can be paid out of deferred taxes as a part of surplus—seems wrong. Treating a deferred tax liability as a credit to a net worth account would amount to giving with one hand what is taken away with the other; it would make little sense for a charge to be made in lieu of taxes, thus reducing net income and ultimately net worth, accompanied by a simultaneous credit to a net worth account in the same amount. We are therefore of the view that statutory surplus should not be construed so as to include the deferred tax account required under present GAAP.

"(6) Under SFAS No. 52, SFAS No. 12, and APB Op. No. 18, increases in equity may be recorded to reflect increases in the carrying value of assets arising out of foreign exchange translation, increases in market value of equity securities (but not above cost), and increases in the investor's equity in earnings of the investee. There is judicial authority on both sides of the question whether unrealized appreciation or depreciation of assets can be taken into account in ascertaining amounts available for dividends. We are here assuming that we are dealing with issuers that are solvent in the equity sense, i.e., that are able to pay their debts as they become due in the ordinary course of business.

"*Randall v. Bailey*[45] dealt with a statutory capital impairment test plus a further statutory prohibition against dividends unless the value

---

42. Basic Concepts and Accounting Principles Underlying Financial Statements of Business Enterprises, APB Statement No. 4 (1980), *reprinted in* Accounting, 3 AICPA Professional Standards AC § 1025, at § 1025.19 (1981).

43. APB Op. No. 11, *reprinted in* AC § 4091, *supra* note 35, at AC § 4091.19; *see*

Black, Interperiod Allocation of Corporate Taxes, AICPA Accounting Research Study No. 9, 13 (1966).

44. APB Op. No. 11, *reprinted in* AC § 4091, *supra* note 35, at AC § 4091.20; Black, *supra* note 43, at 14.

45. 288 N.Y. 280, 43 N.E.2d 43 (1942).

of the remaining assets shall at least equal liabilities and capital. The decision was that unrealized appreciation of fixed assets could be included as surplus by directors and available for dividends.[46] *Berks Broadcasting Co. v. Craumer,*[47] containing a strong dictum to the contrary under general principles of corporate law and the rules of accounting, was decided under a statute that specifically prohibited dividends from unrealized appreciation or revaluation or fixed assets. Paragraph 17 of APB Op. No. 6 expressed disapproval of write-ups to reflect appraisal, market, or current values that are above cost, except in quasi-reorganizations or reorganizations.[48]

"A number of statutes expressly provide that unrealized appreciation cannot be taken into account in determining surplus or earned surplus, although in some respects the statutes are confusing. Indiana prohibits dividends out of surplus from unrealized appreciation or revaluation of assets.[49] Illinois prohibits dividends in cash or property from unrealized appreciation or revaluation but permits stock dividends.[50] Minnesota law states that in determining fair value of assets for a distribution, unrealized appreciation cannot be included except that marketable securities may be valued at not more than market value, and also requires deduction for 'depreciation and depletion for losses of every character whether or not realized' (suggesting that diminutions in value must be recognized).[51] Ohio permits directors to revalue physical assets to create capital surplus,[52] but only stock dividends may be paid therefrom.[53]

"Historically, the prohibitions against recording upward revaluation in assets arose during the 1930s as a result of suspicion and hostility toward what were perceived as doubtful values that were being added arbitrarily to balance sheets. The SEC was strongly against such values and a staunch advocate of historical cost.[54] While historical cost is the generally measured attribute of inventories and property, plant, and equipment, it has never been the exclusive measurement technique. For example, current cost (i.e., market) is used in accounting for inventories in the application of the lower-of-cost-or-market rule; net realizable value is used in accounting for trade accounts receivable and under certain conditions for inventories representing agricultural and mineral products; and present values of long-term receivables and payables under APB 21 are used for measuring cost in a variety of transactions.[55]

46. For a recent recognition of this principle, see Vowteras v. Argo Compressor Service Corp., 77 A.D.2d 945, 431 N.Y.S.2d 136 (1980), *modified* 83 A.D.2d 834, 441 N.Y.S.2d 562 (1981).

47. 356 Pa. 620, 52 A.2d 571 (1947).

48. Depreciation on Appreciation, APB Op. No. 6, para. 17 (1965), *reprinted in* Accounting, 3 AICPA Professional Standards AC § 4072.01 (1981).

49. Ind.Code § 23–1–2–15(a) (1972).

50. Ill.Rev.Stat. Ch. 151.41(c) (1981).

51. Minn.Stats. § 302A.551 (1982).

52. Ohio Rev.Code Ann. § 1730.32(D) (Baldwin 1979).

53. *Id.* § 1730–.33(A).

54. Kripke, The SEC and Corporate Disclosure 179–84 (1979); Loss, Securities Regulation 339 (2d ed. 1961).

55. This subject is discussed extensively in Conceptual Framework for Financial

"The task force believes that the accounting under discussion is not of the kind at which the statutes prohibiting revaluation surplus and APB Op. No. 6, Par. 17, are directed. Currency translation adjustments are based on objectively verifiable exchange rates and are a way of expressing carrying cost where several currencies are involved; marketable equity securities adjustments can never exceed cost and are based on objectively verifiable market quotations; and the equity method of accounting for investments is an asset measuring device based on objectively verifiable facts. None appears to involve the kind of changes in valuation against which the general statutes are directed. For example, SFAS No. 12 addresses the question of reversing write-downs to the extent that the carrying amount does not exceed cost:

> The Board does not regard the reversal of the write-down as representing recognition of an unrealized gain. Rather, the Board views the write-down as establishing a valuation allowance representing the estimated reduction in the realizable value of the portfolio, and it views a subsequent market increase as having reduced or eliminated the requirement for such an allowance. In the Board's view, the reversal of the write-down represents a change in an accounting estimate of an unrealized loss. . . .[56]

"The 1979 revision of the distribution provisions of the Model Act permits determinations of the accounting concepts to be based upon 'a fair valuation or other method that is reasonable in the circumstances.'[57] The commentary states that the Act 'specifically authorizes departure from historical cost accounting and sanctions the utilization of appraisal methods for the purpose of determining the fund available for distributions.'[58] This, of course, is directly contrary to many of the statutes discussed above and would permit revaluations of assets in the circumstances outlined. For a going concern it apparently would permit creation of an extra-GAAP surplus from which dividends could be paid.

"SHOULD DIRECTORS HAVE A SAFE HARBOR WHEN DECLARING DIVIDENDS?

"A number of states now afford directors protection in relying on financial statements when declaring dividends. For example, New York and Delaware permit directors to rely on financial statements prepared or presented by officers or public accountants where the directors believe in the competency of the preparer (New York) or rely in good faith on the preparer (Delaware).[59]

Accounting and Reporting, *supra* note 21, at 196–237.

56. SFAS No. 12, *supra* note 12, *reprinted in* Accounting, 3 AICPA Professional Standards AC § 5132, at AC § 5132.29.

57. Model Business Corp. Act § 45 (1979). The task force understands that the Committee on Corporate Laws is restating the Model Act, but that the sub-

stance of the provisions herein discussed is not being changed.

58. Committee on Corporate Laws, *Changes in the Model Business Corporations Act—Amendments to Financial Provisions,* 34 Bus.Law. 1867, 1885 (1979) [hereinafter cited as Committee Report].

59. Del.Code Ann. tit. 8, § 141(e) (1975); N.Y.Bus.Corp.Law § 717 (McKinney 1963

"It appears to the task force that when it comes to applying statutory financial tests to dividend declarations, corporate directors are in the same position as the courts: they are generally not trained or competent to be responsible for accounting standards that represent extremely complex assumptions and judgments. The task force believes directors should be entitled in good faith to rely on the most recent regular corporate financial statements when declaring dividends except, of course, where an equity insolvency test would not be met.[60]

"While section 35 of the Model Act has a provision similar to those noted above as to distributions, the 1979 Model Act amendments changing the capital and distribution provisions contain ambiguities that may be read to undercut the reliance protections of section 35. The new section 45 provides that determinations may be based upon financial statements prepared on the basis of accounting practices and principles 'that are reasonable in the circumstances.' [61]

"That this is not intended to constitute a safe harbor is made quite clear by the commentary:

> While the directors will normally be entitled to use generally accepted accounting principles and to give presumptive weight to the advice of professional accountants with respect thereto, it is important to recognize that the new Section requires the use of accounting practices and principles that are reasonable in the circumstances, and does not constitute a statutory enactment of generally accepted accounting principles. In the view of the Committee, the widespread controversy concerning various accounting principles, and their constant reevaluation, requires a statutory standard of reasonableness, as a matter of law, recognizing that there may be equally acceptable alternative solutions to specific issues as well as areas requiring judgment in interpreting such principles. This does not mean that the statute is intended to reject the use and reliance upon generally accepted accounting principles; on the contrary, it is expected that their use would be the basic rule in most cases. The statutory language does, however, require informed business judgment in the entire circumstances in applying particular accounting principles to the circumstances that exist at the time, for purposes of the ultimate legal measurement of the validity of distributions.

> If a corporation's financial statements are not presented in accordance with generally accepted accounting principles, however, a board of directors should normally carefully consider the extent to which the assets may not be fairly stated or the liabilities may be understated, to

& Supp.1982–1983); *see* Cal.Corp.Code § 309 (1977). For a general description of this sort of statute, see Model Business Corp. Act § 35 annot. (2d ed. & Supp.1977).

60. For a discussion of additional problems that could be presented to boards of directors if there were different accounting

standards for small and large businesses, see Stanger and Gunther, *"Big GAAP—Little Gap": Should There Be Different Financial Reporting for Small Business?*, 56 N.Y.U.L.Rev. 1209, 1217–21.

61. Model Act, § 45 (1979).

determine the fairness of the aggregate amount of assets and the aggregate amount of liabilities.[62]

"We recognize that the official commentary states that generally accepted accounting principles 'would be the basic rule in most cases,' and that this must be read to create the practical equivalent of a safe harbor in most situations. However, it is also clear that some judgment beyond acceptance of GAAP is required by the commentary. In considering whether there should be a safe harbor for GAAP-based financial statements a number of questions are apparent.

"Where GAAP affords alternatives, should there be a statutory safe harbor if the board of directors in good faith selects one of them? To take a brief example, in December 1977 the FASB promulgated SFAS No. 19 [63] requiring a successful efforts method for oil and gas producing activities. In August 1978 the SEC in Accounting Release 253 [64] announced it intended to develop a reserve recognition method of accounting (RRA) and, meanwhile, issuers could either use the FASB successful efforts method or an SEC prescribed form of full cost accounting (which method had been rejected by the FASB). Each of these three methods frequently produces quite different results from the other two. The FASB in SFAS No. 25 [65] suspended successful efforts as a requirement, and the SEC has ceased attempting to develop RRA, described in its 1978 release as the only way of significantly improving measurement of assets and earnings of oil and gas producing companies.[66] The prior choice of successful efforts or full cost thus remains. Other obvious examples might include LIFO or FIFO and accelerated or straight-line depreciation. These are situations where two methods are permitted and raise the question of whether directors should be required to choose unless under a safe harbor both choices are protected if the directors act in good faith.

"Must directors consider non-GAAP accounting alternatives? Many examples, including the accounting principles discussed in the first part of this paper, could be cited where, if directors were responsible for choosing among accounting standards when considering proposed distributions, they would have to consider non-GAAP alternatives in very complicated accounting issues: How should foreign currency adjustments be made and deferred taxes be carried? Apart from an equity insolvency test, should the directors be expected to explore some sort of asset and liability valuation as an alternative to a GAAP balance sheet?

62. Committee Report, *supra* note 58, at 1884.

63. Financial Accounting and Reporting by Oil and Gas Producing Companies, FASB Statement of Fin. Standards No. 19, (1977).

64. SEC Acc't Release No. 253, [1937–82 Transfer Binder] Fed.Sec.L.Rep. (CCH) ¶ 72,275 (August 31, 1978).

65. Suspension of Certain Accounting Requirements for Oil and Gas Producing Companies, FASB Statement of Fin. Standards No. 25, (1979).

66. SEC Accounting Release No. 289, [1937–82 Transfer Binder] Fed.Sec.L.Rep. (CCH) ¶ 72,311 (Feb. 26, 1981).

"Once initiated, the inquiry could reach far afield from generally accepted accounting principles. One assumes that a decision on what accounting practices were reasonable would not require directors to consider the fair valuation concept of the Bankruptcy Law, where property so valued is compared to debts in order to determine insolvency,[67] or a fair salable value standard under the Uniform Fraudulent Conveyance Act.[68] Fair value has been a very difficult concept under bankruptcy law.[69] Moreover, fair value (with an exception for such items as marketable securities) is essentially a liquidation standard and does not seem an appropriate standard for a going concern that expects to proceed to realize on its assets in an orderly way over time.

"For the reasons discussed elsewhere in this paper, we question whether it is reasonable for the statute to require a director to make a judgment among accounting principles. We believe that, where GAAP statements are presented, they ought to be conclusively deemed to be reasonable in the circumstances in determining compliance with the balance sheet test without the necessity for further judgment by the directors.

"At the same time, we recognize that a vast majority of corporations in the United States are small ones that in many cases do not have either independent accountants or financial statements presented on the basis of GAAP. Reliance by directors on statements prepared on a basis other than GAAP should be allowed if reasonable in the circumstances, without the benefit of a conclusive safe harbor. The draftsmen revising the Model Act apparently thus felt it necessary to create flexibility by permitting, as one alternative, liabilities and assets to be determined by 'a fair valuation or other method that is reasonable in the circumstances'.[70]

    *   *   *"

As the Task Force Report and Hackney make clear, unless GAAP are followed for dividend law purposes, courts will be involved in the morass of fixing accounting principles much as state regulatory agencies in rate-making and the FASB in financial accounting; and, worse yet, courts must act *ad hoc*, not comprehensively, so that as time passes, the slow accretion of court-established principles will be constantly changing, with chaos resulting.

If this is the case, two of several alternatives are for statutes to:

    (a) simply adopt GAAP for dividend law purposes; or

    (b) allow directors wide discretion in developing their own accounting principles, including merely adopting GAAP.

The California statute adopts the first alternative and the Revised Model Business Corporation Act, the second.

67. 11 U.S.C.A. § 101(26) (Supp. III 1979).

68. Uniform Fraudulent Conveyance Act § 2 (1918).

69. *See, e.g.,* 2 Collier on Bankruptcy § 101(26)[4] (15th ed. 1982).

70. Model Business Corp. Act § 45, *supra* note 7.

Cal.Corp.Code § 114 reads:

All references in this division to financial statements, balance sheets, income statements and statements of changes in financial position of a corporation and all references to assets, liabilities, earnings, retained earnings and similar accounting items of a corporation mean such financial statements or such items prepared or determined in conformity with generally accepted accounting principles when applicable, fairly presenting in conformity with generally accepted accounting principles the matters which they purport to present, subject to any specific accounting treatment required by a particular section of this division. Unless otherwise expressly stated, all references in this division to such financial statements mean, in the case of a corporation which has subsidiaries, consolidated statements of the corporation and such of its subsidiaries as are required to be included in such consolidated statements under generally accepted accounting principles then applicable and all references to such accounting items mean such items determined on a consolidated basis in accordance with such consolidated financial statements. Financial statements other than annual statements may be condensed or otherwise presented as permitted by authoritative accounting pronouncements.

One weakness of the first alternative is that despite the Conceptual Framework's aspirations noted in the above Task Force Report, GAAP are basically for purposes of providing disclosures to potential users of financial information[ll] and not for purposes of protection of creditors and shareholders from distributions. Therefore, the effects of some GAAP may be to designate something as income which a reasonable legislator would be unlikely to perceive as appropriate for distribution. (E.g., imputed income from use of equity funds in construction, supra p. 261.)

Many statutes today in effect adopt the second alternative under provisions like Revised MBCA § 6.40(d).[mm] Under that provision the accounting practices and principles followed in determining the dividend pool must be "reasonable in the circumstances." Even if GAAP are observed, they must be independently assessed in light of this standard; the comments to § 6.40 are clear on this. Nevertheless, those same comments note that GAAP usually will be used in applying § 6.40. Will the courts find them to be presumptively reasonable in

ll. FASB, Financial Acctg. Concepts, No. 1 pp. 24–30 (1978).

mm. See Report of Committee on Corporate Laws: Changes in the Model Business Corporation Act, 30 Bus.Law. 501 (1975).

The Maryland statute provides that determinations are "prima facie proper if made in good faith in accordance with generally accepted accounting practices and principles." Md.Corps & Ass'ns Code Ann. § 1–402 (1975).

North Carolina permits carrying assets "in accordance with generally accepted principles of sound accounting practice applicable to the kind of business conducted by the corporation." N.C.Gen.Stat. § 55–49(b) (1982).

Michigan permits valuing assets either at book value "in accordance with generally accepted accounting principles" or at "current fair value." Mich.Comp.Laws Ann. §§ 450, 1106–1110 (West 1973 and Supp. 1982).

the circumstances, or will they embark on their own search for reasonable accounting principles?

When Pennsylvania adopted the Revised MBCA, the legislative committee comments supporting the adoption of § 6.40(d) stated the "reasonable in the circumstances" language addresses the different problem of changing GAAP, noting:

> To avoid the problem encountered under the prior law as the statutory provisions diverged from developing accounting principles, this section does not incorporate technical accounting terminology or specific accounting concepts. Accounting terminology and concepts are constantly under review and subject to revision by the Financial Accounting Standards Board, the American Institute of Certified Public Accountants, the Securities and Exchange Commission, and others. In making determinations under this section, the board of directors may make judgments about accounting matters, taking into account its right to rely upon professional or expert opinion and its obligation to be reasonably informed as to pertinent standards of importance that bear upon the subject at issue.
>
> * * *
>
> The directors will normally be entitled to use generally accepted accounting principles and to give presumptive weight to the advice of professional accountants with respect to their application. The statutory language requires simply informed business judgment applying particular accounting principles to the entire circumstances that exist at the time. [15 Pa.CSA § 1551, Comm.Comment.]

E. TREASURY STOCK—RESTRICTIONS ON A CORPORATION'S ACQUISITION OF ITS OWN SHARES

This part E is irrelevant under the Revised MBCA which treats treasury stock like unissued shares. Revised MBCA § 6.31.

Does the purchase by a corporation of its own shares dissipate the cushion of legal capital intended to exist for the benefit of creditors and preferred stockholders? Yes. Therefore, the treasury stock so purchased usually is not an asset. *ARB No. 43, Chapter 1A,* ¶ 4 and *Chapter 1B* (1953); *APB Op. No. 6,* ¶¶ 12–13 (1965).

While ¶ 4 above cited and ¶ 12 of *APB Op. No. 6* entertain the possibility that under certain circumstances treasury stock may be an asset, those circumstances are very rare—e.g., where treasury stock has been purchased and is about to be delivered in compliance with an obligation of the corporation to make contributions to a pension plan for employees. In other cases, treasury stock in the corporation's hands has no more characteristics of an asset just because it was once issued and outstanding than does the authorized but unissued stock of the corporation, which obviously is not a corporate asset. Compare

United States v. Simon, 425 F.2d 796 (2d Cir. 1969), where the facts taught the lesson that corporate stock which was in essence indirectly pledged to the corporation to secure indebtedness to the corporation is not collateral because the corporate stock itself is of no value to the corporation or its creditors different from unissued stock. For this reason, one clear GAAP is that income or revenue is not to be affected by treasury stock transactions. *ARB 43, Chapter 1B* (1953).

Because the acquisition by a corporation of some of its common stock depletes the cushion for creditors and for preferred stockholders to the extent of the consideration paid, it is, therefore, obvious that a restriction on the purchase by a corporation of its own shares is necessary and that it should be substantially the same as the restriction on dividends.

MBCA § 6, prior to the 1979 amendments, provided that a corporation shall have the right to purchase its own shares only to the extent of unreserved and unrestricted earned surplus available therefor. It further provided that if the articles of incorporation so permit, or with the vote of the holders of at least a majority of all shares entitled to vote thereon, the corporation may purchase its own shares to the extent of unreserved and unrestricted capital surplus. In addition, it provided that to the extent that earned surplus or capital surplus is used as the measure of this right, such surplus shall be restricted so long as the shares are treasury shares, and on the disposition thereof, the restriction shall be removed *pro tanto*.

We shall see examples of the MBCA restriction technique in the accounting entries below. The new provisions of the Revised MBCA presumably would result in reducing the Capital Stock account by the cost of the repurchased shares.

NYBCL § 513 mandates a different technique. It provides that a corporation may purchase its own shares or redeem its redeemable shares out of surplus, except when the corporation is insolvent or would be made insolvent. There is here no distinction between capital surplus and earned surplus. While ordinarily on a resale of treasury stock any selling price in excess of par or stated value would create capital surplus, § 517(a)(5) provides that where a corporation has applied its earned surplus to the acquisition of treasury shares and the shares have subsequently been disposed of for a consideration, the corporation may restore to earned surplus on an appropriate basis all or part of the amount by which earned surplus was reduced at the time of acquisition of the shares. Thus, the New York system requires a direct reduction of earned surplus, in contrast to the MBCA technique of restriction, but on a resale both statutes permit the restoration of earned surplus.

Del.C.L. § 160 permits a corporation to purchase its own stock so long as its capital is not impaired or would not thereby be impaired. In other words, stock may be purchased out of any available surplus. This is consistent with the Delaware dividend law, which did not distinguish between earned surplus and capital surplus.

How does treasury stock affect stockholders' equity?

One might reason that when shares are purchased, there is a reduction of the capital stock account and that to the extent of par (or stated) value, treasury stock should be shown as a deduction from that account directly or through a contra account.

A generation or so ago this was the way in which treasury stock was portrayed. Since most state corporation statutes expressly or impliedly define capital stock to include all issued stock, whether or not outstanding, until legally cancelled, that treatment is less widely used than formerly, but we continue to show it because it is authorized by *APB Op. No. 6*, ¶ 12, unless the applicable state law prescribes other treatment. ¶ 13. This sometimes is called the "par" method, but we call it the "direct capital reduction method."

In the following discussion we consider the restriction technique of the MBCA and the direct reduction of surplus method (which is required by NYBCL) in the basic presentation.

We begin with an assumed Stockholders' Equity as follows:

Capital Stock (100 shares, par value $100 each, issued and outstanding)	$10,000
Earned Surplus	7,500
	$17,500

We shall first consider the easy cases where the purchase price of the treasury stock is equal to the par (or stated) value thereof.

1.　PURCHASE AT PAR

(A) Direct Capital Reduction Method

Where applicable state law does not otherwise require, *APB Op. No. 6*, ¶ 12, provides that on the repurchase by the corporation of ten shares of $100 par value for $1,000, the entry might be:

(1) Capital Stock	$1,000	
Cash		$1,000

However, unless the shares are being cancelled promptly and legal capital thus reduced, it is more appropriate to use a contra debit account called treasury stock and to make the following entry in lieu of the foregoing:

(2) Treasury Stock	$1,000	
Cash		$1,000

The Stockholders' Equity section of the balance sheet might then read:

Capital Stock	$10,000
Less: Treasury Stock	1,000
	$9,000
Earned Surplus	7,500
	$16,500

Note that this statement (where the purchase was at par) does not affect any surplus account, even though most state corporation statutes limit treasury share purchases in much the same way that they limit dividends.

(B) Surplus Restriction Method

Where the law does limit purchases to the amount of earned surplus and requires the restriction thereof, like old MBCA § 6, *APB Op. No. 6,* ¶ 13, requires the reporting company to show that $1,000 of earned surplus is now no longer available for dividends or other stock purchases. We must make an entry in addition to (2) above to restrict earned surplus to that extent, as follows:

(3) Earned Surplus	$1,000	
Restricted Earned Surplus		$1,000 [nn]

The Stockholders' Equity section of our balance sheet might then appear:

Capital Stock		$10,000
Less: Treasury Stock		1,000
		$9,000
Earned Surplus		
Restricted	$1,000	
Unrestricted	6,500	
		$7,500
		$16,500

But even after this restriction, we still show Capital Stock at a net figure of $9,000 although legal capital is $10,000. Therefore, we should leave the Capital Stock account intact, and deduct Treasury Stock from the total Net Worth, as authorized by *APB Op. No. 6,* ¶ 12(b):

Capital Stock		$10,000
Earned Surplus:		
Restricted	$1,000	
Unrestricted	6,500	
		7,500
		$17,500
Less: Treasury Stock		1,000
Total Stockholders' Equity		$16,500 [oo]

nn. Professor Stanger asserts that the MBCA requires only the excess paid for treasury stock over par or stated value to be charged to a surplus account, and permits the par or stated value to be charged to capital account. Stanger, Comparative Accounting Treatment Mandated by the Model Business Corporation Act and the New York Business Corporation Law Regarding Share Reacquisitions and the Related Effect on Surplus, 24 Bus.Law. 115, 120 (1968). But he is so stating in the context of intended immediate retirement, as discussed, infra, pp. 417–418.

oo. Sprouse, Accounting for Treasury Stock Transactions; Prevailing Practices and New Statutory Provisions, 59 Colum.L. Rev. 882, 883–890 (1959), argues that the MBCA was intended to permit but does not actually permit the deduction of the treasury stock from the unallocated total of stockholders' equity. He argues that since treasury stock is not an asset, some stockholders' equity account must be reduced; and since earned surplus is merely restricted and capital is not reduced, capital surplus must be reduced. He even talks, in a case like our example where there was no capital surplus, of the possibility of negative capital surplus. We have preferred to show the unallocated deduction method, which, as Professor Sprouse admits, "does not do great violence" to legal status under MBCA.

(C) Direct Surplus Reduction Method

Under the NYBCL the exclusive entry would be:

(4) Earned Surplus	$1,000	
Cash		$1,000

and Stockholders' Equity would read:

Capital Stock, issued 100 shares, $100 par each, of which 10 are held in the Treasury	$10,000
Earned Surplus	6,500
	$16,500

2. RESALE OF TREASURY STOCK AT PAR

(A) Direct Capital Reduction Method

If the treasury shares were resold for $1,000 the appropriate entry would be:

(5) Cash	$1,000	
Treasury Stock		$1,000

(B) Surplus Restriction Method

This method would also use entry (5). Then, since under MBCA § 6 the restriction on surplus has been removed by the resale of the shares, the restriction should now be reversed, as follows:

(6) Restricted Earned Surplus	$1,000	
Earned Surplus		$1,000

The Stockholders' Equity section of the balance sheet would then appear exactly as it was originally.

(C) Direct Surplus Reduction Method

Under the NYBCL earned surplus was *reduced* by the purchase of treasury stock (entry (4), supra). Accounting would in general take the position that no earned surplus can result on resale of treasury stock any more than earned surplus can result from the sale of original issue stock, and the credit would have to be capital surplus. But NYBCL § 517(a)(5) authorizes the restoration of the reduction of earned surplus, i.e., a reversal of entry (4), upon resale of the treasury stock. It thus achieves the same result as the MBCA does by its technique of imposing and removing a restriction (journal entries (3) and (6), supra).

3. CANCELLATION OF TREASURY STOCK

(A) Direct Capital Reduction Method

If instead of reselling the treasury stock, it is cancelled under the statutory procedure (usually involving a report to the Secretary of State following a directors' resolution), the reduction of legal capital may now be shown, as follows:

(7) Capital Stock	$1,000	
Treasury Stock		$1,000

(B) Surplus Restriction Method

Under the old MBCA, the entry is:

    (8) Capital Stock $1,000

         Treasury Stock $1,000

The restriction on Earned Surplus is now no longer necessary and may be eliminated:

    (9) Restricted Earned Surplus $1,000

         Earned Surplus $1,000

The Stockholders' Equity section of the balance sheet under both sets of entries in (A) and (B) here would look like this:

Capital Stock	$9,000
Earned Surplus	7,500
Total Stockholders' Equity	$16,500

Several writers have viewed with alarm the situation by which earned surplus, having been restricted under the MBCA by the purchase of treasury stock, is restored by the cancellation of that stock, so that a small amount of earned surplus could be used again and again to cancel capital stock. Hackney, *The Financial Provisions of the Model Business Corporation Act*, 70 Harv.L.Rev. 1357, 1396 (1957); Rudolph, *Accounting for Treasury Shares Under the Model Business Corporation Act*, 73 Harv.L.Rev. 323, 328 (1959). Professor Herwitz argues otherwise. He reads old MBCA § 70 as providing that upon the reduction of stated capital the resulting surplus shall be capital surplus. D. Herwitz, *Business Planning* 425–426 (1966). So it does, but it seems to us that Herwitz overlooks the italicized words: "The surplus, *if any*, created by a reduction of stated capital," and it further seems that there is no surplus created where Stockholders' Equity has undoubtedly been reduced by the expenditure of cash for the treasury stock, and the reduction is not permanently reflected except by the reduction of capital stock. Thus there is no argument for the creation of a capital surplus which would negate the express provision of MBCA § 6 that earned surplus is restored, however justified Hackney and Rudolph may be in deploring it. At any rate, Herwitz seems to suggest that in addition to the foregoing entries, the surplus must be reclassified by an entry like this:

    (10) Earned Surplus $1,000

         Capital Surplus $1,000

(C) Direct Surplus Reduction Method

Since the expenditure of cash has already been reflected as a reduction of earned surplus, when the treasury stock is cancelled, NYBCL § 517(a)(5) is inapplicable to permit restoration of earned surplus, and the resulting reduction of capital stock is merely a reclassification which must create a surplus, and NYBCL § 517(a)(3) makes clear that it must be capital surplus.

The entry would be:

    (11) Capital Stock $1,000

          Capital Surplus $1,000

4. ACQUISITION OF TREASURY STOCK ABOVE OR BELOW PAR

Our discussion so far has assumed that the shares have been purchased and resold at a price equal to par (or stated) value. This assumption is, of course, unrealistic. When shares are reacquired at other prices, the accountant's and lawyer's decisions are more complicated.

Assume that ten shares of $100 par value were issued by the corporation for $110 each, a total of $1,100, thus creating a capital surplus of $100. Now they are reacquired by the corporation for $120 each, a total of $1,200.

APB Op. No. 6, ¶ 12, distinguishes between two different factual situations which may exist when a corporation purchases its own shares:

(a) The corporation may have no present intention to contract its net assets by the purchase of the shares. This includes the situation where the directors have not decided what their intentions are.

(b) The corporation may have the intent to permanently contract its net assets by the purchase of the shares.

We shall first consider the case where there is no present intent to contract net assets. In this case it is instructive to work out the entries for all of the methods.

(A) Direct Capital Reduction Method

In earlier days, when the par or stated value of Treasury Stock was deducted from Capital Stock on the balance sheet, the accountant separated the par and cost in excess of par on acquisition.

    (12) Treasury Stock (at par) $1,000

          Capital Surplus   100

          Earned Surplus   100

          Cash $1,200

(B) Surplus Restriction Method

MBCA § 6 (and hence ¶ 13 of *APB Op. No. 6*) would require the following treatment, unless the articles of incorporation or the holders of a majority of shares entitled to vote thereon permitted $100 of entry (14) to go against the related Capital Surplus.

    (13) Treasury Stock (at cost) $1,200

          Cash $1,200

    (14) Earned Surplus   1,200

          Restricted Earned Surplus   1,200

These entries are identical with entries (2) and (3) except for the amounts.

(C) Direct Surplus Reduction Method

NYBCL § 513(a) would require this entry:

(15) Earned Surplus	$1,100	
Capital Surplus	100	
Cash		$1,200

Note that like entry (4), this charges the entire amount as a *reduction* of Earned Surplus, except to the extent that Capital Surplus is available for the purpose. While § 513(a) does not seem to restrict surplus by sources, *APB Op. No. 6,* ¶ 12, restricts the amount of Capital Surplus that is available for this use.

The three different methods would result in the Stockholders' Equity section of the balance sheet appearing as follows (assuming initial Capital Stock issued and outstanding of $10,000, Earned Surplus of $5,000, and Capital Surplus of $1,000).

	Direct Capital Reduction Method	Surplus Restriction Method (MBCA)	Direct Surplus Reduction Method (NYBCL)
Stockholders' Equity			
Capital Stock	$10,000	$10,000	$10,000
Less Treasury Stock	(1,000)	——	——
Capital Stock Outstanding	$ 9,000	$10,000	$10,000
Capital Surplus	900	1,000	900
Earned Surplus			3,900
Restricted		1,200	
Unrestricted	4,900	3,800	
		$16,000	
Less Treasury Stock		(1,200)	
Total Stockholders' Equity	$14,800	$14,800	$14,800

Where a corporation purchases treasury stock and proceeds to formally retire it, *APB Op. No. 6,* ¶ 12, authorizes use of the direct capital reduction method—i.e., the Capital Stock account and Capital Surplus should be diminished to the extent they are attributable to the shares repurchased, and any remaining excess of cost over par should be charged to Earned Surplus. See entry (12), which would be followed by entry (8), thus closing out the Treasury Stock contra account against the Capital Stock account. The APB Opinion seems to authorize the same treatment if at the time of repurchase the corporation has a present intention not to reissue the stock (which is presumably what the APB Opinion means by "constructive retirement").

5. RESALE OF TREASURY STOCK ACQUIRED ABOVE OR BELOW PAR

We have already considered under Caption 2 the journal entries where treasury stock acquired at par was resold at par.

Assume that our ten shares (par value $100 each) which were purchased for $1,200 are resold as follows:

Case 1: at $1,000 (i.e., at par)

Case 2: at $1,500

Case 3: at $200

The entries under the surplus restriction method would be:

Case 1:

(16)	Earned Surplus	$ 200	
	Cash	1,000	
	Treasury Stock		$1,200
(17)	Restricted Earned Surplus	1,200	
	Earned Surplus (to reverse entry 14)		1,200

Case 2:

(18)	Cash	1,500	
	Treasury Stock		1,200
	Capital Surplus Contributed in Excess of Cost of Treasury Stock		300
(19)	Restricted Earned Surplus	1,200	
	Earned Surplus		1,200

Case 3:

(20)	Earned Surplus	1,000	
	Cash	200	
	Treasury Stock		1,200
(21)	Restricted Earned Surplus	1,200	
	Earned Surplus		1,200

Notice that in Cases 1 and 3 the restriction on Earned Surplus is not fully lifted, but is in effect made permanent in part by the new debits to Earned Surplus.

One generalization may be obtained from all these entries: earned surplus was never increased as a result of purchase and sale of treasury stock on any method. This is in keeping with the principle that transactions in shares give rise to no income to the corporation.

But modern corporation laws (MBCA and NYBCL) do permit, upon resale, the restoration of earned surplus restricted or reduced on the purchase of the treasury stock.

F. REDEMPTION OF PREFERRED STOCKS

Although all of the foregoing discussion of Treasury Stock contemplates a statute under which a corporation may acquire its own stock only out of some kind of surplus, such statutes all make special provision for the retirement of redeemable shares out of the capital represented thereby. MBCA § 6; NYBCL § 513(c); Del.C.L. § 160. (Of course the Revised MBCA does not require such a special provision.) Since redeemable shares always have some kind of preferential right against common stock, these provisions do not involve the destruction of a cushion which senior stockholders or common stockholders could have expected. Yet it is obvious that the statutes make it totally unsound for creditors or senior preferred stocks to rely on the net worth represented by redeemable shares unless they freeze this net worth by contract (infra sub-part K).

G. WASTING ASSET COMPANIES

In the leading case of Wittenberg v. Federal Mining and Smelting Co., 15 Del.Ch. 147, 133 A. 48 (1926), affirmed 15 Del.Ch. 409, 138 A. 347, 55 A.L.R. 1 (1927), the courts of Delaware refused to hold that a mining company or other "wasting asset" company could ignore the depletion of its properties in determining the legality of dividends, when there was a preferred stock entitled to protection whose owners had brought suit to enjoin dividends on the common stock. The courts invited legislative correction of the situation and the Delaware legislature promptly responded. Other states have similar provisions for wasting assets corporations. See W.L. Cary, *Corporations*, 1548 et seq. (4th ed. unabridged, 1969). Cary covers the large number of these statutes, the variety of their provisions, and difficulties in construction.

Old MBCA § 45(b) authorizes companies engaged in exploiting natural resources to pay dividends out of depletion reserves if the articles of incorporation so provide, but each such dividend shall be identified as to its source. This option is not permitted by Revised MBCA § 6.40. NYBCL § 510(b) provides that a corporation engaged in the exploitation of natural resources or other wasting assets, including patents, may pay dividends in excess of its surplus after taking account of depletion and amortization, to the extent that the cost of the wasting asset has been recovered by depletion reserves, amortization or sale, if the remaining net assets cover the liquidation preferences of shares having such preferences in involuntary liquidation. Del.C.L. § 170(b) provides that corporations engaged in the exploitation of natural resources or other wasting assets, including patents, may determine net profits derived from the exploitation of such assets without taking into consideration depletion.

Problem

8–5. Problem. What is the relationship between the worth of the assets and the capital stock when the company reaches final liquidation, if all earnings reported without any provision for depletion have been distributed in dividends? What would be the company's financial condition if half the original cost of the mine had been financed by debt?

H. REDUCTION OF CAPITAL IN ORDER TO PAY DIVIDENDS

Suppose that a corporation not having the benefits of the Revised MBCA has no surplus available for use for dividend purposes or for purchase of its own capital stock. Can it create such surplus by reducing its capital? The answer is, "Yes." Charter amendment or other action can reduce the par or stated capital of the capital stock. Old MCBA §§ 58, 69; NYBCL §§ 516, 802; Del.C.L. §§ 242, 244. See Note, *Capital Stock Reduction as Affecting the Rights of Creditors,* 47 Harv.L.Rev. 693 (1934); Comment, *Writing Down Fixed Assets and Stated Capital,* 44 Yale L.J. 1025 (1935).

In fact, where there is a stated capital, it may be reduced by action of the board of directors without even stockholder vote under some circumstances. NYBCL § 516; Del.C.L. § 244; D.R. Herwitz, *Business Planning* 350 et seq. (1966). If the corporation has already purchased its shares and thus restricted or applied surplus, it can free up or restore surplus by retiring the treasury shares so purchased.[pp]

We have already seen that Delaware does not distinguish between capital surplus and earned surplus for dividend or stock purchase purposes; and that both the MBCA and the NYBCL permit the use of capital surplus for dividend purposes, so long as the fact is disclosed.

We have also noted that creditors seem to have almost no protection against reduction of capital except for some older statutes no longer in force which seemed to say that capital could not be reduced without paying off all debt. Such statutes were obviously so restrictive that they could not survive.

What is the position of preferred stockholders if the capital applicable to common stock is reduced? It was held in Matter of Kinney, 279 N.Y. 423, 18 N.E.2d 645 (1939), that a change reducing the stated capital attributable to the common stock fell within a New York statute entitling preferred stockholders to receive the appraised value of their shares because it altered a "preferential" right. This reasoning would likewise under many statutes entitle the preferred stockholders to a class vote on the question. This subject is now dealt with by NYBCL § 806(b)(6)(A). These voting rights are touched off only by a charter amendment; and yet common stock capital may be reduced under some circumstances, especially when it is represented by the stated value of no-par stock, simply by board of directors' action without a stockholder vote or charter amendment. NYBCL § 516; Del.C.L. § 244.

I.   QUASI–REORGANIZATION

Again assuming the Revised MBCA is not applicable, suppose that it is desired to have earned surplus available for dividend purposes or other purposes and not merely a capital surplus arising from reduction

---

pp. But an interesting question exists whether the retirement of treasury shares recreates the earned surplus which was restricted or applied, or whether it creates capital surplus. Some of the statutes are clear to the effect that the reduction of capital creates a reduction surplus which is capital surplus. MBCA § 70; NYBCL § 517(a)(3). Whether this is consistent with the provisions of MBCA § 6 and NYBCL § 517(a)(5) to the effect that earned surplus may be restored *pro tanto* on resale of treasury stock is discussed supra p. 418.

in capital? May capital surplus be used to cure an earned surplus deficit, so that subsequent earnings will build earned surplus? See *ARB No. 43, Chapter 1A,* ¶ 2 (1953). It suggests that while capital surplus may not be used to protect the income account against proper charges, it might be used to eliminate an earned surplus deficit which would otherwise have to be made up out of income, if the change accomplishes the same thing as a reorganization. This is called a "quasi-reorganization".

The SEC had previously worked out its concepts of the circumstances under which a quasi-reorganization was permissible as described below.

SEC, CODIFICATION OF FINANCIAL REPORTING POLICIES § 210
Fed.Sec.L.Rep. (CCH) ¶ 73,025, p. 62,706.

"Inquiry has been made from time to time as to the conditions under which a quasi-reorganization has come to be applied in accounting to the corporate procedures in the course of which a company, without the creation of new corporate entity and without the intervention of formal court proceedings, is enabled to eliminate a deficit whether resulting from operations or the recognition of other losses or both and to establish a new earned surplus account for the accumulation of earnings subsequent to the date selected as the effective date of the quasi-reorganization.

"It has been the Commission's view for some time that a quasi-reorganization may not be considered to have been effected unless at least all of the following conditions exist:

(1) Earned surplus, as of the date selected, is exhausted;

(2) Upon consummation of the quasi-reorganization, no deficit exists in any surplus account;

(3) The entire procedure is made known to all persons entitled to vote on matters of general corporate policy and the appropriate consents to the particular transactions are obtained in advance in accordance with the applicable law and charter provisions;

(4) The procedure accomplishes, with respect to the accounts, substantially what might be accomplished in a reorganization by legal proceedings—namely, the restatement of assets in terms of present conditions as well as appropriate modifications of capital and capital surplus, in order to obviate so far as possible the necessity of future reorganizations of like nature.

"It is implicit in such a procedure that reductions in the carrying value of assets at the effective date may not be made beyond a point which gives appropriate recognition to conditions which appear to have resulted in relatively permanent reductions in asset values; as for example, complete or partial obsolescence, lessened utility value, reduction in investment value due to changed economic conditions, or, in the case of current assets, declines in indicated realization value. It is also implicit in a procedure of this kind that it is not to be employed recurrently but only under circumstances which would justify an actual reorganization or formation of a new corporation, particularly if the sole or principal purpose of the quasi-reorganization is the elimination of a deficit in earned surplus resulting from operating losses.

"In the case of the quasi-reorganization of a parent company, it is an implicit result of such procedure that the effective date should be recognized as having the significance of a date of acquisition of control of subsidiaries. Likewise, in consolidated statements, earned surplus of subsidiaries at the effective date should be excluded from earned surplus on the consolidated balance sheet."

Following the SEC's activism in this matter, the accountants followed suit with *ARB No. 43, Chapter 7A* (1953), modified by *ARB No. 46* (1956). These pronouncements go on the theory that when a company has reached the state of financial difficulty in which a complete reestablishment of its accounting records might occur in a judicial reorganization, it may be appropriate to accomplish the same accounting readjustment without a judicial reorganization—i.e., by a quasi-reorganization. The concept contemplates that a deficit in earned surplus may be eliminated against capital surplus either existing or created by capital reduction; but that in connection therewith, the assets should be restated at sound values, recognizing the unrealized losses which led to the need for reorganization.

Some have urged that Chapter 7A of *ARB No. 43* should be construed to authorize a general revaluation resulting in a net write-up of assets and, consequently, an increase in net worth resulting solely from the revaluation. That position is contrary to the language of Chapter 7A, and to a fairly rigid policy of the SEC. Paragraph 3 of Chapter 7A, in outlining certain procedures to be followed in a quasi-reorganization speaks of a corporation which elects a quasi reorganization and thus seeks "to relieve its future income account or earned surplus account of *charges* which would otherwise be made thereagainst * * *" (Emphasis added.) Paragraph 6 speaks of "the amounts to be *written off*" and of charges "*against* earned surplus" and "*against* capital surplus." (Emphasis added in each quote.) Finally, Paragraph 12 concludes with this sentence: "In this statement the committee has dealt only with that type of readjustment in which either the current income or earned surplus account or the income account of future years is *relieved of charges* which would otherwise be made thereagainst." (Emphasis added.) There is simply no basis in Chapter 7A of *ARB No. 43* to justify a net write-up of assets.

However, net write-ups have been permitted in a very few cases where there has been a sufficient change of ownership of a deficit-ridden company to an identifiable cohesive group of new stockholders having a common interest to permit the company to invoke *APB Op.*

No. 16 accounting on the theory that there has been a "purchase" of the company. An example would be a company coming out of bankruptcy with an age-old and unrealistically low LIFO inventory basis and near-fully depreciated plant and equipment, where new common shares constituting a majority of the outstanding common stock are issued to unaffiliated creditors. See the Form 10–K Annual Report of Continental Steel Corporation for the year ended December 31, 1982.

With the very limited exceptions of this type, SEC policy consistently has been to permit in quasi-reorganizations only the write-ups which do not exceed the total of write-downs, so that there cannot remain any net increase in assets or net worth. The apparent theory of this policy is the rejection of appraisals as a basis for asset write-ups. This policy of the SEC has tended to reinforce the somewhat obliquely stated accounting principle prescribed in Chapter 7A of *ARB No. 43*.

Several state laws contain special provisions in the definition of earned surplus designed to accommodate the concept of quasi-reorganization. MBCA §§ 2(*l*), 70; NYBCL § 517(a)(1) and (4). The New York statute has a special provision for disclosure to stockholders.

The usual pattern of quasi-reorganizations in recent years appears to involve a company with a substantial deficit resulting from several years of operating losses which has turned the corner and is now profitable. Frequently there has been a divesture of the unprofitable business and entry into a new line of business. Sometimes there has been a change in management or ownership. The purposes appear to be (a) to be able to pay dividends out of earned surplus and (b) to present to the marketplace a balance sheet no longer ailing from the substantial losses of the past. The earned surplus is required to be "dated" for a period of ten years from the date of the quasi-reorganization to put the reader on notice that such a restatement did occur.

Also, usually, the only accounting entry in the quasi-reorganization is to wipe out the accumulated operating deficit against contributed capital. The reason for not revaluing assets is that the over-valued assets have been consumed or sold off and management of the company is able to state that in its opinion no revaluation would be appropriate. Note that, since the advent of imputed interest and *APB Op. No. 21*, it is now necessary to revalue liabilities as well as assets where revaluation takes place.

There is also a question, nowadays, as to the accounting propriety of using a quasi-reorganization to indirectly charge to contributed capital a decline in value of operating assets subject to future depreciation charges or held for resale solely because of a decline in market or utility value. Such write-downs normally should go to income and be reported as operating losses, bankruptcy reorganizations being a prime exception. Consideration of wiping out an accumulated operating deficit against contributed capital is a separate issue from revaluation of assets.

J. STOCK DIVIDENDS AND SPLITS

1. ACCOUNTING TREATMENT BY THE RECIPIENT

Accounting thinking follows tax thinking in holding that a common stock dividend distributed pro rata to common stockholders is not income to them—it simply gives them more but smaller pieces of the same pie which in the aggregate constitute no increase from prior holdings. Yet many corporations regularly pay small common stock dividends on common stock, and the policy seems to be well-received by stockholders. Why?

For one thing, if the corporation needs increasing stockholders' equity for expanding business, it is obviously better to retain earnings than to distribute them, have stockholders pay a tax thereon, and then have the corporation restore the funds with the expense and burden of some kind of a security flotation.

But some stockholders need regular cash receipts. How does the stock dividend fit into this picture?

Suppose, to take a simple case, that a corporation has outstanding 10,000 shares of common stock of a par value of $100 each, or a total capital of $1,000,000, and (just to simplify our problem) let us assume that it has no surplus. Suppose that Sam Stockholder has 100 of the outstanding shares, which he purchased at $100 each, an investment of $10,000. In the next year of operations the corporation earns $100,000 net after taxes. Now, if the corporation declares the full $100,000 of earnings as a dividend, the dividend will be taxed to the stockholders. If Sam's tax rate is 20%, he will pay $200 in taxes.

If, on the other hand, the corporation declares a dividend of 1,000 shares of common stock, and transfers the entire earned surplus of $100,000 to capital to provide the par value of these shares, the stockholders will each receive a dividend of ten shares on each 100 shares held, and Sam Stockholder will receive ten shares. Sam now has a total of 110 shares, which cost him $10,000, and his tax "basis", instead of $100 per share, is now approximately $90.91 per share. If he sells ten shares for $1,000 his gain will be only $91 and the tax (assuming a 20% rate) will be $18.18.

True, by selling the dividend the stockholder diminishes his proportionate ownership of the corporation, but in the normal case of the small stockholder in a corporation with millions of shares, the proportions involved are too small to be significant anyway.

Notes

8–6. *Stock Dividends of a Different Class.* Does this reasoning apply equally to a stock dividend of a different class, e.g., a preferred stock dividend to common stockholders? If there was nothing but common stock outstanding before the dividend, the stockholders have gotten nothing that

Fiflis, Acctg. 4th Ed. ACB—16

they did not have before, but they have it in a different form which would facilitate cashing in on it and then owning a smaller percentage of a corporation that is larger by the earnings it has retained. Accordingly, federal tax law has elaborate provisions to the effect that preferred stock which was issued as a dividend on common stock becomes taxable, usually at ordinary rates, if it is sold. See IRC § 306. Such stock is known as § 306 stock. Further study of this very troublesome and intricate problem, which shows up in numerous corporate sales and reorganizations, is beyond the scope of this book.

8–7. *Stock Dividends—Principal or Income.* There is one other principal problem relating to a stock dividend in the hands of the recipient. That is the case where the corporation for some special reason capitalizes a large amount of accumulated earned surplus by a large stock dividend. We then have a problem (which also exists in the case of special large cash dividends) in the law of trusts and estates. In that field the general principle is that where there is a life tenant (or other temporary holder) and remaindermen, income goes to the life tenant and principal is preserved for the benefit of the remaindermen. What is the nature of a dividend paid to the life tenant, either in stock or in cash, which utilizes a large amount of earned surplus built up over many years, even before the creation of the trust? This problem is beyond the scope of this book. Although the problem is frequently stated as one of trust "accounting" and therefore sometimes finds its way into books on accounting for lawyers, the author believes that the problem is not one of accounting at all, but one of trust law and the use of the term "accounting" is a mere coincidence.

2. ACCOUNTING TREATMENT BY THE ISSUER

When a corporation issues new shares pro rata to its existing shareholders, without requiring payment by them, it must credit capital stock account with the par or stated value of the shares issued and debit some capital surplus or earned surplus account in a like sum.

Typically, the dividend will be out of earned surplus and the entry will at least be:

Earned Surplus	$X	
Capital Stock		$X

where X equals the par or stated value of the issued shares.

The further question is whether additional debits and credits should be made capitalizing earned surplus; i.e., debiting additional earned surplus and crediting capital surplus. What circumstances present this problem?

See *ARB No. 43, Chapter 7B,* ¶¶ 10–16, and the dissents. Also note the rules of the stock exchanges quoted in the following.

SEC, CODIFICATION OF FINANCIAL REPORTING POLICIES § 214

Fed.Sec.L.Rep. (CCH) ¶ 73,055, p. 62,712.

"Several instances had come to the attention of the Commission in which registrants made pro rata stock distributions which were misleading. These situations arise particularly when a registrant makes distributions at a time when its retained earnings or its current earnings are substantially less than the fair value of the shares distributed. Under present GAAP, if the ratio of distribution is less than 25 percent of shares of the same class outstanding, the fair value of the shares issued must be transferred from retained earnings to other capital accounts. Failure to make this transfer in connection with a distribution or making a distribution in the absence of retained or current earnings is evidence of a misleading practice. Distributions of over 25 percent (which do not normally call for transfers of fair value) may also lend themselves to such an interpretation if they appear to be part of a program of recurring distributions designed to mislead shareholders.

"It has long been recognized that no income accrues to the shareholder as a result of such stock distributions or dividends, nor is there any change in either the corporate assets or the shareholders' interests therein. However, it is also recognized that many recipients of such stock distributions which are called or otherwise characterized as dividends, consider them to be distributions of corporate earnings equivalent to the fair value of the additional shares received. In recognition of these circumstances, the AICPA has specified in ARB 43, Chapter 7, paragraph 10, that '. . . the corporation should in the public interest account for the transaction by transferring from earned surplus to the category of permanent capitalization (represented by the capital stock and capital surplus accounts) an amount equal to the fair value of the additional shares issued. Unless this is done, the amount of earnings which the shareholder may believe to have been distributed will be left, except to the extent otherwise dictated by legal requirements, in earned surplus subject to possible further similar stock issuances or cash distributions.'

"The Commission also considers that if such stock distributions are not accounted for in this manner, the shareholders may be misled. In a stop order proceeding,* the Commission found that a registration statement was materially misleading because a series of four stock distributions made between 1966 and 1968 '. . . were 'part of a frequent recurrence of issuances of shares' . . . [and] . . . under generally accepted accounting principles they should have been accounted for as stock dividends.'

"If, in addition to failing to account for the distribution properly, the registrant does not have sufficient retained earnings or current income to cover the appropriate transfer to permanent capital, a question immediately arises whether these factors may be part of a manipulative or fraudulent scheme, and as such are proscribed under Rule 10b–5 of the Exchange Act. The Commission has stated in

---

* *Monmouth Capital Corporation*, Securities Act Release No. 5169 (July 14, 1971).

published opinions,** in situations where companies did not have retained or current earnings, that the declaration of a dividend not warranted by the business condition of a company is characteristic of a manipulative scheme.

"The Commission emphasizes that it will deem the types of transactions noted above to be misleading if the accounting is improper or disclosure is inadequate, and if there is a question of whether the condition of the business warrants the distribution, a further investigation will be considered to determine whether such distribution may be part of a manipulative or fraudulent scheme."

———

The corporation laws do not go as far as the accounting and regulatory authorities cited in their requirement for capitalization of surplus in connection with dividends. Old MBCA § 45(d) requires a capitalization of surplus only equal to par or stated value. The Revised MBCA requires nothing. A split-up without any increase in the stated capital of the corporation is authorized by old MBCA § 45(e) without any transfer of surplus. Old MBCA § 46 refers to distributions from capital surplus, and may authorize the capitalization of capital surplus by stock dividends. NYBCL § 511(a) authorizes stock dividends and requires only the transfer from surplus of an amount equal to par or stated value. Del.C.L. § 173 authorizes stock dividends, without any consideration of the capitalization problems.

Questions

8–8. **Question.** Assume that a 10% stock dividend is declared by X Corp., a publicly held company. Further assume the following facts:

	Company	Per Share
Issued and outstanding prior to stock dividend	100,000 shares	$10 par value each
Earned surplus	$500,000	$5 per share
Book value before the stock dividend		$15 per share
Fair market value before the stock dividend		$20 per share

The appropriate entry on issuance of the shares would be, according to *ARB No. 43, Chapter 7B:*

Earned Surplus	$200,000	
Capital Stock		$100,000
Capital Surplus		100,000

(a) What would be the entry if X Corp. was a closely held corporation?

** *Gob Shops of America, Inc.*, 39 S.E.C. 92 (1959); *Mac Robbins & Co., Inc.*, 41 S.E.C. 116 (1962).

(b) What would be the entry if the distribution consisted of 50,000 shares?

What is the book value per share after the stock dividend? What is the earned surplus per share after the stock dividend? What is the combined surplus per share after the stock dividend?

8–9. *Question.* Do you agree with the following? "The market-price formula has no logical basis * * *. The market value per share at any time represents the current appraisal in the financial market of the *entire* equity per share, including both capital and retained earnings. Accordingly, there is no rhyme or reason in a proposal to use the market value of *both* sections as a unit of measure in effecting a transfer from *one* section to the other." W.A. Paton and W.A. Paton, Jr., *Corporation Accounts and Statements* 125 (1955).

8–10. *Question.* Suppose a company built up an enviable earned surplus making buggy whips up to 1920, but since then has been looking for a business in which it could compete, has paid no dividends, and has managed to cover its overhead and break even from interest on its idle cash. It comes under the control of one of our modern market operators who decides to give the stock a whirl in legal fashion and begins to pay handsome stock dividends, capitalizing the ancient earned surplus. Is there anything in *ARB No. 43, Chapter 7B*, to restrict this? The original *ARB No. 11* did provide that no more surplus should be capitalized by a stock dividend than was available from "current income"—i.e., from recent periods from which normal dividends could be expected to come.

Though this possibility for abuse seems to be a significant point, the omission of the above provision of *ARB No. 11* is not mentioned among the changes of substance listed in Appendix B to *ARB No. 43*. Does the failure to impose such a limitation create an opportunity for deception as to the significance of a stock dividend?

Could the same opportunity for deception arise from cash dividends from ancient earned surplus?

8–11. *Question.* Would a corporation want to pay a stock dividend and charge it to capital surplus? Why would it want to call a "dividend" a mere transfer from capital surplus to capital? Such a transfer has been called a "weird performance, and one having no relation whatever to the capitalization of earnings". W.A. Paton and W.A. Paton, Jr., *Corporation Accounts and Statements* 124 (1955).

Does not such a stock dividend present most acutely the danger of deception about which *ARB No. 43, Chapter 7B*, the stock exchanges and the SEC are concerned?

K. CONTRACTUAL LIMITATIONS ON DIVIDENDS

The market substantiates the belief that statutory restrictions on shareholder distributions are largely ineffective to protect creditors' interests. Those creditors who are in a position to require safeguards do not depend on the statutes but instead require various covenants in the debt instruments limiting shareholder distributions, dispositions of assets, and incurrence of additional debt and encumbrances. Thus banks insert such covenants in long-term notes and underwriters insist on them for bonds, debentures and preferred stocks. Here a knowledge of accounting concepts is clearly essential for the lawyer engaged in negotiating and drafting the terms of these documents.

A bank note or trust indenture typically will restrict the borrower in disposing of assets, incurring secured and unsecured debt [qq] and, further, often will contain restrictions on disbributions, although many of the very largest borrowers will not have such covenants imposed on them. As a rule, the smaller the company, the greater the restrictions relative to the amount of future earnings.

Here we shall examine only this type of covenant—the restriction on distributions—so as to compare it with the statutory limitations already described.

According to the American Bar Foundation's Commentaries on Debentures, 410–11 (1971), "the covenant restricting distributions to shareholders is generally expressed in terms of limiting such distributions to an amount comprised of three items *   *   * first, all or part of the accumulated net earnings of the borrower after the peg date [usually the beginning of the fiscal year in which the debt is issued] until the time of the declaration or payment, taken as one accounting period; second, the proceeds from the issuance or sale of stock after the peg date; and third, an additional dollar amount which in effect allows the borrower the flexibility of making distributions to shareholders out of a portion of the net earnings previously accumulated and existing as earned surplus at the peg date. The third item, permitting the use of a specified amount of existing earned surplus, is sometimes referred to as the "dip".

A sample covenant, together with definitions of certain terms is reproduced below from the Bar Foundation Commentaries.

§ 10–12. Limitations on Dividends and Other Stock Payments.

The Company will not declare any dividends on any class of its stock or make any payment on account of, or set apart money for a sinking or other analogous fund for, the purchase, redemption or other retirement of any shares of such stock, or make any distribution in respect thereof, either directly or indirectly, and whether in cash or property or in obligations of the Company (such dividends, payments and distributions being herein called "*Stock Payments*"), unless such dividends are declared to be payable not more than 60 days after the date of declaration, and unless, after giving effect to such proposed Stock Payment, all of the conditions set forth in the following *Subsections A to D,* inclusive, shall exist at the date of such declaration (in the case of a dividend) or at the date of such setting apart in the case of any

qq. For samples and explanations of the various restrictive covenants found in indentures, see Am. Bar Foundation, Commentaries on Indentures, Art. Ten (1971).

such fund, or the date of such other payment or distribution in the case of any other Stock Payment (each such date being herein called a *"Computation Date"*):

A.　no Event of Default has occurred which has not been cured.

B.　the sum of

(1) $ [the dip];

(2) plus (or minus in the case of a deficit) the Consolidated Net Income of the Company and its Consolidated Subsidiaries computed for the period beginning [the peg date] to and including the Computation Date;

(3) plus the aggregate amount of all contributions to capital (including the fair value of property other than cash) received by the Company during such period;

(4) plus the aggregate net proceeds (including the fair value of property other than cash) received by the Company from the issue or sale of any class of its stock during such period;

shall be greater than all Stock Payments declared (in the case of dividends) or set apart (in the case of any such fund) or made (in the case of any other Stock Payment) during such period.

C.　the Consolidated Working Capital [Consolidated Net Tangible Assets] [Consolidated Tangible Net Worth] of the Company and its Consolidated Subsidiaries shall be at least $_____.

D.　after deducting from both Consolidated Current Assets and Consolidated Current Liabilities of the Company and its Consolidated Subsidiaries an amount equal to the aggregate amount included in Consolidated Current Liabilities

(1) as provision for taxes (to the extent not then due, or if due, payable without penalty) measured by income or profits or by salaries or wages, and

(2) as liabilities to the federal or any state government, or to any subdivision or agency of any thereof, on account of amounts withheld or collected from salaries or wages of persons in its employ under any income tax law or any social security law applicable to such persons, or on account of amounts withheld or collected from employees for the purpose of purchasing obligations of the federal government,

the remaining Consolidated Current Assets of the Company and its Consolidated Subsidiaries shall be at least _____% of the remaining Consolidated Current Liabilities of the Company and its Consolidated Subsidiaries.

Provided, however, that this Section shall not apply to, and the term "Stock Payment" shall not include, dividends payable solely in any class of stock of the Company, or the purchase, redemption or other retirement of any stock of any class of the Company by exchange for, or out of the proceeds of the substantially concurrent sale of, shares of any other class of stock of the Company, or the application to the redemption, purchase or other retirement of any such stock of any moneys previously and properly set apart for and then held in a sinking or other analogous fund established for such stock.

For the purposes of this Section, the amount of any Stock Payment declared or paid or distributed in property of the Company shall be deemed to be the book value of such property (after deducting related reserves for depreciation, depletion and amortization) at the Computation Date, and the amount of any Stock Payment declared or paid or distributed in obligations of the Company shall be deemed to be the value of such obligations as of the date of the adoption of the Board Resolution authorizing such Stock Payment, as determined by such Board Resolution. The fair value of any obligations of the Company received by the Company as a contribution to capital or as the consideration for the issuance of stock of the Company (whether upon conversion of such obligations or otherwise) shall be the principal amount of such obligations.

Without regard to the foregoing restrictions of this Section, the Company may pay regular dividends upon shares of the _____ Preferred Stock of the Company outstanding on _____, and may set apart money and apply the same to the purchase or redemption of shares of said Preferred Stock through the operation of the sinking fund provided for by the Company's Certificate of Incorporation as in effect on _____, but all amounts so paid, set apart and/or applied shall be included in all subsequent computations of Stock Payments for the purposes of this Section.

The Company will not permit any Subsidiary to purchase any stock of any class of the Company.

"Net Income" of [the Company] for any period means the net income (or the net deficit, if expenses and charges exceed revenues and other proper income credits) * * * for such period, determined in the following manner:

(1) The gross revenues and other proper income credits * * * shall be computed for such period in accordance with generally accepted accounting principles, *provided, however,* that in any event there shall not be included in such gross revenues and income credits any of the following items: (i) any proceeds of any life insurance policy; (ii) any gain arising from any sale, exchange or other disposition of capital assets, or from the acquisition or retirement or sale of securities of [the Company] or any of its Subsidiaries in excess of an aggregate amount of $_____ for any period of twelve months; or (iii) any restoration to income of any contingency reserve, except to the extent of amounts restored to income to offset losses or charges against income arising out of the contingency for which such reserve was established, or except to

the extent that provision for such contingency reserve was made out of income accrued subsequent to _____, 19__.

(2) From the amount of such gross revenues and other proper income credits for such period determined as provided in the preceding subparagraph (1), there shall be deducted an amount equal to the aggregate of all expenses and other proper income charges (exclusive of losses from the sale, exchange, abandonment or other disposition of capital assets in excess of an aggregate amount of $_____ for any period of twelve months) for such period, determined in accordance with generally accepted accounting principles but in any event including, without limitation, the following items: (i) all interest and rental charges; (ii) amortization of debt discount and expense and amortization of all other deferred charges properly subject to amortization; (iii) provision for all taxes in respect of property and in respect of income, excess profits or otherwise and additions to reserves therefor (including reserves for deferred income taxes), other than taxes or tax credits upon any gain or loss arising from any sale of capital assets or from the acquisition, retirement or sale of any securities of such corporation which is not included for the purpose of determining "Net Income" as provided in this definition; (iv) provision for all contingency reserves, whether general or special; and (v) provision for depreciation, depletion, obsolescence or amortization (including depreciation and amortization of leasehold improvements), in amounts in the aggregate not less than those actually deducted on the books of such corporation and, if not yet actually deducted on such books, then at not less than the rates and not less than the amounts which would be deducted in accordance with the practice last employed.

"Consolidated Net Income" of the [Company] means the aggregate of the Net Income of the Company and its Consolidated Subsidiaries after eliminating all intercompany items and portions of earnings properly attributable to minority interests, if any, in stocks of the Consolidated Subsidiaries, all computed in accordance with generally accepted accounting principles [*provided, however,* that the Net Income of any Person accrued prior to the date such Person either becomes a Consolidated Subsidiary of [the Company] or is consolidated with or merged into [it] shall be excluded, and *provided, further,* that the Net Income of any Person (other than a Consolidated Subsidiary) in which [the Company] or one or more of its Consolidated Subsidiaries has an ownership interest shall be included only to the extent that such Net Income of such Person shall have been actually received by [the Company] or such Consolidated Subsidiary in the form of dividends or similar distributions].

———

Notice that creditors who are able to protect their interests not only restrict distributions but also limit, in other covenants, asset dispositions and changes in indebtedness and in encumbrances. And in the limitations on distributions, instead of tying the limitations to the concept of legal capital—the arbitrary number subject to the control of directors and shareholders—creditors tie the limitations to earnings of the debtor and tailor the terms to their particular concerns. For example, stock dividends are not limited by the covenant because they do not result in a real distribution of assets but only in a new set of paper held by shareholders. Also, note that consolidated accounts are controlled and that subsidiaries' purchases of the parent's shares are specifically prohibited. (In the covenants regulating additional debt or encumbrances, subsidiaries are also specifically regulated since any debt of a subsidiary may take priority over even secured debt of the parent. And in the sample above, in the definition of consolidated net income is an illustration of the ability of creditors to satisfy peculiar concerns for the particular case; there, income accruing to a merged company prior to the merger is excluded from net income, contrary to GAAP for a "pooling of interests." This is not a typical provision but it shows that each covenant is subject to negotiation.)

One more word, of special concern for this course is in order. As put by Dean Manning, in his book on *Legal Capital*, at 106:

> The whole formula restricting shareholder distributions is based fundamentally on the earnings rate of the borrowing enterprise. The definition of "net earnings of the Company" is thus absolutely critical to its administration and the draftsmen of the indenture have consequently elaborated it in considerable detail. Even so, a careful reading of the definition will reveal that it contains many terms and references that are themselves hardly self-executing and that could in turn have been further refined in the covenant. The question of where the lawyer should stop in the process of specification in the document is a matter for negotiating and drafting judgment in each situation, line-by-line and term-by-term; there are no automatic stopping places; and no matter where one stops, the provision will contain open ended unresolved questions, breeding pools for later dispute.

Notes on the Effect of Changing GAAP on Contracts Implicating GAAP

The effect of changes in accounting principles on existing contracts, especially long-term debt and preferred stock, may be cataclysmic. The person who drafts the terms of the debt or stock may ignore the issue as the above example does, or may provide for the problem by incorporating GAAP at the effective date (or from time to time) or by spelling out the accounting to be used. But anticipating every accounting change which could arise would be impossible. And if GAAP at any particular date are contractually frozen, multiple accounting records would be required to observe the contract. One could envision some nightmarish record-keeping problems.

This concern has often caused lawyers, usually speaking through a Committee of the American Bar Association's Section of Corporation, Banking and Business Law, to oppose changes by the FASB and its predecessors.

James H. Fogelson, a prominent and thoughtful corporate lawyer, described some of the difficulties in the following article.

FOGELSON, THE IMPACT OF CHANGES IN ACCOUNTING PRINCIPLES ON RESTRICTIVE COVENANTS IN CREDIT AGREEMENTS AND INDENTURES

33 Bus.Law. 769 (1978).*

"I. INTRODUCTION

"The typical institutional or public debt agreement contains numerous financial covenants designed to protect the loan and assure repayment. An institutional loan agreement may require the borrower to maintain a specified excess of current assets over current liabilities, a specified current ratio and a specified amount of net tangible assets ('NTA'). In addition, the borrower may be prohibited from incurring (or permitting to have outstanding) current or funded indebtedness in excess of a specified percentage of NTA. The borrower may also be prohibited from incurring lease liabilities in excess of a specified percentage of NTA and may be permitted to pay dividends or repurchase its securities only out of net income earned subsequent to a 'peg' date (usually the end of the fiscal year immediately preceding the date of the loan) plus an agreed amount.

"A typical public debt issue will have a dividend restriction tied to net income and may have a senior debt restriction tied to NTA as well as a secured debt and sale and lease back provision tied to NTA.

"NTA, net income, current assets and current and funded indebtedness are normally defined with reference to generally accepted accounting principles ('GAAP').[1] As a result of several significant develop-

1. The typical debt instrument defines NTA to mean all assets appearing on a balance sheet prepared in accordance with GAAP after deducting intangible assets, current liabilities, accumulated depreciation and other similar reserves, write-ups in assets resulting from a revaluation thereof and other negotiated items such as restricted investments in excess of a specified limit, deferred charges and non-current prepaid expenses. "Net Income" is defined as net income determined in accordance with GAAP with occasional reference to specific items of revenue and expense. "Current Assets" are defined to mean current assets determined in accordance with GAAP. "Indebtedness" is typically defined to mean all items which in accordance with GAAP would be included in determining total liabilities as shown on the liability side of a balance sheet, including obligations secured by mortgages (whether or not the obligation has been assumed) and guarantees. "Current Indebtedness" is defined with reference to GAAP but to specifically include liabilities maturing within one year or on demand (excluding revolving credit indebtedness). "Funded Indebtedness" is defined as all indebtedness other than current indebtedness.

ments during the last few years and the likelihood of continued major changes, the effect of a change in an accounting principle on the definitions of accounting terms and therefore on the covenants contained in a debt agreement, and the resulting possible need for amendment has become a matter of real concern, particularly with public debt issues which require a cumbersome process for amendment.

* * *

"Where an enterprise is unable to revise its covenants prior to the effectiveness of a change in a principle, the results can be disastrous. For example, the recently adopted statement relating to accounting for marketable securities required in certain cases a charge to equity and in certain cases a charge to net income in the year the statement became effective. This caused a virtual immediate default by Aristar, Inc. under its loan agreements since it was required to charge net worth by $3,400,000, representing the lower market value of its investments. Note 6 to its Financial Statements for the year ended March 31, 1976, states:

> During the nine months ended March 31, 1976, the Company was in technical default under several of its long-term debt agreements. The default occurred because the Financial Accounting Standards Board adopted on December 27, 1975, a statement of financial accounting standards . . ., which required a reduction of stockholders' equity for unrealized losses on marketable equity securities. This required change in accounting caused stockholders' equity to be reduced below an amount necessary to maintain defined debt ratios in such agreements. The agreements have been amended to allow computation of such ratios without regard to unrealized losses on marketable equity securities.

* * *

"An interesting question raised as a result of SFAS No. 13 is whether capitalized leases should be treated as secured assets and secured debt. If so, there would probably be an impact on covenants limiting secured debt which may be limited to a greater extent than funded indebtedness covenants.

"It is to be noted that leases required to be capitalized under SFAS No. 13 should not be included within a lease covenant, and this point should be made clear in drafting the agreement. In addition, SFAS No. 13 will be helpful to a borrower who is subject to a covenant requiring the maintenance of a specified amount of NTA since, as illustrated above, the leased assets presumably would increase total tangible assets. However, these results are of little solace to a borrower whose leases, which are now balance sheet debt, have put him in default.[19]

---

19. Other recently adopted Statements of Financial Accounting Standards which could impact debt agreements include the following:

SFAS No. 2, "Accounting for Research and Development Costs" (1974), requires an enterprise to expense all research and development costs encompassed by the statement. SFAS No. 2 is effective for fiscal years beginning on or after January 1, 1975, with retroactive application by prior period adjustment so that financial statements for prior periods must be re-

"Where changes in accounting principles cause disruption in loan agreement covenants, institutional lenders have in the past waived defaults and modified the affected covenants to accommodate the new principles. Amendments and waivers of institutional debt agreements are relatively easy to accomplish, since the borrower need only communicate with the lender, or the lead lender of a group of institutional lenders, and negotiate the amendment or waiver.

"On the other hand, it is a more difficult task to amend a public debt instrument since such action requires a meeting of the public debt holders and normally the approval of the holders of two-thirds of the outstanding debt. Consideration also must be given to whether the amendment of a restrictive financial covenant represents the sale of a new security subject to registration under the Securities Act of 1933 (the "1933 Act") in the absence of exemption, such as the recapitalization exemption of section 3(a)(9) of the 1933 Act. Moreover, if a purchase or sale of a security is involved, such transaction would be subject to the antifraud provisions of section 17(a) of the 1933 Act and Section 10(b) of the Securities Exchange Act of 1934 and rule 10b–5 thereunder. The question to be determined is whether the amendment affects the rights of the holders substantially enough so as to give rise to the sale of new security. For example, in *SEC v. Associated Gas & Elec. Co.*,[20] the Second Circuit held that the extension of the maturity

stated to reflect the prior period adjustment.

SFAS No. 5, "Accounting for Contingencies" (1975), requires the accrual of a contingency by a charge to income when it is "probable" (defined to mean "likely to occur") that the contingency has caused an asset to be impaired or a liability to be incurred and the amount of the loss can reasonably be estimated. Even if no accrual is required, the existence of the contingency must be disclosed when there is at least a "reasonable possibility" (defined to mean that the chance of the future event or events occurring is more than remote— such chance is not slight—but less than likely) that a loss may have been incurred. SFAS No. 5 is effective for fiscal years beginning on or after July 1, 1975 with restatement of prior period financial statements where practicable or restatement of as many prior period statements presented as practicable and the cumulative effect of applying SFAS No. 5 on retained earnings at the beginning of the earliest period restated included in determining net income of such period. In a related area, the FASB recently adopted SFAS No. 16, "Prior Period Adjustments" (1977), which generally requires all items of profit and loss to be recognized during the current period, i.e., the period in which the amount of the loss or profit is established. Accruals for estimated losses arising from events occurring in prior periods but the amount of which is not determined until a later period must be charged against income in the later period and may not be treated as an adjustment to income of prior periods. SFAS No. 16 is effective for years beginning on or after October 15, 1977.

SFAS No. 6, "Classification of Short-Term Obligations Expected to be Refinanced" (1975), permits short-term debt obligations intended to be refinanced on a long-term basis to be shown as long-term debt if certain requirements relating to the intention to refinance, the commitment of the lender and the absence of a default are satisfied. This Statement is effective for fiscal years ending on or after December 31, 1975 with prior period reclassification permitted.

SFAS No. 15, "Accounting by Debtors and Creditors for Troubled Debt Restructurings" (1977), prescribes the standards for accounting for asset swaps and renegotiations in connection with debt restructurings. The standard is effective for restructurings occurring after December 31, 1977, with no retroactive application required.

20. 24 F.Supp. 899 (S.D.N.Y.), *aff'd*, 99 F.2d 795 (2d Cir. 1938).

date of an issue of debt constituted the issuance of a security within the meaning of the Public Utility Holding Company Act of 1935.

* * *

"IV.   THE RESPONSE TO CHANGES IN ACCOUNTING PRINCIPLES

"In light of the significant impact changes in accounting principles can have, borrowers would do well to focus on this problem at the time debt is incurred. They should be aware of the matters pending before the FASB and the Commission at the time the debt is incurred and of pronouncements anticipated to become effective after the debt is issued.

* * *

"The Indenture of Macmillan, Inc. in connection with its 1976 public issue of $50,000,000 of 8.85 percent Sinking Fund Debentures, due November 1, 2001, provides in effect that all the restrictions contained therein are to be determined on the basis of GAAP in effect at the time the indenture was executed.

* * *

"Because no one can predict the unknown, to accommodate the problem of possible changes in GAAP which are not under consideration at the time the transaction is negotiated and which therefore are not subject to specific negotiation, borrowers might consider seeking to limit GAAP in a credit agreement to GAAP in effect at the time the debt is incurred. The Macmillan indenture referred to above, which not only provides for changes in GAAP relating to lease accounting but also provides for other possible changes, is an example. The borrower must determine whether to stay with existing GAAP or go with something unknown, although, presumably, given the current climate and experience, any new principles would be more conservative than existing GAAP. It should be noted that such a provision would require the borrower, in effect, to maintain two sets of books. Furthermore, a provision such as that in the Macmillan indenture requires the issuer to maintain an awareness in the future of the accounting principles which were in effect at the time of the transaction.

"In the alternative, a borrower might consider seeking to provide that any change in an accounting principle which would otherwise become effective and which would adversely impact the operation of a restrictive covenant not become effective for purposes of the agreement for a stated period of years, thus deferring any such adverse impact and allowing time for its resolution.

"Failing a specific limitation to existing GAAP (and institutional lenders are frequently reluctant to agree to a provision of such nature) or a provision deferring the application of a change in an accounting principle, consideration should be given to the specific problems which are emerging or are in existence at the time of the loan which can be anticipated in the documentation. Some of these problems may not be capable of treatment and there is really nothing that can be done with respect to them. For example, it is possible that historical cost may be replaced by some form of replacement cost or current value accounting.

Clearly, any change to any other measurement system will have a disruptive effect on covenants but there does not appear to be any logical way to handle this problem—at least until we have some idea as to where we are going. Presumably, if such a drastic change is adopted, appropriate transition rules will be adopted.

"V.   CONCLUSION

"Changes in accounting principles can have an enormous impact on the restrictive covenants contained in credit agreements. In some cases, particularly where a new principle will either become effective shortly after the credit agreement is signed or where the new principal appears to be imminent, borrowers and lenders can negotiate the application of the principle. In other situations, unless a lender is willing to provide generally that the term generally accepted accounting principles is to mean such principles as in effect on the date of the agreement (and the borrower desires treating the problem in this manner), it may be unrealistic to attempt any negotiation since neither party is in a position to know what will happen in the future. Particularly in such cases, the FASB and the Commission must be cognizant of the possible effect of a proposed change on restrictive covenants and consider deferring the effect of the new principle to give enterprises time to accommodate agreements to the new environment. Borrowers, on the other hand, must be alert to proposed changes and new principles and be prepared to argue for deferral of effectiveness and/or retroactivity where necessary.[31]"

William P. Hackney in 1981 proposed a tentative draft clause for discussion by an ABA committee addressing some of these concerns:

Model Provisions
Covering Future Changes in Accounting Principles
for Credit Agreements

[Include in Definitions:]

"GAAP"—Generally accepted accounting principles as such principles shall be in effect at the time of the computation or determination or as of the date of the relevant financial statements, as the case may be (the "Relevant Date"), subject to Section 1.03 hereof.

"Relevant Date"—Defined in the definition of "GAAP".

* * *

1.03. Accounting Principles. (a) Except as otherwise provided in this Agreement, all computations and determinations as to accounting or financial matters and all financial statements to be delivered pursu-

---

31. An example is SFAS No. 15 which applies to debt restructurings. At the time of its proposal, many creditors were concerned that it would be applied retroactively to enormous amounts of renegotiated loans. As adopted, SFAS No. 15 is effec-tive prospectively for periods commencing after December 31, 1977.

An analogous example is SFAS No. 8 relating to foreign currency translation which is being reconsidered by the FASB.

ant to this Agreement shall be made and prepared in accordance with GAAP (including principles of consolidation where appropriate), and all accounting or financial terms shall have the meanings ascribed to such terms by GAAP.

(b) If any change in GAAP after the date of this Agreement shall be required to be applied to transactions then or thereafter in existence, and a violation of one or more provisions of this Agreement shall have occurred or in the opinion of the Borrower would likely occur which would not have occurred or be likely to occur if no change in accounting principles had taken place,

(i) The parties agree that such violation shall not be considered to constitute an Event of Default or a Conditional Default for a period of [specify period] from the date the Borrower notifies the Agent of the application of this subsection 1.03(b);

(ii) The parties agree in such event to negotiate in good faith an amendment of this Agreement which shall approximate to the extent possible the economic effect of the original financial covenants after taking into account such change in GAAP; and

(iii) If the parties are unable to negotiate such an amendment within [specify period], the Borrower shall have the option of (A) prepaying the Loan (pursuant to applicable provisions hereof) or (B) submitting the drafting of such an amendment to a firm of independent certified public accountants of nationally recognized standing acceptable to the parties, which shall complete its draft of such amendment within _____ days of submission. If the Borrower and the Agent cannot agree upon the firm, it shall be selected by binding arbitration in the City of _____, _____ in accordance with the rules then obtaining of the American Arbitration Association. If the Borrower does not exercise either such option within said period, then as used in this Agreement, "GAAP" shall mean generally accepted accounting principles in effect at the Relevant Date. The parties agree that if the Borrower elects the option in clause (B) above, until such firm has been selected and completes drafting such amendment, no such violation shall constitute an Event of Default or a Conditional Default.

(c) If any change in GAAP after the date of this Agreement shall be required to be applied to transactions or conditions then or thereafter in existence, and the Agent shall assert that the effect of such change is or shall likely be to distort materially the effect of any of the definitions of financial terms in Article I hereof or any of the covenants of the Borrower in [Sections _____ hereof] (the "Financial Provisions"), so that the intended economic effect of any of the Financial Provisions will not in fact be accomplished,

(i) The Agent shall notify the Borrower of such assertion, specifying the change in GAAP which is objected to, and until otherwise determined as provided below, the specified change in

GAAP shall not be made by the Borrower in its financial statements for the purpose of applying the Financial Provisions; and

(ii) The parties shall follow the procedures set forth in paragraph (ii) and the first sentence of paragraph (iii) of subsection (b) of this Section. If the parties are unable to agree on an amendment as provided in said paragraph (ii) and if the Borrower does not exercise either option set forth in the first sentence of said paragraph (iii) within the specified period, then as used in this Agreement "GAAP" shall mean generally accepted accounting principles in effect at the Relevant Date, except that the specified change in GAAP which is objected to by the Agent shall not be made in applying the Financial Provisions. The parties agree that if the Borrower elects the option in clause (B) of the first sentence of said paragraph (iii), until such independent firm has been selected and completes drafting such amendment, the specified change in GAAP shall not be made in applying the Financial Provisions.

(d) All expenses of compliance with this Section 1.03 shall be paid for by the Borrower.

*

Part E

MERGERS, ACQUISITIONS
AND INVESTMENTS

Chapter IX

ACCOUNTING FOR MERGERS, ACQUISITIONS AND INVESTMENTS *

OBJECTIVES

1. Comprehend the accounting for acquisitions of businesses and for pooling two or more businesses.

2. Understand consolidation of financial statements of parent and subsidiary entities.

3. Observe "one-line-consolidation," or the "equity method" of accounting for an entity which exercises "significant influence" over another entity.

4. Relate each of these three with the others.

RELEVANCE FOR LAWYERS

Lawyers are involved in virtually all mergers and acquisitions transactions and frequently find that they are required not only to explain the financial effects in disclosure documents but also to negotiate financial terms and often to participate in rendering financial advice to the client. Sophisticated corporate practitioners must have some understanding of the accounting described in this chapter in order to adequately perform their tasks.

* Copyright 1981 by the American Bar Association. All rights reserved. Reprinted with the permission of the American Bar Association and its Section of Corporation, Banking and Business Law.

Most of the essential features of this chapter first appeared in 37 Bus.Law. 89 (1981) and was reprinted in the 1981 Business Law Annual of the National Law Review Reporter. Paul Foster contributed greatly to the original article.

A major change was necessitated by adoption of SFAS No. 94, Consolidation of All Majority-owned Subsidiaries (1987). Original footnote numbers are preserved here.

This chapter is divided into two main parts. In part A, dealing with assets acquisitions, there are two principal categories, acquisitions of isolated assets not a "business" and acquisitions of "businesses" (i.e., "business combinations"). Business combinations are to be treated as "poolings of interests" if the requisite degree of continuity of the rights and risks of their original investments exists for the original owners of both the acquiring company and the acquired company. All other acquisitions are treated as "purchases." In part B, where both companies continue as legal entities, we shall note that if one controls the other, both entities' financial statements will be consolidated, on either the purchase or pooling basis.

Part B also describes the accounting where no control is held by either legal entity over the other. In this case one of three methods of accounting is required, depending on whether certain criteria are met. These methods are:

    (a) The "cost" method;

    (b) A variation thereof, "cost or market;" or

    (c) The "equity" method.

The accounting described in this chapter applies generally whether the entities are corporations, partnerships, trusts or other associations.

A. ACCOUNTING FOR BUSINESS ACQUISITIONS RESULTING IN ONE SURVIVING ENTITY

The simplest situation, and one for which the accounting is familiar to most business lawyers, is that in which an entity acquires substantially all the assets and liabilities of a second business entity, by merger, consolidation or purchase of assets, and remains as the sole survivor in the economic unit—the so-called assets acquisition. The question in this case is: should the acquisition be accounted for as a "purchase," or as a "pooling of interests"?

Before examining these two alternatives, we should make certain that the accounting for purchase of assets not constituting a "business" is clearly in mind.

1. ACCOUNTING FOR THE PURCHASE OF ISOLATED ASSETS NOT A "BUSINESS"

If *A* Corp. were to buy unused raw land from *B* Corp. (carried by *B* Corp. on its books at $35,000) at a price of $20,000 in cash plus assumption of an $80,000 note bearing interest at the current market rate, that purchase would be accounted for in *A*'s journal as follows:

Land	$100,000	
Cash		$20,000
Note Payable		80,000 [9]

---

9. APB St. No. 4, ¶ 145 (1970). If the interest on the note is below the going rate, the assumed liability may be de- creased accordingly. See APB St. No. 4, ¶ 181 M–1C and Discussion (1970). And

The important result to notice here is that the acquired asset is shown at its $100,000 cost to *A*, regardless of the $35,000 book carrying value of the seller, *B*.

Every acquisition must be either the acquisition of a "business" or not. In this case the raw land is clearly not a "business" since it is unused and unimproved. A "business" may be in corporate form, a partnership, sole proprietorship, a trust account, an estate, etc. Thus even the purchase of land could constitute the entire business of operating a parking lot, a ranch, etc. Or a business could be purchased with a view to its liquidation or the disbursal of its assets among the departments of an acquirer, thereby terminating the acquired business in which case it is not an acquisition of a business for accounting purposes.

The accountant must ascertain whether a "business" or a "non-business" will be operated by the acquirer by addressing numerous questions. He or she would focus principally on the economic aspects of the assets and liabilities received, including utilization, management, control benefit, etc. Some of the questions considered would be:

1. Is it a self-sufficient economic entity?

2. Can it be self-sufficient?

3. Is there real economic potential?

4. Does the acquirer intend to operate the consideration received as a business enterprise?

5. Does the acquirer intend to merely use the consideration received to supplement or enhance her existing business enterprise?

6. What changes in operation does the acquirer intend to accomplish?

7. Were any operating personnel concurrently acquired or employed by the acquirer?

8. Does the acquirer intend mere liquidation of the consideration acquired?

There are, of course, many other attributes that would be proper for inclusion in the accountant's thought processes depending upon the circumstance of any particular acquisition.

If several individual assets not constituting a business were to be acquired from *B* for a lump sum in what is often referred to as a "basket purchase," they also would be carried by *A* at their cost to *A*, although a problem would arise concerning allocation of the lump sum among the several items. In this situation GAAP provide that the total price should be allocated among the assets proportionately to their individual fair values. In subsequent income statements, those assets which are depreciable or amortizable will be charged to expense as the assets are used up.[11]

___

see APB Op. No. 21 (1971) (discount or premium in certain cases).

11. APB St. No. 4, ¶ 181 M–1A(2) (1970). To illustrate: If *A* buys three items, with fair values of $300, $400 and $900 respec-

For an income tax case distinguishing purchase of a business from purchase of assets, see Concord Control, Inc. v. Commissioner, 35 T.C.M. 1345 (1976).

2. "PURCHASE" ACCOUNTING FOR AN ASSETS ACQUISITION OF A "BUSINESS"

What should be the method of accounting when, instead of the purchase of isolated assets, control is acquired over a business?

(A) Measurement at Current Cost to Acquiring Company

By our hypothesis, control is acquired by A Corp., B Corp. disappears from the economic entity, and B or B's shareholders receive either A Corp. stock or other property. This will result in a "business combination" which, to accountants, means A Corp.'s acquisition of control, in any form, over the business of B Corp.

Assuming for the moment that the acquisition will be accounted for as a "purchase," this means that the acquired assets will be entered on the acquirer's books at their current cost to it and liabilities will be credited at their current values; i.e., the total purchase price will be allocated among the individual assets and liabilities acquired to the extent of their fair market values. This is one of the two most important consequences of accounting for the combination as a purchase, for it means that, in the usual case, where current cost is higher than the seller's book carrying value, the buyer's future income statements will be charged with greater expenses than the seller's statements would have shown as these assets are depreciated or amortized. The result is that the increment in the buyer's income resulting from the acquisition usually will be less than the seller's income would have been without the combination.

(B) Goodwill Arising on a Purchase

If the combination is to be accounted for as a purchase, there may be a second important impact on accounting income after the combination. When the purchase is of a business rather than of merely isolated assets, the parties typically will have determined a total price not based on values of individual assets but on the going-concern value, which frequently will be in excess of the fair values attributable to the isolated assets net of liabilities. In these circumstances, instead of allocating the full purchase price among only the assets appearing on B's books, accountants recognize that intangible assets, usually called "goodwill," should appear on the books of A Corp.[16]

tively, for an aggregate price of $1,200, the first asset will be entered on A's books at 300/1,600 × $1,200, or $225, the second at 400/1,600 × $1,200, or $300, and the third at 900/1,600 × $1,200, or $675. If the first item is nondepreciable land, it will not affect subsequent income. If the second item is a depreciable desk, its cost less salvage value will be "depreciated" periodically over the term of its useful life by expense charges in some systematic pattern. Intangibles such as a patent will be amortized. See Figure 2, boxes 3 and 4, infra at text following n. 53 for a diagram of these results.

16. APB Op. No. 16, ¶ 68 (1970).

Here again a problem arises concerning allocation of the lump sum purchase price among the acquired assets, including the goodwill, but it is resolved by a two-step process different from the one-step technique described for the basket purchase of a non-business. First the purchase price is allocated among the tangible and identifiable intangible assets (e.g., patents) acquired according to their fair value; then any residue is debited to the new intangible asset account, goodwill.[17]

To illustrate, assume balance sheets in columnar form for corporations A and B prior to A's acquisition of B, as below:

Balance Sheets (000's omitted)

	A Corp.	B Corp.
Assets:		
Cash	$ 50,000	$ 0
Inventory	20,000	10,000
Plant	70,000	15,000
Land		5,000
Totals	$140,000	$30,000
Liabilities and Equity:		
Accounts payable	$ 24,000	$15,000
Equity:		
Capital stock	$ 30,000	$ 6,000
Capital surplus	39,000	4,200
Earned surplus	47,000	4,800
Totals	$140,000	$30,000

Further, assume that A Corp. buys the assets and assumes the liabilities of B for cash paid to B in the amount of $30,000,000 and that no new identifiable assets appear. The form of journal entry for A, omitting all but one of the figures, will be (000's omitted):

Inventory	a	
Plant	b	
Land	c	
Goodwill	d	
Accounts payable		e
Cash		$30,000

---

17. APB Op. No. 16, ¶¶ 68, 87 (1970); APB Op. No. 17, ¶ 26 (1970); APB St. No. 4, ¶ 181 M–1A(3) (1970).

If aggregate fair values of identifiable tangible and intangible assets exceed the purchase price, the value of noncurrent assets (other than marketable securities) to be debited on A's books, is reduced pro rata as necessary. Only after the carrying values of those assets are reduced to zero will an excess of remaining fair value of current assets and marketable securities over the price paid be balanced by a credit sometimes termed "negative goodwill."

APB Op. No. 16, ¶¶ 87, 91 (1970). This negative goodwill, like positive goodwill, will be amortized, but that will result in a credit to revenues, thereby enhancing future income (id. ¶ 91), in contrast to the debit against revenues by amortization expense, required for positive goodwill. [See supra Chapter VI.]

Amortized negative goodwill probably is not taxable income but, by the same token, the asset values above their cost are not depreciable for tax purposes since their tax basis is cost. I.R.C. § 1012. See box in Figure 2 infra, in text following n. 53.

The values, a, b and c, to be attributed to the three identifiable assets will be determined as the fair market value of each. Then the accounts payable will be valued at $15,000,000 if there is no reason to decrease or increase them.[18] Any excess of credits over debits will be balanced by a debit to goodwill. Thus, if the inventory has a fair market value of $12,000,000, plant, $18,000,000, and land, $10,000,000, goodwill will be debited in the amount of $5,000,000, assuming accounts payable are valued at $15,000,000.[20]

On these assumptions the result of accounting for the combination as a "purchase" can be illustrated as follows:

Balance Sheets (000's omitted)

	A Corp.	B Corp.	Fair market value of B's assets and liabilities, and balancing debit to goodwill	Cash paid by A	A Corp. balance sheet after purchase
Assets:					
Cash	$ 50,000	$ 0	$ 0	($30,000)	$ 20,000
Inventory	20,000	10,000	12,000		32,000
Plant	70,000	15,000	18,000		88,000
Land		5,000	10,000		10,000
Goodwill			5,000		5,000
Totals	$140,000	$30,000			$155,000
Liabilities and Equity:					
Accounts Payable	$ 24,000	$15,000	$15,000		$ 39,000
Equity:					
Capital Stock	30,000	6,000			30,000
Capital Surplus	39,000	4,200			39,000
Earned Surplus	47,000	4,800			47,000
Totals	$140,000	$30,000			$155,000

Manifestly, future periods' income for *A* will then be chargeable for the aggregate cost of goods sold in the amount debited to inventory and for depreciation of the fair market value of the former *B* Corp. plant. As we have seen, amortization of the goodwill account is required, over

---

18. See APB Op. No. 16, ¶¶ 72, 89g, h & i (1970), describing when liabilities will be revalued.

20. Throughout this illustration and subsequent illustrations we shall assume no intercorporate dealings had occurred prior to the combination. If there had been intercorporate transactions, our explanation would include additional details. For example, if *B* previously had purchased goods from *A* on credit, *B*'s liabilities would include an account payable to *A* and *A*'s assets would include an account receivable from *B*. On the balance sheet,

the receivable (asset) and liability (payable) would cancel each other and neither would be shown. Similarly if *A*'s income statement for the year of the sale were to be consolidated with *B*'s, the revenue to *A* and cost to *B* should be eliminated with the result that the consolidated income should be less than the sum of the separate incomes of *A* and *B* by the amount of the profit of the sale. These would present merely routine technical accounting problems to eliminate their effects, which we need not consider here.

not more than forty years by periodic charges to expense. Notice that this amortized goodwill has a greater impact on reported net income than do most other expense charges; since amortization of goodwill is not tax deductible,[23] there is no partially offsetting reduction in tax expense on the income statement.

(C) The Concept of Goodwill

Although these mechanics for treating the purchase of a business are settled, at least for the time being,[24] the conceptualization of goodwill is by no means the subject of a consensus. Goodwill means different things to different people. See Chapter VI.

(D) Form of Purchase

Returning to our illustration, and still assuming purchase accounting, even if the consideration given by *A* Corp. is other than cash, the acquired assets and liabilities will be entered on *A* 's books at their cost to *A*, although the consideration paid will be credited to some account other than the cash account.[27] For example, if $10,000,000 par value of *A* 's preferred stock having a current value of $30,000,000, were the consideration in the above illustration, the credit, instead of being to cash account, would be to a capital stock account in the amount of $10,000,000, plus some capital surplus account for $20,000,000, aggregating the net cost of the acquisition. (Of course, the assumption of the $15,000,000 liability is also part of the price paid and will be credited, as well.) The journal entry would be (000's omitted):

23. Treas.Reg. § 1.167(a)(3) (1960) states that Goodwill is not "depreciable" (sic) for federal income tax purposes.

One must further note, however, that if the corporate combination, although accounted for as a purchase, is a tax-free reorganization, the enhanced depreciation and cost of goods sold expense on the financial statements also will not be partially offset by any income tax saving since there is no related tax deduction for these enhanced values.

Although a taxable reorganization will usually be accounted for as a purchase on the financial statements, the criteria for imposing the tax and for purchase accounting are not identical. Hence, a transaction might be tax-free, yet accounted for as a purchase, or taxable, yet accounted for as a pooling of interests. For example, acquisition of another company's subsidiary solely for voting stock is ineligible for pooling (APB Op. No. 16, ¶ 46a (1970)) but would be tax-free under I.R.C. § 368(a)(1)(B); Treas. Reg. § 1.368–2(c) (1976). On the other hand, acquisition for voting stock of ninety percent or more of the voting stock of another corporation plus "boot" for dissenters could be a pooling (See APB Op.

No. 16, ¶ 47b (1970)) but would not be tax-free under I.R.C. § 368(a)(1)(B), although some dissent from this view of the availability of the (B) reorganization when boot is involved has been expressed and some qualifications to the bald proposition may be required. For the refinements, see Note, The "Solely for Voting Stock" Requirement in a (B) Reorganization After Reeves v. Commissioner and Pierson v. United States, 66 Va.L.Rev. 133 (1980); B. Bittker & J. Eustice, Federal Income Taxation of Corporations and Shareholders ¶ 14.13 n. 73 (4th ed. 1979) & 1980 Cum. Supp. n. 3.

For a comparison of the tax and accounting provisions before APB Op. No. 16 (1970), see Gunther, Pooling of Interests and Tax–Free Reorganizations: A Comparison of Philosophy and Operation, 21 Me.L. Rev. 27 (1969).

24. The compromises worked out in APB Op. No. 16 (1970) and No. 17 (1970) have been the subject of continuing debate, resulting in extensive refinement of APB Op. No. 16 (1970).

27. APB Op. No. 16, ¶ 67c (1970).

Inventory	$12,000	
Plant	18,000	
Land	10,000	
Goodwill	5,000	
Accounts payable		$15,000
Capital stock—$10 par preferred stock		10,000
Capital surplus		20,000

This treatment applies to any acquisition by *A* Corp. if it is to be accounted for as a purchase, whether the transaction is a merger, consolidation, or purchase of assets and an assumption of liabilities on the one hand, or, on the other hand, is an acquisition of *B* Corp.'s shares followed by: a statutory merger of *A* and *B;* a liquidating dividend by *B;* or any other set of transactions which would result in *A* holding the assets and liabilities of *B* and *B* disappearing as a separate entity.[28]

3. "POOLING OF INTERESTS" FOR AN ASSETS ACQUISITION OF A BUSINESS

(A) Pooling Accounting

Accounting standards purport to find a fundamental difference between a "purchase" of a business by another entity and a combination whereby the shareholders of the acquired business continue in interest by receiving voting common stock in the surviving entity—a "pooling of interests."[29] "In accounting theory, a 'pooling' is conceptualized as a flowing together of two continuing separate entities, becoming one, with a substantial continuity of ownership, properties and management, whereas a 'purchase' of one by the other is thought of as more closely akin to a termination of one enterprise and the acquisition of its component parts by another."[30] A classic case for "pooling"

---

28. See APB Op. No. 16, ¶ 5 (1970).

Moreover, as we shall see, (text, infra, following n. 55) even if *B* Corp. remains a separate legal entity, its financial statements will be consolidated with those of *A* Corp., and the consolidated financial statements will be identical with those just described.

As will be seen, the accounting entries may be affected by statutory requirements of the governing corporation code. The entries here set forth assume that there are either no such legal provisions, or that if there are, the attorney addressing a particular problem will be able to consider them with the text descriptions as a starting point.

See text at n. 46 et seq. infra.

29. APB Op. No. 16, ¶¶ 8, 42–44 (1970).

30. Hackney, Financial Accounting for Parents and Subsidiaries—A New Approach to Consolidated Statements, 25 U.Pitt.L.Rev. 9, 11 (1963).

CCH, Financial Accounting Standards Board, Accounting Principles Board and Committee on Accounting Procedure Financial Accounting Standards 245 (1977), describes poolings and purchases as follows:

Pooling of Interests Method

The pooling of interests method accounts for a business combination as the uniting of the ownership interests of two or more companies by exchange of equity securities. No acquisition is recognized because the combination is accomplished without disbursing resources of the constituents. Ownership interests continue and the former bases of accounting are retained. The recorded assets and liabilities of the constituents are carried forward to the combined corporation at their recorded

would be the statutory merger of two corporations of similar size with the common shareholders of each holding common stock in similar amounts in the surviving entity.

The accounting for such a pooling of interests is radically different from purchase accounting and rests on the notion that when two entities come together, with the interests in rights and rewards of the owners of each continuing, neither has "acquired" the other and the old basis of accounting for each should continue. This means that the book carrying values of the assets and liabilities of each entity are continued on the books of the new or surviving entity and the earned surpluses of the two are combined.[32] Subsequent income statements, of course, are charged with depreciation and amortization expenses based on the old recorded amounts.[33] Further, accounting for income under pooling is different from purchase accounting in that, irrespective of when the combination occurs during the year, the income of the two entities for the year of the combination is combined on the income statement of the new or surviving entity.[34] Finally, if any prior years' income statements of A are restated, the incomes of A and B will be combined retroactively on those restated income statements although the two entities were independent at that time.[35]

To illustrate, assume the same data for A and B as before,[36] but that this time, instead of A purchasing B's assets for cash and assumption of the liability, it acquires them for 1,000,000 shares of $10 par value common stock, valued at $30,000,000, plus assumption of the liability. The journal entry, on a pooling basis, on A's books at the time of the acquisition of B's net assets will be (000's omitted):

Inventory	$10,000	
Plant	15,000	
Land	5,000	
Accounts payable		$15,000
Capital stock		10,000
Earned surplus		4,800
Capital surplus		200

amounts. Income of the combined corporation includes income of the constituents for the entire fiscal period in which the combination occurs. The reported income of the constituents for prior periods is combined and restated as income of the combined corporation.

Purchase Method

The purchase method accounts for a business combination as the acquisition of one company by another. The acquiring corporation records at its cost the acquired assets less liabilities assumed. A difference between the cost of an acquired company and the sum of the fair values of tangible and identifiable intangible assets less liabilities is recorded as goodwill. The reported income of an acquiring corporation includes the operation of the acquired

company after acquisition, based on the cost to the acquiring corporation.

32. APB Op. No. 16, ¶¶ 51–53 (1970).

For limitations on the carryforward of B's Earned Surplus, see n. 37, infra.

33. "However, the separate companies may have recorded assets and liabilities under differing methods of accounting and the amounts may be adjusted to the same basis of accounting if the change would otherwise have been appropriate for the separate company." APB Op. No. 16, ¶ 52 (1970).

34. APB Op. No. 16, ¶ 56 (1970).

35. Id. ¶ 57. See Figure 2, boxes 8, 9, infra.

36. See text following n. 17, supra, for the data.

Note that B's assets, liabilities and earned surplus are simply transferred at the same carrying value as on B's books—as called for by the pooling concept that this is a marriage of two entities with neither one acquiring the other; just as A's old carrying values and earned surplus continue, so do B's. The credit to capital stock is to evidence the issuance of the A shares and is in the amount of the aggregate par (or stated) value of the shares issued. The capital surplus credit is in the amount necessary to balance the other credits with the debits. Also note that if the net assets acquired in excess of capital stock issued were *less* than B's earned surplus, [and A had no capital surplus] only an amount of earned surplus equal to that excess would have been credited on A's books.[37]

Looking at the separate balance sheets of A and B, infra, pooling calls for combining them as noted without regard to A's current cost of $45,000,000 for the assets of B. Contrast this with our prior accounting (as shown in the last column infra) when stock was issued but the accounting was on a purchase basis.[38]

Balance Sheets (000's omitted)

	A Corp.	B Corp.	Combined in pooling	Fair market values of B's assets and liabilities and balancing debit to goodwill	Combined in purchase (for preferred stock)
Assets:					
Cash	$ 50,000	$ 0	$ 50,000	$ 0	$ 50,000
Inventory	20,000	10,000	30,000	12,000	32,000
Plant	70,000	15,000	85,000	18,000	88,000
Land		5,000	5,000	10,000	10,000
Goodwill				5,000	5,000
Totals	$140,000	$30,000	$170,000		$185,000
Liabilities and Equity:					
Accounts payable	$ 24,000	$15,000	$ 39,000	$15,000	$ 39,000
Equity:					
Capital stock (common and preferred)	30,000	6,000	40,000		40,000
Capital surplus	39,000	4,200	39,200		59,000
Earned surplus	47,000	4,800	51,800		47,000
Totals	$140,000	$30,000	$170,000		$185,000

37. This could be viewed as the result of the mechanics of double-entry bookkeeping. Many would quarrel, however, with the assertion that these results are mechanically dictated by double-entry bookkeeping requirements. See APB Op. No. 16, ¶ 53 (1970) which describes a principled basis for the bookkeeping. It states that the capital (i.e., stated value or par value plus capital surplus) of A and B are added together as are the earned surplus amounts on the combined corporations' balance sheet; if the new combined capital stock exceeds that of A and B together, the excess first reduces combined capital surplus and then reduces combined earned surplus. Implicit is the rationale that this is the equivalent of capitalizing B's surplus, first the capital surplus and then earned surplus to the extent necessary to cover the par or stated value.

38. See text following n. 27 supra.

As already noted, under pooling a unique accounting for income also appears: for the period in which the combination occurs, the income of *B* is added to the surviving corporation's income statement and on restatement of any prior period's income, the combined income of both corporations must be set forth. Finally, of course, as a consequence of *B*'s assets being carried at the old book carrying value of *B*, which is typically lower than the value paid by *A*, *A*'s future income statements typically will show lesser amounts for costs of goods sold, depreciation, and other deferred costs than they would under purchase accounting—and no expense whatsoever for amortization of goodwill, since none arises. Put another way, the increment to *A*'s income on a pooling tends toward being equal to what *B*'s individual income is or would have been for that same period.

(B) Reasons for Pooling

These accounting results are believed by many to be the major motivation for the invention of pooling and the reason for its continued existence.[39] Thus, many corporate acquirers desire, and perhaps could not succeed without, accounting for acquisitions which result in (a) lower reported depreciation and amortization expenses than would be shown under purchase accounting with the consequential higher income and rate of return, (b) carryover of the acquired firm's earned surplus, and (c) combination of earnings in the income statements for the year of acquisition and for restatements of prior years' earnings.[40]

It should be noted that if pooling were not an available accounting choice, acquirers would make decisions about acquisitions independently of the choice of accounting treatment, and presumably would structure some acquisitions to minimize the actual costs—something which is not always done now because of the corrupting influence of pooling accounting.[41] Perhaps for that reason, resources are being inefficiently allocated today.

39. E.g., see A. Wyatt, A Critical Study of Accounting for Business Combinations (Accounting Research Study No. 5) ch. 6 (1963).

40. "Frequently, a business combination is not considered economically feasible unless it may be accounted for as a pooling of interests." Arthur Andersen & Co., SEC Case re Effect of Treasury Stock Transactions on Accounting for Business Combinations 101 (1974), *quoted in* Briloff & Engles, Accountancy and the Merger Movement: A Symbiotic Relationship, 5 J.Corp.L. 81, 82–83 (1979).

However, there is some empirical support for the view that investors are not affected by the choice of accounting alternatives. E.g., Hong, Kaplan & Mandelker, Pooling vs. Purchase; The Effects of Accounting for Mergers on Stock Prices, 53 Acct.Rev. 31–47 (1978).

41. It has frequently been pointed out that some corporate managers have sought to maximize reported earnings rather than to maximize true economic gain. E.g., see Staff Report of the SEC to the Special Subcomm. on Investigations, Comm. on Interstate and Foreign Commerce, The Financial Collapse of the Penn Central Company, H.R. 33–83, 92d Cong., 1st Sess. (1972). The most dramatic illustration of this might be the acquisition of *B* Corp. by *A* Corp. near the end of a poor year for *A* in order to combine *B*'s reported earnings with *A*. This could be done by issuance of *A*'s shares for a value less than what the *A* shares could fetch in cash.

One asserted ground for legitimization of pooling treatment has been the tax-free reorganization rules under the Internal Revenue Code.[42] Under the code, many statutory mergers and consolidations, exchanges of shares and sales of assets for shares have been defined as reorganizations which are "tax-free" to investors and the corporations involved. Consistent with the tax-free treatment for the corporate constituents, however, the corporations' tax bases for assets remain and are carried over to the reorganized company, as is the tax area's near-kin to earned surplus, "earnings and profits." Proponents of pooling have urged that this is similar to pooling's treatment of the assets and surplus of both constituents—which retain their old book carrying values. They urge in effect that what is good for Uncle Sam is good for corporate accounting, but the logic of this assertion is not apparent— especially since pooling accounting is not limited to tax-free reorganizations and purchase accounting is not limited to taxable ones.[43]

Other theoretical underpinnings may exist for pooling accounting, especially when in fact A and B are equally matched; in this situation, it would require some deviation from the historical cost convention to require B but not A to reflect new values in its accounts. The battle over pooling rages unabated in the literature.

(C) Criteria for Pooling

The questionable legitimacy of pooling, based as it is, largely in the attractiveness to managers of its financial statement results and the illogical implication that imperfect parallelism with the Internal Revenue Code is desirable, indicates a weak-principled basis for distinguishing situations where either pooling or purchase accounting should be prescribed. *APB Op. No. 16* nevertheless purports to find twelve criteria for a pooling.[45] Figure 1 is a decision chart which provides a guide for determining whether to account for a transaction as a purchase or a pooling by reference to the twelve requirements, each of which must be met for pooling treatment. Rather than restate the criteria in the text here, see Fig. 1.

42. IRC §§ 354, 361, 368(a)(1), most importantly.

43. See n. 23, supra.

45. APB Op. No. 16, ¶¶ 46–48 (1970).

Figure 1.   Accounting for Business Combinations
A Decision Chart (References are to paragraph numbers of APB Op. No. 16)

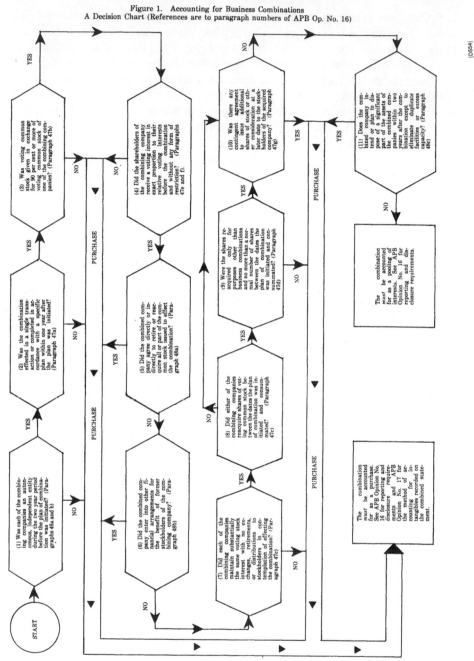

Adapted from: Robert E. Hamilton and James W. Pratt, Accounting (Planning) for Business Combinations, J. of Accounting 83 (Jan. 1972).

4.   A NOTE ON ACCOUNTING FIXED BY LAW

Without attempting a full-scale analysis of the relationship of law to accounting,[46] it should be noted at this point that corporation code provisions regulating dividends (including the effect of corporate combi-

46.   E.g., see Hackney, Accounting Principles in Corporation Law, 30 Law and Contemp.Prob. 791 (1965) for a fine analysis from the law point of view.

nations on capital and surplus) may alter, in the view of a small minority of accountants, the above-described presentation of accounting data on financial statements.[47] For example, the governing corporation statute may prescribe that on a merger, the earned surplus of the merging corporation shall be available to the survivor for dividend purposes.[48] Some accountants may believe that under such a statute, even if the merger would not be considered a pooling for any reason,[49] the earned surplus required to be available for dividends should be presented on the audited balance sheet as part of the survivor's earned surplus.[50] Other accountants disagree.[51]

Notwithstanding, it would seem that dividend law, once a more powerful influence on accounting presentation, now has merely a vestigial effect.[52] At the present time lawyers must follow accounting for the most part in ascertaining dividend limitations.[53]

---

47. E.g., see id. at 800. Wyatt, n. 12, supra, states at 66:

Some accountants contend that while the pooling of interests is an accounting concept rather than a legal concept, it should not violate the applicable state laws. Others contend that the earned surpluses may be combined even if the state law does not permit this, with the surplus available for dividends being shown parenthetically or disclosed in some other manner in the financial statements.

And see Melcher, Stockholders' Equity (ARS No. 15) (1973), at 17 ("* * * corporate statutes often influence the accounting for the issuance of stock"); at 21–22 ("* * * statutory definitions and designations of components of equity continue to influence, if not control, the accounting for shares of stock * * *"). See also, N. Bedford, K. Perry, & A. Wyatt, Advanced Accounting 647 (3d ed. 1973) and G. Catlett & N. Olson, Accounting for Goodwill (ARS No. 10) 65–66 (1968).

48. See, e.g., Model Business Corporation Act Annotated § 76 comment 3.03(8) (2d ed. 1971). For older examples, see Baker, Dividends of Combined Corporations: Some Problems Under Accounting Research Bulletin No. 48, 72 Harv.L.Rev. 494, 497 (1959).

49. E.g., if twenty-five percent of the merged corporation's shareholders were "cashed out," pooling would not be permitted under APB Op. No. 16, ¶ 47b (1970).

50. See n. 47 supra. In actuality, the audited balance sheet would use the caption "retained earnings" or the like, not "earned surplus."

For a case upholding a shareholder's right to demand and receive financial

statements comporting with the governing dividend statute, see Burguierres v. J.M. Burguierres Co., Ltd., 312 So.2d 179 (La.Ct. App. 1975), cited in D. Herwitz, Accounting for Lawyers 170 (1980).

51. See e.g., n. 47 supra.

52. Hackney, Accounting Principles in Corporation Law, 30 Law and Contemp. Prob. 795 n. 13 (1965) stated as early as 1965:

In prior years, the law was considered one of the essential sources dictating in part the development of good accounting practice. Dicksee's pioneering work entitled *Goodwill (1900)* commenced with an introductory chapter consisting of an "outline of the law relating to good will." Hatfield's and May's writings are sprinkled with case citations and quotations from opinions. Dean spoke in 1949 of the circuitry of reference when a lawyer, "asked to pass upon a legal concept deriving its meaning, in whole or part, from accounting concepts, in the absence of statutory authority or case law, turns to the accountant for help in determining ['g.a.a.p.']," while he in turn is met with a request from the accountant for advice as to "the applicable legal principles to be followed" in the same determination. Arthur H. Dean, An Inquiry into the Nature of Business Income Under Present Price Levels 49 (1949). The current view is that

"broad [accounting] principles must transcend the historical limitations of profits 'available for dividends' or 'subject to income tax.' This is not to say that the effects of dividends and of taxes should be ignored; to do so

---

53. See note 53 on page 460.

However, the movement in corporation law is away from tying law to GAAP. As the latest revisions of the MBCA's financial provisions become more widely adopted (as they are now by about fifteen states), both accounting and dividend law will be divorced and thereby be vastly improved.[54]

That being so, this chapter informs lawyers of accounting practices rather than informing accountants as to dividend law.

5. SUMMARY

The skeletal outline, described in Part A of the accounting for the case of a single survivor after an acquisition, may be simply diagramed as in Figure 2.

would ignore a significant part of the environment in which accounting operates. Rather the task is to formulate those principles which will enable us to measure the resources held by specific entities and the related changes *before* consideration of taxes and dividends. The measurements should be independent of the dividend and the tax questions but, at the same time, should facilitate the solution of those questions. * * * "
Robert T. Sprouse & Maurice Moonitz, A Tentative Set of Broad Accounting Prin-ciples for Business Enterprises 10 (AICPA Accounting Research Study No. 3, 1962).

53. Cf., Hackney, 245, supra at 813–23. See the prescient statement of Ralph Baker in Hildebrand on Texas Corporations—A Review, 21 Tex.L.Rev. 169, 190 (1942).

54. See Report of Comm. on Corp.Laws, Changes in the Model Business Corporation Act—Amendments to Financial Provisions, 34 Bus.Law. 1867 (1979) and Chapter VIII.

Figure 2.

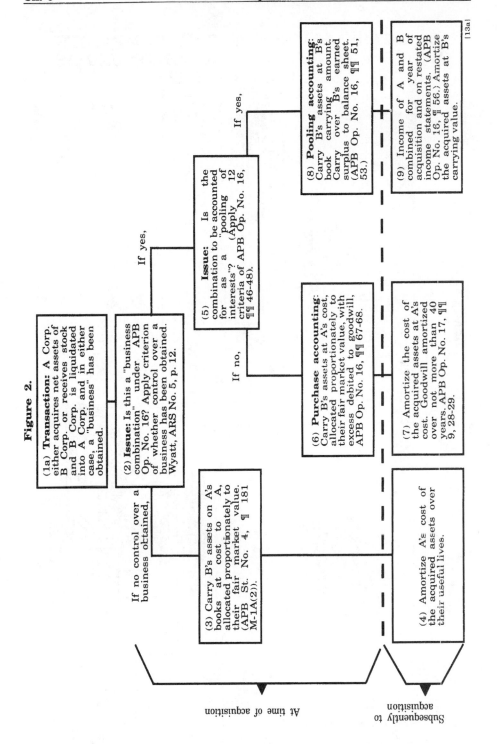

B. SHARE ACQUISITIONS OF COMPANIES WHICH ARE THEREAFTER CONTINUED AS SEPARATE ENTITIES

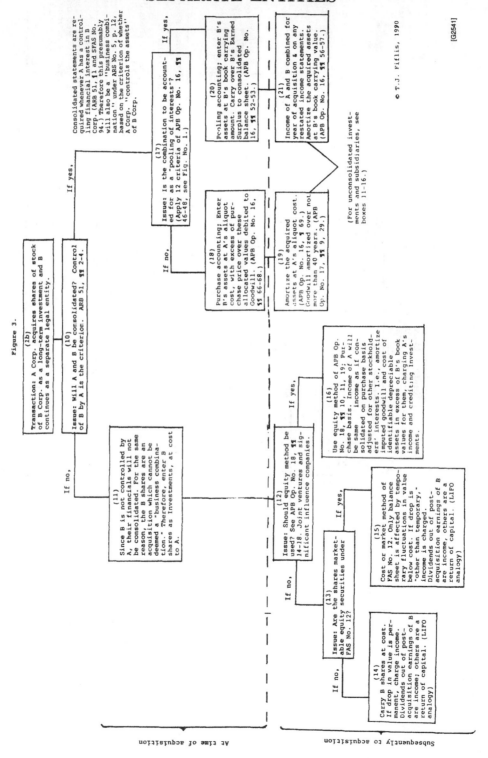

Figure 3.

When, instead of *B* Corp.'s assets being absorbed by *A* on purchase, *A* and *B* remain separate legal entities and *B*'s shares are held by *A*, a host of additional accounting issues arise. To help isolate the questions to be discussed here, a diagram (Figure 3) correlating the transactions, accounting issues posed, and accounting treatments prescribed by GAAP may be a helpful analytic and mnemonic device if set forth in advance of the explanation instead of at the end as we did in part A. Experts may find Figure 3 to be a useful summary of GAAP in this area. The explanation follows in the remainder of part B.

Inspection will reveal that the diagram has two main divisions. These result from dividing those acquisitions by *A* of *B* Corp. which are required to be accounted for on consolidated statements [58] from those which must be accounted for by parent-company-only statements.[59]

To begin, consistently with our scheme of treating simpler matters first, we shall consider cases in which consolidated statements are required.[62]

1. ACCOUNTING FOR A BUSINESS COMBINATION IN CONSOLIDATED STATEMENTS

Consolidated statements ordinarily are called for by GAAP [although *required* only presumptively [63]] when two or more separate legal entities constitute a single economic enterprise—i.e., when one of the companies has a "controlling financial interest" in the other or others.[64] As a rule of thumb, accountants consider ownership of a majority voting interest to be a basis for consolidation,[65] but even with such majority interest, consolidation will not be proper when there is no real control in *A*, as when that control is temporary, does not rest with the majority vote (as when a receivership exists), or when the owner's control over a foreign subsidiary is limited by a foreign government's restrictions.

In 1987 the FASB adopted SFAS No. 94, *Consolidation of All Majority-owned Subsidiaries*, to eliminate an exception for "non-homogeneous subsidiaries"; i.e., subsidiaries whose business was deemed by

58. See Figure 3, boxes 17–21, supra.

59. Id. boxes 11–16.

62. Id. boxes 10, 17–21.

63. ARB No. 51, ¶ 1 (1959) speaks of the "presumption that consolidated statements are more meaningful" and "usually necessary for a fair presentation" when there is a "controlling financial interest." Convention calls for consolidation in these circumstances.

64. APB Op. No. 18, ¶ 3c (1970) states: "the usual condition for control is ownership of a majority (over 50%) of the outstanding voting stock. The power to control may also exist with a lesser percentage of ownership, for example, by contract, lease, agreement with other stockholders

or by court decree." And see N. Bedford, K. Perry & A. Wyatt, Advanced Accounting 295–96, 587–88 (1973) for further discussion of the accountants' concept of control.

In sum, the accountants' concept of control, like that of the securities law, is basically one of fact, although in practice, accountants feel that majority voting ownership is an overwhelming consideration.

The author is the "law" member of an FASB Task Force on consolidations which has been reconsidering this matter for nearly a decade.

65. ARB No. 51, ¶ 2.

management to be so different from that of the parent as to make consolidated statements misleading. This was the basis for a common practice of not consolidating finance and insurance company subsidiaries, in the discretion of management, thereby resulting in off-balance sheet accounting just as under the old practice of not showing lease and pension benefit liabilities. In *SFAS No. 94* the FASB decreed that all companies in which a majority voting interest is held should be consolidated regardless of lack of homogeneity.

Since control is the criterion now for both consolidation and finding a business combination, our explanation is much less complex than it was prior to 1987. Now presumably any business combination (which by definition requires control over the assets of the combined companies) where *B* Corp.'s separate legal status continues will also require consolidation of *A*'s and *B*'s accounts.

When consolidated statements are called for, the books of account of the separate legal entities are not affected merely by virtue of the consolidation, but consolidated statements, including income statements, balance sheets, and cash flow statements, as they are now called, are prepared for the entire economic enterprise. In the process, intercompany transactions and intercompany claims are eliminated from the consolidated statements, as is that peculiar intercompany claim, the parent's investment in the subsidiary.[67]

Because of this the consolidated statements of *A* and *B* after a business combination (still assuming no minority shareholders' interest) will appear identical to those of *A* Corp. when *A* Corp. acquired the net assets of *B,* as described, supra, part A, subparts 2 and 3.[68] That is to say, the acquisition of *B* Corp. will be treated as a "business combination" to be accounted for on either a "purchase" or a "pooling" basis depending on whether the twelve criteria of *APB Op. No. 16,* set forth in Figure 1, are met. It is a business combination because, by our hypothesis, *A* Corp. has control of *B* Corp. (otherwise their statements would not be consolidated), and this, we have seen, is virtually the criterion for treating an acquisition as a business combination.[69]

To illustrate the consolidation process let us use the same data as in our prior illustration of purchase and pooling when the net assets of

---

67. There are two discrete underlying theories of consolidated statements, based on two different perspectives:

   (a) that of the stockholders of the parent company (known as the "proprietary theory"); and

   (b) that of the management of the parent company (known as the "entity theory").

Different formats of financial statements will result, depending on which theory is followed, when there is a minority shareholder interest in the consolidated subsidiary.

Under the proprietary theory, those minority shareholders of the consolidated subsidiary are treated as outsiders, like creditors, whereas under the entity theory, they are treated as co-owners. The former, proprietary theory, is predominant in practice. For a description see n. 77, infra. And see e.g., N. Bedford, K. Perry & A. Wyatt, Advanced Accounting 301–03 (3d ed. 1973).

68. See text at n. 20, and n. 38, *et seq.* supra. Compare Figure 3, boxes 17–21 and Figure 2, boxes 5–9, supra.

69. See text following n. 11, supra.

Some may quarrel with this assertion, pointing out the "controlling financial interest" condition for consolidated statements is contained in formal GAAP (ARB No. 51, ¶ 1) whereas the "control over assets" test of ARS 5 for determining wheth-

B were acquired. Assume *A* Corp. buys all of *B*'s outstanding shares for $30,000,000 value in stock plus assumption of the $15,000,000 liability, and the fair market values of *B*'s assets and liabilities and the balance sheet carrying values of *A* and *B* appear as follows:

Balance Sheets (000's omitted)

	A Corp.	B Corp.	Fair market values of *B*'s assets and liabilities
Assets:			
Cash	$ 50,000	$ 0	$ 0
Inventory	20,000	10,000	12,000
Plant	70,000	15,000	18,000
Land		5,000	10,000
Totals	$140,000	$30,000	
Liabilities and Equity:			
Accounts payable	$ 24,000	$15,000	$15,000
Equity:			
Capital stock (common and preferred)	$ 30,000	$ 6,000	
Capital surplus	39,000	4,200	
Earned surplus	47,000	4,800	
Totals	$140,000	$30,000	

(A) Consolidation on a Purchase Accounting Basis

If the *A* stock used in the combination is preferred stock, the accounting must be on the "purchase" basis,[73] recognizing the fair market value of *B*'s assets as well as goodwill on the consolidated balance sheet at the time of acquisition. Even on *A*'s unconsolidated balance sheet, *A*'s investment in *B* of $10,000,000 par value preferred having a value of $30,000,000, will be carried at *A*'s cost, $30,000,000. The journal entries on *A*'s books will be (000's omitted):

Investments	$30,000	
Capital stock—preferred		$10,000
Capital surplus		20,000

A Corp.'s unconsolidated balance sheet will then appear (000's omitted):

	A Corp.
Assets:	
Cash	$ 50,000
Inventory	20,000
Investments	30,000
Plant	70,000
Total	$170,000
Liabilities and Equity:	
Accounts payable	$ 24,000
Equity:	
Capital stock (preferred and common)	40,000
Capital surplus	59,000
Earned surplus	47,000
Total	$170,000

er a business combination exists is not only literally different, but also is not contained in formal GAAP; APB Op. No. 16, ¶ 1 (1970), dealing with business combinations, refers only to "one accounting entity" being formed.

73. See Figure 1, box 3.

Now the problem is, how will A's and B's balance sheets at the date of acquisition be consolidated?

In consolidation, since we have assumed there is no minority shareholder interest in B Corp. and there are no intercompany transactions or accounts between A and B, the only necessary step is to substitute B's assets and liabilities for the "investments" account on A's individual balance sheet. Since the combination with B is to be accounted for as a "purchase," this entails bringing the assets into the consolidated balance sheet at fair market values with any excess carried as goodwill. The result will be just as if A Corp. had purchased the net assets of B instead of B's shares of stock.[74] On a worksheet this reallocation process may be set forth as follows:

Balance Sheets (000's omitted)

	A Corp.	B Corp.	Eliminations and adjustments: Debits	Eliminations and adjustments: Credits	Consolidated balance sheet
Assets:					
Cash	$ 50,000	$ 0			$ 50,000
Inventory	20,000	10,000	$ 2,000[*]		32,000
Plant	70,000	15,000	3,000[*]		88,000
Investments	30,000			$30,000[***]	
Land		5,000	5,000[*]		10,000
Goodwill			5,000[**]		5,000
Totals	$170,000	$30,000			$185,000
Liabilities and Equity:					
Accounts payable	$ 24,000	$15,000			$ 39,000
Equity:					
Capital stock (preferred and common)	40,000	6,000	6,000[****]		40,000
Capital surplus	59,000	4,200	4,200[****]		59,000
Earned surplus	47,000	4,800	4,800[****]		47,000
Totals	$170,000	$30,000	$30,000	$30,000	$185,000

[*]   To allocate the excess of fair market value of identifiable tangible and intangible assets.

[**]   To enter goodwill.

[***]   To eliminate the investments account.

[****]   To eliminate B's equity accounts.

It will be observed that the consolidated balance sheet is identical with the balance sheet resulting after the purchase of net assets, previously set forth in the text following note 38.[75]

74. If A had purchased B's net assets, as we have seen, the journal entry would have been (000's omitted):

Inventory	$12,000	
Plant	18,000	
Land	10,000	
Goodwill	5,000	
Accounts payable		$15,000
Capital stock		10,000
Capital surplus		20,000

See text at n. 27 supra.

75. This result would be altered had A purchased less than 100% of B Corp.'s shares. In that event, the B Corp. minority shareholders' interest would appear on the consolidated balance sheet. See n. 77, infra. See Figure 3, boxes 18 and 19, supra.

In periods after the purchase, consolidated statements of income will, of course, include charges against income for cost of goods sold, depreciation, and amortization of goodwill and these charges will be greater than the charges on *B* Corp.'s income statements because the related asset accounts on the consolidated balance sheet are greater (since equal to the higher fair market value paid by *A*) than they are on *B*'s balance sheet. Therefore, the consolidated income on the purchase basis will be diminished to this extent from the aggregate of the separate incomes of *A* and *B*.

To illustrate, assume *B*'s income statement for the first year of operations after the purchase showed $4,000,000 of net income, *B* paid a $1,000,000 dividend to *A*, *B*'s plant is being depreciated at a 10 percent rate, goodwill is amortized at the minimum 2.5 percent rate (over forty years) allowed by *APB Op. No. 17*, and the *B* inventory is carried on the first-in, first-out basis and has been turned over at least once during the year.

On these assumptions, *B*'s contribution to the consolidated earning statement would not be $4,000,000, but would be diminished by:

    (a) $2,000,000 additional expense because of the additional inventory amount which will be charged to cost of goods sold as that inventory is sold off;

    (b) Additional plant depreciation expense in the amount of 10 percent of the $3,000,000 write-up in plant on the consolidated balance sheet (or $300,000); and

    (c) An amortization charge for the $5,000,000 of goodwill, in the annual amount of $125,000.

The $1,000,000 dividend would be an intercorporate transfer affecting nothing in the consolidated statements, just as if the cash had been transferred from one corporate bank account to another. Hence, the net contribution by *B* Corp. to consolidated income will be:

B Corp.'s earnings	$ 4,000,000
Less adjustments on consolidation:	
Extra cost of goods sold	(2,000,000)
Extra depreciation	(300,000)
Amortization of goodwill	(125,000)
Net contribution to consolidated income	$ 1,575,000 [76]

(B) Consolidation on a Pooling of Interests Basis

The distinctive features of a pooling of interests, we have seen, are:

    (a) No new valuations are accorded the assets and liabilities of *B* Corp. after the pooling of interests;

    (b) No goodwill arises;

    (c) The earned surplus of *B* Corp. usually is carried over to the financial statements of the combined entities;

---

76. We have ignored accounting for income tax expense or benefits which could entail additional complexity beyond the purposes of this paper.

(d) Income of the two entities for the year of the combination is aggregated; and

(e) If prior years' income statements are presented the incomes of *A* and *B* will be combined although the two entities were separate at that time.

These attributes apply whether *B* Corp.'s net assets are acquired by *A,* as in our part A, subpart 3, or *B* Corp.'s shares are acquired and *B*'s statements are consolidated with *A*'s. If *A*'s and *B*'s balance sheets are consolidated at the time of acquisition, they will appear as illustrated in the "combined in pooling" column, at text following note 38, supra. Thereafter, unlike the case of a purchase, the sums of the consolidated entities' separate charges for depreciation, etc., will be charged on the consolidated income statements.[77]

77. See Figure 3 boxes 20 and 21, supra. If, contrary to our assumptions, *A* owns less than 100 percent of *B* Corp., the consolidated balance sheet will portray the minority interest in the subsidiary as a liability just before net worth in the same amounts whether *A*'s acquisition is accounted for as a purchase or a pooling. If the minority holds a 10 percent interest, and it is common stock, it would be carried at 10 percent of *B*'s net worth (capital stock plus all surpluses). If preferred stock of *B* instead is held by the minority, the amount will be the par value of the preferred held by them, or, the liquidation preference of that holding, if greater, on the theory that the minority preferred does not participate in surplus, which instead redounds to the benefit of the common, except to the extent of any liquidation preference in excess of par.

On a pooling, only *A*'s proportionate share of *B*'s earned surplus will appear as such. (The minority's proportionate share of earned surplus of *B* will be netted-in as part of the liability for minority interests.) The capital surplus account of *A* will be credited to the extent the net worth of *B* exceeds the aggregate of the amounts credited to the liability for minority interests, earned surplus and capital stock.

If the combination is accounted for as a purchase, the capital surplus will be credited for the purchase price paid by *A* less the amount credited to *A*'s capital stock account.

To illustrate, let us assume the same data as shown in the balance sheets in the text preceding note 73, except that 10 percent of the common stock of *B* is held by minority shareholders. It will appear that the 10 percent minority interest will be shown as a liability of $1,500,000 on the consolidated balance sheet whether the accounting is as a purchase or a pooling (since that 10 per-

cent is neither purchased nor pooled—it has not been acquired by *A*).

Similarly, if only 90 percent of the common is acquired, the consolidated balance sheet will show acquisition of an undivided 90 percent interest in *B*'s assets and liabilities. The remaining 10 percent undivided interest will be carried in consolidation at *B*'s carrying value. Thus, assuming a 90 percent acquisition for $27,000,000, assets would be diminished by 10 percent of the write-up in each asset as follows: inventory—$200,000, plant—$300,000, land—$500,000 and goodwill—$500,000, totalling $1,500,000 reduction in asset values. The minority interest in *B*'s earnings is determined on the basis of *B*'s carrying value, i.e., the 10 percent undivided interest.

Giving effect to the foregoing:

	If purchased:	If pooling:
Assets		
Cash	$ 50,000	$ 50,000
Inventory	31,800	30,000
Plant	87,700	85,000
Land	9,500	5,000
Goodwill	4,500	—0—
	$183,500	$170,000
Liabilities		
Accounts payable	$ 39,000	$ 39,000
Minority interest in subsidiary	1,500	1,500
Equity		
Capital stock	39,000	39,000
Capital surplus	57,000	39,180*
Earned surplus	47,000	51,320
	$183,500	$170,000

* Of the $15,000,000 net worth of *B* Corp., $1,500,000 is credited to minority interest, $4,320,000 is credited to earned surplus, and $9,000,000 is credited to capital stock, leaving $180,000 to be credited to capital surplus.

2. ACCOUNTING FOR AN INVESTMENT BY THE INVESTOR WHEN CONSOLIDATED STATEMENTS ARE NOT APPROPRIATE

In comparison with the prior subpart 1, where the criteria for consolidated statements were met, the accounting for a second category of situations, those in which the criteria for consolidation are not met, is more complicated.[78] Here, as can be seen from Figure 3, after box 11, there are no business combinations involved.

By our hypothesis, *B* Corp.'s financial statements will not be consolidated with those of *A* Corp. For these acquisitions, depending on the facts, one of three types of accounting treatment will be accorded *B* Corp. on *A*'s published financial statements:

      (1) The "cost" method;

      (2) The "cost or market" method; or

      (3) The "equity" method.

If *A* Corp. invests in equity shares of *B* Corp. without obtaining control, the acquisition will not be considered a "business combination"[80] and, further, the financial statements will not be consolidated.[81] The criteria for determining when one of the three methods, cost, cost or market, or equity, will be applied to these published statements, and the description of each, when there is no business combination or consolidation of statements, follows.

(1) The Cost Method

At the instant when the *B* Corp. shares are first acquired, the accounting for a noncontrolling interest under all three methods is identical. *A* Corp. will simply debit an investment account for the cost and credit cash or whatever else it uses to pay for the investment. But thereafter the three methods diverge.

The simplest to describe is the "cost" method, which will be applicable if *A* Corp. is not engaged with another in a joint venture in *B* Corp., has no "significant influence over operating and financial policies" of *B* Corp. (the criterion for use of the "equity" method), and the *B* shares are not "marketable equity securities" (the criterion for use of the "cost or market" method, regulated by *SFAS No. 12*).[83]

---

78. Where *A* Corp. has investments in two or more companies, one or more of them may be consolidated and others may not. Thus, in our Figure 3 we might have diagramed the situation where consolidated statements for *A* Corp. and *B* Corp. include one or more unconsolidated investees, *C, D,* and *E.* Since the accounting for unconsolidated investees on consolidated statements is identical with the accounting for unconsolidated investees on parent-company-only statements, Figure 3 simply includes the former at boxes 14–16. The explanation which follows applies equally to unconsolidated investees whether in consolidated statements or parent-company-only statements.

SFAS No. 94 will minimize such cases.

80. See text at n. 12 supra. Regarding the meaning of "control," see n. 63, supra. See Figure 3 boxes 11–14, supra.

81. See text at n. 64, supra.

83. FASB, Statement of Financial Accounting Standards No. 12, Accounting for Certain Marketable Securities (1975).

The cost method simply calls for carrying the *B* shares at cost like any other long-term investment,[84] with a write-down for a permanent decline in value below cost (although write-downs are not common).[85] In addition, income is recognized by *A* Corp. when dividends are declared by *B* Corp. out of post-acquisition earnings of *B*,[86] and other dividends are considered returns of capital and reduce the carrying amount of the investment.[87]

(2) The "Cost or Market" Method of SFAS No. 12

If, instead, the *B* shares still are not to be accounted for on the equity method, but do fit the criteria of *SFAS No. 12* (which covers marketable equity securities whether held for the short or long-term),[88] they initially will be entered at cost, but on subsequent balance sheets of *A* will be carried at the lower of cost or market at the balance sheet date.[89]   Under *SFAS No. 12*, the income statement of *A* will not be

---

84.   APB St. No. 4, ¶¶ 163–64 (1970).

85.   Id. ¶ 183 S–5E.

86.   See APB Op. No. 18, ¶¶ 6(a), 7 (1971) and ARB No. 43, ch. 1, ¶ 3 (1953). Although not stated in these authorities, they support the apparent practice assuming a LIFO basis for these dividends; i.e., payment of dividends is deemed to be out of the most recent earnings. See Hackney, Financial Accounting for Parents and Subsidiaries—A New Approach to Consolidated Statements, 25 U.Pitt.L.Rev. 9, 18 n. 19 (1963).

87.   Ibid.

88.   This chapter is not concerned with short-term investments held as a more profitable substitute for cash. Short-term investments in securities are carried either at cost, or, if they are within the terms of SFAS No. 12 governing marketable equity securities, at "cost or market" as therein described. See notes 89 and 90, infra, regarding such short-term holdings. The equity method is inapplicable to short-term investments. Cf. APB Op. No. 18, ¶¶ 2, 14–17 & n. 4 (1971); FAS No. 12, ¶ 6 (1971).

SFAS No. 12, ¶ 7 (1971) defines "marketable" as follows:

(b) Marketable, as applied to an equity security, means an equity security as to which sales prices or bid and ask prices are currently available on a national securities exchange (i.e., those registered with the Securities and Exchange Commission) or in the over-the-counter market. In the over-the-counter market, an equity security shall be considered mark-

etable when a quotation is publicly reported by the National Association of Securities Dealers Automatic Quotations System or by the National Quotations Bureau Inc. (provided, in the latter case, that quotations are available from at least three dealers). Equity securities traded in foreign markets shall be considered marketable when such markets are of a breadth and scope comparable to those referred to above. Restricted stock does not meet this definition.

89.   SFAS No. 12, ¶ 8 (1971).

The discussion in the text here is based on the simple case of a long-term investment in only one company.

If two or more companies are investees or two or more companies' stocks are held as short-term substitutes for cash, the accounting is complicated slightly by FAS No. 12's use of the portfolio concept. And the application of that concept will vary depending on whether the investor's balance sheet is "classified" (i.e., divided into current and noncurrent assets and liabilities). At the risk of getting off into a complex tangent, this may be briefly illustrated.

Assuming a classified balance sheet and holdings for the short-term of stocks in three companies, A, B and C, purchased at costs of $10, $12 and $6, respectively, and long-term holdings of X, Y and Z, purchased respectively at the same costs, further assume that at the end of the accounting period the values have changed as follows:

affected by any write-down to market for long-term investments [90] unless it is judged to be an "other than temporary" decline.[91] Consistent with this treatment of temporary declines (not being charged against income), if the market value rebounds at a subsequent balance sheet date, the investment will be written up again (but not above original cost) and the recoupment will not be counted as income. In this latter respect the cost or market method differs from other cases in which the written-down value becomes the new "cost" figure for future purposes and is not written up on recoupment—as in the case of inventory write-downs. Finally, as with the cost method, dividends out of post-acquisition earnings of B are income to A; other dividends are a return of capital which diminish the carrying value of the investment account.[92]

(3) The Equity Method

The equity method is far more complex and is subject to much misunderstanding, even among sophisticated lawyers. One of its features is well-enough known—that the balance sheet value of the investment account will be written up or down in proportion to A's ownership share as the shareholders' equity of the investee rises or falls, and that the write-up or write-down will be added to or subtracted from A's

Holding: Short-term:	Cost:	End-of-period-value:
A	$10	$ 8
B	12	14
C	6	3
Totals	$28	$25
Long-term:		
X	10	8
Y	12	14
Z	6	3
Totals	$28	$25

The short-term and long-term holdings each will be treated as a portfolio and the *aggregate* costs and market values compiled. The lower of the aggregate cost or market value for each portfolio will be carried on the balance sheet. Thus each portfolio above will be shown at $25, the lower of the aggregates of cost or market.

Because SFAS No. 12 provides no criteria for distinguishing short-term from long-term holdings, and ARB 43, c3A, ¶ 4 states only that "marketable securities representing the investment of cash available for current operations" should be considered short-term, there is much freedom in constituting the two portfolios. See L. Heath, Financial Reporting and the Evaluation of

Solvency 81 (AICPA, Accounting Research Monograph 3) (1978).

90. Id. ¶ 11 requires that writedowns of long-term investments by-pass income accounts. Instead, the debit will be to an equity account and the credit to a "contra-asset" account. If the value later increases and is higher at a subsequent balance sheet date, the contra-asset account will be debited for the increase to the extent of the investments' original cost and equity will be recredited.

The term "contra-asset account" refers to an account which is part of the main asset account but is segregated in a separate ledger account for the purpose of preserving the main account intact. Other examples of contra-asset accounts are what lawyers know as reserves for bad debts and reserves for depreciation. (Accountants now eschew the term "reserves" for all but reserves out of surplus. See AICPA, Accounting Terminology Bulletin No. 1, ¶¶ 57–64 (1953).)

For short-term investments, on the other hand, changes in the contra-asset account will be debited (for losses) or credited (for gains) against income.

91. SFAS No. 12, ¶ 21.

92. Cf. APB Op. No. 18, ¶ 9 (1971).

income. But few are aware that a significant adjustment to that write-up or write-down is required.[93] It will be explained shortly.

Although *APB Op. No. 18,* para. 19, as amended by *SFAS No. 94* (1987), states the accounting details for the equity method,[94] one who is not already familiar with the practices, like the reader of Dr. Johnson's dictionary,[95] will find little meaning in these prescripts. Before explaining those mechanical steps in the equity method, we shall determine in subtopic (a), following, when the equity method is required by GAAP. Then in subtopic (b) we shall consider the mechanics, including the adjustment, which will be illustrated in (c).

93. See text at n. 119, *et seq.* infra.

94. The more significant portions of which are here quoted:

19. Applying the equity method. * * * The procedures set forth below should be followed by an investor in applying the equity method of accounting to investments in common stock of * * * corporate joint ventures, and other investees which qualify for the equity method:

a. Intercompany profits and losses should be eliminated until realized by the investor or investee as if a * * * corporate joint venture or investee company were consolidated.

b. A difference between the cost of an investment and the amount of underlying equity in net assets of an investee should be accounted for as if the investee were a consolidated subsidiary.

c. The investment(s) in common stock should be shown in the balance sheet of an investor as a single amount, and the investor's share of earnings or losses of an investee should ordinarily be shown in the income statement as a single amount * * *.

* * *

e. A transaction of an investee of a capital nature that affects the investor's share of stockholders' equity of the investee should be accounted for as if the investee were a consolidated subsidiary.

f. Sales of stock of an investee by an investor should be accounted for as gains or losses equal to the difference at the time of sale between selling price and carrying amount of the stock sold.

* * *

h. A loss in value of an investment which is other than a temporary decline should be recognized the same as a loss in value of other long-term assets. Evi-dence of a loss in value might include, but would not necessarily be limited to, absence of an ability to recover the carrying amount of the investment or inability of the investee to sustain an earnings capacity which would justify the carrying amount of the investment. A current fair value of an investment that is less than its carrying amount may indicate a loss in value of the investment. However, a decline in the quoted market price below the carrying amount or the existence of operating losses is not necessarily indicative of a loss in value that is other than temporary. All are factors to be evaluated.

i. An investor's share of losses of an investee may equal or exceed the carrying amount of an investment accounted for by the equity method plus advances made by the investor. The investor ordinarily should discontinue applying the equity method when the investment (and net advances) is reduced to zero and should not provide for additional losses unless the investor has guaranteed obligations of the investee or is otherwise committed to provide further financial support for the investee. If the investee subsequently reports net income, the investor should resume applying the equity method only after its share of that net income equals the share of net losses not recognized during the period the equity method was suspended.

95. S. Johnson, Preface to the English Dictionary, *reprinted in* II The Works of Samuel Johnson, LL.D. 446, 450–51 (1837): "[E]very art is obscure to those that have not learned it; * * * it must be remembered that I am speaking of that which words are insufficient to explain. * * * The solution of all difficulties, and the supply of all defects, must be sought in the examples."

(a) Criteria for Use of the Equity Method

One key to understanding the equity method is to note that it is a parallel to consolidated statements. Just as financial statements usually will be consolidated if *A* Corp. *controls B* Corp., so too, the equity method usually will be applied if the statements are not consolidated but nevertheless, *A* has at least *"significant influence"* over operating and financial policies of *B* Corp.,[96] and, moreover, *A*'s income, net assets, and net worth will be the same under the equity method, with a minor exception, as they would be if consolidated statements were prepared. The changes in *A*'s net assets will be included in the single investment account on *A*'s balance sheet. Because of these characteristics, the equity method is frequently referred to as "one-line consolidation." For an illustration see the General Electric financials in Chapter X, where GE's finance subsidiary is both consolidated on one set of financials and accounted for by this equity method on another set. This is an extremely rare case providing a real life comparison of the equity method and consolidation. [If you find this exciting, you are a born (sp?) accountant.] The equity method is required where *B* Corp. is a joint venture corporation, such as when *A* and *C* each own 50 percent of *B* and operate it cooperatively.[100] It also applies even if *B* Corp. is not a joint venture but *A* Corp. has "significant influence" over *B*'s operating and financial policies.[101] Since adoption of *SFAS No. 94* in 1987, the equity method is no longer allowed for majority owned subsidiaries which are non-homogeneous. In those cases full consolidation is now required. For a majority owned subsidiary not in fact controlled by the majority shareholder, consolidation is proscribed, as we have seen, and ¶ 24 of *SFAS No. 94* indicates that the FASB intentionally remained silent on this issue; however it is likely that the significant influence test applies. According to *Opinion No. 18* there is a rule of thumb presumption that significant influence exists if there is 20 percent or greater ownership by *A* of *B*'s voting power.[102] However it may be noted that the subjectivity of the "significant influence" standard has enabled several firms to use the equity method when ownership of shares is at a much lower level but significant influence is claimed because of other factors such as interlocking directorates.[103] The FASB in May, 1981, issued an interpretation addressed to the latter abuse, further explaining the criterion, and the SEC has been reconsidering the criterion in large part because of its subjectivity and potential for abuse.[104]

96. APB Op. No. 18, ¶ 17 (1971).

100. APB Op. No. 18, ¶ 16 (1971).

101. Id. ¶ 17.

102. APB Op. No. 18, ¶ 17 (1971).

103. E.g., Leasco Corp., holding about 3 percent of Reliance Group in 1979 used the equity method on the grounds that the two firms were operated by the same officers and directors. See Briloff, Leveraged Leasco, Barron's 10/20/80 at 4.

104. See Briloff, supra n. 103, and FASB Interpretation No. 35, Criteria for Applying the Equity Method of Accounting for Investments in Common Stock (May, 1981), emphasizing that "significant influence" is a question of fact although the presumptions in ¶ 17 of APB Op. No. 18 (1971) are intended to provide a reasonable degree of uniformity.

Paragraph 4 of the Interpretation reads:

An ambiguity arises as to those unconsolidated subsidiaries which are not consolidated for the reason that there is no real control in *A Corp.*[106]

Footnote 4 to ¶ 14 of *APB Op. No. 18,* as amended by *SFAS No. 94* (1987), states, with respect to these subsidiaries, that the equity method may not apply to them.

4. Examples of indications that an investor may be unable to exercise significant influence over the operating and financial policies of an investee include:

a. Opposition by the investee, such as litigation or complaints to governmental regulatory authorities, challenges the investor's ability to exercise significant influence. (Sic)

b. The investor and investee sign an agreement under which the investor surrenders significant rights as a shareholder.

c. Majority ownership of the investee is concentrated among a small group of shareholders who operate the investee without regard to the views of the investor.

d. The investor needs or wants more financial information to apply the equity method than is available to the investee's other shareholders (for example, the investor wants quarterly financial information from an investee that publicly reports only annually), tries to obtain that information, and fails.

e. The investor tries and fails to obtain representation on the investee's board of directors. (Footnotes omitted.)

In SEC v. McLouth Steel Corporation, [1981 Current Vol.] Fed.Sec.L.Rep. (CCH) ¶ 98,032 (D.D.C. 1981), the Commission announced a consent decree stating that the Complaint in that case alleged use of the equity method by McLouth to account for its holdings in Jewell Coal and Coke Company despite an inability to exercise significant influence, identifying seven supporting factors:

1. McLouth was not represented on the Jewell Board of Directors, despite its request to be represented;

2. McLouth did not participate in Jewell's policy making process;

3. There was no significant interchange of managerial personnel between McLouth and Jewell;

4. The remaining 80.13 percent of Jewell's outstanding common stock was owned or controlled by one family;

5. McLouth was forced to resort to three separate lawsuits against Jewell to exert any influence;

6. McLouth was unable to win shareholder support for a dividend proposal; and

7. The relationship between the managements of McLouth and Jewell was overtly hostile.

106. ARB No. 51, ¶ 2, as amended by SFAS No. 94, ¶ 13, states:

2. The usual condition for a controlling financial interest is ownership of a majority voting interest, and, therefore, as a general rule ownership by one company, directly or indirectly, of over fifty per cent of the outstanding voting shares of another company is a condition pointing toward consolidation. However, there are exceptions to this general rule. A majority-owned subsidiary shall not be consolidated if control is likely to be temporary, or if it does not rest with the majority owner (as, for instance, if the subsidiary is in legal reorganization or in bankruptcy or operates under foreign exchange restrictions, controls, or other governmentally imposed uncertainties so severe that they cast significant doubt on the parent's ability to control the subsidiary.)

ARB No. 43, ch. 12, ¶ 8 (1968) states:

8. In view of the uncertain values and availability of the assets and net income of foreign subsidiaries subject to controls and exchange restrictions and the consequent unrealistic statements of income that may result from the translation of many foreign currencies into dollars, careful consideration should be given to the fundamental question of whether it is proper to consolidate the statements of foreign subsidiaries with the statements of United States companies. Whether consolidation of foreign subsidiaries is decided upon or not, adequate disclosure of foreign operations should be made.

The limitations ＊ ＊ ＊ in paragraph 2 of ARB No. 51 [see footnote 106], should also be applied as limitations to the use of the equity method.

This means that the equity method may not be used even for 50 percent-plus subsidiaries which are not consolidated because control is temporary, or control does not rest with the majority (e.g., because the company is in receivership), or a foreign government in fact prevents control, viz., because control does not in fact exist. But "significant influence" nevertheless may exist as to these noncontrolled subsidiaries and, if it does, it would seem the equity method should be used. Further, in subsequent footnotes (6 and 7), *Opinion No. 18* also states that the equity method may not be used for joint ventures or less-than-50 percent-owned companies over which *A* Corp. has significant influence, "insofar as the limitations on the use of the equity method outlined in footnote 4 would be applicable to investments other than those in subsidiaries." This may mean simply that the equity method does not apply when in fact *A*'s "significant influence" over *B* is merely temporary or does not exist. But this is not clear.[107]

(b) The Mechanics of the Equity Method

If the criteria for application of the equity method are met, *APB Op. No. 18* spells out in further nearly incomprehensible detail the mechanics.[108] We may translate and summarize these as follows:

(a) On acquisition. As noted previously, on acquisition of the *B* Corp. shares, they are entered at cost on *A*'s books, by a debit to an account which may be labelled "Investments," and a credit to cash or whatever was used to pay the seller.

(b) During the holding of the *B* shares. When the *B* Corp. shares are accounted for by the equity method, *A* Corp. must:

(i) Recognize *A*'s proportionate share of *B*'s post-acquisition earnings by debiting (on *A*'s financial statements) "investments" and crediting a revenue account. Any intercompany transactions must be eliminated, as for consolidated statements. This will result in *A*'s balance sheet assets (and consequently net worth) being increased for profits of *B*, or decreased for losses of *B*, and *A*'s income statement being similarly affected.

(ii) Recognize a charge against revenues for certain imputed depreciation, cost of sales, and amortization expense. (This is the little-known adjustment referred to above which will be explained immediately following ¶ (c) below).[109]

---

107. There is a further ambiguity. APB Op. No. 18 n. 4 (1971) says that where the equity method and consolidation of financial statements are not allowed, the cost method must be followed. Since SFAS No. 12 (1975) postdates APB Op. No. 18 (1971), it is likely that either the "cost or market" method of FAS No. 12 (1975) or the cost method will apply, depending on whether or not the *B* Corp. shares are "marketable equity securities" as defined at ¶ 7(a)–(b) of SFAS No. 12 (1975). See text at n. 87, et seq. supra.

108. APB Op. No. 18, ¶ 19. See n. 94 supra.

109. And see APB Op. No. 18, ¶ 19(b) (1971) quoted at n. 94 supra.

(iii) When dividends are received from *B*, whether or not from post-acquisition earnings, treat as a return of capital by a debit to "cash" and credit to "investments" on *A*'s financial statements, thereby not reflecting dividends in income (since *A*'s proportionate share of *B*'s earnings has already been recognized—at (i) above).

(iv) If there is an "other than a temporary decline" in the value of the *B* shares, debit a loss account and credit "investments."

(c) On resale. On resale of the *B* shares, *A* Corp. must charge the loss or credit revenue in the ordinary manner as for any asset by crediting investments at the current carrying value and debiting "cash" (or whatever is received) and charging or crediting the difference to loss or gains, as the case may be.

What is the explanation of item (b)(ii), "recognize a charge against revenues for imputed depreciation, cost of sales and amortization expense?" The crux of the matter is this:

When *A* Corp. purchases a sufficient portion of *B* Corp. to exert significant influence over *B*, *A* often pays more than a proportionate share of the fair market value of identifiable tangible and intangible assets, and an even greater amount more than a proportionate share of the book value of net worth shown on *B*'s books. We have seen that the cost of an isolated asset (presumably equal to fair market value) in excess of the seller's book value is recognized on the buyer's books when purchased, and depreciated or amortized (if a depreciable or amortizable asset), as time passes.[110] We have also seen that when a going concern is acquired in a business combination and the purchase price is in excess of the aggregate fair market values of the identifiable tangible and intangible assets, under the "purchase" mode of accounting, goodwill is required to be recognized and amortized over not more than forty years. Similarly when *A* acquires significant influence over *B* Corp. so that the equity method must be used, the excess of purchase price over fair market value of identifiable assets is required by GAAP to be imputed as goodwill and amortized as expense and the excess of fair value of the identifiable depreciable or amortizable assets over *B*'s book carrying values must be depreciated or amortized so as to reduce *A*'s revenues. This debit against revenues is balanced by a credit against the investment account.

(c) Illustration

For this purpose, and to permit comparisons, let us assume the same data as in our first illustration of purchase accounting [111] except that instead of purchasing 100 percent of the net assets of *B* Corp. for $30,000,000, *A* purchases 20 percent of the voting shares of *B* for $6,000,000.

On these assumptions, the balance sheets of *A* and *B* and the market value of *B*'s assets will be as follows:

110. See text at n. 9 supra.   111. See text at n. 17 supra.

Balance Sheets (000's omitted)

	A Corp.	B Corp.	Fair market value of B's assets and liabilities
Assets:			
Cash	$ 50,000	$ 0	$ 0
Inventory	20,000	10,000	12,000
Plant	70,000	15,000	18,000
Land		5,000	10,000
Totals	$140,000	$30,000	
Liabilities and Equity:			
Accounts payable	$ 24,000	$15,000	$15,000
Equity:			
Capital stock	30,000	6,000	
Capital surplus	39,000	4,200	
Earned surplus	47,000	4,800	
Totals	$140,000	$30,000	

At this point A's accounting, using the equity method, is simple. Merely add a new asset to the balance sheet, "Investment in B Corp., $6,000,000" and diminish A's cash by crediting that account the $6,000,000 paid.

However, the complexities of the equity method, its parallelism to consolidated statements, and its differences from the cost and cost or market methods, arise subsequently as B Corp. operates and pays dividends.

To keep this primer efficient, let us continue to assume no inter-corporate transactions have occurred but that during the first year B's operations resulted in earnings of $4,000,000, $1,000,000 in dividends was paid to all shareholders ($200,000 to A Corp.), that the plant is being depreciated at 10 percent, and that any goodwill would be amortized over the maximum forty years allowed by APB Op. No. 17. Further assume that inventory is carried on the first-in, first-out method and that the inventory was turned over at least once during the year so that B's entire opening inventory was sold during the year. On these assumptions, if A had owned 100 percent of B, and A's and B's financial statements were fully consolidated, as we have seen,[112] B's contributions to profits would have been less than B's reported $4,000,000 because:

    (a) The cost of goods sold on the consolidated statements would have been increased by the $2,000,000 excess of value of the inventory contributed by B over its book carrying value;

---

112.   See text at n. 76 supra.

(b) Depreciation (at 10 percent) would have been increased by $300,000 for the excess of the plant's $18,000,000 value over its $15,000,000 book carrying value; and

(c) Amortization of the $5,000,000 goodwill at 2.5 percent per year would have increased expenses by $125,000.

Thus, the contribution of B to the consolidated income of A and B, as we have seen, would have been calculated (ignoring related tax effects):

B's reported earnings	$4,000,000
Less: Additional cost of goods sold	(2,000,000)
Additional depreciation	(300,000)
Amortization of goodwill	(125,000)
	$1,575,000

Since A does not own 100 percent of B's shares, but owns only 20 percent, A's share of undistributed income (before dividends) therefore is 20 percent of $1,575,000, or $315,000. Since A's receipt of $200,000 cash, as a dividend, is not revenue to A, but diminishes A's investment, A's investment account will be written up by the net $115,000, A's cash account will be increased by the $200,000 received, and A's income account will be written up the $315,000 total, consisting of $200,000 realized in cash and the $115,000 increased equity in B Corp.—hence the name, "equity" method.[113]

C. SUMMARY

A summary of parts A and B of this chapter is fully contained in Figures 1–3. It is suggested that these are the best mnemonic device

---

113. For those who prefer to see the accountant's work, the following may be more readily understandable:

Observing the mechanics outlined in the text above (text at n. 108), the following debits and credits would properly reflect the effects on A's financial statements:

(a) On acquisition at January 1:

Investments	$6,000,000	
Cash		$6,000,000

To enter A's purchase of 20 percent voting interest in B Corp.

(b) At end of first year of A's ownership:

Investments	$800,000	
Investment Revenues		$800,000

To enter A's 20 percent share of B Corp.'s $4,000,000 net income for year

(c) At this point it becomes necessary to pretend that A acquired B Corp. and that purchase accounting would be followed, meaning that 20 percent of the fair market value of B's assets and liabilities would be entered on A's balance sheet with the balance of the purchase price entered as goodwill.

The calculation of the amounts to be allocated among the assets and goodwill proceeds thusly:

Purchase price paid for 20 percent of B	$6,000,000
Less—20 percent of B's book value (net assets)	(3,000,000)
Equals investment excess	$3,000,000

Allocation of investment excess:

20 percent of the $5,000,000 excess in value of Land over its book value on B's books	$1,000,000
20 percent of the $3,000,000 excess in value of Plant over its book value on B's books	600,000
20 percent of the $2,000,000 excess in inventory over that shown on B's books	400,000
Balance to goodwill	1,000,000
Investment excess	$3,000,000

for fully comprehending that subject matter. The following verbal summary of both parts may be a helpful supplement.

We have seen that when a single economic entity is formed by two legal entities coming together (i.e., *A* controls *B*), accountants ordinarily believe it more informative to present a single set of financial statements. Thus whether net assets of one legal entity are acquired by another legal entity, or instead shares of stock of the first, sufficient to provide control, are acquired by the second, a single set of financial statements usually will cover both. In the assets acquisition, these are statements of the acquiring legal entity whereas in the controlling share acquisition these are the consolidated statements of both legal entities.[133]

In any of these cases in which a single economic entity is formed, whether an assets acquisition or a controlling shares acquisition, one issue is whether a new basis of accountability arises for the acquisition. If so, "purchase accounting" will be required, with a write-up of the acquired company's assets, including goodwill, and amortization of goodwill and the written-up assets thereby diminishing the subsequent net income of the combined entity correspondingly.[135]

If instead the two sets of owners of the companies making up the single economic entity are envisioned as merely pooling their interests, with each set maintaining a continuing interest in rights and risks, no new basis of accountability arises, and the book carrying values of each will carry over to the balance sheets and be amortized on the income statements of the new entity.[136]

In cases where there is not a single economic entity formed because *A* does not control *B*, the financial statements of each will be separately published and the acquiring company will account for its investment on the cost basis [137] unless (a) the investment consists of marketable equity securities, in which case they will be accounted for on the "cost or market" basis,[138] or (b) the investor is involved in a joint venture in the investee or holds significant influence over operating and financial policies of the investee. In the latter case, (b), the equity method must be used with a new basis of accountability for the acquired company, and the investor will include in its net worth and income its proportionate share of the investee's income, adjusted to reflect depreciation and amortization of the fair market value of the investee's net assets and goodwill at the date of acquisition.[139]

133. See Parts B and C1, supra.

135. See Parts A2, B1(A) and B2(A)(1), supra.

136. See Parts A3, B1(B) and B2(B)(3), supra.

137. See Part B2(A)(1), supra.

138. See Part B2(A)(2), supra.

139. See Part B2(C)(3), supra.

*

Part F

ANALYSIS OF FINANCIAL INFORMATION

Chapter X

FINANCIAL STATEMENTS AND AN INTRODUCTION TO FINANCIAL ANALYSIS, THE CASH FLOW STATEMENT AND THE MD & A

OBJECTIVES

1. Comprehend the concept of cash flows, the statement of cash flows, and the SEC's required Management Discussion and Analysis of the financial statements.

2. Observe some fundamentals of financial and credit analysis.

RELEVANCE FOR LAWYERS

Lawyers regularly engage in advising their clients and others in financial matters. More importantly, in order to understand many legal obligations it is necessary to understand how financial data is used. For example, when a question arises as to whether a preferred stock should be issued with a mandatory redemption feature, the issuer's lawyer should be aware that a debt covenant based on financial concepts may be violated, which in turn could cause insolvency.

Accounting is the most important source of the raw data for investment and credit analysis, a subject which, like much else in modern life, is in a period of rapid change. We shall introduce you to some of the major themes so that the evolving changes may be placed in context by you as developments occur. This chapter is designed to initiate a lawyer's working knowledge of investment and credit analysis based on accounting information and to further explain financial statements, including the third required statement, the "statement of cash flows."

482

A. THE USERS AND USES OF FINANCIAL STATEMENTS—FUTURE CASH GENERATION FOR DISTRIBUTION TO CREDITORS AND OWNERS AS THE ULTIMATE GOAL

Economic decision-makers in our society are important users of accounting information. The FASB, in its *Statement of Financial Accounting Concepts No. 1,* points out that "[a]mong the potential users are owners, lenders, suppliers, potential investors and creditors, employees, management, directors, customers, financial analysts and advisors, brokers, underwriters, stock exchanges, lawyers, economists, taxing authorities, regulatory authorities, legislators, financial press and reporting agencies, labor unions, trade associations, business researchers, teachers and students, and the public." [a]

FASB *Concepts Statement No. 1* further points out that these users divide naturally into two categories. The first category consists of those in a position to demand and receive from the particular enterprise whatever data is deemed desirable. That group includes business managers, governmental agencies with statutory power to require information, and lenders and investors with bargaining power to compel production of data. The second category are those with little or no power to require specific information. This category includes small shareholders and debtholders of corporations whose shares or debt instruments are publicly traded, or suppliers and employees of businesses whether or not that business's equity and debt instruments are publicly traded.

Of this second category,

[i]nvestors and creditors and their advisors are the most obvious * * * external groups. [T]heir decisions significantly affect the allocation of resources in the economy. In addition, information provided to meet investors' and creditors' needs is likely to be generally useful to members of other groups who are interested in essentially the same financial aspects of business enterprises as investors and creditors.[b]

Before proceeding further, a question may be posed by those who are familiar with portfolio theory: [c] Of what utility is firm-specific financial information for investors in publicly traded firms?

a. FASB, Financial Accounting Concepts Statement No. 1, ¶ 24 (1978).

b. Id. ¶ 30.

c. For descriptions of portfolio theory, see:

R. Brealey, An Introduction to Risk and Return on Common Stocks (1969);

J. Cohen, E. Zinburg & A. Zeikel, Investment Analysis and Portfolio Management (3d ed. 1973), Part IV;

B. Lev, Financial Statement Analysis, A New Approach (1974) (Prentice–Hall, Inc.);

J. Lorie & M. Hamilton, The Stock Market, Theories and Evidence (1973) (Richard D. Irwin, Inc.);

F. Modigliani & G. Pogue, An Introduction to Risk and Return, Concepts and Evidence, 30 Fin.Analysts J. 68 (March–April 1974), 30 Fin.Analysts J. 69 (May–June 1974).

Those unfamiliar with portfolio theory should know that that theory holds that a diversified portfolio of efficiently traded securities virtually eliminates firm-specific risks (such as poor health of the CEO, excessive dependence on a single customer or supplier, etc.) and leaves the portfolio subject only to system-wide risks (those risks which cause a general rise or fall in the securities markets). That is because such things as the CEO's poor health will be bad for one firm but only to the extent it is good for another in the portfolio.

Without rewriting the book on portfolio theory, we here answer the question about utility, albeit cryptically, to indicate that it has not been ignored:

(a) First off, not all investors, creditors, suppliers and employees invest in diversified portfolios;

(b) Not all publicly traded securities are traded in efficient markets;

(c) Portfolio theory, like all models, is not a perfect model of the real world;

(d) Not all investors utilize portfolio theory; and

(e) A well-known "paradox" of the efficient market hypothesis is that unless at least some investors attempt to gather and analyze firm-specific information, the market will not reflect this information and therefore prices will not be efficiently established. Hence, firm-specific information does underlie the efficient market hypothesis which, in turn, is the foundation of portfolio theory.

See in general R. Posner & K. Scott, *Economics of Corporation Law and Securities Regulation*, Ch. 10 (1980). For these reasons, the SEC does impose firm-specific disclosure requirements and hence lawyers must understand firm-specific analysis. For another, only slightly less cryptic, answer, see W. Beaver, *Financial Reporting: An Accounting Revolution* 33–39 (1981).

All of the consumers of accounting information mentioned above are concerned with the economic condition of the enterprise, which the FASB has concluded means the ability to generate cash flows:

> To investors, lenders, suppliers, and employees, a business enterprise is a source of cash in the form of dividends or interest and perhaps appreciated market prices, repayment of borrowing, payment for goods or services, or salaries or wages. They invest cash, goods, or services in an enterprise and expect to obtain sufficient cash in return to make the investment worthwhile. They are directly concerned with the ability of the enterprise to generate favorable cash flows and may also

Study of these volumes is assisted by a minimal knowledge of algebra and business statistics, but one need not be intimidated if not familiar with these subjects as an entirely adequate understanding of algebra and statistics can be obtained from standard undergraduate texts. The business statistics involves an elementary understanding of frequency distributions, measures of their central tendency and dispersion, including the concept of standard deviation, and simple correlation of two variables.

Another volume, for which a knowledge of calculus is probably necessary is W. Sharpe, Portfolio Theory and Capital Markets (1970) (McGraw–Hill Book Company).

be concerned with how the market's perception of that ability affects the relative prices of its securities. To customers a business enterprise is a source of goods or services, but only by obtaining sufficient cash to pay for the resources it uses and to meet its other obligations can the enterprise provide those goods or services. To managers, the cash flows of a business enterprise are a significant part of their management responsibilities, including their accountability to directors and owners. Many, if not most, of their decisions have cash flow consequences for the enterprise. Thus, investors, creditors, employees, customers, and managers significantly share a common interest in an enterprise's ability to generate favorable cash flows.[d]

How does the enterprise's cash flow relate to the cash flow of the investor? The FASB has stated in Exposure Draft, Proposed SFAC, *Reporting Income, Cash Flows and Financial Position of Business Enterprises* (1981):

> 6. Investors invest cash in an enterprise with the expectation of receiving a greater amount of cash in return. For publicly owned enterprises, the amount of cash to be invested is normally determined by the stock market price. Similarly, the investors' return for a period may be computed as the stock market price at the end of the period, plus dividends paid during the period, less the stock market price at the beginning of the period (adjusted for stock splits, rights issues, and similar special events). A rate of return for the period may be computed by dividing the return by the price at the start of the period. The current stock market price of an equity security incorporates the market estimate of the discounted amount of future cash distributions from the enterprise to investors and future stock market prices. Since distributions from the enterprise to present and future investors ultimately depend on the cash flow of the enterprise, the market's assessment of future cash distributions must necessarily entail an assessment by the market as to the amounts, timing, and uncertainty of enterprise cash flows. As a consequence, the stock market price for an equity security may be regarded, at least in part, as a market estimate of the discounted amount of expected future cash flows of the enterprise. Those estimates of cash flows are commonly based on the enterprise's past performance, its present financial position, its liquidity and financial flexibility, and other information available to those who make investment decisions. As a consequence, there is a link—often complex and indirect ＊ ＊ ＊—between an investor's rate of return on an investment in an enterprise and the enterprises' cash flows.

We here consider some uses, for this purpose, of the balance sheet and income statement, and the statement of cash flows. We shall describe traditional financial statement analysis and note some major current developments. First let us note the meaning of the concepts of "liquidity" and "financial flexibility."

d.   Supra n. a, ¶ 25.

B. HISTORICAL NOTE ON THE CHANGING FOCUS OF ACCOUNTING INFORMATION

In the early decades of this century, public investment in common stock was not as widespread as it is now and accounting principles were designed principally to serve creditors—mainly bank lenders who had the bargaining power to demand balance sheets and did so. These banks, concerned largely with the borrower's liquidity, developed a system of analysis of the balance sheet based primarily on the "pounce principle." Thus a lender wanted to know the ability of a borrower to liquidate and repay the loan if pounced upon by the lender at any particular time. Lenders seemed generally agreed on the notion that the "pounce value" of the borrower was primarily composed of the firm's cash plus the immediate sale value of its other most liquid (or "current") assets: receivables, inventory, and marketable securities. This is the concept accountants have long called "liquidity," i.e., an asset's or liability's nearness to cash. An asset or liability is considered more, or less, liquid depending on the length of time after the balance sheet date at which it is expected to be received or paid in cash.

However, this early, nearly exclusive concern of creditors for liquidity has changed to include a concern for "financial flexibility" for the purpose of estimating the debtor's anticipated cash flow from operations, investment activity and financing transactions.[e]

"Financial flexibility" is the firm's adaptability to unforeseeable circumstances, so as to meet cash needs. For example, a firm with a large amount of marketable securities has the ability to generate cash by sale of these securities and is said to have a degree of financial flexibility for this reason. Financial flexibility is related to liquidity as can be seen from this very illustration, but these are not identical concepts. Thus accounts receivable of the same company, like the marketable securities, are also liquid assets, but unlike the securities, they may not evidence financial flexibility if the firm must maintain a consistent level of accounts receivable outstanding in order to keep up

---

e. According to L. Heath, Financial Reporting and the Evaluation of Solvency (AICPA Accounting Research Monograph No. 3, 1978) (hereafter sometimes cited as "Heath"), in discussing financial position, accountants divide a business's activities into three major categories:

Operating activities are those activities directly related to the purchase and sale of raw materials, supplies, and merchandise, the conversion of raw material and supplies into finished goods and services, the sale of finished goods and services, and the servicing of goods and services sold previously. *Financing* activities are those activities directly related to obtaining capital including, for example, the borrowing and repayment of debt, the issuance and reacquisition of a company's stock, the conversion of securities into common stock, and the payment of dividends. *Investment* activities include the purchase and sale of securities of various types (excluding a company's own securities) and the purchase and sale of plant and equipment that is used in the production, distribution, and maintenance of other goods and services. The lines between those different types of activities are not clear, but the distinction is, nevertheless, useful for this discussion. (Italics supplied.)

its sales level.[f] However, accounting has lagged behind finance. Even today, little formal information concerning financial flexibility is required to be disclosed.

Beginning in the 1930s perhaps as a result of the federal securities acts and other forces, accounting began to be guided by the perceived needs of creditors and investors in corporate securities for data on profitability of the firm, with a consequential emphasis on income. The income statement came to be considered more important than the previously predominant balance sheet which came to virtually dominate accounting thought until recently.

At present financial statement analysis consists both of credit analysis, concerned largely with liquidity, financial flexibility and cash flow, and investment analysis concerned with all of these but also largely with profitability. However, all of these aspects of financial analysis are closely related. Professor Heath, who uses the term "solvency" to denote the concerns of credit analysts for liquidity, flexibility and cash flow, states: "[l]ong-run solvency depends on long-run profitability. No method of obtaining money to pay debts will be available in the long run to an enterprise that is not profitable. In the long run, however, profitability and solvency do not necessarily go together. A profitable enterprise in need of cash to finance increasing receivables, inventory, and plant may tie itself to an unrealistic debt repayment schedule that results in its insolvency."[g]

In the past decade many of our largest businesses have undergone radical changes in their capital structure to take on enormous debt as a proportion of total capital. This has been largely caused by the takeover movement which launched leveraged buyouts and recapitalizations as a response. But debt and interest on it must be repaid when due. As a result, fixed cash demands have made these companies much more risky and cash flow has now assumed primacy if not exclusivity in the minds of financial analysts.

Let us briefly illustrate modern financial analysis, for both profitability and solvency, by analyzing some actual recent financial statements. This is an analysis by lawyers, not financial analysts. Its purpose is to illustrate use of the financial statements, not to exhaust the possibilities.

f. FASB, Discussion Memorandum, Reporting Funds Flows, Liquidity, and Financial Flexibility (hereafter in this Chapter cited as "FASB Discussion Memorandum") ¶ 184 (Dec. 15, 1980).

g. L. Heath 1, supra. For a dramatic illustration of such an insolvency, see SEC, Report of Investigation in the Matter of National Telephone Co., Inc. [1977–1978 Transfer Binder] Fed.Sec.L.Rep. (CCH) ¶ 81,410 (1978).

C. FINANCIAL STATEMENTS OF GENERAL ELECTRIC COMPANY CONTAINED IN ITS 1989 ANNUAL REPORT TO SHAREHOLDERS

First, peruse very lightly the financial statements, notes and auditor's repor thereon, for GE in the Appendix to this chapter.

D. SOME GENERAL OBSERVATIONS CONCERNING FINANCIAL STATEMENTS

The GE financial statements are far more complicated than the simple statements we have been using for illustrations, yet many modern corporations have become so incredibly complex, and their history so intricate, that financial statements cannot hold all of the necessary accounting information. The explanatory footnotes frequently run several pages, as in the case of GE, and contain a great deal of information necessary to understand the basis on which the financial statements are constructed.

These statements were chosen for illustration because the arrangement is good and the captions and footnotes serve to illustrate a number of points that are discussed in this book. They were chosen before they were analyzed. Let us see what analysis can and cannot tell us about this enterprise.

One unusual aspect of GE's presentation is that it has first consolidated all its subsidiaries as required by *SFAS No. 94*. The consolidated statements are those headed "General Electric Company and consolidated affiliates." Then the company has separated out General Electric Financial Services, Inc. (GEFS) because it believes that will be more meaningful to users. These additional statements are the columns headed "GE" and "GEFS." The "GE" financials are on the equity method. Thus, on the "GE" balance sheet, there is a "one line consolidation" of GEFS carried as "Investment in GEFS" at $6,069,000,000 for 1989. Similarly the "GE" income statement includes in one line, "Earnings of GEFS." The "GEFS" statements are for the financial services company alone.

Note that the businesses in which the company is engaged are not disclosed in the body of the statements, although some reference to them is made in the footnotes. This illustrates that accounting is a universal language that reduces all the varied activities of the manufacturing, mining, transportation, mercantile, publishing, financial and service industries to the single common denominator of monetary measurement. This very universality is also a patent weakness which is only partially remedied by footnotes 33 and 34 which do reveal the thirteen lines of business engaged in by the company as well as geographic segments of the company. Of course other, unaudited parts of the Annual Report to Shareholders, of which these statements are a major portion, contain a good deal of further information concerning the business segments. Other portions of the typical Annual Report are the President's letter, Financial Highlights, and, most importantly, the Management's Discussion (infra p. 530).

Also note that all figures on the GE statements (other than per share data) are rounded off to millions of dollars, which is permissible under accounting and SEC practice. One virtue claimed for this practice is that it helps to avoid readers thinking that accounting has a precision which it does not claim.

The statements of two or more years side-by-side are known as "comparative" statements. It has become customary to set them forth in this fashion in corporate annual reports to stockholders. Indeed, SEC Rule 14a–3 [h] requires it in annual reports to shareholders for companies subject to SEC proxy regulation.

Finally, notice that the assets portion of the balance sheet is arranged with the most current and liquid assets toward the top: Cash first, then Marketable securities, then Current receivables, then Inventories, and then Other receivables.

The next item is not liquid, Property, plant and equipment, sometimes referred to as "fixed assets" followed by Investment in GEFS and Intangible assets.

Finally, there is a category for "All other assets" which include investments in other companies and long-term receivables, etc. (see n. 20).

The liabilities portion of the balance sheet is similarly arranged with the most current payables first. After the liabilities is shown equity.

These two progressions from current to less current items are a customary arrangement of most balance sheets. In many cases the balance sheet is more specifically classified into current and non-current assets and liabilities (termed "classified" balance sheets).

E. RATIO ANALYSIS GENERALLY

One technique of analysis of financial statements is to find the ratios [i] between various pairs of elements of the financial statements so as to obtain a common denominator for comparison with the same company's ratios in prior years and with the ratios of other companies in the same or different industries. The ratios may be between a pair of elements of a single financial statement. E.g., the current ratio, which we shall consider shortly, is the ratio of two sets of balance sheet

h. 17 C.F.R. § 240.14a–3.

i. A ratio may be expressed by a phrase (say, 3 to 1), or a numerator and denominator (say, 3/1) or by the same thing under the decimal system (say, 3.0). The decimal expression is used typically only for ratios where the numerator is smaller than the denominator. The ratio expresses relative size of the two quantities. In our illustration the numerator is three times the denominator. If the ratio is a current ratio, it would mean current assets are three times as much as current liabilities.

items, current assets and current liabilities. Or the two elements of the ratio may be taken from two different statements. E.g., the ratio of sales revenues to accounts receivable is based on an income statement element and a balance sheet element. Similarly ratios may be based on an element of the statement of cash flows and an element of the balance sheet (e.g., cash flow to debt). The number is virtually unlimited.[j] Auditors analyze these ratios in what they refer to as an "analytical review" for the purpose of detecting possible errors and irregularities because of variances from prior periods' statements or those of other firms in the industry.

Creditors and investors do continue to use ratio analysis.[k] One study found that analysts consider ratio analysis to be of "moderate-to-strong" importance to lenders. The following chart summarizes the ratios considered most significant by those interviewed in the study.

Financial Ratios Considered Most Significant
(Based on Interview Results) [*]

Financial Ratios	Short Term Bank Loans Seasonal	Trade Credit	Intermediate Term Bank Loans	Long Term Bonds
Accounts receivable turnover	X	X	X	X
Cash flow to total debt			X	X
Current liabilities to tangible net worth		X		
Current ratio	X	X		
Fixed-charge coverage				X
Inventory to working capital		X		
Quick ratio		X		
Return on sales			X	
Total debt to tangible net worth	X	X	X	X
Working capital to sales			X	

[*] Interviews conducted with senior executives at 3 bond rating agencies, 11 leading investment banking firms, 2 large life insurance companies, Dun and Bradstreet, 24 leading banks in 8 cities, and Robert Morris Associates.

[Ed's. Note: Most of these ratios are explained in the following materials.]

The real question, however, is whether the significance attached is well-founded; i.e., do the ratios provide predictive value? Apparently it is believed that they do and there is evidence that this belief is well-founded.[l]

j. See Beaver, Financial Ratios as Predictors of Failure, Empirical Research in Accounting, Selected Studies, 1966 Supp., J. Acctg. Res. 71, which examined thirty ratios.

k. See Backer & Gosman, Financial Reporting and Business Liquidity (Nat. Assoc. of Accountants) 1978.

l. Beaver, supra, considers the utility of various ratios in predicting insolvency, and finds utility in some of them. See also, to similar effect, Altman, Haldeman, and Narayan, Zeta Analysis: A New Model to Identify Bankruptcy Risk of Corporations, J. of Banking and Finance 29 (Spring 1977).

Let us in the remainder of this chapter analyze the GE statements for liquidity, profitability, historical cash flow of the company, and financial flexibility. Following GE's lead, we shall make this analysis solely for the "GE" columns which account for GEFS by the "equity method."

F. LIQUIDITY ANALYSIS

1. SHORT–TERM LIQUIDITY—WORKING CAPITAL ANALYSIS

ACCOUNTING RESEARCH BULLETIN NO. 43, CHAPTER 3A

AICPA, 1953.*

Working Capital, Current Assets and Current Liabilities

"1. The working capital of a borrower has always been of prime interest to grantors of credit; and bond indentures, credit agreements, and preferred stock agreements commonly contain provisions restricting corporate actions which would effect a reduction or impairment of working capital. Many such contracts forego precise or uniform definitions and merely provide that current assets and current liabilities shall be determined in accordance with generally accepted accounting principles. Considerable variation and inconsistency exists, however, with respect to their classification and display in financial statements. In this section the committee discusses the nature of current assets and current liabilities with a view toward a more useful presentation thereof in financial statements.

"2. The committee believes that, in the past, definitions of current assets have tended to be overly concerned with whether the assets may be immediately realizable. The discussion which follows takes cognizance of the tendency for creditors to rely more upon the ability of debtors to pay their obligations out of the proceeds of current operations and less upon the debtor's ability to pay in case of liquidation. It should be emphasized that financial statements of a going concern are prepared on the assumption that the company will continue in business. Accordingly, the views expressed in this section represent a departure from any narrow definition or strict *one year* interpretation of either current assets or current liabilities; the objective is to relate the criteria developed to the operating cycle of a business.

"3. Financial position, as it is reflected by the records and accounts from which the statement is prepared, is revealed in a presentation of the assets and liabilities of the enterprise. In the statements of manufacturing, trading, and service enterprises these assets and liabilities are generally classified and segregated; if they are classified logically, summations or totals of the *current* or *circulating* or *working* assets, hereinafter referred to as *current assets,* and of obligations currently payable, designated as *current liabilities,* will permit the ready determination of working capital. *Working capital,* sometimes called *net working capital,* is represented by the excess of current assets over current liabilities and identifies the relatively liquid portion of total enterprise capital which constitutes a margin or buffer for meeting obligations within the ordinary operating cycle of business. If the conventions of accounting relative to the identification and presentation of current assets and current liabilities are made logical and consistent, the amounts, bases of valuation, and composition of such assets and liabilities and their relation to the total assets or capital employed will provide valuable data for credit and management purposes and afford a sound basis for comparisons from year to year. It is recognized that there may be exceptions, in special cases, to certain of the inclusions and exclusions as set forth in this section. When such exceptions occur they should be accorded the treatment merited in the particular circumstances under the general principles outlined herein.

"4. For accounting purposes, the term *current assets* is used to designate cash and other assets or resources commonly identified as those which are reasonably expected to be realized in cash or sold or consumed during the normal operating cycle of the business. Thus the term comprehends in general such resources as (a) cash available for current operations and items which are the equivalent of cash; (b) inventories of merchandise, raw materials, goods in process, finished goods, operating supplies, and ordinary maintenance material and parts; (c) trade accounts, notes, and acceptances receivable; (d) receivables from officers, employees, affiliates, and others, if collectible in the ordinary course of business within a year; (e) installment or deferred accounts and notes receivable if they conform generally to normal trade practices and terms within the business; (f) marketable securities representing the investment of cash available for current operations; and (g) prepaid expenses such as insurance, interest, rents, taxes, unused royalties, current paid advertising service not yet received, and operating supplies. Prepaid expenses are not current assets in the sense that they will be converted into cash but in the sense that, if not paid in advance, they would require the use of current assets during the operating cycle.

"5. The ordinary operations of a business involve a circulation of capital within the current asset group. Cash is expended for materials, finished parts, operating supplies, labor, and other factory services, and such expenditures are accumulated as inventory cost. Inventory costs, upon sale of the products to which such costs attach, are converted into trade receivables and ultimately into cash again. The average time intervening between the acquisition of materials or services entering this process and the final cash realization constitutes an *operating cycle.* A one-year time period is to be used as a basis for the segregation of current assets in cases where there are several operating cycles occurring within a year. However, where the period of the operating cycle is more than twelve months, as in, for instance, the tobacco, distillery, and lumber businesses, the longer period should be used. Where a particular business has no clearly defined operating cycle, the one-year rule should govern.

"6. This concept of the nature of current assets contemplates the exclusion from that classification of such resources as: (a) cash and claims to cash which are restricted as to withdrawal or use for other than current operations, are designated for expenditure in the acquisition or construction of noncurrent assets, or are segregated [1] for the liquidation of long-term debts; (b) investments in securities (whether marketable or not) or advances which have been made for the purposes of control, affiliation, or other continuing business advantage; (c) receivables arising from unusual transactions (such as the sale of capital assets, or loans or advances to affiliates, officers, or employees) which are not expected to be collected within twelve months; (d) cash surrender value of life insurance policies; (e) land and other natural resources; (f) depreciable assets; and (g) long-term prepayments which are fairly chargeable to the operations of several years, or deferred charges such as * * * bonus payments under a long-term lease, costs of rearrangement of factory layout or removal to a new location, * * *.

"7. The term *current liabilities* is used principally to designate obligations whose liquidation is reasonably expected to require the use of existing resources properly classifiable as current assets, or the creation of other current liabilities. As a balance-sheet category, the classification is intended to include obligations for items which have entered into the operating cycle, such as payables incurred in the acquisition of materials and supplies to be used in the production of goods or in providing services to be offered for sale; collections received in advance of the delivery of goods or performance of services; [2] and debts which arise from operations directly related to the operating cycle, such as accruals for wages, salaries, commissions, rentals, royalties, and income and other taxes. Other liabilities whose regular and ordinary liquidation is expected to occur within a relatively short period of time, usually twelve months, are also intended for inclusion, such as short-term debts arising from the acquisition of capital assets,

1. Even though not actually set aside in special accounts, funds that are clearly to be used in the near future for the liquidation of long-term debts, payments to sinking funds, or for similar purposes should also, under this concept, be excluded from current assets. However, where such funds are considered to offset maturing debt which has properly been set up as a current liability, they may be included within the current asset classification.

2. Examples of such current liabilities are obligations resulting from advance collections on ticket sales, which will normally be liquidated in the ordinary course of business by the delivery of services. On the contrary, obligations representing long-term deferments of the delivery of goods or services would not be shown as current liabilities. Examples of the latter are the issuance of a long-term warranty or the advance receipt by a lessor of rental for the final period of a ten-year lease as a condition to execution of the lease agreement.

serial maturities of long-term obligations, amounts required to be expended within one year under sinking fund provisions, and agency obligations arising from the collection or acceptance of cash or other assets for the account of third persons.

"8. This concept of current liabilities would include estimated or accrued amounts which are expected to be required to cover expenditures within the year for known obligations (a) the amount of which can be determined only approximately (as in the case of provisions for accruing bonus payments) or (b) where the specific person or persons to whom payment will be made cannot as yet be designated (as in the case of estimated costs to be incurred in connection with guaranteed servicing or repair of products already sold). The current liability classification, however, is not intended to include * * * debts to be liquidated by funds which have been accumulated in accounts of a type not properly classified as current assets, or long-term obligations incurred to provide increased amounts of working capital for long periods. When the amounts of the periodic payments of an obligation are, by contract, measured by current transactions, as for example by rents or revenues received in the case of equipment trust certificates or by the depletion of natural resources in the case of property obligations, the portion of the total obligation to be included as a current liability should be that representing the amount accrued at the balance-sheet date.

"9. The amounts at which various current assets are carried do not always represent their present realizable cash values. Accounts receivable net of allowances for uncollectible accounts, and for unearned discounts where unearned discounts are considered, are effectively stated at the amount of cash estimated as realizable. However, practice varies with respect to the carrying basis for current assets such as marketable securities and inventories. In the case of marketable securities where market value is less than cost by a substantial amount and it is evident that the decline in market value is not due to a mere temporary condition, the amount to be included as a current asset should not exceed the market value. The basis for carrying inventories is stated in chapter 4. It is important that the amounts at which current assets are stated be supplemented by information which reveals, for temporary investments, their market value at the balance-sheet date, and for the various classifications of inventory items, the basis upon which their amounts are stated and, where practicable, indication of the method of determining the cost—e.g., *average cost, first-in first-out, last-in first-out,* etc."

(A) The Current Ratio

As we have noted, credit analysts traditionally have been concerned with the "pounce value" of the debtor company. To help determine this, they focussed attention on the current assets and current liabilities on the classified balance sheet. They developed the "current ratio," that is the ratio of current assets to current liabilities. It is obvious that the assets to which short-term creditors will look for the payment of their debts are the current assets, namely cash, receivables that will become cash, and inventories which later may become first receivables and then cash. In most industries several years ago it was considered that a 2 to 1 current ratio, i.e., twice as many current assets as current liabilities, was a reasonably strong ratio. A higher ratio was still better. For companies with inventories, anything much lower raised a question. However in recent years a desirable current ratio has diminished far below the old traditional norm for several reasons. For example, financial management will call for minimizing cash on hand whenever a company can earn more on productive assets than what the bank will pay for cash funds. And inventories will be minimized by improved handling and transportation if that is cost efficient. Thus a lower current ratio may be evidence of good management.

GE has not supplied "classified balance sheets" clearly designating current and non-current assets and liabilities. Doubtless one strong reason for this must have been that this would make the fully consolidated statements into a mish-mash because they include the peculiar assets of a finance subsidiary, GEFS. Nevertheless we can fairly make our own classifications for the "GE" data on the equity method. In current assets we would count the Cash, Marketable securities, Current receivables and Inventories and exclude the others even though note 20 indicates the final item, "All other assets," may include some current assets. We exclude these because note 20 shows many are non-current and for others it is unclear. Furthermore, they are of such a character as to be very unlike the other current assets. We include in current liabilities the first five items.

On this basis, the GE current ratios for 1988 and 1989 were 1.16 and 1.12 respectively. From the "Management's Discussion of Financial Resources and Liquidity" reprinted at p. 536 infra, we find that management has improved the turnover of both receivables and inventory, thereby minimizing them, making for a lower ratio. We also see that inventories are valued mainly on the lower LIFO basis. On the other hand, from note 1 of the financials we find that GE's inventory includes much overhead which it had formerly excluded and which increased the ratio. Nevertheless additional analysis below indicates nothing of concern regarding GE's current ratio although it is far below the old norm. Perhaps the most persuasive reason is that with its finance subsidiary, GEFS, GE has great financial flexibility.

The current ratio traditionally has been the most widely used of an extensive series of ratios that can be applied to the figures in the financial statements for various purposes. We point out, however, that every ratio must be used with some circumspection, some awareness of the circumstances of the particular company, and the possible lack of appropriateness of usual rules of thumb like the 2 to 1 figure mentioned. For instance, are the inventories really available for the payment of short-term debt? When inventories are reduced below the level needed for profitable operations, they may produce receivables and cash, which might seem available to pay debt, but a company will go out of business unless the inventories are restored. This means new debts; therefore nothing will have been accomplished by liquidation of inventory. A permanent amount of inventory is as necessary a part of the permanent assets of a company as is its land and buildings. This becomes even more clear when, as in the present case, inventory already has been pared down, especially if the least salable inventory may be what remains, although there is no indication of that circumstance in the GE case.

Should not the same reasoning be applied to receivables?

Suppose that a current creditor says that he is not interested in the ability of the debtor to replace its inventory or receivables. He wants to know that if matters become desperate and the debtor becomes insolvent, he could force a liquidation sufficient to pay the current liabilities without regard to replacement and continuation of the business, and he would argue that from that point of view the inventory and receivables are sound current assets. There are three things wrong with this argument. In the first place, on a forced liquidation, inventories (unless on LIFO as in GE's case) have a tendency to bring a great deal less than their cost, and the cost figure on the balance sheet cannot be relied upon as a forced liquidation value. In the second place, if there really were an insolvency, the long-term debt would be accelerated under the typical terms of debt agreements; i.e., it would become due and payable immediately by reason of some default, and would thus become a current liability competing for immediate payment with those creditor claims that are listed as current liabilities on the financial statements. Finally, if matters reached the stage of efforts to force a liquidation, such actions could be thwarted by a petition in bankruptcy.

Suppose that instead of being a manufacturer, GE were a trucking company. It would then have no inventories; its working assets (trucks) would be classified not as current assets but as fixed assets. Its only current assets would be cash, marketable securities, receivables, and prepaid expenses, and yet its current liabilities might be the usual amounts. Thus, its current ratio may be less than 1.15, or so, and, indeed, sometimes less than 1.0. A person who uses ratios without intelligent understanding might therefore readily conclude that the company was in bad shape for that reason alone. On the contrary, this different kind of current asset picture is typical for companies without inventories, which use fixed assets as their earning resources.

(B) The "Acid Test" (or the "Quick Asset Ratio")

Because of these considerations many credit grantors have for several years used a different ratio, known as the "quick asset ratio" or the "acid test"—i.e., the ratio of cash, marketable securities, and receivables to the current liabilities. That is, inventories and prepaid expenses are not included in this test. A ratio of 1 to 1 is the typical target marked for the acid test. GE's acid test ratios for 1988 and 1989 were .67 and .64, respectively, not terribly alarming in light of the additional factors already noted.

Notes

10–1. *Classification of Accounts.* There are some difficult questions of classification between the current and non-current categories.

If a debt is due say, in a single amount, twenty years from now, it is carried as a fixed liability. If, however, it is payable in installments and some portion thereof is payable within one year, that portion is classified as a current liability under current practice. Notice the explanation of the short-term debt liability in GE's n. 21 indicating "Current portion of long-term borrowings."

Until a few years ago, practices varied in classifying short-term debt which is not intended to be paid off except by "rolling over"; i.e., replacement with new short-term debt. Is this more realistically to be considered long-term debt, or is the short-term legal liability and the risk of non-renewal a basis for requiring classification as a current liability? The consequences under contractual limitations as to working capital can be important.[m]

SFAS No. 6, *Classification of Short–Term Obligations Expected to be Refinanced* (1975), adopts the working capital definition of *ARB No. 43, Chapter 3A,* and states that certain items such as trade accounts payable and other normal accruals must always be shown as current liabilities, but that borrowings which the company intends to, and demonstrably can, refinance may be shown as long-term obligations. Demonstrability is subject to stringent standards; it means either that refinancing was actually obtained before the statements were published or that a good commitment from some lender has been obtained.

10–2. *A Critique of Current Account Analysis.* For the history of the development of *ARB No. 43, Chapter 3A* on working capital and a severely critical evaluation, which finds the definitions of current assets and liabilities to be inconsistent, confusing, irrational and misleading, see L. Heath, *Financial Reporting and the Evaluation of Solvency* (AICPA Accounting Research Monograph 3) (1978).

Professor Heath, finds the criterion for current assets, those to be "realized in cash or sold or consumed during the normal operating cycle," to be overly broad. He points out that some portion of plant and equipment will be used during the operating cycle and hence that portion would

m. For an example of a restrictive covenant for a loan agreement, see Am.Bar Foundation, Commentaries on Model Debenture Indenture Provisions 456 (1971): The Company will not permit (i) Consolidated Working Capital at any time to be less than _____ or (ii) Consolidated Current Assets to be less than ___% of Consolidated Current Liabilities.

be included in current assets under the criterion. However, that is not the practice.

Further he notes that the operating cycle concept is poorly defined. He states, "John W. Coughlan [*Working Capital and Credit Standing,* Accountancy 110 (November, 1960)] argued that the definitions of the operating cycle and of current assets are completely circular because the operating cycle is defined as the period money is "tied up" in current assets, and current assets are defined as those that would be converted into cash within the operating cycle. He illustrated by a numerical example involving a company that sells a portion of its output on open account with terms of forty-five days and a portion on installment terms payable over four and one-half years. He then reasoned—Consider the above attempt to determine whether installment receivables were current assets. Installment receivables were current if they would be realized in cash within the operating cycle; but whether they were so realized depended on whether the period for their collection was included in the computation of this cycle. Installment receivables are a current asset if, in computing the normal operating cycle, they are assumed to be current assets."

Current liabilities, Heath continues, are also poorly defined. The concept of Chapter 3A of *ARB No. 43* is "based on an assumed relationship between specific assets and specific liabilities that does not exist. * * * It is meaningless to try to determine which of a company's many assets were the source of the cash used to pay a particular liability. * * * Similarly, it is meaningless to try to determine which of a company's liabilities 'is reasonably expected to require the use of existing resources properly classifiable as current assets.' "

10–3. *Conclusiveness of the Classification of Accounts on the Financial Statements.* Lawyers concerned with drafting restrictive covenants in notes and indentures may not be totally aware of these ambiguities of current assets and liabilities. Those concerned with debtors allegedly in default because working capital has fallen below the covenant limits may find fruitful sources of argument in Chapter 3A instead of taking the firm's accountant's determination of the client's current assets and liabilities as conclusive. That determination is, of course, usually required to be made in accordance with "generally accepted accounting principles."

2. EVALUATION OF LIQUIDITY ANALYSIS THROUGH WORKING CAPITAL RATIOS

Does working capital analysis focus on the real concerns of creditors? What is the issue to be addressed?

One writer has stated the shortcomings of analysis in terms of current accounts:

> In the development of an integrated structure at least three points merit consideration. One is that the true source of funds which underlies net cash flows is sales. A second is that current liabilities (as of January 1) do not represent the sum total of cash outlays anticipated within the forthcoming period. The third point is that acceptance of

the going concern hypothesis [n] implies that neither current assets nor current liabilities are reducible to zero. * * *

Current liabilities are never wholly discharged; nor—by analogous reasoning—are current assets ever entirely available to meet currently maturing obligations.[o]

Professor Heath explains that the important thing is the timing of and ability to adjust cash flows. "The central question in solvency analysis today is whether the cash expected to be received within a given period will equal or exceed required cash payments within that same period." [p]

He goes further and says that the current practice of classifying assets as current and noncurrent is not only useless, but is misleading to users of financial statements and should be discontinued as GE has done.[q] In determining cash availability Professor Heath suggests two things should be considered:

(a) timing and amount of expected cash inflows and outflows; and

(b) adaptability of the firm to changing conditions so as to cut down on outflows when inflows diminish, or to increase inflows when outflows increase, which he calls "financial flexibility."

He recommends a simple and straight-forward substitute for traditional current ratio analysis. His suggestion is to merely increase disclosure of the attributes of the various balance sheet accounts which are relevant to liquidity.[r]

Since GE's cash flow is very good, much of our working capital analysis above would be taken lightly by most analysts.

The SEC in its requirements for the Management Discussion part of the annual report to shareholders (see the GE statement infra p. 536) has largely embraced Heath's disclosure suggestion. See the material there captioned "Management's Discussion of Financial Resources and Liquidity."

Does this disclosure make more sense than does the current ratio analysis as explained above? Would a ratio analysis still be useful?

Although Heath points to a study by Professor William Beaver [s] to support his position that the analysis of working capital accounts is counterproductive, that may not be a fair conclusion. Beaver did find that three ratios had a *higher* predictive power than the current asset ratio, but he did not find the latter to be useless. The five ratios he found to be the best predictors of failure, in this order, were:

(a) Cash flow (defined as net income plus depreciation, depletion and amortization) to total debt (including preferred stock)

(b) Net income to total assets

---

n. See Chapter I, subpart M1.

o. James E. Walter, Determination of Technical Solvency, J.Bus. 30, No. 1 (January, 1957) 32, 38, and 43.

p. See Heath, supra at 17.

q. Id. at 8.

r. Id. at 74–86.

s. Beaver, Alternative Accounting Measures as Predictors of Failure, Acctg.Rev. 118 (Jan. 1968).

(c) Total debt to total assets

(d) Current assets to current liabilities

(e) Cash to current liabilities.

3. LONG–TERM LIQUIDITY ANALYSIS

(A) The Long–Term Debt to Fixed Assets Ratio

A ratio frequently considered in determining the longer term prospects for liquidity is long-term debt to fixed assets. The notion seems to be that fixed assets will ultimately be turned into cash from operations, or from sale or refinancing to pay the long-term debt.

For the GE statements the analyst would have to make several decisions as to which assets to include in his denominator for fixed assets and which liabilities to include in the numerator for long-term debt. E.g., should "Intangible Assets" or "All other assets" be included in fixed assets? Should "All other liabilities" be included in long-term debt? Is enough information given about them to decide?

But what of the debit balance for the item captioned "Deferred Income Taxes," which usually floats below liabilities and above stockholders' equity but is sometimes partially included in current liabilities? [t] And the mysterious caption without a dollar figure appended, "Commitments and contingent liabilities"? For the latter, see Chapter VII supra; regarding deferred taxes, see Chapter V.

(B) The Long–Term Debt to Capitalization [Long–Term Debt Plus Equity] Ratios

Another comparison thought to be useful in assessing long-term liquidity is the ratio of long-term debt to total capitalization (i.e., the sum of long-term debt and equity), or some variation of this ratio, such as equity to total capitalization (the complement to total debt to total capitalization) or long-term debt to equity. [u] Here, too, the same classification problems and questions just raised in (A) above apply and need not be reiterated.

Counting as long-term debt not only the $3,947,000,000 Long-term borrowings of GE but also the $5,635,000,000 of "All other liabilities" for 1989, but excluding "Deferred income taxes," the ratio is .31, which most analysts would consider excellent for an industrial company. Notice that GE's management in its Management Discussion (infra p.

---

t. See APB Opinion No. 11, Accounting for Income Taxes, ¶ 57 (1967) and SFAS No. 37, Balance Sheet Classification of Deferred Income Taxes (1980).

Although the analyst is not bound by these rules, they may be "the law" for purposes of interpreting restrictive covenants in debt agreements.

u. The ratio considered in the preceding section, long-term debt to fixed assets, is also a variation of this ratio. Essentially

the expectation is that current assets and current liabilities will fluctuate together, and that the long-term picture of the company is shown by fixed assets balanced by capitalization, i.e., long-term debt and shareholders' equity. Each of the variations of this ratio shows how much of the capitalization (or how much of the fixed assets) is represented by equity and how much is debt.

538) excluded "All other liabilities" to derive a .21 debt to capitalization ratio and said, "This relationship of debt and equity capital is sound and is well within the range of what would be expected of a strong industrially oriented firm."

An outside analyst might add, "Given the permanency of high inflation and the financial flexibility and excellent cash flow of GE, don't worry about whether this ratio is too high—perhaps it is too low to take full advantage of leverage."

What does that mean? What is "leverage"?

Leveraging is the use of debt in combination with equity capital. If the rate of return on the whole investment is higher than the interest rate, the equity owners get the benefit of that excess. If lower, they suffer the detriment. Thus if a firm can earn 10% return on investment, has borrowed at 6%, and is capitalized with $5,000 of debt and $5,000 of equity, the $1,000 return (10% of $10,000) will go to pay $300 (6% of $5,000) to the debt holders and $700 to the equity holders. It can be said that through the use of debt, the equity geared up or leveraged a 10% return ($1,000 on $10,000) to 14% ($700 on $5,000).

If the return on total investment falls below the debt interest rate, the leverage works in reverse. Thus if a company with the same capitalization were paying 20% interest for all of its debt, but it was earning only 10% on its capitalization, it would find that the entire $1,000 return on the total $10,000 of debt and equity must be used to pay the interest on the debt only, leaving a zero return on the equity.

There is another limit to appropriate leverage. It would not be wise to finance 100% with debt (perhaps retaining equity through a penny's investment in no-par value capital stock) even if the firm's return exceeds the interest rate. An external limitation on the amount of debt will be imposed by the potential lender, who wants a significant amount of equity as a "cushion" for his debt, i.e., an investment in the corporation which will suffer any losses before the lender. The smaller the ratio of debt to equity, or to total capitalization, or to assets, the more comfortable the cushion, and the better the company's ability to borrow, and the lower the interest rate.

No aspect of a company's equity or of its financial condition can be judged simply by computing a ratio, and the condition of a company's capitalization cannot be determined from the debt-to-total capitalization alone. As the foregoing simple illustrations showed, the burden of the debt depends in large part on its overall annual interest cost relative to the firm's return on its capital.

The burden of the debt also depends on its maturity—when funds will have to be provided for its payment. Most of GE's debt has maturities of ten years or less, or installment or sinking fund maturities.

Another consideration in 1991 is the fact that there is tremendous uncertainty about such things as prospective interest rates, a potential recession, the Middle East crisis, the impact of the trend toward free markets in former Iron Curtain countries, a united Germany, and the 1992 European Economic Community integration. All of these yield a mixed conclusion on whether a company like GE with its international consumer products (appliances) and technical products such as medical systems may be well advised to not await developments before increasing its leverage.

In addition, GE is heavily involved in defense production which may suffer large cuts. This counterbalances and diversifies GE's risks so that one might conclude that GE must be alert to change and be careful to make the right choices in the future. In considering this factor, the most important consideration is the quality and depth of GE's management—a factor on which a few years' financial statements can hardly be edifying. The analyst will look elsewhere to consider this quality.

Furthermore the all important cash flow factor here comes in to make it clear that GE is already well poised. In 1989 it announced a program to repurchase $10 billion of its own shares over five years but it was careful to say this program could be interrupted should the need arise. Thus GE could easily keep the remaining unspent portion of the $10 billion for expansion in Europe and elsewhere without adverse consequences.

(C) The Cash Flow to Debt Ratio

Recent studies have indicated that an important datum for creditors and investors is the ratio of cash flow to debt.[v] Further, Professor Beaver found it to be the most relevant to predicting future insolvency.[w] For his study, cash flow was defined as net income plus depreciation, depletion, and amortization. (We shall see that this is not real cash flow.) Total debt includes all liabilities plus preferred stock. We believe real cash flow is clearly the most important datum in today's economy but defer its study until later in this chapter.

G. PROFITABILITY RATIOS

A large number of ratios among elements of the income statement, or between elements of the income statement and elements of the balance sheet or other financial statements have been devised to help analyze profitability of the enterprise. We will again sample only a few.

1. "TIMES–INTEREST–EARNED"

A useful computation is the coverage of fixed charges by income available for that purpose. In most companies the principal fixed charge is interest expense, and we shall first consider its coverage by

v. Backer & Gosman, Financial Reporting and Business Liquidity (Nat. Assoc. of Accountants, 1978).

w. Beaver, Alternative Accounting Measures as Predictors of Failure, Acctg. Rev. 118 (Jan. 1968).

income. This is a profitability ratio because it depends on earnings and an expense.

GE's earnings before income taxes for 1989 were $3,939,000,000. For 1989 there was $726,000,000 in interest expense included in this calculation. Therefore, before interest and income taxes, earnings were $4,665,000,000. Since interest must be covered before taxes are due, we can use that figure as the numerator for our calculation and the $726,000,000 interest expense for the denominator, to find interest is "covered" about 6.4 times. This is a quite comfortable margin.[x]

2. COVERAGE OF OTHER FIXED CHARGES

Creditors and investors may be interested in more than the coverage of interest by net income. As we may see in Chapters IX, XI and XII on consolidated statements, leases and pensions, a company may engage in "off-balance-sheet financing". For instance, it can obtain the use of fixed assets in a way other than buying them and borrowing part of the cost; it can lease them, and agree to reimburse the lessor for his cost and a profit thereon over a period of years in the form of lease rentals.

At the end of 1989, per n. 18, the equity method accounts of GE show that it, as lessee, had only operating leases (no financing leases) with an aggregate of $3,069,000,000 of rentals due for their entire terms ($2,057,000,000 due in the five years 1990–1994). For a company of GE's size, these amounts are deemed minimal. GE's projected pension obligations are also not out of line.

3. RETURN ON SALES

One conclusion that can be drawn from a statement of income is whether the company is adequately profitable.

According to one study, the return on sales ratio is an important ratio for intermediate term bank lenders.[y]

In small businesses, accountants frequently prepare "long form" reports for their clients in which the components of the statement of income are set forth in much greater detail than shown here, and each

---

x. A sample restrictive covenant based on the times-interest-earned concept is contained in Am.Bar Foundation, Commentaries on Model Debenture Indenture Provisions 397 (1971). It reads:

(b) Neither the Company nor any Subsidiary will incur any Debt unless

(1) Consolidated Income Available for Interest for any 12 consecutive calendar months within the 15 calendar months immediately preceding the date on which such additional Debt is so incurred shall have been not less than _____ times the annual interest charges on the Consolidated Debt to be

outstanding immediately after the incurring of such additional Debt; and

(2) Consolidated Income Available for Debt Service for said 12 months' period shall have been not less than _____ times the Maximum Annual Service Charge on the Consolidated Debt to be outstanding immediately after the incurring of such additional Debt.

Debt service would include principal payments as well as interest.

y. Backer & Gosman, Financial Reporting and Business Liquidity (Nat. Assoc. of Accountants, 1978).

item is calculated as a percentage of sales. Experienced businessmen, accountants, bankers and financial analysts can spot weaknesses in the operation from a ratio (that is, a percentage of sales) which is out-of-line compared to the ratios of other companies in that type of business, and similarly can spot favorable or unfavorable trends in a company from the movement of these ratios from year to year in comparative statements.

The ratio of net profits from sales to sales revenue is a useful common denominator between companies and between years for the same company. For GE this calculation would be as follows:

(In $000,000)	1987	1988	1989
Revenues from sales of goods	$29,937	$28,958	$31,326
Revenues from sales of services	9,378	9,866	9,693
Totals	$39,305	$38,824	$41,019
Operating profits from sales before income taxes:			
Earnings before income taxes, etc.	$ 3,207	$ 4,482	$ 5,492
Adjusted to remove:			
Other income	(609)	(680)	(704)
Earnings of GEFS	(552)	(788)	(927)
Interest and other financial charges	645	669	726
Minority interest in net earnings	1	29	38
Totals	$ 2,652	$ 3,712	$ 4,625
Ratios of profits from sales to revenues from sales	6.7%	9.5%	11.3%

The increases are tremendously high and the analyst would look further at Management's Discussion, infra p. 530, because the SEC requires disclosure there of changes in income statement line items. Management claims the increase to 11.3% in 1989 is due to "productivity improvements and revenue gains"; i.e., that costs were reduced and sales were increased—not very revealing. Reading on we strike real pay dirt as we are told various facts from which we may draw certain conclusions:

FACTS	CONCLUSIONS
—volume of sales increased 6% in 1989 after having decreased 2% in 1988 but after removing the effects of acquisitions, the 1989 increase was only 3% and 1988 would have shown a 4% increase.	The volume of sales increased only 3% for 1989, less than in 1988, indicating a lower trend.

FACTS	CONCLUSIONS
—the 9.6% ratio for 1988 would have been 10.7% but for abnormally high refrigerator warranty expense; the normal margin previously was 8–10%.	The 11.3% record for 1989 was good but not as great in comparison with the 8–10% norm as it looks in comparison with 1987—a poor year.
—cost productivity improved 5% in each of the last two years.	Cost savings may have resulted from cutting corners; this could cause higher costs in the future—as for warranties. This must be viewed with skepticism.
—in 1987 there was $1,118 million expensed for business restructuring, thereby depressing 1987 earnings and making 1988 and 1989 look relatively better.	1989 is not as good in relation to 1988 and 1987 as first appears.
—defense spending cuts may be expected and GE earns about ⅛ of its consolidated revenues (⅙ of GE's equity method revenues) from defense contracts.	Revenues will be substantially diminished in 1990.
—management plans to eliminate 6,000 more jobs in the next two years.	GE has 300,000 employees, hence this is not of great materiality.
—GE's broadcasting business (NBC) accounts for over $600 million of GE's 1989 profits. GE has a small cable TV investment.	It is common knowledge that cable TV is hurting the three former major networks, of which NBC is one. Hence profits from broadcasting may be softer in the future. However, GE has already moved heavily into cable TV and that will diversify the risk.
—orders for major appliances weakened during the second half of 1989.	Profits for 1990 will fall.
—incoming order rates for Plastics slackened in the latter part of 1989 reflecting a slowing in automotive and appliance markets.	Profits for 1990 will fall.
—GEFS contributed about $1 billion to 1989 profit.	This is a business vulnerable to interest rate changes and stock market conditions and therefore represents high risk.
—$2.8 billion, about 40% of 1989 earnings were from international operations with rapid increases in Europe.	What will be the effect of the EEC integration in 1992 and a united Germany?

4. RETURN ON INVESTMENT

GE's return on average shareowner's equity is said by management to have been 20% in 1989, 19.4% in 1988 and 18.5% in 1987. The 1989 calculation is:

(1) Average shareowner's equity equals end of 1988 year equity ($18,466 million) plus end of 1989 year equity ($20,890 million) divided by two.

(2) $$\frac{\text{Net Earnings}}{\text{Average Share-owner's Equity}} = \frac{\$\ 3,989\text{M}}{\$19,678\text{M}} = 20\%$$

But you already know enough to avoid being confused into believing that a shareholder will earn 20% of his stock market purchase price for GE shares. The equity is GE's equity not the shareowners'.

This ratio is the end product of a long complicated accounting system which you have studied in detail; and you understand some of the hard and sometimes conventional or even arbitrary choices that go into the making of the figures of income and stockholders' equity. One insight, which the authors want the student and young lawyer to understand from this book, appears in a quotation about this ratio in an English journal, The Accountant, November 14, 1964:

> Given time to reflect on the doubtful validity of our accounting conventions, it would seem that, having made nonsense of profits and nonsense of capital employed, we deduce, by expressing one nonsense as a percentage of the other, a return on capital employed, by which we may compare the performance of one company's index of nonsense with that of another.

> H. Ross, *The Elusive Art of Accounting* (1966).

This same insight applies to our entire analysis. Clearly if the raw materials of the ratios are not what they seem to be, the results of comparisons will not be what is intended. One of the objectives of this course is to make you aware that the measurements built into the present accounting system may be very misleading in some situations and that use of ratio comparisons based on these measurements must be done with alertness and caution.

5. THE "PAYOUT RATIO"

GE's Statement of Earnings, near the bottom, shows a common phenomenon: only a fraction of earnings typically is paid out as dividends, here 39% in 1989 (the "payout ratio"). This is because the rest is deemed necessary to expand or replace plant and equipment, retire debt, and fill other needs. In inflationary times such as the present, and with the capital markets in poor shape, the pressure is to retain more, rather than less, earnings for these purposes.

In 1988 the payout ratio was 38% and in 1987, 41%. Although one may draw the obvious conclusions about GE's dividend policy from these data, that is obviously risky. A better datum would be an express statement by management concerning its dividend policy.

H. THE STATEMENT OF CASH FLOWS—THE THIRD FINANCIAL STATEMENT

1. THE IMPORTANCE OF CASH FLOW

One of America's largest and oldest retailers went bankrupt some years ago in 1975 causing huge losses to investors who, in 1973, had been paying as much as twenty times earnings for its stock. The sad thing for those investors was that their trip was hardly necessary. To begin to understand why, we chart below in Fig. 1 data from the published financial statements of the company through 1973, prepared in accordance with then existing GAAP. "Working Capital Provided by Operations" was the increase from operations each year in net current assets.

What if those investors had also been supplied with data as to net cash flow for those same years? That data is charted in Fig. 2.

With this information an investor would at least have had reason to question, two years before 1975, the ultimate profitability of his or her investment. One who read it correctly might even have been able

Fig. 1

W.T. Grant Company Net Income and Working Capital From Operations For Fiscal Years Ending January 31, 1966 to 1973.

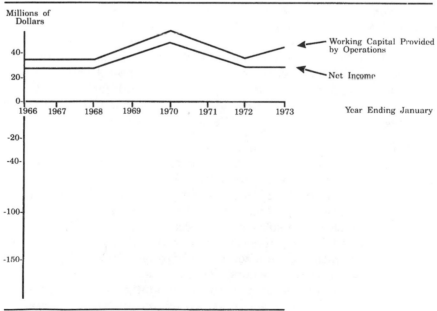

Fig. 2

W.T. Grant Company Net Income, Working Capital and Cash Flow From
Operations For Fiscal Years Ending January 31, 1966 to 1973.

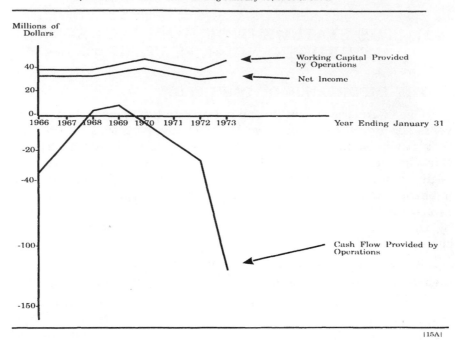

to extrapolate into 1974 or 1975 and perhaps have foreseen what happened then, as appears in Fig. 3.

What the W.T. Grant statements had failed adequately to show was that the generation of net income and working capital had been based on a sales drive involving the acceptance of installment receivables of very poor quality in lieu of cash payment, and that the situation had been aggravated by very poor collection practices.

But knowing what you know about accounting for estimated bad debts, you might ask, should not this circumstance raise questions concerning the adequacy of provisions for doubtful accounts in the years ending January 31, 1969 to January 31, 1973? If the provision for doubtful accounts in those years had anticipated the losses on receivables which would subsequently occur during the 1974 recession, the Company would likely have shown substantial net losses, at least in the later years, rather than a continued high level of earnings, thereby providing a warning to investors. However, since there is no way to reliably predict future economic trends, accounting recognition at any point in time must necessarily be based on information *presently* available. In the absence of information to the contrary one must

Fig. 3

W.T. Grant Company Net Income, Working Capital and Cash Flow
From Operations For Fiscal Years Ending January 31, 1966 to 1975.

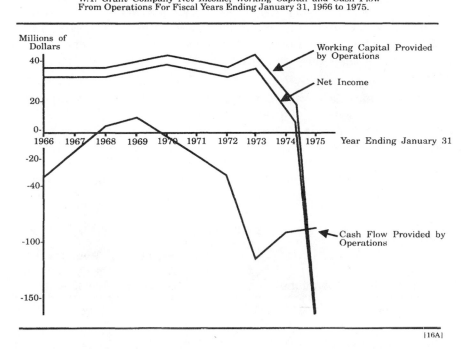

assume that the Company's officers and the auditors did recognize and properly evaluate in their deliberation process all information available at each financial statement date concerning the status of receivables, including delinquent accounts and the Company's collection practices, and that proper bad debt accounting would not (and did not) bring home the problem.

GAAP now do require firms to supply the cash flow data, a statement of cash flows, and presumably intelligent investors will not be fooled again by circumstances such as W.T. Grant's. SFAS No. 95, *Statement of Cash Flows* (1987). See the GE statement supra p. 528.

The cash flow statement is gaining in importance for investors as against the income statement.[z] The reason is that the income statement, compiled on the accrual basis, is not tied to cash receipts and disbursements, but financial analysis is ultimately concerned with cash. Thus the income statement includes non-cash accruals but defers to future periods current cash transactions as well as several types of cash receipts and disbursements not affecting income. It also excludes

z. Hawkins & Campbell, Equity Valuation: Models, Analysis and Implications (Fin.Exec.Res.Found., 1978); Louis Harris and Associates, Inc., A Study of the Attitudes Toward and an Assessment of the Financial Accounting Standards Board (Financial Accounting Foundation 1980) (67% of 415 executives, analysts, and academics believed cash flow information was "highly important" while only 49% felt the same way about earnings per share. And see J. Accountancy 108 (July, 1981).

capital items and balance sheet transactions such as receipts on issuance of stock or borrowing, and disbursements for dividends or bond redemptions.[aa] From such a statement how is a manager, investor or creditor to know when a company making good profit is getting into a cash bind? The question that the income statement does not answer is: what was the cash flow and what are the prospects for future cash flow?

To answer this question, past experience with cash receipts and disbursements may be of predictive value. The analyst might start with an accrual income statement and alter it to reflect cash receipts and disbursements from operations plus investment and financing transactions. The following illustration for a mythical company shows the relationship between an accrual income statement and a statement on a cash basis so adjusted:

Exel Corp.

Income from Operations		Statement of Cash Receipts and Disbursements from Operations, Financing and Investments	
Sales revenues	$115,000	$58,000	Cash received from sales
Less:		Less:	
Cost of goods sold	(42,500)	(35,000)	Cash paid for raw material purchases
Depreciation	(5,000)	–	
Salary expense	(27,500)	(15,000)	Cash paid for salaries
Rent expense	(20,000)	(20,000)	Cash paid for rent
Net income	$20,000	($12,000)	Net Cash (Deficit) from Operations
		10,000	Receipt from sale of stock
		15,000	Receipt from bank loan
		(3,000)	Disbursement for investment in equipment
		$10,000	Net cash received from operations, financing, and investment

At the time of the W.T. Grant events, described above, GAAP permitted cash flow statements or an alternative form, the one used by Grant, which described instead changes in all working capital accounts including not only cash but also receivables, inventories and payables. Grant apparently believed that more is better. To better understand W.T. Grant's statements, consider the statement on the right, below, compared to the cash statement on the left:

aa. Much of the explanation in these first few pages is modeled on the excellent treatment in S. Davidson, J. Schindler, C. Stickney, & R. Weil, Financial Accounting, An Introduction to Concepts, Methods, and Uses, Chapter XX (1976), although there are minor differences of concept with that presentation.

Statement of Cash Receipts and Disbursements from Operations, Financing, and Investing			Statement of Changes in Working Capital from Operations, Financing, and Investing
Cash received from sales	$58,000	$105,000	Cash and current accounts receivable from sales
Less:			
Cash paid for raw material purchases	(35,000)	(42,500)	Inventory sold
Cash paid for salaries	(15,000)	(27,500)	Salaries paid or accrued
Cash paid for rent	(20,000)	(20,000)	Rent paid
Net Cash (Deficit) from Operations	($12,000)	$15,000	Increase in working capital from operations
Receipt from sale of stock	10,000	10,000	Increase in working capital from sale of stock
Receipt from bank loan	15,000	10,000	Increase in working capital from long-term bank loan ($10,000) ($5,000 of loan is due in short-term)
Disbursement for investment in equipment	(3,000)	(3,000)	Decrease in working capital for equipment acquired
Net cash received from operations, financing, and investment	$10,000	$32,000	Net increase in working capital from operations, financing, and investment

From these data alone, one could not assess the future cash prospects of the company, but *if*, upon investigation, it appears:

    (a) Sales were obtained in the volume shown only because they are on credit, permitting installment payments over as long as ten years;

    (b) The $7500 unpaid for raw materials is 60 days past due;

    (c) Employees have resigned because of non-payment of salaries;

    (d) The bank loan has exhausted the personal credit of the president, who guaranteed the loan;

    (e) There is little likelihood of further sales of stock or bank credit;

we may conclude that this company is in trouble.

    Presumably additional meaning could be obtained from having two or more years' statements available. See the three years' comparative statements of GE, supra, p. 528.

    Now we see that a substantial portion of the accounts receivable from sales are currently receivable and the salaries payable are currently due. Also we find that sales probably were made from $7,500 inventory held in stock from a prior period as well as $35,000 from current purchases. In addition, notice a difference in the non-operational transactions—of the $15,000 received as a loan from the bank, $5,000 is currently due to be repaid to the bank, so that the net increase in liquidity from this transaction is $5,000 less than the $15,000 cash receipt shown. Showing only $10,000 as a positive increase in current accounts seems appropriate since the next year only the $10,000 will be available to pay other than the bank loan itself.

Each of these statements is a simplified form of statement of changes in the liquidity of the company for the prior period, in one of which the concept of "funds" is based on cash and in the other of which it is based on working capital.

Notice the three types of changes in each:

(a) Changes from operation of the firm's business;

(b) Changes from financial transactions (sale of stock and receipt of bank loan);

(c) Changes from investments; i.e., transactions in fixed assets (purchase of equipment).

The sources and uses of funds, (defined as cash in the above left hand statement and as working capital in the right hand one) may be from any of these three.

APB Op. No. 19 (1971) which was superseded by *SFAS No. 95,* gave the option to companies to prepare a statement based either on sources and uses of cash or on sources and uses of working capital, or anything between them.

In addition, although both of these concepts and the concept of "funds" itself refer to current assets and liabilities, *APB Op. No. 19,* ¶ 8, required disclosure of financing and investment activities that do not affect current assets or liabilities, for example, purchase of plant by issuing a long-term note to the seller. Davidson, et al., supra, refer to this as the "dual transactions assumption" because in our example, it could be treated as equivalent to issuance of the long-term note for cash and a purchase of plant for a cash payment thus causing both transactions to include a working capital element. But in reality the APB Opinion expanded the Statement to include changes in certain assets and liabilities other than cash or other current elements.

Professor Loyd Heath, after a study of *APB Op. No. 19,* developed the view which has now prevailed in *SFAS No. 95,* which has as its motto, "Less is more."

HEATH, LET'S SCRAP THE "FUNDS" STATEMENT
J. Accountancy 94 (Oct. 1978).*

"Funds statements found in practice today are a hodgepodge of miscellaneous information presented in a confusing and misleading way.

"Many accountants * * * attribute the confusion over the funds statement to confusion over what is meant by the term 'funds.' R.A. Rayman, for example, argued:

> The fact that funds analysis has not made more headway may be attributable to the absence of a definition of funds which is generally accepted. There is, in fact, a variety of definitions ranging over the whole spectrum of liquidity, from cash at one extreme to total resources at the other, with compromises like working capital somewhere in between.[1]

"In my opinion, the * * * solution does not lie in redefining funds; it lies in scrapping the funds statement, identifying the objectives it tries but fails to meet and designing statements that achieve those objectives.

"Specious Objectives

"The stated objectives of funds statements in Accounting Principles Board Opinion No. 19, * * * are specious.

" * * * According to the opinion, the objectives are '(1) to summarize the financing and investing activities of the entity, including the extent to which the enterprise has generated funds from operations during the period, and (2) to complete the disclosure of changes in financial position during the period.'

" * * * (T)he first objective begs the question of what effects of financing and investing activities should be summarized. Financing and investing activities, like all business activities, have many different effects. A single transaction may affect cash, working capital, total assets, capital structure, net assets and so forth. Obviously not all those effects can be portrayed in a single statement, but the opinion is silent as to which one or ones are the object or objects of attention in the statement. Paragraph 8 says only that the statement 'should be based on a broad concept embracing all changes in financial position' without even saying a broad concept of what! The problem reflects more than just poor draftsmanship; it reflects the absence of an underlying concept.

"The second objective is unattainable. As noted, business activities have many effects. No statement can possibly 'complete the disclosure of changes in financial position' (par. 4) or 'disclose all important changes in financial position for the period covered' (par. 11). A

* Copyright © 1978 by the American Institute of Certified Public Accountants, Inc.

1. R.A. Rayman, "Is Conventional Accounting Obsolete?" J. Accountancy, June 1970, p. 423.

meaningful statement must focus on a specific aspect or dimension of financial position such as cash, working capital, net assets, monetary assets and so forth. The possibilities are almost limitless. No statement can portray in an understandable way all effects of all activities on all possible measures of financial position.

"Relevant Objectives

"Changes in all three of the measures of financial position discussed in the last section [operations, financing and investing] are clearly of interest to investors, creditors and other external users of financial statements. Changes in debt-paying ability are of such obvious interest to creditors and investors that the matter hardly requires comment; the only real issue is which measure of debt-paying ability is likely to be most useful. Changes in the size and composition of a company's capital structure are also clearly of interest. One of the most widely used financial ratios in credit analysis is the ratio of debt to equity. That ratio would obviously be affected by changes in the composition of a company's capital structure such as the conversion of debentures into common stock and various kinds of refinancing operations. The nature of those activities and a report of how they affect a company's capital structure would, therefore, also be of interest. Changes in the amount or composition of long-term assets are likely to signal changes in a company's future profits and future cash needs so that they, too, are likely to be of interest to investors and creditors.

"Conflicting Objectives

"The basic problem with Opinion No. 19 is not, therefore, that it requires disclosure of unimportant or irrelevant information but that it requires too many different types of information to be disclosed on the same statement. The result is a confusing statement.

"Financial statements are maps of economic territory; they portray the financial characteristics of business enterprises. Different maps are needed for different purposes because only a limited amount of information can be portrayed on a single map. A single geographic map designed to portray changes in annual rainfall, changes in education level of the population, changes in agricultural crops and changes in unemployment is not likely to portray any of that information clearly. Similarly, a single financial statement designed to portray many different types of changes in the financial position of a business enterprise is not likely to portray any of that information clearly. That, however, is exactly what Opinion No. 19 requires of the funds statement.

"Recommendation

"Once the basis of the confusion over the funds statement is diagnosed, the general nature of a solution becomes obvious; several different statements are needed to communicate clearly the information now crammed into a single statement. Specifically, three statements are needed to replace the funds statement and achieve its objectives: a statement of cash receipts and payments, a statement of financing activities and a statement of investing activities.

"Statement of Cash Receipts and Payments

"One of the relevant objectives of funds statements is to report changes in some measure of debt-paying ability. Both historically and currently the measure of debt-paying ability used most frequently in funds statements has been working capital. That measure is rejected here in favor of cash.

"The central question in credit analysis today is not whether a company's working capital is 'adequate' but whether the cash expected to be received within a given time period will equal or exceed required cash payments within that same period. Analysis of working capital position does not provide that information. A company's principal sources of cash are from sale of its products or services to its customers, from borrowing and from issuance of stock to investors. Its principal uses are payments to employees, suppliers and governments, repayment of debt and purchase of plant and equipment. Most of the cash a company will receive within the following year is not represented by assets classified as current, and most of the obligation it will have to pay are not represented by liabilities classified as current.

"The rationale for recommending a statement of cash receipts and payments as one of the statements to replace the funds statement is implicit in the above discussion. If a financial statement user's primary object of attention is the future cash receipts and payments of a company, then it follows that a statement of past cash receipts and payments would be useful for the same reason that historical income statements are useful in predicting the future income of a company: both provide a basis for predicting future performance."

Note

10–4. *Cash Flow Per Share.* The SEC consistently has prohibited publication of cash flow per share on the basis that this could be misleading. The FASB follows this lead in SFAS No. 95. However, in 1989 the SEC began to reconsider the question of whether cash flow per share may be more informative than earnings per share in many cases. (Some would urge that the issue is not so much whether one figure is more meaningful than the other as it is which figure is less misleading. Put in this form the thought naturally comes to mind, why not prohibit both?)

2. THE RELATIONSHIP OF THE THREE PRINCIPAL FINANCIAL STATEMENTS

In Chapter I it was pointed out that annual income under GAAP is identical with the change in equity from the beginning to the end of the year with adjustments for capital contributions (deducted) and distributions through dividends (added). Putting the income calculation in logical terms, using the Greek delta to denote "difference" and the subscripts "o" and "c" to denote "opening balance" and "closing balance," respectively:

Opening balances: $A_o - L_o = NW_o$

Less closing balances: $A_c - L_c = NW_c$

Yields the difference between opening and closing assets and liabilities on the left and equity on the right, the difference in each being

Net Income: $\Delta A - \Delta L = \Delta NW$

The relationship of the income statement to the balance sheet is simply stated: the income statement depicts the change in equity (adjusted) and explains all changes in assets and liabilities in the period resulting from the firm's income earning operations.

From that we also see that the change in any of the three elements of the balance sheet equation over the year may be similarly measured. E.g.:

$$A_o = L_o + NW_o$$
$$\text{Less } A_c = L_c + NW_c$$
$$\Delta A = \Delta L + \Delta NW$$

This says the change in all assets equals the change in all liabilities and net worth.

By the same token we can measure the change in any sub-element of the balance sheet such as cash:

$$Cash_o = L_o + NW_o - \text{Other than Cash Assets}_o$$
$$\text{Less } Cash_c = L_c + NW_c - \text{Other than Cash Assets}_c$$
$$\Delta Cash = \Delta L + \Delta NW - \Delta \text{Other than Cash Assets}$$

The statement of cash flows states this change in cash by stating the changes in all the other balance sheet accounts. Thus it explains cash flows (in and out) from all the firm's activities in operations, financing and investing.

The accountant makes precisely this calculation to make up the statement of cash flows although the mechanical details are somewhat complex because of the thousands of changes during a year for even the smallest business, and because the changes in account balances are the result of both increases and decreases in each account which must be separated. We need not explore this technology.

3. PORTRAYAL OF CASH FLOWS

SFAS No. 95 permits the statement of cash flows to portray cash flow from operations in two different ways, known as the "direct" method and the "indirect" method.

Under the direct method the statement lists each category of revenue and expense on the income statement and the amount of cash flow (as opposed to accruals or deferrals) for each item. See the right hand statement at p. 510.

Under the indirect method, sometimes referred to as the "add back" method, which is used by GE (see its statement of cash flows at p.

528) and most firms, the statement starts with net income from the income statement prepared on the accrual basis and lists adjustments for operational revenues and expenses that are non-cash items. E.g., GE adds back depreciation of $2,256 million in 1989 because that is a non-cash expense which reduced accrual basis income but did not reduce cash.

4. SUPPLEMENTAL DISCLOSURE IN THE STATEMENT OF CASH FLOWS

SFAS No. 95, ¶ 32, recognizing that the cash flow statement provides only limited data for analysts, requires supplemental disclosure in footnotes or otherwise of additional data concerning investing and financing activity. Examples include conversion of debentures to common stock, buying fixed assets by means of a purchase money mortgage, entering into a capital lease as lessee, and like-kind exchanges.

I. MANAGEMENT'S DISCUSSION AND ANALYSIS

Professor Heath went on to recommend separate statements of financing and investing activities illustrated below:

Exhibit 2
Example, Inc.
Statement of Financing Activities
Year Ending December 31, 1977

Debt Financing	**Increase or (decrease)**
Notes payable to banks	
Borrowed	$ 50,000
Repaid	(16,908)
Net amount borrowed	33,092
Mortgage repaid	(2,000)
Net increase in debt financing	31,092

Equity Financing	
Convertible preferred	
Conversion of 300 shares $100 par value 5% convertible preferred for 1,500 shares $10 par value common stock	(30,000)
Common stock and capital in excess of par	
Issued 1,500 shares on conversion of 300 shares 5% convertible preferred	30,000
Issued 500 shares for $7,495 cash	7,495
Retained earnings	
net increase	3,983
Net increase in equity financing	$ 11,478

Exhibit 3
Example, Inc.
Statement of Investing Activities
Year Ending December 31, 1977

Plant and Equipment

Land, buildings and equipment, December 31, 1976	$319,101
Plus purchase	62,119
	381,220
Less cost of properties disposed of	31,595
Land, buildings and equipment, December 31, 1977	$349,625

However these have not been adopted unlike his proposed cash flow statement. Nevertheless the need for more information on financing and investing is clear and the SEC has mandated disclosure of this and much more information in shareholders' annual reports and other SEC disclosure documents.

FINANCIAL STATEMENTS, THE MANAGEMENT'S DISCUSSION AND ANALYSIS (MD & A) AND THE ACCOUNTING PROVISIONS OF THE FOREIGN CORRUPT PRACTICES ACT ("FCPA")

by Ted J. Fiflis
ALI–ABA Post Graduate Course in Securities Regulation, 1990.

"The two central bodies of disclosure required in SEC documents are the financial statements and managements' analyses thereof, known as the MD & A or the MDA, for Management's Discussion and Analysis of Financial Condition and Results of Operations, described in Reg. S–K, Item 303.

"Both are required in all the registration statements, periodic reports, proxy statements and [shareholders' annual reports] and both have received extraordinarily heavy enforcement emphasis by the Commission in recent years.

*   *   *

"I. The MD & A

"*Introduction*

"The principal interest of any investor is in optimizing his or her financial prospects. The question is how best to fashion a plan of investment for the future which causes his or her wealth to be maximized. Risk and expected return are the relevant factors. Investment decisions made on the basis of fundamental analysis, technical analysis or modern portfolio theory all have firm-specific financial information relevant to risk and return as their basic underpinning, although the desired information may vary, as will its application.

"At the heart of firm-specific disclosure on risk and return are the financial statements. For these statements to be reliable they must be based on accurate books and records and the assets, books and records must be safeguarded against misappropriation. Further, these financial statements must speak in a single language. Therefore they must be based on generally accepted conventions. These have taken the form of [GAAP]. [GAAS] are applied by independent auditors to maximize the probability that books and records are reliable and that GAAP have been properly applied.

"However, even then, financial statements are 'but the skin of a living thought' and subject to great misinterpretation as to their import for the future. A balance sheet presents only a snap-shot picture of certain assets and liabilities included and measured on the basis of these generally accepted conventions and hence does not portray the future. Even income and cash flow statements which present more of a moving picture, do so only for the past. Of course, the past is prologue and extrapolation from these statements is what investors have always done to determine the prospective risk and return for their investments.

"Because of this use of financials to project into the future, the SEC has sought to improve the reliability of this extrapolation by mandating disclosure in the MD & A of an insider's view of the financial statements. The MD & A is intended to reveal trends and uncertainties and other material facts not apparent to an outsider.   *   *   *

"The contents and explanation of the MD & A are prescribed in Item 303 of Reg. S–K (CCH Fed.Sec.L.Rep. ¶ 71,033), most recently explained further in Release No. 33–6835, 54 Fed.Reg. 22427 (May 25, 1989), (CCH Fed.Sec.L.Rep. ¶ 72,436), also known as Financial Reporting Release No. 36.

*   *   *

"*Brief History of the MD & A*

"Beginning in 1968 as mere summary statements about percentage variations in income statement items, the MD & A evolved by 1980 to a comprehensive discussion of items on and off the three principal financial statements concerning:

—liquidity,

—capital resources,

—results of operations, and

—trends, demands, commitments and uncertainties.

It has now developed to being the single most important disclosure item in SEC filings and disclosure documents.

"Carl Schneider, in an especially enlightening article describing the SEC's 1989 Release explaining the MD & A, stated: 'It would be only slight hyperbole to state that the MD & A is currently interpreted by the SEC as if it read as follows, thus superseding many other parts of the mandated disclosures having any financial relevance: 'Disclose on a quarterly basis all material information, historical or prospective, that has impacted or might foreseeably impact on the financial affairs of the registrant.'[2]

"More precisely the 1989 Release stated the purpose is to provide:

[i]n one section of a filing material historical and prospective textual disclosure enabling investors and other users to assess the financial conditions and results of operations of the registrant, with particular emphasis on the registrant's prospects for the future.

The Commission has long recognized the need for a narrative explanation of the financial statements, because a numerical presentation and brief accompanying footnotes alone may be insufficient for an investor to judge the quality of earnings and the likelihood that past performance is indicative of future performance. MD & A is intended to give the investor an opportunity to look at the company through the eyes of management by providing both a short and long-term analysis of the business of the company. The Item asks management to discuss the dynamics of the business and to analyze the financials.

. . . [I]t is the responsibility of management to identify and address those key variables and other qualitative and quantitative factors which are peculiar to and necessary for an understanding and evaluation of the individual company.   *   *   *

"A few of the more significant elements [of the MD & A] are discussed below.

"A.   Forward–Looking Information

"The general notion that forward-looking information is encouraged but not required by the SEC is substantially altered by Item 303 as construed in the 1989 Release to mandate much of that data.

"Concerning liquidity, Item 303 requires disclosures for any known trends or 'any known demands, commitments or uncertainties that . . . are reasonably likely to result in the registrant's liquidity increasing or decreasing in any material way.' For capital resources disclosure of 'known . . . trends' is mandated. For net sales, revenues and income, 'known trends or uncertainties' must be described.

"This is mandatory, not just permissive disclosure. The distinction drawn in the Release between permissive disclosure of forward-looking information and mandatory disclosure of 'presently known data which will impact upon future operating results . . .' is elusive. However, it has its antecedents in the auditor's distinction between 'projections,' by which is meant extrapolations from historic data, and 'forecasts,' meaning strictly hypothetically assumed future events. Although the MD & A distinction is not identical, the underlying natures of the MD & A and accounting concepts are similar.

"The Release purports to illustrate and distinguish mandated and permissive data as it may affect future financial matters such as:

2. Schneider, MD & A Disclosure, 22 Rev.Sec. & Commod.Reg. 149 (Aug. 23, 1989).

[a] reduction in the registrant's product prices; erosion in the registrant's market share; changes in insurance coverage; or the likely non-renewal of a material contract. In contrast, optional forward-looking disclosure involves anticipating a future trend or event or anticipating a less predictable impact of a known event, trend or uncertainty.

"The calculus for determining whether the disclosure is mandated is stated as follows in the Release (text at note 27):

Where a trend, demand, commitment, event or uncertainty is known, management must make two assessments:

(1) Is the known trend, demand, commitment, event or uncertainty likely to come to fruition? If management determines that it is not reasonably likely to occur, no disclosure is required.

(2) If management cannot make that determination, it must evaluate objectively the consequences of the known trend, demand, commitment, event or uncertainty, on the assumption that it will come to fruition. Disclosure is then required unless management determines that a material effect on the registrant's financial condition or results of operations is not reasonably likely to occur.

Each final determination resulting from the assessments made by management must be objectively reasonable, viewed as of the time the determination is made.

"The Release illustrates this process with the now common case in which a reporting company is named a 'potentially responsible party' ('PRP') by the EPA under the Superfund statute—the Comprehensive Environmental Response, Compensation and Liability Act of 1980 ('CERCLA'). CERCLA created sweeping liability for costs of the clean-up of hazardous waste sites. It is retroactive and applies to any person who generated or transported the waste or owned or operated the site any time after dumping. After noting that mere designation as a PRP does not trigger MD & A disclosure the Release illustrates the operation of the calculus:

FACTS: A registrant has been correctly designated a PRP by the EPA with respect to cleanup of hazardous waste at three sites. No statutory defenses are available. The registrant is in the process of preliminary investigations of the sites to determine the nature of its potential liability and the amount of remedial costs necessary to clean up the sites. Other PRPs also have been designated, but the ability to obtain contribution is unclear, as is the extent of insurance coverage, if any. Management is unable to determine that a material effect on future financial condition or results of operations is not reasonably likely to occur.

Based upon the facts of this hypothetical case, MD & A disclosure of the effects of the PRP status, quantified to the extent reasonably practicable, would be required. For MD & A purposes, aggregate potential cleanup costs must be considered in light of the joint and several liability to which a PRP is subject. Facts regarding whether insurance coverage may be contested, and whether and to what extent potential sources of contribution or indemnification constitute reliable sources of recovery may be factored into the determination of whether a material future effect is not reasonably likely to occur.

*   *   *

"C.   Liquidity—Capital Resources

"Discussions of liquidity and capital resources are combined by most companies in their MD & A's.

"Material commitments for capital resources at year-end and known trends in acquisition or disposition of capital resources as well as changes in their mix and relative cost is required. Changes in financing by debt, equity or off-balance sheet financing (such as by leasing) must also be disclosed.

"Moreover, amounts and certainty of cash flow must be evaluated as must prospective long (over 12 months) and short term (within 12 months) sources and needs of capital.

"Here again an accountant's concept is employed as the Release states that more than conventional liquidity is involved—'financial flexibility' is what is required to be disclosed. Financial flexibility has to do with all available means of obtaining cash such as by sale of an unused parcel of real estate held for future development. Here the impact on future development from a necessary sale would have to be disclosed along with the availability of this resource.

*   *   *

"In addition, the issuer must disclose plans to remedy any cash shortfall, or that it has not got a plan, etc.

"Discussion is called for for such items as:

a) discretionary operating expenses such as expenses relating to advertising, research and development or maintenance of equipment; b) debt refinancings or redemptions; or c) levels of financing provided by suppliers or to customers.

"In short, it appears that disclosure is required of all the things which give a corporate treasurer either nightmares or pleasant dreams. (Good news about financial flexibility must also be disclosed.) For this reason the treasurer's office must be closely involved in drafting the MD & A.

*   *   *

"D.   Material Changes

"The Release requires a thorough trend analysis. It states:

Instruction 4 to Item 303(a) requires a discussion of the causes of material changes from year-to-year in financial statement line items 'to the extent necessary to an understanding of the registrant's businesses as a whole.' An analysis of changes in line items is required where material and where the changes diverge from changes in related line items of the financial statements, where identification and quantification of the extent of contribution of each of two or more factors is necessary to an understanding of a material change, or where there are material increases or decreases in net sales or revenue.

Discussion of the impact of discontinued operations and of extraordinary gains and losses is also required where these items have had or are reasonably likely to have a material effect on reported or future financial condition or results of operations. Other non-recurring items should be discussed as 'unusual or infrequent' events or transactions 'that materially affected the amount of reported income from continuing operations.'

* * *

"E.   Segment Analysis (Disaggregation by Line of Business)

"Unitary treatment of consolidated data for a company operating two or more lines of business is often misleading.

* * *

"The Release states:

In formulating a judgment as to whether a discussion of segment information is necessary to an understanding of the business, a multi-segment registrant preparing a full fiscal year MD & A should analyze revenues, profitability, and the cash needs of its significant industry segments. To the extent any segment contributes in a materially disproportionate way to those items, or where discussion on a consolidated basis would present an incomplete and misleading picture of the enterprise, segment discussion should be included. This may occur, for example, when there are legal or other restrictions upon the free flow of funds from one segment, subsidiary or division of the registrant to others; when known trends, demands, commitments, events or uncertainties within a segment are reasonably likely to have a material effect on the business as a whole; when the ability to dispose of identified assets of a segment may be relevant to the financial flexibility of the registrant; and in other circumstances in which the registrant concludes that segment analysis is appropriate to an understanding of its business.

"The problems of segment analysis are hardly hinted at. According to Fiflis, Kripke & Foster, op. cit. supra, at pp. 590–91, 594–95:

Just as consolidated statements are deemed necessary to present a unified view of a single business enterprise conducted through several corporations, there is a need to "disaggregate" diverse business lines conducted through a single enterprise—whether it be a single corporation or many—to enable the reader to appraise the operations of each line of business. For example, the appraisal of risks of a manufacturer of nuclear cores will differ from that of a retail grocery chain. And foreign operations are different from domestic operations from a risk standpoint. Indeed segmented reporting may be necessary to avoid liability for misrepresentation. See Republic Technology Fund, Inc. v. The Lionel Corp., 483 F.2d 540, 546 (2d Cir.1973).

Appendix to Chapter 10

GENERAL ELECTRIC COMPANY

Statement of Earnings

For the years ended December 31 (In millions)	General Electric Company and consolidated affiliates		
	1989	1988	1987
Revenues			
Sales of goods	$31,314	$28,953	$29,937
Sales of services	9,673	9,840	9,370
Other income (note 3)	690	675	655
Earnings of GEFS	—	—	—
GEFS revenues from operations (note 4)	12,897	10,621	8,196
Total revenues	54,574	50,089	48,158
Costs and expenses (note 5)			
Cost of goods sold	22,827	21,155	22,359
Cost of services sold	6,873	7,676	7,290
Interest and other financial charges (note 7)	6,591	4,817	3,912
Insurance policy holder losses and benefits	1,614	1,501	1,560
Provision for losses on financing receivables (note 8)	527	434	290
Other costs and expenses	10,355	9,724	8,406
Unusual expenses, including provisions for business restructurings (note 9)	—	—	1,118
Minority interest in net earnings (loss) of consolidated affiliates	84	61	(4)
Total costs and expenses	48,871	45,368	44,931
Earnings before income taxes, extraordinary item and cumulative effect of accounting changes	5,703	4,721	3,227
Provision for income taxes (note 10)	(1,764)	(1,335)	(1,108)
Earnings before extraordinary item and cumulative effect of accounting changes	3,939	3,386	2,119
Extraordinary item (note 25)	—	—	(62)
Cumulative effect to January 1, 1987 of accounting changes			
Initial application of Statement of Financial Accounting Standards No. 96 — "Accounting for Income Taxes" (note 1)	—	—	577
Change in overhead recorded in inventory (note 1)	—	—	281
Net earnings	$ 3,939	$ 3,386	$ 2,915
Net earnings per share (in dollars)			
Before extraordinary item and cumulative effect of accounting changes	$ 4.36	$ 3.75	$ 2.33
Extraordinary item (note 25)	—	—	(.07)
Cumulative effect to January 1, 1987 of accounting changes			
Initial application of Statement of Financial Accounting Standards No. 96 — "Accounting for Income Taxes" (note 1)	—	—	.63
Change in overhead recorded in inventory (note 1)	—	—	.31
Net earnings per share	$ 4.36	$ 3.75	$ 3.20
Dividends declared per share (in dollars)	$ 1.70	$ 1.46	$ 1.32

The notes to consolidated financial statements on pages [____] are an integral part of this statement.   [G3615]

	GE			GEFS	
1989	1988	1987	1989	1988	1987
$31,326	$28,958	$29,937	$ —	$ —	$ —
9,693	9,866	9,378	—	—	—
704	680	649	—	—	—
927	788	552	—	—	—
—	—	—	12,945	10,655	8,225
42,650	40,292	40,516	12,945	10,655	8,225
22,839	21,160	22,359	—	—	—
6,893	7,702	7,298	—	—	—
726	669	645	5,912	4,177	3,277
—	—	—	1,614	1,501	1,560
—	—	—	527	434	290
6,662	6,250	5,979	3,708	3,484	2,440
—	—	1,027	—		91
38	29	1	46	32	(5)
37,158	35,810	37,309	11,807	9,628	7,653
5,492	4,482	3,207	1,138	1,027	572
(1,553)	(1,096)	(1,088)	(211)	(239)	(20)
3,939	3,386	2,119	927	788	552
—	—	(62)	—	—	(62)
—	—	577	—	—	518
—	—	281	—	—	—
$ 3,939	$ 3,386	$ 2,915	$ 927	$ 788	$ 1,008

In the supplemental consolidating data on this page, "GE" means the pre-1988 basis of consolidation as described in note 1 to the consolidated financial statements; "GEFS" means General Electric Financial Services, Inc. and all of its affiliates and associated companies. Transactions between GE and GEFS have been eliminated from the "General Electric Company and consolidated affiliates" columns on the preceding page. Eliminations are shown on page [544].

[G3616]

Statement of Financial Position

At December 31 (In millions)	General Electric Company and consolidated affiliates	
	1989	1988
Assets		
Cash and equivalents (note 11)	$ 2,258	$ 2,456
Marketable securities carried at cost (note 12)	6,799	5,510
Marketable securities carried at market (note 13)	8,488	5,089
Securities purchased under agreements to resell	16,020	13,811
Current receivables (note 14)	6,976	6,780
Inventories (note 15)	6,655	6,486
GEFS financing receivables (investment in time sales, loans and financing leases) — net (note 16)	41,779	35,832
Other GEFS receivables (note 17)	5,476	4,699
Property, plant and equipment (including equipment leased to others) — net (note 18)	15,646	13,611
Investment in GEFS	—	—
Intangible assets (note 19)	8,822	8,552
All other assets (note 20)	9,425	8,039
Total assets	**$128,344**	**$110,865**
Liabilities and equity		
Short-term borrowings (note 21)	$ 37,200	$ 30,422
Accounts payable (note 22)	6,666	6,004
Securities sold under agreements to repurchase	16,555	13,864
Securities sold but not yet purchased, at market (note 23)	4,090	2,088
Progress collections and price adjustments accrued	3,315	3,504
Dividends payable	426	369
All other GE current costs and expenses accrued (note 24)	5,650	5,549
Long-term borrowings (note 25)	16,110	15,082
Reserves of insurance affiliates	5,032	4,177
All other liabilities (notes 17 and 26)	7,866	6,986
Deferred income taxes (note 27)	3,543	3,373
Total liabilities	106,453	91,418
Minority interest in equity of consolidated affiliates (note 28)	1,001	981
Common stock (926,564,000 shares issued)	584	584
Other capital	826	823
Retained earnings	20,352	17,950
Less common stock held in treasury	(872)	(891)
Total share owners' equity (notes 29 and 30)	20,890	18,466
Total liabilities and equity	**$128,344**	**$110,865**
Commitments and contingent liabilities (note 31)		

The notes to consolidated financial statements on pages [____] are an integral part of this statement.

[G3617]

	GE		GEFS	
	1989	1988	1989	1988
	$ 1,749	$ 1,823	$ 509	$ 633
	49	80	6,750	5,430
	—	—	8,488	5,089
	—	—	16,020	13,811
	7,218	7,110	—	—
	6,655	6,486	—	—
	—	—	41,779	35,939
	—	—	5,856	4,806
	9,666	9,360	5,980	4,251
	6,069	4,819	—	—
	7,048	6,984	1,774	1,568
	5,653	4,621	3,772	3,418
	$ 44,107	$ 41,283	$ 90,928	$ 74,945
	$ 1,696	$ 1,861	$ 35,740	$ 28,731
	2,901	2,136	4,144	4,132
	—	—	16,555	13,864
	—	—	4,090	2,088
	3,315	3,504	—	—
	426	369	—	—
	5,650	5,549	—	—
	3,947	4,330	12,165	10,862
	—	—	5,032	4,177
	5,635	5,481	2,236	1,505
	(636)	(641)	4,179	4,014
	22,934	22,589	84,141	69,373
	283	228	718	753
	584	584	1	1
	826	823	1,702	1,379
	20,352	17,950	4,366	3,439
	(872)	(891)	—	—
	20,890	18,466	6,069	4,819
	$ 44,107	$ 41,283	$ 90,928	$ 74,945

In the supplemental consolidating data on this page, "GE" means the pre-1988 basis of consolidation as described in note 1 to the consolidated financial statements; "GEFS" means General Electric Financial Services, Inc. and all of its affiliates and associated companies. Transactions between GE and GEFS have been eliminated from the "General Electric Company and consolidated affiliates" columns on the preceding page. Eliminations are shown on page [544].   [G3618]

Statement of Cash Flows

	General Electric Company and consolidated affiliates		
For the years ended December 31 (In millions)	1989	1988	1987
Cash flows from operating activities			
Net earnings	**$ 3,939**	$ 3,386	$ 2,915
Adjustments to reconcile net earnings to cash provided from operating activities			
Extraordinary item and cumulative effect of changes in accounting principles	—	—	(796)
Depreciation, depletion and amortization	**2,256**	2,266	1,913
Earnings retained by GEFS	—	—	—
Deferred income taxes	**281**	124	37
Decrease (increase) in GE current receivables	**(100)**	123	138
Decrease (increase) in GE inventories	**(167)**	(209)	375
Increase (decrease) in accounts payable	**503**	303	149
Increase in insurance reserves	**486**	315	669
Provision for losses on financing receivables	**527**	434	290
Net change in certain broker-dealer accounts	**(872)**	(573)	(103)
All other operating activities	**(230)**	933	252
Cash provided from operating activities	**6,623**	7,102	5,839
Cash flows from investing activities			
Property, plant and equipment including equipment leased to others			
Additions	**(5,474)**	(3,681)	(2,277)
Dispositions	**1,294**	470	890
Net increase in GEFS financing receivables	**(6,649)**	(6,057)	(4,575)
Payments for principal businesses purchased, net of cash acquired	**(1,860)**	(3,504)	(555)
Proceeds from principal business dispositions	—	880	646
All other investing activities	**(400)**	(1,620)	(1,097)
Cash used for investing activities	**(13,089)**	(13,512)	(6,968)
Cash flows from financing activities			
Net change in borrowings (less than 90-day maturities)	**7,360**	3,868	2,519
Debt having maturities more than 90 days			
Newly issued	**8,078**	11,324	8,219
Repayments and other reductions	**(7,710)**	(8,801)	(6,883)
Sale of preferred stock by GE Capital	—	600	—
Disposition of GE shares from treasury (mainly for employee plans)	**509**	356	361
Purchase of GE shares for treasury	**(490)**	(387)	(846)
Dividends paid to GE share owners	**(1,479)**	(1,263)	(1,177)
Cash provided from (used for) financing activities	**6,268**	5,697	2,193
Increase (decrease) in cash and equivalents during year	**(198)**	(713)	1,064
Cash and equivalents at beginning of year	**2,456**	3,169	2,105
Cash and equivalents at end of year	**$ 2,258**	$ 2,456	$ 3,169

The notes to consolidated financial statements on pages [——] are an integral part of this statement.   [G3619]

GE			GEFS		
1989	1988	1987	1989	1988	1987
$ 3,939	$ 3,386	$ 2,915	$ 927	$ 788	$ 1,008
—	—	(796)	—	—	(456)
1,524	1,522	1,544	732	744	369
(927)	(788)	(552)	—	—	—
178	(215)	(158)	103	339	195
(12)	(170)	111	—	—	—
(167)	(209)	375	—	—	—
693	(342)	21	(75)	693	48
—	—	—	486	315	669
—	—	—	527	434	290
—	—	—	(872)	(573)	(103)
(468)	440	413	256	751	159
4,760	3,624	3,873	2,084	3,491	2,179
(2,217)	(1,884)	(1,698)	(3,257)	(1,797)	(579)
205	118	410	1,089	352	480
—	—	—	(6,542)	(5,943)	(4,627)
(759)	(2,963)	—	(1,101)	(541)	(555)
—	880	646	—	—	—
115	444	(6)	(801)	(2,007)	(1,282)
(2,656)	(3,405)	(648)	(10,612)	(9,936)	(6,563)
850	(466)	(961)	6,576	4,249	3,515
204	934	396	7,874	10,291	7,818
(1,772)	(30)	(238)	(6,046)	(8,771)	(6,645)
—	—	—	—	600	—
509	356	361	—	—	—
(490)	(387)	(846)	—	—	—
(1,479)	(1,263)	(1,177)	—	—	—
(2,178)	(856)	(2,465)	8,404	6,369	4,688
(74)	(637)	760	(124)	(76)	304
1,823	2,460	1,700	633	709	405
$ 1,749	$ 1,823	$ 2,460	$ 509	$ 633	$ 709

In the supplemental consolidating data on this page, "GE" means the pre-1988 basis of consolidation as described in note 1 to the consolidated financial statements; "GEFS" means General Electric Financial Services, Inc. and all of its affiliates and associated companies. Transactions between GE and GEFS have been eliminated from the "General Electric Company and consolidated affiliates" columns on the preceding page. Eliminations are shown on page [—].   [G9620]

Management's Discussion of Operations

Overview

General Electric Company's consolidated financial statements include the detailed effects of adding to the Company's manufacturing and industrial services businesses the accounts of General Electric Financial Services, Inc. (GEFS).

Note 1 to the consolidated financial statements explains the consolidation procedure. Among other things, that note also explains how the terms "GE" or "GE except GEFS" and "GEFS" are used in this report to help readers understand the various data. These terms are used frequently in this Management Discussion for clarification or emphasis.

Consolidated net earnings for 1989 were $3.939 billion, or 16% more than for 1988. This was the third consecutive year of strong double-digit earnings increases. Operating margin for GE of 11.3% of sales — an all-time record — reflected continuing widespread productivity improvements and revenue gains in both domestic and international markets. While virtually all key businesses contributed to the higher earnings, particularly good 1989 performances were reported in GE Financial Services, Plastics and Medical Systems. See Industry Segments beginning on page [532] for additional detail about performance by various businesses of the Company.

Net earnings for 1989 and 1988 did not include corporate provisions for business restructuring expenses, nor did either year include any impact from accounting changes. Net earnings in 1987 also reflected solid operating performance, but analysis of results for that year was complicated by two types of transactions that essentially equaled each other in net earnings. These were a reduction in pre-tax and after-tax earnings caused by unusual and extraordinary expenses ($747 million after taxes), mainly for business restructurings to improve future profitability; and an increase in after-tax earnings ($720 million) from two accounting changes, one involving income taxes and the other involving overhead recorded in inventories, as explained in note 1.

The following paragraphs discuss various aspects of the consolidated Statement of Earnings on page [524].

Consolidated revenues of $54.6 billion in 1989 were 9% more than the $50.1 billion for 1988 following a 4% increase from 1987. The principal components of consolidated revenues are "sales of goods and services" by GE and "revenues from operations" or "earned income" from GEFS.

■ GE's sales of goods and services for 1989 totaled $41.0 billion, a 6% increase from the year before. Virtually all of the 1989 increase came from a higher volume of shipments, with slightly higher overall prices having only a minor effect. Sales in 1988 were down about 1% from 1987, with the effect of about 2% lower shipment volume

partly offset by modestly higher prices. If sales for the three years 1987-1989 were adjusted for the effect of acquisitions and dispositions, the increase in 1989 from 1988 would have been about 3% and 1988 would have been up about 4% from 1987.

■ GE's other income from a wide variety of sources has totaled between about $650 million and $700 million for each of the last three years. See note 3.

■ GEFS revenues, or earned income, from operations for 1989 were $12.9 billion, up 21% from 1988's $10.7 billion, which was 30% more than 1987's $8.2 billion. The principal reason for the increases has been higher levels of assets in GE Capital, including the effect of acquisitions. Yields (i.e., prices or interest rates paid to GE Capital by its customers for its financing of their needs) increased from the prior period in both 1989 and 1988. Note 4 shows GEFS revenues from operations by principal type of activity.

Principal costs and expenses for GE are those classified as costs of goods and services sold and selling, general and administrative expense.

■ "Operating margin" is sales of goods and services less the costs of sales and selling, general and administrative expenses. Operating margin was 11.3% of sales in 1989, up from 9.6% in 1988. Excluding abnormally high refrigerator compressor warranty expense provisions in 1988, operating margin for that year would have been about 10.7%. These recent improvements follow several years during which the margin rate was in the 8-10% range and stem directly from the ongoing focus throughout the Company on improving productivity. GE's total cost productivity, which excludes the effects of inflation, averaged 5% for the last two years compared with results in the 1-2% range in the early years of the 1980s. There were no corporate-level business restructuring expense provisions in 1989 and 1988 to compare with the $1 billion

GE/S&P earnings per share increase/decrease compared with 1984

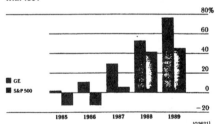

[G3621]

provided in 1987. Those provisions in 1987, and for several years prior to that, were largely targeted at improving cost structures.

■ GE's interest expense in 1989 was $726 million, up 9% from $669 million in 1988, which was 4% more than in 1987. Higher interest expense in 1989 was due to a higher average level of borrowings stemming from 1988 acquisition activity. The effect of this was partly offset by somewhat lower average 1989 interest rates. The increase in interest expense in 1988 from 1987 was mainly from higher average interest rates partly offset by a somewhat lower average level of borrowings.

GEFS' principal cost is interest expense.

■ GEFS' interest expense totaled $5.9 billion in 1989, 42% more than in 1988, which had been 27% more than in 1987. The increased interest expense reflects the higher level of borrowings that have been used mainly to invest in earning assets involved in a wide variety of financings made available to third parties. The composite interest rate incurred for GEFS' finance activities was 9.60% in 1989 compared with 8.39% in 1988 and 8.11% in 1987. The "spread," or difference between interest rates GEFS pays to its lenders and rates it charges to its customers, narrowed in 1989 after increasing somewhat in the previous two years.

■ Among GEFS' other costs, the provision for losses on financing receivables of $527 million in 1989 was up $93 million from 1988, which had been $144 million more than 1987. At year-ends 1989 and 1988, GEFS' reserve coverage was equal to 2.63% of financing receivables compared with 2.59% at the end of 1987. Insurance policy holder losses and benefits expense increased by 8% to $1.6 billion in 1989 after having declined modestly the previous year. The current-year increase was principally due to increased losses on life reinsurance, partially offset by lower losses due to the reduced property and casualty insurance business.

The interest of minority share owners in the equity of consolidated affiliates is relatively small but has been growing in recent years. For GE, the increase represents mainly the impact of recent aggressive formation of joint ventures and alliances aimed at increasing global competitiveness. For GEFS, the increase resulted principally from GE Capital's sale of variable rate preferred stock to third parties in 1988 to augment its equity base. There were no further sales of such stock in 1989.

The consolidated effective income tax rate was 30.9% in 1989 compared with 28.3% in 1988 and 34.3% in 1987. (The U.S. federal statutory rate was 34% for both 1989 and 1988 compared with 40% in 1987.) The decrease in the U.S. federal statutory rate was the main reason for the lower effective consolidated rates in 1989 and 1988 compared with 1987. There are, however, numerous reasons

Constant dollar sales per GE employee
(In thousands)

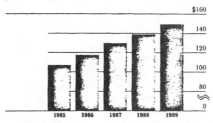

for differences between the statutory and effective rates. Together with other information about income tax provisions, an analysis of the differences between the U.S. federal statutory rate and the consolidated rate can be found in note 10.

Dividends declared totaled $1.537 billion in 1989, or $1.70 per share. At the same time, the Company retained sufficient earnings to support enhanced productive capability and to provide adequate financial resources for internal and external growth opportunities. The fourth-quarter 1989 increase of 15% in dividends declared marked the 14th consecutive year of dividend growth.

Return on average share owners' equity reached 20.0% in 1989, up from 19.4% in 1988 and one and one-half points better than for 1987. Information about the five-year GE common share repurchase program announced in November 1989 can be found in this report in the section that discusses Financial Resources and Liquidity starting on page [536].

The global economic and political outlook has numerous uncertainties. For example, it is well known that the U.S. government is seriously considering reductions in defense spending. It is also well known that there is no consensus on how much and what types of reductions there will be or how and when such reductions will be implemented. About one-eighth of GE's consolidated revenues might be affected by such reductions. (See Industry Segments on the next page.) Longer range, reduced defense spending could result in a lower federal budget deficit, lower interest rates, and consequent stimulation of domestic investment and economic growth. Further, global opportunities for market growth such as that anticipated from the scheduled European economic integration in 1992 appear plentiful. Despite these uncertainties, management believes that the strength of GE's diversity and worldwide leadership in key businesses position the Company to continue good performance into 1990 and beyond.

[G3822]

Industry Segments

Consolidated industry segment revenues and operating profit for the last five years appear on the opposite page. The presentation of consolidated industry segments is in two parts, one for GE except GEFS and one for GEFS. Consistent with years before 1988, GE revenues and operating profit continue to include earnings of GEFS. Revenues and operating profit for GEFS by the industry segments in which it conducts business are presented separately with appropriate elimination of GEFS' earnings as well as the minor effect of transactions between GE and GEFS segments. Additional financial data plus detailed descriptions of each segment can be found in note 33.

Consolidated operating profit is the principal source of GE's net earnings, and the relationship between the two is depicted in the chart on this page. Consolidated operating profit exceeded $7 billion in 1989 with three segments — Aircraft Engines, Materials and Financing — each surpassing $1 billion for the first time. As shown in the chart, operating profit had dipped some in 1986, although net earnings continued a steady increase. Operating profit in 1987 was after absorbing $1.069 billion of unusual corporate-level expenses as noted earlier in this Management's Discussion. There were no such unusual expenses in 1989 or 1988. Comments on each segment follow.

■ *Aerospace* revenues have been at about the $5.3 billion level for the past three years, and operating profits have ranged between $600 million and $650 million for the same years. New orders received of $6 billion in 1989 were up 8% from 1988, bringing the backlog of firm unfilled orders at December 31, 1989 to $8.0 billion, of which approximately 40% is scheduled for completion in 1990.

Although there was a significant increase in orders from international customers in 1989, much of the Aerospace business is performed under contract for the U.S. government, mainly for the Department of Defense. Despite orders growth over the past two years leading to a record backlog consisting of hundreds of different contracts, management expects that some defense industry adjustments will take place in response to changing levels of defense spending. Management has developed long-range contingency plans to anticipate such possible changes, including a contemplated reduction of approximately 10,000 positions (about 25%) in the work force over a three-year period. In 1989, approximately 4,000 of this reduction occurred — through attrition, a business disposition and layoffs. The need for similar actions, if necessary, will be determined over the next two or more years on a business-by-business/location-by-location basis as business conditions evolve. No specific decisions have yet been made regarding potential additional actions.

■ *Aircraft Engines* revenues were up 6% in 1989 following a small decrease in 1988 from 1987. Operating profit continued to increase through 1989. New engine orders of $8 billion in 1989, following the very strong 1988 performance of $9.7 billion, brought firm backlogs to $13.3 billion at the end of 1989 compared with $12.4 billion the year before. Of the 1989 backlog, about 45% is scheduled for completion in 1990. In addition, customers have options that total $22 billion. Although military programs are important to Aircraft Engines' business, the surge in commercial engines and accelerating growth in parts and services provide a sound base as the decade of the 1990s begins.

■ *Broadcasting* operating profit increased 12% in 1989 over 1988, continuing the improvements since GE acquired NBC in mid-1986. The 7% decline in 1989 revenues reflected the lack of a counterpart to coverage of the 1988 Olympic Games. A principal reason for better operating profit was higher productivity, which was partly offset by start-up costs associated with launching CNBC, the Consumer News and Business cable channel and related cable activities.

■ *Industrial* operating profits increased 6% in 1989 to $847 million with improvements in most ongoing businesses. Flat revenues reflected a number of business dispositions, principally the semiconductor business sold in late 1988. Improved operating profits in 1989 were led by Electrical Distribution and Control, which included the consolidation for part of the year of results for GE's European controls ventures with GEC of the United Kingdom. Transportation Systems 1989 operating profits were substantially higher on a strong increase in shipments. Lighting operating profits were up somewhat from the prior year on slightly higher sales. Factory Automation, including Drive Systems, had a good increase in operating profit and sales. Motors operating profits for 1989 were about

Consolidated operating profit and net earnings
(In billions)

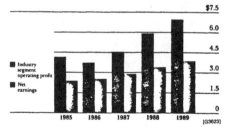

[G3623]

Summary of Industry Segments

	General Electric Company and consolidated affiliates				
For the years ended December 31 (In millions)	1989	1988	1987	1986	1985
Revenues					
GE					
Aerospace	$ 5,282	$ 5,343	$ 5,262	$ 4,318	$ 3,085
Aircraft Engines	6,863	6,481	6,773	5,977	4,712
Broadcasting	3,392	3,638	3,241	1,888	51
Industrial	7,059	7,061	6,662	6,770	6,946
Major Appliances	5,620	5,289	4,721	4,352	3,617
Materials	4,929	3,539	2,751	2,331	2,119
Power Systems	5,129	4,805	4,995	5,262	5,824
Technical Products and Services	4,545	4,431	3,670	3,021	2,317
Earnings of GEFS	927	788	552	504	413
All Other	319	394	3,176	3,379	1,071
Corporate Items and Eliminations	(1,415)	(1,477)	(1,287)	(1,077)	(903)
Total GE	42,650	40,292	40,516	36,725	29,252
GEFS					
Financing	7,333	5,827	3,507	2,594	2,469
Insurance	2,710	2,478	2,217	2,026	1,332
Securities Broker-Dealer	2,897	2,316	2,491	1,176	—
All Other	5	34	10	18	4
Total GEFS	12,945	10,655	8,225	5,814	3,805
Eliminations	(1,021)	(858)	(583)	(526)	(433)
Consolidated revenues	$54,574	$50,089	$48,158	$42,013	$32,624
Operating profit					
GE					
Aerospace	$ 646	$ 640	$ 603	$ 608	$ 437
Aircraft Engines	1,050	1,000	940	869	673
Broadcasting	603	540	500	240	20
Industrial	847	798	302	575	658
Major Appliances	399	61	490	462	399
Materials	1,057	733	507	424	330
Power Systems	507	503	199	354	740
Technical Products and Services	589	484	275	112	22
Earnings of GEFS	927	788	552	504	413
All Other	176	168	72	162	376
Total GE	6,801	5,715	4,440	4,310	4,068
GEFS					
Financing	1,152	899	636	(99)	501
Insurance	407	334	183	132	48
Securities Broker-Dealer	(53)	64	(23)	83	—
All Other	(368)	(270)	(224)	(177)	(125)
Total GEFS	1,138	1,027	572	(61)	424
Eliminations	(903)	(802)	(562)	(513)	(420)
Consolidated operating profit	7,036	5,940	4,450	3,736	4,072
GE interest and financial charges (net of eliminations)	(703)	(655)	(635)	(616)	(354)
GE items not traceable to segments	(630)	(564)	(588)	7	(287)
Earnings before income taxes, extraordinary item and cumulative effect of changes in accounting principles	$ 5,703	$ 4,721	$ 3,227	$ 3,127	$ 3,431

The notes to consolidated financial statements on pages __–__ are an integral part of this statement. "GE" means the pre-1988 basis of consolidation as described in note 1 to the consolidated financial statements; "GEFS" means General Electric Financial Services, Inc. and all of its affiliates and associated companies. Operating profit of GE segments excludes interest and other financial charges; operating profit of GEFS includes the effect of interest and discount, which is the largest element of GEFS' operating costs.   [G3624]

even with 1988 on modestly higher sales.

■ *Major Appliances* revenues were $5.6 billion in 1989, a 6% increase from 1988. The current year included sales from the European venture beginning in the second quarter. This increase was partially offset by the absence of revenues of businesses that have been sold, mainly Roper's outdoor power products. Order rates weakened during the second half of 1989 although core product lines showed some market-share gains. The substantial increase in 1989 operating profit was primarily because prior-year results were impacted severely by refrigerator compressor-related warranty provisions.

■ *Materials* revenues were up $1.4 billion in 1989 from the year before, an increase of 39%. A large part of the increase was due to having a full year of Borg-Warner's chemicals operations in 1989 compared with only the last quarter of 1988. Incoming order rates for Plastics slackened in the latter part of 1989 reflecting a slowing in automotive and appliance markets. The 44% increase for 1989 operating profit reflected higher physical volume of Plastics' shipments, including a solid contribution from the Borg-Warner Chemicals acquisition. Superabrasives also contributed to the higher operating profit for 1989. Silicones and Ladd Petroleum profitability were about the same in 1989 and 1988.

■ *Power Systems* revenues were up 7% in 1989 — the first upswing in five years. Operating profit improved slightly. Power Generation had improved operating profit reflecting higher shipments of gas turbines and widespread productivity improvements. Other businesses in the segment had somewhat lower results than last year. Spurred by strengthening demand by domestic utilities and a $750 million order for the world's largest combined-cycle power plant to be built by Tokyo Electric Power Company, Power Generation recorded new orders of almost $4 billion in 1989 — over 40% ahead of 1988. The Power Generation backlog was $5 billion at December 31, 1989, about 45% of which is scheduled for completion in 1990.

■ *Technical Products and Services* operating profits were up 22% in 1989, continuing the good increases of prior years. The revenue increase of only 3% in 1989 reflected the impact of some miscellaneous business dispositions. Higher operating profit was sparked by Medical Systems, where a sharp increase in operating profit reflected higher volume in x-ray, computed tomography and magnetic resonance imaging, as well as good productivity improvements. Medical Systems equipment orders

were very strong in the second half of 1989. The backlog of unfilled orders was $1.5 billion at year-end 1989, about 75% of which is scheduled to be shipped in 1990. Communications and Services had a good increase in operating profit with particularly good contributions by GE Americom, Information Services and Mobile Communications.

■ *Earnings of GEFS* continued to increase in 1989. Comments on GEFS industry segments appear below. Of GEFS' 1989 net earnings, GE Capital's contribution was $816 million, 36% more than 1988's $600 million, which was 28% more than 1987's $470 million. (The 1987 amount excludes the cumulative effect of the income tax accounting change and extraordinary loss discussed in note 1).

■ *Financing* operating profits continued to increase very substantially as they have each year since 1986. The level of earning assets and the impact of changes in interest rates on borrowing costs and financing yields are important factors in Financing operating profits. Total assets of GE Capital increased by 23% in 1989 from 1988, which had been 30% more than 1987. Financing yields increased again in 1989 following an increase in 1988. GE Capital's composite annual interest rate increased 119 basis points in 1989 compared with a 43 basis-point increase in 1988. These increases in composite interest rates reflected principally the effect of higher short-term interest rates on commercial paper borrowings. GE Capital's lending "spread" (difference between interest rates charged to customers and interest rates paid to lenders) decreased somewhat during 1989. The spread had increased somewhat during 1988.

■ *Insurance* operating profit increased 22% in 1989 from 1988. Principal reasons for the 1989 improvement were the inclusion of all operations of FGIC Corporation as a result of completing its acquisition early in 1989 and improvement in the mortgage insurance market.

Total assets of GE Capital
(In billions)

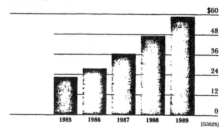

[G3625]

Employers Reinsurance Corporation, which is the largest single business in the insurance segment, had modestly higher net earnings in 1989. ERC has increased revenues each year since 1986.

■ *Securities Broker-Dealer* (Kidder, Peabody) had an operating loss for 1989 compared with a profit in 1988. Most of the 1989 loss was incurred during the first quarter of the year, and, as revenues improved and costs were reduced, the last six months were about break-even. Kidder, Peabody took steps during 1989 to exit certain businesses, to upgrade staff in others and to streamline the organization.

■ *All other GEFS* consists principally of acquisition-related interest expense not allocated to the segments.

■ *GE items not traceable to segments* include expenses such as the Corporate R&D Center and corporate staffs and income from corporate treasury activities.

International operations

■ *Total international operations* (consisting of all exports from the United States plus the results of operations located outside the United States) had revenues aggregating $13.9 billion and operating profit of $2.8 billion in 1989. International revenues were $10.8 billion in 1988, up from $9.2 billion in 1987. International operating profit in 1988 was $2.1 billion compared with $1.7 billion in 1987.

The chart (above right) shows the growth in GE's revenues for international operations by areas of the world over the last five years. An especially significant increase in European operations is evident, especially in the last two years. This is the result of significant increases in exports of Aircraft Engines; a much higher volume of shipments of Plastics products; the establishment of an increasing presence in European Medical Systems markets related to acquisitions beginning in 1988; and, in 1989, the impact of venture activities, especially in Major Appliances and Controls.

■ *GE's exports from the United States* to external customers escalated to $6.2 billion in 1989, up from $4.9 billion in 1988 and $4.0 billion in 1987. The chart (on the right) shows the substantial growth in GE's exports for the last five years, led by the strong increases in Aircraft Engines. Export sales by major world areas follow.

GE's exports from the United States to external customers
(In millions)

	1989	1988	1987
Europe	$2,915	$1,805	$1,253
Pacific Basin	1,926	1,357	1,146
Americas	596	531	625
Other	724	1,177	1,000
	$6,161	$4,870	$4,024

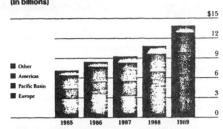

Total international revenues
(In billions)

In addition, exports from GE operations in the United States to GE affiliates offshore were $1.107 billion in 1989, $874 million in 1988 and $801 million in 1987.

■ *GE again sharply increased its positive contribution to the U.S. balance of trade.* In 1989, this contribution netted to about $4.8 billion compared with $3.1 billion in 1988 and $2.1 billion in 1987. This improvement is attributable to the higher level of export activity, as depicted below.

GE contribution to U.S. balance of trade (estimated)
(In billions)

	1989	1988	1987
Export sales from the United States			
To external customers	$6.2	$4.9	$4.0
To GE affiliates	1.1	0.8	0.8
Total exports from the United States	7.3	5.7	4.8
Imports into the United States			
From GE affiliates	0.7	1.0	1.1
Directly from other suppliers	1.8	1.6	1.6
Total imports into the United States	2.5	2.6	2.7
GE positive contribution to U.S. balance of trade	$4.8	$3.1	$2.1

GE's exports from the United States to external customers (In billions)

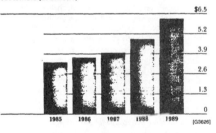

[G3626]

Management's Discussion of Financial Resources and Liquidity

Overview

This discussion of financial resources and liquidity focuses on the Statement of Financial Position (page [526]) and the Statement of Cash Flows (page [528]). As with the Statement of Earnings, the content of these two statements is so different for GE and GEFS that most of the asset, liability and cash flow categories do not lend themselves to simple combination. This, of course, reflects the differences in the nature of the businesses.

Although GE's manufacturing and nonfinancial services activities involve a variety of different businesses, their underlying characteristics are the developing, preparing for market and selling of tangible products and services. Risk and reward are directly related to the ability to manage those activities. Financial leverage comes from realizing an adequate return on share owners' equity with judicious use of borrowed funds.

GEFS is not a "captive finance company" or a vehicle for "off-balance-sheet financing" for GE. In fact, very little of its business is directly related to other GE operations. Its principal businesses provide financing, reinsurance and broker-dealer services to third parties. The underlying characteristics of these businesses involve the management of financial risk. They do not develop, manufacture or sell products and services such as, for example, an aircraft engine or the delivering of a message over a TV network. Their risk and reward are related to the ability to provide funds at competitive rates coupled with creative value-added services.

These fundamental differences are reflected in the measurements commonly used by investors, rating agencies and financial analysts. These differences will become clearer in the discussion that follows with respect to the more significant items in the two financial statements.

Statement of Financial Position

■ *Marketable securities carried at cost* for each of the last two years were mainly debt securities held by GEFS' insurance affiliates in support of their obligations to policy holders. The increase to $6.8 billion in 1989 from $5.5 billion in 1988 reflects the acquisition of FGIC.

■ *Marketable securities carried at market* represent primarily the investing and trading portfolio of Kidder, Peabody and, to a lesser degree, similar insurance affiliate activities. The increase to $8.5 billion in 1989 from $5.1 billion in 1988 reflects a higher level of activity in these businesses as well as higher market prices at the end of 1989 compared with 1988.

■ *Securities purchased under agreements to resell* ("reverse repurchase agreements") are related to the liability account: Securities sold under agreements to repur-

chase ("repurchase agreements"). These typically represent highly liquid, short-term investments of excess funds or borrowing of such funds from others. At year-ends 1989 and 1988, the balances (both assets and liabilities) were solely those of Kidder, Peabody in connection with its broker-dealer activities.

■ *GE's current receivables* are mainly amounts due from customers and were $5.3 billion at the end of each of the last two years. Customer receivables "turned over" 7.50 times in 1989 compared with 7.01 times in 1988. ("Turnover" relates receivables to sales and is a measurement of collection efficiency. Higher turnover indicates faster collections.) GE's trend in this area has been improving since 1985, primarily as a result of vigorous management attention to credit and collections. Other receivables measurements, such as delinquency ratios and amounts past due, also have been improving, and the overall condition of customer receivables remained excellent at the end of 1989. Current receivables other than amounts owed by customers are amounts that did not originate from sales of GE products or services, such as advances to suppliers in connection with large contracts.

■ *Inventories* of $6.7 billion at the end of 1989 were slightly higher than the $6.5 billion at the end of 1988. Inventories turned over 4.44 times in 1989 compared with 4.38 times in 1988. As with receivables, this is a measurement of efficient use of resources and has been showing steady improvement in recent years. There were no significant changes in inventory levels in the key businesses between the last two year ends. Last-in first-out (LIFO) revaluations decreased $37 million in 1989 compared with an increase of $150 million in 1988. LIFO revaluations increased $324 million in 1987, mostly related to the accounting change described in note 1. Included in these changes were decreases of $68 million, $23 million and $22 million (1989, 1988 and 1987, respectively) due to lower inventory levels. In each of the last three years, there was a net current-year price increase.

GE/S&P dividends per share increase compared with 1984

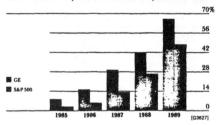

[G3627]

■ *GEFS' financing receivables* grew to $41.8 billion in 1989, a $5.9 billion (16%) increase. Note 16 includes additional information and details about these receivables, which are GEFS' single most important earning asset.

GEFS provides time sales and loans on various bases with varying levels of security and differing maturities, and it also makes preferred stock investments and occasionally receives warrants convertible into common stock. Time sales and loans grew $4.1 billion to $30.9 billion. Increases were in retailer and auto financing ($2.1 billion); commercial real estate financing ($1.2 billion); and commercial and industrial loans ($1.1 billion). Home and recreation financing decreased by $666 million.

Included in time sales and loans and other assets were fundings and investments, principally by GE Capital, for leveraged corporate restructurings, management buyouts and recapitalizations — so-called leveraged buyouts or LBOs. GE Capital structures these transactions to afford itself sufficient collateral protection with approximately 75% of investment positioned at the senior debt level. The GEFS portfolio at December 31, 1989 was widely dispersed throughout the United States and, to a lesser degree, Canada and Europe; it included a number of different industries; and it consisted of approximately 100 accounts aggregating approximately $8.3 billion. Receivable losses from these transactions have averaged about 1% of investment over the past three years and have been much more than offset by the equity gains that are an integral part of LBO financings.

Also included in GEFS' time sales and loans were $8.8 billion invested in approximately 800 real estate loans, virtually all for commercial properties. Typically, such loans were structured so that existing cash flows more than covered debt service and were secured by first mortgages largely on multitenant office buildings and apartment projects. Loans for land acquisition and development and project construction were not an important part of the portfolio. At year-end 1989, the portfolio was geographically balanced with investments throughout the United States and, to a much lesser extent, Canada and Europe. Receivable losses on commercial real estate loans have averaged significantly less than 1% of investment over the past three years.

Investment in financing leases reached $12.8 billion at the end of 1989, up from $11.1 billion at the prior year end. Details of these balances can be found in note 16.

The allowance for losses deducted in arriving at the net balance of $41.8 billion increased from $972 million at the end of 1988 to $1.127 billion at December 31, 1989. Included were additions by charging operations ($527 million in 1989, $434 million in 1988 and $290 million in 1987) and write-offs of $420 million in 1989, $294 million in 1988 and $171 million in 1987. Overall, net loss experi-

Dividends per share

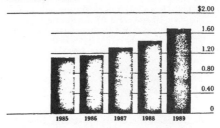

ence as a percent of average financing receivables was 0.98% in 1989, 0.81% in 1988 and 0.62% in 1987. The increases in 1989 and 1988 reflect significant growth in credit card operations whose loss rates, as expected, are relatively high in comparison with other GE Capital businesses. At the end of both 1989 and 1988, the reserve coverage on financing receivables was equal to 2.63% of the receivables balances outstanding. The relationship was equal to 2.59% at the end of 1987.

Although the nature of GE Capital's business is such that an economic downturn or increasing level of interest rates could result in financial stress to customers, management believes that the diversified nature of the portfolio affords reasonable protection against any material negative impact on GEFS' operating results or financial condition. In summary, GEFS' financing receivables are in good condition and reserve protection is appropriate.

■ *Property, plant and equipment* (including equipment leased to others) aggregated $15.6 billion at December 31, 1989, up $2.0 billion from $13.6 billion a year earlier. GE's property, plant and equipment consists of investments for its own productive use, whereas the largest element of GEFS' investment is in equipment that is provided to third parties on operating leases. Details by categories of investment can be found in note 18.

GE's total expenditures for new plant and equipment during 1989 were $2.3 billion, bringing the total of the last five years (excluding the unusually large addition by acquisition of RCA in 1986) to $10.3 billion. Of that five-year total, 32% was to increase capacity; 25% was to increase productivity; 12% was to support new business start-ups; 14% was to replace and renew older equipment; and 17% was for such other purposes as improving R&D facilities and safety and environmental protection.

GEFS added $3.1 billion to its equipment leased to others in 1989. Current-year amortization was $647 million.

[G3628]

■ *Intangible assets* aggregated $8.8 billion at December 31, 1989. The majority of this consolidated total is GE's intangibles, which were $7.0 billion at that date, about the same as a year earlier. The largest portion of GE's balance (in both goodwill and other intangibles) arose from the acquisition of RCA Corporation in 1986. Other balances were mainly related to acquisitions of Borg-Warner's chemicals businesses, Roper Corporation, a TV station in Miami, Fla., and CGR medical business assets. The increase in 1989 included completion of Borg-Warner valuations.

GEFS' intangible assets were $1.8 billion at the end of 1989 compared with $1.6 billion a year earlier, principally reflecting the 1989 completion of the acquisition of FGIC Corporation.

■ *All other assets* totaled $9.4 billion at December 31, 1989 compared with $8.0 billion a year earlier. These include a wide variety of items as detailed in note 20. GE's all other assets increased $1.1 billion during 1989, principally because of new investments in joint ventures classified as "associated companies."

■ *Total borrowings* on a consolidated basis aggregated $53.3 billion at December 31, 1989 compared with $45.5 billion at the end of 1988. However, borrowings must be looked at separately for GE and GEFS. The major debt-rating agencies evaluate the financial condition of the entities separately because of their distinctly different business characteristics. Using criteria appropriate to each, those major rating agencies continue to give top ratings to debt of both GE and GEFS.

GE's total borrowings were $5.6 billion at the end of 1989, a decrease of $548 million from the end of 1988. Long-term borrowings of $3.9 billion were down from $4.3 billion a year earlier, and short-term borrowings declined to $1.7 billion from $1.9 billion. The current portion of long-term borrowings included in short-term borrowings dropped about $1.1 billion during 1989 reflecting mainly reductions related to debt involving the 1986 acquisition of RCA Corporation. By the end of 1989, all debt of RCA Corporation that had been assumed by GE had been retired. GE's total debt at the end of 1989 equaled 21.0% of total capital, or a decrease of 3.9 points from 24.9% at the end of 1988. This relationship of debt and equity capital is sound and is well within the range of what would be expected of a strong industrially oriented firm.

GEFS' total borrowings were $47.9 billion at December 31, 1989, of which $35.7 billion is due in 1990 and $12.2 billion is due in subsequent years. The comparable amounts at the end of 1988 were: $39.6 billion total; $28.7 billion due within one year; and $10.9 billion due beyond that. The increases were to support the growth in

GEFS' earning assets. GEFS' composite interest rates were discussed in connection with the Statement of Earnings. A large portion of GEFS' borrowings is in the form of commercial paper ($30.5 billion and $24.6 billion at the ends of 1989 and 1988, respectively). Most of this commercial paper is issued by GE Capital. Its commercial paper has maturities of up to nine months. The average remaining terms of GE Capital's commercial paper were 23 days at the ends of 1989 and 1988. Average interest rates on GE Capital's commercial paper were 8.81% and 9.32% at the end of those respective years. "Leverage," the relationship of debt to equity capital, is expected by investors to be much higher in a financial enterprise than in an industrial enterprise. GE Capital's ratio of debt to equity was 7.80 to 1.00 at the end of 1989 compared with 7.67 to 1.00 at the end of 1988. This relationship of debt to equity capital is believed to be sound and is appropriate for a highly rated financial services enterprise.

Notes 21 and 25 provide details of short-term and long-term borrowings.

Statement of Cash Flows

The Statement of Cash Flows (page[528]) emphasizes the analysis of cash flows from three broad categories — operating activities, investing activities and financing activities. Inasmuch as the cash management activities of GE and GEFS are separate and distinct, it is more useful to review the separate cash flow statements than the consolidated statement.

GE

GE's cash and equivalents aggregated $1.7 billion at the end of 1989, slightly lower ($74 million) than at the end of 1988. During 1989, GE generated $4.8 billion in cash from its operating activities. This provided resources to invest over $2 billion in new plant and equipment; to make acquisitions, the principal ones of which required cash outlays of

Consolidated total assets
(In billions)

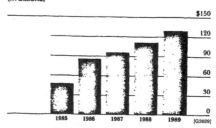

almost $800 million; to reduce total debt by $500 million; and to pay $1.5 billion in dividends to share owners.

Operating activities are the principal source of GE's cash flows. Over the past three years, operating activities have provided more than $12 billion of cash. Principal ongoing applications usually are to invest in new plant and equipment ($5.8 billion total over the last three years) and to pay dividends to share owners ($3.9 billion total over the last three years). Expenditures for new plant and equipment are again expected to be in the $2 billion-plus range for 1990, and dividends are expected to increase with earnings.

Based on past performance and current expectations, in combination with the financial flexibility that comes with the highest credit ratings, GE is in a sound position to continue making long-term investments for future growth, including selective acquisitions and investments in joint ventures. The five-year share repurchase program discussed separately on this page is a direct result of GE's solid financial condition and cash-generating capability.

GEFS

GEFS' principal source of cash is financing activities that involve continuing rollover of short-term borrowings and appropriate addition of long-term borrowings with a reasonable balance of maturities. Over the past three years, GEFS' outstanding borrowings with 90-day or less maturities have increased a total of $14.3 billion. New borrowings of $26.0 billion having maturities longer than 90 days were added during those years while $21.5 billion of such longer-term borrowings were paid off.

GEFS' principal application of cash has been in investing activities to grow the business. Of the $27.1 billion of net investments by GEFS over the past three years, $17.1 billion was devoted to additional financing receivables. Other principal investments during these years were $2.2 billion to acquire new businesses as GEFS expands its activities and $5.6 billion for new equipment, which is mainly for lease to others.

Cash used for new investments in excess of cash provided from additional borrowings has been provided mainly by generation of $7.8 billion of cash from operating activities for the years 1987-1989 and from issuance of $600 million cumulative variable preferred stock by GE Capital in 1988. GEFS' cash and equivalents balance has remained relatively stable throughout the period — again in keeping with its business mission.

In summary, based on past performance and current expectations, in combination with the financial flexibility that comes with excellent credit ratings, GEFS is well positioned to continue growing its assets and to produce a good rate of return on GE share owners' investment in GEFS.

Return on share owners' equity

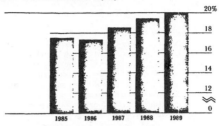

Five-year share repurchase program

In November 1989, GE's Board of Directors authorized the repurchase of up to $10 billion of the Company's common stock over the next five years. This authorization was made after evaluating various alternatives to enhance long-term share owner value. Based on the financial and competitive positions of the Company, its debt capacity and the cash-generating characteristics now present in its key businesses, management believes GE has the flexibility to continue increasing dividends in line with earnings, to maintain a high degree of internal reinvestment, to make selective acquisitions complementary to existing business — and also to repurchase a significant amount of stock. Such repurchases will result in higher earnings per share and returns on equity than would otherwise be the case.

The repurchase plan is designed to be flexible. Shares will be acquired with funds from a combination of free cash flows and new borrowings while keeping GE's debt-to-capital ratio in the 25% range. Should world economic conditions, a major acquisition or other circumstances warrant, the Company would modify the pace and dimension of the plan to maintain GE's solid financial position. This repurchase plan was reviewed with debt rating agencies, who confirmed GE's Triple-A debt rating.

During the last six weeks of 1989, about 3.8 million shares were reacquired at a cost of $236 million.

[G3630]

Management's Discussion of Selected Financial Data

Selected financial data summarizes on the opposite page some data frequently requested about General Electric Company and provides a record that may be useful for reviewing trends. The data are divided into three sections: upper portion — consolidated information, middle portion — GE data that reflect various conventional measurements for industrial enterprises, and lower portion — GEFS data that reflect key information and ratios pertinent to financial services.

GE's total research and development expenditures were a record $3.931 billion in 1989, up 9% from 1988's $3.601 billion. Of the 1989 expenditures, $1.334 billion was from GE's own funds, an increase of 15% from 1988's $1.155 billion. Expenditures from funds provided from customers (mainly the U.S. government) were $2.597 billion in 1989, or 6% more than $2.446 billion the year before. Aircraft Engines and Aerospace account for the largest share of GE's R&D expenditures from both Company and customer funds. Other significant expenditures of Company funds were for Medical Systems, Plastics and Power Systems.

GE's total backlog of firm unfilled orders at the end of 1989 was $30.5 billion. Orders constituting this backlog may be canceled or deferred by customers (subject in certain cases to cancellation penalties). Comments on unfilled orders for businesses with relatively long manufacturing cycles can be found in the discussion of Industry Segments, which begins on page [532] About 46% of the 1989 total unfilled orders is scheduled to be shipped in 1990 with most of the remainder to be shipped in the two years after that. For comparison, about 49% of the 1988 backlog was expected to be shipped in 1989.

Unfilled orders for export of all types of products and services from the United States were $9.9 billion at December 31, 1989, up from $8.2 billion the year before. The backlog of Aircraft Engine orders is a major portion of the export backlog, but significant increases were recorded in 1989 by Aerospace and Power Systems.

Inflation has not been a significant factor in consolidated earnings growth in recent years because of the relatively modest rate of price increases in the economies of the United States and of the principal foreign countries where the Company has operations.

Regarding environmental matters, the operations of the Company, like those of other companies engaged in similar businesses, involve the use, disposal and cleanup of substances regulated under environmental protection laws.

In 1989, GE had capital expenditures of about $110 million for projects related to the environment. The comparable amount for 1988 was about $70 million. These amounts exclude expenditures for remedial actions, which are discussed on this page. Capital expenditures for environmental purposes have included pollution control devices

such as waste-water treatment plants, ground-water monitoring devices, air strippers or separators, and incinerators at new and existing facilities constructed or altered in the normal course of business. Consistent with GE's policies stressing environmental responsibility, average annual capital expenditures for nonremedial projects are presently expected to range between $150 million and $200 million over the next two years. The principal reasons for this expected increase from existing levels are new or expanded programs to build or modify manufacturing processes so they can use alternative methods that will result in minimizing environmental waste and reducing emissions.

The Company also is involved in a sizable number of remedial actions to clean up hazardous wastes as required by federal and state laws. Such statutes require that responsible parties fund remedial actions regardless of fault, legality of original disposal or ownership of a disposal site. In 1989, GE spent approximately $75 million on remedial cleanups and related studies compared with approximately $48 million spent for such purposes in 1988. It is presently expected that remedial cleanups and related studies will require average annual expenditures in the range of $80 million to $120 million over the next two years.

It is difficult to estimate reasonably the ultimate level of environmental expenditures due to a number of uncertainties, including uncertainties about the status of law, regulation, technology, insurance coverage of GE costs and information relating to individual sites. Subject to the foregoing, Company management believes that capital expenditures and remedial actions to comply with the present laws governing environmental protection will not have a material effect upon its capital expenditures, earnings or competitive position.

Consolidated employment at year end
(In thousands)

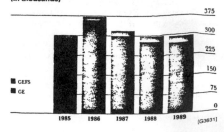

[G3631]

Selected Financial Data

(Dollar amounts in millions; per-share amounts in dollars)	1989	1988	1987	1986	1985
General Electric Company and consolidated affiliates					
Revenues	$ 54,574	$ 50,089	$ 48,158	$ 42,013	$ 32,624
Earnings before extraordinary loss and cumulative					
effect of accounting changes	3,939	3,386	2,119	2,492	2,277
Net earnings	3,939	3,386	2,915	2,492	2,277
Dividends declared	1,537	1,314	1,209	1,081	1,020
Earned on average share owners' equity	20.0%	19.4%	18.5%	17.3%	17.5%
Per share					
Net earnings	$ 4.36	$ 3.75	$ 3.20	$ 2.73	$ 2.50
Dividends declared	1.70	1.46	1.32½	1.18½	1.11½
Stock price range	64¾-43½	47⅞-38⅜	66⅜-38¾	44⅜-33¼	36⅞-27¾
Total assets	128,344	110,865	95,414	84,818	49,123
Long-term borrowings	16,110	15,082	12,517	10,001	5,577
Shares outstanding — average (in thousands)	904,223	901,780	911,639	912,594	910,762
Share owner accounts — average	526,000	529,000	491,000	492,000	506,000
Employees at year end					
Domestic	243,000	255,000	277,000	302,000	243,000
Foreign	49,000	43,000	45,000	71,000	56,000
Total employees	292,000	298,000	322,000	373,000	299,000
GE data					
Short-term borrowings	$ 1,696	$ 1,861	$ 1,110	$ 1,813	$ 1,297
Long-term borrowings	3,947	4,330	4,491	4,351	753
Minority interest	283	228	190	189	126
Share owners' equity	20,890	18,466	16,480	15,109	13,671
Total capital invested	$ 26,816	$ 24,885	$ 22,271	$ 21,462	$ 15,847
Return on average total capital invested	17.0%	16.4%	14.7%	13.9%	16.2%
Borrowings as a percentage of total capital invested	21.0%	24.9%	25.1%	28.7%	12.9%
Current assets	$ 15,671	$ 15,499	$ 15,739	$ 14,288	$ 12,546
Current liabilities	13,988	13,419	12,671	11,461	8,919
Working capital	$ 1,683	$ 2,080	$ 3,068	$ 2,827	$ 3,627
Property, plant and equipment additions (other than					
by acquisition of RCA)	$ 2,251	$ 2,288	$ 1,778	$ 2,042	$ 1,953
Year-end orders backlog	30,473	27,265	22,737	23,943	23,117
GEFS data					
Earnings before extraordinary loss and cumulative					
effect of accounting change	$ 927	$ 788	$ 552	$ 504	$ 413
Net earnings	927	788	1,008	504	413
Share owner's equity	6,069	4,819	3,980	2,994	2,302
Earned on average share owner's equity	17.6%	18.0%	18.0%	19.7%	19.9%
Borrowings from others	$ 47,905	$ 39,593	$ 30,885	$ 23,397	$ 16,393
Ratio of debt to equity (GE Capital)	7.80:1	7.67:1	7.98:1	7.83:1	7.89:1
Total assets of GE Capital	$ 58,696	$ 47,766	$ 36,644	$ 27,970	$ 22,469
Reserve coverage on financing receivables	2.63%	2.63%	2.59%	2.59%	2.57%
Insurance premiums written	$ 1,819	$ 1,809	$ 1,729	$ 1,704	$ 1,092
Securities broker-dealer earned income	2,897	2,316	2,491	1,176	—

See notes 1 and 25 to the consolidated financial statements for information about 1987 accounting changes and extraordinary loss and note 2 for information about certain acquisitions and related matters. In addition, RCA Corporation and Kidder, Peabody & Co. were acquired in June 1986. "GE" means the pre-1988 basis of consolidation as described in note 1 to the consolidated financial statements; "GEFS" means General Electric Financial Services, Inc. and all of its affiliates and associated companies. Transactions between GE and GEFS have been eliminated from the "consolidated data." Share data reflect the 2-for-1 stock split in April 1987.   [G3632]

Management's Discussion of Financial Responsibility

The financial information in this report, including the audited financial statements, has been prepared by management. Preparation of financial statements and related data involves estimates and the use of judgment. Accounting principles used in preparing the financial statements are those that are generally accepted in the United States. These principles are consistent in most important respects with standards issued to date by the International Accounting Standards Committee. Where there is no single specified accounting principle or standard, management makes a choice from reasonable, accepted alternatives, using methods that it believes are prudent for General Electric Company and its consolidated affiliates.

To safeguard Company assets, it is important to have a sound but dynamic system of internal financial controls and procedures that balances benefits and costs. One of the key elements of internal financial controls has been the Company's success in recruiting, selecting, training and developing professional financial managers. Their responsibilities include implementing and overseeing the financial control system, reporting on management's stewardship of the assets entrusted to it by share owners, and performing accurate and proper maintenance of the accounts.

Management has long recognized its responsibility for conducting the affairs of the Company and its affiliates in an ethical and socially responsible manner. General Electric Company is dedicated to the highest standards of integrity. Integrity is not an occasional requirement but a continuing commitment that is reflected in key written policy statements. These cover, among other subjects, environmental protection, potentially conflicting outside business interests of employees, compliance with antitrust laws, and proper domestic and international business practices. Management insists on maintaining the highest standards of conduct and practices with respect to transactions with the United States government. There is continuing emphasis to all employees that even the appearance of impropriety can erode public confidence in the Company and in the government procurement process. Ongoing education, communication and review programs are designed to create a strong compliance environment and to make it clearly understood that deviation from Company policies will not be tolerated.

KPMG Peat Marwick provide an objective, independent review of management's discharge of its obligations relating to the fairness of reported operating results and financial condition. Their report for 1989 appears on the opposite page.

The Audit Committee of the Board (consisting solely of Directors from outside GE) maintains an ongoing appraisal — on behalf of share owners — of the effectiveness of the independent auditors, the Company's staff of corporate auditors and management, with respect to the financial reporting process, and of the adequacy of internal financial controls. The committee also reviews the Company's accounting policies, compliance with key policies, and the Annual Report and proxy material.

John F. Welch, Jr.
Chairman of the Board and
Chief Executive Officer

Dennis D. Dammerman
Senior Vice President
Finance

February 16, 1990

[G3633]

Notes to Consolidated Financial Statements

Index

Note 1   Summary of Significant Accounting Policies

Consolidation and financial statement presentation

Consolidation. The consolidated financial statements represent the adding together of all companies in which General Electric Company directly or indirectly has a majority ownership or otherwise controls ("affiliated companies"). Prior to 1988, results of financial services affiliates — the principal one being General Electric Financial Services, Inc. (GEFS or GE Financial Services) and its affiliated companies — were included on the equity basis as one line in total earnings and net assets. This was permissible under accounting rules in effect before 1988. Because financial services operations are so different in nature from and essentially unrelated to operations of other GE businesses, management believed that financial statements were more understandable if GEFS' statements were shown separately. It should be emphasized that, under both current and prior procedures, consolidated net earnings and share owners' equity are the same for all periods presented. However, substantially more detail is required under the current standard than under rules previously in effect. Also as a result of this change, the Company adopted an unclassified consolidated statement of financial position.

Management believes it is important to preserve as much as possible the identity of the principal financial data and related measurements to which share owners and others have become accustomed over the years. Accordingly, consolidated financial statements and notes now are generally presented in a format that includes data grouped basically as follows.

- *GE* — this is essentially the pre-1988 basis of consolidation except that it includes some very small financial services affiliates previously not consolidated. The effect of transactions among companies within this group has been eliminated. Where appropriate for clarification or emphasis, particularly in the notes, this group of entities also is referred to as "GE except GEFS."

- *GEFS* — this affiliate owns all of the common stock of General Electric Capital Corporation (GECC or GE Capital) and of Employers Reinsurance Corporation (ERC), and 80% of the stock of Kidder, Peabody Group Inc. (Kidder, Peabody). These affiliates and their respective affiliates are consolidated in the GEFS columns with the effect of transactions among them eliminated before the consolidated presentation.

[G3635]

■ *Consolidated* — these columns represent the adding together of GE and GEFS. However, it is necessary to remove the effect of transactions between GE except GEFS and GEFS to arrive at a consolidated total. The "eliminations" used to arrive at these consolidated totals are summarized below.

Eliminations

(In millions)	1989	1988	1987
Statement of Earnings			
Sales of goods	$ (12)	$ (5)	$ —
Sales of services	(20)	(26)	(8)
Other income	(14)	(5)	6
Earnings of GEFS	(927)	(788)	(552)
GEFS revenues from operations	(48)	(34)	(29)
Total revenues	(1,021)	(858)	(583)
Cost of goods sold	(12)	(5)	—
Cost of services sold	(20)	(26)	(8)
Interest and other financial charges	(47)	(29)	(10)
Other costs and expenses	(15)	(10)	(13)
Total costs and expenses	(94)	(70)	(31)
Earnings before income taxes, extraordinary item and cumulative effect of accounting changes	(927)	(788)	(552)
Extraordinary item	—	—	62
Income tax accounting change	—	—	(518)
Net earnings	$ (927)	$ (788)	$(1,008)
Statement of Financial Position			
GE current receivables	$ (242)	$ (330)	
GEFS financing receivables	—	(107)	
Other GEFS receivables	(380)	(107)	
Investment in GEFS	(6,069)	(4,819)	
Total assets	$(6,691)	$(5,363)	
Short-term borrowings	$ (236)	$ (170)	
Accounts payable	(379)	(264)	
Long-term borrowings	(2)	(110)	
All other liabilities	(5)	—	
Total liabilities	(622)	(544)	
GEFS equity	(6,069)	(4,819)	
Total liabilities and equity	$(6,691)	$(5,363)	
Statement of Cash Flows			
Net earnings (operating activities)	$ (221)	$ (13)	$ (213)
Investing activities	179	(171)	243
Financing activities	42	184	(30)
Total	$ —	$ —	$ —

Results of companies in which GE or GEFS owns between 20% and 50% ("associated companies") are included in the financial statements on a "one-line" basis.

Cash flows. During 1989, the definition of "cash and equivalents" for GE except GEFS was modified to exclude marketable securities having original maturities between 90 and 365 days. GEFS' cash and equivalents, which includes only cash and very short-term (only a few days' maturities), is not affected by this modification.

Pensions and other retirement benefits. Accounting policies for pensions and other retirement benefits are discussed in note 6.

Income taxes. SFAS No. 96 — "Accounting for Income Taxes" was issued by the Financial Accounting Standards Board in December 1987. A requirement of SFAS No. 96 is that deferred tax liabilities or assets at the end of each period be determined using the tax rate expected to be in effect when taxes are actually paid or recovered. Accordingly, under SFAS No. 96 rules, income tax expense provisions will increase or decrease in the same period in which a change in tax rates is enacted. Previous rules required providing deferred taxes using rates in effect when the tax asset or liability was first recorded without subsequent adjustment solely for tax-rate changes (except with respect to leveraged leases).

In conformity with SFAS No. 96 transition rules, the Company elected to adopt the new income tax accounting during 1987. The cumulative effect to January 1, 1987 ($577 million, including $518 million for GEFS) of the change is shown in the 1987 columns of the Statement of Earnings.

GE accounting policies

Sales. A sale is recorded when title passes to the customer or when services are performed in accordance with contracts.

Investment tax credit (ITC). The ITC was repealed, with some transitional exceptions, effective January 1, 1986. However, for financial reporting purposes, GE has deferred recognition of the ITC each year and continues to amortize ITC as a reduction of the provision for income taxes over the lives of the facilities to which the credit applies.

Inventories. The values of most inventories are determined on a last-in first-out, or LIFO, basis and do not exceed realizable values. Effective January 1, 1987, GE changed its accounting procedures to include in inventory certain manufacturing overhead costs previously charged directly to expense. The more significant types of manufacturing overhead included in inventory as a result of the change are: depreciation of plant and equipment; pension and other benefits of manufacturing employees; and certain product-related engineering expenses. The Company believes this change was preferable because it provides a better matching of production costs with related revenues

[G3636]

in reporting operating results. In accordance with generally accepted accounting principles, the cumulative effect of this change for periods prior to January 1, 1987 ($281 million after providing for taxes of $215 million) is shown separately in 1987 in the Statement of Earnings on page 524. There was virtually no effect from this change on 1987 results after recording the cumulative effect.

Depreciation, depletion and amortization. The cost of most manufacturing plant and equipment is depreciated using an accelerated method based primarily on a sum-of-the-years digits formula. If manufacturing plant and equipment is subject to abnormal economic conditions or obsolescence, additional depreciation is provided.

GEFS accounting policies

Methods of recording revenues ("earned income"). Income on all loans is earned on the interest method. For loan contracts on which finance charges are precomputed, finance charges are deferred at the time of contract acquisition. For loan contracts on which finance charges are not precomputed but are billed to customers, income is recorded when earned. Accrual of interest income is suspended when collection of an account becomes doubtful, generally after the account becomes 90 days delinquent.

Financing lease income that includes related investment tax credits and residual values is recorded on the interest method so as to produce a level yield on funds not yet recovered. Unguaranteed residual values included in lease income are based primarily on independent appraisals of the values of leased assets remaining at expiration of the lease terms.

Origination, commitment and other nonrefundable fees related to fundings are deferred and recorded in earned income on the interest method. Commitment fees related to loans not expected to be funded and line-of-credit fees are deferred and recorded in earned income on a straight-line basis over the period to which the fees relate. Syndication fees are recorded in earned income at the time the related services are performed unless significant contingencies exist.

Kidder, Peabody's proprietary securities and commodities transactions are recorded on a trade-date basis. Trading and investment securities are valued at market or estimated fair value. Unrealized gains and losses on open contractual commitments, principally financial futures, when-issued securities and forward contracts on U.S. government and federal agency securities, are reflected in the Statement of Earnings on a trade-date basis. Customers' transactions and the related revenues and expenses are reflected in the financial statements on a settlement-date basis. Revenues and expenses on a trade-date basis are not materially different. Investment banking revenues from management fees, sales concessions and underwriting fees are recorded on settlement date. Advisory fee revenue is recorded when services are substantially completed and the revenue is reasonably determinable.

See "insurance affiliates" on page 546 for information with respect to earned income of these businesses.

Allowance for losses on financing receivables. GE Capital maintains an allowance for losses on financing receivables at an amount that it believes is sufficient to provide adequate protection against future losses in the portfolio. For small-balance and certain large-balance receivables, the allowance for losses is determined principally on the basis of actual experience during the preceding three years. Further allowances also are provided to reflect management's judgment of additional loss potential. For other receivables, principally the larger loans and leases, the allowance for losses is determined primarily on the basis of management's judgment of net loss potential, including specific allowances for known troubled accounts.

All accounts or portions thereof deemed to be uncollectible or to require an excessive collection cost are written off to the allowance for losses. Small-balance accounts are progressively written down (from 10% when more than three months delinquent to 100% when more than 12 months delinquent) to record the balances at estimated realizable value. However, if at any time during that period an account is judged to be uncollectible, such as in the case of a bankruptcy, the remaining balance is written off. Larger-balance accounts are reviewed at least quarterly, and those accounts that are more than three months delinquent are written down, if necessary, to record the balances at estimated realizable value.

Marketable securities. Marketable securities of Kidder, Peabody are carried at market value with the difference between cost and market value included in operations. Marketable debt securities held by all other GEFS affiliates are carried at amortized cost. Marketable equity securities of insurance affiliates are carried at market value, and unrealized gains or losses, less applicable deferred income taxes, are recognized in equity.

Securities purchased under agreements to resell (reverse repurchase agreements) and securities sold under agreements to repurchase (repurchase agreements). Repurchase and reverse repurchase agreements are treated as financing transactions and are carried at the contract amount at which the securities subsequently will be resold or reacquired. Repurchase agreements relate either to marketable securities, which are carried at market value, or to securities obtained pursuant to reverse repurchase agreements. It is GEFS' policy to take possession of securities subject to reverse repurchase agreements. GEFS monitors the market value of the underlying securities in relation to the related receivable, including accrued interest, and requests additional collateral if appropriate.   [G3637]

Depreciation and amortization. The cost of equipment leased to others on operating leases is amortized, principally on a straight-line basis, to estimated net salvage value over the lease term or over the estimated economic life of the equipment. Depreciation of property and equipment for GEFS' own use is recorded on either a sum-of-the-years digits or a straight-line basis over the lives of the assets.

Investment tax credit (ITC). ITC associated with equipment on operating leases and with buildings and equipment is deferred and amortized over the lives of the underlying assets.

Insurance affiliates. Premiums on short-duration insurance contracts are reported as earned income over the terms of the related reinsurance treaties or insurance policies. In general, earned premiums are calculated on a pro-rata basis or are determined based on reports received from reinsureds. Premium adjustments under retrospectively rated reinsurance contracts are recorded based on estimated losses and loss expenses, including both case and incurred-but-not-reported (IBNR) reserves. Revenues on long-duration contracts are reported as earned when due.

Deferred insurance acquisition costs are amortized as the related premiums are earned for property and casualty business. Deferred insurance acquisition costs for the life insurance business are amortized over the premium-paying periods of the contracts in proportion either to anticipated premium income or to gross profit, as appropriate. Deferred insurance acquisition costs are reviewed for recoverability, and for short-duration contracts, anticipated investment income is considered in making recoverability evaluations.

The estimated liability for outstanding losses and loss expenses consists of case reserves based on reports and estimates of losses and an IBNR reserve based primarily on experience. Where experience is not sufficient, industry averages for the particular insurance products are used. Estimated amounts of salvage and subrogation recoverable on paid and unpaid losses are deducted from outstanding losses. The liability for future policy benefits of the life insurance affiliates has been computed mainly by a net-level-premium method based on assumptions for investment yields, mortality and terminations that were appropriate at date of purchase or at the time the policies were developed, including provisions for adverse deviations.

Note *2*   Acquisitions and Related Matters

GE

Although there were a number of acquisitions and dispositions during 1989, the larger transactions involved completion of arrangements for several joint ventures. These included the combining of interests in European appliances and electrical controls with General Electric plc, (GEC), an unrelated corporation in the United Kingdom. (GE also acquired GEC's medical systems sales and service in the United Kingdom.) Besides the businesses and resources contributed by the parties in these transactions, GE paid cash of $570 million to GEC in the second quarter of 1989. Other new joint ventures included an arrangement with Ericsson of Sweden (mobile communications businesses). Legal form and percentage ownerships in these alliances vary.

During 1988, GE completed a number of acquisitions. The largest of these were:

Roper Corporation, acquired in April for $507 million cash. Roper's principal businesses were the manufacture and sale of gas and electric ranges and outdoor power garden equipment. In December, GE sold Roper's garden equipment business for $295 million cash. Roper's kitchen appliance business prior to acquisition had annual sales of about $375 million.

Borg-Warner's chemicals businesses, acquired in September for $2.3 billion cash. These businesses (annual sales of about $1.6 billion prior to acquisition) manufacture and sell products complementary to GE's plastics businesses.

Both of these acquisitions were accounted for as purchases with the excess of purchase price over the estimate of fair values of net assets acquired recorded as goodwill. See note 19.

Business dispositions during 1988 included most of the GE Solid State (semiconductor) business; seven of NBC's eight radio stations; RCA Global Communications, Inc. (a provider of international communications services); and Sadelmi-Cogepi, a foreign construction firm. Cash proceeds from these transactions aggregated about $700 million. Aggregate annual sales of these businesses were about $900 million.

On December 31, 1987, GE and a French electronics company, Thomson, S.A., completed a transaction in which GE acquired Thomson's medical equipment business (CGR) and Thomson acquired most of GE's consumer electronics business. The total transaction included cash received by GE of about $560 million. CGR's 1987 sales of

[G3636]

about $800 million came mainly from digital x-ray, mammography, computed tomography, ultrasound, and related sales and service in Europe and Latin America. GE's consumer electronics business included mainly GE and RCA brand television sets, VCRs and audio products with sales of about $3 billion annually. GE will continue for some time to receive royalty income from patents related to consumer electronics products. Other related closings, principally for offshore consumer electronics operations, took place in 1988.

Also during 1987, activities involving a "new products" division and NBC's radio networks were sold for cash aggregating about $90 million and a note for $3 million. In addition, GE donated RCA's David Sarnoff Research Center to a not-for-profit organization in 1987.

There was no material effect on GE's operating results or financial position from the above transactions in the year when they occurred.

GEFS

During 1989, GE Capital acquired for $407 million cash the remaining 62% of the common stock it had not previously owned in FGIC Corporation (FGIC), a company principally engaged in providing financial guarantee insurance on selected securities. FGIC, which had annual revenues prior to acquisition of about $125 million, is now consolidated with GE Capital. The aggregate effect of this acquisition and a number of asset acquisitions from other financial services businesses during 1989 was not material.

In June 1988, as part of the management-led acquisition of Montgomery Ward & Co., Incorporated (Montgomery Ward) from Mobil Corporation, GE Capital acquired Montgomery Ward's credit operations comprising Montgomery Ward Credit Corporation (MW Credit) and certain related assets (collectively with MW Credit, MW Credit Operations) for a cash purchase price of $718 million. GE Capital and Kidder, Peabody acquired 40% and 10%, respectively, of Montgomery Ward's common stock for a cash purchase price of $4 million and $1 million, respectively. In addition, GE Capital and Kidder, Peabody paid cash of $82 million and $8 million, respectively, for preferred stock in Montgomery Ward. The management-led acquisition of Montgomery Ward was partially financed by GE Capital in the form of a $275 million subordinated loan.

The acquisition of the MW Credit Operations was accounted for as a purchase, and, accordingly, the purchase price was allocated to the assets and liabilities of MW Credit Operations based on estimates of fair value. The excess purchase price over estimated fair value of net assets acquired (goodwill) is being amortized on a straight-line basis over 20 years.

If the preceding 1988 transactions had occurred on January 1, 1988 or January 1, 1987, management estimates that GEFS results of operations for the years ended December 31, 1988 and 1987 would have been as follows.

(In millions)	1988	1987
Revenues	$10,889	$8,702
Earnings before extraordinary item and cumulative effect of change in accounting principle	784	579
Net earnings	784	1,035

The above unaudited pro forma information has been prepared based on assumptions that management deems appropriate, but the results are not necessarily indicative of those that might have occurred had the acquisitions taken place at the beginnings of the respective years. The results of MW Credit Operations have been consolidated with GEFS since the date of acquisition. There would not have been any significant pro forma effect on consolidated net earnings per share from this transaction.

In July and December 1987, GE Capital acquired the outstanding capital stock of D&K Financial Corporation (D&K) and Gelco Corporation (Gelco), respectively, for an aggregate purchase price of approximately $535 million. Both entities are in the business of leasing vehicle fleets and other equipment. The acquisitions were accounted for as purchases. Results of operations of the acquired corporations have been included in GE Capital since their respective dates of acquisition and are not material.

Note 3   GE Other Income

Other income of GE except GEFS is summarized in the table below.

(In millions)	1989	1988	1987
Royalty and technical agreements	$359	$359	$283
Marketable securities and bank deposits	106	155	133
Associated companies	14	62	61
Customer financing	30	38	52
Other investments			
Interest	11	13	15
Dividends	2	8	4
Other sundry items	182	45	101
	$704	$680	$649

[G3639]

Note 4   GEFS Revenues from Operations

GEFS revenues from operations (earned income) are summarized in the table below.

(In millions)	1989	1988	1987
Time sales, loan, investment and other income	$ 8,113	$ 5,986	$ 4,475
Financing leases	1,078	870	738
Operating lease rentals	1,426	1,372	536
Premium and commission income of insurance affiliates	1,810	1,802	1,748
Commissions and fees of securities broker-dealer	518	625	728
	$12,945	$10,655	$ 8,225

Details of certain items included in earned income from financing leases are shown below.

(In millions)	1989	1988	1987
Deferred investment tax credit amortized			
Direct financing leases	$16	$20	$31
Leveraged leases	21	3	16
Total financing leases	$37	$23	$47
Gains on sale of residual values at lease completion			
Direct financing leases	$38	$39	$44
Leveraged leases	12	29	4
Total financing leases	$50	$68	$48

Noncancelable future rentals due from customers for equipment on operating leases as of December 31, 1989 totaled $2,354 million and are due as follows: 1990 — $734 million; 1991 — $484 million; 1992 — $353 million; 1993 — $254 million; 1994 — $164 million; and $365 million thereafter.

Note 5   Supplemental Cost Details (excluding unusual expenses)

Supplemental cost details are shown in the table below.

Supplemental cost details	1989			1988			1987		
(In millions)	GE	GEFS	Total	GE	GEFS	Total	GE	GEFS	Total
Employee compensation, including Social Security taxes and other benefits	$11,960	$1,103	$13,063	$11,690	$1,052	$12,742	$12,139	$959	$13,098
Selling, general and administrative expense	6,662	—	6,662	6,250	—	6,250	5,979	—	5,979
Company-funded research and development	1,334	—	1,334	1,155	—	1,155	1,194	—	1,194
Maintenance and repairs	821	—	821	839	—	839	840		840
Rental expense	709	176	885	700	160	860	657	123	780
Advertising	415	75	490	413	66	479	495	51	546
Taxes, except payroll and income taxes	298	110	408	374	77	451	289	82	371

Total employee compensation data include Social Security taxes of $804 million in 1989, $819 million in 1988 and $796 million in 1987.

[G3640]

Note *6*   Pensions and Other Retiree Benefits

GE and its affiliates sponsor a number of pension and other retiree benefit plans. This note summarizes important financial aspects of GE's obligations for these plans. Measurements of obligations and costs are based on actuarial calculations involving various assumptions as to future events.

Principal pension plans

The principal pension plans are the GE Pension Plan (GE Plan) and the GE Supplementary Pension Plan (Supplementary Plan). The RCA Retirement Plan (RCA Plan) was merged with the GE Pension Plan at the end of 1988. Amounts and comments about the GE Plan in this note include the RCA Plan for all periods shown. Other pension plans are sponsored by domestic and foreign affiliates, but these are not considered to be significant individually or in the aggregate to the consolidated financial position.

The GE Plan covers substantially all employees in the United States, including approximately 50% of GEFS employees. Generally, benefits are based on the greater of a formula recognizing career earnings or a formula recognizing length of service and final average earnings. Benefits are funded through the GE Pension Trust. At the end of 1989, approximately 208,900 employees were covered, approximately 122,900 former employees with vested rights were entitled to future benefits and approximately 154,500 retirees or beneficiaries were receiving benefits.

The Supplementary Plan is an unfunded plan providing supplementary retirement benefits primarily to higher-level, longer-service management and professional employees in the United States. At the end of 1989, about 3,400 employees were eligible for this plan, and about 4,100 retirees or beneficiaries were receiving benefits.

Statement of Financial Accounting Standards (SFAS) No. 87 requires use of the projected unit credit cost method to determine the projected benefit obligation and plan cost. The projected benefit obligation is the actuarial present value of the portion of projected future benefits that is attributed to employee service to date. The benefit cost for service during the year is the portion of the projected benefit obligation that is attributed to employee service during the year. This cost method recognizes the effect of future compensation and service in projecting the future benefits.

In addition, SFAS No. 87 establishes a "transition gain." This is the excess at January 1, 1986 (when the Company adopted SFAS No. 87) of the current fair market value of plan assets over the plan's projected benefit obligation. This transition gain is being amortized over 15 years except that such excess for the RCA Plan was recognized as an asset in accounting for the RCA acquisition in 1986.

Gains and losses that occur because actual experience differs from that assumed are amortized over the average future service period of employees. Prior-service cost for changes in pension benefits that are allocable to previous periods of service are amortized in the same manner.

Actuarial assumptions for the principal pension plans include 8.5% for both the assumed discount rate used to determine the present value of future benefits and the expected long-term rate of return on plan assets. The assumed rate of average future increases in pension benefit compensation is 6.5%.

Employer costs for the principal pension plans in 1989 and 1988 recognized the impact of continued favorable investment performance. Benefit costs for service during the year recognize plan design changes in 1988. For example, beginning in 1989, employee contributions no longer reduce pension costs because such contributions are used to provide additional pension benefits. Details of cost for the principal pension plans follow.

Cost for principal pension plans (In millions)	1989	1988	1987
Benefit cost for service during the year — net of employee contributions	$ 413	$ 300	$ 385
Interest cost on projected benefit obligation	1,259	1,232	1,187
Recognized return on plan assets	(1,574)	(1,460)	(1,293)
Net amortization	(339)	(299)	(254)
Net pension cost	$ (241)	$ (227)	$ 25
Details of return on plan assets			
Actual return on plan assets	$ 4,026	$ 2,261	$ 1,237
Recognized return on plan assets	(1,574)	(1,460)	(1,293)
Unrecognized return on plan assets	$ 2,452	$ 801	$ (56)

Recognized return on plan assets is determined by applying the expected long-term rate of return to the market-related value of assets.

Funding policy for the GE Plan is to contribute amounts sufficient to meet minimum funding requirements set forth in U.S. employee benefit and tax laws plus such additional amounts as GE may determine to be appropriate from time to time. GE made no contribution for 1989 and 1988 because the funding status of the GE Plan precluded current tax deduction and a contribution would have generated an excise tax.

The funding status of an ongoing plan may be measured by comparing the market-related value of assets with the projected benefit obligation. The market-related value of assets is based on amortized cost plus recognition of market appreciation and depreciation in the portfolio over five years. GE believes the market-related value of assets is a more realistic measure than current fair market value

[G3641]

because the market-related value reduces the impact of short-term market fluctuations. The funding status for the principal pension plans follows.

Funding status for principal pension plans

December 31 (In millions)	1989	1988
Market-related value of assets	$20,794	$19,308
Projected benefit obligation	16,057	15,473

A schedule reconciling the projected benefit obligation for principal pension plans with GE's recorded pension liability is shown below.

Reconciliation of projected benefit obligation with pension liability for principal pension plans

December 31 (In millions)	1989	1988
Projected benefit obligation	$16,057	$15,473
Less current fair market value of trust assets	(24,211)	(21,502)
Unrecognized SFAS No. 87 transition gain	1,693	1,847
Other unrecognized net experience gains	5,333	3,303
Unrecognized prior-service cost	90	114
Recorded prepaid pension assets	1,469	1,177
Recorded pension liability	$ 431	$ 412

The portion of the projected benefit obligation representing the accumulated benefit obligation amounted to $14,940 million and $14,073 million at the ends of 1989 and 1988, respectively. The vested benefit obligation was $14,721 million and $13,895 million at the ends of 1989 and 1988, respectively. These amounts are based on compensation and service to date.

Trust assets consist mainly of common stock and fixed income investments. Trust assets included GE common stock valued at $201 million at year-end 1989 ($139 million at year-end 1988) mainly held in connection with an indexed portfolio.

Other unrecognized net experience gains resulted principally from favorable investment performance.

Principal retiree health care and life insurance plans

GE and its affiliates sponsor a number of plans providing retiree health care and life insurance benefits. GE's aggregate cost for the principal plans, which cover substantially all employees in the United States, was $283 million in 1989, $302 million in 1988 and $278 million in 1987.

Generally, employees who retire after qualifying for optional early retirement under the GE Plan are eligible to participate in retiree health care and life insurance plans. Health care benefits for eligible retirees under age 65 and eligible dependents are included in costs as covered expenses are actually incurred. For eligible retirees and spouses over age 65, the present value of future health care benefits is funded or accrued and is included in costs in the year the retiree becomes eligible for benefits. The present value of future life insurance benefits for eligible retirees is funded and is included in costs in the year of retirement.

Most retirees outside the United States are covered by government health care programs, and GE's cost is not significant.

Note 7　Interest and Other Financial Charges

GE. Interest capitalized, principally on major property, plant and equipment projects, was $48 million in 1989, $11 million in 1988 and $23 million in 1987.

GEFS. GEFS interest and discount expense reported in the Statement of Earnings is net of interest income on temporary investments of excess funds ($160 million, $285 million and $165 million in 1989, 1988 and 1987, respectively) and capitalized interest of $13 million, $16 million and $4 million, respectively, for 1989, 1988 and 1987.

Note 8　GEFS Allowance for Losses on Financing Receivables

GEFS allowance for losses on financing receivables represented 2.63% of total financing receivables at both year-ends 1989 and 1988. The table below shows the activity in the allowance for losses on financing receivables during each of the last three years.

(In millions)	1989	1988	1987
Balance at January 1	$ 972	$ 743	$ 603
Additions charged to operations	527	434	290
Net transfers related to companies acquired and sold	48	89	21
Amounts written off	(420)	(294)	(171)
Balance at December 31	$1,127	$ 972	$ 743

Amounts written off in 1989 were approximately 0.98% of average financing receivables outstanding during the year, compared with 0.81% and 0.62% of average financing receivables outstanding during 1988 and 1987, respectively.

Note 9　Unusual Expenses

GE. Unusual expenses in 1987 were provisions for corporate restructurings. These were for the expenses of refocusing a wide variety of business and marketing activities and reducing foreign and domestic risk exposures. These provisions included costs of rationalizing and improving a large number of production facilities; rearranging production activities among a number of existing plants; and reorganizing, phasing out or otherwise concluding other activities no longer considered essential to the conduct of the Company's business.

GEFS. GEFS unusual expenses in 1987 included amounts related to insider trading charges and business restructuring activities of Kidder, Peabody.

[G3642]

Note 10   **Provision for Income Taxes (excluding 1987 extraordinary item and cumulative effect of changes in accounting principles)**

Provision for income taxes	1989			1988			1987		
(In millions)	GE	GEFS	Total	GE	GEFS	Total	GE	GEFS	Total
Estimated amounts payable (recoverable)	$1,375	$ 48	$1,423	$1,311	$ (32)	$1,279	$1,246	$ (212)	$1,034
Deferred tax expense (benefit) from "temporary differences"	242	144	386	(152)	274	122	(71)	231	160
Investment credit deferred (amortized) — net	(64)	19	(45)	(63)	(3)	(66)	(87)	1	(86)
	$1,553	$ 211	$1,764	$1,096	$ 239	$1,335	$1,088	$ 20	$1,108

"Estimated amounts payable" includes amounts applicable to foreign jurisdictions of $272 million, $344 million and $197 million in 1989, 1988 and 1987, respectively.

General Electric Company files a consolidated U.S. federal income tax return that includes GEFS. GEFS' provision for estimated taxes recoverable (payable) includes its effect on the consolidated tax return. The amount reported by GEFS has been reduced to the extent of consolidated investment tax credit carryforwards of $168 million at December 31, 1987. Investment tax credit carryforwards of $168 million and $107 million realized in 1988 and 1987, respectively, were reflected as reinstatements of deferred tax balances.

Deferred income taxes reflect the impact of "temporary differences" between the amount of assets and liabilities for financial reporting purposes and such amounts as measured by tax laws and regulations. See note 27 for details of the balances in deferred income taxes at the ends of 1989 and 1988.

The U.S. investment tax credit (ITC) was repealed, with some transitional exceptions, effective January 1, 1986. However, because of its use of the deferral method of accounting for the ITC, GE has an unamortized balance remaining. As a result of the accounting change in 1987, unamortized ITC is treated as a temporary difference for deferred tax accounting. GE's remaining unamortized ITC balance was $112 million, net of deferred tax at year-end 1989, and will be added to income in future years.

The U.S. federal statutory tax rate on corporations was 34% in 1989 and 1988, down from 40% in 1987. Data about "effective tax rates," i.e., provision for income taxes as a percentage of earnings before income taxes, extraordinary item and cumulative effect of accounting changes, follow.

Effective tax rates (before extraordinary item and cumulative effect of accounting changes)	1989	1988	1987
GE	28.3%	24.5%	33.9%
GEFS	18.6	23.3	3.5
Consolidated	30.9	28.3	34.3

A reconciliation from the consolidated provision for income taxes that would have resulted using the U.S. federal statutory rate to the actual provision is shown below.

Differences between expected U.S. federal statutory tax-rate provision and actual tax provision (In millions)	1989	1988	1987
Expected consolidated tax provision at statutory rates	$1,939	$1,605	$1,291
Increase (reduction) in taxes resulting from GE			
Inclusion of GEFS earnings (before extraordinary item and cumulative effect of accounting change in 1987) in before-tax income on an after-tax basis	(315)	(268)	(221)
Varying tax rates of other affiliates (principally foreign)	(60)	(76)	(117)
Amortization of investment tax credit	(64)	(70)	(88)
Current-year effect of income tax accounting change	—	—	133
All other — net	125	(14)	98
	(314)	(428)	(195)
Increase (reduction) in taxes resulting from GEFS			
Amortization of investment tax credit on financing and operating leases	(22)	(17)	(27)
Dividends received which are not fully taxable	(27)	(17)	(13)
Income from tax-exempt marketable securities	(131)	(104)	(112)
Income taxes at capital gains rate	—	—	(14)
Adjustment of tax-deductible claim reserves of insurance affiliates	(21)	(22)	—
Change in tax-rate assumptions for leveraged leases	(23)	(14)	(31)
All other — net	18	64	(12)
	(176)	(110)	(209)
Eliminations	315	268	221
Actual consolidated tax provision	$1,764	$1,335	$1,108

Provision has been made for substantially all U.S. federal income tax liabilities applicable to undistributed earnings of affiliates and associated companies.   [G3643]

Based on the location (not tax jurisdiction) of the business providing goods or services, consolidated domestic income before taxes, extraordinary item and cumulative effect of changes in accounting principles was $4,930 million in 1989, $3,936 million in 1988 and $2,710 million in 1987. The corresponding amounts for foreign-based operations were $773 million, $785 million and $517 million in each of those years, respectively.

Note 11 Cash and Equivalents

Deposits restricted as to usage and withdrawal or used as partial compensation for short-term borrowing arrangements were not material for either GE except GEFS or GEFS. See note 21 for related information about credit lines and compensating balances.

Note 12 Marketable Securities Carried at Cost

Carrying value of marketable securities for GE except GEFS was substantially the same as market value at year-ends 1989 and 1988. Market value of GEFS' securities carried at amortized cost was $6,952 million and $5,537 million at December 31, 1989 and 1988, respectively.

Note 13 GEFS Marketable Securities Carried at Market

December 31 (In millions)	1989	1988
U.S. government and federal agency securities	$4,399	$2,433
State and municipal securities	191	215
Corporate stocks, bonds and foreign securities	3,898	2,441
	$8,488	$5,089

At December 31, 1989, the carrying value of equity securities carried at market value included unrealized gains and unrealized losses of approximately $32 million and $37 million, respectively.

A significant portion of securities carried at market value at December 31, 1989 was pledged as collateral for bank loans and repurchase agreements.

Note 14 GE Current Receivables

December 31 (In millions)	1989	1988
Receivable from:		
Customers	$5,298	$5,289
Associated companies	190	160
Others	1,897	1,857
	7,385	7,306
Less allowance for losses	(167)	(196)
	$7,218	$7,110

Note 15 GE Inventories

December 31 (In millions)	1989	1988
Raw materials and work in process	$ 5,492	$ 5,603
Finished goods	3,103	2,863
Unbilled shipments	249	246
	8,844	8,712
Less revaluation to LIFO	(2,189)	(2,226)
LIFO value of inventories	$ 6,655	$ 6,486

LIFO revaluations decreased $37 million in 1989 compared with an increase of $150 million in 1988. LIFO revaluations increased $324 million in 1987, mostly related to the accounting change described in note 1. Included in these changes were decreases of $68 million, $23 million and $22 million (1989, 1988 and 1987, respectively) due to lower inventory levels. In each of the last three years, there was a current-year expense for price increases.

[G3644]

Note 16   GEFS Financing Receivables (investment in time sales, loans and financing leases)

December 31 (In millions)	1989	1988
Time sales and loans		
Retailer and auto financing	$ 9,606	$ 7,465
Commercial real estate financing	8,890	7,725
Commercial and industrial loans	8,599	7,476
Equipment sales financing	2,562	2,171
Home and recreation financing	1,222	1,888
Other	—	45
	30,879	26,770
Deferred income	(737)	(983)
Time sales and loans — net of deferred income	30,142	25,787
Investment in financing leases		
Direct financing leases	9,827	8,433
Leveraged leases	2,937	2,691
	12,764	11,124
	42,906	36,911
Less allowance for losses	(1,127)	(972)
	$41,779	$35,939

"Time sales and loans" represents transactions in a variety of forms, including time sales, revolving charge and credit, mortgages, installment loans, intermediate-term loans, and revolving loans secured by business assets and mandatorily redeemable preferred stock. The portfolio includes time sales and loans carried at the principal amount on which finance charges are billed periodically, and time sales and loans acquired on a discount basis carried at gross book value, which includes finance charges.

"Financing leases" consists of direct financing and leveraged leases of aircraft, railroad rolling stock, automobiles and other transportation equipment, data processing equipment, medical equipment, and other manufacturing, power generation, mining and commercial equipment and facilities.

As the sole owner of assets under direct financing leases and as the equity participant in leveraged leases, GEFS is taxed on total lease payments received and is entitled to tax deductions based on the cost of leased assets and tax deductions for interest paid to third-party participants. GEFS also is entitled generally to any investment tax credit on leased equipment and to any residual value of leased assets.

Investments in direct financing and leveraged leases represent unpaid rentals and estimated unguaranteed residual values of leased equipment, less related deferred income and principal and interest on notes and other instruments representing third-party participation. Because GEFS has no general obligation on such notes and other instruments representing third-party participation, such notes and other instruments have not been included in liabilities but have been offset against the related rentals receivable. GEFS' share of rentals receivable is subordinate to the share of the other participants who also have a security interest in the leased equipment.

Additional detail about investment in financing leases at December 31, 1989 and 1988 is shown below.

Investment in financing leases	Direct financing leases		Leveraged leases		Total financing leases	
December 31 (In millions)	1989	1988	1989	1988	1989	1988
Total minimum lease payments receivable	$12,009	$10,109	$11,444	$10,745	$23,453	$20,854
Less principal and interest on third-party nonrecourse debt	—	—	(8,207)	(7,893)	(8,207)	(7,893)
Rentals receivable	12,009	10,109	3,237	2,852	15,246	12,961
Estimated unguaranteed residual value of leased assets	1,250	1,102	883	817	2,133	1,919
Less deferred income (a)	(3,432)	(2,778)	(1,183)	(978)	(4,615)	(3,756)
Investment in financing leases (as shown above)	9,827	8,433	2,937	2,691	12,764	11,124
Less amounts to arrive at net investment						
Allowance for losses	(214)	(121)	(48)	(74)	(262)	(195)
Deferred taxes arising from financing leases	(1,207)	(1,218)	(2,444)	(2,406)	(3,651)	(3,624)
Net investment in financing leases	$ 8,406	$ 7,094	$ 445	$ 211	$ 8,851	$ 7,305

(a) Total financing lease deferred income is net of deferred initial direct costs of $37 million and $33 million for 1989 and 1988, respectively.

[G3645]

Contractual maturities of time sales and loans and rentals receivable at December 31, 1989 are shown below.

Contractual maturities (In millions)	Total	1990	1991	1992	1993	1994	1995 and after
Time sales and loans							
Retailer and auto financing	$ 9,606	$ 7,336	$ 1,980	$ 196	$ 57	$ 29	$ 8
Commercial real estate financing	8,890	403	619	1,105	2,088	1,599	3,076
Commercial and industrial loans	8,599	1,326	1,026	1,006	803	758	3,680
Equipment sales financing	2,562	908	654	400	230	131	239
Home and recreation financing	1,222	686	77	69	64	60	266
	30,879	10,659	4,356	2,776	3,242	2,577	7,269
Investment in financing leases							
Direct financing leases	12,009	2,788	2,651	1,879	1,371	783	2,537
Leveraged leases	3,237	141	156	162	166	181	2,431
	15,246	2,929	2,807	2,041	1,537	964	4,968
	$46,125	$13,588	$ 7,163	$ 4,817	$ 4,779	$ 3,541	$12,237

Experience has shown that a substantial portion of receivables will be paid prior to contractual maturity. Accordingly, the maturities of time sales and loans and rentals receivable shown in the table above are not to be regarded as forecasts of future cash collections.

Note 17 Other GEFS Receivables from and Payables to Brokers and Dealers

Included in other receivables and other liabilities of GEFS are amounts receivable from and payable to brokers and dealers in connection with Kidder, Peabody's normal trading, lending and borrowing of securities. At December 31, 1989 and 1988, such amounts consisted of the following.

December 31 (In millions)	1989	1988
Included in other receivables		
Securities failed to deliver	$ 215	$ 132
Deposits paid for securities borrowed	1,030	1,226
Other, principally clearing organizations	17	32
	$1,262	$1,390
Included in other liabilities		
Securities failed to receive	$ 484	$ 451
Deposits received for securities loaned	665	903
Other, principally clearing organizations	24	48
	$1,173	$1,402

Note 18 Property, Plant and Equipment (including equipment leased to others)

December 31 (In millions)	1989	1988
Original cost		
GE		
Land and improvements	$ 266	$ 260
Buildings, structures and related equipment	4,600	4,250
Machinery and equipment	13,756	12,957
Leasehold costs and manufacturing plant under construction	1,051	1,126
Oil and gas properties	749	764
	20,422	19,357
GEFS		
Buildings and equipment	1,206	745
Equipment leased to others		
Vehicles	2,076	1,564
Railroad rolling stock	1,347	1,038
Marine shipping containers	816	857
Aircraft	1,324	618
Data processing equipment	461	355
Other	816	634
	8,046	5,811
	$28,468	$25,168
Accumulated depreciation, depletion and amortization		
GE	$10,756	$ 9,997
GEFS		
Equipment leased to others	1,745	1,321
Buildings and equipment	321	239
	$12,822	$11,557

GEFS' increase in buildings and equipment includes the effect of the transfer of GE Americom from GE at year-end 1989. Current-year amortization of GEFS' equipment on lease to others was $647 million, $665 million and $316 million in 1989, 1988 and 1987, respectively.

At December 31, 1989, GE except GEFS had minimum rental commitments under noncancelable operating leases

[G3646]

aggregating $3,069 million. Amounts payable over the next five years are: 1990 — $537 million; 1991 — $480 million; 1992 — $394 million; 1993 — $338 million; and 1994 — $308 million.

At December 31, 1989, GEFS had minimum rental commitments under noncancelable operating leases aggregating $942 million. Amounts payable over the next five years are: 1990 — $168 million; 1991 — $143 million; 1992 — $106 million; 1993 — $65 million; and 1994 — $68 million.

Note *19* Intangible Assets

December 31 (In millions)	1989	1988
GE		
Goodwill	$6,517	$6,423
Other intangibles	531	561
	7,048	6,984
GEFS		
Goodwill	1,587	1,364
Other intangibles	187	204
	1,774	1,568
	$8,822	$8,552

Accumulated amortization of GE's goodwill was $484 million and $318 million at December 31, 1989 and 1988, respectively. Accumulated amortization of other intangibles for GE was $474 million and $455 million at December 31, 1989 and 1988, respectively. The largest GE goodwill and other intangibles were from the RCA acquisition, for which goodwill is being amortized on a straight-line basis over 40 years. Other amounts of goodwill being amortized over 40 years arose from a number of acquisitions in 1987 and 1988. All other GE intangibles and goodwill are being amortized over shorter periods as appropriate, ranging from one year to 20 years.

Accumulated amortization of GEFS' goodwill was $181 million and $133 million at December 31, 1989 and 1988, respectively. Accumulated amortization of GEFS' other intangibles was $90 million and $73 million at December 31, 1989 and 1988, respectively. The principal sources of GEFS goodwill include acquisitions of FGIC Corporation; Gelco; MW Credit Operations; Kidder, Peabody; ERC; and a number of auto auctions. Amortization is being recorded over various periods, none more than 30 years. GEFS' other intangibles represent principally the value of insurance-in-force related to ERC's property and casualty reinsurance business, which is being amortized on a straight-line basis over its estimated life of approximately 16 years.

Note *20* All Other Assets

December 31 (In millions)	1989	1988
GE		
Investments		
Associated companies (including advances of $54 million and $29 million)	$1,448	$ 647
Miscellaneous investments		
Government and government-guaranteed securities	144	202
Other	167	175
Marketable equity securities	54	72
Less allowance for losses	(113)	(100)
	1,700	996
Prepaid pension assets	1,469	1,177
Recoverable engineering costs on government contracts	782	752
Long-term receivables	608	675
Television program costs	410	352
Deferred charges	372	318
Real estate development projects	31	73
Customer financing	62	73
Other	219	205
	5,653	4,621
GEFS		
Investment in associated companies (including advances of $277 million and $389 million)	1,045	1,145
Miscellaneous investments	1,539	1,034
Broker-dealer cash and securities segregated by regulation	134	383
Deferred insurance acquisition costs	410	262
Deferred charges	274	225
Real estate properties	151	122
Other	219	247
	3,772	3,418
	$9,425	$8,039

For GE, aggregate market value of marketable equity securities, which are carried at cost, was $67 million and $72 million at year-ends 1989 and 1988, respectively. Gross unrealized gains and losses were $19 million and $6 million, respectively, at December 31, 1989.

The National Broadcasting Company (NBC, an affiliate of GE) capitalizes program costs (including rights to broadcast) when paid or when a program is ready for broadcast, if earlier. These costs are amortized based upon projected revenues or expensed when a program is determined to have no value.

At year-end 1989, NBC had approximately $1.70 billion of commitments to acquire broadcast material or the rights to broadcast television programs that require payments over the next six years.

For GEFS, miscellaneous investments included $1.149 billion and $641 million at December 31, 1989 and 1988, respectively, of items at estimated realizable values previously included in financing receivables.

[G3647]

Note 21 Short-Term Borrowings

Amount and average rate at December 31

(In millions)	1989 Amount	Rate	1988 Amount	Rate
GE				
Commercial paper	$ 597	8.5%	$ —	
Notes with trust departments	313	8.2	337	8.5%
Affiliate bank borrowings (principally foreign)	436	18.8	261	25.7
Current portion of long-term borrowings	150		1,233	
Other	200		30	
	1,696		1,861	
GEFS				
Commercial paper	30,452	8.80	24,591	9.32
Banks	2,702	8.58	1,987	9.34
Current portion of long-term borrowings	1,365		790	
Notes with trust departments	847	8.29	990	8.48
Passbooks and investment certificates	374		373	
	35,740		28,731	
Eliminations	(236)		(170)	
	$37,200		$30,422	

The average balance of short-term borrowings for GE except GEFS, excluding the current portion of long-term borrowings, was $2,284 million in 1989 compared with an average balance of $1,416 million in 1988. (Except for commercial paper, the average balance is calculated by averaging month-end balances for the year; commercial paper average borrowings are based on daily balances for the year.) The maximum balances in these calculations were $2,791 million at the end of June 1989 and $2,444 million at the end of September 1988. The average worldwide effective interest rate for the year 1989 was 11%; for 1988, it was 15%. These average rates represent total short-term interest incurred divided by the average balance outstanding. Although the total unused credit available to GE through banks and commercial credit markets is not readily quantifiable, confirmed credit lines of about $1.3 billion had been extended by 47 banks at year-end 1989. Substantially all of these lines also are available for use by GE Capital and GEFS in addition to their own credit lines.

The average daily balance of GEFS' borrowings, excluding the current portion of long-term borrowings, was $31,154 million in 1989 compared with $27,889 million for 1988. The December 28, 1989 balance of $34,769 million was the maximum balance in 1989. The December 5, 1988 balance of $30,385 million was the maximum balance in 1988. The average short-term interest rate, excluding the current portion of long-term debt, was 9.44% for 1989, representing short-term interest expense divided by the average daily balance, compared with 7.96% for 1988.

At December 31, 1989, GE Capital had established lines of credit aggregating $13,445 million with 187 banks, including $10,370 million of revolving credit agreements with 118 banks pursuant to which GE Capital has the right to borrow funds for periods exceeding one year. In addition, at December 31, 1989, approximately $1,256 million of GE's credit lines was available for use by GE Capital. A total of $4,430 million of these lines also was available for use by GE Financial Services. During 1989, GEFS did not borrow under any of these credit lines.

GEFS compensates banks for credit facilities in the form of fees or a combination of balances and fees as agreed to with the bank.

At December 31, 1989, Kidder, Peabody had established lines of credit aggregating $5,727 million, of which $3,862 million was available on an unsecured basis. Borrowings from banks were primarily unsecured demand obligations, at interest rates approximating broker call loan rates, to finance inventories of securities and to facilitate the securities settlement process.

[G3648]

Note 22   Accounts Payable

December 31 (In millions)	1989	1988
GE		
Trade accounts	$2,606	$1,939
Collected for the account of others	195	180
Other (including associated companies)	100	17
	2,901	2,136
GEFS		
Accounts and drafts payable	4,144	4,132
Eliminations	(379)	(264)
	$6,666	$6,004

Note 23   GEFS Securities Sold but Not Yet Purchased, at Market

December 31 (In millions)	1989	1988
U.S. government and federal agency securities	$3,508	$1,560
State and municipal securities	4	9
Corporate stocks, bonds and foreign securities	578	519
	$4,090	$2,088

Note 24   GE All Other Current Costs and Expenses Accrued

At year-ends 1989 and 1988, this account included taxes accrued of $1,521 million and $1,568 million, respectively, and compensation and benefit accruals of $948 million and $982 million, respectively. Also included are amounts for product warranties, estimated costs on shipments billed to customers and a wide variety of other sundry items.

Note 25   Long-Term Borrowings

December 31 (In millions)	1989	1988
GE	$ 3,947	$ 4,330
GEFS	12,165	10,862
Eliminations	(2)	(110)
	$16,110	$15,082

Outstanding balances in long-term borrowings for GE at December 31, 1989 and 1988 are as follows.

December 31 (In millions)	Weighted average interest rate	Maturities	1989	1988
Notes	6.97%	1991-1992	$1,056	$1,163
Extendible notes (a)	7.69	1998-2006	600	800
Debentures/sinking fund debentures	8.43	1992-2016	513	545
Foreign currency notes (b)	8.14	1992-1993	900	900
Deep discount notes (c)	7.51	1993-1994	350	350
Industrial development/ pollution control bonds	6.17	1991-2019	236	262
Other	(d)		292	310
			$3,947	$4,330

(a) GE will reset interest rates at end of initial and each subsequent interest period. At each rate-reset date, notes are redeemable in whole or in part at GE's option or repayable at option of the holders at face value plus accrued interest. Current interest periods range from May 1, 1991 to April 8, 1993. Notes are included in the current portion of long-term debt when the interest-rate-reset date is within one year.

(b) In connection with a European Currency Unit 150 million note issue (7⅞% coupon rate) due in 1992, GE entered into a currency and interest-rate swap agreement under which GE assumes a fixed Japanese yen liability (22,262 million) for payment of principal in 1992 and pays interest in yen at a rate somewhat below the six-month yen LIBOR.

A Euro-yen 35 billion note issue due in 1993 is equal to US $194 million at a fixed exchange rate of yen 180.41 = US $1.00.

In connection with a US $500 million note issue (9¼% coupon rate) due in 1993, GE entered into currency and interest-rate swap agreements under which GE assumes a fixed Dutch guilder liability (632 million) and a fixed German mark liability (373 million) for payment of principal in 1993. GE pays interest in the respective currencies at somewhat below the respective currency three-month LIBOR.

(c) Including amortization of original issue discount, the effective interest rates are: 4½% Euro-dollar notes (US $200 million) – 7.41%, 2¾% U.S. dollar notes ($150 million) – 7.66%.

(d) "Other" includes original issue premium and discounts and a variety of borrowings by affiliates and parent components with various interest rates and maturities. Through 1988, "other" also included an adjustment to bring RCA borrowings at acquisition date to fair market value. Such RCA borrowings have now all been retired.

Long-term borrowing maturities during the next five years, including the portion classified as current, are $150 million in 1990, $861 million in 1991, $442 million in 1992, $982 million in 1993 and $179 million in 1994. These amounts are after deducting debentures that have been reacquired for sinking-fund needs.

[G3649]

Outstanding balances in long-term borrowings for GEFS at December 31, 1989 and 1988 are as follows.

December 31 (In millions)	Weighted average interest rate	Maturities	1989	1988
Senior notes				
Master notes	(a)	1991	$ 165	$ 181
Foreign currency notes (b)	9.64%	1991-1998	1,493	757
Zero coupon/deep discount notes	14.08	1992-2001	2,270	2,270
Extendible, reset or remarketed notes (c)	8.25	1991-2018	2,456	2,998
Floating rate notes	(d)	2049	269	164
Other notes	8.99	1991-2009	6,209	5,304
Less unamortized discount/premium			(984)	(1,136)
Total senior notes			11,878	10,538
Subordinated notes	9.32	1991-1997	287	324
			$12,165	$10,862

(a) Notes have a rolling 13-month or 15-month maturity and bear floating interest rates based principally on GE Capital's 180-day open-market notes.

(b) For notes denominated in pounds sterling (equal to US $158 million), European Currency Units (US $499 million) and Canadian dollars (US $315 million), GEFS has entered into currency swap or interest-rate swap agreements under which GEFS assumes a fixed principal liability and pays fixed or floating rate interest to a commercial bank counterparty. For the notes denominated in Swiss francs (US $153 million), there is no stated maturity date but issuer calls and investor puts are available at 10-year intervals. GEFS can limit the ultimate retirement to US $153 million and interest is fixed for the first 10-year period. In connection with a US $125 million note issue due in 1998, GEFS entered into a currency swap agreement under which GEFS assumes a fixed pound sterling liability (74 million) for payment of principal in 1993.

(c) GEFS will reset interest rates at end of initial and each subsequent interest period. For Extendible notes, at each rate-reset date, holders may redeem notes at face value plus accrued interest. Current interest periods range from February 20, 1990 to March 4, 1993. Notes are included in the current portion of long-term debt when the interest-rate-reset date is within one year.

(d) The rate of interest payable on each note is a variable rate based on the commercial paper rate each month. Interest is payable at the option of GEFS either monthly or semiannually.

Long-term borrowing maturities during the next five years, including the current portion of notes payable after one year, are: 1990 — $1,365 million; 1991 — $1,427 million (including $165 million of notes having a rolling 13-month or 15-month maturity); 1992 — $1,678 million; 1993 — $1,890 million; and 1994 — $1,073 million.

In December 1987, GE Capital initiated a debt extinguishment program to use the proceeds from the issuance of new long-term debt to repurchase or redeem approximately $1.1 billion of existing debt at market prices or redemption premiums in excess of the net carrying amounts. This resulted in an after-tax loss of $62 million (net of $39 million tax credit) that was reported as an extraordinary item in the consolidated Statement of Earnings for the year 1987. The extinguishments were completed during the first quarter of 1988.

Note 26   GE All Other Liabilities

For GE except GEFS, this account includes noncurrent compensation and benefit accruals at year-ends 1989 and 1988 of $1,511 million and $1,516 million, respectively. Other noncurrent liabilities include amounts for product warranties, deferred incentive compensation, deferred investment tax credit, deferred income and a wide variety of other sundry items.

Note 27   Deferred Income Taxes

The tax effects of principal temporary differences between the carrying amounts of assets and liabilities and their tax bases are summarized below.

December 31 (In millions)	1989	1988
GE except GEFS		
Provisions for expenses	$(1,785)	$(1,723)
Accumulated depreciation	929	852
Assets and liabilities related to pensions	409	331
Other — net	(189)	(101)
Net deferred tax asset	(636)	(641)
GEFS		
Financing leases	3,651	3,624
Tax transfer leases	332	335
Operating leases	331	177
Provision for losses	(392)	(377)
Other — net	257	255
Net deferred tax liability	4,179	4,014
Net deferred tax liability	$ 3,543	$ 3,373

Note 28   Minority Interest in Equity of Consolidated Affiliates

December 31 (In millions)	1989	1988
GE	$ 283	$ 228
GEFS	718	753
	$1,001	$ 981

Minority interest in equity of consolidated GEFS affiliates includes the issuance by GE Capital in 1988 of six thousand shares of $100 par value variable cumulative preferred stock for net proceeds of approximately $600 million. No additional preferred shares were issued in 1989. Dividend rates on this preferred stock during 1989 ranged from 6.42% to 7.85%.

[G3650]

Note 29   Share Owners' Equity

GE preferred stock up to 50,000,000 shares ($1.00 par value) is authorized, but no such shares have been issued. Authorized shares of common stock (par value $0.63) total 1,100,000,000.

Shares of GE common stock

December 31 (In thousands)	1989	1988	1987
Issued	926,564	926,564	926,564
In treasury	(21,783)	(24,448)	(23,611)
Outstanding	904,781	902,116	902,953

GE share owners' equity is as follows.

GE share owners' equity

(In millions)	1989	1988	1987
Common stock issued			
Balance at January 1	$ 584	$ 584	$ 579
Adjustment for stock split	—	—	5
Balance at December 31	$ 584	$ 584	$ 584
Other capital			
Balance at January 1	$ 823	$ 878	$ 733
Adjustment for stock split	—	—	(5)
Foreign currency translation adjustments	(4)	(39)	145
Unrealized gains (losses) on securities held by insurance affiliates	5	18	(33)
Gains (losses) on treasury stock dispositions	2	(34)	30
Other	—	—	8
Balance at December 31	$ 826	$ 823	$ 878
Retained earnings			
Balance at January 1	$17,950	$15,878	$14,172
Net earnings	3,939	3,386	2,915
Dividends declared	(1,537)	(1,314)	(1,209)
Balance at December 31	$20,352	$17,950	$15,878
Common stock held in treasury			
Balance at January 1	$ 891	$ 860	$ 375
Purchases — net	362	387	846
Dispositions			
Employee savings plans	(124)	(213)	(148)
Stock options and appreciation rights	(212)	(77)	(96)
Employee stock ownership plan	—	(11)	(39)
Dividend reinvestment and share purchase plan	(47)	(49)	(42)
Contribution to GE Pension Trust	—	—	(25)
Conversion of long-term debt	—	(1)	(24)
Incentive compensation plans	2	(5)	13
Balance at December 31	$ 872	$ 891	$ 860

In November 1989, GE's Board of Directors authorized the repurchase of up to $10 billion of Company common stock over a five-year period. This repurchase program is designed to be flexible. Shares will be acquired with funds from a combination of borrowings and free cash flow. Should world economic conditions, a major acquisition or other circumstances warrant, the Company would modify the pace and dimension of the repurchase program to maintain the solidity of its financial position. As of December 31, 1989, 3,765 thousand shares having an aggregate cost of $236 million had been repurchased under the program and placed in treasury.

In April 1987, GE share owners authorized: (a) an increase in the number of authorized shares of common stock from 550,000,000 shares each with a par value of $1.25 to 1,100,000,000 shares each with a par value of $0.63; (b) the split of each previously issued common share, including shares held in treasury, into two shares of common stock each with a par value of $0.63; and (c) an increase in the number of authorized shares of preferred stock from 2,000,000 shares with a par value of $1.00 per share to 50,000,000 shares with a par value of $1.00 per share. All share data have been adjusted for this change.

The effects of translating to U.S. dollars the financial statements of foreign affiliates whose functional currency is the local currency are included in other capital. Cumulative foreign currency translation adjustments were $133 million, $137 million and $176 million of additions to other capital at December 31, 1989, 1988 and 1987, respectively.

Note 30   Other Stock-Related Information

Stock option plans, appreciation rights and performance units are described in the Company's current Proxy Statement. Requirements for stock option shares may be met within certain restrictions either from unissued or treasury shares. During 1989, options were granted to 3,800 employees and 15 nonemployee Directors. As of December 31, 1989, a total of 456 individuals were eligible to receive class-grant options, and all exempt salaried employees were eligible for special option grants. A total of 4,633 persons held options exercisable at the end of 1989 or in the future.

Stock option information

(Shares in thousands)	Shares subject to option	Average per share — Option price	Average per share — Market price
Balance at January 1, 1989	19,936	$36.41	$44.75
Options granted	5,038	57.19	57.19
Options exercised	(3,954)	28.28	55.64
Options surrendered on exercise of appreciation rights	(712)	30.77	56.37
Options terminated	(217)	44.45	—
Balance at December 31, 1989	20,091	43.34	64.50

Outstanding options and rights expire and the award period for outstanding performance units ends on various dates from January 1, 1990 to December 15, 1999. Shares available for granting additional options at the end of 1989 were 6,473,950 (11,936,568 at the end of 1988).   [G36511]

Note 31 Commitments and Contingent Liabilities

At December 31, 1989, there were no known contingent liabilities (including guarantees, pending litigation, taxes and other claims) that, in the opinion of management, would be material in relation to General Electric Company and consolidated affiliates' financial position, nor were there any material commitments outside the normal course of business.

Note 32 Supplemental Cash Flows Information

"All other operating activities" in the Statement of Cash Flows consists principally of adjustments to current and noncurrent accruals of costs and expenses, amortization of premium and discount on debt, and adjustments to assets such as amortization of goodwill and intangibles.

Information about acquisitions and dispositions can be found in note 2. The Statement of Cash Flows excludes certain noncash transactions that had no significant effects on the investing or financing activities of GE or GEFS. The transfer of GE Americom from GE to GEFS at the end of 1989 increased GEFS' equity by $332 million.

Cash used in each of the last three years included:

(In millions)	1989	1988	1987
Interest (paid)			
GE	$ (793)	$ (640)	$ (577)
GEFS	(5,876)	(4,030)	(3,301)
	$(6,669)	$(4,670)	$(3,878)
Income taxes (paid) recovered (federal, foreign, state and local)			
GE	$(1,163)	$(1,284)	$(1,096)
GEFS	(168)	251	403
	$(1,331)	$(1,033)	$ (693)

"Net change in certain broker-dealer accounts" included:

(In millions)	1989	1988	1987
Marketable securities of broker-dealer	$(3,356)	$(1,009)	$ 1,826
Securities purchased under agreements to resell	(2,209)	(922)	72
Securities sold under agreements to repurchase	2,691	677	117
Securities sold but not yet purchased	2,002	681	(2,118)
	$ (872)	$ (573)	$ (103)

"Net increase in GEFS financing receivables" included:

(In millions)	1989	1988	1987
Increase in loans to customers	$(24,699)	$(23,731)	$(18,990)
Principal collections from customers	21,350	19,802	15,370
Investment in equipment for financing leases	(4,766)	(5,031)	(3,117)
Principal collections on financing leases	3,214	3,974	2,291
Net change in credit card receivables	(1,641)	(957)	(181)
	$ (6,542)	$ (5,943)	$ (4,627)

GEFS' "all other investing activities" included:

(In millions)	1989	1988	1987
Purchases of marketable securities by insurance affiliates	$(4,879)	$(3,188)	$(3,769)
Dispositions of marketable securities by insurance affiliates	4,481	2,334	2,624
Other	(403)	(1,153)	(137)
	$ (801)	$(2,007)	$(1,282)

GEFS' "debt having maturities more than 90 days" included:

(In millions)	1989	1988	1987
Newly issued debt			
Short-term (91-365 days)	$ 4,571	$ 5,916	$ 5,546
Long-term senior	2,842	3,936	1,927
Long-term subordinated	—	58	—
Proceeds – nonrecourse, leveraged lease debt	461	381	345
	$ 7,874	$10,291	$ 7,818
Repayments and other reductions			
Short-term	$ (5,556)	$ (6,220)	$ (5,836)
Long-term senior	(230)	(2,284)	(526)
Long-term subordinated	(7)	(6)	(20)
Principal payments – nonrecourse, leveraged lease debt	(253)	(261)	(263)
	$ (6,046)	$ (8,771)	$ (6,645)

Note 33   Industry Segment Details

Revenues
For the years ended December 31

(In millions)	Total revenues			Intersegment revenues			External revenues		
	1989	1988	1987	1989	1988	1987	1989	1988	1987
GE									
Aerospace	$ 5,282	$ 5,343	$ 5,262	$ 77	$ 166	$ 78	$ 5,205	$ 5,177	$ 5,184
Aircraft Engines	6,863	6,481	6,773	69	119	48	6,794	6,362	6,725
Broadcasting	3,392	3,638	3,241	1	—	—	3,391	3,638	3,241
Industrial	7,059	7,061	6,662	701	706	708	6,358	6,355	5,954
Major Appliances	5,620	5,289	4,721	—	—	—	5,620	5,289	4,721
Materials	4,929	3,539	2,751	33	40	32	4,896	3,499	2,719
Power Systems	5,129	4,805	4,995	128	126	125	5,001	4,679	4,870
Technical Products and Services	4,545	4,431	3,670	194	161	337	4,351	4,270	3,333
Earnings of GEFS	927	788	552	—	—	—	927	788	552
All Other	319	394	3,176	—	—	4	319	394	3,172
Corporate Items and Eliminations	(1,415)	(1,477)	(1,287)	(1,203)	(1,318)	(1,332)	(212)	(159)	45
Total GE	42,650	40,292	40,516	—	—	—	42,650	40,292	40,516
GEFS									
Financing	7,333	5,827	3,507	—	—	—	7,333	5,827	3,507
Insurance	2,710	2,478	2,217	—	—	—	2,710	2,478	2,217
Securities Broker-Dealer	2,897	2,316	2,491	—	—	—	2,897	2,316	2,491
All Other	5	34	10	—	—	—	5	34	10
Total GEFS	12,945	10,655	8,225	—	—	—	12,945	10,655	8,225
Eliminations	(1,021)	(858)	(583)	—	—	—	(1,021)	(858)	(583)
Consolidated revenues	$54,574	$50,089	$48,158	$ —	$ —	$ —	$54,574	$50,089	$48,158

(In millions)	Assets At December 31			Property, plant and equipment (including equipment leased to others) For the years ended December 31					
				Additions			Depreciation, depletion and amortization		
	1989	1988	1987	1989	1988	1987	1989	1988	1987
GE									
Aerospace	$ 3,806	$ 3,838	$ 3,943	$ 173	$ 208	$ 178	$ 153	$ 170	$ 151
Aircraft Engines	5,341	5,164	5,066	341	234	242	273	251	242
Broadcasting	4,428	4,104	3,948	81	147	115	79	70	64
Industrial	4,016	3,729	4,041	354	301	274	248	249	315
Major Appliances	2,825	2,284	1,529	149	215	118	112	105	93
Materials	8,023	7,130	3,901	722	757	378	319	252	202
Power Systems	2,604	2,531	3,266	138	127	118	136	138	162
Technical Products and Services	2,772	3,183	3,873	219	203	235	154	168	170
Investment in GEFS	6,069	4,819	3,980	—	—	—	—	—	—
All Other	951	1,122	2,046	3	5	72	—	17	62
Corporate Items and Eliminations	3,272	3,379	2,707	71	91	48	50	102	83
Total GE	44,107	41,283	38,300	2,251	2,288	1,778	1,524	1,522	1,544
GEFS									
Financing	54,056	44,874	34,163	3,174	1,738	503	679	695	325
Insurance	9,663	8,025	6,577	17	26	3	8	6	4
Securities Broker-Dealer	27,118	21,891	20,041	33	19	60	32	32	28
All Other	91	155	625	33	14	13	13	11	12
Total GEFS	90,928	74,945	61,406	3,257	1,797	579	732	744	369
Eliminations	(6,691)	(5,363)	(4,292)	—	—	—	—	—	—
Consolidated totals	$128,344	$110,865	$95,414	$5,508	$4,085	$2,357	$2,256	$2,266	$1,913

[G3653]

Revenues include income from all sources: i.e., for GE, both sales of products and services to customers and "other income"; for GEFS, "earned income" as described in note 1. In general, it is GE policy to price sales from one Company component to another as nearly as practical to equivalent commercial selling prices. About one-sixth of GE's consolidated revenues are from agencies of the U.S. government, GE's largest single customer. Most of these were for aerospace and aircraft engine products and services.

Operating profit by industry segment is on page[533] of this report.

A description of each of General Electric Company and consolidated affiliates' industry segments follows.

GE

■ *Aerospace* products and services encompass electronics, avionic systems, military vehicle equipment, automated test systems, computer software, armament systems, missile system components, simulation systems, spacecraft, communication systems, radar, sonar and systems integration. Most aerospace sales are to agencies of the U.S. government, principally the Department of Defense and the National Aeronautics and Space Administration.

■ *Aircraft Engines* and replacement parts are manufactured and sold by GE for use in commercial and military aircraft, in naval ships and as industrial power sources. GE's military engines are used in a wide variety of aircraft that includes fighters, bombers, tankers and helicopters. GE's large CFM56 and CF6 engines power all categories of commercial aircraft: short/medium, intermediate and long-range. Applications for GE's CFM56 engine, produced jointly by GE and SNECMA of France, include: Boeing's 737-300/-400/-500 series; Airbus Industrie's A320, A321 and A340 series; and military aircraft such as the KC-135, E/KE-3 and E-6. The CFM56-3-powered 737 has become the fastest selling aircraft/engine combination in commercial aviation history. GE's CF6 family of engines powers intermediate and long-range aircraft such as Boeing's 747 and 767 series, Airbus Industrie's A300, A310 and A330 series, and McDonnell Douglas' DC-10 and MD-11 series. GE also produces jet engines for executive aircraft and regional commuter airlines.

■ *Broadcasting* consists primarily of the National Broadcasting Company (NBC), which is the current leader in network television. NBC's principal businesses are the furnishing within the United States of network television services to affiliated television stations, the production of live and recorded television programs, and the operation, under licenses from the Federal Communications Commission (FCC), of seven VHF television broadcasting stations. The NBC Television Network is one of three competing major national commercial broadcast television networks and serves more than 200 regularly affiliated stations within the United States. The television stations NBC owns and operates are located in Chicago, Cleveland, Denver, Los Angeles, Miami, New York and Washington, D.C. Broadcasting operations are subject to FCC regulation and station licensing. NBC is currently expanding its operations, including investment and programming activities in cable television.

■ *Industrial* encompasses factory automation products, motors, electrical equipment for industrial and commercial construction, GE Supply Company, transportation systems and lighting products. Customers for many of these products and services include electrical distributors, original equipment manufacturers and industrial end users. Motors and motor-related products serve the appliance, commercial, industrial, heating, air conditioning and automotive markets. Motor products are used within GE and also are sold externally. Electrical distribution and control equipment, for which European operations were expanded with a new joint venture in 1989, is sold for installation in commercial, industrial and residential facilities. Factory automation products cover a broad range of electrical and electronic products, including drive systems, with emphasis on manufacturing and advanced engineering automation applications. GE Supply operates a nationwide network of electrical supply houses. Transportation systems include diesel-electric and electric locomotives, transit propulsion equipment, motorized wheels for off-highway vehicles, such as those used in mining operations, and drilling devices. Locomotives are sold principally to domestic and foreign railroads, while markets for other products include state and urban transit authorities and industrial users. Lighting products include a wide variety of lamps — incandescent, fluorescent, high intensity discharge, halogen and specialty — as well as wiring devices and quartz products. Markets and customers are principally in the United States, although foreign markets are becoming increasingly important. Markets are extremely varied, ranging from household consumers to commercial and industrial end users and original equipment manufacturers. Until the fourth quarter of 1988, the Industrial segment also included semiconductor operations that have since been sold. [G3654]

■ *Major Appliances* includes kitchen and laundry equipment such as refrigerators, ranges, microwave ovens, freezers, dishwashers, clothes washers and dryers, and room air conditioners. These are sold under GE, Hotpoint and Monogram brands and, increasingly, under private brands for retailers. Distribution of appliances using the RCA brand began in 1989. GE microwave ovens and room air conditioners are mainly sourced from foreign suppliers while investment in Company-owned domestic facilities is focused on refrigerators, dishwashers, ranges and home laundry equipment. Acquisition of Roper Corporation in 1988 added to GE's productive capacity and broadened its product offerings, including gas ranges. A large portion of major appliance sales is to a variety of retail outlets with a significant portion of sales of certain products such as laundry equipment and refrigerators being for replacement of older products. The other principal market consists of residential building contractors who install major appliances in new dwellings. A nationwide service network supports GE's appliance business. European market participation was expanded significantly in 1989 with the formation of a new joint venture.

■ *Materials* includes high-performance engineered plastics used in applications such as substitutes for metal and glass in automobiles and as housings for computers and other business equipment; silicones; superabrasives such as man-made diamonds; and laminates. Market opportunities for many of these products are created by functional replacement that provides customers with an improved material at lower cost. These materials are sold to a diverse customer base (mainly manufacturers) in the United States and abroad. Acquisition of the chemicals businesses of Borg-Warner Corporation at the end of 1988's third quarter provided GE with another product — ABS resins, a family of thermoplastic resins used by custom molders and major original equipment manufacturers for use in a variety of applications, including fabrication of automotive parts, telecommunications equipment, computer enclosures, major appliance parts and pipe. The acquisition also added technical and manufacturing strength and domestic and offshore marketing facilities and expertise that complement GE's other plastics businesses. Materials also includes Ladd Petroleum Corporation, an oil and natural gas developer and supplier with operations mainly in the United States.

■ *Power Systems* serves worldwide utility, industrial and governmental customers with products for the generation, transmission and distribution of electricity and with related installation, engineering and repair services. GE has remained the leader in most power systems products in the face of a decline in domestic and foreign markets for a number of years. Worldwide competition continues to be

intense. During 1989, there were tangible signs of market improvement. GE management continues vigorous efforts to improve cost-competitiveness and to adapt products and marketing to the changing environment. Steam turbine-generators are sold to the electric utility industry, to the U.S. Navy and, for cogeneration, to private industrial customers. Marine steam turbines and propulsion gears also are sold to the U.S. Navy. Gas turbines are used principally as packaged power plants for electric utilities and for industrial cogeneration and mechanical drive applications. Centrifugal compressors are sold for application in gas reinjection, pipeline services and process applications such as refineries and ammonia plants. Although there have been no nuclear plant orders in the United States since the mid-1970s and international activity has been very low, GE continues to invest in advanced technology development and to focus its resources on refueling and serving its installed boiling-water reactors. Power delivery products include transformers, relays, electric load management systems, power conversion systems and meters, principally for electric utilities. Installation, engineering and repair services include management and technical expertise for large projects, such as power plants; maintenance, inspection, repair and rebuilding of electrical apparatus produced by GE and others; on-site engineering and upgrading of already installed products sold by GE and others; and environmental systems for utilities.

■ *Technical Products and Services* consists of technology operations providing products, systems and services to a variety of customers. Businesses in this segment include medical systems and services, communications and information services, and certain other specialized services. Medical systems include magnetic resonance (MR) scanners, computed tomography (CT) scanners, x-ray, nuclear imaging, ultrasound, and other diagnostic equipment and supporting services sold to domestic and foreign hospitals and medical facilities. Acquisitions and joint ventures in recent years have expanded GE's medical systems activities in world markets. GE Americom, a leading domestic satellite carrier, operates seven domestic satellites providing distribution services for cable television, broadcast television and radio, and voice, video and wideband data services to agencies of the federal government. Common carrier services of Americom are subject to regulation by the FCC. (As of December 31, 1989, GE Americom was transferred to GE Capital. GE Americom's operating results will be included in GEFS beginning in 1990.) Information services are provided both to internal and external customers by GE Information Services, GE Consulting Services and the GE Computer Service operation. These include

{G3655}

enhanced computer-based communications services, such as data network services, electronic messaging and electronic data interchange, which are offered to commercial and industrial customers through a worldwide network; application software packages; custom system design and programming services; and independent maintenance and rental/leasing services for minicomputers and microcomputers, electronic test instruments and data communications equipment. A separate services component provides a variety of specialized services to government customers. In December 1989, GE's mobile communications business was placed in a joint venture with Ericsson of Sweden. This venture combines GE's mobile radio manufacturing and distribution strength in North America with Ericsson's European market strength and position in digital cellular technology.

■ *Earnings of and Investment in GEFS* are shown on a "one-line" basis in GE's segment data but are eliminated in consolidation. A separate discussion of GEFS segments appears below.

■ *All Other* for periods prior to 1988 consists mostly of former consumer electronics operations (principally video and audio products, including operations acquired from RCA in 1986) and results of miscellaneous other activities no longer part of GE's business. Ongoing operations mainly involve licensing use of GE know-how to others.

GEFS

The business of General Electric Financial Services, Inc. (GEFS) consists of the ownership of three affiliates that, together with their affiliates and other investments, constitute General Electric Company's principal financial services activities. GEFS owns all of the common stock of General Electric Capital Corporation (GECC) and of Employers Reinsurance Corporation (ERC) and owns 80% of Kidder, Peabody Group Inc. (the other 20% is held by or on behalf of certain Kidder, Peabody officers).

For industry segment purposes, Financing consists solely of activities of GE Capital; Insurance consists principally of activities of ERC but also includes certain insurance entities owned by GE Capital; Securities Broker-Dealer consists entirely of Kidder, Peabody's operations; and All Other is mainly GEFS' corporate activities not identifiable with specific industry segments.

Additional information about each GEFS segment follows.

■ *Financing* activities of GE Capital include time sales, revolving credit and inventory financing for retail merchants (major appliances, television sets, furniture and other home furnishings, and personal computers); automobile leasing and automobile inventory financing; home and recreation financing (principally time sales and dealer inventory financing of mobile homes); commercial and industrial loans and equipment sales financing provided through leases, time sales and loans; leasing services for

third-party investors; and commercial and residential real estate financing. Acquisition of Montgomery Ward & Co.'s credit operations in mid-1988 added to GE Capital's earning assets, particularly in credit card operations, which continue to expand. GE Capital also is an equity investor in certain other service and financial services organizations and participates in leveraged buyouts. Although leasing has been a major factor in GE Capital's growth over the years, GE Capital has actively changed its investment portfolio to place greater emphasis on asset ownership, management and operation. Virtually all products financed by GE Capital are manufactured by companies other than GE.

■ *Insurance* consists mainly of ERC, a multiple-line property and casualty reinsurer that writes all lines of reinsurance other than title and annuities. ERC reinsures property and casualty risks written by more than 1,000 domestic and foreign insurers and augments its foreign business through subsidiaries located in the United Kingdom and Denmark. By way of other subsidiaries, ERC writes property and casualty reinsurance through brokers and provides reinsurance brokerage services. ERC also writes certain specialty lines of insurance on a direct basis, principally excess workers' compensation for self-insurers, libel and allied torts, and errors and omissions coverage for insurance agents and brokers. It is licensed in all states of the United States, the District of Columbia, certain provinces of Canada and in other jurisdictions. ERC's business is generally subject to regulation by various insurance regulatory agencies. Other insurance activities of GEFS include GE Capital affiliates that provide financial guarantee insurance on selected securities, private mortgage insurance, life reinsurance and, for GE Capital customers, credit life and certain types of property/casualty insurance.

■ *Securities Broker-Dealer* represents Kidder, Peabody, which is a major investment banking and securities firm. Principal businesses include securities underwriting; sales and trading of equity and fixed income securities; financial futures activities; advisory services for mergers, acquisitions and other corporate finance matters; merchant banking; research services; and asset management. These services are provided in the United States and abroad to domestic and foreign business entities, governments, government agencies, and individual and institutional investors. Kidder is a member of the principal domestic securities and commodities exchanges and is a primary dealer in U.S. government securities. Certain affiliates of Kidder, Peabody are subject to the rules and regulations of various federal, state and industry regulatory agencies that apply to securities broker-dealers, including the U.S. Securities and Exchange Commission, U.S. Commodity Futures Trading Commission, New York Stock Exchange, National Association of Securities Dealers and the Chicago Board of Trade. [G3656]

Note 34 Geographic Segment Information (consolidated)

Revenues
For the years ended December 31

(In millions)	Total revenues			Intersegment revenues			External revenues		
	1989	1988	1987	1989	1988	1987	1989	1988	1987
United States	$48,912	$46,364	$45,160	$ 1,107	$ 874	$ 801	$47,805	$45,490	$44,359
Other areas of the world	7,458	5,576	4,894	689	977	1,095	6,769	4,599	3,799
Intercompany eliminations	(1,796)	(1,851)	(1,896)	(1,796)	(1,851)	(1,896)	—	—	—
Total	$54,574	$50,089	$48,158	$ —	$ —	$ —	$54,574	$50,089	$48,158

	Operating profit For the years ended December 31			Assets At December 31		
	1989	1988	1987	1989	1988	1987
United States	$ 6,070	$ 4,941	$ 3,715	$117,109	$102,327	$89,480
Other areas of the world	974	1,009	725	11,346	8,641	6,027
Intercompany eliminations	(8)	(10)	10	(111)	(103)	(93)
Total	$ 7,036	$ 5,940	$ 4,450	$128,344	$110,865	$95,414

U.S. revenues include GE exports to external customers, and royalty and licensing income from foreign sources.

Exports to external customers by major areas of the world are shown on page [535].

Note 35 Quarterly Information (unaudited)

(Dollar amounts in millions; per-share amounts in dollars)	First quarter		Second quarter		Third quarter		Fourth quarter	
	1989	1988	1989	1988	1989	1988	1989	1988
Consolidated operations								
Net earnings	$ 849	$ 725	$ 972	$ 835	$ 945	$ 815	$1,173	$1,011
Net earnings per share	0.94	0.80	1.08	0.93	1.04	0.90	1.30	1.12
Dividends declared per share	0.41	0.35	0.41	0.35	0.41	0.35	0.47	0.41
Common stock market price								
High	49	47⅞	56¼	44½	59⅛	44¾	64¾	46⅝
Low	43½	40	44½	38⅝	51⅜	39	52¾	42⅛
Selected data								
GE								
Sales of products and services	8,868	7,975	10,188	9,245	9,616	9,306	12,347	12,298
Gross profit from sales	2,392	1,978	2,989	2,365	2,499	2,349	3,407	3,270
GEFS								
Revenues from operations	2,824	2,411	3,261	2,465	3,230	2,717	3,630	3,062
Operating profit	259	246	231	223	341	230	307	328

For GE, gross profit from sales is sales of goods and services less cost of goods and services sold. These costs of sales accounted for a relatively smaller proportion of GE operating costs in 1989 than in 1988, reflecting differences between the periods from acquisitions and dispositions as well as ongoing refinements among broad cost classifications. For GEFS, operating profit is as presented on page [525] of this report.

Second-, third- and fourth-quarter 1988 net earnings included negative effects ($23 million — 2 cents per share, $43 million — 5 cents per share and $231 million — 26 cents per share, respectively) of expenses and accruals for abnormally high warranty costs for certain refrigerator compressors.

[G3657]

Independent Auditors' Report

**To Share Owners and Board of Directors of
General Electric Company**

We have audited the accompanying statement of financial position of General Electric Company and consolidated affiliates as of December 31, 1989 and 1988 and the related statements of earnings and cash flows for each of the years in the three-year period ended December 31, 1989. These consolidated financial statements are the responsibility of the Company's management. Our responsibility is to express an opinion on these consolidated financial statements based on our audits.

We conducted our audits in accordance with generally accepted auditing standards. Those standards require that we plan and perform the audit to obtain reasonable assurance about whether the financial statements are free of material misstatement. An audit includes examining, on a test basis, evidence supporting the amounts and disclosures in the financial statements. An audit also includes assessing the accounting principles used and significant estimates made by management, as well as evaluating the overall financial statement presentation. We believe that our audits provide a reasonable basis for our opinion.

In our opinion, the aforementioned financial statements appearing on pages [_____ and _____] present fairly, in all material respects, the financial position of General Electric Company and consolidated affiliates at December 31, 1989 and 1988, and the results of their operations and their cash flows for each of the years in the three-year period ended December 31, 1989, in conformity with generally accepted accounting principles.

As discussed in note 1 to the consolidated financial statements, in 1987 the Company changed its methods of accounting for income taxes and overhead recorded in inventory. We concur with these accounting changes.

KPMG Peat Marwick

KPMG Peat Marwick
Stamford, Connecticut

February 16, 1990   [G3634]

Part G

ADVANCED PROBLEMS

Chapter XI

ACCOUNTING FOR LEASES

OBJECTIVES

1. Comprehend "off-balance sheet financing" through leasing.

2. Understand the business practices and economic substance of lease financing and the compromises of that substance resulting in current GAAP for leases.

RELEVANCE FOR LAWYERS

Leases constitute a very substantial portion of the financing of fixed assets by U.S. firms. GAAP for leases therefore result in significant impacts on financial statements which are of concern to business lawyers in many contexts, including negotiating and drafting the leases, advising on disclosure, and tax counselling.

A. BACKGROUND IN OFF–BALANCE SHEET FINANCING

A user of funds may obtain an apparent great advantage if he or she receives the funds in a form other than a conventional loan or other debt instrument, so that the obligation may be kept off the balance sheet. Suppose that the user had borrowed 70 to 100% of the cost of assets used in the business. This would tend to make the balance sheet look "heavy"—i.e., the ratios of debt to assets, and of debt to stockholders' equity, would seem high to a prospective investor or creditor. Moreover, such high debt ratios might actually violate covenants in the debtor's loan agreements fixing ratios of debt to assets or to capital; and if the loan was secured by the assets, the security arrangement might violate covenants against secured borrowing. How much better everything would look if the debt could be kept off the balance sheet, even at the price of also keeping the asset off. Devices for accomplishing this result are called "off-balance sheet financing."

Of these, the most significant in dollar amounts is the use of the lease by the lessee to obtain property without paying cash for it and without being formally a debtor. One might suppose that this device borders on the fraudulent, because it deceives creditors. However, frequently the prospective creditors cooperate with the debtor in kidding themselves. Thus loan officers of banks have often told borrowers to go to a leasing company to obtain equipment by lease because if they borrowed the money to purchase equipment, they would lose their credit lines, while under a leasing transaction the debt would not show on the balance sheet, and the credit lines would be maintained. Similarly, surety companies have told a contractor that if he or she bought the equipment, borrowing most of the money, the balance sheet would be too heavy to permit the writing of surety bonds for the jobs; but if the contractor would protect his balance sheet by obtaining the equipment through leasing, the surety company would be glad to issue the bond.

A full financial analysis of leasing is beyond the scope of this book, but in general, it may be said that most of the other advantages have disappeared, if they ever really existed, and that the principal remaining advantages of leasing are three: (1) it may still permit off-balance sheet financing; (2) the tax advantages of owning property may be obtained by a lessor who may be able to use those advantages more advantageously than the lessee, under leases properly structured; and (3) it enables the lessee to "buy" the use of the asset for a short period of time—a day, a month or perhaps a year—and then turn it back to its owner for the remainder of its useful life for less than the cost of acquiring, maintaining and owning.

Let us consider a ten-year lease of a single store in a large building. Accounting takes the position that this is a forward contract for the temporary use of the store, and neither the liability to pay rent nor the asset consisting of the right to use the store need be recorded, except to the extent rents are paid in advance. The result is that certain chain stores and other businesses have enormous obligations to pay rent in the future which are not included in the books of account or as liabilities in the financial statements. During the Great Depression creditors of chain stores and investors in them learned the hard way that lease liabilities could provide enormous claims, and many chain stores went bankrupt because they could not meet their lease liabilities. This led, after a long period of bankruptcy litigation on the provability of lease claims, to limitations thereon in bankruptcy. It also led to an SEC requirement, which later became a GAAP, that the obligations under long-term leases be disclosed in a footnote to the financial statements.

Now let us take a lease of a chattel. If it is a six-month lease of a chattel whose life is ten years, e.g., the ordinary short-term rental of a piece of construction equipment by a contractor who needs it temporarily for a special job, obviously the accounting will be the same as in the case of the store lease.

But now suppose the lease of the chattel is for the estimated useful life of the property, say, ten years. Or suppose the building lease is for forty years, requires the lessee to pay all taxes, insurance and maintenance and includes an option for the lessee to purchase the building at the end of the lease period for a nominal price. Is the balance sheet of the lessee fairly presented if it fails to include both asset and liability covered by such a lease? Compare each lease with a similar transaction structured as an installment sale by the lessor and purchase by the lessee. Should the accounting be different?

Now imagine the spectrum of lease transactions arranged in order on a horizontal scale. Where should accountants draw the line between lease transactions that should be capitalized and those that should not? Herein is the one pervasive question regarding lease accounting. Accounting literature on leases is directed primarily to this line-drawing question.

The process of fixing GAAP for leases has been laborious. The basic rules are in SFAS No. 13, *Accounting for Leases* (1976). After more than two dozen amendments and interpretations, made over the intervening fourteen years, the FASB recently issued a one volume codification of this vast array, FASB, *Accounting for Leases, FASB Statement No. 13 as Amended and Interpreted* (Jan. 1990).

B. ACCOUNTING FOR LESSEES AND LESSORS

1. ACCOUNTING FOR LESSEES

In *SFAS No. 13* the FASB formally differentiated "capital leases," which are displayed on the balance sheet, from ordinary "operating leases," which are off the balance sheet, and set forth the criteria to be used in that classification. For the lessee a capital lease is one which meets any one of four criteria. The first two are easy enough to comprehend: (1) the lease transfers ownership to the lessee by the end of the term; or (2) the lease contains a bargain purchase option. The third is that the lease term equals 75% or more of the economic life of the property. The fourth covers leases under which the present value of the lease payments equal or exceed 90% of fair value to the lessor of the leased property.

To illustrate the application of these alternative criteria, assume that a truck manufacturer produces a truck, costing $45,000, which it offers either to sell for $50,000 cash or to lease on terms indicated below. The useful life is fifteen years with zero estimated salvage value. The leasing option is on the following terms:

Lease term	10 years
Annual rental due December 31 each year	$ 8,280
Estimated value of truck at end of ten years	$10,000
"Implicit interest rate of the lease"	12% [a]

Obviously neither of the first two criteria for a capital lease is met. Nor is the third because the lease term is only 66⅔% of the estimated life of the truck. But is the present value of the lease payments equal to or in excess of 90% of the $50,000 value of the truck, $45,000? From Table 2 of the Appendix to this book we find that at a 12% discount rate the present value of the lease payments is the value of an annuity of $8,280 for ten years, or 5.65 × $8,280 which is $46,782. Therefore the fourth criterion is met since $46,782 exceeds 90% of $50,000, and the lease is to be accounted for as a capital lease.

SFAS No. 13 requires capitalization of capital leases, showing an asset and a liability equal to the present discounted value of the rents, ($46,782 here) and it requires depreciation of the asset in a manner consistent with the lessee's normal depreciation policy, not necessarily straight line although most firms do use the straight line method. The discount is treated as interest and is to be recognized as expense in proportion to the remaining balance of the obligation, like interest on any obligation.

If a lease does not meet the FASB's standards for a capital lease, and is therefore termed an operating lease, rent shall be charged as expense on a straight line basis, unless some other systematic and

a. The "implicit rate" is defined in SFAS No. 13 as the rate that causes the present value of the lease payments plus the residual value of the asset at the end of the lease to equal the fair market value of the leased item, here $50,000. One can see that at a 12% discount rate (from the Appendix at the end of this book) the ten annual payments of $8,280 and the residual value of $10,000 together have a present value equal to the $50,000 fair market value. Therefore 12% is the implicit rate of the lease.

Revised SFAS No. 13 permits a lessee to use his or her own cost of funds for these calculations if the lessor's implicit rate is unknown. Thus some other rate, say 13% or 14% might have been used here if that is what the lessee must pay on its borrowings. These rates would alter the following numbers substantially. The lessor must always use the lessor's implicit rate whereas the lessee must use it only if it is known to the lessee.

rational basis is more representative of the time pattern of use benefit. The FASB also incorporates some disclosure requirements for operating leases.

To illustrate accounting for a capitalized lease, using the preceding example, on inception of the lease, the entry is to show as an asset (and therefore also a liability) the present value of the lease payments:

1/1/X1	Leased Equipment	$46,782	
	Payable		$46,782

Then at the end of Year 1:

12/31/X1	Depreciation Expense	4,678	
	Accumulated Depreciation		4,678
	Payable	2,666	
	Interest Expense	5,614	
	Cash		8,280

The Interest Expense of $5,614 for the first year is 12% of the unpaid balance of the Payable, $46,782. For year 19X2, the unpaid balance is $46,782 minus $2,666 or $44,116, of which 12% is $5,294. This process shows that in the end the level payments of rent of $8,280 for ten years total $82,800 which is the same as the aggregate of Interest and Depreciation Expense (less rounding errors) for the ten years. See the following table. The difference between debiting the level $8,280 rent expense each year and the changing charges for Interest plus the Depreciation is in the pattern of annual amounts, graphically portrayed by the chart following the table.

Table of Depreciation and Principal and Interest Payments

	(a) Depreciation	(b) Interest	(c) Total (a) + (b)	(d) Principal	(e) Rental
19X1	$ 4,678	$ 5,614	$10,292	$ 2,666	$ 8,280
19X2	4,678	5,294	9,972	2,986	8,280
19X3	4,678	4,936	9,614	3,344	8,280
19X4	4,678	4,534	9,212	3,746	8,280
19X5	4,678	4,085	8,763	4,195	8,280
19X6	4,678	3,581	8,259	4,699	8,280
19X7	4,678	3,017	7,695	5,263	8,280
19X8	4,678	2,386	7,064	5,894	8,280
19X9	4,678	1,679	6,357	6,601	8,280
19Y0	4,678	886	5,564	7,394	8,280
Totals	$46,780	$36,012	$82,792 (round to $82,800)	$46,780	$82,800

The pattern of expenses for the operating lease shows a steady Rent Expense of $8,280 annually whereas the capital lease expense for Depreciation and Interest shows a decreasing amount. These may be illustrated:

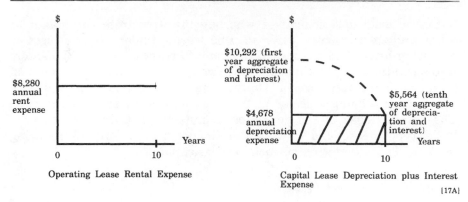

Operating Lease Rental Expense

Capital Lease Depreciation plus Interest Expense

[17A]

2. ACCOUNTING FOR LESSORS

SFAS No. 13 also authorizes two different forms of accounting for lessors. On the one hand is the lessor of a building, e.g., an apartment building, who has a group of tenants, either without leases or with short-term leases. She is clearly running the risks of the owner of a building and her accounting follows conventional property accounting. She shows the ownership of the assets; she takes depreciation; and she records the lease rentals as revenue only when properly accrued. Similar accounting is followed by an owner of chattels who operates a rent-a-car service or construction equipment rental fleet for daily or short-term leasing. These lessors are taking the risks of ownership. They use the "operating method" of lease accounting.

On the other hand are lessors in the capital leases described above. These lessors have the right to receive under a firm lease substantially the equivalent of the purchase price, plus a charge for the use of money. These lessors are either the manufacturers or dealers themselves or are frequently banks or insurance or finance companies which, in another department or through an affiliate, are engaged in installment sale financing. They are department stores of finance, and they offer the potential user of machinery a choice of acquiring it either on an installment sale basis or on a leasing basis. General Electric's finance subsidiary whose financial statements are set out in the Appendix to Chapter X is such a firm. Usually, because the lease pay-outs may be something less than complete, the financing charge may be perhaps ½% higher per annum than the rate would be if the transaction were frankly treated as an installment purchase obligation.

Under *SFAS 13* leases are to be capitalized by the lessor if they meet one of the four criteria above discussed for the lessee and both of two others: collection is reasonably predictable; and there are no important uncertainties as to non-reimbursable costs of the lessor. These conditions are familiar to you as necessary for the recognition of revenue generally. Hence it is no surprise that they apply only to lessors, not lessees.

Unlike lessees, as we have stated, lessors are of two types: those who make or sell the leased item, and financial intermediaries such as banks or insurance companies who buy the item from the maker or seller and then lease it. Both may be leasing under capital leases or operating leases. In the case of the manufacturer or dealer who enters into a capital lease, it will be making two types of profit: (1) the gain on sale, and (2) interest income. On the other hand, the bank or insurance company, not being a dealer in the item, makes interest income only. The capital lease of the dealer or manufacturer is referred to as a "sales-type" lease and that of the financier as a "direct financing lease." The accounting of each will be explained.

(A) Sales–Type Leases

The task is to show the two items of profit and to do that requires the following data:

(1) The "gross investment"; i.e., the sum of the lease payments and the residual value:

Lease payments, 10 × $8,280 or	$82,800
Residual value	10,000
Total gross investment	$92,800

(2) The "net investment"; i.e., present value of these two items:

Lease payments ($8,280 × 5.65 [b])	$46,782
Residual value ($10,000 × .322 [c])	3,220
	$50,002 [d]
	(rounded to $50,000)

(3) The difference is the unearned interest which will become earned income over the ten years:

Gross investment	$92,800
Less: Net investment	50,000
Unearned interest income	$42,800

In year one the earned income is 12% of the net investment of $50,000, or $6,000. Here note the lessor's interest income is more than the lessee's interest expense. This is because the lessee's investment here does not include the residual value.

In years two through ten the remaining interest at 12% earned on the declining balance will be credited to income.

(4) The lessor's gross gain on the sale in year one is the difference between the $50,000 present value of the lease payments and residual value, on the one hand, and the $45,000 cost, or $5,000.

(B) Direct Financing Leases

Here the bank has no $5,000 profit from sale but presumably had paid $50,000 for the item and will lease it on the stated terms.

b. From Table 2 of the Appendix.

c. From Table 1.

d. The $50,002 results from multiplying a rounding error. We shall use the $50,000 amount.

Here the entries will merely result in allocating the $42,800 of unearned income declining from $6,000 in year one as above.

3. DISCLOSURE BY LESSORS AND LESSEES

Footnote disclosures by lessors and lessees are required to supplement the accounts. The following are two examples of the details required by Revised *SFAS No. 13*. The first is from AT&T's 1989 financials describing AT&T's operating, direct financing, and sales type leases as lessor of manufactured products and under capital and operating leases as lessee of properties used in its business. The second illustration is from General Electric's 1989 financials and illustrates, in note 16, disclosure of direct financing and leveraged leases [e] by GE's financial services unit and, in note 18, disclosures for operating leases.

From AT&T footnotes to financial statements:

(H) Leases [in millions]

As Lessor: The Company leases equipment to others through operating leases; the majority of these are cancellable. The minimum future rentals on noncancellable leases are $301 in 1990, $151 in 1991, $57 in 1992, $9 in 1993, $3 in 1994 and $7 in later years. AT&T's net investment in equipment used to support leasing operations, included in property, plant and equipment, was as follows:

At December 31	1989	1988
Machinery, electronic and other equipment ..	**$2,978**	$2,839
Less: Accumulated depreciation	1,875	1,666
Net investment	**$1,103**	$1,173

AT&T also provides direct financing and other leasing programs for its products and those of other companies and leases its products to others under sales-type leases. The Company's net investment in finance assets arising from these leasing arrangements amounted to $2,145 and $1,393, including residual values of $306 and $144 and is reflected net of unearned income of $656 and $387, in 1989 and 1988, respectively. Finance service revenues are recognized over the life of the respective leases using the interest method and are included in sales of services. The future maturities of these finance assets are $836 in 1990, $641 in 1991, $441 in 1992, $248 in 1993, $99 in 1994 and $79 in later years.

As Lessee: AT&T leases land, buildings and equipment through contracts that expire in various years. Future minimum lease payments at December 31, 1989 are as follows:

e. "Leveraged leases" are direct financing leases under which the lessor is also using financing on the asset, usually with a financial institution and secured only by the property or the lease payments.

	Capital Leases	Operating Leases
1990	$ 136	$ 531
1991	106	392
1992	58	281
1993	49	199
1994	35	157
Later years	92	669
Total minimum lease payments	476	$ 2,229
Less: Estimated executory cost	1	
Imputed interest	144	
Present value of net minimum lease payments	$ 331	

Rental expense for operating leases was $1,114 in 1989, $1,106 in 1988 and $887 in 1987.

From GE's 1989 footnotes to financial statements:

Note 16   GEFS Financing Receivables (investment in time sales, loans and financing leases)

December 31 (In millions)	1989	1988
Investment in financing leases		
Direct financing leases	9,827	8,433
Leveraged leases	2,937	2,691
	12,764	11,124
	42,906	36,911
Less allowance for losses	(1,127)	(972)
	$41,779	$35,939

"Financing leases" consists of direct financing and leveraged leases of aircraft, railroad rolling stock, automobiles and other transportation equipment, data processing equipment, medical equipment, and other manufacturing, power generation, mining and commercial equipment and facilities.

As the sole owner of assets under direct financing leases and as the equity participant in leveraged leases, GEFS is taxed on total lease payments received and is entitled to tax deductions based on the cost of leased assets and tax deductions for interest paid to third-party participants. GEFS also is entitled generally to any investment tax credit on leased equipment and to any residual value of leased assets.

Investments in direct financing and leveraged leases represent unpaid rentals and estimated unguaranteed residual values of leased equipment, less related deferred income and principal and interest on notes and other instruments representing third-party participation. Because GEFS has no general obligation on such notes and other instruments representing third-party participation, such notes and other instruments have not been included in liabilities but have been offset against the related rentals receivable. GEFS' share of rentals receivable is subordinate to the share of the other participants who also have a security interest in the leased equipment.

Additional detail about investment in financing leases at December 31, 1989 and 1988 is shown below.

Investment in financing leases	Direct financing leases		Leveraged leases		Total financing leases	
December 31 (In millions)	1989	1988	1989	1988	1989	1988
Total minimum lease payments receivable	$12,009	$10,109	$11,444	$10,745	$23,453	$20,854
Less principal and interest on third-party nonre- course debt	—	—	(8,207)	(7,893)	(8,207)	(7,893)
Rentals receivable	12,009	10,109	3,237	2,852	15,246	12,961
Estimated unguaranteed residual value of leased as- sets	1,250	1,102	883	817	2,133	1,919
Less deferred income (a)	(3,432)	(2,778)	(1,183)	(978)	(4,615)	(3,756)
Investment in financing leases (as shown above)	9,827	8,433	2,937	2,691	12,764	11,124
Less amounts to arrive at net investment						
Allowance for losses	(214)	(121)	(48)	(74)	(262)	(195)
Deferred taxes arising from financing leases	(1,207)	(1,218)	(2,444)	(2,406)	(3,651)	(3,624)
Net investment in financing leases	$8,406	$7,094	$445	$211	$8,851	$7,305

(a) Total financing lease deferred income is net of deferred initial direct costs of $37 million and $33 million for 1989 and 1988, respectively.

Contractual maturities of rentals receivable at December 31, 1989 are shown below.

Contractual maturities (In millions)	Total	1990	1991	1992	1993	1994	1995 and after
Investment in financing leases							
Direct financing leases	12,009	2,788	2,651	1,879	1,371	783	2,537
Leveraged leases	3,237	141	156	162	166	181	2,431
	15,246	2,929	2,807	2,041	1,537	964	4,968

Experience has shown that a substantial portion of receivables will be paid prior to contractual maturity. Accordingly, the maturities of rentals receivable shown in the table above are not to be regarded as forecasts of future cash collections.

Note 18   Property, Plant and Equipment (including equipment leased to others)

December 31 (In millions)	1989	1988
Original cost		
GE		
Land and improvements	$ 266	$ 260
Buildings, structures and related equipment	4,600	4,250
Machinery and equipment	13,756	12,957
Leasehold costs and manufacturing plant under construction	1,051	1,126
Oil and gas properties	749	764
	20,422	19,357
GEFS		
Buildings and equipment	1,206	745
Equipment leased to others		
Vehicles	2,076	1,564
Railroad rolling stock	1,347	1,038
Marine shipping containers	816	857
Aircraft	1,324	618
Data processing equipment	461	355
Other	816	634
	8,046	5,811
	$28,468	$25,168

Accumulated depreciation, depletion and amortization

GE	$10,756	$ 9,997
GEFS		
Equipment leased to others	1,745	1,321
Buildings and equipment	321	239
	$12,822	$11,557

GEFS' increase in buildings and equipment includes the effect of the transfer of GE Americom from GE at year-end 1989. Current-year amortization of GEFS' equipment on lease to others was $647 million, $665 million and $316 million in 1989, 1988 and 1987, respectively.

At December 31, 1989, GE except GEFS had minimum rental commitments under noncancellable operating leases aggregating $3,069 million. Amounts payable over the next five years are: 1990—$537 million; 1991—$480 million; 1992—$394 million; 1993—$338 million; and 1994—$308 million.

At December 31, 1989, GEFS had minimum rental commitments under noncancelable operating leases aggregating $942 million. Amounts payable over the next five years are: 1990—$168 million; 1991—$143 million; 1992—$106 million; 1993—$65 million; and 1994—$68 million.

4. THE LESSOR AS TOOL OF THE LESSEE

Another series of problems arises when the lessor is merely a subsidiary or other entity created by the lessee for the primary purpose of borrowing from an institution the money with which to buy the equipment, and then leasing it to the lessee. Since such a lessor might have only nominal net worth of its own, a lender would make such a loan (which might be for 100% of the cost of the machine from the manufacturer) only because the lessee guaranteed the loan or because the lender was assured of recovery of its loan plus interest out of the rentals, with the rentals from the "high credit lessee" assigned by the lessor to the lender as security. In this kind of case, the APB took the position that the lease should be treated as purchase financing, with the lessee treating itself as debtor on the loan. See *APB Op. No. 5*, ¶ 12 (1964). Even if there was no guarantee, the APB took the position that the lessee must consolidate a lessor-subsidiary and thus show the debt in consolidated statements. *APB Op. No. 10*, ¶ 4 (1966). Even if arrangements are carefully constructed so that the lessor is not technically a subsidiary of the lessee, *Opinion No. 5*, ¶ 12, took the same position where the parties were related and the lessor was created directly or indirectly by the lessee and was substantially dependent on the lessee for its operations. The SEC indicated in *ASR 132* (1972) that it intended to enforce this provision, which had been frequently disregarded in practice.

Now *SFAS No. 13* requires in Paragraph 31 that the accounts of subsidiaries which engage in leasing to parent or affiliated companies should be fully consolidated. It holds that the equity method of one line consolidation is not adequate for fair presentation of those subsidiaries because their assets and liabilities are significant to the consolidated financial position of the enterprise. *SFAS No. 13* does not sufficiently deal with non-subsidiary lessors which have no economic substance except to act as lessors to lessees which caused their creation, and SEC *ASR 132,* supra, is the latest authoritative expression on that point.

C. THE COOKBOOK APPROACH IN LEASE ACCOUNTING

Throughout the years of debate and rule making concerning leases the regulators and rule makers have sought to prescribe a distinction between sales and rentals so as to always obtain the "right" answer in the sense that the statements of financial position (balance sheet) and results of operation (income statements) will report all leases in accordance with their economic substance and effect. On the other side, entrepreneurs, salesmen, purchasing agents, lenders, professionals and company controllers have sought to design lease transactions around the specified criteria in a manner that achieves as much for their particular party as possible without having the lease fall into the unwanted accounting category, whether it be capital lease accounting or operating lease accounting, that they are trying to avoid. For example, property can be leased for 74% or 76% of its estimated useful life depending on whether the desired accounting result is to have an operating lease or a capital lease. Similarly, lease payments can be built into the lease that will yield a present value of 89% or 91% of the fair value of the property. In practice, some designers of leases, where the percentage is close, tend to stay about one point away from the magic numbers of 75% of economic useful life and 90% of fair value of the property.

Can it be said that presenting all leases falling on one side of such a narrow line as operating leases and all leases falling on the other side as capital leases achieves fairness in the resulting financial statements? The accounting difference is so substantial that it far overdramatizes the difference of a percentage point, or perhaps less, in estimated salvage value or in estimated present value of minimum lease payments.

No matter what criteria are prescribed, this activity, i.e., tailoring transactions around the accounting requirements, will continue as long as our private enterprise system continues. The task for the regulators and rule makers will continue to be to cope with the ingenuity of business people in structuring leasing transactions motivated by competition for the sale (or "lease") of products or the unabated desire to present, within GAAP, the most desirable financial statements to lenders and investors. While the criteria are arbitrary, and may thus be criticized in particular situations, *SFAS No. 13* has moved any control over accounting for leases from the controller's office to the bargaining table where specified conditions must be achieved to produce the desired accounting.

D. A WORD ON SYMMETRY

One of the principal criticisms of the predecessors to *SFAS No. 13* was that they prescribed different criteria for classifying leases as regards the lessee and the lessor resulting in a lack of symmetry. That weakness, along with ambiguities and generally loose application made it fairly easy to have the lessee accounting for the lease one way and the lessor the other way. The FASB sought to achieve a high degree of symmetry by decreeing that the four criteria imposed upon the lessee in Paragraph 7 of *SFAS No. 13* for classifying a lease would also apply to the lessor. The Board, however, left two areas where there can be departures from symmetry in classification.

The first is in Paragraph 7d which prescribes that the lessor shall compute the present value of minimum lease payments using the *interest rate implicit in the lease,* whereas the lessee may compute the present value of minimum lease payments using its *incremental borrowing rate,* except in certain circumstances where the lessee knows the lessor's implicit rate. This difference can result in different classification for the lessee and the lessor, particularly where the ¶ 7d computation is close to 90% and there is a material difference between the rate implicit in the lease and the lessee's incremental borrowing rate. The other area leading to a departure from symmetry is in Paragraph 8 which requires the lessor, in order to have capital lease accounting on its end of the transaction, to meet one of the four criteria in Paragraph 7d (same as the lessee) and, in addition, to meet the further criteria of collectibility of minimum lease payments and no important uncertainties.

These possibilities for lack of symmetry in classification suggest that there may continue to be circumstances where, in this highly complex cookbook approach, a skillful designer of leases might tailor a lease to be accounted for as a capital lease for one party and an operating lease for the other, thus meeting the accounting desires of both. This result may not have been intended by the Board but it is a necessary result of the cookbook approach and the specific requirements imposed in Paragraphs 7d and 8 of *SFAS No. 13.*

Given the same classification, however, true symmetry of accounting is still not achieved in the sales-type lease because the lessor front-ends the profit on the sale (Paragraph 17c) (the $5,000 in our illustration) whereas the lessee spreads the cost of the asset over its estimated life (Paragraph 11).

E. FOR MASTER CHEFS ONLY

We have lulled the reader to some extent by explaining only the simplest concepts of lease accounting. Given the billions of dollars involved, and the great rewards already noted for accounting in one way instead of another, together with the revolution in financial services, one might correctly suspect that intricate devices exist for avoiding accounting disadvantages.

Accounting for leases has become so intricate that, as we have intimated, a specialized industry exists in advising on how to design and account for leasing transactions. Thus in the prior edition of this book we included another ten pages describing the intricacies of accounting for the problems of real estate leases, including sales and leasebacks, subleases, and leveraged leases.

For an explanation of GAAP for sales and leasebacks, see Arcady, Herdman & Strianese, *Real Estate Sale–Leasebacks Under FASB 98,* J. Accountancy 101 (June 1989). Regarding leverage leases, see, e.g., Kieso & Weygandt, *Intermediate Accounting* 945–49 (1977).

Chapter XII

PENSION BENEFITS

OBJECTIVES

Understand the economic substance of pension obligations of firms and the many compromises of that substance resulting in current GAAP.

RELEVANCE FOR LAWYERS

Because of the vast sums being invested in retirement funds, which provide the overwhelming bulk of security for Americans today, lawyers must understand the costs to employers in order to knowledgeably advise employees, employers, investors and others. This chapter provides an introduction to this complex realm.

A. INTRODUCTION

In excess of a trillion and a half dollars is now invested in private retirement plans in the United States. The AT&T plan alone had over $33 billion in assets at the end of 1989. Some of these plans are insurance contracts but most are trusts which have been established by one or a group of employers or labor unions as settlors (often referred to as "sponsors") with employees as beneficiaries.

In the typical plan, the sponsor agrees to pay amounts according to some formula to the trustees of the plan, to fund the plan and enable it to pay the plan's benefits when due. These benefits sometimes include health and death benefits as well as other welfare payments. The pension benefits ordinarily are related to the amount of wages or salaries earned by the beneficiaries and each one's length of service, although this is not always so.

There are two major classes of plans: (1) "defined contribution" plans, wherein the contributions of the sponsor to the trustees are fixed by a formula such as a percentage of the sponsor's profits or the employee's earnings, and benefits depend as well on the investment earnings from these contributions, and (2) "defined benefit" plans wherein the contributions are undefined but are based on how much is deemed necessary to meet a defined amount of benefits (taking into account the investment performance of the plan) to be paid to the employee or his or her estate on retirement or death.

In a defined contribution plan, the employee has the full risk of gain or loss on portfolio investments. In a defined benefit plan, the employer bears those benefits or detriments and must adjust its contributions accordingly. The employee, of course, bears the ultimate risk of the employer's insolvency, except to the extent of insurance by the Pension Benefit Guaranty Corporation, a federal agency established under the Employees' Retirement Income Security Act ("ERISA"),[a] about which more later. The overwhelming majority of plans are defined benefit plans, although it is more common to find defined contribution plans for multi-employer situations where employees go from one employer to another such as in teaching or the construction and trucking industries.

B. ACCOUNTING FOR PENSION PLANS

Because the assets of these plans are placed in various types of investments in trust for the benefit of the employees, the accounting for the trusts is very important to the employees who should be interested in knowing how well their investments are doing. GAAP for defined benefit plans themselves, to be distinguished from GAAP for the sponsors, are found in *SFAS No. 35*, which was issued in March 1980,

a. Pub.L. No. 93–406, 88 Stat. 829 (1974).

and is entitled *Accounting and Reporting by Defined Benefit Pension Plans*. Requirements applicable to other types of plans such as defined contribution plans and health and welfare plans are contained in AICPA Audit Guides. Since the major source of capital for these funds is continuing contributions by the employer or labor union settlor, the financial status of the sponsor also should be of interest to the employee-beneficiaries.

We have said that plan beneficiaries "should be" interested in pension plan disclosures. Unfortunately, pension plan rights are taken for granted until an expected benefit is denied, as in the case of one Mr. Daniel, a Teamsters' Union member who paid union dues for most of his working life expecting a pension which he never received. Mr. Daniel fought for his pension all the way to the Supreme Court but mercifully died (presumably of old age) a week before the decision was issued, not knowing he had finally failed. In International Brotherhood of Teamsters v. Daniel, 439 U.S. 551 (1979), the Court provided some useful learning on the characteristics of pension plans and also held that an interest in the Teamsters' Union plan did not involve a "security" and therefore was not regulated by the securities laws. However, the SEC later issued two exhaustive releases in which it took the position that some plans may involve securities even after *Daniel*. See Sec.Act Rel. 6188, 19 SEC Dkt. 465 (1980); Sec.Act Rel. 6281, 21 SEC Dkt. 1372 (1981). Disclosure obligations under the securities laws may be more demanding than under other laws, notably the Internal Revenue Code and ERISA, as well as the common law. In any event, one may expect the adequacy of disclosure to be tested in such *post hoc* fashion when the scrutiny of the courts may be close. Hence *SFAS No. 35* can be expected to be tested rigorously.

In keeping with our major purpose of considering accounting for business entities, we shall not further consider accounting for these pension plans, but shall consider accounting by the sponsoring employer or other person.

C. ACCOUNTING BY THE PENSION PLAN'S SPONSOR

1. THE FACTORS IN ACCOUNTING FOR SPONSORS OF PENSION PLANS

The accounting questions for the financial statements of the employer sponsors of these plans are: how much should be charged to expense or deferred cost each year for pension obligations, and how much, if any, should be reflected as a liability (or asset) when payments to the plan trustees are less than (or more than) the sponsor's ultimate obligations?

The employer's accounting for its payments and obligations to defined contribution plans is fairly simple since those plans essentially call for a certain liability to arise each year which does not change with subsequent events; hence the payments or obligations to pay are determined ("defined") and are simply treated like additional wage or salary payments.

The accounting for payments and obligations to defined benefit plans, on the other hand, is completely dependent on the particular conceptualization adopted. This is because the plans have several complex features:

(a) Eligibility. The plan will state which employees are eligible, e.g., full-time salaried persons with at least one year of service.

(b) Prior service costs. Typically employees in service at the time of adoption or amendment will receive credit for at least some years of prior service under various terms of the plan including eligibility (above), benefits, vesting, etc. (below).

(c) Vesting. Employees who quit after only a few years of service may not be fully vested with benefits. E.g., the plan may require that employees work a minimum of two years before any vesting and vesting of 10% for each year of service thereafter; i.e., 100% vesting after at least twelve years of service.

(d) Benefits formula. The benefit may be defined as, say, 3% of the employee's highest salary before resignation or retirement multiplied by each year of service, payable beginning at age sixty-five and for the lives of the employee and spouse.

(e) Funding. Under a defined benefit plan there is a liability of the sponsor to the employee and an arrangement for funding the trust res to provide some assurance to the employee. But the amount of cash or property agreed to be paid in to the trust will usually be different from the sponsor's total obligation at least in the early years, largely because of the liability for prior services. Thus the plan will specify annual or other funding requirements different from the sponsor's ultimate obligation.

(f) Plan performance. The funds paid in will be invested in order to earn income. As already indicated, under a defined benefit plan the employee gets a certain (defined) amount regardless of the investment performance of the trust and any shortfall must be made up by the sponsor. Therefore the investment performance will be credited to the sponsor.

Clearly until the unrealistic event that all employees have retired and the sponsor is out of business, many questions cannot be answered precisely; e.g.:

— what employees (and spouses) will survive to retirement?

— what will be survival rates thereafter?

— what will each employee's maximum salary be prior to retirement?

— what vesting will have occurred?

— what will have been the plan's investment performance?

Realistically what is required is that estimates be made for these matters.

You are probably aware that most of these same questions have been dealt with for many decades by insurance actuaries. Hence actuarial techniques will be relevant. Similarly the questions involving expected returns on investments of the plan and anticipated wage and salary levels involve a knowledge of finance. Added to these are the fact that pension plans, as trusts, require a knowledge of the law of trusts and contracts for their interpretation, although more significantly, pensions, as an important element of our social welfare system, have drawn the attention of Congress, which a few years ago adopted ERISA, summarized below.

Thus, the fields of actuarial science, finance, law and accounting are all involved in the accounting for pension obligations and payments. A major legal impact on pension costs is the federal ERISA, explained briefly below.

2. ERISA

EXCERPT FROM FASB, DISCUSSION MEMORANDUM, EMPLOYERS' ACCOUNTING FOR PENSIONS AND OTHER POSTEMPLOYMENT BENEFITS

App.C., pp. 123, 128–36 FASB, 1981.[*]

"ERISA—Before and After

"C–21. Prior to the enactment of ERISA, statutory law governing pension plans in the United States was largely contained in the Internal Revenue Code. The old law set forth requirements to be met in order to be classified as a 'qualified' plan. Technically, a qualified pension plan is a plan that meets the requirements of Section 401 of the Internal Revenue Code. Tax advantages provided by a qualified plan include:

a. The employer is allowed to deduct contributions as a business expense.

b. The employee pays no tax on the employer's contributions or on the earnings or appreciation of the fund until the funds are actually distributed or made available in the form of retirement or other deferred benefits.[b]

c. The trust, which is a part of the qualified plan, is exempt from taxes on the earnings and appreciation of the fund.

* Copyright © 1981, by Financial Accounting Standards Board, High Ridge Park, Stamford, Conn. 06905, U.S.A. Reprinted with permission. Copies of the complete document are available from the FASB.

b. Ed's. Note—The income tax laws of certain states (e.g., New York and New Jersey) permit exclusion from gross income for purposes of state income tax of limited amounts of pension benefits received by retired employees.

Hence, as a practical matter, most pre-ERISA pension plans were qualified plans.

"C–22. Qualification requirements under the old law focused primarily on the 'exclusive benefit of employees or their beneficiaries' and 'anti-discriminatory' provisions of a plan. The Code was essentially silent on matters such as standards for participation, vesting, and funding. ERISA not only established standards in these and other areas, but also amended the Internal Revenue Code of 1954 by adding those standards to the qualification section of the Code.

"Coverage

"C–23. In general, ERISA applies to any employee benefit plan established or maintained:

a. By any employer engaged in commerce or in any industry or activity affecting commerce or

b. By any employee organization representing employees engaged in commerce or in any business or activity affecting commerce or

c. By both.

"ERISA does not apply to governmental plans (federal, state, or local), church plans, and certain special-purpose plans.

"Participation

"C–24. The old law did not mandate any particular eligibility requirements in qualified plans. Generally, any eligibility requirement was satisfactory provided that either (a) at least 70 percent of all employees who had completed 5 years of service were covered, or (b) the Internal Revenue Service (IRS) found that eligibility requirements did not result in discrimination in favor of officers, stockholders, or highly compensated employees.

"C–25. ERISA provides that an employee who has attained the age of 25 years and has completed 1 year of service may not be excluded from coverage under a qualified plan, with certain exceptions. However under ERISA, if a plan provides for 100–percent vesting after not more than 3 years, the plan can defer participation until the employee has completed 3 years of service. Also, an employee may not be excluded from coverage under a qualified plan because of age, except that under a defined benefit pension plan an employee may be excluded if, on the date employed, the employee is within 5 years of normal retirement date.

"Vesting

"C–26. The old law did not require vesting prior to normal retirement date. However, qualified plans customarily granted substantial vested rights prior to attainment of normal retirement age. Under the old law, a qualified plan could provide that a participant's vested benefit be forfeited if the participant entered the employ of a competitor, committed a crime, or was disloyal to the employer.

"C–27. Plans covered by ERISA must contain a vesting provision that is at least as liberal as one of the three minimum vesting standards specified in that Act. Those standards are (a) full vesting after 10 years of service, or (b) full vesting after 15 years of service on a prescribed graduated basis, or (c) full vesting under a combination of age and service (the 'Rule of 45'—Section 203(a) of ERISA). In the event of plan termination, nonvested accrued benefits become nonforfeitable but are not covered by the payment guarantee of the PBGC.

"Funding

"C–30. The old law required that defined benefit pension plans fund only the normal cost and interest on the past service cost. The past service cost itself was not required to be funded. However, the common practice was to fund such costs, generally over a 30– or 40–year period. That practice was encouraged by the fact that only amounts funded were deductible for federal income tax purposes.

"C–31. The old law contained no requirement regarding the manner in which assets of a pension trust were to be valued, nor did it prescribe actuarial certification of the annual contribution to such plans. Actuarial assumptions were required to be reasonable in the aggregate, but each individual actuarial assumption by itself was not required to be reasonable.

"C–32. ERISA establishes a minimum funding standard (or alternative minimum funding standard) that every covered defined benefit pension plan must satisfy. Under the minimum funding standard, as amended by the Multiemployer Pension Plan Amendments Act of 1980, plans are required to fund not only normal cost for the plan year, but also amounts necessary to amortize, in equal annual installments these past service costs over a period of several years.

"C–33. In determining the minimum funding standards, ERISA provides that normal costs, accrued liability, past service liabilities, and experience gains and losses shall be determined under the funding method used to determine costs under the plan. Plan assets may be valued based on any reasonable actuarial method of valuation that takes into account fair market value and that is permitted under regulations prescribed by the Secretary of the Treasury. If the plan administrator so elects, bonds and other evidences of indebtedness may be valued on an amortized basis to maturity or earliest call date. Actuarial assumptions are required to be reasonable in the aggregate rather than individually.

"C–34. To implement the new funding rules, each plan is required to establish a funding standard account, which will be debited with all annual contributions required to meet the minimum standard and will be credited with actual contributions. If a debit balance exists in the funding standard account, an excise tax [penalty] is imposed.

"Fiduciary Responsibility

"C–36. In order to attain and retain qualified status, the old law required a plan to demonstrate that:

    a. Local law was being followed in matters relating to the trust. If the state in which the trust was operated had 'a prudent man' rule, that rule had to be considered.

    b. The plan was operated for the benefit of the participants or their beneficiaries. This requirement is contained in Section 401 of the Code. The rule was broad enough to permit a trust to enter into transactions with the employer so long as the transactions were commercially fair and reasonable (i.e., 'arm's-length' transactions).

    c. The plan did not enter into a 'prohibited transaction' with the employer. In general, a prohibited transaction is one in which property is transferred between the employer and the plan at a price that is not at arm's length, or money is lent without adequate security or at an unreasonable rate of interest.

The only sanction contained in the old law for violation of these fiduciary standards was the disqualification of the plan. Since disqualification affected primarily the plan participants, it was rarely invoked.

"C–37. ERISA officially established a federal 'prudent man' rule. That act requires that fiduciaries act 'with the care, skill, prudence, and diligence under the circumstances then prevailing that a prudent man acting in a like capacity and familiar with such matters would use in conducting an enterprise of like character and with like aims.'

"C–38. ERISA requires that a fiduciary diversify the investments of the pension fund assets, with the purpose of minimizing the risk of large losses. Diversification must rule unless it is 'clearly prudent' not to do so. In general, a plan may invest in the securities of an employer up to a limit of 10 percent of plan assets, based on fair market value. With the exception of that 10–percent investment rule, a plan is prohibited from engaging directly or indirectly, with a party-in-interest, [in transactions].

"C–39. ERISA also imposes severe sanctions. Fiduciaries who breach any of their obligations are personally liable to the plan for its losses resulting from the breach and for profits they made through use of plan assets. Exculpatory provisions are not permitted. Parties-in-interest who participate in prohibited transactions are subject to a nondeductible five-percent excise tax on the amount involved in the transaction. If the transaction is not corrected in timely fashion after notice from the IRS, the party-in-interest is subject to a 100 percent excise tax, also nondeductible.

"Plan Termination Insurance and Employer Liability

"C–40. There is no counterpart in the old law to the plan termination insurance provisions of ERISA. Under the old law, there were several ways in which an employer's liability could be limited under the terms of the plan.

a. The employer could reserve the unilateral right to modify or terminate the plan at any time. This right might be limited by a collective bargaining agreement. Also, the Internal Revenue Code limited the reasons why a plan could be terminated (or modified) and stipulated loss of tax deductions when a plan was terminated in the early years of existence for reasons other than business necessity.

b. The employer could reserve the right to suspend contributions to the plan at any time and for any reason. Again, the employer's freedom might be limited by a collective bargaining agreement or IRS regulations.

c. Upon plan termination, the employer's liability could be limited to amounts already contributed and held in trust or under insurance company contracts.

d. Neither the employer nor any agents could be held liable for their acts or failures to act, except in the event of willful termination.

"C–41. ERISA created the Pension Benefit Guaranty Corporation (PBGC) within the Department of Labor for the purpose of guaranteeing the payment of covered vested benefits under defined benefit pension plans in the event of plan termination, subject to [several] limitations.

"C–42. ERISA established a premium rate schedule for the PBGC for the first two years, after which the PBGC may revise the rates within prescribed limits. The limits can be exceeded only with congressional approval.

"C–43. Upon termination of a covered plan, the employer is liable to the PBGC for the excess of the liability for guaranteed benefits over accumulated plan assets, but not in excess of 30 percent of the employer's net worth. The PBGC is to determine the employer's net worth at a selected date up to 120 days prior to plan termination. Net worth is determined on whatever basis best reflects, in the determination of the PBGC, the current status of the employer's operations and prospects at the time chosen for determining the net worth."

3. GAAP FOR PENSION ACCOUNTING BY EMPLOYERS

To witness the longstanding controversy that has always surrounded this subject, note that the requirements for pension accounting by employers were set out as a temporary measure in 1966 in APB Opinion No. 8, *Accounting for the Cost of Pension Plans,* and that in 1985, two decades later, the FASB finally issued a final pronouncement which it described as one which "continues the evolutionary search for more meaningful and more useful pension accounting." SFAS No. 87, *Employers' Accounting for Pensions* (1985). A supplementary statement dealing with plan terminations is SFAS No. 88, *Employers' Accounting for Settlements and Curtailments of Defined Benefit Pension Plans and for Termination Benefits* (1985).

The following article is one of the most comprehensible explanations available of this most complex of all accounting pronouncements.

It may not be clear from the article that the accounting as here described for defined contribution plans is that required after *SFAS No. 87,* although that SFAS relates almost entirely to defined benefit plans. Since pension plans are intricate contracts it is often difficult to ascertain where the line is drawn between the two types. *SFAS No. 87* leaves for separate treatment the accounting for post-retirement health care benefits, which is now undergoing FASB scrutiny. Nor does *SFAS No. 87* replace *SFAS No. 35,* regulating the accounting for the retirement plan itself.

MILLER, THE NEW PENSION ACCOUNTING
J. Accountancy, Jan. 1987, pp. 98–108.*

"After six years of debate about accounting for pensions, and after due process, the Financial Accounting Standards Board issued Statement no. 87, *Employers' Accounting for Pensions,* late in December 1985 and closed what may be the most controversial project in its history. Much opposition came from the board's constituents who believed that Accounting Principles Board Opinion no. 8, *Accounting for the Cost of Pension Plans,* was satisfactory. Many of them used the familiar expression, 'If it ain't broke, don't fix it!'

"The controversy caused the board to incorporate many compromises and unusual features in its complex standard. This article * * * seek[s] to explain these complexities [and] describe why reform was needed.

"WHAT WAS BROKEN?

"The FASB identified two major problems: (1) annual pension costs were inappropriately measured, and (2) significant assets and liabilities were omitted from the statement of financial position. Given the importance of financial statements, these defects caused the FASB and other parties to consider generally accepted accounting principles in need of fixing.

"These problems can be traced to the APB's reliance on two flawed premises: (1) that defined contribution pension plans and defined benefit pension plans have equivalent economic effects on the employer and (2) that the defined benefit pension fund trust is a separate entity from the employer, in both legal form and economic substance. It is now clear that accounting practices based on these flawed premises weren't reflecting the underlying economic substance.

"WHAT GOT FIXED?

"The FASB relied on the opposite premises: (1) that defined benefit plans have different economic effects from defined contribution plans and (2) that the pension trust fund is not completely separate from the employer. The board's intent was to produce a more uniform and consistent calculation of the annual pension cost in contrast to the various measures allowed under APB Opinion no. 8. These premises also led to the recognition of some new balance sheet items in some situations.

"This article focuses on the requirements related to these problems. To make the requirements more comprehensible, let's look at the economics of pensions more closely.

"POSSIBLE PENSION ARRANGEMENTS

"There is a bewildering array of pension arrangements, but this complexity is simplified by looking at the two most basic arrangements—defined contribution and defined benefit plans. Further, defined benefit arrangements can be looked at in terms of their legal form or their economic substance.

"*Defined contribution plans.* The employer invests a specified amount on behalf of the employees and benefits are paid out of the accumulated contributions and investment income. To protect the employees, virtually all defined contribution plans establish a separate trust entity that takes control of the assets. The employees are the beneficiaries of the trust, and the employer merely contributes funds to it. [Here] the employees, the employer and the trust fund are three separate entities.

"*Defined benefit plans—legal form.* This looks much the same as a defined contribution plan. On the surface, the only difference is that the agreement defines the amounts paid out instead of the amounts contributed * * *.

"*Defined benefit plans—economic substance.* In this view, the pension trust fund provides only limited protection for the employees and the employer remains fully liable for the payment of the defined benefits. The trust is legally separate from the employer, but they are connected in economic substance. The employer is the real beneficiary [of the investment performance] not the employees.

"In substance, the fund assets [are available to pay the employer's] debt to the employees. Any excess in the fund belongs to the employer, and any deficiency must eventually be made up. * * * Two implications should be clear: (1) the employer [continues to be] liable for the promised benefits and (2) funding [of the trust] merely shifts assets [from the employer to the trust].

"FORM VERSUS SUBSTANCE

"APB Opinion no. 8 reflected the legal form perspective and concluded that the employer's pension obligation is primarily to the trust fund and that the obligation is settled by funding the current year's expense.

"Statement no. 87 [which supersedes APB *Opinion No. 8*] reflects the substance perspective and concludes that the employer remains obligated to the employees because funding is merely collateralization of the debt. This view also implies that the employer's pension expense is best measured as the change in the liability. However, various influences caused the board to settle for less than a full implementation of this view.

"The rest of this article looks at accounting requirements [for defined contribution plans and] under each of the [form and substance] views of [defined benefit plans] and under Statement no. 87 for the following four areas:

> Ongoing pension expense.
>
> Prior service costs.
>
> Statement of financial position items.
>
> Unexpected gains and losses.

"The chart [below] summarizes the key points of this discussion.

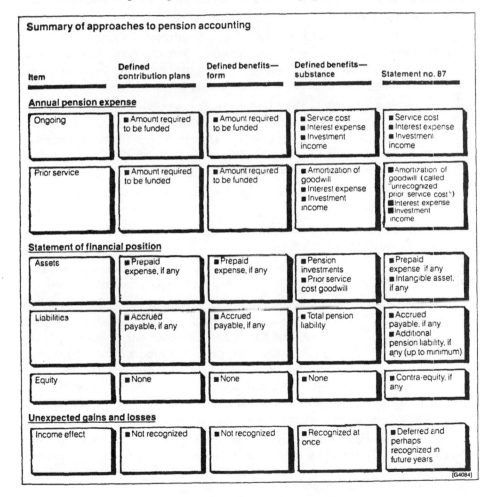

Summary of approaches to pension accounting

Item	Defined contribution plans	Defined benefits— form	Defined benefits— substance	Statement no. 87
Annual pension expense				
Ongoing	▪ Amount required to be funded	▪ Amount required to be funded	▪ Service cost ▪ Interest expense ▪ Investment income	▪ Service cost ▪ Interest expense ▪ Investment income
Prior service	▪ Amount required to be funded	▪ Amount required to be funded	▪ Amortization of goodwill ▪ Interest expense ▪ Investment income	▪ Amortization of goodwill (called "unrecognized prior service cost") ▪ Interest expense ▪ Investment income
Statement of financial position				
Assets	▪ Prepaid expense, if any	▪ Prepaid expense, if any	▪ Pension investments ▪ Prior service cost goodwill	▪ Prepaid expense if any ▪ Intangible asset, if any
Liabilities	▪ Accrued payable, if any	▪ Accrued payable, if any	▪ Total pension liability	▪ Accrued payable, if any ▪ Additional pension liability, if any (up to minimum)
Equity	▪ None	▪ None	▪ None	▪ Contra-equity, if any
Unexpected gains and losses				
Income effect	▪ Not recognized	▪ Not recognized	▪ Recognized at once	▪ Deferred and perhaps recognized in future years

[G4084]

"ONGOING PENSION EXPENSE

"Ongoing pension expense is the annual cost incurred by the employer because of its pension plan. This cost may be expensed outright or capitalized as part of the cost of an asset, such as inventory. Thus, the words 'cost' and 'expense' can be used interchangeably.

"*Defined contribution plans.* Ongoing expense for a defined contribution plan is simply the amount that the employer is obligated to contribute to the pension fund. For example, if the agreement calls for 10 percent of total salary to be paid in, and if total salaries are $15 million, pension expense is $1.5 million.

"*Defined benefit plans—form.* Because a defined benefit plan looks so much like a defined contribution plan, reliance on the legal form bases expense on the amount that can be funded to provide the promised benefits. This amount in turn is derived from the selected actuarial method, which is usually based on decisions about funding. The FASB believed GAAP needed fixing because it was based on the legal form perspective.

"*Defined benefit plans—substance.* According to the substance view, pension expense is tied to the liability and the fund assets. This view leads to using three factors to measure ongoing pension cost: service cost, interest expense and investment income.

1. Service cost is the increase in the employer's liability to the employees for their services rendered during the year. It is the same as accrued payroll cost, except that it is imprecisely estimated and deferred for a long time. It equals the present value of the additional benefits that the employer is obliged to pay.

2. Interest expense is the growth of the liability from the passage of time.

3. Investment income is earned by the fund assets and reduces pension expense.

"Because they reflect market events, the combined amount of these three items is virtually certain to differ from the amount funded.

"*Statement no. 87.* The new standard reflects the essence of the substance view. The employer is required to use the above three items to measure ongoing expense and to disclose their amounts separately in the footnotes. Service cost equals the present value of the additional expected benefits. Interest expense is found by applying the selected discount rate to the beginning balance of the liability. Investment income is the actual return earned on the fund assets. (As discussed later, the actual return is modified to become the expected return.)

"To accomplish the change from APB Opinion no. 8 practices, Statement no. 87 includes a transition component of pension expense. This item is an allocation of the net asset or net liability existing when the standard is first implemented.

"PRIOR SERVICE PENSION EXPENSE

"Prior service pension expense is created when the employer grants new or increased benefits for work in earlier periods; it arises when a pension plan is amended or a company offers a new plan. Prior service cost has been a stumbling block for standard setters, and the controversies were magnified by the unusual nature of the expense and its typically large size.

"*Defined contribution plans.* Under a defined contribution plan, prior service expense equals the additional amount that the employer agrees to contribute to the trust. For example, if an employer decides to contribute $1 million each year over the next three years to increase benefits to the employees, $1 million would be added to each year's expense when the funding occurs.

"*Defined benefit plans—form.* The legal form view of a defined benefit plan would report the prior service expense as the amount that the employer agrees to fund in each year. This practice was allowed under APB Opinion no. 8, which also allowed management to elect to fund prior service costs at a pace different from the one used to recognize the expense. The total pension cost eventually equaled the amount funded but differed in each year.

"These practices caused controversy because they spread the original cost and subsequent interest expense over the funding period selected by management instead of more meaningful and objective periods.

"*Defined benefit plans—substance.* In this view, granting new benefits for prior service is seen as the acquisition of pension goodwill in exchange for the employer's liability for the new benefits. * * *

"When this view is applied to pensions, granting the new benefits does not immediately affect income. However, income is subsequently reduced by amortizing the goodwill over its useful life and by accruing interest expense on the debt. Funding is merely a shift of resources within the entity, and the liability is reduced only when benefits are actually paid. Thus, income earned from the funded assets is offset against the amortization and the interest expense.

"*Statement no. 87.* The FASB implemented the substance perspective, as reflected in the chart. The goodwill (called unrecognized prior service costs) is amortized with an accelerated pattern based on the 'service years' expected from the affected employees. It is also acceptable to use straight-line amortization over the average remaining service life of these employees. Unlike the other three components of expense, the amount of amortization does not have to be separately disclosed.

[The great differences between economic substance and *SFAS No. 87* arise in balance sheet items and unexpected gains and losses.]

"BALANCE SHEET ITEMS

"Depending on the perspective taken, various pension items may or may not be recognized on the employer's statement of financial position.

"*Defined contribution plans.* Because the trustee of a defined contribution trust assumes the liability and assumes control of the assets, the employer should not recognize either the obligation or the investments on its statement of financial position. However, if the amount funded differs from the expense, the statement should have a prepaid expense (if funding exceeds expense) or an accrued expense (if funding falls below the expense).

"*Defined benefit plans—form.* Because a defined benefit trust looks like a defined contribution trust, a form-based analysis treats them the same. Thus, a prepaid or accrued expense appears when the amount funded is not the same as the expense. This perspective was the foundation of much of APB Opinion no. 8, and these accounts were essentially all that was recognized.

"*Defined benefit plans—substance.* Looking at economic substance gives a different picture. The trust nominally assumes the liability, but the real burden is still on the employer. Thus, it should recognize a pension liability equal to the present value of the promised benefits. Further, the fund assets belong in substance to the employer. Even though legal title rests with the trustee, the investments are committed for paying the employer's obligation and should be included among its assets. A third item that should appear on the balance sheet is the prior service pension goodwill described earlier.

"*Statement no. 87.* Much controversy about the FASB project centered on the employer's statement of financial position. Because of disagreements over what items should appear and how they should be measured, the board struck compromises that mixed form and substance practices.

"Under the new standard, the employer maintains an account called prepaid [or alternatively, accrued] pension cost, with a balance equal to the difference between the amount funded and the amount expensed. If it has a debit balance, it is like an asset; if it has a credit balance, it is like a liability.

"Each year, the employer determines if it should establish an *additional pension liability.* The test compares the fair value of the pension fund assets with the accumulated benefit obligation (ABO), which is a middle-of-the-road measure of the liability.* If the ABO is

---

* ALTERNATIVE MEASURES OF THE PENSION OBLIGATION

The FASB also faced the controversial question of how to measure the employer's defined benefit obligation.

The contractual cash flows for pensions are highly contingent on future events for their size and timing. Consequently, traditional measurement techniques are not suitable and it is necessary to fall back to predicting the future actuarially and then discounting the expected cash outflows.

A critical issue in this process is the determination of which future cash flows are present obligations of the employer.

Some people argue that only vested benefits should be included because they constitute the only legally unavoidable cash payments. This measure includes the estimated benefits to be paid to only some of the employees and is based on their present salaries. This amount is criticized for its adherence to legal form instead of substance. Perhaps not unexpectedly, the vested benefit measure played a central role in APB Opinion no. 8.

Others argue that some nonvested benefits are virtually certain to become vested and conclude that the pension liability should include the present value of some portion of them, based on actuarial projec-

greater than the plan assets' value, the difference is the minimum liability level. Depending on the relationship between the size of the minimum liability and the direction and balance of the prepaid (accrued) pension cost account, the employer may have to recognize an additional liability to get up to the minimum.

"If the additional liability must be recognized, something with an equal debit balance also must be recognized. On this point, Statement no. 87 requires the employer to recognize a *pension intangible asset*. However, this asset is not amortized.

"If there were no constraints, an employer could report a pension intangible without having any underlying goodwill because the intangible is created whenever the plan is underfunded, which can happen

tions of turnover. People within this group disagree whether the calculation should be based on the employees' current or expected salaries.

Proponents of the smaller accumulated benefit obligation (ABO) argue that the employer can be obligated only for benefits based on the current salaries. They assert that the future salary levels are established by future events, whereas a liability can exist only for past events. The ABO is the fundamental measure of the pension liability in statements no. 35, *Accounting and Reporting by Defined Benefit Pension Plans*, and no. 36, *Disclosure of Pension Information*. It is used in Statement no. 87 only for determining the size of the minimum liability, and its amount is disclosed in the footnote.

Proponents of the larger projected benefit obligation (PBO) argue that the employer has a larger liability because it is obligated to pay a percentage of the employee's final salary, which is reasonably expected to be greater than the current salary. The PBO plays a central role in Statement no. 87, particularly in measuring the ongoing service cost, the prior service cost and the interest components of annual pension expense. The PBO is also used in measuring gains and losses, and its amount is disclosed in the footnote.

The accompanying diagram illustrates the size relationships among the vested, accumulated benefit and projected benefit obligations.

Additional benefits for all employees at future salaries

Additional benefits for all employees at present salaries

Benefits for vested employees at present salaries

Vested benefits obligation

Accumulated benefits obligation (ABO)

Projected benefits obligation (PBO)

[G5986]

with or without the granting of prior service costs. Accordingly, Statement no. 87 requires that the intangible be no larger than the balance of unamortized prior service costs that have not yet been allocated to annual expense.

"If the additional liability is greater than the maximum intangible, the employer needs another debit. For example, if the additional liability is $1 million and unrecognized prior service costs are only $800,000, the employer needs another $200,000 debit. One approach would simply debit a loss and eventually reduce retained earnings. Statement no. 87 requires an alternative that debits a *contra-stockholders' equity* account—a nonarticulated reduction in equity that bypasses the income statement. (Similar items are created under Statement no. 12, *Accounting for Certain Marketable Securities,* for losses on such securities and under Statement no. 52, *Foreign Currency Translation,* for certain currency translation gains and losses.) The board went further by requiring the employer to defer taxes because it considered this nonarticulated debit to be a timing difference.

"UNEXPECTED GAINS AND LOSSES

"Another controversial issue was what to do about the volatility of pension expense. Many accountants believe that volatility is something to be avoided. Some don't like it for pensions because they think that the agreement is long term in nature and that the employer's progress should be evaluated without pollution from short-term swings. Others don't like it because they think that actuarial measurement methods are more volatile than the real underlying economic activity and conditions. Others simply don't like volatility because it makes the company appear more risky. Whatever the reasons, concerns about volatility focused attention on unexpected gains and losses from changes in the market value of pension fund assets and from changes in actuarial estimates of the liability.

"*Defined contribution plans.* For defined contribution pension plans, there is nothing to worry about because any unexpected gains and losses affect only the employees' trust fund and its financial statements.

"*Defined benefit plans—form.* If only the form of defined benefit plans is considered, they look like defined contribution plans and unexpected gains and losses can be ignored.

"In practice, however, most agreements require the employer to make larger contributions if unexpected events lead to underfunding, and may allow reduced funding if an excess accumulates. These gains and losses could then be reflected in higher or lower pension expense in the future, in accordance with the funding policy. The end result is that the unexpected gains and losses are smoothed out.

"*Defined benefit plans—substance.* Under the substance view, changes in the market value of the assets and the estimate of the pension liability immediately affect the employer's financial condition.

The simplest approach merely revalues the assets and the liability for expected and unexpected gains and losses, and the net change in equity is reported in income for the same year.

"*Statement no. 87.* The board compromised on this issue and created what are probably the most unusual practices in the standard.

"First, the combined expected and unexpected changes in the value of the fund assets are disclosed in the footnotes as the actual return earned during the year. However, the effect of the unexpected gains and losses is backed out in coming to the bottom-line pension expense reported on the income statement. Consequently, the income statement reports net expense based on only the expected gains and losses. Second, unexpected gains and losses from changes in the estimated pension liability created by new actuarial assumptions are not recognized on the income statement and are not separately reported in the footnotes.

"All the unrecognized gains and losses are pooled in a memo record kept outside the formal accounts. However, the FASB wanted to keep this amount from getting so large that its absence would distort the financial statements.

"This concern led the board to invent 'corridor amortization.' The employer is required to monitor the balance accumulated in the memo record. When it gets too large, part of it is funneled back into pension expense for the year. The board determined that the balance gets too large when it exceeds 10 percent of the larger of the projected benefit obligation (PBO) or the value of the plan assets. (This choice is clearly arbitrary, but there were no nonarbitrary choices available.)

"If this limit is exceeded, the employer divides the excess by the number of years in the average remaining service life of the active employees. This result is then added to pension expense if the memo record shows more deferred losses than gains or deducted if it shows more deferred gains than losses.

"For example, suppose that the PBO is $10 million, the fund assets are $9 million and the employer has deferred $1.5 million of unexpected losses. Because the PBO is larger than the plan assets, the limits of the corridor are plus or minus 10 percent of $10 million, or $1 million. Thus, the employer has an excess deferred loss of $500,000. If the average remaining service life of its employees is 20 years, $25,000 of the loss should be added to pension expense.

"The board acknowledged the arbitrariness of this approach by allowing the employer to use any amortization method as long as it produces an effect equal to or greater than the one described.

"MORE REPAIRS NEEDED

"This article provides a highly condensed overview of Statement no. 87. Because of the standard's complexity, many of its features have not been covered, including the required disclosures, which are more extensive than those established in Statement no. 36, *Disclosure of*

Pension Information. The ✱ ✱ ✱ main goal of this ✱ ✱ ✱ article is to explain why the FASB considered GAAP 'broken' and in need of fixing. It also shows what was considered a suitable repair job.

"Even though the board considers pension accounting 'fixed,' its members were not completely convinced that they had made GAAP as good as new. Consider this quote from paragraph 5 of Statement no. 87: 'The FASB believes that the conclusions it has reached are a worthwhile and significant step in that direction, but it also believes that those conclusions are not likely to be the final step in that evolution. Pension accounting in 1985 is still in a transitional stage. . . . '

"Despite this disclaimer, however, the FASB has not made another appointment for further repairs. Based on my experience with the project and its controversies, I do not think it likely that the issues will come back until the board has a new set of members and a new generation of constituent representatives. Thus, at this juncture, accountants need to understand Statement no. 87 and know how to put it into practice."

Perhaps because Professor Miller was involved in working on *SFAS No. 87,* he does not make clear that under this standard not only are liabilities shown at less than they are in substance, but also charges to expense are substantially deferred. Both of these consequences, as Miller states, were due to the concerns of sponsors that their income statements and balance sheets would look bad otherwise, and perhaps various legal and economic disabilities were anticipated [e.g., from violation of debt covenants]. These fears caused intense pressure and the ultimate compromises of *SFAS No. 87* which have left no one satisfied.

For the tenacious, the following is a basic illustration of the accounting process just described.

EXCERPT FROM M. BACKER, P. ELGERS, AND R. ASEBROOK, FINANCIAL ACCOUNTING
pp. 496–501 (1988).*

"Measuring and Reporting of Pension Expense

"On January 1, 1987, the One Hoss Shay Company was established by 40 members of the graduating MBA class of State University. The entire group plans to retire at the end of 20 years. At that time, the pension will be calculated as follows: for each year of employment, each individual will receive a lump sum pension equal to ten percent of the salary earned during the year of retirement. (An employee with 20 years of service will receive 200 percent of the final year's salary when he retires.) Presently, each employee earns $40,000 per year. Salaries are expected to grow at a rate of six percent each year, and the time value of money is eight percent per year. On January 1, 1987, the company made a $150,000 contribution to the pension plan, which has been invested in assets expected to earn eight percent each year. At the end of the first year, the plan assets have a market value of $170,000. The pertinent actuarial assumptions include the discount rate (eight percent), the rate of salary increase (six percent), and employee turnover (none).

"For 1987, the interest cost and service cost components of pension expense are computed as follows:

Interest cost, 1987: Because there were no future benefits earned at the beginning of the year, there is no interest cost in this year. Interest cost for the second year of the plan will be calculated later.

Service cost, 1987:

Present salary, covered employees ($40,000 × 40)	$1,600,000
Future value factor at 6 percent, $(1.06)^{19}$ [Appendix Table 3]	× 3.026
Salary projected for year preceding retirement	$4,841,600
Percentage earned in current period	× .10
Projected future pension benefit earned in current period	$ 484,160
Present value factor at 8 percent, $(1.08)^{-19}$ [Appendix Table 1]	× .232
Service cost, current period	$ 112,325

The calculation has required that the projected change in future benefits due to the current period's employment ($484,160) be discounted to the present; that is, the 19 years remaining until retirement.

Return on plan assets, 1987: This negative component of pension cost is computed at the *expected* return rate of eight percent:

Beginning balance in plan assets	$ 150,000
Expected rate of return	× .08
Return on plan assets	$ 12,000

Amortization of unrecognized gains and losses, 1987: There is an unrecognized gain of $8,000 in the One Hoss Shay Company's pension plan, because the plan's assets of $170,000 are greater than the $162,000 ($150,000 beginning balance plus $12,000 return) that was expected. Because this gain does not exceed 10 percent of the beginning-of-the-year pension plan assets ($150,000), no amortization is required.

Amortization of unrecognized prior service cost, 1987: There are no prior service costs, because all services from covered employees are received after the date of plan adoption. If there were prior service costs, they would be recognized as expense evenly over the remaining service lives of the employees covered.

As a result of all of the preceding pension calculations, One Hoss Shay's 1987 net pension cost is $100,325, as follows:

Service cost	$ 112,325
Interest cost	0
Return on plan assets	(12,000)
Amortization of unrecognized gains or losses	0
Amortization of unrecognized prior service cost	0
Net pension cost	$ 100,325

"It is useful to extend this example through the second year—1988—to illustrate the interest cost calculation and the change in the present value of the pension obligation. Assume that One Hoss Shay Company contributes an additional $150,000 to the pension plan on January 1, 1988, and that the plan assets have a market value of $340,000 at the end of 1988.

Second year, 1988 pension cost

Interest cost, 1988: The present value of the projected pension obligations was $112,325 at the beginning of 1988 (equal to the balance at the end of 1987). If no additional benefits were earned during 1988, the present value of the projected obligations would have increased by eight percent due solely to the passage of time.

Present value at the beginning of the year, of projected benefits earned in prior years	$ 112,325
Discount rate	× .08
Interest cost	$ 8,986

Service cost, 1988:

Salary projected for the year of retirement (same as that computed in 1987)	$4,841,600
Percentage earned in current period	× .10
Projected future pension benefit earned in current period	$ 484,160
Present value factor at 8 percent, $(1.08)^{-18}$ [Appendix Table 1]	× .250
Service cost, current period	$ 121,040

"The present value of the projected pension obligation at the end of 1988 may be computed in one of two ways:

Present value of present projected pension obligation at beginning of the year	$ 112,325
Interest cost on beginning balance	8,986
Service cost, current year	121,040
Present value of projected pension obligation	$ 242,351

Alternative calculation:

Salary projected for the year of retirement (same as computed in 1987)	$4,841,600
Percentage earned through end of 1988	× .20
Projected future pension benefit earned through end of 1988	$ 968,320
Present value factor at 8 percent, $(1.08)^{-18}$ [Appendix Table 1]	× .250
Present value of projected pension obligation (slight difference due to rounding)	$ 242,080

Return on plan assets: At the beginning of 1988 the plan assets had a market value of $320,000 ($170,000 end of 1987 value, plus $150,000 additional contribution).

Beginning balance in plan assets	$ 320,000
Expected rate of return	× .08
Return on plan assets	$ 25,600

Amortization of unrecognized gains and losses, 1988: During 1988, there is an unrecognized loss of $5,600 because the plan's assets of $340,000 are less than the expected amount of $345,600 ($320,000 beginning balance plus $25,600 expected return). The net unrecognized gain is $2,400 ($8,000 gain in 1987, and $5,600 loss in 1988), which is not large enough to require amortization.

Amortization of unrecognized prior service costs, 1988: Not applicable.

"Consequently, the net pension costs for 1987 and 1988 may be compared as follows:

Net Pension Cost	1987	1988
Service cost	$112,325	$121,040
Interest cost	0	8,986
Return on plan assets	(12,000)	(25,600)
Amortization, gains and losses	0	0
Amortization, prior service cost	0	0
	$100,325	$104,426

"In general, for an employee group with little turnover and a pension plan that is funded currently (that is, employer contributions approximately match current service costs), the service cost, interest cost, and returns on plan assets will increase over time.

"The remaining portion of this chapter describes the measurement and reporting of pension assets and liabilities.

"Measuring and Reporting of Pension Assets and Liabilities

"If management decides to contribute to the pension plan in an amount that differs from the period's net pension expense, pension assets or liabilities will result. For example, recall that the One Hoss Shay Company decided to fund its plan at the rate of $150,000 per year in 1987 and 1988. Net pension expenses (computed previously) were

$100,325 in 1987 and $104,426 in 1988, and the following journal entries were recorded:

1987:	dr.	Pension Expense	100,325	
	dr.	Prepaid Pension Cost	49,675	
		cr. Cash		150,000
1988:	dr.	Pension Expense	104,426	
	dr.	Prepaid Pension Cost	45,574	
		cr. Cash		150,000

"As a result, at the end of 1988 the company would report a balance of $95,249 ($49,675 + $45,574) as an asset on the balance sheet, reflecting the excess of its cumulative contributions over its cumulative net pension expenses. If, on the other hand, the cash funding is less than the pension expense, a liability for accrued pension cost will be created.

"In many cases, the FASB's new rules require that firms recognize additional liabilities beyond those created by differences between cumulative contributions and cumulative expenses. These additional liabilities are due primarily to three factors: (1) substantial prior service costs at the time of the adoption or amendment of pension plans, (2) methods used to compute pension expenses and fund pension plans prior to the adoption of SFAS No. 87 in late 1985, and (3) lower than expected returns on plan assets. If at the balance sheet date the accumulated pension benefit obligation of the pension plan exceeds the value of the plan's assets (plus or minus any pension liabilities or assets appearing on the balance sheet), an additional liability must be recorded. To illustrate, assume that Golden Harvester, Inc., provides the following information at December 31, 1987:

Pension plan assets, at fair value	$520 million
Accrued pension cost (liability)	$ 45 million
Accumulated pension benefit obligation	$600 million

"In this case, Golden Harvester, Inc., would be required to recognize an additional liability of $35 million, computed in this manner:

Accumulated pension benefit obligation	$ 600 million
Less: Accrued pension cost (liability)	(45 million)
Unrecognized pension obligation	$ 555 million
Less: Pension plan assets, at fair value	(520 million)
Net pension liability	$ 35 million

"If the recording of such an additional liability is required, offsetting amounts must be recorded. The offsetting amount is recorded as an intangible asset not to exceed the amount of the firm's unrecognized prior service cost. If the amount of the additional liability recorded is greater than the firm's unrecognized prior service cost, the excess of this liability over prior service cost is recorded as a negative shareholders' equity account. If Golden Harvester has unrecognized prior service costs of $21 million, the required adjustment would be:

dr. Intangible Pension Asset   21,000,000

dr. Excess Additional Pension   14,000,000
      Liability over
      Unrecognized Service
      Cost

    cr. Pension Liability   35,000,000

"The rationale for recording the intangible pension asset at a value not to exceed the amount of unrecognized prior service cost is that prior service costs are intended to benefit future periods. Accordingly, the intangible pension asset will be amortized over the service life of the employee group to which it applies.[4] There is no clear interpretation of the negative shareholders' equity account, however; it is employed mainly as the result of inadequate pension funding or lower than expected returns on plan investments in previous periods.

"The accumulated benefit obligation used in these calculations does not correspond to the present value of the projected pension benefits that was used earlier in computing the service cost component of net pension expense. The difference between these amounts stems from the fact that the accumulated benefit obligation ignores future compensation changes and instead assumes that pension benefits will be based on present salary levels. The rate used in discounting the pension benefits in order to compute the accumulated benefits obligation, on the other hand, is based on prevailing market rates of interest, which incorporate investor expectations concerning inflation. This is a basic inconsistency, because in computing the present value of the accumulated benefit obligation, the numerator of the present value calculation assumes no inflation, while the denominator of the calculation assumes the level of inflation reflected in prevailing interest rates. As a consequence, if prices (and salary levels) are expected to increase, then the accumulated benefit obligation will be less than the present value of the projected pension obligation.

"The extent to which the accumulated benefit obligation differs from the present value of projected pension liabilities depends on both the discount rate selected and the rate of salary growth to be expected. If the accumulated benefit obligation is computed using a relatively low rate (five or six percent per annum), then the difference is likely to be minor because the rate of inflation assumed in the discount rate is low. If on the other hand, relatively high rates of discount are used, then the difference is likely to be substantial."

4. This intangible asset is amortized in a unique way through the prior service cost portion of the net pension expense. There is no individual entry made to debit amortization expense and credit an intangible asset account.

D. DISCLOSURE

SFAS No. 87, ¶ 54, prescribes disclosure of the following in addition to the accounting described above.

a. A description of the plan including employee groups covered, type of benefit formula, funding policy, types of assets held and significant nonbenefit liabilities, if any, and the nature and effect of significant matters affecting comparability of information for all periods presented

b. The amount of net periodic pension cost for the period showing separately the service cost component, the interest cost component, the actual return on assets for the period, and the net total of other components

c. A schedule reconciling the funded status of the plan with amounts reported in the employer's statement of financial position, showing separately:

(1) The fair value of plan assets

(2) The projected benefit obligation identifying the accumulated benefit obligation and the vested benefit obligation

(3) The amount of unrecognized prior service cost

(4) The amount of unrecognized net gain or loss (including asset gains and losses not yet reflected in market-related value)

(5) The amount of any remaining unrecognized net obligation or net asset existing at the date of initial application of this Statement

(6) The amount of any additional liability recognized pursuant to paragraph 36

(7) The amount of net pension asset or liability recognized in the statement of financial position pursuant to paragraphs 35 and 36 (which is the net result of combining the preceding six items)

d. The weighted-average assumed discount rate and rate of compensation increase (if applicable) used to measure the projected benefit obligation and the weighted-average expected long-term rate of return on plan assets

e. If applicable, the amounts and types of securities of the employer and related parties included in plan assets, and the approximate amount of annual benefits of employees and retirees covered by annuity contracts issued by the employer and related parties.

To illustrate ¶ 54 as well as the SEC's requirements for the Management's Discussion and Analysis ("MD&A") section of the annual report, we reproduce a portion of AT&T's MD&A and a footnote to its 1989 financials.

Excerpt from AT&T's MD&A:

In the fourth quarter of 1989, we amended our management pension plan to make more managers service pension-eligible with improved pension benefits. For managers with five or more years of service as of December 30, 1989, the amendment added five years of age and service to determine service pension-eligibility as well as a frozen minimum pension benefit. The changes apply until pensions calculated using actual age and service are higher. We also offered a special retirement option which further increased pension payments for all managers who chose to retire on December 30, 1989. The 12,500 managers who elected to retire on that date will receive an additional 15 percent pension benefit for five years or until age 65, whichever is earlier. This option was accounted for as a termination payment and increased total costs and expenses for the fourth quarter of 1989 by $163 million. Payments will be made from pension plan assets. Our future pension fund contributions will be higher because of the plan amendment and the special retirement option. * * *

Increases in total costs and expenses over the past two years also came from higher expenditures for employee and retiree health care benefits. To control growth in this area, we established a cap on the health care insurance premiums we will pay on behalf of employees who retire on or after March 1, 1990. The cap may require those retirees to contribute to health care costs for themselves and their dependents beginning July 1, 1995.

The Financial Accounting Standards Board has issued an exposure draft of a new standard on accounting for postretirement benefits other than pensions. The standard is expected to be issued in 1990 and, beginning in 1992, would require companies to accrue postretirement expenses during the years employees are working. Presently, AT&T and most other American businesses expense these benefits as the costs are incurred by retirees. The effect of the new standard would be to increase reported expenses when adopted.

Excerpt from footnotes to financial statements of AT&T:

(M) Employee Benefit Plans

Pension Plans

The Company sponsors non-contributory defined benefit plans covering substantially all management and non-management employees. Benefits for management employees are based on a career average pay plan; benefits for non-management employees are based on a plan that is not directly pay-related.

The Company's pension contributions are made to trust funds that are held for the sole benefit of pension plan participants. Contributions are determined using the aggregate cost method, an acceptable funding method under the Employee Retirement Income Security Act of 1974, and in accordance with appropriate Internal Revenue Service regulations.

Pension cost is computed using the projected unit credit method in accordance with FAS No. 87, "Employers' Accounting for Pensions."

Pension cost includes the following components:

	1989	1988	1987
Service cost—benefits earned during the period	$ 415	$ 425	$ 447
Interest cost on projected benefit obligation	1,583	1,438	1,356
Amortization of unrecognized prior service costs*	73	39	22
Credit for expected return on plan assets†	(2,072)	(1,785)	(1,651)
Amortization of transition asset	(480)	(480)	(480)
Charge for special retirement option	163	—	—
Net pension cost (credit)	$ (318)	$ (363)	$ (306)

* These costs pertain to plan amendments in 1989 and prior years and are amortized on a straight line basis over the average remaining service period of active employees.

† The actual return on plan assets was $5,871, $3,363, and $1,499 in 1989, 1988 and 1987, respectively.

The funded status of the plan was as follows:

At December 31	1989	1988
Actuarial present value of accumulated benefit obligation, including vested benefits of $19,325 and $15,260, respectively	$21,395	$17,146
Plan assets at market value	$33,397	$28,477
Less: Actuarial present value of projected benefit obligation	21,988	18,315
Excess of assets over projected benefit obligation	11,409	10,162
Unrecognized prior service costs	1,537	663
Unrecognized transition asset	(5,718)	(6,198)
Unrecognized net gain	(5,120)	(3,255)
Adjustment to recognize minimum liability for non-qualified plan	(41)	–
Prepaid pension cost in balance sheet	$ 2,067	$ 1,372

The projected benefit obligation was determined using discount rates of 8.25% and 8.75% at December 31, 1989 and 1988, respectively, and an assumed long-term rate of compensation increase of 5.0%. The expected long-term rate of return on plan assets used in determining pension cost was 8.5% for 1989 and 8.0% for 1988 and 1987. The unrecognized transition asset is being amortized over 15.9 years. Plan assets consist primarily of listed stocks, corporate and governmental debt, and real estate investments.

In October 1989, the Company amended its management pension plan to make more managers service pension-eligible with improved pension benefits. For all management employees with at least five years service as of December 30, 1989, the amendment adds five years of age and service to determine service pension-eligibility as well as a frozen minimum pension benefit. The changes apply until pensions calculated using actual age and service are higher. The Company also offered a special retirement option for employees eligible to retire on December 30, 1989. Those employees who elected to retire on that date will receive an additional 15% benefit as part of their monthly pension for five years or until age 65, whichever is earlier. The special retirement option was accounted for as a termination benefit in accordance with FAS No. 88, "Employers' Accounting for Settlements and Curtailments of Defined Benefit Pension Plans and for Termination Benefits". Accordingly, pension cost for fourth quarter 1989 included a one-time charge of $163 million. Payments will be made from pension plan assets.

Savings Plans

The Company sponsors savings plans for substantially all employees. These plans allow employees to contribute a portion of their pretax or after-tax income in accordance with specified guidelines. AT&T matches a percentage of these contributions up to certain limitations. Such costs amounted to $277 in 1989, $274 in 1988 and $248 in 1987.

General Electric's 1989 financials include the following note.

Note 6 Pensions and Other Retiree Benefits

GE and its affiliates sponsor a number of pension and other retiree benefit plans. This note summarizes important financial aspects of GE's obligations for these plans. Measurements of obligations and costs are based on actuarial calculations involving various assumptions as to future events.

Principal pension plans

The principal pension plans are the GE Pension Plan (GE Plan) and the GE Supplementary Pension Plan (Supplementary Plan). The RCA Retirement Plan (RCA Plan) was merged with the GE Pension Plan at the end of 1988. Amounts and comments about the GE Plan in this note include the RCA Plan for all periods shown. Other pension plans are sponsored by domestic and foreign affiliates but these are not considered to be significant individually or in the aggregate to the consolidated financial position.

The GE Plan covers substantially all employees in the United States, including approximately 50% of GEFS employees. Generally, benefits are based on the greater of a formula recognizing career earnings or a formula recognizing length of service and final average earnings. Benefits are funded through the GE Pension Trust. At the end of 1989, approximately 208,900 employees were covered, approximately 122,900 former employees with vested rights were entitled to future benefits and approximately 154,500 retirees or beneficiaries were receiving benefits.

The Supplementary Plan is an unfunded plan providing supplementary retirement benefits primarily to higher-level, longer-service management and professional employees in the United States. At the end of 1989, about 3,400 employees were eligible for this plan, and about 4,100 retirees or beneficiaries were receiving benefits.

Statement of Financial Accounting Standards (SFAS) No. 87 requires use of the projected unit credit cost method to determine the projected benefit obligation and plan cost. The projected benefit obligation is the actuarial present value of the portion of projected future benefits that is attributed to employee service to date. The benefit cost for service during the year is the portion of the projected benefit obligation that is attributed to employee service during the year. This cost method recognizes the effect of future compensation and service in projecting the future benefits.

In addition, SFAS No. 87 establishes a "transition gain."

This is the excess at January 1, 1986 (when the Company adopted SFAS No. 87) of the current fair market value of plan assets over the plan's projected benefit obligation. This transition gain is being amortized over 15 years except that such excess for the RCA Plan was recognized as an asset in accounting for the RCA acquisition in 1986.

Gains and losses that occur because actual experience differs from that assumed are amortized over the average future service period of employees. Prior-service cost for changes in pension benefits that are allocable to previous periods of service are amortized in the same manner.

Actuarial assumptions for the principal pension plans include 8.5% for both the assumed discount rate used to determine the present value of future benefits and the expected long-term rate of return on plan assets. The assumed rate of average future increases in pension benefit compensation is 6.5%.

Employer costs for the principal pension plans in 1989 and 1988 recognized the impact of continued favorable investment performance. Benefit costs for service during the year recognize plan design changes in 1988. For example, beginning in 1989, employee contributions no longer reduce pension costs because such contributions are used to provide additional pension benefits. Details of cost for the principal pension plans follow.

Cost for principal pension plans (In millions)	1989	1988	1987
Benefit cost for service during the year—net of employee contributions	$ 413	$ 300	$ 385
Interest cost on projected benefit obligation	1,259	1,232	1,187
Recognized return on plan assets	(1,574)	(1,460)	(1,293)
Net amortization	(339)	(299)	(254)
Net pension cost	$ (241)	$ (227)	$ 25
Details of return on plan assets			
Actual return on plan assets	$4,026	$2,261	$1,237
Recognized return on plan assets	(1,574)	(1,460)	(1,293)
Unrecognized return on plan assets	$2,452	$ 801	$ (56)

Recognized return on plan assets is determined by applying the expected long-term rate of return to the market-related value of assets.

Funding policy for the GE Plan is to contribute amounts sufficient to meet minimum funding requirements set forth in U.S. employee benefit and tax laws plus such additional amounts as GE may determine to be appropriate from time to time. GE made no contribution for 1989 and 1988 because the funding status of the GE Plan precluded current tax deduction and a contribution would have generated an excise tax.

The funding status of an ongoing plan may be measured by comparing the market-related value of assets with the projected benefit obligation. The market-related value of assets is based on amortized cost plus recognition of market appreciation and depreciation in the portfolio over five years. GE believes the market-related value of assets is a more realistic measure than current fair market value because the market-related value reduces the impact of short-term market fluctuations. The funding status for the principal pension plans follows.

Funding status for principal pension plans

December 31 (In millions)	1989	1988
Market-related value of assets	$ 20,794	$ 19,308
Projected benefit obligation	16,057	15,473

A schedule reconciling the projected benefit obligation for principal pension plans with GE's recorded pension liability is shown below.

Reconciliation of projected benefit obligation with pension liability for principal pension plans

December 31 (In millions)	1989	1988
Projected benefit obligation	$ 16,057	$ 15,473
Less current fair market value of trust assets	(24,211)	(21,502)
Unrecognized SFAS No. 87 transition gain	1,693	1,847
Other unrecognized net experience gains	5,333	3,303
Unrecognized prior-service cost	90	114
Recorded prepaid pension assets	1,469	1,177
Recorded pension liability	$ 431	$ 412

The portion of the projected benefit obligation representing the accumulated benefit obligation amounted to $14,940 million and $14,073 million at the ends of 1989 and 1988, respectively. The vested benefit obligation was $14,721 million and $13,895 million at the ends of 1989 and 1988, respectively. These amounts are based on compensation and service to date.

Trust assets consist mainly of common stock and fixed income investments. Trust assets included GE common stock valued at $201 million at year-end 1989 ($139 million at year-end 1988) mainly held in connection with an indexed portfolio.

Other unrecognized net experience gains resulted principally from favorable investment performance.

Chapter XIII

FOREIGN CURRENCY TRANSLATION IN INTERNATIONAL BUSINESS

OBJECTIVES

Grasp the basics of measuring rights and obligations in accounting for international trade.

RELEVANCE TO LAWYERS

As business has become international in character for all but the smallest firms, practicing lawyers have been increasingly mystified by foreign currency translation problems and often fail to understand the consequences of drafting contracts in one form or another. This short chapter should clarify the issues to enable a lawyer to be more comfortable in dealing with accounting and international financial transactions.

Unfortunately for today's law students the world of business has become more complex geographically as well as in most other respects. Whereas international business transactions were an exotic rarity in a business practice many years ago, today they are commonplace for most medium-sized law firms. Doubtless they will become even more common over the coming decade as the U.S. economy becomes more interdependent with those of foreign nations. Even in inland cities, many local companies have dealings in the Americas, Europe, and Asia. A large majority of the 500 largest business corporations have foreign subsidiaries. Tapping of the international financial markets is not uncommon even for a strictly local business like cement manufacturing or steel processing. Hence it is impossible to ignore the accounting problems posed.

While the issue of foreign currency translation can be complex, there are only two underlying questions:

(a) How should the foreign currency financial statements of a foreign subsidiary be translated to U.S. dollars?

(b) How should any of the accounts of a domestic company that are originally expressed in units of foreign currency, e.g., a U.S. company that has borrowed money overseas, be translated into U.S. dollars?

Of course, there is a fundamental question about whether the financial statements of a foreign subsidiary should be consolidated with the financial statements of the domestic parent (or even included on the equity method). This question raises some complex issues which are not dealt with in this book.

For the most part, multi-national U.S. companies do include their foreign operations in consolidated financial statements. This is done by multiplying the foreign currency amounts by an exchange rate. If the exchange rate for U.S. dollars and German marks is 2.6510 marks to the dollar, one might think it a simple matter to translate the statements of a German subsidiary. And so it would be if the ratio were constant over time. But anyone who has traveled is well aware that the exchange rate fluctuates from day to day and, over any period of time, may vary widely. Coupled with the fact that transactions take place at various times, the problem is posed as to which dates' exchange rates should be applied.

Until 1981, foreign currency financial statements were translated based on the principles of SFAS No. 8, *Accounting for the Translation of Foreign Currency Transactions and Foreign Currency Financial Statements* (1975). That statement required that the cost of plant and inventories and other similar nonmonetary assets be translated according to the exchange rate at the date of acquisition of the particular asset while monetary assets and liabilities (cash, accounts payable, etc.) were translated at the year-end current exchange rate. This method is still in use for a large portion of foreign operations. We refer to this as the "dual monetary-nonmonetary rate" method here, although this is not a commonly used term.

To illustrate the effects of this dual translation process before 1981, assume that a U.S. firm had a Canadian subsidiary which not only conducted business in Canada but basically ran that business as a Canadian company and used its profits there to expand its operations rather than exchanging its Canadian funds for U.S. funds and transferring them to the U.S. *SFAS No. 8* required monetary assets to be translated at the rate in existence at the statement date but nonmonetary assets at the rate in existence at the transaction date. Therefore, the purchase of a Canadian plant for $10,000 (Canadian) when the rate was $1.00 (Canadian) = $.80 (U.S.) would result in the plant being translated at $8,000 (U.S.) both at acquisition and at year end. Assuming that the plant was acquired entirely by funds borrowed in Canada, and the year end rate was $1.00 (Canadian) = $.81 (U.S.), the liability, which originally was the equivalent of $8,000 (U.S.), would be translated at $8,100 (U.S.), thus resulting in a reported loss of $100, when in fact the loan will be paid in Canadian funds generated from the profits of the Canadian plant and no loss will be incurred. Thus real economic effects were not being portrayed in the translated financial statements in this situation.

To illustrate this treatment we may establish comparative balance sheets using Canadian dollars in comparison with U.S. dollars:

"Dual Monetary–Nonmonetary Rate" Method:

Balance Sheet at Date of Transaction
(Rate: $1 (Can.) = $.80 (U.S.))

	$(Canadian)	$(U.S.)
Assets:		
Plant	$10,000	$8,000
Liabilities and Equity:		
Notes Payable	10,000	8,000
Equity	–0–	–0–

Balance Sheet at Year End
(Rate: $1 (Can.) = $.81 (U.S.))

	$(Canadian)	$(U.S.)
Assets:		
Plant	$10,000	$8,000
Liabilities and Equity:		
Notes Payable	10,000	8,100
Equity (Deficit)	–0–	(100)

On the parent's consolidated or equity method income statement the $100 would be depicted as a loss, reducing net income. Notice that on the Canadian subsidiary's books there is, of course, no gain or loss just as no translation gain or loss appears on the U.S. parent's books for its other, U.S., operations.

SFAS No. 52, *Foreign Currency Translation* (1981) was issued to overcome this result. The objective of *SFAS No. 52* is to achieve accounting results that reflect the diversity of economic circumstances surrounding foreign operations. In particular, the standard recognizes that because foreign operations differ greatly in structure and substance, no single method of translation is appropriate in all circumstances. *SFAS No. 52* instead established two basic treatments. First, foreign operations are translated using either the same dual monetary-nonmonetary translation method (the method formerly required in all cases by *SFAS No. 8*) or the "single current rate" method, to be explained below, depending on the circumstances. Second, translation gains and losses that result from applying the current rate method are recorded in a separate shareholders' equity account rather than in net income.

The Canadian subsidiary discussed above can be used to illustrate the changes made to the translation rules. Since the Canadian subsidiary is a self-contained foreign operation, the local currency financial statements would be translated using the new single current rate method. Under this method the plant as well as the loan would be translated at the statement date exchange rate, resulting in a balance of $8,100 (U.S.) for each of the asset, Plant, and the liability, Notes Payable, at year end. Income would not be affected, thus eliminating the accounting loss that was created by the use of mixed historical rates and closing rates that were required by *SFAS No. 8.*

To illustrate:

"Single Current Rate" Method:

Balance Sheet at Date of Transaction
(Rate: $1 (Can.) = $.80 (U.S.))

	$(Canadian)	$(U.S.)
Assets:		
Plant	$10,000	$8,000
Liabilities and Equity:		
Notes Payable	10,000	8,000
Equity	–0–	–0–

Balance Sheet at Year End
(Rate: $1 (Can.) = $.81 (U.S.))

	$(Canadian)	$(U.S.)
Assets:		
Plant	$10,000	$8,100
Liabilities and Equity:		
Notes Payable	10,000	8,100
Equity	–0–	–0–

Any translation gain or loss that would result from using the single current rate method would bypass the income statement and not be reported in the translated income statement. In our Canadian subsidiary example, assets equaled liabilities and equity was zero, and so a change in exchange rates merely changed the U.S. dollar translated amounts without creating a translation gain or loss. If, as in the more normal case, assets exceeded liabilities, as would occur, say, if only

$7,000 (Can.) had been borrowed, the translation gain or loss on net worth ($30 (U.S.) gain) would be recorded in a separate component of equity account, thereby excluding any erratic unrealized translation gains and losses from affecting consolidated income.

To illustrate:

"Single Current Rate" Method:

Balance Sheet at Date of Transaction
(Rate: $1 (Can.) = $.80 (U.S.))

	$(Canadian)	$(U.S.)
Assets:		
Plant	$10,000	$8,000
Liabilities and Equity:		
Notes Payable	7,000	5,600
Equity	3,000	2,400
Total Liabilities and Equity	$10,000	$8,000

Balance Sheet at Year End
(Rate: $1 (Can.) = $.81 (U.S.))

	$(Canadian)	$(U.S.)
Assets:		
Plant	$10,000	$8,100
Liabilities and Equity:		
Notes Payable	7,000	5,670
Equity	3,000	2,430
Total Liabilities and Equity	$10,000	$8,100

The $30 "gain" in equity will not be reflected as income in the income statement.

It should be noted that in some cases under *SFAS No. 52*, the dual monetary-nonmonetary method instead would be the appropriate translation method to use. For example, consider that the Canadian subsidiary, instead of being self-contained, was an extension of the U.S. parent and depended on the parent for financing and that the subsidiary relies on the parent for the product it sells in the Canadian market and sales proceeds are remitted back to the parent. *SFAS No. 52* in this case would require that the dual rate monetary-nonmonetary translation method be used.

Problem

13-1. Problem. What would the accounting results be under the last set of facts posed, using the dual rate monetary-nonmonetary method?

Multi-national companies are often affected by movements in foreign exchange rates for reasons that go beyond their ownership of foreign operations. With today's complex forms of international trade and finance, U.S. companies may themselves either have monetary assets or liabilities that are ultimately receivable or payable in foreign currency. If, for example, a U.S. company borrows one million Swiss francs when the exchange rate is S fr 1 = $.40, the U.S. dollar equivalent of the loan is $400,000. If the exchange rate changes to S fr 1 = $.45, the U.S. dollar equivalent of the loan becomes $450,000. *SFAS No. 8* required that a $50,000 loss be charged to income. There was little quarrel over the accounting for this type of transaction. The U.S. firm had indeed suffered a loss of $50,000 because one million Swiss francs will have to be acquired to settle the liability. *SFAS No. 52* continues to require gains and losses on foreign currency balances to be recorded in income.

A further elaboration of the underlying concepts of *SFAS No. 52* and the crucial question of how to choose between the "single current rate" and the "dual monetary-nonmonetary rate" method is criticized in the following.

EXCERPT FROM STANGER, ACCOUNTING DEVELOPMENTS
5 Corp.L.Rev. 276–280 (1982).

" * * * The promulgation [of *SFAS No. 52*] emphasizes the term 'functional currency,' which is defined roughly as the currency of the primary economic environment in which the foreign entity operates, which is normally that in which it primarily operates and generates cash. The definition is further refined as discussed below.

"With respect to foreign currency transactions, that is, transactions of the reporting entity itself which are denominated in a currency other than its functional currency, as, for example, when a U.S. entity makes purchases or sales giving rise to payables and receivables fixed in terms of such other currency, the new standards make no change from the prior requirement that a change in the current exchange rate between the transaction date (or most recent intervening balance sheet date, if that is later) and the balance sheet date shall be recognized in the income statement for the reporting period. This is conceptually consonant with the emphasis in SFAS No. 52 that financial statements should provide information to reflect the effect of rate changes upon the entity's cash flows and equity.[8] Moreover, the prior rule [*SFAS No. 8*] was not subjected to meaningful criticism in this area since it was consistent with the reality of the transactions within the entity engaged in the specific activities being affected by the rate of changes.

"What the New Mandate Says

"The new standards mandate, however, that the following gains and losses on foreign currency transactions of the reporting entity not be included in determining periodic net income, but shall be accumulated in a separate component of shareholders' equity and accounted for, as hereinafter described, with respect to translation adjustments of foreign currency statements:

    a. Foreign currency transactions that are designated as, and are effective as, economic hedges of a net investment in a foreign entity, commencing as of the designation date.

---

8. SFAS No. 52, ¶ 4; cf. Statement of Financial Accounting Concepts (SFAC) No. 1, "Objectives of Financial Reporting by Business Enterprises" (FASB, 1978).

b. Intercompany foreign currency transactions that are of a long-term-investment nature (that is, settlement is not planned or anticipated in the foreseeable future), when the entities to the transaction are consolidated, combined, or accounted for by the equity method in the reporting enterprise's financial statements.

"The real problem existed with respect to translation of foreign currency statements of foreign entities accounted for by the reporting entity by consolidation or the equity method of accounting. Since the prior standards required translation gains and losses, albeit under the temporal method,[12] [Ed's. note—the dual monetary-nonmonetary method] to be included in the income of the current period, the impact upon the income statement of the reporting entity was direct, irrespective of whether the currency fluctuations had any true impact upon the operations or cash flows of the reporting entity. One example will suffice. If a foreign subsidiary borrowed in a foreign currency for its own operating needs and if it generated its own cash flows in that currency to meet that debt when due, no economic impact resulting from the transaction of the subsidiary would affect the parent. Yet, because foreign currency statements had to be translated as a prior step to consolidation, the translation gain or loss so generated appeared upon the income statement of the reporting entity. The same was true where foreign currency statements of corporate joint ventures or investees were translated prior to the application of the equity method.

"Current Exchange Rate Should Be Used

"SFAS No. 52 requires that the current exchange rate rather than the temporal rate be used in translating foreign currency statements of foreign entities whose functional currency is not the reporting currency, as follows: '(a) For assets and liabilities—the exchange rate at the balance sheet date, (b) For revenues, expenses, gains and losses—a weighted average rate for the period.'[13] The rationale for adopting the current exchange rate was that the objective of translation was not to determine individual elements of the foreign currency financial statements as they would have been in the reporting currency, as under the temporal method, but rather to treat the foreign entity as a net investment of the reporting entity.[14]

"To address the valid criticism concerning the inclusion of translation gains and losses on the income statement, the new standards

---

12. Under the temporal method, elements of foreign financial statements denominated in a functional currency other than the reporting currency are described as follows:

(1) Cash and accounts receivable—at the current exchange rate in effect at the balance sheet date.

(2) Other assets and liabilities—at historical or current exchange rates depending, respectively, upon whether they are carried, in accordance with generally accepted accounting principles, at historical cost or current prices.

(3) Revenues and expenses—at the average rate for the period except for revenues and expenses relating to assets and liabilities translated at historical rates which are likewise to be translated at the historical rates used to translate the related assets and liabilities.

SFAS No. 8, ¶¶ 11–13.

13. SFAS No. 52, ¶ 12.

14. Id., ¶¶ 70, 74.

accumulate these gains and losses in a separate component of equity until sale or substantially complete liquidation of the investment in the foreign entity at which time such accumulated amount is reported as part of the gain or loss on such sale or liquidation.[15]

"Where the Flaw Arises

"The flaw in the new standards arises, however, from the establishment of criteria to determine the functional currency. SFAS No. 52 states that if the operations of a foreign entity are relatively self-contained and integrated within a particular country, the functional currency would generally be the currency of the country.[16] However, the promulgation concedes that if a foreign operation is a direct or integral component of the reporting entity's operations (i.e., it buys or sells mostly from or to the parent), the functional currency would be the reporting currency. It goes on to emphasize that the determination of the functional currency is basically a factual determination and that in some instances the observable facts will not clearly identify a single functional currency but that management's judgment will be required.[17] Moreover, if the functional currency is determined by management to be the reporting currency, the remeasurement process is to be such as to produce the same result as if the foreign entity's books were kept in the reporting currency [18] (i.e., the temporal method [19]). In such latter case, the translation gains and losses are deemed incurred by the reporting entity and are to be accounted for and appear on the income statement in the same manner as internal foreign currency transactions.[20] In addition, in order to deal with the highly unsatisfactory results that arise with respect to foreign entities in highly inflationary economies, the promulgation requires that in such economies (defined as those having cumulative inflation of approximately 100 percent or more over a three-year period), the foreign currency financial statements shall be remeasured as if the functional currency were the reporting currency.[21]

"What the New Standard Has Accomplished

"What has SFAS No. 52 achieved? It has eliminated the gyrating effect of translation gains and losses on the income statement, unless the foreign entity's functional currency is the reporting currency [i.e., not the foreign currency] or unless the foreign entity operates in a highly inflationary economy. Yet, management of the reporting entity makes the judgmental decision as to whether the functional currency is or is not the reporting currency. It is submitted that the promulgation

15. Id., ¶¶ 13, 14.

16. Id., ¶ 6.

17. Id., ¶ 8. Appendix A sets forth six major indicators to aid in selecting the functional currency but concedes there may be others and that in any event the readings derived from the indicators could be mixed or inconclusive.

18. Id., ¶ 10.

19. SFAS No. 52, Appendix B, makes it quite clear that the temporal method applies in such a case, by listing specific elements of the financial statements and their respected methods of translation. See Greene, "The Monster Lives," Forbes, Jan. 4, 1982, p. 43.

20. SFAS No. 52, ¶¶ 15, 16.

21. Id., ¶ 11.

may be inconsistent with the qualitative characteristics of reliability and neutrality.[22] While a decision by management concerning the functional currency, once made, is to be applied consistently unless significant changes in economic facts and circumstances occur indicating clearly that the functional currency has changed, restatement of prior financial statements is not required.[23] The last word in this area has not yet been written. It is not without significance that the standards were adopted by the FASB by only a 4–3 vote!"

22. SFAC No. 2, "Qualitative Characteristics of Accounting Information," (FASB, May 1980).

23. SFAS No. 52, ¶¶ 9, 45.

Chapter XIV

THE AUDITOR'S RESPONSIBILITIES IN PREVENTING MISLEADING FINANCIAL STATEMENTS THROUGH "COOKED BOOKS"

OBJECTIVES

Comprehend the auditor's new responsibilities under GAAS for uncovering fraud and errors in financial reports.

RELEVANCE FOR LAWYERS

Lawyers are heavily involved in litigation involving misrepresentations in financial statements. More importantly, they advise business clients on disclosure obligations under securities laws and otherwise and must understand the nature of the auditor's involvement in preventing negligent or intentional misrepresentations in financial statements.

Revolutionary changes were made in 1988 concerning the auditor's duty to uncover and prevent such misrepresentation. This was due in part to the massive financial frauds of the 1980s, capped off by the largest financial scandal of all history—the savings and loan debacle whose cost to taxpayers is currently estimated at one-quarter to one-half trillion dollars and is likely to defer many needed social programs for decades. This chapter describes the changes in auditors' duties as perceived by the profession itself. However, it does not cover legal principles applicable to auditors' liabilities to clients or others.

A. "COOKED BOOKS"

In early 1983, SEC Commissioner James C. Treadway, Jr. made several speeches on the subject of "Cooked Books". Following are some excerpts from his April 13, 1983 Remarks to the American Society of Corporate Secretaries, Inc., Cleveland, Ohio. These continue to be pithily descriptive of numerous cases occurring in the intervening years.

Financial statement frauds and outright falsifications of books and records are not new. But the problem is persistent; the new cases are egregious; and they have involved major, blue chip companies * * *.

While "cooked books" may not be a new problem, the recent cases have some aspects worth noting. First, these new cases seem to arise in a corporate atmosphere which tolerates or encourages reporting profits, even if they do not exist. Three factors seem to create that atmosphere: (1) aggressive and arbitrary demands by top management that divisions and subsidiaries achieve unrealistic profit goals; (2) poor communications between headquarters and the divisions; and (3) the failure or absence of adequate internal controls or checks and balances in the corporate structure.

The next aspect I would focus on is the fact that the employees who have participated in "cooking the books" apparently believed they were acting in the best interest of the company. In some cases, it was an admitted feeling of "team effort" rather than an effort to realize immediate personal gain, such as from theft, kickbacks or bribes.

The third general factor emerging from these cases is the lack of creativity in "cooking the books." The methods have been startlingly simple—pre-recognize revenue; falsify or totally concoct inventory; ship without invoices or issue invoices without shipping; and play games with a variety of expenses. Sometimes third parties, such as suppliers, have been enlisted to defer or redate invoices. But creativity has been almost totally missing. Indeed, the methods have been so crude that I wonder why the participants thought their activities would remain undetected for any length of time.

But I believe the *single most significant factor* to emerge from these cases is the organizational structure of the companies involved. I refer to a decentralized corporate structure, with autonomous divisional management. Such a structure is intended to encourage responsibility, productivity, and therefore profits—all entirely laudable objectives. But the unfortunate corollary has been a lack of accountability. The situation has been exacerbated when headquarters has unilaterally set profit goals for a division or, without expressly stating goals, applied steady pressure for increased profits. Either way, the pressure has created an atmosphere in which falsification of books and records at middle and lower-levels became possible, even predictable. This pressure-filled atmosphere has caused middle and lower level managers and entire divisions to adopt the attitude that the outright falsification of books and records on a regular, on-going, pervasive basis is an entirely appropriate way to achieve profit objectives, as long as the falsifications get by the independent auditors, who are viewed as fair game to be deceived.

Considering the number of parties actually or potentially involved or responsible—lower-level employees, mid-level managers, officers, directors, and sometimes third parties—I could dwell at length upon the respective liabilities of various parties. But that exercise would serve little purpose unless it were to identify a more important problem—a dysfunction or break-down in corporate structure. That is my focus today—structure. If corporate managers, operating under constant pressures from above to report profits, are allowed to believe that the corporate structure will tolerate reporting questionable or non-existent profits at the expense of the integrity of the company's financial statements, "cooked books," a devastating kind of fraud seems bound to occur in massive proportions.

* * *

* * * [W]hat is the impact of "cooked books" on our system of disclosure, which is largely based on voluntary compliance and minimal governmental interference? "Cooked books" cause false financial statements; if the financial statements are false, it is impossible for the narrative portion of any disclosure document to be accurate; and the entire disclosure process is therefore totally undermined.

So back to my original question. What do "cooked books" have to do with corporate governance? I would characterize corporate governance as an approach to management of a public company which has as its essential premise the idea that the corporation should institute and enforce adequate controls and procedures to assure that the corporation is operated solely for the benefit of stockholders. Sound corporate governance requires a structure and procedures which will preclude undesirable activity prior to its occurrence or, if it does not preclude it, will detect and remedy it with promptness. More specifically, corporate governance means oversight of management by an active and questioning Board of Directors and the use of whatever other mechanisms of oversight, reporting and review—such as independent Audit and other Committees at the Board of Directors' level and appropriate counterparts at other levels within the corporation—as are necessary to assure that corporate managers at all levels are properly sensitive to and discharge their paramount duty to stockholders. And the duty of managers to stockholders surely must include accurately accounting for the management of the corporate assets by not "cooking the books."

* * *

IN RE ERNST & WHINNEY

SEC, Admin.Proceeding (1990)
[CCH] Fed.Sec.L.Rep. ¶ 84,610.

INTRODUCTION

On October 15, 1985, the Commission issued an Order for Private Proceedings ("Order") pursuant to Rule 2(e)(1)(ii) of the Commission's

Rules of Practice (17 C.F.R. § 201(e)(1)(ii)) naming as respondents Ernst & Whinney ("E & W"), Michael J. Ferrante, C.P.A., ("Ferrante") and Michael S. Hope, C.P.A., ("Hope" or "the engagement partner").

The Order is based upon allegations of the Commission's Office of the Chief Accountant ("OCA") that respondents had engaged in "unethical or improper professional conduct" arising out of audits performed by E & W of the 1980 and 1981 financial statements of United States Surgical Corporation ("Surgical") resulting in the issuance of unqualified audit reports on statements which were incorrect for significantly over-stating income. OCA charges that E & W's examinations were not made in accordance with generally accepted auditing standards ("GAAS"), as certified by E & W, and challenges its further certification that the financial statements were prepared by Surgical in conformity with generally accepted accounting principles ("GAAP").

* * *

The Parties

E & W, an international accounting firm, is one of the eight largest public accounting firms in the world. It maintains 122 offices in the United States, having approximately 1,150 partners and employing a professional staff of 13,000 individuals. It is the auditor for more than 1,400 corporations whose financial statements are filed with this Commission.

* * *

[Ferrante] was first assigned to the Surgical engagement in 1977 and participated in each of the Surgical audits from that time on through December 1983. He was the audit partner on the 1980 and 1981 audits involved in this proceeding.

Surgical is a publicly held New York operation organized in 1975 as the successor by merger to another corporation. Its executive offices are in Norwalk, Connecticut. Surgical is primarily engaged in designing, developing, manufacturing, and marketing a proprietary line of surgical products which are either manufactured by Surgical directly or by other companies on a sub-contractual basis. These products include surgical stapling and other wound-closing instruments as a substitute for conventional suturing with needle and thread. Its stapling instruments consist of reusable models as well as disposable models that are discarded after a single use.

Between 1969 and 1981, Surgical experienced dramatic growth. In 1969, total assets were $1,272,790 and sales were $573,615. By 1981, its total assets had grown to $207,339,000 and annual sales amounted to $111,800,000. Operations which resulted in a loss of $932,000 in 1969 showed a reported profit of $12,904,000 by 1981.

Another company involved in these proceedings is the *Barden Corporation* ("Barden"), a publicly held Connecticut corporation engaged in the engineering, design, manufacture and sale of precision ball bearings, surgical assemblies and high-precision dies. Its principal executive offices are in Danbury, Connecticut. *Lacey Manufacturing Company* ("Lacey") is a division of Barden located in Bridgeport, Connecticut, and, as pertinent hereto, has manufactured, among other things, surgical staplings and components and high precision dies for Surgical since 1971.

At all times relevant to these proceedings, E & W was the independent auditor of Surgical and as such issued unqualified audit reports on Surgical's financial statement for that company's fiscal years ended December 31, 1980 and 1981. Each of these reports was incorporated in a Form 10–K filed with the Commission on or about February 3, 1981 and March 17, 1982, respectively.

E & W was also the auditor of Barden and issued audit reports on Barden's financial statements for each of that company's fiscal years ended September 30, 1980, 1981, and 1982. Each of those reports was incorporated in a Form 10–K filed with the Commission.

Background

In 1980 and 1981, Surgical experienced for the first time sharply increased competition for its products. Although Surgical's stapling devices were protected by patents, in 1980 the company began to face serious competition from other companies trying to enter this market, which Surgical had long dominated. In addition, a former dealer of its products in Australia, Alan Blackman, began to manufacture and market identical versions of Surgical's staplers in Australia, a country where Surgical held no patents, and in several other countries. Moreover, several of Surgical's most fundamental patents were to expire in the next several years.

In order to counter these pressures, Surgical undertook to develop, manufacture and market entire new lines of surgical stapling products. Thus, whereas before 1980 Surgical had introduced an average of only 1 or 2 new products annually, it introduced 10 new products in 1980 and 14 new products in 1981. Additionally, Surgical also began a legal campaign to contain Blackman. It spent more than $5 million in legal fees and related expenses litigating against Blackman and his companies all over the world.

The Order charges that Surgical, faced with the additional expenses stated above, adopted a number of "fraudulent and manipulative" accounting changes intended to show the continuance at about the same levels of pre-tax income, resulting in an overstatement of pre-tax income by about 18 percent in 1980 and 67.8 percent in 1981. These reported earnings approximated in excess of $12 million each year.

The basis of these allegations against respondents by OCA in connection with the audits of Surgical's 1980 and 1981 financial statements is that they repeatedly ignored or failed to perceive material facts involving Surgical, a so-called "aggressive" company in a state of transition, failed to plan their audit procedures to test proper assertions, relied unduly on client representations, and failed to resolve material conflicts in the audit evidence, all of which resulted in the issuance by respondents of incorrect audit reports, i.e., that the 1980 and 1981 audits were performed in accordance with GAAS and that Surgical's financial statements were fairly represented in accordance with GAAP.

Respondents, on the other hand, contend that the audits involved were conducted by experienced staff personnel exercising their sound and considered professional judgment with full knowledge and awareness of the business activities and practices of Surgical, and that where in some areas accounting decisions were made and auditing procedures were performed whose appropriateness might be debatable, such conduct did not amount to "unethical or improper professional conduct". Respondents further argue that Rule 2(e)(1)(ii) by its terms does not permit the disciplining of accountants absent a showing of willful misconduct and that mere negligent conduct offers no basis for imposing the sanctions called for in Rule 2(e).[7]

Audit Planning

The financial statements of a company are prepared by its managers and constitute assertions made by management that the statements are truthful presentations of the company's financial condition and the results of its financial operation. The purpose of an audit is to make an examination that will, in accordance with GAAS, put the auditor in a position to express an opinion as to whether the financial statements are presented fairly and in conformity with GAAP, applied on a consistent basis. (SAS 1, AU 350.1).

Most of the auditor's work during an audit consists of obtaining and evaluating evidential matter concerning the assertions in the financial statements. The relationship between clients and accountants during the audit process is one of healthy skepticism. GAAS requires the auditor at the outset to plan an overall strategy for testing management's assertions by considering, among other things, the company's business, its accounting policies and procedures, and the company's own internal controls over the accounting data. Since audits are fluid processes, transactions and events may occur during the course of the audit that cause the auditors to plan and perform additional audit procedures.

*   *   *

As part of their planning, and before doing the actual audit steps, the auditors must determine the risk of material errors in particular accounts or transactions and plan appropriate audit steps in light of that determination. In addition, the auditors must evaluate the company's internal controls in order to establish a basis for reliance thereon

7. Rule 2(e)(1) provides, in pertinent part, (subparagraph ii) that the Commission may deny, temporarily or permanently, the privilege of appearing or practicing before it in any way to any person who is found by the Commission after notice of and opportunity for hearing to have engaged in "improper professional conduct."

in determining the nature, extent and timing of audit tests to be applied.

If a conclusion has been reached that the system can be a source of reliance, the auditors then determine, by performing compliance tests, whether the system is being followed. Compliance tests are an important prerequisite of audit reliance on a client's internal controls. Analytic review, a comparison of balances from one year to the next, is a type of substantive test.

The concept of materiality plays a significant role in planning the audit and assessing audit risk. Auditors generally consider amounts that are less that 5 percent of pre-tax income to be immaterial, and anything more than 10 percent of pre-tax income to be clearly material. Auditors must plan the audit to detect errors in the financial statements that individually or in the aggregate are material to the financial statements. They must consider materiality of errors in individual accounts as well as in the aggregate of all the accounts.

In starting out on the 1980 and 1981 Surgical audits, the respective E & W audit teams consisted of the engagement partner (Hope), the audit partner (Ferrante) and other members of the respective engagement staffs. In addition, every E & W engagement has an "independent review partner" who reviews selected audit documents at the conclusion of the field work and whose concurrence with the auditors' conclusion that sufficient procedures had been planned and performed to support the auditors' report is required before that report can be issued. During the audits in question herein, William Hufferd was the independent review partner assigned to them by E & W. Robert Hammond also performed a second review of the audit papers.

The 1980 and 1981 Surgical audits were planned in accordance with the E & W audit approach based upon "specific risk analysis" ("SRA") designed to evaluate the risk of material error for related groups of accounts.

E & W approaches an audit in three phases: initial planning, program development and program execution. The objective of initial planning is to update the auditor's knowledge with respect to all facets of the company's internal and external operating environment that may bear upon audit risk. Thus, for the 1980 audit, the auditors reviewed Surgical's 1979 10–K and Annual Report to shareholders and the 10–K's filed by competitors, re-reading Surgical's quarterly reports (Form 10–Q) for the first three quarters of 1980; and performing an overall analytical review of major financial statement amounts to determine whether they raised questions to be addressed by appropriate audit procedures.

During the program development phase of the 1980 audit (as well as the 1981 audit) the auditors performed detailed analytical reviews, evaluated the company's internal control systems; considered the likelihood of error in related groups of accounts and developed a preliminary audit approach.

As a result of the auditors' evaluation of the foregoing factors, they expressed their conclusion as to risk by selecting one of three broad descriptions: "high", "moderate", or "low". After risk was assessed for each specific control objective, testing procedures were formulated as set forth in the preliminary audit approach section of the SRA workpapers which were then incorporated into the audit program. E & W contends that the audit approach used in the planning of the 1980 and 1981 audits was "thorough, comprehensive and in complete compliance with professional standards" * * *.

On the other hand, it is the contention of the OCA that in planning for and executing the audits for the 1980 and, more significantly for the 1981 Surgical financial statements, the E & W auditors failed to consider a number of accounting changes which were put into effect by Surgical solely for the purpose of increasing reported income (assertedly a violation of GAAP) in anticipation of lower income resulting from efforts to meet increased domestic competition by developing additional product lines, and by instituting protective litigation against the Australian competition. OCA further alleges that E & W failed to plan appropriate procedures, failed to obtain sufficient competent evidential matter, and failed to recognize and deal appropriately with accounting issues that arose during the audits. In sum, OCA charges E & W with lack of due care in execution of the audits, particularly in the face of the new aggressive accounting stance taken by Surgical's management.

The Specific Audit Failures Alleged

The Order for Proceedings herein alleges various GAAP and GAAS violations in E & W's audits of Surgical's financial statements for 1980 and 1981 with respect to the following matters:

(1) The recognition of revenue on sales of product to salespeople.

(2) The allocation of overhead cost to inventories (1980 audit only).

(3) The capitalization of costs incurred in the "tooling qualification process".

(4) The manner of recording "Leased and Loaned" instruments (1980 audit only).

(5) The capitalization of legal fees as patent costs (1981 audit only).

(6) Changes in accounting estimates, particularly with respect to the estimated useful lives of patents, molds and dies, and recognition of a 10% salvage value on certain fixed assets (1981 audit only).

(7) The tooling confirmation Problems-other Vendors (1981 audit).

(8) The Lacey–Barden Premium Billings Issue (1981 audit only).

(1) Sales to Salespersons

Prior to 1980, Surgical marketed virtually all of its products via its "Auto–Suture Division", almost entirely through a network of independent dealers who purchased product from Surgical and then resold it to doctors and hospitals. Between 1975 and 1981, Surgical gradually changed over from the dealer marketing system to one relying exclusively on employee salespersons, so that by the end of 1981 all of the independent dealers had been replaced.

* * * Newly hired sales people are shipped an initial inventory of demonstration ("demo") product, and later of new products as they are introduced. The salespersons are charged for the initial supply, receiving a discount of 20 percent on the sterile items, and at actual cost for non-sterile items.

* * * In addition to this contractual obligation, it was also Surgical's practice and policy to buy back demo product in the possession of terminated sales persons. * * *

Surgical reported these "sales" as current income at the time the merchandise was shipped to the salespeople, later entering offsets for the amount of product repurchased, even though the product was to be paid for over a period of time out of commissions earned.

This accounting method of recognizing revenues on the sale of goods where the right of return exists not only by contract but by policy, is not in accord with GAAP as expressed in "Statement of Position (S.O.P.) 75–1, issued by the AICPA. Basically, it states that where there is a right of return, either by policy or in practice, transactions should not be recognized currently as sales unless certain conditions are met. It is clear that these conditions were not met under the practices of Surgical.[15]

(2) The Allocation of Overhead Costs to Inventories (1980 Audit)

From 1976 through 1979, Surgical applied overhead costs to its inventory of both manufactured and purchased finished goods and of work in process, by product line, primarily on the basis of direct labor hours incurred in manufacturing the products. The method used was a common one for allocating overhead to inventory for manufacturing companies. However, it did not allocate any overhead cost to Surgical's raw materials inventory during this period. The unallocated overhead was applied to the cost of goods sold.

After the physical inventory was done, the auditors became aware that during the last two months of 1980, as a result of a year-end "sales push", Surgical's raw materials inventories had increased and its finished goods inventory had decreased thereby causing significant distortions. Consequently, Surgical and the auditors jointly decided to allocate overhead for the first time to the raw materials inventory as well as to finished goods and work in process. Thus, unlike in 1979 when overhead associated with raw materials inventory was charged to cost of sales, the change for the 1980 audit increased the amount of overhead costs allocated to inventory with the ultimate effect of overstating pre-tax income for 1980.

15. Thus, S.O.P. 75–1 permits the recording of sales and to account for returns as they are received but only where future returns and losses are expected to be clearly insignificant. No such expectation has been demonstrated.

* * * [A]ccording to OCA's calculations, overhead applicable to Surgical's inventory using the same overhead allocation method as used in 1979 amounted to $6,275,000 whereas under the revised 1980 method of allocating overhead to raw materials the overhead allocations increased to $8,592,000 for a difference of approximately $2,300,000. Based upon the record herein, it is found that the OCA's calculations as shown in Exhibit 333 to be (sic) more accurate.

The OCA asserts that the allocation for the first time of overhead costs to raw materials costs resulted in a "change in accounting principle" under Accounting Principles Board Opinion Number 20 ("APB–20"), which requires that where such a change occurs, the nature and justification for the change and its effect on income should be disclosed in the financial statements for the period in which it is made. Specifically, the disclosure should state why the newly adopted accounting principal is preferable to the former one.

The 1980 financial statements of Surgical (Form 10–K) do not disclose this change in accounting principle. Moreover, the 1980 audit work papers do not show that this matter was discussed in the light of APB–20 by the auditors.

Respondents assert that the allocation of overhead to inventory was not the change contemplated by APB–20, and, even if it were, the matter was not material. They also contend that the question was in fact considered by the auditors who merely made a "judgment call" as to whether it was required to be justified or disclosed.

APB–20 (Paragraph 7) states that "a change in accounting principle results from adoption of a generally accepted accounting principle different from the one used previously for reporting purposes," and that the "term *accounting principle* includes not only accounting principles and practices but also the methods of applying them".

In Paragraph 8 of the opinion, it is pointed out that a characteristic of such a change is that it concerns a choice from among two or more generally accepted accounting principles.

> "However, neither (a) initial adoption of an accounting principle in recognition of events or transactions occurring for the first time or that previously were immaterial in their effect nor (b) adoption or modification of an accounting principle necessitated by transactions or events that are clearly different in substance from those previously occurring is a change in accounting principle."

It is clear from the circumstances herein that the decision to allocate overhead to raw materials inventory for the first time constituted "a change in accounting principle" as contemplated under APB–20, and should have been disclosed in the accounting statements. The change from the prior method (since 1977) of allocating inventory overhead only to finished goods and work in process, which at first was approved by the auditors for 1980, but then changed to include raw materials following the sales push during the last two months of that year, created what to the auditors and to Surgical seemed a "distortion" in the inventory account as a result of which net profits would have been reported proportionately lower.

Both methods of allocating inventory were in accordance with GAAP. Since under APB–20, (Paragraph 7) the term "accounting principle" includes not only such principles and practice but also the methods of applying them, the change in allocation during 1980 would be an appropriate change as contemplated by APB–20, unless the situation falls within either of the two exceptions set forth in paragraph 8 of APB–20.

* * * Surgical's increased in-house manufacturing capacity and the consequent increase in manufacturing overhead costs, do not fall within the exceptions of para. 8.

In any event, E & W did not consider this issue in the light of APB–20 during the 1979 audit nor during the 1980 audit. Consequently, the auditors failed to discern that an accounting issue existed in connection with Surgical's change in method of application of overhead to inventory. This failure to recognize and deal appropriately with an important accounting concept was a violation of GAAS. Even if the issues had been considered, the auditors could not have relied on the exclusions contained in APB–20 to justify the failure to require Surgical to disclose the change in accounting principles or to qualify the audit report.

* * *

(4) The Manner of Recording "Leased and Loaned" Instruments (1980 Audit Only)

Many of Surgical's products, such as reusable stainless steel stapling instruments and electronic instruments, were not held for sale in the ordinary course of business, but were either leased or loaned to customers. As at December 31, 1980, Surgical's leased and loaned assets had a recorded cost of 3.65 million dollars.

Under all of the circumstances, it is concluded that respondents violated GAAS by not planning and performing audit tests to gather sufficient evidence concerning the existence and valuation of the leased and loaned instruments, and Surgical's assertion that the TPR assets had with no apparent justification increased in value by $1 million. Those steps that were taken, particularly the use of only 8 confirmation letters, were woefully inadequate both in sample size and in the proportionately large number of exceptions reported. Thus, there was a wholly insufficient statistical basis for concluding that the account was fairly stated under GAAP.

(5) The Capitalization of Legal Fees As Patent Costs (1981 Audit)

Alan R. Blackman was Surgical's former Australian distributor who, beginning in 1979, embarked upon a program of manufacturing and marketing stapling products that were copies of and in competition with Surgical's products, first in Australia and, in 1980, in the United States and other parts of the world. Surgical responded to Blackman's conduct by commencing litigation in 1980 against Blackman in a number of jurisdictions throughout the world. By 1981 there were nine law suits pending between Blackman and Surgical. Only three of them directly involved patents held by Surgical * * *.

In its 1981 financial statements, Surgical capitalized as patents all legal fees and related costs amounting to $5.8 million incurred in connection with the Blackman litigation, including over $2 million incurred in connection with the suits in Australia. Under GAAP, only those costs incurred in successfully establishing or defending the validity of a patent are properly capitalizable as patents. The theory behind this rule is that these expenditures are directly related to the asset, the patent, and will make that asset more valuable. On the other hand, GAAP holds that legal fees incurred in defending a company's business in general are not properly capitalizable but should be expensed, as are all legal fees.

Respondents' claim that the nine law suits heretofore described were all bundled together as part of one global strategy to wear down Blackman and force him out of business may be true, but the strategy was not for protection of patents but rather the protection of Surgical's business. Looking to the substance of the lawsuits as a whole rather than the form in which they were presented in the various jurisdictions makes it clear that they were not patent related. They were primarily designed to drive out Blackman as a business competitor.

(6) Changes in Accounting Estimates and Recognition of Salvage Value (1981 Audit).

In 1981, Surgical adopted changes in accounting estimates that had the effect of increasing reported pre-tax income by $1,280,000, as follows:

    (a) Change in the estimated useful life of patents from 5 to 10 years—$476,000.

    (b) Changing the estimated useful life of new additions to molds and dies from 7 to 10 years—$270,000.

    (c) Recognizing an estimated salvage value of 10% on certain fixed assets to which no salvage value had previously been applied—$402,000.

    * * *

The OCA contends that respondents violated GAAS by performing insufficient audit procedures to test the reasonableness of these changes. OCA further asserts that there is an accounting presumption that entities will not change their accounting estimates unless justified by new events or new or better information, and argues that it is the duty of the auditors to review the company's evidence supporting the changes and satisfy themselves that management had a reasonable and sound basis for making them. This interpretation of APB–20 would seem to create a presumption against changes in estimates and place a burden upon a company to overcome that presumption by appropriate evidence.

While it is true that APB–20 recognizes a presumption against changes in accounting *principles* (Paragraphs 7 through 9), there is no such presumption against changing accounting *estimates* (Paragraphs 10 and 11). APB–20, paragraph 10, states that changes in estimates used in accounting "are necessary consequences of periodic presentations of financial statements," and that "accounting estimates change as new events occur, as more experience is acquired, or as additional information is obtained".

To accept the client's justification for a change in accounting estimate, the auditor need only conclude that it is reasonable and supported by the evidence. The client is not required to show that the change is for the better or is an improvement.

OCA contends that three considerations should have caused the auditors to increase their level of skepticism with respect to these changes, namely, (1) that Surgical did not volunteer to its auditors the fact that it had made the changes in estimates; (2) that three of the four changes were all made in the fourth quarter of 1981; and (3) Surgical's fourth quarter earnings had fallen dramatically, (and hence presumably exerting pressure upon the company to seek off-setting increases in profits elsewhere). These factors are said to have presented an unambiguous picture of a company manipulating its accounting to inflate its income, particularly since Surgical had also, during the fourth quarter, adopted a policy of capitalizing other expenses such as, as seen above, tooling qualification costs. As a result, it is argued that the auditors should have examined carefully their decision to accept each change in estimate, and that there was some duty imposed upon management to justify the changes by showing to the auditors that they were better than the estimates being replaced. However, APB–20 does not place such a burden.

In coming to the conclusion concerning these disputed items, the auditors relied upon their knowledge of the client's business and upon the representations made to them by management. There is nothing unusual or suspicious about a company's adopting changes in estimates without first consulting with its auditors. Moreover, it is logical for a company to adopt changes in estimates in the fourth quarter of a fiscal year when it is in preparation of its annual financial statements. The fact that the changes in estimates had the effect of increasing reported income is not significant, in most cases, since estimates, when they are initially adopted, tend to be conservative due to the lack of experience on which to base them. The auditors were aware that in 1981, Surgical had adopted five other changes in asset or liability reserves that had the effect of *decreasing* pre-tax income by a total of $900,000.

Surgical's business was undergoing profound changes in 1981. The amount of its tangible assets had increased more than threefold over what they were in 1979. In 1980 and 1981, Surgical introduced some 20 new products as compared with prior years when it had introduced, at most, two. It sold off a division and product line. Its fixed assets accounts had increased by approximately $51 million and its patents account by $5.8 million.

In light of the changes in Surgical's business and the material additions to its asset accounts, it was not unreasonable to expect that management would reassess and, if appropriate, revise accounting estimates that pertain to those accounts. Since some of Surgical's revised estimates relating to asset reliability reserves had the effect of decreasing income by a substantial amount, as shown above, the fact that the proposed estimates had the effect of increasing net income would not, by itself, be cause for raising the level of skepticism on the part of the auditors.[33]

Estimates by nature are imprecise projections as to future events. In order to evaluate a change in estimate, auditors must look to the past to determine where the changed estimate is reasonable in light of experience, and into the future to determine whether there is a legitimate reason to believe that what was true in the past will no longer hold true in the future.

(a) Patent Lives

Prior experience showed that product manufactured by Surgical under patent had economic lives of some 15 years or more. The patents had a legal life of 17 years. Hence, it would appear that a change in estimated patent life from 5 to 10 years was conservative.

Additionally, another firm, Delmed, Inc., paid Surgical nearly $2 million for a fully amortized (for 5 years) patent which indicated that they had a useful life beyond their 5–year accounting life. Moreover, a research report by Sanford C. Bernstein & Co., concluded that Surgical would remain the market leader in its field for a substantial period into the future despite the fact that several strong competitors were about to enter into the manufacture and distribution of similar products.

(b) Molds and Dies

It would appear from the record that the change in the estimated useful lives of molds and dies was reasonable. The molds and dies had an economic life of at least ten years and they physically lasted approximately that period. This estimation was also supported by tests made by respondents of Schedule V of Surgical's Forms 10–K during each audit for the duration of the Surgical engagement.

(c) Salvage Values

Salvage value is the estimate of the amount recoverable upon disposition of an asset at the end of its useful life. The recognition of a

---

33. When Surgical did propose accounting conventions or changes in estimates that were inconsistent with GAAP or were not reasonable in light of the evidence, the auditors did not permit Surgical to adopt such changes which had to do with attempts to capitalize rent, refinements in the method of calculating average interest rates, changes in estimated useful life of leasehold improvements, and over-capitalization of interest expenses on construction of a facility. Surgical's pre-tax income would have been $528,000 higher but for the auditor's refusal to concur in Surgical's adoption of these changes.

salvage value decreases the depreciable cost of an asset and increases income. It would appear that the assets to which the salvage value was applied did, in fact, have a recoverable value at the conclusion of their usual lives, of which the auditors were aware, and that many companies employ a 10 percent salvage value as a matter of convention.

It is agreed by OCA and counsel for respondents that Surgical violated GAAP by applying the 10 percent salvage value retroactively. GAAP requires that such a change in estimate be applied prospectively only.

The effect of applying the salvage value retroactively was to increase 1981 reported pre-tax income by $260,000. Since this amount was approximately 2 percent of pre-tax income, it becomes an immaterial amount to which GAAP would ordinarily not apply. However, it could be taken into consideration in determining whether respondents were guilty of improper professional conduct in not recognizing a campaign by Surgical's management to unduly inflate its net profits, and whether respondents, in carrying out their auditing functions under GAAS, should not have noted and called attention to this allegedly violative conduct.

Under the circumstances herein, the change in estimates and the imposition of the salvage charge were not sufficient in and of themselves to increase the level of skepticism with which respondents should have conducted the audit.

(7) The Tooling Confirmations Problems—Other Vendors (1981 Audit)

In its 1981 financial statements, Surgical reported owning molds and dies costing about $32 million, or about 15 percent of its total assets, most of which were physically in the possession of outside vendors who used them to make parts for Surgical. One critical assertion that GAAS required E & W to test was that these molds and dies physically existed. Accordingly, E & W selected nine vendors, each of which according to Surgical's books held over $1 million of Surgical's molds and dies, and sent them confirmation letters itemizing by tool number the molds and dies which Surgical's records showed the vendors had in their possession. The letters requested the recipients to confirm the holding of the listed items. The net book value of the tooling at the nine locations was $12,100,000.

Only six of the nine confirmation letters were returned, four of which contained exceptions. These six provided the auditors with a sample that consisted of 479 individual tools and dies representing 43 percent of all tooling at outside locations. These returned confirmations contained about 127 exceptions, some 56 of which were followed up by the audit staff and disclosed evidence of either the tools' actual or probable existence or that the error in the vendor's records arose from some aberration in the vendor's response procedures. There was no follow-up on the remaining 71 exceptions, the book value of which was almost one million dollars.

* * *

Respondents isolated for testing the nine vendors that held material amounts of Surgical's tooling. Under E & W's own internal guidance, this selection was a test of "key items" that were individually material. Thus, the auditors were required to validate or confirm each vendor's confirmation and to follow them up in some manner, especially the three that were not returned. This failure constituted a violation of GAAS, and, in view of the amount of the total book values of the molds and dies listed in the confirmations, a material one.

* * *

(8) The Lacey–Barden Premium Billing Issue (1981 audit).

As noted heretofore, Barden, through its Lacey manufacturing division, was a major supplier to Surgical of parts for its stapling instruments. The tooling necessary to produce these parts was also built by Lacey to Surgical's design and specifications.

On or about January 27, 1982, E & W completed its field work on the audit of Surgical's 1981 financial statements. On February 3, 1982 E & W authorized Surgical to issue a press release disclosing its sales and earnings figures for the calendar year 1981, specifically that its earnings rose from $.89 per share in 1980 to $1.13 in 1981.[38]

* * *

During the same week that Surgical's earnings were released, Paul Yamont, Senior Vice President and Treasurer of Barden, called William Burke, the E & W partner in charge of the Barden audit, and advised him that in excess of $300,000 in Lacey billings to Surgical appeared to have been improperly recorded by Barden during the first quarter of Barden's fiscal year, and more importantly, that Surgical may have paid Lacey over $1 million for production work, with the purchase orders and invoices mislabeled as being for "tooling modifications." Since Surgical capitalized its tooling payments and expensed its product costs as "cost of sales" this presented the question as to whether Surgical might have deliberately misstated its molds and dies account and thus its pre-tax earnings, by a material amount.

Yamont told Burke that Barden's accounting department was not aware of any costs underlying the invoices, and Yamont suggested that the work described on the invoices might not have been performed. He further suggested that the facts might indicate a "kickback" scheme involving individuals at Barden or Lacey, and someone at Surgical.

Burke visited Barden twice during that week to discuss the issue with Yamont and two other members of the Barden accounting department, Thomas Loughman and Russell Moore, who were united in their analysis that the premium charge billings were for product and not for tooling.

---

38. Surgical's executive officers could earn bonuses ranging from 15 percent to 75 percent of their base salaries if the earnings per share growth ranged from 15 percent to 30 percent over the previous year, which provided an incentive to these officials to keep earnings per share at a higher level.

Recognizing that the information Burke received from Yamont warranted his consulting with Norman Strauss, E & W's regional director of accounting and auditing, on February 10, 1982, Burke and Strauss met and discussed the fact that the amount of billings of about $300,000 recorded in the wrong period was immaterial to Barden's fiscal 1981 financial statements, but was material to the first quarter of 1982 for Barden. It was agreed that Burke should recommend to Barden that it disclose this item in its quarterly financial statements.

Burke also discussed with Strauss the fact that the billings to Surgical for alleged tooling modification was not supported by any records of tooling costs and that if this were so, Surgical would be improperly capitalizing as tooling amounts expended for parts.

That same day Strauss informed Bruce Dixon, E & W's managing partner for the New York region, that Yamont had reported finding tooling invoices to Surgical with no associated costs, suggesting that the descriptions on the invoices might be incorrect.

After receiving this information from Burke, Strauss ascertained that Surgical's financial statements for the year ending December 31, 1981 were scheduled to be issued shortly. Consequently, Dixon advised Hope not to release the accountants' report on Surgical's 1981 Form 10–K unless and until the questions relating to those billings were resolved. Hope then informed Surgical that for reasons he was not in a position to disclose, the accountants' report could not be issued at that time.[39]

On February 11, 1982, Dixon and Strauss discussed Burke's information with Robert Neary, E & W's national director of accounting and auditing as well as with E & W's in-house lawyers. This order not to sign off on the Surgical audit came at a time when it was expected that E & W would do so.

Several days prior, on February 8, 1982, Barden's board of directors asked E & W, Barden's corporate accounting department and Barden's outside counsel to investigate the Lacey billings to Surgical. During the period February 12 to 15, Burke and Robert Kempenich, the manager of the Barden engagement, reviewed and analyzed documents provided by Barden's accounting department and visited Lacy to interview Robert More, Lacey's general manager.

Burke and Kempenich were told by More that beginning in 1980, Lacey (Barden's manufacturing division) had been billing Surgical base prices for certain products, particularly for DTA and TA(P), plus "premium charges" intended to compensate Lacey for manufacturing steps that were being performed manually.[41]

---

39. This inability to tell Surgical why its report was delayed was because it would have been ethically bound not to disclose Barden's confidential information to Surgical.

41. The base price for the product represented the cost at which Surgical thought Lacey would ultimately be able to produce the product once cost-saving equipment or manufacturing changes enumerated in the agreement came on line. Lacey

More told the auditors that tooling costs involving the modification program had not been significant. Nevertheless, in early 1981 Lacey began invoicing Surgical for "the design and modification of tooling", with the amounts of the invoices calculated in the same manner as were the premium charges for the production of the same parts.

By February 15, Burke and Kempenich had concluded that invoices in the amount of approximately $1,050,000 that were described as being for "tool modification" work at Surgical's direction were in fact for production work on parts. They also concluded that some of the premium charge billings amounting to $300,000 had been issued in the wrong accounting period. The auditors recorded their conclusions in a memorandum and on February 18, 1982, Burke reported them at a meeting of the Barden board of directors. (Yamont, although not a director, was present at the meeting).[42]

At that meeting, Irving Berelson, chairman of Barden's executive committee stated that Barden's outside counsel (in which firm he was also a senior partner) reported that their own investigation corroborated E & W's auditors' findings.

Once the auditors had learned about the Barden information, the crucial issue became whether Surgical was improperly recording the premium billing payments as capital items, rather than expensing them as purchases of product (which, in turn, inflated the net profits). This raised a fundamental question of the integrity of Surgical's management, and that the integrity issue might affect other items in Surgical's financial statements as well.

Lacey calculated and Surgical paid monthly premium charges for the product in accordance with this agreement from November 1980 through January 1982. Only in the first two months did the billing descriptions describe the work as "premium charges" and these payments were not capitalized. Beginning with the premium charge amounts Lacey assessed for products produced in January 1981, the Surgical purchase orders and the billing descriptions began calling the work "tooling modifications" and the costs then were being capitalized by Surgical. A similar pricing arrangement was negotiated with respect to manufacturing new products, the DTA and TA(P) cartridges.

At this point, E & W and its staff were not only faced with the problem of client confidentiality but also one of client integrity. The information that Yamont disclosed to the Barden auditors raised the distinct possibility that Surgical had concealed material information from them and that this, in turn, had profound implications for the entire Surgical audit. If the representations of Surgical's highest management could not be trusted, GAAS would at least require its

and Surgical agreed to reduce the premium charges as the manual operations were discontinued.

42. Burke also told the board that the fact that Robert More had exclusive knowl-

edge and control with respect to Lacey's relations with its customers, including Surgical, was a control weakness.

auditors to revisit the audit field work and might also require them to resign from the audit itself. (SAS 16, AU 327, deals with errors and irregularities in financial statements and sets forth GAAS requirements for auditors when a client's integrity is questioned). SAS 16 also directs auditors who "remain uncertain" whether the financial statements are materially misstated to consider resigning from the engagement.

The client confidentiality problem affecting E & W lay in the fact that the firm and its counsel believed they could not use information learned from the Barden audit to resolve their problem with Surgical's financial statements unless and until Barden gave E & W permission to do so.[43] Thus, although the auditors knew the issue was whether Barden had made products for Surgical and billed them as capitalizable tooling, because of the perceived client confidentiality problem, they could not tell Surgical the reason E & W would not sign off on its Form 10–K.

At the same time Surgical was pressing very forcefully for a prompt signing off without change on its financial reports since its purported net profits for 1981 had already been reported in the media. Having learned of possible client fraud from its audit of Barden, E & W had to straighten out that matter before it could sign off on Surgical by either reviewing the "premium billing" and other instances of Surgical's capitalizing expense items or withdrawing from the engagement. However, E & W could not ethically justify either action with respect to the Surgical audit since both would have been based upon information learned from the Barden audit. Moreover, either course would have been time consuming. If E & W did not resolve the matter promptly, Surgical threatened to bring action for any delay in issuing its financial reports which, if nothing else, would have caused the disclosure of E & W's ethics situation arising from its representation of two audit clients and possible misusing of information with respect to both of them. In fact, E & W's concern was so great it brought in its highest officials including Robert Neary, its national director of accounting and auditing, and Joseph Keller, its national co-chairman to help resolve the dilemma.

It is quite clear that Surgical, Barden's principal customer, because of its economic clout over Barden and to some extent over E & W,[44] and the threat of public disclosure of E & W's ethical posture, was in a strong position to insist upon prompt disposition of the matter. Hence, the only satisfactory solution would have been one involving the obtaining of Barden's consent and resolving the accounting issue arising from the premium billings in a way allowing E & W to sign off on the audit without delay, including delay resulting from protracted inquiry

43. Barden was reluctant to give such consent since it did not want to disclose business secrets to Surgical, its most important customer.

44. Surgical was one of the top five revenue producing clients in E & W's White Plains Office.

into Surgical's accounting methods, or, should E & W have withdrawn from the engagement, from an audit by another auditor.

On February 22, 1982, E & W personnel Dixon, Burke and Hope met at Berelsen's law offices with Berelsen, Yamont and two other attorneys for Barden in an unsuccessful effort to persuade Barden to let E & W use information obtained by its Barden auditors in its audit of Surgical. (Prior thereto it was thought that Yamont had met with Hirsch, Surgical's president, to tell him the full story as Yamont understood it).

On February 23, 1982, Dixon and Hope for E & W met with Hirsch, (President) Rosenkrantz (Comptroller) and Korthoff (Vice–President of operations) of Surgical at which meeting Dixon told them that Barden had refused to permit information developed in connection with audit work to be used in the Surgical audit. Hope further informed the group that E & W would not sign off on Surgical's financial statements until the matter was resolved. At this point Hirsch became angry and verbally abusive of the auditors, causing Dixon to walk out of the meeting.

Hirsch retrieved Dixon from the lobby of the building, and apologized to him for his conduct, and the meeting resumed.

In an effort to open up communication between Surgical and Barden without breaching Barden's confidentiality requirements, the E & W representatives had Surgical send a confirmation letter to Yamont, Barden's treasurer, on February 23, 1982, asking Barden to agree or disagree that the tooling invoices issued to Surgical from April 1981 through January 1982 (and attached to the letter) represented valid charges for services actually performed in the design, development and modification of Surgical's tooling. Because of Yamont's prior contentions that these invoices represented premium labor charges, they did not expect him to confirm, but offered him the opportunity to have denied the allegations in the letter. He did neither. Hence, the line of communication remained closed.

Previous statements by Berelsen, chairman of Barden's executive committee, had made it clear that he did not want Barden involved in the Surgical audit. Hence, the auditors were probably not surprised that Berelsen expressed displeasure at receiving the confirmation request and that Yamont was also unhappy about it. Nevertheless, following a meeting between Hirsch and Rosenkrantz of Surgical, and Berelsen and Yamont of Barden, Berelsen abruptly changed his mind (apparently as the result of pressure by Hirsch) and agreed to allow the E & W Surgical team access to his company's records.

On March 3, 1982, E & W staff met with officers of Surgical to discuss the issue of the premium billings and the labeling of them as "tool modifications". Korthoff, Surgical's operations chief, submitted that since November 1980, Lacey and Surgical had agreed upon a standard, or base price for the manufacture by Lacey of certain of Surgical's new-generation stapling products and a "premium charge" representing additional manual work that Lacey had to do before tooling could be put in place. Korthoff stated that in April 1981, Surgical informed Lacey that it would no longer pay the agreed-to premium charges, but that it would instead pay for tooling modifications that would eliminate the need for future manual operations.

The auditors asked Korthoff to reconcile this statement with the fact that the documentation showed no change in the premium-type billing after April. He explained that Robert More, Lacey's general manager, asked that the premium billing methodology be continued for the convenience of Lacey's accounting system. Korthoff said that because the tooling modifications were taking place at the same time that the tools were turning out product, and since Surgical's engineers were at Lacey on a daily basis monitoring the program, he was confident that Surgical was being billed fairly for the tooling work being performed.

The auditors noted that the final monthly premium billings for January, February and March, 1981 (plus an estimated $70,000 for April) added up to exactly $400,000.00. Although these invoices were labeled for premium charges, Korthoff told the auditors that the amount resulted from a negotiated settlement to end the tooling modification program rather than for work done under the premium billing arrangement.

The E & W auditors present were not persuaded by Korthoff's explanations. His statements flew in the face of the substantial amount of audit evidence assembled by Burke and Kempenich leading to the conclusion that the billings had been mislabeled. This, then, raised the very serious question of client integrity, i.e., as to whether Surgical management's representations were truthful.

Concerned with the fact that Surgical may have been trying to improperly capitalize payments to other vendors as tooling, just as with Lacey, the auditors reviewed Surgical's purchase orders (POs) to other vendors who were manufacturing both tooling and product for Surgical, including purchase order requisitions ("PORs") and capital expenditure request ("CERs"). The review revealed eight Surgical purchase orders to two of its vendors, "Tenax" and "PMP", where the purchase order price exceeded substantially but in exact round numbers the prices detailed in the accompanying POR and CER. The sum of these differences amounted to a very round and exact $90,000.00. Moreover, one of the PORs appeared to have been purposely altered from $25,000 to $50,000. The auditors also found one $340,000 purchase order to PMP that bore a strong resemblance to the Lacey "cost reduction" program of premium charges in which the PO described a "cost reduction program".

As a follow-up to these other vendor issues, Ferrante and Hope discussed the matter with Korthoff and Rosenkrantz. Korthoff told Ferrante that he was personally responsible for changing one of the Tenax purchase orders from $25,000 to $50,000 as a premium for expedited delivery. This despite the fact that Surgical had already agreed to pay an expedited delivery charge of $5,631 for the same product. Korthoff was unable to explain the above discrepancies. The two auditors agreed to put these "other vendors" issues on hold, pending the outcome of the Lacey investigation. However, Hope and Ferrante never performed these additional audit steps, nor never mentioned the matters again to Surgical.

On March 5, 1982, a meeting was held in E & W's White Plains office at which representatives of Surgical (Korthoff, Rosenkrantz and Surgical's general counsel), of Barden (More and an attorney), and of E & W (Hope, Burke and Strauss) attended.

At the meeting, Korthoff gave the same explanation he gave to Hope and Ferrante two days earlier as to the way the premium billings were set up. More was generally silent and by his silence, seemed to confirm Korthoff's story. As pointed out heretofore, just three weeks earlier More had explained in great detail to Burke and Kempenich that the billings were for manual labor operations incurred in production and that the billings were mislabeled "tooling modifications" at Surgical's direction. The auditors stated that in view of More's prior story they were surprised at his acquiescence to Korthoff's version at the meeting, and that they had expected the clients, Surgical and Barden, to disagree concerning the nature of the work underlying the billings. It is quite apparent, however, that More was outgunned and standing alone facing the principal customer of his employer without the support of those in his accounting department who had an understanding similar to his earlier one. The auditors were apparently satisfied, since More's turnabout in his story eliminated one of the chief problems preventing them from signing off on the audit. Under the circumstances, the failure of the auditors to more vigorously question More at that meeting is hard to understand.

Still somewhat skeptical of the explanations given by Korthoff, the E & W auditors, Hope and Dixon, on March 8, 1982 met with Jay Huffard, chairman of Surgical's audit committee, accompanied by Surgical's general counsel. The auditors told Huffard that they found three inconsistencies with the position of Surgical (Korthoff) that the premium billings were actually for tooling, mainly, (1) More's initial version had characterized tooling costs as relatively insignificant; (2) Lacey's internal financial records did not evidence a substantial tooling effort; and (3) the documentation showed that billings even after April, 1981, continued to be based on product shipped and premium labor charges despite Korthoff's allegations that this practice ceased on April 1. They also told Huffard that they had discovered additional problems with Surgical's purchases of tooling from other vendors.

Although chairman of Surgical's audit committee and presumed to be independent, Huffard expressed his opinion that Surgical did not have a problem, accused the auditors of "overreacting", and attempted to pressure them into signing Surgical's 10–K.[48]

Having acceded to Korthoff's story as to how the premium labor billings became tooling billing, particularly in view of the significant evidence the other way, there remained a further step with respect thereto before respondents felt they could sign off on Surgical's Form 10–K. Specifically, this was the question raised by Yamont and others on Barden's accounting staff that Barden's books did not reflect any expenditures for tooling modifications by Barden on behalf of Surgical.

On March 10, 1982, Hope and Burke, the respective engagement partners, met with More, Korthoff and Lee Stremba (an attorney from Berelsen's firm), first at the Lacey plant and later at Barden. While examining the books of Lacey and Barden they found an account called "Surgical production" for labor costs involved in tooling work done by Barden's tool makers for Surgical.

The tool and die makers ordinarily charged their time to two types of direct labor accounts: (1) Where Lacey had a separate purchase order for a particular tool or modification and thus planned to bill the customer separately for tooling, Lacey would open a job order and charge time to a job-order account called "Product Group Six". (2) Toolmakers also modified tools when there was no specific purchase order for tooling, in which case the toolmakers charged their time to the account known as "Product Group Eight".

More told the auditors that Lacey toolmakers never worked on production. The auditors inferred from this that all toolmaker time under the so-called "tooling program" which was supposedly paid for through the premium billings must have been charged to Group Eight, because of the absence of special job orders (Group Six). The auditors further inferred that since More was now telling them that the Lacey toolmakers never worked on production, all of the time charged in Group Eight had to be for tooling only and not for production.

At the request of the auditors, Loughman, of Barden's accounting section, pulled from the Barden records all toolmaker time under Group Eight amounting to $217,000 and the auditors concluded therefrom that this represented the Surgical tooling charges which Yamont and Loughman previously were unable to find in Barden's books.

However, the record is clear that the Barden tool and die makers did, in fact, perform substantial duties that were solely for production and hence not capitalizable, such as repairs, maintenance, sharpening and aligning of tools and dies and that these costs should be charged to

48. At this point it can be observed that when the premium charge issue was raised, E & W responded appropriately. It instructed the engagement partner not to sign Surgical's audit report, assembled a consultative team including regional and national office partners, investigated relevant documentation, interviewed appropri- ate personnel, documented the result of its investigation with detailed memoranda and workpapers, and confronted Surgical.

Yet, as will be seen, the audit inquiry ultimately resulted in a failure by E & W adequately to address and resolve the important client integrity issues presented.

production. Thus, in order for the auditors to be able to reasonably conclude that substantially all of the time charged to Group Eight was properly capitalizable or whether any part thereof should be charged to production, it would have been appropriate for them to find out just what jobs were performed by the toolmakers and what percent of their time, if any, was in production work. Rather than to ask this simple question of the toolmakers themselves, or of the Barden accountants, or to physically visit and watch the toolmakers at work, or to see even one tool that had been modified, the auditors chose to rely upon contradictory management assertions that toolmakers do not work on production, which in turn became the basis for their assigning the entire $217,000 of toolmakers services performed for Surgical in 1981 to modification and production of tools and dies.

It became important to accept this figure without any diminution since it permitted the auditors through some rough calculations by Hope to conclude that the sum of $1,050,000 was the correct amount to be capitalized as tooling modification, thereby removing one of the obstacles critical to E & W's signing off on Surgical's 1981 financial statements.

Hope's calculations started with the sum of $217,000 as representing direct labor costs. He added to this a charge for overhead of $325,000, computed by using a general overhead rate of 150 percent shown in Lacey's financial statements as applicable to all production. Hope then added an estimated $117,000 for engineering labor which he computed from a ratio which Product Group Eight toolmaker costs bore to total toolmaker costs. Finally, by subtracting the total of these costs from $1,050,000, Hope obtained an estimated gross profit on the billing of $391,000, or 37% of the total billings, which he considered to be "not inappropriate".[50]

However, in actuality Barden had varying overhead rates for different departments, and in 1981, tool room rate was 90%, not 150% as utilized by Hope. Moreover, this 90% rate *included* overhead for engineering labor, rather than as a separate additional charge in Hope's calculations. This must have been known to the E & W auditors doing the Barden audit.

It is obvious that Hope's calculations would have resulted in significantly different results if he had taken the trouble to seek out the correct tool room overhead rate and its embracing of engineering labor overhead, both of which could have been readily ascertained by inquiry which apparently the auditors did not do.

50. To summarize Hope's calculations:

Tool and die labor charged to Surgical production orders during calendar 1981	$217,000	
Lacey engineering labor allocated to Surgical product support in the same proportion as tool and die labor ($284,000 × 41.2%)		117,000
		659,000
Lacey overhead rate (exclusive of engineering labor) of 150% × $217,000	325,000	
Indicated gross profit (37.2%)		391,000
Total billings		$1,050,000

On March 11, 1982, the E & W "working group" convened in Dixon's office to consider Hope's results. Present in person or by telephone from the lowest to the highest in the E & W audit echelon were Hope, Burke, Strauss, Dixon, Neary, lawyers from E & W's general counsel's office, two attorneys from E & W's outside law firm, and Joseph Keller, then E & W's co-chairman. All of them agreed that the facts developed by Hope supported his conclusion that the toolmaker labor costs accumulated in the Group Eight production account at Lacey reasonably supported the payment to Barden and the capitalization by Surgical of $1,050,000. However, in the interest of extra caution they concluded that E & W should obtain from Korthoff on behalf of Surgical a written version of his story, and from Barden a confirmation that the invoices for premium billings were actually for tooling work performed.

As noted heretofore, a confirmation letter had been sent to Yamont on February 23 asking both More and Yamont to sign the confirmation, which they both declined to do. In conformity with the request of the E & W working group, a second confirmation was prepared similar in form and content to the first, except that it only asked for an affirmative confirmation that the "premium billing" was actually for tooling.

Some time between March 10 and 16, Burke and Dixon asked Yamont to sign the second confirm as Barden's "chief financial officer". It was important that Yamont sign because of his known disagreement that there was tooling involved in the billing. Yamont refused to sign in that capacity since that was not his title, nor in any capacity, since he had no personal knowledge of the transactions. The Barden auditors knew of Yamont's position all along and that he never had changed it.

On March 16, 1982 Burke met with Berelsen and a lawyer for Barden and related the result of E & W's second investigation, i.e., that the premium charge of $1,050,000 really was for tooling modification. Berelsen then authorized More to sign the confirmation as a representative of Lacey. The next day, Berelsen in a separate letter attested to More's authority to sign the confirm.[52]

The auditors now had in hand what they felt was sufficient evidentiary matter to justify signing off on the Form 10–K which they did promptly. On one day, March 17, 1982, they received Korthoff's written explanations, a letter signed by Surgical's general counsel

---

52. Normally, it is unusual in seeking confirmations involved with an audit to require more than the signature of an officer attesting to the contents of the confirmation letter. Here, however, the auditors were insisting upon two signatures, one of which was to be Berelsen's. However, Berelsen refused to confirm directly the contents of the letter but agreed to and did, *in a separate writing*, merely confirm that More was a vice-president of Barden and as such authorized to sign the confirmation. Berelsen's attestation letter was totally superfluous and added nothing except window-dressing. It is clear that Berelsen, an experienced and careful attorney, was distancing himself and keeping his name off the confirm while satisfying E & W's desires for a second signature. His excuse that he would not have allowed More to sign the confirmation if he thought it were untrue is rather weak.

attesting to Korthoff's authority to sign his memorandum, More's signed confirmation, Berelsen's attesting letter, and a detailed report from Hope in which he set forth his calculations that $1,050,000 of premium labor billing could have reflected tooling costs only. Also on the same day, Hope signed off E & W's unqualified audit report on Surgical's 1981 financial statements and they were filed with the Commission.

Since the auditors were satisfied concerning the Lacey/Barden matter, they decided not to pursue any further the other evidence suggesting that Surgical was padding its tooling billing with several of its vendors. Thus, the auditors performed no further work on the $340,000 PMP purchase order for a "cost reduction program" nor on the eight purchase orders from other vendors that exceeded the amounts on the purchase order requisitions by rounded-off amounts. They also were willing not to pursue further the PO/POR discrepancies on the grounds that although explanations with respect thereto were incomplete, the amounts were deemed immaterial. Concededly, immateriality does not justify an auditor to ignore an issue of client integrity, an issue which is very much involved herein.

Hence, at the conclusion of the March investigation, the E & W auditors had lost their proper audit skepticism, ignored and disregarded comprehensive documentation that was inconsistent with Surgical's story, ignored the earlier audit conclusions, relied upon unwarranted and untested assumptions, and disregarded the clear objections of the Barden accounting department.

Subsequent to the filing of Surgical's financial report for 1981, there were other events by which E & W was made aware that the Barden accountants continued in their belief that the premium billings of $1,050,000 were for production and not for tooling. Thus, on March 26, 1982, Richard Larsen, E & W's tax partner for both Surgical and Barden, visited Barden and was told by the accounting staff of their belief.

Again, in the E & W Audit Management Letter dated June 14, 1982 to Barden resulting from the 1981 audit, E & W expressed concern over the fact that a senior member of Barden management was allowed sole authority and responsibility for business transactions with a major customer (Surgical) and who entered into "unusual billing arrangements" with that customer during the first quarter of fiscal 1982. Despite respondents' protestations to the contrary, the language of the letter and the context in which it is stated make it clear that E & W was referring to Robert More as the Barden official, and that the "unusual billing arrangements" referred to the manner in which More had entered into the premium billing arrangements with Surgical for payment of additional labor charges. This meaning of the term "premium charges" had been quite clear to E & W in February 1982, as appears in the Burke and Kempenich memorandum following their examination of Barden's books.

In Hope's memorandum of March 17, 1982, which wrapped up all of the information E & W deemed necessary to sign off on Surgical's financials, he recognizes that the amount of $1,050,000 as charges for "tooling" had been arrived at on the same basis as amounts previously billed by Lacey as "premium prices" for production. Nothing was changed except the nomenclature. At the time, Hope had before him Korthoff's memorandum of March 12, 1982 referring to the practice of Lacey billing Surgical for "premium charges" the costs of the extra direct labor required to perform additional manned operations to the various component product parts.

Additional post-filing developments relate to Barden, as the holder of an industrial revenue bond issued by the Connecticut Developing Authority (CDA) covering its Lacey facility in Bridgeport, being required to periodically file with CDA schedules of its expenditures for capital items. Barden retained E & W to perform the required audit examination of these schedules. Prior to January 1983, the schedule of capital expenditures filed by Barden did not contain any of the items involved in the "premium billing" arrangement. However, E & W decided that because of the changes in nomenclature on the billing, they should be listed as capital expenditures.

So, on February 23, 1983, E & W filed with CDA an audit opinion and a new "Exhibit B" including the $1,050,000 in premium charge billings as a capital expense for tooling modifications. The schedule submitted, *as prepared by the Barden accounting department,* was under a heading reading as follows:

"THE BARDEN CORPORATION SCHEDULE OF PREMIUM BILLING CHARGES INCLUDED IN MANUFACTURING PRODUCTS COST *BILLED AT CUSTOMER REQUEST AS MODIFICATION OF MOLDS, TOOLS AND DIES.*

(Emphasis added).

The auditors would not interpret the wording of the caption by the Barden accountants as reflecting that Barden was taking a position that the "premium billings" were not for capitalizable tooling. The language of the heading and the surrounding circumstances demonstrate otherwise. In fact, the Barden auditors insisted upon including the language: "Billed at customer request . . ." because of their continuing belief that the billing charges related to production, not tooling expense.

In November 1983, Burke, after giving testimony in connection with the commission's investigation of Surgical, got the impression that Loughman did not agree that the Lacey billings to Surgical represented work done on Surgical's tooling. E & W, therefore, decided that Burke and Bruce Rosen should go to Barden to perform additional procedures. There they met with Lacey's engineering vice president, Robert Werner, who advised that while toolmakers spend more than half their time doing modification and design work, that the rest is spent doing non-capitalizable maintenance. He also advised that Lacey performed substantial tool and die modification and design work which was charged to Product Group Eight. At this point, it should have been clear to the auditors that not all of the labor costs in the sum of $217,000 were for tooling. Although the auditors never learned how much non-capitalizable toolmaking labor was included in this account, E & W decided not to pursue the question further because E & W resigned from the Surgical audit in December 1983 having become aware by this time of Surgical's deception relating to its arrangements in 1981 with certain vendors for the cost of defective parts to be billed to Surgical as tooling rather than expensed. * * * Finally, on November 29, 1984, Barden terminated its engagement with E & W.

SAS 16, AU 327, ¶ 14 (1977) states that when an independent auditor's examination causes him to be believe that irregularities may exist, he should attempt to obtain sufficient evidential matter to determine whether, in fact, material errors or irregularities do exist and, if so, their effect.

The most serious of the audit failures found in this case, is the Lacey/Barden client integrity investigation. In the face of the apparent implications involved in the premium billing issue pointing to a conclusion that the two corporations and officials thereof were engaged in a scheme to permit Surgical to improperly capitalize product costs relating to the new items manufactured for Surgical by Lacey, the initial reaction by the auditors after investigation was that invoices in the amount of some $1,050,000, described therein as being for "tool modification" work at Surgical's direction, were in fact for production work on parts. It was even suspected that fraud or some "kickback" dealings may have been going on. By that time, respondents, recognizing the seriousness of the issue involved, proceeded with a further investigation to resolve these questions, as outlined heretofore.

Yet, some six weeks later there developed a complete change in E & W's conclusions made on February 15, 1982, based upon Korthoff's representations as to the "premium billings," the change in More's assertion that there were only nominal costs for engineering and tooling associated with the premium billing program, and the discovery of an account "Surgical production", showing toolmaker labor costs of $217,000. The fact that More had changed his statement and that Lacey's internal bookkeeping did not appear to reflect a significant Surgical tooling program were deemed unresolved questions by Hope in his wrap-up memorandum of March 17, 1982 to the E & W working group.

Under the circumstances, it should have been quite clear to the auditors that More's change in statement was made in the face of severe pressure by Surgical at the meeting of March 5, 1982, which surely called for a more searching investigation than was made herein. The assumption by the E & W auditors that the $217,000 toolmaker costs for Surgical reflected only tooling modification labor was unwarranted. The auditors should have clarified this fact either in the tool room itself with the toolmakers or in the record and documents of Barden. As it turned out in fact, almost half of the toolmakers' work was involved with production not toolmaking and had the $217,000 figure been proportionately amended, it would have shown that there was no basis for E & W's assumption that Surgical paid Barden in 1981 $1,050,000 for tooling modification. Moreover, Hope's calculations in arriving at this latter sum was also based on erroneous assumptions concerning overhead and engineering labor, the correctness of which was readily available rather than from guesswork.

Discussion and Conclusions of Law

The authority of the Commission to discipline accountants and bar them from practice before the Commission under Rule 2(e) has been expressly upheld in the federal courts. See *Davy v. S.E.C.*, 792 F.2d 1418, 1421 (9th Cir. 1986) citing *Touche Ross v. S.E.C.*, 609 F.2d 570 (2nd Cir. 1979). As stated in *Davy*, "no court has since disagreed with *Touche Ross*".

The Second Circuit in *Touche Ross*, in sustaining the validity of the Rule as a necessary adjunct to the Commission's power to protect the integrity of its administrative procedures and the public in general, stated at page 581:

"＊ ＊ ＊ the Commission necessarily must rely heavily on both the accounting and legal professions to perform their tasks diligently and responsibly. Breaches of professional responsibility jeopardize the achievement of the objectives of the securities laws and can inflict great damage on public investors."

Respondents contend that in order to make a finding under Rule 2(e) of "improper professional conduct" by accountants and the imposition of a sanction therefor, there must also be a showing of "wilful" misconduct. They argue that to discipline "merely negligent" conduct would not be "reasonably related" to preserving the integrity of the Commission's processes.

The provisions of Rule 2(e)(1), call for the imposition of sanctions in situations wherein the Commission finds *inter alia* that the respondents:

"(i) not to possess the requisite qualifications to represent others, or

"(ii) to be lacking in character or integrity or to have engaged in unethical or improper professional conduct, or

"(iii) to have wilfully violated ＊ ＊ ＊ any provision of the Federal Securities Laws, or the rules and regulations thereunder."

The Order for Proceedings herein charges only violations of subparagraph (ii), specifically that respondents have "engaged in unethical or improper professional conduct".

Respondents, however, argue this way: that the charge of failure to comply with GAAS should be governed by the "wilfully violated" requirements of subparagraph (iii) of the Rule, since such failure amounts to a violation of the Commission's Regulation S–X (17 C.F.R. 210) which requires that all financial statements filed with the Commission be audited in accordance with GAAS; and that the Commission cannot proceed under subparagraph (ii) of Rule 2(e) thereby to avoid the "wilfully violated" requirements of subparagraph (iii).

This argument is specious. There is nothing in the administrative process that prevents the Commission from proceeding based upon violations of subparagraph (ii) even though the conduct of respondents might also come out to a violation of subparagraph (iii) or some other provision of law.

Respondents further urge that a reading of Rule 2(e) in its entirety demonstrates that its provisions contemplate sanctioning only *wilful* or deliberate wrongdoing, and that subparagraph (ii) is embraced within the "willfully violated" language of subparagraph (iii).

This argument is likewise insupportable; the allegation of "improper professional conduct" can very well stand on its own as a basis for proceeding against respondents.

Respondents advance in support of their contentions the Commission's decision in *Matter of William R. Carter,* 47 S.E.C. 471 (1981) in which the Commission dismissed proceedings under Rule 2(e) against two lawyers because there had not been then adopted applicable standards of professional conduct, and because generally accepted standards of professional conduct did not then unambiguously cover the actions of the lawyers in that case.

Carter, however, is inapplicable to the instant situation. It involves the question of when an attorney must disclose to a corporate client evidence of corporate misconduct. The Commission specifically directed itself only "to the narrow range of lawyers engaged in a federal securities practice, to the specific factual context of an ongoing disclosure program of a corporate client, and to the limited question of when it is appropriate for a lawyer to make further efforts within the corporation to forestall continuing violative conduct." (at page 476 of 47 S.E.C.) The Commission specifically differentiated between lawyers and accountants noting that the latter "issue audit reports that speak directly to the investing public and publicly represent that the code of conduct embodied in the statements of auditing standards promulgated by the AICPA has been followed" (at page 478). Lawyers, on the other hand, speak to their clients, not to the public, and are governed by generally recognized professional standards.

Finally, in *Carter,* the Commission expressly elected to analyze respondents' actions in the context of the "wilfully violated" provisions of subparagraph (iii) rather than under subparagraph (ii) of Rule 2(e)(1). Thus, the dicta quoted by respondents in their brief are unrelated to the situation which exists in this proceeding and do not give support to the respondents' contentions.

In the same vein, respondents contend that Rule 2(e) cannot be construed as to permit the imposition of sanctions on accountants' mere negligence arising from the good faith exercise of their professional judgment, that the language in subparagraph (ii) is vague, and that the Commission has never clearly articulated the meaning of the phrase "unethical or improper professional conduct" with reference to non-specific auditing and accounting standards. They urge that since the application of accounting and auditing standards to unique factual circumstances requires the subjective exercise of professional judgment, when this judgment is exercised in good faith, even erroneously, they cannot be the basis for an adverse finding under subparagraph (ii).

None of these arguments relates to the fact that the conduct of the auditors, whether through negligence, good faith, incompetence or ignorance, may subject accountants to the discipline of subparagraph (ii) in order to preserve thereby the integrity of the Commission's processes.

These contentions by respondents are not persuasive and should be rejected. Accounting and auditing standards do exist in the pronouncements of AICPA, and in the setting out of auditing standards and accounting principles in the decisions of the Commission. As was stated in *Carter:*

> At the same time, however, we perceive no unfairness whatsoever in holding those professionals who practice before us to generally recognized norms of professional conduct, whether or not such norms had previously been explicitly adopted or endorsed by the Commission. To do so upsets no justifiable expectations, since the professional is already subject to those norms. (page 508 of 47 S.E.C.).

Under all of the circumstances hereinbefore described it is concluded that the unqualified signing of the 1980 and 1981 Surgical's financial statements by E & W constituted a violation of the GAAS requirements and improper professional conduct under the provisions of Rule 2(e)(1)(ii) with respect to the respondents herein. The auditors failed to plan appropriate procedures, failed to obtain sufficient competent evidential matter, failed to recognize and deal appropriately with accounting issues that arose during the audits, failed to exercise due care in the execution of the audits, failed to maintain the proper level of professional skepticism, and failed to resolve the serious question of client integrity before certifying the 1981 financial statements.

The auditors unduly relied on the representation of Surgical's management with respect to matters of major significance in the audit. SAS 19 states that:

> "representations from management are part of the evidential matter the independent auditor obtains, but they are not a substitute for the application of those auditing procedures necessary to afford a reasonable basis for his opinion on the financial statements".

Without being repetitious of what has been stated hereinbefore, it is concluded that the auditors did not perform the necessary audit procedures to confirm the representations of management.

Respondents assert as a defense that they have been the victims of Surgical and Barden managements' fraud and deception, particularly with respect to the premium billings arrangements. That they were deliberately deceived is clear. Such deception however, did not relieve them of their responsibility to perform audits in conformity with GAAS and it does not matter that the accountant had been intentionally deceived by the party being audited. See *Matter of S.D. Leidesdorf & Company,* 46 S.E.C. 776 (1977) and *Matter of Ernst and Ernst,* 46 S.E.C., 1234, 1272 (1978), although the fact that auditors are deliberately deceived by management may be viewed as a mitigating factor, particularly in assessing a sanction. But such deception does not relieve the auditors of their responsibility to perform audits in conformity with GAAS (see *Ernst & Ernst, supra*). In fact, had the auditors properly conducted such routine audit procedures as following up on confirmation exceptions, they might well have discovered sooner Surgical's fraudulent practices regarding the vendor tooling purchase order scheme.

———

After Commissioner Treadway (whose speech is excerpted before the *E & W* case) left the SEC, the AICPA, the American Accounting Association, the Financial Executives Institute, the Institute of Internal Auditors and the National Association of Accountants appointed him chair of a blue ribbon panel to study and make recommendations to limit financial frauds. The result was the Report of the National Commission on Fraudulent Financial Reporting, 1987—the "Treadway Commission Report."

The Report makes specific recommendations to public companies, auditors, the SEC, Congress, and educators.

As to public companies, it endorsed the already widespread use of audit committees and internal auditing as well as the publication of management and audit committee reports. See the GE reports in the Appendix to Chapter X.

For external auditors, increased responsibility was urged. As a result, the Auditing Standards Board of the AICPA adopted radical changes described in the next section.

B. THE "EXPECTATIONS GAP" AUDITING STANDARDS

As relentless waves of ever-larger business frauds washed over the American economy during the past two decades, the public grew increasingly indignant at the perpetrators and those who were paid very well to guard against such wrongs. Scandal after scandal made it more and more apparent that auditors were not doing the job which investors were paying them for. The savings and loan disaster is the best-known example.

Because the accounting profession as it now exists would soon disappear without public support, the profession realized that it must reform. In 1988 the AICPA, through its Auditing Standards Board, radically altered GAAS with the purpose of increasing the auditor's responsibilities in detecting intentionally and negligently misleading financial statements.

The ASB adopted nine Statements of Auditing Standards to eliminate the expectations gap. We have already described in Chapter II the new form of auditor's report, designed to better inform investors of what the auditor does.

SAS No. 53, *The Auditor's Responsibility to Detect and Report Errors and Irregularities,* and SAS No. 54, *Illegal Acts by Clients,* are the substantive heart of the effort to cut back on misrepresentations. These two pronouncements deal with the question of the auditor's standard in uncovering negligent and intentional misrepresentations as well as illegality. The other seven SASs may be divided into three more groups.

(1) Those designed to cause more effective audits:

    (a) SAS No. 55, *Consideration of the Internal Control Structure in a Financial Statement Audit*

    (b) SAS No. 56, *Analytical Procedures*

    (c) SAS No. 57, *Auditing Accounting Estimates*

(2) Those designed to improve public reports:

    (a) SAS No. 58, *Reports on Audited Financial Statements*

    (b) SAS No. 59, *The Auditor's Consideration of an Entity's Ability to Continue as a Going Concern*

(3) Those designed to improve communications within the reporting entity:

    (a) SAS No. 60, *Communication of Internal Control Structure Related Matters Noted in an Audit*

    (b) SAS No. 61, *Communications with Audit Committees.*

1. THE CENTERPIECE; SASs NOs. 53 AND 54

SAS NO. 53, THE AUDITOR'S RESPONSIBILITY TO DETECT AND REPORT ERRORS AND IRREGULARITIES

I AICPA, Professional Standards AU § 327 (1988).

1. This Statement provides guidance on the independent auditor's responsibility for the detection of errors and irregularities in an audit of financial statements in accordance with generally accepted auditing standards. It describes factors that influence the auditor's ability to

detect errors and irregularities and explains how the exercise of due care should give appropriate consideration to the possibility of errors or irregularities. It also provides guidance on the auditor's responsibility to communicate detected matters both within and outside the entity whose financial statements are under audit.

Definition of Errors and Irregularities

2. The term *errors* refers to *unintentional* misstatements or omissions of amounts or disclosures in financial statements. Errors may involve—

> Mistakes in gathering or processing accounting data from which financial statements are prepared.

> Incorrect accounting estimates arising from oversight or misinterpretation of facts.

> Mistakes in the application of accounting principles relating to amount, classification, manner of presentation, or disclosure.

3. The term *irregularities* refers to *intentional* misstatements or omissions of amounts or disclosures in financial statements. Irregularities include fraudulent financial reporting undertaken to render financial statements misleading, sometimes called management fraud, and misappropriation of assets, sometimes called *defalcations*. Irregularities may involve acts such as the following:

> Manipulation, falsification, or alteration of accounting records or supporting documents from which financial statements are prepared.

> Misrepresentation or intentional omission of events, transactions, or other significant information.

> Intentional misapplication of accounting principles relating to amounts, classification, manner of presentation, or disclosure.

4. The primary factor that distinguishes errors from irregularities is whether the underlying cause of a misstatement in financial statements is intentional or unintentional. Intent, however, is often difficult to determine, particularly in matters involving accounting estimates or the application of accounting principles. For example, an unreasonable accounting estimate may result from unintentional bias or may be an intentional attempt to misstate the financial statements.

The Auditor's Responsibility to Detect Errors and Irregularities

5. The auditor should assess the risk that errors and irregularities may cause the financial statements to contain a material misstatement. Based on that assessment, the auditor should design the audit to provide reasonable assurance of detecting errors and irregularities that are material to the financial statements.[2,3]

2. The concept of reasonable assurance is recognized in the third standard of fieldwork, "Sufficient competent evidential matter is to be obtained through inspection, observation, inquiries and confirmation to afford a reasonable basis for an opinion regarding the financial statements under examination" and is discussed in

3. See note 3 on page 656.

6. The auditor's assessment of the risk of material misstatement of the financial statements requires the auditor to understand the characteristics of errors and irregularities that are discussed in the Appendix and the complex interaction of those characteristics. Based on that understanding, the auditor designs and performs appropriate audit procedures and evaluates the results.

7. Because of the characteristics of irregularities, particularly those involving forgery and collusion, a properly designed and executed audit may not detect a material irregularity. For example, generally accepted auditing standards do not require that an auditor authenticate documents, nor is the auditor trained to do so. Also, audit procedures that are effective for detecting a misstatement that is unintentional may be ineffective for a misstatement that is intentional and is concealed through collusion between client personnel and third parties or among management or employees of the client.

8. The auditor should exercise (a) due care in planning, performing, and evaluating the results of audit procedures, and (b) the proper degree of professional skepticism to achieve reasonable assurance that material errors or irregularities will be detected. Since the auditor's opinion on the financial statements is based on the concept of reasonable assurance, the auditor is not an insurer and his report does not constitute a guarantee. Therefore, the subsequent discovery that a material misstatement exists in the financial statements does not, in and of itself, evidence inadequate planning, performance, or judgment on the part of the auditor.

Consideration of the Possibility of Material Misstatements in Audit Planning

9. In developing an audit plan, the auditor should consider factors influencing audit risk that relate to several or all account balances and obtain an understanding of the internal control structure.[4] These matters often have effects pervasive to the financial statements taken as a whole and also influence the auditor's consideration of risk at the account balance or class-of-transactions level.

Consideration of Audit Risk at the Financial Statement Level

10. An assessment of the risk of material misstatements should be made during planning. The auditor's understanding of the internal control structure should either heighten or mitigate the auditor's concern about the risk of material misstatements. The factors consid-

Statement on Auditing Standards No. 31, *Evidential Matter* (AICPA, *Professional Standards*, vol. 1, AU sec. 326) and SAS No. 39, *Audit Sampling* (AICPA, *Professional Standards*, vol. 1, AU sec. 350).

3. The auditor's responsibility for detecting misstatements resulting from illegal acts, as defined in SAS No. 54, *Illegal Acts by Clients*, having a direct and material effect on the determination of financial statement amounts is the same as that for other errors and irregularities.

4. See SAS No. 55, *Consideration of the Internal Control Structure in a Financial Statement Audit*.

ered in assessing risk should be considered in combination to make an overall judgment; the presence of some factors in isolation would not necessarily indicate increased risk. Factors such as those listed below may be considered.

Management Characteristics

Management operating and financing decisions are dominated by a single person.

Management's attitude toward financial reporting is unduly aggressive.

Management (particularly senior accounting personnel) turnover is high.

Management places undue emphasis on meeting earnings projections.

Management's reputation in the business community is poor.

Operating and Industry Characteristics

Profitability of entity relative to its industry is inadequate or inconsistent.

Sensitivity of operating results to economic factors (inflation, interest rates, unemployment, etc.) is high.

Rate of change in entity's industry is rapid.

Direction of change in entity's industry is declining with many business failures.

Organization is decentralized without adequate monitoring.

Internal or external matters that raise substantial doubt about the entity's ability to continue as a going concern are present. (See SAS No. 59, *The Auditor's Consideration of an Entity's Ability to Continue as a Going Concern.*)

Engagement Characteristics

Many contentious or difficult accounting issues are present.

Significant difficult-to-audit transactions or balances are present.

Significant and unusual related party transactions not in the ordinary course of business are present.

Nature, cause (if known), or the amount of known and likely misstatements detected in the audit of prior period's financial statements is significant.

It is a new client with no prior audit history or sufficient information is not available from the predecessor auditor.

11. The size, complexity, and ownership characteristics of the entity have a significant influence on the risk factors considered to be important. For example, for a large entity, the auditor would ordinarily give consideration to factors that constrain improper conduct by senior management, such as the effectiveness of the board of directors, the audit committee or others with equivalent authority and responsi-

bility[5], and the internal audit function. Consideration would also be given to the measures taken to enforce a formal code of conduct and the effectiveness of the budgeting or responsibility reporting system. For a small entity some of these matters might be considered inapplicable or unimportant, particularly if the auditor's past experience with the entity has been that effective owner-manager or trustee involvement creates a good control environment.

12. The auditor should assess the risk of management misrepresentation by reviewing information obtained about risk factors and the internal control structure. Matters such as the following may be considered:

> Are there known circumstances that may indicate a management predisposition to distort financial statements, such as frequent disputes about aggressive application of accounting principles that increase earnings, evasive responses to audit inquiries, or excessive emphasis on meeting quantified targets that must be achieved to receive a substantial portion of management compensation?

> Are there indications that management has failed to establish policies and procedures that provide reasonable assurance of reliable accounting estimates, such as personnel who develop estimates appearing to lack necessary knowledge and experience, supervisors of these personnel appearing careless or inexperienced, or there is a history of unreliable or unreasonable estimates?

> Are there conditions that indicate lack of control of activities, such as constant crisis conditions in operating or accounting areas, disorganized work areas, frequent or excessive back orders, shortages, delays, or lack of documentation for major transactions?

> Are there indications of a lack of control over computer processing, such as a lack of controls over access to applications that initiate or control the movement of assets (for example, a demand deposit application in a bank), high levels of processing errors, or unusual delays in providing processing results and reports?

> Are there indications that management has not developed or communicated adequate policies and procedures for security of data or assets, such as not investigating employees in key positions before hiring, or allowing unauthorized personnel to have ready access to data or assets?

13. The auditor should consider the effect of the matters described in paragraphs 10 to 12 on the overall audit strategy and the expected conduct and scope of the audit.

The Auditor's Response to Risk at the Financial Statement Level

14. The auditor's overall judgment about the level of risk in an engagement may affect engagement staffing, extent of supervision,

---

5. For entities that do not have audit committees, the phrase "others with equivalent authority and responsibility" may include the board of directors, the board of trustees, or the owner in owner-managed entities.

overall strategy for expected conduct and scope of audit, and degree of professional skepticism applied. Thus, the auditor's assessment of risk may affect audit planning in one or more of the following ways. The experience and training of personnel assigned significant engagement responsibilities should be commensurate with the auditor's assessment of the level of risk for the engagement. Ordinarily, higher risk requires more experienced personnel or more extensive supervision by the auditor with final responsibility for the engagement during both the planning and the conduct of the engagement. Higher risk may cause the auditor to expand the extent of procedures applied, apply procedures closer to or as of the balance sheet date, particularly in critical audit areas, or modify the nature of procedures to obtain more persuasive evidence. Higher risk will also ordinarily cause the auditor to exercise a heightened degree of professional skepticism in conducting the audit (see paragraphs 16 to 21).

The Auditor's Consideration of Audit Risk at the Balance or Class Level

15. The following matters are examples of factors that may influence the auditor's consideration of risk of material misstatement related to particular assertions at the balance or class level: [6]

Effect of risk factors identified at the financial statement or engagement level on the particular account balance or transaction class.

Complexity and contentiousness of accounting issues affecting balance or class.

Frequency or significance of difficult-to-audit transactions affecting balance or class.

Nature, cause, and amount of known and likely misstatements detected in the balance or class in the prior audit.

Susceptibility of related assets to misappropriation.

Competence and experience of personnel assigned to processing data that affect the balance or class.

Extent of judgment involved in determining the total balance or class.

Size and volume of individual items constituting the balance or class.

Complexity of calculations affecting the balance or class.

Professional Skepticism

16. An audit of financial statements in accordance with generally accepted auditing standards should be planned and performed with an attitude of professional skepticism. The auditor neither assumes that

6. Additional factors relating to risk assessment are found in SAS No. 47, *Audit Risk and Materiality in Conducting an Au-* *dit* (AICPA, *Professional Standards*, vol. 1, AU sec. 312).

management is dishonest nor assumes unquestioned honesty. Rather, the auditor recognizes that conditions observed and evidential matter obtained, including information from prior audits, need to be objectively evaluated to determine whether the financial statements are free of material misstatement.

17. Management integrity is important because management can direct subordinates to record transactions or conceal information in a manner that can materially misstate financial statements. When approaching difficult-to-substantiate assertions, the auditor should recognize the increased importance of his consideration of factors that bear on management integrity. A presumption of management dishonesty, however, would be contrary to the accumulated experience of auditors. Moreover, if dishonesty were presumed, the auditor would potentially need to question the genuineness of all records and documents obtained from the client and would require conclusive rather than persuasive evidence to corroborate all management representations. An audit conducted on these terms would be unreasonably costly and impractical.

Professional Skepticism in Audit Planning

18. Whenever the auditor has reached a conclusion that there is significant risk of material misstatement of the financial statements, the auditor reacts in one or more ways. The auditor should consider this assessment in determining the nature, timing, or extent of procedures, assigning staff, or requiring appropriate levels of supervision. The auditor may identify specific transactions involving senior management and confirm the details with appropriate external parties and review in detail all material accounting entries prepared or approved by senior management.

19. The auditor should consider whether accounting policies are acceptable in the circumstances. However, when the auditor has reached a conclusion that there is significant risk of intentional distortion of financial statements, the auditor should recognize that management's selection and application of significant accounting policies, particularly those related to revenue recognition, asset valuation, and capitalization versus expensing, may be misused. Increased risk of intentional distortion of the financial statements should cause greater concern about whether accounting principles that are otherwise generally accepted are being used in inappropriate circumstances to create a distortion of earnings. For example, management might use the percentage of completion method in circumstances that do not justify its use to misstate operating results.

20. When evaluation at the financial statement level indicates significant risk, the auditor requires more or different evidence to support material transactions than would be the case in the absence of such risk. For example, the auditor may perform additional procedures to determine that sales are properly recorded, giving considera-

tion to the possibility that the buyer has a right to return the product. Transactions that are both large and unusual, particularly at year-end, should be selected for testing.

Professional Skepticism in Performance of the Audit

21. In performing procedures and gathering evidential matter, the auditor continually maintains an attitude of professional skepticism. The performance of auditing procedures during the audit may result in the detection of conditions or circumstances that should cause the auditor to consider whether material misstatements exist. If a condition or circumstance differs adversely from the auditor's expectation, the auditor needs to consider the reason for such a difference. Examples of such conditions or circumstances are as follows:

> Analytical procedures disclose significant differences from expectations.

> Significant unreconciled differences between reconciliations of a control account and subsidiary records or between a physical count and a related account are not appropriately investigated and corrected on a timely basis.

> Confirmation requests disclose significant differences or yield fewer responses than expected.

> Transactions selected for testing are not supported by proper documentation or are not appropriately authorized.

> Supporting records or files that should be readily available are not promptly produced when requested.

> Audit tests detect errors that apparently were known to client personnel, but were not voluntarily disclosed to the auditor.

When such conditions or circumstances exist, the planned scope of audit procedures should be reconsidered. As the number of differences from expectations or the frequency with which the auditor is unable to obtain satisfactory explanations increases, the auditor should consider whether the assessment of the risk of material misstatement of the financial statements made in the planning stage of the engagement is still appropriate.

Evaluation of Audit Test Results

22. The auditor should evaluate the significance of differences between the accounting records and the underlying facts and circumstances detected by the application of auditing procedures. The auditor should consider both the quantitative and qualitative aspects of these matters and whether they are indicative of an error or an irregularity. Often a particular matter considered in isolation cannot be identified as an error or irregularity; nevertheless, this evaluation is important. Because irregularities are intentional, they have implications beyond

their direct monetary effect and the auditor needs to consider the implications for other aspects of the audit.

23. The auditor's objective is to reach a conclusion on whether the financial statements, taken as a whole, are materially misstated. The auditor should accumulate potential audit adjustments during the audit and summarize and evaluate the combined effect. In this regard, the auditor may designate an amount below which potential audit adjustments need not be accumulated. This amount would be set so that any such adjustments, either individually or when aggregated with other adjustments, would not be material to the financial statements.

24. If the auditor has determined that an audit adjustment is, or may be, an irregularity, but has also determined that the effect on the financial statements could not be material, the auditor should—

    a. Refer the matter to an appropriate level of management that is at least one level above those involved.

    b. Be satisfied that, in view of the organizational position of the likely perpetrator, the irregularity has no implications for other aspects of the audit or that those implications have been adequately considered.

For example, irregularities involving misappropriation of cash from a small imprest fund would normally be of little significance because both the manner of operating the fund and its size would tend to establish a limit on the amount of loss and the custodianship of such a fund is normally entrusted to a relatively low-level employee.

25. If the auditor has determined that an audit adjustment is, or may be, an irregularity and has either determined that the effect could be material or has been unable to evaluate potential materiality, the auditor should—

    a. Consider the implications for other aspects of the audit.

    b. Discuss the matter and the approach to further investigation with an appropriate level of management that is at least one level above those involved.

    c. Attempt to obtain sufficient competent evidential matter to determine whether, in fact, material irregularities exist and, if so, their effect.

    d. If appropriate, suggest that the client consult with legal counsel on matters concerning questions of law.

The Effect of Irregularities on the Audit Report

26. If the auditor has concluded that the financial statements are materially affected by an irregularity, the auditor should insist that the financial statements be revised and, if they are not, express a qualified or an adverse opinion on the financial statements, disclosing all substantive reasons for his opinion.

27. If the auditor is precluded from applying necessary procedures, or if, after the application of extended procedures, the auditor is

unable to conclude whether possible irregularities may materially affect the financial statements, the auditor should—

     a. Disclaim or qualify an opinion on the financial statements.

     b. Communicate his findings to the audit committee or the board of directors.

If the client refuses to accept the auditor's report as modified for the circumstances described above, the auditor should withdraw from the engagement and communicate the reasons for withdrawal to the audit committee or board of directors. Whether the auditor concludes that withdrawal from the engagement is appropriate in other circumstances depends on the diligence and cooperation of senior management and the board of directors in investigating the circumstances and taking appropriate remedial action. For example, if the auditor is precluded by the client from obtaining reasonably available evidential matter, withdrawal ordinarily would be appropriate. However, because of the variety of circumstances that may arise, it is not possible to describe all those circumstances when withdrawal would be appropriate.

Communications Concerning Errors or Irregularities

    28. For the audit committee[7] to make the informed judgments necessary to fulfill its responsibility for the oversight of financial reporting, the auditor should assure himself that the audit committee is adequately informed about any irregularities of which the auditor becomes aware during the audit unless those irregularities are clearly inconsequential.[8] For example, a minor defalcation by an employee at a low level in the organization might be considered inconsequential. However, irregularities involving senior management of which the auditor becomes aware should be reported directly to the audit committee. Irregularities that are individually immaterial may be reported to the audit committee on an aggregate basis, and the auditor may reach an understanding with the audit committee on the nature and amount of reportable irregularities.

    29. Disclosure of irregularities to parties other than the client's senior management and its audit committee or board of directors is not ordinarily part of the auditor's responsibility, and would be precluded by the auditor's ethical or legal obligation of confidentiality unless the matter affects his opinion on the financial statements. The auditor should recognize, however, that in the following circumstances a duty to disclose outside the client may exist:

     a. When the entity reports an auditor change under the appropriate securities law on Form 8–K.[9]

---

7. See note 5.

8. The auditor's responsibility to communicate errors within certain entities whose financial statements are under audit is described in SAS No. 61, *Communication With Audit Committees.*

9. Disclosure to the Securities and Exchange Commission may be necessary if, among other matters, the auditor withdraws because the board of directors has not taken appropriate remedial action. Such failure may be a reportable disagreement on Form 8–K.

    b. To a successor auditor when the successor makes inquiries in accordance with SAS No. 7, *Communications Between Predecessor and Successor Auditors* (AICPA, *Professional Standards,* vol. 1, AU sec. 315).[10]

    c. In response to a subpoena.

    d. To a funding agency or other specified agency in accordance with requirements for the audits of entities that receive financial assistance from a government agency.

Because potential conflicts with the auditor's ethical and legal obligations for confidentiality may be complex, the auditor may wish to consult with legal counsel before discussing irregularities with parties outside the client.

Responsibilities in Other Circumstances

    30. This Statement describes the auditor's responsibilities to detect and report errors and irregularities in an audit of a complete set of financial statements made in accordance with generally accepted auditing standards. In other engagements, the auditor's responsibilities may be more extensive or more restricted, depending on the terms of the engagement.

    31. The auditor may accept an engagement that necessitates a more extensive responsibility to detect or report irregularities. For example, in an audit in accordance with *Standards for Audit of Governmental Organizations, Programs, Activities, and Functions, 1981 Revision,* issued by the U.S. General Accounting Office, the auditor should be aware that such standards go beyond generally accepted auditing standards as they relate to notification when the audit indicates that irregularities may exist. These standards require the auditor not only to promptly report instances of irregularities to the audited entity's management, but also to report the matter to the funding agency or other specified agency.

    32. When an examination does not encompass a complete set of financial statements or a complete individual financial statement, or when the scope is less extensive than an audit in accordance with generally accepted auditing standards, the auditor's ability to detect material misstatements may be considerably reduced. For example, in an engagement to report on specified elements, accounts, or items of financial statements, the auditor's procedures focus on the specific element, account, or item and the special purpose of the engagement. In these circumstances, the auditor's assessment of risk at the financial statement level and other aspects of the examination that relate to the entity and its financial statements taken as a whole is necessarily more restricted.

10. In accordance with SAS No. 7, communications between predecessor and successor auditors require the specific permission of the client.

Effective Date

33. This Statement is effective for audits of financial statements for periods beginning on or after January 1, 1989. Early application of the provisions of this Statement is permissible.

Appendix

Characteristics of Errors and Irregularities

1. Characteristics of errors and irregularities that are relevant because of their potential influence on the auditor's ability to detect such matters are materiality of the effect on financial statements, level of management or employees involved, extent and skillfulness of any concealment, relationship to established specific control procedures, and the specific financial statement affected.

Materiality

2. SAS No. 47, *Audit Risk and Materiality in Conducting an Audit* (AICPA, *Professional Standards,* vol. 1, AU sec. 312.04), states that "financial statements are materially misstated when they contain errors or irregularities whose effect, individually or in the aggregate, is important enough to cause them not be presented fairly in conformity with generally accepted accounting principles." SAS No. 47, paragraph 13, also states: "The auditor generally plans the audit primarily to detect errors that he believes could be large enough, individually or in the aggregate, to be quantitatively material to the financial statements." As used in SAS No. 47, the term *errors* refers to both errors and irregularities.

3. In planning the audit, the auditor is concerned with matters that could be material to the financial statements. An audit in accordance with generally accepted auditing standards may detect errors or irregularities that are not material to the financial statements, but such an audit can provide no assurance of detecting immaterial errors or irregularities. In this regard, there is no important distinction between errors and irregularities. There is a distinction, however, in the auditor's response to detected matters. Generally, an isolated, immaterial error in processing accounting data or applying accounting principles is not significant to the audit. In contrast, detection on an irregularity requires consideration of the implications for the integrity of management or employees and the possible effect on other aspects of the audit.

Level of Involvement

4. An irregularity may be caused by an employee or by management and, if by management, by a relatively high or low level of management. The experience of auditors indicates that the level of involvement often combines with other characteristics in ways that have an influence on the auditor's ability to detect.

5. Defalcations by employees are often immaterial in amount and concealed in a manner that does not misstate net assets or net income. This type of irregularity can be more efficiently and effectively dealt with by an effective internal control structure and fidelity bonding of employees.

6. Material irregularities perpetrated by senior levels of management, including an owner-manager of a small business, are infrequent, but when they do occur they often engender widespread attention. These irregularities may not be susceptible to prevention or detection by specific control procedures because senior management is above the controls that deter employees or may override these controls with relative ease. Culture, custom, and the corporate governance system inhibit irregularities by senior management, but are not infallible deterrents. For this reason, an audit in accordance with generally accepted auditing standards necessarily gives due consideration to factors that bear on management integrity and the control environment.

Concealment

7. Concealment is any attempt by the perpetrator of an irregularity to reduce the likelihood of detection. Concealment usually involves manipulation of accounting records or supporting documents to disguise the fact that the accounting records are not in agreement with the underlying facts and circumstances. Concealment can be skillful and elaborate or clumsy and limited. The auditor's ability to detect a concealed irregularity depends on the skillfulness of the perpetrator, the frequency and extent of manipulation, and the relative size of individual amounts manipulated.

8. Forgery may be used to create false signatures, other signs of authenticity, or entire documents. Collusion may result in falsified confirmations or other evidence of validity. Also, unrecorded transactions are normally more difficult to detect than concealment achieved by manipulation of recorded transactions. However, the effect of concealment on the ability to detect an irregularity is dependent on the particular circumstances. For example, an attempt to mislead users of financial statements by recording large, fictitious revenue transactions late in the period without supporting documentation would be more readily detected than fictitious revenue transactions spread throughout the period, individually immaterial in amount, and supported by legitimate-appearing invoices and shipping documents. Moreover, both of these irregularities might be extremely difficult, if not impossible, to detect if collusion of customers is added to the concealment scheme.

Internal Control Structure

9. A lack of control procedures could permit an error or irregularity to occur repeatedly and the repeated occurrence could accumulate to a material amount. However, the auditor may not detect an error or

irregularity that results from a nonrecurring breakdown of a specific control procedure because a rare item permitted by temporary conditions may not come to light in the performance of analytical or other procedures.

10. Irregularities may also be perpetrated or concealed by circumvention of specific control procedures or may be perpetrated by a level of management above specific control procedures. These types of irregularities are generally more difficult for an auditor to detect. However, the auditor should consider whether there are circumstances or factors that indicate a higher risk of these types of irregularities and modify auditing procedures accordingly.

Financial Statement Effect

11. Other matters remaining equal, errors or irregularities that involve overstatement will generally be more readily detected than those that involve understatement because the audit evidence available is more reliable for detecting such errors or irregularities. Also, misstatements that are charged to the income statement are less likely to be detected than those that are concealed in the balance sheet, because the process of comparing recorded accountability with the existing assets should detect significant errors concealed in the balance sheet.

Summary

12. The foregoing discussion considers characteristics of errors and irregularities individually and explains the effect an individual characteristic tends to have on the auditor's detection ability. However, these characteristics may interact in particular circumstances in ways that also affect the auditor's ability to detect a specific error or irregularity.

The Statement entitled The Auditor's Responsibility to Detect and Report Errors and Irregularities *was adopted by the assenting votes of twenty members of the board, of whom one, Mr. Clancy, assented with qualification. Mr. Gunther dissented.*

Mr. Clancy qualifies his assent to the issuance of this Statement because, although he endorses the extension of the auditor's responsibilities to detect and report material misstatements of the financial statements, he believes that the inclusion of the reasonable assurance concept in the auditor's responsibility statement diminishes an otherwise affirmative acknowledgement that the audit should be designed to detect material misstatements of the financial statements.

Mr. Gunther dissents because he has not seen evidence that SAS No. 16, *The Independent Auditor's Responsibility for the Detection of Errors or Irregularities,* is inadequate.

CARMICHAEL, THE AUDITOR'S NEW GUIDE TO ERRORS, IRREGULARITIES AND ILLEGAL ACTS

J. Accountancy 40 (Sept. 1988).*

* * *

"SAS no. 53, *The Auditor's Responsibility to Detect and Report Errors and Irregularities,* updates and revises SAS no. 16, *The Independent Auditor's Responsibility for the Detection of Errors or Irregularities,* to say that an audit should be designed to provide reasonable assurance of detecting material misstatements—both material errors and material irregularities. SAS no. 53 imposes many new requirements, including a responsibility to assess specifically the likelihood of material misstatement at the entity level and the likelihood of management misrepresentation.

"SAS no. 54, *Illegal Acts by Clients* revises SAS no. 17, *Illegal Acts by Clients,* in regard to illegal acts that have a direct effect on the financial statements but retains the position that the auditor should be aware of the possibility that illegal acts with an *indirect* effect on financial statements may have occurred.

"WHY TWO SEPARATE SASs?

"The main reason for two separate SASs is that the auditing standards board wanted to make a sharp distinction between auditors' responsibilities for detecting *irregularities* and their responsibilities for uncovering *illegal* acts.

"The ASB believed it simply isn't feasible to design an audit to provide reasonable assurance of detecting *all* illegal acts that could have a material effect on the financial statements. U.S. businesses are subject to a host of laws and regulations that, if violated, lead to very material consequences in their financial statements. These include laws governing securities issuance and trading, occupational safety and health, food and drug administration, environmental protection, equal employment, price fixing and antitrust violations. Auditors usually aren't trained to spot violations of such laws and regulations and, as a practical matter, they have little, if any, chance of detecting them unless informed of them by their clients or their clients' attorneys or if there's evidence of a government investigation or enforcement proceeding in the corporate minutes or correspondence made available to the auditor.

"For these reasons, the auditor doesn't plan the audit to include audit procedures specifically designed to detect illegal acts.

"There is, however, one very important exception to this generalization. For illegal acts that have both a *direct* and a *material* effect on financial statement line-item amounts, auditors have exactly the same responsibility they have for detecting material errors and irregularities.

"For example, assume a client obtains a government contract requiring compliance with certain specified laws and regulations in order for revenue to be earned. Also assume that the amount of revenue earned is material. The auditor needs to test compliance with the laws and regulations on which the revenue stream is dependent.

"Violation of other laws and regulations also might cause the government to suspend the contract. These laws and regulations, however, have an indirect effect on the financial statements and this indirect contingency may need to be disclosed. Nevertheless, auditors have no responsibility to design the audit to detect violations of laws and regulations that could have a material effect only through the need to disclose a contingency.

"DO THE NEW SASs IMPOSE NEW MATERIALITY STANDARDS?

"Does the notion of an illegal act with a direct and material effect on a financial statement line item mean that materiality is judged in relation to the individual amount? Definitely not! Materiality should be evaluated in relation to the financial statements taken as a whole, as explained in SAS no. 47, *Audit Risk and Materiality in Conducting an Audit.* The ASB didn't intend to change any of the guidance in SAS no. 47.

* * *

"HOW IS RESPONSIBILITY FOR DETECTION CHANGED?

"SAS no. 16 required the auditor to plan the audit *to search for* material errors and irregularities. SAS no. 53, in contrast, requires the auditor to design the audit *to provide reasonable assurance* of detecting errors and irregularities that are material to the financial statements.

"The difference in the words is subtle; to a casual reader there might be little distinction. But the ASB had an important message for auditors: Be more sensitive to the possibility of material irregularities in every audit. Carefully consider and evaluate the risk that financial statement assertions may be materially misstated because of intentional misconduct by senior management or employees.

"The difference between SAS no. 16 and SAS no. 53 is exemplified by the auditor's attitude about the possibility of management dishonesty. Most auditors believed that SAS no. 16 entitled them to assume that management was honest unless information came to their attention that specifically contradicted that assumption.

"SAS no. 53 throws that comfortable notion on the heap of discarded audit folklore. Auditors can't assume management is honest or dishonest. They should take a hard, cold look at the possibility of management misrepresentation at the start of the audit and reexamine the likelihood of management misrepresentations as the audit progresses.

"Another difference between SAS no. 53 and SAS no. 16 is that SAS no. 53 expresses the auditor's responsibility in a much more affirmative fashion. SAS no. 16 stressed the inherent limitations of an audit. The new SAS, however, still acknowledges that forgery or collusion may result in failure to detect a material irregularity.

"DO THE LETTERS CHANGE?

"*Engagement letters.* Because auditors can't altogether guarantee the detection of material irregularities, they have included a disclaimer of responsibility in engagement letters. This caveat points out that an audit isn't specifically designed, and can't be relied on, to detect irregularities—although they may be discovered.

"Apparently, some auditors believed the language of the engagement letter was an accurate description of their responsibility. SAS no. 53 clearly invalidates this misguided belief. An audit should be designed to provide reasonable assurance of detecting material irregularities.

"Does this mean the wording of the typical engagement letter should be modified? Probably. The ASB didn't take a position on this issue because an engagement letter is a business device for the auditor's protection and not a professional requirement. Engagement letters should be revised along the lines of the new description of an audit in the scope paragraph of the new standard report presented in SAS no. 58, *Reports on Audited Financial Statements.*

"*The management representation letter.* Does the professional skepticism mandated by SAS no. 53 mean a management representation letter is worthless? Certainly not. Obtaining certain representations from management is required by SAS no. 19, *Client Representations,* and SAS nos. 53 and 54 don't change this requirement.

"If the auditor exercises professional skepticism in planning and performing the audit and in evaluating audit test results, the worth of management's representations is actually enhanced rather than reduced. Management's representation letter is signed near the conclusion of the audit and by that point the auditor should have resolved any significant doubts about management's integrity. Moreover, obtaining management's representations is never a substitute for applying audit procedures.

"Does the typical representation letter need to be modified because of SASs nos. 53 and 54? No. The representations ordinarily obtained under SAS no. 19 already include appropriate representations about the absence of illegal acts and irregularities.

"*The legal representation letter.* Should the written representations ordinarily obtained from the client's lawyer be modified because of SASs nos. 53 or 54? For example, should the attorney be asked to provide comfort on the absence of illegal acts? No. The lawyer doesn't conduct a legal audit and wouldn't be able to provide such broad assurance on the legality of the client's conduct. The ordinary legal representation letter requires no modification.

"In some cases, however, the client's attorney may be asked to provide an opinion on the legality of a *specific* matter. Whether such documentation is needed is left to the auditor's professional judgment. However, such documentation is usually a separate matter and not part of the ordinary legal representation letter.

"WHAT ABOUT EMPLOYEE FRAUD?

"SAS no. 53 deals with irregularities—including misappropriation of assets by employees. However, most of the discussion is directed to management misrepresentations. This is because management misrepresentations are an area of potential conflict between the auditor's objectives and management's objectives. For example, there's a risk that management may, in some circumstances, override controls designed to produce reliable accounting estimates. Nevertheless, management should always desire to maintain effective controls to prevent or detect employee defalcations.

"Employee frauds usually don't materially affect the financial statements. If, however, an employee fraud does result in a material misstatement, the audit should be designed to provide reasonable assurance of detecting that employee fraud.

"DETECTING ERRORS

"The key difference between errors and irregularities is intent: An irregularity involves *intentional* misconduct. Although SAS no. 53 doesn't come right out and say so, it implies that a material error should be easier to detect than a material irregularity. Although SAS no. 53 covers the responsibility for detecting both errors and irregularities, its focus is clearly on irregularities and what the auditor should do to detect them.

"HOW IS AUDIT PERFORMANCE AFFECTED?

"One important potential change in practice is a specific requirement to review client characteristics that might increase the risk of material misstatements. Three examples of red-flag client characteristics identified by SAS no. 53 are

1. The client's operating and financing decisions are dominated by a single person.

2. The client's organizational structure is decentralized and monitored inadequately.

3. There are many contentious or difficult accounting issues.

"Auditors should consider the effect of red flags on the overall audit strategy. Note that the auditor makes a general judgment: The mere presence of one or two red flags might not be considered important in particular circumstances. Also, the red flags the auditor considers significant or important depend on several factors including the size, complexity and ownership characteristics of the client company.

"Auditors also should consider the red flags in conjunction with information about the client's internal control structure. The auditor first gives consideration to the internal control structure when assessing the risk of material misstatement at the financial statement or engagement level. Understanding the internal control structure should either heighten or mitigate the auditor's concern about the risk of material misstatements. The auditor's overall judgment about the level of risk of material misstatements in the financial statements is then considered in developing the audit plan.

"*The risk questionnaire.* SAS no. 53 doesn't specifically require use of a generalized form to document the auditor's assessment of the risk of material misstatement. However, because SAS no. 53 does specifically require auditors to make that assessment, it's prudent to document it. Page [673] presents a general risk questionnaire that documents specific management, entity, industry and engagement characteristics to assess the risk of material irregularities, including the likelihood of management misrepresentations.

"Note that the form provides space for adding risk factors. A variety of factors may point to a higher-than-normal risk of material misstatement at the engagement level: competitive pressures, litigation closely related to survival, significant related-party transactions, management compensation arrangements that depend heavily on earnings or stock performance and discretionary accounting changes that significantly increase income.

"The questionnaire doesn't include information related to illegal acts except those treated like errors or irregularities—that is, those that have a direct and material effect on a line-item amount. Other illegal acts may come to the auditor's attention by reading minutes and contracts and conferring with legal counsel.

"*Auditing in a high-risk environment.* When the risk of material misstatement is higher than normal, the audit plan may be modified in several general ways. Higher risk usually requires more experienced personnel or more extensive supervision. Higher risk may cause auditors to attempt to obtain more persuasive evidence and exercise a heightened degree of professional skepticism in critical audit areas.

"SAS no. 53 indicates that in planning the audit program for a particular account balance or transaction class, auditors should consider the red flags identified during the general planning stage for each account balance. For example, high-technology companies usually feature several characteristics indicative of higher-than-normal engagement risk: The industry's rate of change is rapid; profitability's inconsistent; and operations are extrasensitive to interest rate and inflation changes. These factors may cause auditors to have increased concern about inventory obsolescence and inventory valuation generally. Other risk factors that may be relevant to an account balance are listed in the [footnote.*]

* "ASSESSING RISK AT THE TRANS-ACTION LEVEL

"SAS no. 53 indicates that in planning an audit program for a particular account balance or transaction class, auditors should consider any red flags identified during the general planning stage for each account balance. Risk factors at the ac-

GENERAL RISK QUESTIONNAIRE

Client _____

Prepared by _____

Date _____

Approved by _____

Date _____

Instructions

This form documents our consideration of the overall level of risk on the engagement. Assessing the engagement risk requires judgment. The particular matters to be considered and the significance of each should be determined based on the circumstances of the engagement. Not all the matters listed will be important in a particular engagement.

If the conditions or circumstances in this engagement indicate higher or lower risk than normal, describe them in the column on the right. If other conditions or circumstances seem important, add them at the end. After all relevant factors are considered, the auditor should make an overall assessment of engagement risk and indicate its effect on the audit plan.

Factor	Indicator		Comment or description
	Lower	Higher	
Management operating style	Effective oversight group	Domination of decisions by single person	
Management attitude on financial reporting	Conservative	Aggressive	
Management turnover, including senior accounting personnel	Nominal	High	
Emphasis on meeting earnings projections	Little	Very high	
Reputation in business community	Honest	Credible allegation of improper conduct	
Profitability relative to industry	Adequate and consistent	Inadequate or inconsistent	
Sensitivity of operations to interest rate changes or inflation	Relatively insensitive	Very sensitive	
Rate of change in industry	Stable	Rapid	
Status of industry	Healthy	Distressed	
Organization of operations	Centralized	Decentralized	
Indicators of going-concern problems	No serious indications	Substantial doubt could exist	
Contentious accounting issues	None	Many	
Difficult-to-audit transactions or balances	Few	Many	
Misstatements detected in prior audits	Few and immaterial	Greater than preliminary judgment about materiality	
Relationship with client	Recurring engagement	New engagement	

Consideration of the risk factors identified above has caused the following modifications of the audit plan in the following critical audit areas:

_____

_____

_____

[G2542]

"HOW SHOULD AUDIT TEST RESULTS BE EVALUATED?

"SAS no. 53 indicates that the auditor's assessment of the risk of material errors and irregularities doesn't end with planning the audit. The results of audit tests may cause the auditor to reassess this risk as the audit progresses. This is particularly appropriate when audit test results differ significantly from the auditor's expectations or when the auditor is unable to obtain satisfactory explanations for audit differences. For example, confirmation requests may yield fewer responses than expected.

"SAS no. 53 also prescribes the auditor's approach when audit differences are detected. An audit difference is simply a discrepancy between the accounting records and the underlying facts and circumstances. For example, there may be a difference between the physical count of an asset—such as securities on hand—and the recorded amount in the account balance. The auditor should evaluate both the quantitative and qualitative aspects of these audit differences and then consider whether these differences indicate an irregularity. This consideration is important because irregularities are intentional.

"The detection of an irregularity has implications beyond the monetary effect of the particular difference and beyond the projected effect of the detected amount. When auditors detect an irregularity, they need to consider how the potential misstatement affects the financial statements as a whole. What's the likelihood of similar items remaining undetected? What's the likelihood of irregularities in other areas?

"When auditors believe the financial statement effect isn't material, they should refer the matter to management at least one level above those involved. They should also be satisfied that because of the organizational position of the likely perpetrator, the irregularity has no implications for other aspects of the audit. For example, theft from a small petty cash fund usually doesn't affect other aspects of the audit because the custodian is usually a low-level employee and the amount isn't material.

"When auditors believe the effect of the irregularity is or could be material, however, additional steps are required. They should discuss

count-balance or transaction-class level include

The complexity and contentiousness of the accounting issues.

The frequency or significance of difficult-to-audit transactions.

The nature, cause and amount of known and likely misstatements detected in the balance or class in prior examinations.

The susceptibility of related assets to misappropriation.

The competence and experience of personnel assigned to processing data that affects the balance or class.

The extent of judgment involved in determining the total balance or class. Estimates, for example, require more judgment.

The size and volume of individual items constituting the balance or class.

The complexity of calculations affecting the balance or class. Revenue of rate-regulated entities, for example, often requires complex calculations."

the matter and the approach to further investigation with management at least one level above those involved. In addition, they should

Consider the implications for other aspects of the audit.

Attempt to resolve any open questions concerning the existence and amount of the irregularity.

Suggest the client consult with legal counsel about possible prosecution of the perpetrator, insurance coverage and the necessity of timely disclosure.

"*Illegal acts.* Evaluation of audit test results may also cause auditors to question whether there's a possible illegal act. For example, illegal acts may be indicated by unauthorized transactions, improperly recorded transactions and large payments for unspecified services to consultants or other affiliated parties.

"SAS no. 54 indicates that when auditors believe there's a possible illegal act, they should obtain sufficient information to evaluate the effect on the financial statements. Such information normally concerns the nature of the act and the circumstances surrounding its occurrence. First, the auditor attempts to obtain this information from management above those involved. If necessary, the auditor consults with the client's legal counsel and applies additional audit procedures.

"Once auditors conclude that an illegal act in fact has occurred, they need to consider its effect on the financial statements and its implications for other aspects of the audit. Is this illegal act indicative of a significant deficiency in the internal control structure? Is the level of management or employees involved indicative of a management integrity problem?

"Indications of lack of management integrity mean an increased risk of material misstatement of the financial statements. In the extreme, if there's widespread lack of management integrity at the top level, the audit usually can't be completed.

"COMMUNICATIONS WITH CLIENTS

"When irregularities or illegal acts are detected, they must be communicated to senior management and to the board of directors or its audit committee. Since both SASs impose essentially the same internal communication requirements for irregularities and illegal acts, they can be considered together.

"Both SASs require the auditor to make sure the audit committee or its equivalent is informed of irregularities or illegal acts unless these are clearly inconsequential. An irregularity or illegal act involving senior management, however, is *never* inconsequential. This type of irregularity or illegal act should be communicated directly to the audit committee or its equivalent.

" * * * If the entity doesn't have an audit committee, the communication is made to the equivalent of the audit committee—that is, an individual or a group with equivalent responsibility for oversight of financial reporting, such as the board of directors, the board of trustees or the owner of an owner-managed business.

* * *

"Although the auditor doesn't ordinarily have a responsibility to communicate directly with anyone outside the client, there are four exceptions.

 1. The entity reports an auditor change on form 8–k [to the SEC].

 2. A successor auditor makes inquiries in accordance with SAS no. 7, *Communications Between Predecessor and Successor Auditors.*

 3. A subpoena is issued.

 4. A government funding agency asks for information in accordance with the requirements for audits of entities that receive financial assistance."

* * *

2. MORE EFFECTIVE AUDITS; SASs NOs. 55, 56 AND 57

TEMKIN & WINTERS, SAS NO. 55: THE AUDITOR'S NEW RESPONSIBILITY FOR INTERNAL CONTROL

J. Accountancy 86 (May 1988).*

"The auditor's responsibility for considering internal control in a financial statement audit has expanded.

* * *

"EXPANDED RESPONSIBILITY

"SAS no. 55 expands the auditor's responsibility in two ways. First, it broadens 'internal control' to 'internal control structure.' Second, it increases the knowledge the auditor must have about internal control.

 "*Internal control structure.*** The internal control structure consists of the control environment, the accounting system and control

---

* Copyright © 1988 by the American Institute of Certified Public Accountants, Inc.

** "DEFINING THE INTERNAL CONTROL STRUCTURE

SAS no. 55 broadens the auditor's responsibility for internal control. Not only must the auditor consider control procedures, but also the control environment and the accounting system. Here are the new definitions.

"*Control environment:* The overall attitude, awareness and actions of the board of directors, management, owners and others concerning the importance of control. The control environment includes:

 Management's philosophy and operating style.

 The entity's organizational structure.

The functioning of the board of directors and its committees—particularly the audit committee.

Methods of assigning authority and responsibility.

Management's control methods for monitoring and following up on performance—including internal auditing.

Personnel policies and practices.

Various external influences that affect an entity's operations and practices, such as examinations by bank regulatory agencies.

"*Accounting system:* The methods and records established to identify, assemble, analyze, classify, record and report an entity's transactions and to maintain accountability for the related assets and liabilities. An effective accounting system includes methods and records that will:

procedures. (See the [marginal note] for complete definitions.) This broader concept recognizes that policies and procedures an entity establishes within each of these areas are forms of control that can have a significant direct effect on several major audit planning matters.

"The three components of internal control structure are an important source of information about the types and risks of potential material misstatements—including management misrepresentations—that could occur in financial statements. Additionally, these policies and procedures are a primary source of information about the specific processes, methods, records and reports used in preparing the entity's financial statements. Both types of information are essential considerations when designing audit procedures.

"For example, the internal control structure affects how the audit is planned to assess whether the company has recorded all revenue. Simply knowing that revenue can be understated isn't sufficient: More specific knowledge about potential causes of possible misstatement is needed. Understanding the control structure explains how sales transactions are initiated, processed and summarized. This knowledge helps identify specific sources of potential misstatement—such as shipping documents that initially aren't prepared to recognize the transaction.

* * *

"*Increased knowledge of internal control.* SAS no. 55 requires the auditor to obtain a sufficient understanding of the control environment, the accounting system and control procedures to plan the audit. This

Identify and record all valid transactions.

Describe in a timely way the transactions in sufficient detail to permit proper classification for financial reporting.

Measure the value of transactions so their proper monetary value can be recorded in the financial statements.

Determine the time period in which transactions occurred to record them in the proper accounting period.

Present properly transactions and related disclosures in the financial statements.

Control procedures: Those policies and procedures (in addition to the control environment and accounting system) that management has established to provide reasonable assurance that specific objectives will be achieved. Control procedures pertain to:

Proper authorization of transactions and activities.

Segregation of duties to reduce opportunities for any person both to perpetrate and conceal errors or irregularities in the normal course of business. Segregation involves assigning different people the responsibilities of authorizing transactions, recording transactions and maintaining custody of assets.

The design and use of adequate documents and records to help ensure proper recording of transactions and events—such as monitoring the use of prenumbered shipping documents.

Adequate safeguards over access to and use of assets and records—such as secured facilities and authorizations for access to computer programs and data files.

Independent checks on performance and proper valuation of recorded amounts—such as clerical checks, reconciliations, comparison of assets with recorded accountability, computer-programmed controls, management review of reports that summarize the detail of account balances (for example, an aged trial balance of accounts receivable) and user review of computer-generated reports.

means understanding how internal control policies and procedures are designed and determining whether they're in operation.

* * *

"SUFFICIENT UNDERSTANDING TO PLAN

"Without doubt, auditors implementing SAS no. 55 will ask, 'What's an understanding of the internal control structure sufficient to plan an audit?' The answer will vary from entity to entity and requires the auditor's judgment. SAS no. 55 provides three major considerations to help auditors formulate their judgments:

"*What knowledge of each element should include.* SAS no. 55 provides specific guidance. For example, it says the auditor should obtain sufficient knowledge of the control environment to understand management's and the board of directors' attitude, awareness and actions concerning the control environment.

"The standard also requires the auditor to obtain sufficient knowledge of the accounting system to understand

The classes of transactions in the entity's operations that are significant to the financial statements.

How those transactions are initiated.

The accounting records, supporting documents, machine-readable information and specific accounts in the financial statements used in processing and reporting transactions.

The accounting process involved from the initiation of a transaction to its inclusion in the financial statements, including how the computer is used to process data.

The financial reporting process used to prepare the entity's financial statements, including significant accounting estimates and disclosures.

"As far as specific control procedures are concerned, SAS no. 55 recognizes that as auditors obtain an understanding of each element, they are also likely to gain insight about control procedures. For example, in learning about the cash accounting system, auditors usually become aware of whether bank accounts are reconciled.

"In some audits, the knowledge of control procedures acquired in understanding the control environment and accounting system will be sufficient; in others, the auditor will need to devote additional effort to understand control procedures. The statement makes it clear, however, that audit planning ordinarily doesn't require understanding control procedures related to *each* account balance, transaction class or disclosure component in the financial statements or to *every* assertion relevant to those components.

"*The auditor's judgment.* In determining whether there's sufficient understanding to plan, auditors consider their assessments of inherent risk, judgments about materiality and the complexity and sophistication of the entity's operations and systems. As inherent risk assessments increase, as amounts the auditor considers material become smaller or as an entity's operations and systems become more complex, it may be necessary to devote more attention to obtaining knowledge of each internal control structure element to gain sufficient understanding to plan the audit. For example, when auditing an entity with a complex, computerized accounting system, the auditor ordinarily would devote more effort to understanding the accounting system and its control procedures than when auditing a smaller company with a simple accounting system.

"*The use of other sources.* An understanding of the internal control structure usually isn't the only source of knowledge the auditor uses to identify the types and risks of possible misstatements and to design substantive tests. Although this understanding is significant, knowledge can also be gained from other sources—such as prior audits. The understanding of the internal control structure needed to plan will vary with the planning knowledge obtained from other sources.

"PROCEDURES TO OBTAIN UNDERSTANDING

"The auditor may use a variety of ways to obtain knowledge about design of policies and procedures and whether they're in operation. These include asking appropriate management, supervisory and staff personnel, inspecting documents and records and observing the company's activities and operations.

"The nature and extent of the procedures the auditor chooses to perform will vary depending on the specific internal control structure policy or procedure involved, his or her assessments of inherent risk, judgments about materiality and the complexity and sophistication of the entity's systems. For example, the auditor may conclude that the inherent risk assessment or the materiality judgment for the prepaid insurance account doesn't require specific procedures to understand the control structure.

"In selecting procedures to obtain the understanding, it's very important to know what 'placed in operation' means and how it differs from 'operating effectiveness.' This distinction is critical to proper implementation of SAS no. 55.

"*Placed in operation* means the entity is actually using the policy or procedure—that is, it doesn't exist only in theory or on paper. Knowing what policy is in use is critical to audit planning because only policies and procedures in use affect the types and risks of misstatements and the design of substantive tests.

"*Operating effectiveness* refers to how a policy or procedure is used, the consistency with which it's used and who's applying it. For example, an auditor may find through interviews with personnel, observing the processing of sales transactions and inspecting sales files that prenumbered sales invoices are used. This may not tell the auditor, however, about operating effectiveness: How often are such invoices not prepared? How often do errors occur in their preparation? Are they sometimes prepared by unauthorized personnel?

"In obtaining a sufficient understanding of the internal control structure to plan an audit, the auditor isn't required to evaluate operating effectiveness. However, as discussed below, such evaluation is essential to assess control risk.

"DOCUMENTATION

"SAS no. 55 requires auditors to document their understanding of the control environment, accounting system and control procedures.

* * *

"ASSESSING CONTROL RISK

"After obtaining the understanding, the auditor assesses control risk. Formally defined, control risk is the risk that a material misstatement that could occur in a financial statement assertion will not be prevented or detected on a timely basis by the entity's internal control structure policies or procedures. Stated simply, control risk is the likelihood that a material misstatement will get through the internal control structure into the financial statements. The auditor assesses this risk by evaluating the effectiveness of the policies and procedures in the control environment, accounting system and control procedures set up to prevent or detect misstatements.

* * *

"DETERMINING THE ASSESSED LEVEL OF CONTROL RISK

"The conclusion from assessing control risk is called the 'assessed level of control risk.' The level may vary from maximum to minimum; it can be stated in quantitative terms—such as percentages—or qualitative terms—for example, maximum, substantial, moderate or low.

"The answers to two questions determine the assessed level of control risk:

     1. Does an entity have internal control structure policies or procedures that pertain to a financial statement assertion?

     2. How effective is the design and operation of those policies or procedures in preventing or detecting misstatements in the assertion?

"Under SAS no. 55, the auditor isn't required to assess control risk at below the maximum level for any assertion. Sometimes auditors may not assess control risk at below maximum because policies or procedures aren't relevant to the assertions or they're unlikely to be effective. Even when potentially effective policies and procedures exist, an auditor may decide not to test their effectiveness because doing so would be inefficient. In such circumstances, the auditor assesses control risk for these assertions at the maximum level. Auditors also assess control risk at the maximum level when they obtain evidence that policies and procedures relevant to an assertion aren't designed or operating effectively.

"When auditors assess control risk at below the maximum level, SAS no. 55 requires them to identify internal control structure policies or procedures relevant to the assertion and perform tests of both design and operation effectiveness. These 'tests of controls' include procedures such as inquiry, observation, inspection of documents and reperforming a policy or procedure by the auditor. The auditor uses the resulting evidence to assess whether control risk for the assertion is below the maximum level.

"The auditor considers two potential sources of evidence about the effectiveness of the design and operation of internal control structure policies and procedures: (1) the understanding of the internal control structure and (2) any planned tests of controls performed concurrently with obtaining the understanding.

"UNDERSTANDING THE INTERNAL CONTROL STRUCTURE

"In many audits, obtaining the understanding requires substantial audit effort that may provide considerable knowledge about the effectiveness of the control environment, accounting system and certain control procedures. Using this understanding in assessing control risk, however, may seem inconsistent with two matters discussed earlier. Some clarifying comments are in order.

"Although SAS no. 55 doesn't specifically require auditors to evaluate effectiveness of the design and operation of policies and procedures when obtaining the understanding, it does require them to obtain evidence about the effectiveness of both design and operation to assess control risk at below the maximum level. This may raise a question about how the understanding can provide evidence to support an assessment of control risk at below the maximum level.

"The answer is that some procedures performed to obtain the understanding may provide evidence about the effectiveness of design or operation for some policies and procedures even though they weren't specifically planned to do so. This evidence may be sufficient to support an assessed level of control risk below the maximum level.

"For example, the auditor may have made inquiries about management's use of budgets and inspected reports about variances between budgeted and actual amounts. These procedures were performed specifically to understand the design of budgeting policies and whether they're in operation. Even so, the auditor should realize this may also provide evidence about how effective the budgeting policies are in preventing or detecting material misstatements in the classification of expenses. In some circumstances, that evidence may be sufficient to support an assessed level of control risk that's below the maximum level.

*   *   *

"DOCUMENTING THE CONTROL RISK ASSESSMENT

"SAS no. 55 requires the auditor also to document the basis for conclusions about the assessed level of control risk. *   *   *

"USING THE ASSESSED LEVEL OF CONTROL RISK

"The assessed level of control risk for an assertion relates directly to the substantive tests the auditor plans and performs. The logic is simple: The more effective the internal control structure, the lower the risk of misstatement. The lower the risk, the less evidence the auditor needs from substantive tests to form an opinion on the financial statements. Consequently, as control risk decreases, the auditor may modify substantive tests by

> Changing the nature of substantive tests from a more effective to a less effective procedure—such as using tests directed toward parties within rather than outside the entity.

> Changing the timing of substantive tests—performing them at an interim date rather than at year-end.

> Changing the extent of substantive tests—to a smaller sample size, for example."

*   *   *

CALLAHAN, JAENICKE & NEEBES, SASs NOs. 56 and 57: INCREASING AUDIT EFFECTIVENESS

J. Accountancy 56 (Oct. 1988).*

"The pervasive presence of accounting estimates in financial statements provides fertile ground for financial statement misstatements that are difficult to detect. Overly optimistic estimates of loan loss reserves, inventory obsolescence, warranty expenses or asset lives can result in material misstatements. Whether those misstatements are the result of honest—but overly optimistic—beliefs on the one hand or deliberate misrepresentations on the other, the result is the same— misleading financial reporting.

"One of the key goals of the auditing standards board's nine new SASs is to improve the auditor's effectiveness in detecting misstatements. Three of the nine SASs—SASs nos. 55, 56 and 57—are designed to achieve this goal.

"This article examines the ways in which SAS no. 56, *Analytical Procedures,* and SAS no. 57, *Auditing Accounting Estimates,* help the auditor detect material financial statement misstatements. These misstatements often are caused by overly optimistic accounting estimates that can be detected through the use of analytical procedures. The article also provides practical guidance for implementing the new standards on both large and small engagements. (For a related article detailing how microcomputers are used to perform analytical procedures, see page 128.)

"WHY SAS no. 56?

"One major reason the ASB issued a new standard on analytical procedures was, of course, the call for one by the Treadway commission and others interested in closing the "expectation gap." Certainly, no one would disagree that properly designed analytical procedures can be powerful tools in uncovering fraudulent financial reporting. However, the ASB revised SAS no. 23, *Analytical Review Procedures,* for a more fundamental reason: SAS no. 23 neither conveyed the importance of analytical procedures as an audit tool nor provided sufficient guidance on their use as a substantive test.

"Auditors have long realized the importance of analytical procedures in an audit. They're used on almost every audit—most often in the planning and final review stages. Many auditors, however, have discovered that analytical procedures are equally important tools when used as substantive tests. For some audit objectives, they represent *the most effective* procedure the auditor can employ. Also, analytical procedures are noted in SAS no. 59, *The Auditor's Consideration of an Entity's Ability to Continue as a Going Concern,* as an example of audit procedures that may identify conditions or events indicative of possible substantial doubt on the part of the auditor about the entity's ability to continue as a going concern for a reasonable period of time.

"WHAT SAS no. 56 SAYS

"SAS no. 56 defines analytical procedures as comparisons of recorded amounts, or ratios developed from recorded amounts, to expectations developed by the auditor. It requires the auditor to use analytical procedures in the planning and final review stages of *all* audits.

"Most auditors already do this to some extent, given the wide variety of analytical procedures that are available. For example, year-to-year comparisons of financial results and ratio analyses are two of the more common forms of analytical procedures. And reading the financial statements for any unexpected items or scanning a cash disbursements or receipts journal for unusual items are also applications of analytical procedures.

"Most important, SAS no. 56 provides guidance on the development, use and evaluation of the results of analytical procedures *as substantive tests.* Although it doesn't require their use in this context, SAS no. 56 certainly encourages it: Thirteen paragraphs are devoted to this subject compared with four on analytical procedures in the planning and final review stages. In many instances, using analytical procedures as substantive tests may be more effective for testing management's assertions related to certain account balances or classes of transactions than some of the more traditional tests of details.

"SAS no. 56 doesn't specify which analytical procedures should be performed in the various stages of an audit. The SAS gives the auditor wide latitude to choose procedures that make the most sense in the particular circumstances. The use of analytical procedures is limited only by the availability of reliable data and the auditor's own creativity." *

---

* "SAS NO. 56: THE EARLIER THE BETTER

"SAS no. 56 requires the auditor to use analytical procedures in the *planning* and *final review* stages of *all* audits. The earlier they are used, the better, however, as this case history involving an accounting estimate indicates.

"The client. A small manufacturer of toys and games.

"The problem. The valuation of excess inventories. No questions were raised un-

3. IMPROVED PUBLISHED REPORTS; SAS NO. 59 ("GOING CONCERN" OPINIONS)

ELLINGSEN, PANY & FAGAN, SAS NO. 59: HOW TO EVALUATE GOING CONCERN
J. Accountancy 24 (Jan. 1989).*

"Business failures have many causes—among them, foreign competition, declining commodity prices and poor management. But when a business fails soon after its financial statements receive a clean opinion, some fingers invariably point to the auditors—even if the failure was due to sudden events after the audit.

"Have auditors assumed enough responsibility to meet public expectations for evaluating whether the companies they audit are able to stay in business?

"The American Institute of CPAs auditing standards board responded to this question by issuing Statement on Auditing Standards no. 59, *The Auditor's Consideration of an Entity's Ability to Continue as a Going Concern.* This new SAS increases the auditor's responsibility and clarifies what *cannot* be expected of auditors. The new standard replaces SAS no. 34, *The Auditor's Consideration When a Question Arises About an Entity's Continued Existence.* (See exhibit 1 below.)

"For auditors, SAS no. 59 presents three fundamental requirements:

1. To evaluate in every audit whether there's substantial doubt about the entity's ability to continue as a going concern for a reasonable period of time.

til the preissuance review by the CPA firm's report reviewer.

"Observations by report reviewer. 'The problem surfaced about two minutes into the final review. My review began with what I consider to be one of the most important analytical procedures—a close reading of the financial statements. That gives me a good sense of the overall financial statement presentation and key areas before I continue with the rest of the review.

'Initial comparisons showed that sales were down while inventory increased substantially. A quick calculation indicated well over a year's supply of inventory at yearend. The client's past experience and readily available industry data suggested that a three- or four-month supply would be more typical.

'The inventory workpapers were extensive and indicated a significant amount of audit work relating to existence, completeness, rights and obligations (pledged and consigned inventory) and even valuation as

it related to the company's method of pricing inventory, but there was no analysis of excess inventory and no consideration of that aspect of the valuation assertion.

'In essence, a two-minute analysis in the final review identified a significant audit issue that simple analytical procedures could have identified in the planning stage. Moreover, the issue wasn't identified by all of the substantive tests of details performed during the course of the audit.'

"Epilogue. 'Fortunately, the valuation problem was corrected before the report was issued—but not without certain costs. Those costs included performing additional procedures that could have been completed more efficiently earlier in the audit. More important, we could have avoided the delays in issuing the report, aggravation to the client and embarrassment to us from raising such a key issue so late in the audit.' "

* Copyright © 1989 by the American Institute of Certified Public Accountants, Inc.

EXHIBIT 1
A comparison of SAS no. 34 and SAS no. 59

	SAS no. 34	SAS no. 59
Overall responsibility	Entity's ability to continue as a going concern is considered in an audit only when contrary information is discovered.	Entity's ability to continue as a going concern is considered in every audit. Results obtained by audit procedures are evaluated to determine going concern ability.
Cause of report modification	Questionable recovery of assets and classification of liabilities.	Inability to continue as a going concern.
Level of doubt needed for report modification	Substantial.	Substantial.
Time frame	Approximately one year.	Not to exceed one year from audited financial statements.
Effect on audit opinion	Qualified 'subject to.'	Unqualified with an explanatory paragraph following the opinion paragraph.

[G2543]

2. To consider the adequacy of financial statement disclosure about the ability to continue as a going concern.

3. To include an explanatory paragraph in the audit report describing the uncertainty when there's substantial doubt about going concern ability.

"This article describes the requirements of SAS no. 59, contrasts them with the requirements of SAS no. 34, tells how to implement the new standard and relates it to other professional standards.

"HOW SAS no. 59 DEFINES A GOING CONCERN

"SAS no. 59 increases the auditor's responsibility vis-à-vis going concern. Auditors now must consider whether there's *substantial doubt* about the entity's ability to continue as a *going concern* for a *reasonable period of time* on every audit engagement.

"Under SAS no. 34, the entity's *continuation was usually assumed* and auditors were required to consider the going concern issue only when the results of other audit procedures brought forth *contradictory information.* This was in a sense a negative duty. On the other hand, the SAS no. 59 requirements are an affirmative duty.

"In describing the auditor's responsibility for evaluating going concern, SAS no. 59 uses three terms that deserve special attention: substantial doubt, going concern and reasonable period of time.

"*Substantial doubt* is *not defined* in accounting or auditing literature. Like beauty, it's intended to be in the eye of the beholder—or in this case, the auditor. The term also appeared in SAS no. 34 without a definition and also was considered a matter of the auditor's judgment.

"*The going concern concept* has long been a tenet of financial accounting. However, there's very little guidance in the accounting literature and, until SAS no. 34, there was also very little guidance in the auditing literature.

"At first glance the meaning of going concern may seem simple—an entity either continues in operation or it does not. Yet this simple distinction may not be an adequate basis for determining the effect on the audit report. For example

Is an entity that has filed for reorganization under chapter 11 but that expects to maintain operations a going concern?

Is a company that doesn't file for reorganization, yet is gradually declining because of annual operating losses, a going concern?

How about a company that has sold 95% of its operations yet continues to function?

"The answer to each of these questions is maybe. Auditors must use judgment in considering all the particulars about the entity's ability to continue as a going concern.

"Therefore, rather than use concepts—such as bankruptcy or the loss of operating control through regulatory or judicial action—to define an entity's inability to continue as a going concern, the new standard, like SAS no. 34, describes examples of what a going concern is *not*.

"Paragraph 1 says: 'Ordinarily, information that significantly contradicts the going concern assumption relates to the entity's inability to continue to meet its obligations as they become due without substantial disposition of assets outside the ordinary course of business, restructuring of debt, externally forced revisions of its operations, or similar actions.'

"Although SAS no. 34 used the same examples as SAS no. 59 to describe information that contradicts the going concern assumption, the old standard intentionally used the term 'continued existence.' This avoided any implication that auditors had a responsibility beyond the consideration of asset recoverability and liability classification. The new standard requires auditors to evaluate whether there's substantial doubt about the entity's ability to continue as a going concern—even when asset recoverability and liability classification aren't in question. Therefore, the term 'going concern' replaced 'continued existence.'

"*Reasonable period of time* is defined in SAS no. 59 as 'a period of time not to exceed one year from the date of the financial statements.' The ASB included this time frame to ensure that auditors were expected to deal only with existing conditions, not to predict future events. The ASB believes that assessing what might happen beyond one year involves more speculation about future events than consideration of current conditions. Thus, auditors should consider whether the company can continue as a going concern for one year from the date of the financial statements.

"Assume, for example, Acme Co. has significant debt maturing two years from the date of the financial statements. Auditors Spike, Lee &

Co. have substantial doubt about Acme's ability to continue as a going concern once the debt matures. However, in that two-year period, management will have time to restructure operations or pursue alternative financing. Also, conditions may improve. Furthermore, if conditions get worse, the auditors will have another opportunity to hoist the red flag before the debt matures.

"Accordingly, under SAS no. 59, Spike, Lee & Co. wouldn't include an explanatory paragraph in its audit report about its substantial doubt about Acme as a going concern. Its substantial doubt isn't related to the new SAS's one-year time frame.

"WHAT SAS no. 59 DOES NOT REQUIRE

"To understand what SAS no. 59 requires of auditors in evaluating going concern ability, it's helpful to understand what it does *not* require:

It does *not* make auditors responsible for predicting future events.

It generally does *not* require auditors to perform more procedures than they currently now do.

"The ASB designed SAS no. 59 so auditors could satisfy public concern about evaluating whether the companies they audit can continue as going concerns—without being in the position of predicting their clients' financial health. Annual audits can be compared to annual physical examinations performed by doctors. Physicians deal with conditions existing at the date of the exam. They can't predict what might happen to the patient tomorrow and, accordingly, aren't accountable for the patient's future good health.

"Auditors function with similar constraints. SAS no. 59 recognizes that auditors can't predict significant factors such as interest rates, the price of oil or a 'Black Monday' in the stock market. Indeed, the new standard points out that even if an entity goes out of business shortly after receiving a clean audit report, this doesn't indicate inadequate audit performance. Furthermore, the standard warns that a clean audit report should *not* be misinterpreted as providing any type of guarantee about the company's continuance as a going concern for one year.

"SAS no. 59 doesn't require auditors to design specific audit procedures to evaluate whether there's substantial doubt about the company's going concern ability. The ASB believes information gathered in the normal course of an audit should provide sufficient information for that purpose. Accordingly, the new standard requires auditors to evaluate the results of audit procedures performed to achieve *other* objectives in considering whether the entity is able to stay in business.

"For example, an auditor may have designed and performed audit procedures—such as analyzing liquidity ratios—to ascertain whether the entity is complying with certain loan covenants. Evaluation of the liquidity ratios not only assists the auditor vis-à-vis the loan covenants but also helps the auditor evaluate whether the ratios raise doubt about

EXHIBIT 2
Conditions and events that may indicate a going concern problem

Negative trends

Recurring operating losses.

Working capital deficiencies.

Negative cash flows from operations.

Adverse key financial ratios.

Other indications

Defaults on loans or similar agreements.

Arrearages in dividends.

Denial of usual trade credit.

Restructuring of debt.

Noncompliance with statutory capital requirements.

Need for new sources or methods of financing.

Need to dispose of substantial assets.

Internal matters

Work stoppages.

Other labor difficulties.

Substantial dependence on a particular project.

Uneconomic long-term commitments.

Need to revise operations significantly.

External matters

Legal proceedings.

Legislation.

Loss of a key franchise, license or patent.

Loss of a principal customer or supplier.

Uninsured or underinsured catastrophe.

[G2544]

the company's ability to continue as a going concern. Exhibit 2 above lists the conditions and events that might indicate there is a going concern problem.

"When evaluating the ability to continue as a going concern, the auditor should consider relevant conditions and events *in the aggregate.*

The significance of particular conditions and events will depend on the circumstances, and some may be significant only when considered with others.

"To illustrate, assume the results of procedures performed to ascertain compliance with loan covenants identified not only unfavorable liquidity ratios but also a significant decline in the company's operating ratios. Further assume that the results of analytical procedures indicated the company experienced significant negative variances when comparing the current year's budget with actual financial results.

"The *aggregate* effect of these conditions and events may cause an auditor to believe there's substantial doubt about the company's going concern ability. The presence of only one of the conditions or events, however, likely wouldn't cause such doubt. If substantial doubt exists, SAS no. 59 directs auditors to consider management's plans for dealing with the adverse condition. * * *

"The new standard does *not* require auditors to consider mitigating factors, a step prescribed by SAS no. 34. SAS no. 59 recognizes that mitigating factors are usually inseparable from management's plans and identifying them is management's responsibility—not the auditor's.

"MANAGEMENT'S PLANS

"In considering management's plans, the auditor should seek evidence about whether the adverse condition or event will be mitigated within a reasonable period of time (not to exceed one year from the date of the financial statements). For example, if management plans to liquidate assets in the normal course of business to ameliorate adverse circumstances, the auditor should ordinarily obtain evidence about

> The marketability of the assets management plans to sell.
>
> Restrictions, if any, on the disposal of the assets.
>
> The effects of the disposal.

"Often management's plans include prospective information that demonstrates the entity's ability to overcome the adverse circumstances. Auditors should consider whether the support for significant assumptions underlying the prospective financial information is adequate. At a minimum, auditors must read the prospective financial information and the assumptions underlying that information. They must also compare information from prior periods and the current period with actual results. * * *

"RESPONSIBILITIES BEYOND ASSET RECOVERY AND LIABILITY CLASSIFICATION

"If, after considering management's plans, the auditor still has substantial doubt about the entity's ability to continue as a going concern, the auditor includes an explanatory paragraph in the audit report.

"The auditor also assesses the sufficiency of financial statement disclosures *whether or not* substantial doubt still remains after considering management's plans. Under SAS no. 34, substantial doubt—taken alone—did not require qualification of the audit report; it merely required an assessment of asset recoverability and amount and classification of liabilities. Under SAS no. 59, substantial doubt is sufficient to require an explanatory paragraph in the audit report—even when asset recoverability and liability amounts and classification are *not* in question. The following example illustrates this.

"Smith, Jones & Co. audits the financial statements of ABC Advertising Co. Ninety percent of ABC's revenues come from one account. Just before yearend it loses that account. ABC's only significant asset, the receivable from that account, is fully collectible, however.

"Under SAS no. 34, Smith, Jones & Co. would not qualify its report. SAS no. 34 required qualification only when there was substantial doubt about asset recovery and the amount and classification of liabilities. Under SAS no. 59, however, Smith, Jones & Co. should modify its report if there's substantial doubt about ABC's ability to continue as a going concern—regardless of the status of assets and liabilities. In this case, depending on management's plans, Smith, Jones & Co. may have to include an explanatory paragraph in its report.

"Thus, SAS no. 59 expands the auditor's traditional role in reporting on the ability of the company to stay in business beyond the effect on assets and liabilities. There's some controversy about this expansion: Critics fear it could lead to unwarranted requests and expectations for additional auditor assurances beyond the auditor's expertise. However, proponents of the new responsibility—including the majority of the 21–member ASB—believe the auditor can and should evaluate whether the client can continue as a going concern beyond the effect on assets and liabilities.

*   *   *

"FINANCIAL STATEMENT DISCLOSURE

"Accounting standards don't specifically address financial statement disclosures about going concern problems. However, the third generally accepted auditing standard of reporting (AU section 150.02 of *AICPA Professional Standards*) says informative disclosures in the financial statements are to be regarded as adequate unless otherwise stated in the audit report. Therefore, in both SASs nos. 34 and 59, the ASB provided guidance about some of the information that might be disclosed in financial statements when there's a going concern problem. SAS no. 59 requires the auditor to consider the adequacy of financial statement disclosure at two thresholds:

     1. When there's substantial doubt about the company's ability to stay in business.

     2. When that doubt is alleviated by the auditor's assessment of management's plans.

"*Substantial doubt.* When the auditor concludes there's substantial doubt about the client's ability to continue as a going concern, SAS no. 59 requires that the auditor ask: How are the financial statements affected? Are related financial statement disclosures adequate? Disclosed information might include

The principal conditions—such as working capital deficiencies, recurring operating losses, liabilities in excess of assets and defaults on debts—that caused the auditor to doubt the company's going concern ability for a reasonable period of time.

The possible effects of these conditions and events—such as a reduction in the size of operations.

Management's evaluation of the significance of these conditions and any mitigating factors.

Possible discontinuance of operations.

Management's plans, including relevant prospective financial information—such as debt restructuring plans to prevent defaults and plans to stop operating losses by cutting unprofitable products or reducing expenses.

Information about the recoverability or classification of recorded asset amounts or the amounts or classification of liabilities. For example, when there's substantial doubt about an entity's continuation in business, inventory may become difficult to sell, even at cost; receivables may become difficult to collect; and long-term liabilities may become due immediately.

"*Management's plans.* When doubt about the company as a going concern is alleviated by the auditor's assessment of management's plans, SAS no. 59 requires the auditor to consider disclosing the principal conditions and events that caused the substantial doubt. If disclosure is necessary and if alleviation of the doubt depends on realizing management's plans, the financial statements may need to

State that the company's ability to continue as a going concern is dependent on the realization of management's plans.

List specific management plans.

"If the auditor determines the financial statements don't adequately disclose the going concern problem, a departure from generally accepted accounting principles exists. This may result in either a qualified ("except for") opinion or an adverse opinion.

"THE ADDED EXPLANATORY PARAGRAPH

" 'Subject to' opinions have been eliminated by SAS no. 58, *Reports on Audited Financial Statements.* However, the red flag feature of alerting the reader to material uncertainties has been retained: Auditors still must address material uncertainties in their audit reports in a required emphasis paragraph.

"Under SAS no. 59, when an auditor concludes there's substantial doubt about the client's ability to stay in business for a reasonable period of time, an explanatory paragraph, describing the uncertainty, should be added following the opinion paragraph. SAS no. 59 provides the following paragraph as an example:

" 'The accompanying financial statements have been prepared assuming that the Company will continue as a going concern. As discussed in Note X to the financial statements, the Company has suffered recurring losses from operations and has a net capital deficiency that raise substantial doubt about its ability to continue as a going concern. Management's plans in regard to these matters are also described in Note X. The financial statements do not include any adjustments that might result from the outcome of this uncertainty.' " [a]

*   *   *

4. IMPROVED INTERNAL COMMUNICATIONS; SASs NOs. 60 and 61

ROUSSEY, TEN EYCK & BLANCO–BEST, [TWO] NEW SASs: CLOSING THE COMMUNICATIONS GAP *

J. Accountancy 44 (Dec. 1988).

*   *   *

"SAS no. 60: INTERNAL CONTROL RELATED COMMUNICATIONS

"Historically, auditors have recommended improvements in their clients' internal controls. In recent years, clients' managements and audit committees have become even more interested in internal controls; therefore, this communication has taken on increased importance. In response, the ASB issued SAS no. 60, *Communication of Internal Control Structure Related Matters Noted in an Audit*. This statement

> Establishes a new threshold for reporting significant deficiencies in the internal control structure—known as "reportable conditions."

> Prescribes new reporting language that addresses many of the concerns raised by report users.

"WHAT'S REPORTABLE?

"SAS no. 60 defines reportable conditions as 'matters coming to the auditor's attention that, in his judgment, should be communicated to the audit committee [or others, including boards of directors, owners in owner-managed entities, etc., with equivalent authority and responsibility in entities that don't have audit committees] because they represent significant deficiencies in the design or operation of the internal control structure which could adversely affect the organization's ability to record, process, summarize and report financial data consistent with the assertions of management in the financial statements.' Such deficiencies can occur in any of the three elements of the internal control structure: the control environment, accounting system or control procedures. That's quite a definition, but what does it mean?

---

a. Apparently some auditors have softened the recommended language through euphemisms for the phrase, "substantial doubt about . . . ability to continue as a going concern." The SEC staff has required use of both "substantial doubt" and "going concern." J. Accountancy 18 (Aug. 1990).

"One easy way to view a 'reportable condition' is by comparing it to the old concept of 'material weakness' as set forth in superseded SAS no. 20, *Required Communications of Material Weaknesses in Internal Accounting Control.* Under the old standard, a material weakness related to deficiencies in internal control *policies and procedures.* A reportable condition also encompasses deficiencies in the control environment and the accounting system. Moreover, a material weakness was limited solely to deficiencies that might affect *material amounts* in the financial statements; a reportable condition isn't so limited. For example, a client is not able to reconcile data stored in a computer file; however, it doesn't result in materially misstated financial statements. Such a deficiency would not have been considered a material weakness under SAS no. 20, but it might be significant enough to be a reportable condition under SAS no. 60.

"The SAS's appendix includes other examples of reportable conditions. As a rule of thumb, the auditor might consider a reportable condition to be a weakness in the internal control structure that, in the auditor's judgment, is of sufficient *magnitude or importance* to be of interest to the client's audit committee. Magnitude and importance are matters that should be decided by the auditor.

"MATERIAL WEAKNESS RETAINED

"Nevertheless, some clients found the material weakness concept in SAS no. 20 useful. For example, audit committees of companies subject to the Foreign Corrupt Practices Act sometimes used information about material weaknesses to evaluate their companies' compliance with the internal control provisions of that act. In addition, certain regulatory authorities ask for information about material weaknesses because they believe the criteria for identifying such weaknesses are more objective than those for identifying reportable conditions. For example, the General Accounting Office's *Government Auditing Standards: Standards for Audit of Governmental Organizations, Programs, Activities, and Functions,* commonly referred to as the 'yellow book,' requires auditors of state and local governments to point out which reportable conditions are also considered material weaknesses.

"Therefore, a material weakness concept similar to that in SAS no. 20 was retained. SAS no. 60 defines a material weakness as 'a reportable condition in which the design or operation of the specific internal control structure elements does not reduce to a relatively low level the risk that errors or irregularities in amounts that would be material in relation to the financial statements being audited may occur and not be detected within a timely period by employees in the normal course of performing their assigned functions.' Therefore, by definition, a material weakness is a reportable condition; however, a reportable condition isn't necessarily a material weakness.

* * *

"COMMUNICATING REPORTABLE CONDITIONS

"Under SAS no. 60, the auditor can communicate reportable conditions to the audit committee either orally or in writing—although writing is preferable. If the auditor communicates these matters orally, the auditor should document the discussions in the workpapers. If the auditor communicates in writing, the SAS prescribes a new format that

> 1. States the purpose of the audit was to report on the financial statements and not to provide assurance on the internal control structure.
>
> 2. Includes the definition of reportable conditions.
>
> 3. Includes a restriction on distribution.

*   *   *

"SAS no. 61: COMMUNICATION WITH AUDIT COMMITTEES

"The growing number of audit committees and their need for more useful information precipitated an expansion of the auditor's communication responsibilities. Other SASs require informing audit committees about reportable conditions and, unless clearly inconsequential, irregularities and illegal acts. The ASB, however, believed there was a host of other information—about audit scope and audit findings—that auditors could provide to audit committees to make it easier for them to fulfill their oversight responsibilities. Exhibit 4 . . . lists the matters that SAS no. 61 requires the auditor to communicate.

*   *   *

EXHIBIT 4
What should the auditor communicate?

SAS no. 61 requires an auditor to make sure the audit committee is informed about

- The level of assurance (reasonable, not absolute) provided by the audit about whether the financial statements are free from material misstatements.
- The auditor's responsibility with respect to internal control structure matters.
- Management's initial selection of and changes in significant accounting policies or their application—especially for unusual transactions or in areas that lack authoritative guidance.
- The process management uses in formulating sensitive accounting estimates and the

basis for the auditor's conclusions about the reasonableness of those estimates.
- Any audit adjustments that, individually or in the aggregate, and whether recorded or not, could have a significant effect on the financial reporting process.
- The auditor's responsibility for other information in documents containing audited financial statements and any procedures performed on other information and the results.
- Disagreements with management, whether satisfactorily resolved or not, about matters that could be significant to the company's financial statements or the auditor's report. These

disagreements might include application of accounting principles, judgments about accounting estimates, audit scope, financial statement disclosures or wording of the auditor's report.
- The auditor's views on significant matters about which management consulted with other accountants.
- The major issues the auditor discussed with management in connection with being retained.
- Any serious difficulties encountered with management in performing the audit—for example, management setting an unreasonable timetable or not providing the information required by the auditor.

[G2545]

Appendix

THE CONCEPT OF PRESENT VALUE OF A FUTURE CASH FLOW; THE "MULTIPLIER"

A. DISCOUNTING TO PRESENT VALUE OF A FUTURE PAYMENT

How much should be loaned on the promise to repay $1 in a year? Or putting the question another way, what is the present value of a dollar to be paid a year from today? Let us assume that only simple interest is to be charged and that the simple interest rate is 10%. ("Simple" interest is to be distinguished from "compound" interest. For simple interest, the calculation of the amount of interest is made at the end of the period, based on the initial principal amount lent. If, however, interest is to be determined periodically during the period of the loan, say, daily, and interest on the principal and on that interest at the end of the first day is calculated and then interest on the sum of those two figures charged for the second day, and so forth, we describe that as daily "compounded" (or "compound") interest.)

In our discussion here we shall compound interest only annually, meaning simple interest shall accrue during the year and then be added to principal for the calculation of simple interest on that sum in year two, and so on. On that assumption, the amount which will be loaned in the posited case is $.909 (rounded to the nearest mill) since $.909 plus 10% of $.909 is $.9999, which rounds off to $1. Hence, it may be said that the present value of $1 one year from now "discounted" at 10% simple interest, is $.909. The word "discounted" is suggested by the fact that we start with, and discount from, the $1 ultimate receipt to derive the *lower* present value. Thus the term "discount rate" involves the process of determining the lower present value of a future known amount, whereas the term "interest rate" involves the opposite process of starting with the initial principal known amount of the loan to arrive at the final payment of principal plus interest.

How was the $.909 figure derived?

The logic is not difficult. Rephrasing our problem, how much principal must be loaned, which when added to the interest earned for one year, will aggregate $1? Stating the same question algebraically, if

$$(1) \quad p_1 + i = \$1$$

(where p_1 is the principal sum, or present value, of the loan, and i is the amount of the interest for the year), what is the value of p_1?

The amount of simple interest to be earned on an investment of principal for one year is the result of multiplying the principal by the annual interest rate and by the time period to which the rate is related, one year. Again, in algebraic terms, (where r is the interest rate and t is the number of time periods involved)

$$(2) \quad i = p_1 rt$$

but since, in this example, $t = 1$, the "t" term may be ignored, and, hence,

$$(3) \quad i = p_1 r.$$

Substituting the value of i from equation (3) in equation (1);

$$(4) \quad p_1 + p_1 r = \$1$$

and factoring out p_1,

$$(5) \quad p_1 (1 + r) = \$1.$$

Dividing both sides of the equation by $(1 + r)$ to solve for p_1,

$$(6) \quad p_1 = \frac{\$1}{(1 + r)}$$

and if $r = .10$,

$$(7) \quad p_1 = \frac{\$1}{(1 + .10)}$$

Therefore,

$$(8) \quad p_1 = \$.909.$$

If we wish instead to determine the present value of $1 to be received *two* years hence (p_2), at the same 10% interest rate, but compounded annually, we can derive p_2 by this logic: If we know that the present value of $1 one year hence, discounted at 10%, is $.909, we also know that the present value of $1 two years hence will be an amount which, if invested for the first year, will result, with interest, in receipt of $.909 at the end of the first year, which upon being reinvested at 10% for the second year, will yield $1 at the end of the second year.

Thus for the first year of the two-year period, we would, instead of asking the present value of $1, ask the present value of $.909 to be received at the end of the first year, since that $.909 reinvested for the second year will yield $1.

Using our above formula, from equation (6),

$$(9) \quad p_2 = \frac{\$.909}{(1 + .10)}$$

and

$$(10) \quad p_2 = \$.826.$$

To derive a generally applicable formula, instead of using our 10% value for r and the $.909 value for p_1, we instead may state equation (9) more generally, as:

$$(11) \quad p_2 = \frac{p_1}{(1 + r)}$$

Then, since

$$(12) \quad p_1 = \frac{\$1}{(1 + r)}$$

substituting this value of p_1 in equation (11),

$$(13) \quad p_2 = \frac{\frac{\$1}{(1 + r)}}{(1 + r)}$$

To eliminate this complexity, multiply equation (13) by $\frac{(1 + r)}{(1 + r)}$

(which, of course, is 1 and therefore does not change either side), as follows:

$$(14) \quad p_2 = \frac{\frac{\$1}{(1 + r)}}{(1 + r)} \times \frac{(1 + r)}{(1 + r)}$$

Then

$$(15) \quad p_2 = \frac{\$1}{(1 + r)(1 + r)}$$

and

$$(16) \quad p_2 = \frac{\$1}{(1 + r)^2}$$

and

$$(17) \quad p_2 = \$.826$$

By this same process, we see that the number of times the term $(1 + r)$ must appear in the denominator of the right hand side of the equation (15) is the number of the year at the end of which the final payment is to be received. Hence, if the number of years is 3, the equation is:

$$(18) \quad p_3 = \frac{\$1}{(1 + r)^3}$$

and

$$(19) \quad p_3 = \$.751$$

All this mathematical work has been done and put in tables such as the following, which give the present value of the sum of $1 received at the end of a particular number of years at particular discount rates.

Table 1

Present Value of $1: What a Dollar at End of Specified Future Year is Worth Today

Year	3%	4%	5%	6%	7%	8%	10%	12%	15%	20%	Year
1	.971	.962	.952	.943	.935	.926	.909	.893	.870	.833	1
2	.943	.925	.907	.890	.873	.857	.826	.797	.756	.694	2
3	.915	.890	.864	.839	.816	.794	.751	.711	.658	.578	3
4	.889	.855	.823	.792	.763	.735	.683	.636	.572	.482	4
5	.863	.823	.784	.747	.713	.681	.620	.567	.497	.402	5
6	.838	.790	.746	.705	.666	.630	.564	.507	.432	.335	6
7	.813	.760	.711	.665	.623	.583	.513	.452	.376	.279	7
8	.789	.731	.677	.627	.582	.540	.466	.404	.326	.233	8
9	.766	.703	.645	.591	.544	.500	.424	.360	.284	.194	9
10	.744	.676	.614	.558	.508	.463	.385	.322	.247	.162	10
11	.722	.650	.585	.526	.475	.429	.350	.287	.215	.134	11
12	.701	.625	.557	.497	.444	.397	.318	.257	.187	.112	12
13	.681	.601	.530	.468	.415	.368	.289	.229	.162	.0935	13
14	.661	.577	.505	.442	.388	.340	.263	.204	.141	.0779	14
15	.642	.555	.481	.417	.362	.315	.239	.183	.122	.0649	15
16	.623	.534	.458	.393	.339	.292	.217	.163	.107	.0541	16
17	.605	.513	.436	.371	.317	.270	.197	.146	.093	.0451	17
18	.587	.494	.416	.350	.296	.250	.179	.130	.0808	.0376	18
19	.570	.475	.396	.330	.277	.232	.163	.116	.0703	.0313	19
20	.554	.456	.377	.311	.258	.215	.148	.104	.0611	.0261	20
25	.478	.375	.295	.232	.184	.146	.0923	.0588	.0304	.0105	25
30	.412	.308	.231	.174	.131	.0994	.0573	.0334	.0151	.00421	30
40	.307	.208	.142	.0972	.067	.0460	.0221	.0107	.00373	.000680	40
50	.228	.141	.087	.0543	.034	.0213	.00852	.00346	.000922	.000109	50

Each column lists how much a dollar received at the end of various years in the future is worth today. For example, at 6 percent a dollar to be received ten years hence is equivalent in value to $.558 now. In other words, $.558 invested now at 6 percent with interest compounded annually, would grow to $1.00 in ten years.

Formula for entry in table is $p = A/(1 + r)^t$.

(This Table is from A. Alchian & W. Allen, University Economics (2d ed. 1967).) See the column headed 10% to compare with the above results. And note the identity of the formula in the footnote of Table 1 with the one we have just derived.

With this table, we may determine the present value of any future annual receipt by multiplying the value in the table by the number of dollars to be received. For example, the present value of $158 received one year from now, at 10% simple interest, is .909 × $158, or $143.62. And the present value of $180 received two years hence, at 10%, compounded annually, is .826 × $180 or $148.68.

B. PRESENT VALUE OF AN ANNUITY

You will find that for many purposes it becomes useful to determine the present value of a series of *equal* annual receipts. To facilitate calculations, another table may be devised, as follows:

(This Table is also from A. Alchian & W. Allen, University Economics (2d ed. 1967).)

Table 2
Present Value of Annuity of $1, Received at End of Each Year

Year	3%	4%	5%	6%	7%	8%	10%	12%	15%	20%	Year
1	0.971	0.960	0.952	0.943	0.935	0.926	0.909	0.890	0.870	0.833	1
2	1.91	1.89	1.86	1.83	1.81	1.78	1.73	1.69	1.63	1.53	2
3	2.83	2.78	2.72	2.67	2.62	2.58	2.48	2.40	2.28	2.11	3
4	3.72	3.63	3.55	3.46	3.39	3.31	3.16	3.04	2.86	2.59	4
5	4.58	4.45	4.33	4.21	4.10	3.99	3.79	3.60	3.35	2.99	5
6	5.42	5.24	5.08	4.91	4.77	4.62	4.35	4.11	3.78	3.33	6
7	6.23	6.00	5.79	5.58	5.39	5.21	4.86	4.56	4.16	3.60	7
8	7.02	6.73	6.46	6.20	5.97	5.75	5.33	4.97	4.49	3.84	8
9	7.79	7.44	7.11	6.80	6.52	6.25	5.75	5.33	4.78	4.03	9
10	8.53	8.11	7.72	7.36	7.02	6.71	6.14	5.65	5.02	4.19	10
11	9.25	8.76	8.31	7.88	7.50	7.14	6.49	5.94	5.23	4.33	11
12	9.95	9.39	8.86	8.38	7.94	7.54	6.81	6.19	5.41	4.44	12
13	10.6	9.99	9.39	8.85	8.36	7.90	7.10	6.42	5.65	4.53	13
14	11.3	10.6	9.90	9.29	8.75	8.24	7.36	6.63	5.76	4.61	14
15	11.9	11.1	10.4	9.71	9.11	8.56	7.60	6.81	5.87	4.68	15
16	12.6	11.6	10.8	10.1	9.45	8.85	7.82	6.97	5.96	4.73	16
17	13.2	12.2	11.3	10.4	9.76	9.12	8.02	7.12	6.03	4.77	17
18	13.8	12.7	11.7	10.8	10.1	9.37	8.20	7.25	6.10	4.81	18
19	14.3	13.1	12.1	11.1	10.3	9.60	8.36	7.37	6.17	4.84	19
20	14.9	13.6	12.5	11.4	10.6	9.82	8.51	7.47	6.23	4.87	20
25	17.4	15.6	14.1	12.8	11.7	10.7	9.08	7.84	6.46	4.95	25
30	19.6	17.3	15.4	13.8	12.4	11.3	9.43	8.06	6.57	4.98	30
40	23.1	19.8	17.2	15.0	13.3	11.9	9.78	8.24	6.64	5.00	40
50	25.7	21.5	18.3	15.8	13.8	12.2	9.91	8.30	6.66	5.00	50

An annuity is a sequence of annual amounts received at the end of each year. This table shows with each entry how much it takes today to buy an annuity of $1 a year at the rates of interest indicated. For example, an annuity of $1 a year for twenty years at 6 percent interest could be purchased today with $11.40. This amount would, if invested at 6 percent, be sufficient to yield some interest which, along with some depletion of the principal in each year, would enable a payout of exactly $1 a year for twenty years, at which time the fund would be completely depleted. And $1,000 a year for twenty years would, at 6 percent compounded annually, cost today $11,400, which is obviously 1,000 times as much as for an annuity of just $1. Formula for entry is $p = [1 - (1 + i)^{-tt}]/i$.

It will be seen that each value in this Table 2 may be derived from Table 1. Thus the present value of equal annual payments of $1 for two years discounted at 10%, shown in Table 2 is the sum of the values from Table 1, .909 and .826, or 1.73 (subject to rounding errors). Similarly the value for three years' payments may be obtained by adding the value for the third year from Table 1.

The "Multiplier" Concept

Table 2 indicates the value of level streams of annuities for up to 50 years. What is the value of an annuity forever (infinity)? Most likely, if you had not been exposed to all the preceding discussions, you could answer this question from common experience. Putting it otherwise, how much must be invested at, say, 10% simple interest to yield $1 at the end of every year? The answer, obviously, is $10, since, as we saw in equation (2) above,

$$(20)\ i = prt$$

and for our problem here i is given at $1 while r is .10 and t is 1 for the first year. Therefore,

$$(21)\ \$1 = p(.10)(1)$$

and

$$(22) \quad p = \frac{\$1}{.10}$$

or

$$(23) \quad p = \$10$$

Logic tells us the same formula applies for year two since the sum of $10 which grew to $11 after one year, was reduced back to $10 by the payment of the $1 annuity, leaving $10 to continue earning for another year at a 10% rate.

Since in equation (22), the value of p was 1/.10 (which is described as the "reciprocal" of the interest rate) and the end result of dividing .10 into 1, 10, is to be used to *multiply* the particular amount of the future annuity of $1 to arrive at the $10 present value of the infinite annuity, we have come to speak in terms of the end result of the division process, i.e., the result of dividing .10 into 1, yielding 10, as the "multiplier." Thus we see that *the multiplier for determining the present value of a perpetual income stream is the reciprocal of the interest rate.* For example, the "multiplier" for an interest rate of 20% is the reciprocal of .20, which is 1/.20, or 5.

The multiplier, in theory, can be used only to value an infinite level stream of annuities. However, in practice, although infinity is too long to expect anything to last, it is reasoned that the practical result of even a stream of annuities for a long, but discrete, period is the same as a perpetual annuity if the initial principal remains available for reinvestment. (In fact, these do not quite work out to be mathematical equivalents, but the approximation is accepted since there are even more inaccuracies in the whole process so that this small mathematical error is inconsequential relative to others and perhaps they are balanced out anyway. We need not belabor this point.)

Another practice has developed of using a multiplier even when the stream of annuities is not equal but has an upward trend or downward trend. In this event the multiplier will be increased for the upward trend or decreased for the downward trend on the rationale that there is an "average" stream of annuities (which of course is higher than current income in an upward trend and vice versa for a downward trend).

C. FUTURE AMOUNTS CORRESPONDING TO GIVEN PRESENT VALUES AT INTEREST

Instead of deriving present values of future amounts, we can derive for any annual rate of interest the future amount that will be exchangeable for any present value. How much will $1 paid now purchase if the future amount is due in one year, or in two years, or in three years? At 15 percent per year, $1 will be worth $1.15 in one year. And at 15 percent for the next year, that $1.15 will in turn grow to \$1.32. Hence, \$1 today is the present price or value of \$1.32 in two years. In terms of our formula, this can be expressed

$$p_2(1 + r)(1 + r) = A,$$

$$\$1(1.15)(1.15) = \$1(1.32) = \$1.32.$$

If the future amount is deferred three years, the term (1.15) enters three times, and if deferred t years, it enters t times. For three years, the quantity (1.15) is multiplied together three times, denoted $(1.15)^3$, and equals 1.52. Therefore, in three years \$1 will grow to \$1.52. In general, the formula is

$$p_t(1 + r)^t = A$$

for any present payment, p_t, that is paid for an amount A available t years later. The multiplicative factor $(1 + r)^t$ is called the *future-value* (or *amount*) *factor*. Values of this future-amount factor for different combinations of t and r are given in Table 3. For example, at 6 percent in five years, the future-amount factor is 1.34, which means that a present payment of \$1 will buy, or grow to, the future amount \$1.34 at the end of five years. Notice that the entries in Table 3 are simply the reciprocals of the entries in Table 1.

For the latest on these matters see FASB, Discussion Memorandum, An Analysis of Issues Related to Present Value—Based Measurements in Accounting (1990).

Table 3

Compound Amount of \$1: Amount to Which \$1 Now Will Grow by End of Specified Year at Compounded Interest

Year	3%	4%	5%	6%	7%	8%	10%	12%	15%	20%	Year
1	1.03	1.04	1.05	1.06	1.07	1.08	1.10	1.12	1.15	1.20	1
2	1.06	1.08	1.10	1.12	1.14	1.17	1.21	1.25	1.32	1.44	2
3	1.09	1.12	1.16	1.19	1.23	1.26	1.33	1.40	1.52	1.73	3
4	1.13	1.17	1.22	1.26	1.31	1.36	1.46	1.57	1.74	2.07	4
5	1.16	1.22	1.28	1.34	1.40	1.47	1.61	1.76	2.01	2.49	5
6	1.19	1.27	1.34	1.41	1.50	1.59	1.77	1.97	2.31	2.99	6
7	1.23	1.32	1.41	1.50	1.61	1.71	1.94	2.21	2.66	3.58	7
8	1.27	1.37	1.48	1.59	1.72	1.85	2.14	2.48	3.05	4.30	8
9	1.30	1.42	1.55	1.68	1.84	2.00	2.35	2.77	3.52	5.16	9
10	1.34	1.48	1.63	1.79	1.97	2.16	2.59	3.11	4.05	6.19	10
11	1.38	1.54	1.71	1.89	2.10	2.33	2.85	3.48	4.66	7.43	11
12	1.43	1.60	1.80	2.01	2.25	2.52	3.13	3.90	5.30	8.92	12
13	1.47	1.67	1.89	2.13	2.41	2.72	3.45	4.36	6.10	10.7	13
14	1.51	1.73	1.98	2.26	2.58	2.94	3.79	4.89	7.00	12.8	14
15	1.56	1.80	2.08	2.39	2.76	3.17	4.17	5.47	8.13	15.4	15
16	1.60	1.87	2.18	2.54	2.95	3.43	4.59	6.13	9.40	18.5	16
17	1.65	1.95	2.29	2.69	3.16	3.70	5.05	6.87	10.6	22.2	17
18	1.70	2.03	2.41	2.85	3.38	4.00	5.55	7.70	12.5	26.6	18
19	1.75	2.11	2.53	3.02	3.62	4.32	6.11	8.61	14.0	31.9	19
20	1.81	2.19	2.65	3.20	3.87	4.66	6.72	9.65	16.1	38.3	20
25	2.09	2.67	3.39	4.29	5.43	6.85	10.8	17.0	32.9	95.4	25
30	2.43	3.24	4.32	5.74	7.61	10.0	17.4	30.0	66.2	237	30
40	3.26	4.80	7.04	10.3	15.0	21.7	45.3	93.1	267.0	1470	40
50	4.38	7.11	11.5	18.4	29.5	46.9	117	289	1080	9100	50

This table shows to what amounts \$1.00 invested now will grow at the end of various years, at different rates of growth compounded annually. For example, \$1.00 invested now will grow in thirty years to \$5.74 at 6 percent. In other words, \$5.74 due thirty years hence is worth now exactly \$1.00 at a 6 percent rate of interest per year. If you invest \$100 now at 10 percent, you will have \$1,740 in thirty years. Isn't that worth it? The entries in this table are the reciprocals of the entries in Table; that is, they are the entries of Table divided into 1. You really don't "need" this extra table, but having it saves some calculations. Formula for entries in table is $A = 1(1 + i)^t$.

*

Index

†